Pharmacy Law and Practice

Fifth Edition

Pharmacy Law and Practice

Fifth Edition

Jon Merrills
BPharm, BA, BA (Law), FRPharmS
Barrister (Middle Temple)

Jonathan Fisher
BA, LLB (Cantab)
Barrister (Grays Inn)
One of Her Majesty's Counsel

AMSTERDAM • BOSTON • HEIDELBERG • LONDON
NEW YORK • OXFORD • PARIS • SAN DIEGO
SAN FRANCISCO • SINGAPORE • SYDNEY • TOKYO
Academic Press is an imprint of Elsevier

Academic Press is an imprint of Elsevier
32 Jamestown Road, London NW1 7BY, UK
225 Wyman Street, Waltham, MA 02451, USA
525 B Street, Suite 1800, San Diego, CA 92101-4495, USA

Fifth edition 2013   10 07/66220

Notice
No responsibility is assumed by the publisher for any injury and/or damage to
persons or property as a matter of products liability, negligence or otherwise,
or from any use or operation of any methods, products, instructions or ideas
contained in the material herein. Because of rapid advances in the medical
sciences, in particular, independent verification of diagnoses and drug dosages
should be made.

British Library Cataloguing-in-Publication Data
A catalogue record for this book is available from the British Library

Library of Congress Cataloging-in-Publication Data
A catalog record for this book is available from the Library of Congress

ISBN: 978-0-12-394289-0

For information on all Academic Press publications
visit our website at www.store.elsevier.com

Typeset by MPS Limited, Chennai, India
www.adi-mps.com

Transferred to Digital Printing in 2013

Working together
to grow libraries in
developing countries

www.elsevier.com • www.bookaid.org

Contents

3.   NHS Pharmaceutical Services in the Community

4. The Drug Tariff

Reimbursement and Remuneration Structure for Community Pharmacy

5. Applications to Dispense NHS Scripts

6.   Rural Dispensing

7.   Prescription Charges

8.   The Interests of the Public

9.   Complaints and Breaches of the Terms of Service

10. Retail Pharmacy

11. The Manufacture and Licensing of Medicinal Products

12. Control on Sales of Medicines

13. Emergency Supplies, Deliveries and Faxed Prescriptions

14. Unlicensed Products

15. Traditional and Alternative Medicines

16. Controlled Drugs

17. Labelling, Leaflets, Packaging and Advertising

18. Poisons and Dangerous Substances

19. Patient Group Directions

20. Non-Medical Prescribing

21. Rights of Access

22. Confidentiality

23. Consent

24. The European Union

25. The Pharmacy Profession

26. Liability in Negligence

27. Business Premises

28. Business Associations

30.   Employment Law

When we wrote the first edition, our objective was to describe the law rather than just list the Acts, regulations and cases that make-up the law applying to community pharmacy.

That is still our objective. There has been an avalanche of new laws affecting pharmacy practice, all of which has had to be considered. The result is that this fifth edition is once again a complete rewrite. As always there has had to be a compromise between including everything we would have liked and producing a readable text.

Once again we have concentrated on the laws which apply to community pharmacy and we have extended into other areas only where we consider it relevant to the community pharmacist. Although community pharmacists sometimes deal with agricultural products and veterinary medicines, we have generally left out the detailed laws in these areas. Instead we have included from those laws, sections which affect the day-to-day practice as a pharmacist.

We have sought to produce an accessible text for both the community pharmacist and the pharmacy student. Any errors are ours – we strived for none.

Jon Merrills
Jonathan Fisher

Chapter 1

The National Health Service

History of the National Health Service from Conception to Latest Changes

INTRODUCTION

The National Health Service (NHS) has been described as the most magnificent feature of the UK's post-Second World War landscape. The National Health Service Act 1946, which created the NHS as we know it, was extensive in scope. It covered the funding of the service and created a national network of hospitals operating in a tiered management structure. Benefits were extended to the whole of the population, which were provided free of charge with medicines and the services of hospitals, doctors, dentists and opticians.

THE NATIONAL INSURANCE ACT 1911

Before 1911 the provision of medical care was haphazard. There were some voluntary health insurance schemes, often based on a particular industry. By 1900 about 7 million people in the country were covered. In return for flat-rate payments they had the services of a doctor and were provided with free medicines.

In 1911 the then Prime Minister, Lloyd George, introduced a compulsory health insurance scheme. It was based on a German scheme which had been introduced in 1883 by Bismarck.

The National Health Insurance Act 1911 covered all employees below a certain income level. The worker paid into a scheme run by a trade union, a friendly society or a commercial insurance company. In return, when the employee was ill he or she received cash, the free services of a doctor and the necessary medicines. However, only about 43% of the population was included. The majority, mainly women and children, were not covered.

A NATIONAL HEALTH SERVICE BEGINS

There remained a number of problems with the provision of health services. The hospitals varied in quality of buildings and quality of care. Many were run by charities. Only those persons who actually paid the insurance were covered for treatment. There was no provision for dependants. The problems,

Pharmacy Law and Practice. DOI: http://dx.doi.org/10.1016/B978-0-12-394289-0.00001-1

especially those of the hospitals, were highlighted during the Second World War.

The 1944 White Paper, 'A National Health Service', set out two guiding principles:

- Firstly, that such a service should be comprehensive, with all citizens receiving all the advice, treatment and care they needed, combined with the best medical and other facilities available.
- Secondly, that the service should be free to the public at the point of use.

The new Socialist government of 1946 immediately implemented the National Health Service Act 1946, which brought the NHS into being on 5 July 1948.

THE NATIONAL HEALTH SERVICE ACT 1946

The words are quoted purely for historical purposes – this Act has been superseded.

Section 1 - (1) It shall be the duty of the Minister of Health to promote the establishment in England and Wales of a comprehensive health service designed to secure improvement in the physical and mental health of the people of England and Wales and the prevention, diagnosis and treatment of illness, and for that purpose to provide or secure the effective provision of services in accordance with the following provisions of this Act

(2) The services so provided shall be free of charge, except where any provision of this Act expressly provides for the making and recovery of charges

The Minister was to provide hospital and other medical and nursing services throughout England and Wales,

to such extent as he considers necessary to meet all reasonable requirements (Section 3)

The Act vested in the Minister a range of facilities and services which had previously been owned or provided by local health authorities, voluntary hospital authorities and other voluntary organisations, by the Government under the 1911 scheme and by doctors practising privately.

The Act covered England and Wales, with separate legislation produced for Scotland and Northern Ireland.

The Act recognised the right of doctors to continue to practise privately, either full time or in combination with certain types of NHS contract. They could admit patients to private beds in NHS hospitals.

The 1946 Act set up a tripartite structure to administer the new arrangements. Different authorities controlled the hospitals, the primary care service and the mental hospitals.

Hospitals

The NHS took over control of 2688 hospitals from local authorities, charities and commercial bodies. The new structure consisted of 14 regional boards. Below them were 388 hospital management committees. The special position of teaching hospitals was recognised by the creation of 36 teaching hospital groups. Within each hospital, the management was in the hands of an administrator, a matron and the senior doctor.

Local health authorities administered ambulance services, midwifery, home nursing and provision of care for the mentally ill.

Primary Care

The primary health care services were run by 134 executive councils. The health professionals – general practitioner (GP), dentist, optician and pharmacist – were (and remain) independent contractors. By contrast staff in the hospital services were (and remain) employees.

The Act embodied the principle of the 1911 Act that medicines were normally to be dispensed at pharmacies, and that normally doctors were not to dispense for their patients. Regulations could lay down the conditions for departing from this.

In the first full year of its operation, the Government spent £11.4 billion (in today's money) on health.

Dispensing by Pharmacists

The 1911 Act gave statutory recognition to the principle, long advocated by pharmacists, that the dispensing of prescriptions should be carried out under normal conditions only by or under the supervision of pharmacists. It applied this principle to the large class of the community which received their medicines under the provisions of the Act. This principle was carried on into the 1946 Act.

The equivalent of around 50 million prescriptions was dispensed annually in England and Wales before the NHS. By 1950 prescription numbers had risen to over 217 million. It is now over 1 billion in the United Kingdom. Around 13,000 pharmacies issue over 90% of these prescriptions, with the rest being issued by over 6500 dispensing doctors.

Changes to the Original Structure

This original structure has been changed over the years as the amending legislation reflected changes in both government and management theory.

THE NATIONAL HEALTH SERVICE ACT 1977 (NOW REPEALED)

This repealed the whole of the 1946 Act and consolidated a number of previous measures into one Act. It was the main NHS Act for many years.

Since then the structure of the NHS has again been altered by both primary and secondary legislations.

THE NATIONAL HEALTH SERVICE ACT 2006

In 2006 most of the health legislation made since 1977 was consolidated into three Acts of Parliament:

(1) The National Health Service Act 2006
(2) The National Health Service (Wales) Act 2006
(3) The National Health Service (Consequential Provisions) Act 2006.

The consolidation repealed and re-enacted in its entirety the National Health Service Act 1977. The three acts received Royal Assent on 8 November 2006 and came into effect on 1 March 2007 (subject to a few exceptions).

The consolidation made no substantial changes to the substance of the law. The statutes contained within the new Acts were reordered, and inconsistencies in the legislation removed. Some obsolete provisions were repealed using a pre-consolidation amendment order.

The 2006 Acts also incorporated provisions from:

- Health Act 2006
- Health and Social Care (Community Health and Standards) Act 2003
- National Health Service Reform and Health Care Professions Act 2002
- Health and Social Care Act 2001
- Health Act 1999
- Primary Care Act 1997
- Health Authorities Act 1995
- National Health Service and Community Care Act 1990.

RECENT CHANGES: THE NHS AND SOCIAL CARE ACT 2012

The incoming coalition government published a White Paper, Equity and Excellence: Liberating the NHS, in July 2010. It proposed the most significant reorganisation of the NHS in its history, and the resulting Health and Social Care Bill finally received Royal Assent in March 2012.

According to the Department of Health, the new Act puts clinicians at the centre of commissioning, frees up providers to innovate, empowers patients and gives a new focus to public health. The Act creates an independent NHS Board, promotes patient choice and reduces NHS administration costs.

Key areas:

- establishes an independent NHS Board to allocate resources and provide commissioning guidance;
- increases GPs' powers to commission services on behalf of their patients;
- strengthens the role of the Care Quality Commission;
- develops Monitor, the body that currently regulates NHS foundation trusts, into an economic regulator to oversee aspects of access and competition in the NHS;
- cuts the number of health bodies to reduce NHS administration costs, including abolishing Primary Care Trusts and Strategic Health Authorities;
- repeals NHS trust legislation;
- removes the cap on income from private patients.

AMENDMENTS TO THE NHS ACT 2006

The Act does not repeal the 2006 NHS Act but instead amends it by replacing huge sections with new text. The new Act is a substantial piece of legislation. It contains 309 sections and 23 schedules.

A large number of regulations will now be laid before parliament in order to amplify the provisions of the Act. These will add to the complexity of the changes.

WHAT THE 2012 ACT DOES

There is a new and enlarged *Section 1*, which contains the Secretary of State's duty to promote a comprehensive health service. The amendments to *Section 1* leave intact the duty of the Secretary of State. However, the duty on the Secretary to provide or secure the provision of services for the purposes of the health service is removed and replaced by a duty 'to promote' the NHS:

(a) to carry out the public health functions; and
(b) to act with a view to securing the provision of services when exercising functions in relation to the NHS Commissioning Board, commissioning consortia and local authorities.

The Act thus draws a distinction between the Secretary of State's public health functions and the role in relation to the securing of services for the purposes of the NHS.

The Act sets out a new framework for the NHS. The Secretary of State retains only those controls necessary to discharge core functions. Clinician-led commissioning forms one of the most radical elements of the Government's NHS reforms. Various organisations, for example, the National Health Service Commissioning Board, separate from the Secretary of State, are responsible for exercising functions in relation to the health service.

Clinical commissioning groups (CCGs), made up of GPs, take over responsibility for commissioning the majority of NHS services in England.

The CCGs will be overseen by the NHS Commissioning Board which will make sure that they have the capacity and capability to commission services successfully and to meet their financial responsibilities.

Section 1 of the NHS Act 2006 now reads:

1. Secretary of State's duty to promote comprehensive health service
  (1) *The Secretary of State must continue the promotion in England of a comprehensive health service designed to secure improvement:*
    (a) *in the physical and mental health of the people of England, and*
    (b) *in the prevention, diagnosis and treatment of physical and mental illness.*
  (2) *For that purpose, the Secretary of State must exercise the functions conferred by this Act so as to secure that services are provided in accordance with this Act.*
  (3) *The Secretary of State retains ministerial responsibility to Parliament for the provision of the health service in England.*
  (4) *The services provided as part of the health service in England must be free of charge except in so far as the making and recovery of charges is expressly provided for by or under any enactment, whenever passed.*

New *Sections 1A–1G* add further duties:

1A. Duty as to improvement in quality of services
The Secretary of State must exercise his functions with a view to securing continuous improvement in the quality of services provided to individuals concerning

  (a) *the prevention, diagnosis or treatment of illness, or*
  (b) *the protection or improvement of public health.*

1B. Duty to have regard to the NHS Constitution
The Secretary of State must have regard to the NHS Constitution set out in Chapter 1 of Part 1 of the Health Act 2009.

1C. Duty as to reducing inequalities
The Secretary of State must have regard to the need to reduce inequalities between the people of England with respect to the benefits that they can obtain from the health service.

1D. Duty as to promoting autonomy
The Secretary of State must have regard to the desirability of securing, so far as consistent with the interests of the health service:

  (a) *that any other person exercising functions in relation to the health service or providing services for its purposes is free to exercise those functions or provide those services in the manner that it considers most appropriate, and*
  (b) *that unnecessary burdens are not imposed on any such person.*

1E. Duty as to research
The Secretary of State must promote:

    (a)   research on matters relevant to the health service, and
    (b)   the use in the health service of evidence obtained from research.

1F. Duty as to education and training
The Secretary of State must ensure an effective system for the planning and delivery of education and training to persons who are employed, or who are considering becoming employed, in connection with the health service in England.

1G. Secretary of State's duty as to reporting on and reviewing treatment of providers
The Secretary of State must by April 2013, report to Parliament on the treatment of NHS health care providers as respects any matter, including taxation, which might affect their ability to provide health care services for the purposes of the NHS or the reward available to them for doing so.
He must recommend how any differences in the treatment of NHS health care providers could be addressed, and must keep such matters under review.

New *Sections 1H and 1I* deal with commissioning.

1H. The National Health Service Commissioning Board and its general functions
    (1)   There is to be a body corporate known as the National Health Service Commissioning Board ("the Board").
    (2)   The Board is subject to the duty under section 1(1) concurrently with the Secretary of State except in relation to the part of the health service that is provided in pursuance of the public health functions of the Secretary of State or local authorities.
    (3)   For the purpose of discharging that duty, the Board:
        (a)   has the function of arranging for the provision of services for the purposes of the health service in England in accordance with this Act, and
        (b)   must exercise the functions conferred on it by this Act in relation to clinical commissioning groups so as to secure that services are provided for those purposes in accordance with this Act.
    (4)   Schedule A1 makes further provision about the Board.
    (5)   In this Act:
        (a)   any reference to the public health functions of the Secretary of State is a reference to the functions of the Secretary of State under sections 2A and 2B and paragraphs 7C, 8 and 12 of Schedule 1, and
        (b)   any reference to the public health functions of local authorities is a reference to the functions of local authorities under sections 2B and 111 and paragraphs 1 to 7B and 13 of Schedule 1.

1I. Clinical commissioning groups and their general functions

    (1)   There are to be bodies corporate known as clinical commissioning groups established in accordance with Chapter A2 of Part 2.

(2) *Each clinical commissioning group has the function of arranging for the provision of services for the purposes of the health service in England in accordance with this Act.*

Abolition of Various Bodies

The Act abolishes:

Strategic Health Authorities (SHAs)
Primary Care Trusts (PCTs)
Health Protection Agency
Alcohol Education and Research Council
Appointments Commission
National Information Governance Board for Health and Social Care
National Patient Safety Agency
NHS Institute for Innovation and Improvement
Office of the Health Professions Adjudicator

Territorial Extent and Application

Section 280 sets out the territorial extent of the Act.

Most of the provisions contained in the Bill extend to England and Wales only, but apply only to England. Some provisions apply only to Wales; others extend to the whole of the United Kingdom. Sections covering the arrangements between the NHS Commissioning Board and Northern Ireland Ministers and Scottish Ministers extend to England, Wales and Northern Ireland or England, Wales and Scotland, respectively.

General Principles, Scope and Nature of the Current NHS

Actual care is provided by NHS staff in general practices, hospitals, treatment centres, pharmacies, NHS walk-in centres and other community settings. The NHS employs around 1.7 million people. Of those, just under half are clinically qualified, including 39,409 GPs, 410,615 nurses, 18,450 ambulance staff and 103,912 hospital and community health service (HCHS) medical and dental staff.

Around 3 million people are treated in the NHS in England every week. According to the Department of Health, 1.2 million people visit a pharmacy every day.

About the NHS – Department of Health website.[1]

Funding

The NHS is funded through central taxation.

When the NHS was launched in 1948 it had a budget of £437 million (roughly £9 billion at today's value). For 2011/2012 it is around £106 billion.

Charges

The services provided as part of the health service in England must be free of charge where legislation expressly allows for charges to be made (e.g., prescription charging).

Special Hospitals

'Special hospitals' must also be provided for persons subject to detention under the Mental Health Act 1983 and who require treatment in high-security institutions.

The Secretary of State also has power to provide:

* invalid carriages
* a microbiological service
* assistance for relevant research.

Pharmaceutical Services

Pharmaceutical services are arranged by the NHS Commissioning Board, using contractors. Under the new provisions the Secretary of State directs the Board to provide pharmaceutical services through pharmacy contracts. Trusts cannot themselves be granted a NHS dispensing contract. They can lease their premises to a pharmacist or a company which can operate a pharmacy and be granted a contract.

Acts of Parliament Mainly Concerned with the NHS

The National Health Service Act 1946*
The National Health Service (Scotland) Act 1947*
The National Health Service (Amendment) Act 1949
The National Health Service Act 1951*
The National Health Service Act 1952*
The National Health Service (Amendment) Act 1957*
The National Health Service Act 1961*
The National Health Service (Hospital Boards) Act 1964*
The National Health Service Act 1966
The National Health Service (Family Planning) Act 1967*
The Health Services and Public Health Act 1968
The National Health Service (Scotland) Act 1972
The National Health Service (Family Planning) Amendment Act 1972*
The National Health Service Reorganisation Act 1973* (repealed by HA Act 1995)
The Health Services Act 1976*
The National Health Service Act 1977*

The National Health Service (Scotland) Act 1978
The Health Services Act 1980
The Health and Social Security Act 1984
The Health and Medicines Act 1988
The National Health Service and Community Care Act 1990
Health Authorities Act 1995
National Health Service (Amendment) Act 1995
Health Service Commissioners (Amendment) Act 1996
National Health Service (Private Finance) Act 1997
National Health Service (Primary Care) Act 1997
Audit Commission Act 1998
Health Act 1999
Health and Social Care Act 2001
NHS Reform & Health Care Professions Act 2002
Health and Social Care (Community Health and Standards) Act 2003
The National Health Service Act 2006
The National Health Service (Wales) Act 2006
The National Health Service (Consequential Provisions) Act 2006
Health Act 2009
Health and Social Care Act 2012

Asterisked Acts have been totally repealed.
Equity and excellence: liberating the NHS.[2]

Self-Assessment Questions

1. Describe the pre-1946 health care provision in the United Kingdom?
   Answer: Rarely free except to working men, patchy provision with varying standards, provided by a mixture of private, local authority and charitable organisation.
2. How is the new post-2013 NHS to be regulated?
   Answer: CCGs will be overseen by the NHS Commissioning Board which will make sure that they have the capacity and capability to commission services successfully and to meet their financial responsibilities.
3. What duties does the Secretary of State for Health have in respect of the NHS?
   Answer: The duties on the Secretary of State for Health are to promote the NHS to carry out the public health functions and to act with a view to securing the provision of services when exercising functions in relation to the NHS Commissioning Board, commissioning consortia and local authorities.

ADDITIONAL RESOURCES

1. http://www.nhs.uk/NHSEngland/thenhs/about/Pages/overview.aspx
2. http://www.dh.gov.uk/en/Healthcare/LiberatingtheNHS/index.htm

Chapter 2

Administration of the NHS

The New Administrative Structure of the NHS

ADMINISTRATION

Although funded centrally from national taxation, NHS services in England, Northern Ireland, Scotland and Wales are managed separately. While some differences have emerged between these systems in recent years, they remain similar in most respects and are often talked about as a single, unified system.

The Secretary of State for Health is the political head of the Department of Health (DH) which sets overall health policy in England, including policy for the NHS. The Secretary of State is assisted by a Minister of Health and a number of junior Ministers.

Following the Health and Social Care Act 2012, Ministers remain responsible for the NHS, will set objectives and retain powers to intervene in emergencies. The department provides an overall budget for the NHS.

The department is staffed by civil servants. The most senior is the Permanent Secretary. He or she is answerable to the Secretary of State and to Parliament for the way the department is run.

The DH is managed by a board. It supports the Permanent Secretary to achieve the department's objectives and ensure its work is conducted efficiently and effectively.

The DH is organised into business groups – referred to as Directorates, each headed by a Director General.

In relation to the NHS, the main functions of the department are to negotiate with the Treasury for funding, to set the policy framework and to monitor the performance of the NHS.

Chief professional officers, including a Chief Pharmaceutical Officer, provide expert knowledge in specialist health and social care disciplines.

Non-Departmental Public Bodies

A number of bodies have been created to assist with the work of the NHS, but which are not part of the DH.

Pharmacy Law and Practice. DOI: http://dx.doi.org/10.1016/B978-0-12-394289-0.00002-3

Overall Governance of the NHS

Five main bodies are responsible for the overall governance of the NHS. They are:

(1) **The DH**: The Secretary of State will provide an overall budget for the NHS. The DH says that, while the Secretary of State will no longer have a 'duty' to provide an NHS, Ministers will remain responsible for the NHS, will set objectives and retain powers to intervene in emergencies.

(2) **NHS Commissioning Board (CB)**: This will develop and support Clinical Commissioning Groups (CCGs) and hold them to account for improving outcomes for patients.

(3) **The National Institute for Health and Clinical Excellence (NICE)**: NICE will continue to provide independent advice and guidance to the NHS, for instance, about whether medications and treatments should be available on the NHS. It will extend its role to social care.

(4) **The Care Quality Commission (CQC)**: NHS providers will no longer be performance managed by Strategic Health Authorities (SHAs) after their abolition. Instead, the CQC will ensure services comply with safety and quality requirements.

(5) **Monitor**: This will promote efficiency within the NHS, set prices and ensure that competition works in the interests of patients.

THE NHS COMMISSIONING BOARD

The 2012 Act establishes the NHS CB as a new non-departmental independent public body, accountable to the Secretary of State for Health.

A new Schedule 1 of the NHS Act 2006 sets out the constitution and establishment of the NHS CB.

It is comprised of:

(a) a chair appointed by the Secretary of State,
(b) at least five other members also appointed by the Secretary of State, and
(c) the chief executive and other members.

The Board was established in shadow form in October 2011, as a Special Health Authority, and became fully operational from April 2012. It takes up its full statutory duties and responsibilities on 1 April 2013.

Below the Board are four regional hubs comprising 27 local teams. There are about 6000 staff.

The Board is nationally accountable for the outcomes achieved by the NHS and provides leadership for the new commissioning system. It is accountable to the Secretary of State via an annual mandate (see below).

The Board has overall responsibility for a budget of around £95 billion, of which it allocates £65 billion directly to CCGs.

The Board supports the groups, allocates resources and commissions certain services, such as primary care, including pharmacy. The Board holds

CCGs to account for the quality of services they commission, the outcomes they achieve for patients and for their financial performance.

The Board has the power to intervene where there is evidence that CCGs are failing or are likely to fail to fulfil their functions.

Other specific functions of the Board, such as commissioning specialised services, are set out in the Act.

The most important of these functions are:

- To agree and deliver improved outcomes and account to Ministers and Parliament.
- To oversee the commissioning budget, ensuring financial control and value for money.
- To develop and oversee a comprehensive system of CCGs.
- To directly commission around £20 billion of services including specialised services and primary care.
- To support quality improvement.
- To promote innovative integrated care systems.
- To promote equality and diversity and the reduction of inequalities in all its activities.
- To develop commissioning guidance, standard contracts, pricing mechanisms and information standards.
- To engage with the public, patients and carers and to champion patient interests.
- To work with Monitor to develop choice and competition for patient services.
- To oversee emergency planning.
- To develop a medium-term strategy for the NHS with its partners.

The services which the Board commissions are:

(a) services which can be more effectively commissioned at national level, such as:
  specialised services for rare conditions
  high secure services
  prison health services
  health services for the armed forces.
(b) primary care services including:
  medical,
  dental,
  ophthalmic, and
  community pharmaceutical services.

From autumn 2012 the national board will start vetting the general practitioner (GP)-led groups to verify that they are ready to start managing local health services.

SHAs and Primary Care Trusts (PCTs) are abolished on 1 April 2013, leaving the GP-led groups and the national board to take on their full functions.

ANNUAL MANDATE TO THE BOARD

Before the start of each financial year, the Secretary of State must publish and lay before Parliament a document to be known as 'the mandate'.

The Secretary of State must specify in the mandate:

(a) the objectives that the Secretary of State considers the Board should seek to achieve in the exercise of its functions during that financial year and such subsequent financial years as the Secretary of State considers appropriate;

(b) any requirements that the Secretary of State considers it necessary to impose on the Board for the purpose of ensuring that it achieves those objectives;

(c) certain financial provisions.

THE NHS CONSTITUTION

The Board must, in the exercise of its functions:

(a) act with a view to securing that health services are provided in a way which promotes the NHS Constitution, and

(b) promote awareness of the NHS Constitution among patients, staff and members of the public.

NHS FOUNDATION TRUSTS

NHS Foundation Trusts (FTs) were originally established in the Health and Social Care (Community Health and Standards) Act 2003, which is now part of the National Health Service Act 2006.

NHS FTs are a new type of NHS organisation, established as independent, not-for-profit public benefit corporations. They are independent legal entities owned by their members who include patients, staff and local people. Their primary purpose is to provide NHS services to NHS patients. These Trusts remain within the NHS although they are not under direct Government control. FTs are accountable to Parliament, where they must lay their annual reports and accounts.

FTs are granted a licence to operate by the Independent Regulator, Monitor. FTs have greater powers and flexibilities than traditional NHS hospitals. In particular they are able to:

- borrow from the private sector
- retain their surpluses
- keep hold of all money from the sale of land and assets
- exercise a greater degree of flexibility in setting pay and benefits packages.

The public, patients and staff can join the FT as members and elect a Council of Governors to represent them.

The Council of Governors is not responsible for the day-to-day management of the organisation, for example, setting budgets, staff pay and other operational matters – that is a matter for the independent Board of Directors. They must be financially viable but are not required to break even each year. However, the Council of Governors appoints the chair and non-executive directors of the Board of Directors.

They can borrow money within limits set by Monitor, retain surpluses and decide on service developments and innovations for their local community. They are not allowed to sell off or mortgage NHS property or resources which are needed to provide key NHS services.

Local CCGs contract with FTs to deliver services.

Although they are free from central government control and performance management, they must meet the standards and be licensed by the CQC.

Changes Made by the Health and Social Care Act 2012

The Health and Social Care Act 2012 made the following changes for FTs:

- All providers are to be placed under a 'duty of candour' requiring them to be open and transparent in admitting mistakes.
- FTs will be required to hold council meetings in public.
- FTs will be required to produce separate accounts for their NHS and privately funded activities.

Private Patient Income Cap

The Private Patient Income Cap is set at 49%. However, an increase in the proportion of an FT's private income of more than 5% would need majority approval by its governors, and every FT must set out how its non-NHS income has benefited NHS services in its annual report.

The legislation also sets out the arrangements for FTs undergoing organisational change in the event of mergers, acquisitions, separations and dissolutions.

At the time of writing there are around 150 NHS FTs in existence. It is anticipated that over the next 3–5 years all NHS Trusts will become FTs.

Model Core Constitution[1]
A short guide to NHS FTs[2]

MONITOR

The Health and Social Care Act 2012 makes provision for the Independent Regulator of NHS FTs to continue in existence and to be known in legislation as 'Monitor'.

It outlines Monitor's overarching duties and constitution.

Monitor:

- assesses NHS Trusts for FT status
- ensures that FTs are financially viable
- ensures that FTs are well led
- licenses providers of NHS services
- protects and promotes the interests of users of health care services.

CLINICAL COMMISSIONING GROUPS

The Act makes provision for the constitution of CCGs. They are groups of GPs and others which are formed into corporate statutory bodies. They are authorised to act by the NHS CB, taking on the previous duties of the Secretary of State.

From April 2013, CCGs are responsible for designing local health services in England. They do this by commissioning or buying the majority of health and care services including:

- elective hospital care
- rehabilitation care
- urgent and emergency care
- most community health services
- mental health and learning disability services.

They are responsible for commissioning the great majority of health services, while the NHS CB is responsible for commissioning services that cannot be solely commissioned by CCGs, such as national specialist services and GP services. CCGs take responsibility for spending around 60% of the NHS budget.

All GP practices must belong to a CCG. The Groups have boundaries within those of local authorities.

CCGs will work with patients and health care professionals and in partnership with local communities and local authorities. They are required to obtain advice from a wider range of health professionals and will be supported by clinical networks and new clinical senates.

Governing bodies of CCGs must include a nurse and a hospital doctor.

At a local level, GPs have been forming themselves into CCGs since 2010. There are now 211 of them, although some of the smaller ones may merge.

CCGs have the power under *Section 2* of the Act to acquire and dispose of property, enter into agreements including contracts, or accept gifts of property. Property in this sense means any possession – it is not limited to buildings or land.[3,4]

Primary Care Services

Primary care services continue to be provided by GPs, dentists, pharmacists and opticians.

EXTRACTS FROM THE HEALTH ACT 2006

The amended NHS Act 2006 now reads:

Role of clinical commissioning groups in the health service in England
  (1)   1 *Clinical commissioning groups and their general functions*
          There are to be bodies corporate known as clinical commissioning groups
          established in accordance with Chapter A2 of Part 2.
  (2)   *Each clinical commissioning group has the function of arranging for the*
          provision of services for the purposes of the health service in England in
          accordance with this Act.

                                      (S11 NHS Act 2006 as amended)

Duties of clinical commissioning groups as to commissioning certain health services
  (1)   *"A clinical commissioning group must arrange for the provision of the*
          following to such extent as it considers necessary to meet the reasonable
          requirements of the persons for whom it has responsibility",
          (a)   hospital accommodation,
          (b)   other accommodation for the purpose of any service provided under this
                Act,
          (c)   medical, dental, ophthalmic, nursing and ambulance services,
          (d)   such other services or facilities for the care of pregnant women, women
                who are breastfeeding and young children as the group considers are
                appropriate as part of the health service,
          (e)   such other services or facilities for the prevention of illness, the care of
                persons suffering from illness and the after-care of persons who have
                suffered from illness as the group considers are appropriate as part of the
                health service,
          (f)   such other services or facilities as are required for the diagnosis and
                treatment of illness.

Transitional Arrangements

Former PCT responsibilities for local health improvement are transferred to local authorities, who will employ Directors of Public Health jointly appointed with the Public Health Service.

Following this transfer of responsibilities PCTs will be abolished in April 2013.

PUBLIC HEALTH

The NHS Act 2012 makes local authorities, along with the Secretary of State, responsible for public health for the first time since the 1970s.

The Act thus draws a distinction between the Secretary of State's public health functions and his or her role in relation to the securing of services for the purposes of the NHS.

Direct responsibility for securing the provision of these services is conferred on the board and CCGs.

The Secretary of State retains only those controls that are necessary to discharge core functions.

Public Health England Operating Structure.[5]

NHS WALK-IN CENTRES

NHS walk-in centres give fast access to health advice and treatment. There are now around 100 centres throughout England. They are open 7 days a week with extended hours and provide:

- treatment for minor illnesses and injuries
- assessment by an experienced NHS nurse
- advice on how to stay healthy
- information on out-of-hours GP and dental services
- information on local pharmacy services
- information on other local health services.

NHS DIRECT

NHS Direct was made a Special Health Authority in April 2004. It delivers user-friendly health care advice and information, often by telephone. NHS Direct is the single largest provider of NHS 111.

NHS 111 is a 24h medical helpline, run on an 'any qualified provider' basis, with a free to call 111 number due to be rolled out nationally by 2013, at which point it will replace the previous NHS Direct 0845 number.

NATIONAL INSTITUTE FOR HEALTH AND CARE EXCELLENCE

The previous NICE is re-established as a non-departmental public body with a new title. It provides independent advice to the NHS including about whether medicines and treatments should be available. From 2013 its role is extended to social care.

CARE QUALITY COMMISSION

The Health and Social Care Act 2008 established the CQC. The CQC[6] regulates most health and adult social care services in England, including those provided by the NHS, local authorities, private companies or voluntary organisation.

It also protects the interests of people detained under the Mental Health Act.

SPECIAL HEALTH AUTHORITIES

These are health authorities which provide a health service to the whole of England. They were set up under *Section 28* of the NHS Act 2006. They are independent but can be subject to ministerial direction.

Section 7 of the amended NHS Act 2006 states:

The Secretary of State may direct a Special Health Authority to exercise any functions of the Secretary of State or any other person which relate to the health service in England and are specified in the direction.

Current SHAs include:

- Health and Social Care Information Centre[7]
- Health Education England[8]
- Health Research Authority[9]
- National Treatment Agency[10]
- NHS Blood and Transplant[11]
- NHS Business Services Authority[12]
- NHS Commissioning Board Authority[13]
- NHS Litigation Authority[14]
- NHS Trust Development Authority[15]
- The NHS Institute for Innovation and Improvement[16]

NHS BUSINESS SERVICES AUTHORITY

The NHS Business Services Authority (NHSBSA) was established on 1 October 2005 as a Special Health Authority and became operational on 1 April 2006. It brought together five previously separate NHS organisations into a single Special Health Authority. NHSBS took over Dental Practice Board, NHS Counter Fraud and Security Management Service, NHS Pensions Agency and Prescriptions Pricing Authority (PPA). It provides central services to NHS organisations, NHS contractors, patients and the public.

NHS PRESCRIPTION SERVICES

NHS Prescription Services, formally the PPA, is part of the NHSBSA.

It calculates how much the pharmacists, appliance contractors and dispensing doctors should be paid as reimbursement and remuneration for medicines and medical devices dispensed to patients from NHS prescription forms. It processes more than 2 million prescription items every working day and payments amount to more than £8 billion a year.

NHSBS also provides information services to 25,000 prescribers and managing organisations within the NHS in England.

HEALTH AND CARE PROFESSIONALS COUNCIL

The Act abolished the General Social Care Council that transferred some of its functions to the Health Professions Council, which was renamed as the Health and Care Professionals Council to reflect its wider remit across health and social care.

PROFESSIONAL STANDARDS AUTHORITY FOR HEALTH AND SOCIAL CARE

This is the renamed 'Council for Healthcare Regulatory Excellence (CHRE)'. Some of its functions are altered.

HEALTH AND SOCIAL CARE INFORMATION CENTRE SPECIAL HEALTH AUTHORITY

The Act re-established this body as non-departmental public body with functions relating to the collection and analysis of data.

NHS TRUSTS

Section 25 of NHS Act 2006 created NHS Trusts as corporate bodies to provide goods and services for the purposes of the health service.

There are many acute NHS Trusts and mental health NHS Trusts, which oversee NHS hospitals and specialist care centres. The Government intends that the majority of the remaining 113 NHS Trusts will become FTs by April 2014.

AMBULANCE TRUSTS

There are 11 ambulance services covering England, which provide emergency access to health care.

Effects of Devolution

The services are organised slightly differently in each of the countries of the United Kingdom. The regional tier is absent, and the functions are provided either by the local health authorities or at national level.

Wales

During 1999 the National Assembly for Wales took on responsibility for the management and performance of the NHS in Wales. The reorganisation of NHS Wales came into effect on 1 October 2009.

The Chief Executive of NHS Wales is responsible for providing the Minister with policy advice and for exercising strategic leadership and management of the NHS.

The Chief Executive chairs the National Delivery Group, part of the Department for Health and Social Services, which is responsible for overseeing the development and delivery of NHS services across Wales.

Single local health organisations are responsible for delivering all health care services within a geographical area, rather than the Trust and Local Health Board (LHB) system that existed previously.

There are seven LHBs which plan, secure and deliver health care services in their areas.

There are three NHS Trusts in Wales with an all – Wales focus. These are:

(1) Welsh Ambulance Services Trust for emergency services
(2) Velindre NHS Trust for specialist services in cancer care
(3) Public Health Wales for public health issues.

NORTHERN IRELAND

In Northern Ireland the DH and Social Services is required to secure the provision of an integrated service designed to promote health and social welfare of the population.

The DH, Social Services and Public Safety is part of the Northern Ireland Executive. It has overall authority for health and social care services.

In 2007 the Health and Social Care Board was merged alongside the Public Health Agency. The agency advises and the board spends the current budget of around £4 billion. Services are commissioned by the Health and Social Care Board and provided by five local health and social care trusts. Each trust manages its own staff and services and controls its own budget.

Ambulance Services in Northern Ireland are provided by the Northern Ireland Ambulance Service HSC Trust.

GPs are represented on local commissioning groups in each of the five health trusts. They have minimal spending power – theirs is more of an advisory role.

The Board is also directly responsible for managing contracts for family health services provided by GPs, dentists, opticians and community pharmacists. These are all services not provided by health and social care trusts.

SCOTLAND

The Scottish Health Service is responsible to the Scottish Parliament.

The NHS in Scotland is led by the Director General of the Health and Social Care Directorate and Chief Executive of NHS Scotland. He or she is responsible to The Cabinet Secretary for Health, Wellbeing and Cities and to The Minister for Public Health.

There is a Health and Social Care Management Board.

The Health and Social Care Directorates has four Chief Professional Officers, including a Chief Pharmacist.

The Health and Social Care Directorate:

- helps people sustain and improve their health, especially in disadvantaged communities
- ensures better, local and faster access to health care
- allocates resources

- sets the strategic direction for NHS Scotland
- develops and implements health and social care policy.

NHS Scotland consists of:

- Fourteen regional NHS Boards that are responsible for the protection and the improvement of their population's health and for the delivery of front line health care services. Each NHS Board is accountable to Scottish Ministers, supported by the Scottish Government Health and Social Care Directorates.
- Seven Special NHS Boards and one public health body who support the regional NHS Boards by providing a range of important specialist and national services.

NHS Health Scotland:[17]

- Promotes ways to improve the health of the population and reduce health inequalities.

NHS National Waiting Times Centre:[18]

- Ensures prompt access to first-class treatment.

NHS 24:[19]

- Provides health advice and information.

Scottish Ambulance Service:[20]

- Responds to accident and emergency calls.

The State Hospitals Board for Scotland:[21]

- Provides assessment, treatment and care in secure hospitals for individuals with a mental disorder and dangerous, violent or criminal behaviour.

NHS National Services Scotland:[22]

- Supplies health protection, blood transfusion and information.

The public health body is Healthcare Improvement Scotland. Its purpose is to support health care providers in Scotland to deliver high-quality, evidence-based, safe, effective and person-centred care, and to scrutinise those services to provide public assurance about the quality and safety of that care.

Self-Assessment Questions

1. Explain the main bodies which are responsible for the governance of the NHS?

   Answer: Five main bodies are responsible for the overall governance of the NHS – The DH, the NHS CB, the NICE, the CQC and Monitor.

2. What is an NHS CB?

   Answer: NHS CB is a new non-departmental independent public body accountable to the Secretary of State for Health. The Board is nationally accountable for the outcomes achieved by the NHS and provides leadership for the new commissioning system. It supports the CCGs, allocates resources and commissions certain services, such as primary care, including pharmacy. It holds CCGs to account for the quality of services they commission.

3. What are CCGs?

   Answer: CCGs are groups of GPs and others which are formed into corporate statutory bodies. They are responsible for designing local health services in England. They do this by commissioning or buying the majority of health and care services.

ADDITIONAL RESOURCES

1. http://www.monitor-nhsft.gov.uk/home/browse-category/guidance-applicants/model-core-constitution
2. http://www.dh.gov.uk/prod_consum_dh/groups/dh_digitalassets/@dh/@en/documents/digital-asset/dh_4126018.pdf
3. http://www.guardian.co.uk/society/2013/mar/12/nhs-commissioning-board-launches
4. http://www.guardian.co.uk/society/2013/mar/12/clinical-commissioning-groups-nhs-direction
5. http://www.hsj.co.uk/Journals/2011/12/20/g/q/e/Public-Health-Englands-Operating-Model-all-factsheets-with-cover.pdf
6. http://www.cqc.org.uk/
7. http://www.nhs.uk/ServiceDirectories/Pages/Trust.aspx?id=T1430
8. http://www.nhs.uk/ServiceDirectories/Pages/Trust.aspx?id=T1510
9. http://www.nhs.uk/ServiceDirectories/Pages/Trust.aspx?id=T1480
10. http://www.nhs.uk/ServiceDirectories/Pages/Trust.aspx?id=T1190
11. http://www.nhs.uk/ServiceDirectories/Pages/Trust.aspx?id=T1460
12. http://www.nhs.uk/ServiceDirectories/Pages/Trust.aspx?id=T1450
13. http://www.nhs.uk/ServiceDirectories/Pages/Trust.aspx?id=T1470
14. http://www.nhs.uk/ServiceDirectories/Pages/Trust.aspx?id=T1150
15. http://www.nhs.uk/ServiceDirectories/Pages/Trust.aspx?id=T1490
16. http://www.nhs.uk/ServiceDirectories/Pages/Trust.aspx?id=T1440
17. http://www.healthscotland.com/
18. http://www.nhsgoldenjubilee.co.uk/home/
19. http://www.nhs24.com/content/
20. http://www.scottishambulance.com/
21. http://www.tsh.scot.nhs.uk/
22. http://www.nhsnss.org/

Chapter 3

NHS Pharmaceutical Services in the Community

Sections 126–169 of the amended NHS Act 2006 now deal with pharmaceutical services (PS). In addition there are a number of regulations dealing with these services in detail.

THE DUTY

Arrangements for Pharmaceutical Services in England

The NHS Commissioning Board (NHS CB) is under a duty to arrange for the supply of pharmaceutical services to patients in England.

According to the amended *Section 126(3)* of the NHS Act 2006, the Board must make arrangements for the provision to persons who are in England of:

(a) *Proper and sufficient drugs and medicines and listed appliances which are ordered for those persons by a medical practitioner in pursuance of his or her functions in the health service, the Scottish health service, the Northern Ireland health service or the armed forces of the Crown.*

(b) *Proper and sufficient drugs and medicines and listed appliances which are ordered for those persons by a dental practitioner in pursuance of:*
  (i) *his or her functions in the health service, the Scottish health service or the Northern Ireland health service (other than functions exercised in pursuance of the provision of services mentioned in paragraph (c)), or*
  (ii) *his or her functions in the armed forces of the Crown.*

(c) *Listed drugs and medicines and listed appliances which are ordered for those persons by a dental practitioner in pursuance of the provision of primary dental services or equivalent services in the Scottish health service or the Northern Ireland health service.*

(d) *Such drugs and medicines and such listed appliances as may be determined by the Secretary of State for the purposes of this paragraph, and which are ordered for those persons by a prescribed description of person in accordance with such conditions, if any, as may be prescribed, in pursuance of functions in the health service, the Scottish health service, the Northern Ireland health service or the armed forces of the Crown.*

(e) *Such other services as may be prescribed.*

Pharmacy Law and Practice. DOI: http://dx.doi.org/10.1016/B978-0-12-394289-0.00003-5

Briefly

In short the Board must arrange for the supply of 'proper and sufficient drugs and medicines and listed appliances' when they are ordered by a medical practitioner or other authorised prescriber under the NHS. The Board cannot provide PS itself.

The Board is responsible for:

- Keeping pharmaceutical lists
- Governing market entry applications
- Commissioning pharmaceutical and local pharmaceutical services
- Dealing with essential small pharmacies

The services which are so provided are known as 'pharmaceutical services'. The details of those arrangements are dealt with by regulations made under *Section 126(2)*. The current regulations are the NHS (PS & LPS) REgulations 2013 SI No.349.

The Secretary of State for Health will retain ultimate accountability for securing the provision of NHS services by holding the NHS CB to account.

PS consist of:

(1) the supply of drugs and medicines as above
(2) the supply of appliances
(3) the provision of certain 'additional professional services'
(4) the supply of contraceptive substances and appliances.

PS may be provided by:

(1) pharmacists
(2) pharmacy companies
(3) appliance contractors.

Authorised Prescribers

The other authorised prescribers referred to in *Section 126(3)(d)* are:

(a) persons who are registered in the register maintained under Article 5 of the Health Professions Order 2001;
(b) registered pharmacists;
(c) registered dental care professionals;
(d) optometrists;
(e) registered osteopaths;
(f) registered chiropractors;
(g) registered nurses or registered midwives;
(h) persons not mentioned above who are registered in any register established, continued or maintained under an Order in Council under *Section 60(1)* of the Health Act 1999 (c. 8);
(i) any other health professionals the Secretary of State specifies.

HEALTH PROFESSIONS COUNCIL REGISTER

The Health Professions Council maintains the register referred to above. The Council regulates 15 health professions. They are:

(1) arts therapists
(2) biomedical scientists
(3) chiropodists/podiatrists
(4) clinical scientists
(5) dietitians
(6) hearing aid dispensers
(7) occupational therapists
(8) operating department practitioners
(9) orthoptists
(10) paramedics
(11) physiotherapists
(12) practitioner psychologists (e.g. clinical psychologists)
(13) prosthetists and orthotists
(14) radiographers
(15) speech and language therapists.

Not all of the health professionals registered by the Health Professions Council have the right to prescribe prescription only medicines (POMs) or to prescribe under the NHS.

Additional Pharmaceutical Services (*Section 127*)

(1) *The Secretary of State may:*
   (a) *give directions to the Board requiring it to arrange for the provision to persons in England of additional PS, or*
   (b) *by giving directions to the Board authorise it to arrange for such provision if it wishes to do so.*
(2) *Directions under this section may require or authorise the Board to arrange for the provision of a service by means such that the person receiving it does so otherwise than at the premises from which it is provided.*
(3) *The Secretary of State must publish any directions under this section in the Drug Tariff (DT) or in such other manner as he considers appropriate.*

Persons Authorised to Provide Pharmaceutical Services

Unless regulations provide otherwise, arrangements for the dispensing of medicines may only be made with pharmacists or pharmacy companies.

The regulations do not provide otherwise.

S132 (1) Except as may be provided for by or under regulations, no arrangements may be made by the Board with a medical practitioner or dental practitioner under which he is required or agrees to provide pharmaceutical services to any person to whom he is rendering primary medical services or primary dental services.

> *(2) Except as may be provided for by or under regulations, no arrangements for the dispensing of medicines may be made under this Chapter with persons other than persons who:*
>
> > *(a) are registered pharmacists or persons lawfully conducting a retail pharmacy business in accordance with section 69 of the Medicines Act 1968 (c. 67), and*
> >
> > *(b) undertake that all medicines supplied by them under the arrangements will be dispensed either by or under the supervision of a registered pharmacist.*

Regulations do, however, provide for general medical practitioners (GMPs) to provide medicines to:

(1) patients living in a rural area, more than 1.6 km from a pharmacy;

(2) patients who have satisfied the Board that they have serious difficulty in obtaining drugs or appliances from a pharmacy because of its distance or the poor communications.

THE CONTRACT

The 'contract' which governs the relationship between the Board and the pharmacy is not contained in any single document, despite the size of the Contract Regulations, but consists of an amalgam of parts from various documents.

The nature of the arrangements between the previous Primary Care Trusts (PCTs) (and their predecessors) and those professionals providing the services to patients has been discussed by the courts. In 1968 the courts decided that the pharmacy had a contract with the Executive Council (a predecessor to the PCT) to provide services (*Appleby v. Sleep, 2 AER 265*). Other views have since been expressed that there is no contract as such, merely an administrative arrangement set out in regulations   (*Roy v. Kensington & Chelsea, FPC 1992 1AER 705 (HL)*).

CONTRACTORS OBLIGATIONS

The contract is made up of three service levels.

Under the 2013 Regulations there are three different levels of service provision:

(1) essential

(2) advanced

(3) enhanced.

Essential services are provided by all contractors, but contractors can choose whether they wish to provide advanced and enhanced services.

Advanced services can be provided by all contractors who have met accreditation requirements. They are currently set out in the Pharmaceutical Services (Advanced and Enhanced Services) (England) Directions 2012.

Enhanced services are commissioned locally by the NHS CB in response to the needs of the local population.

Components of Essential Service

Under their contract with a PCT pharmacists are obliged to:

(a) dispense all NHS prescriptions presented to them, within a reasonable time;

(b) maintain certain minimum hours of opening;

(c) provide on request an estimate of the time when the prescription will be ready;

(d) where required check evidence of entitlement to exemption or remission of charges;

(e) give advice to patients about the medicines;

(f) maintain patient medication records;

(g) dispose of unwanted drugs;

(h) promote healthy lifestyle messages to the public;

(i) provide information about other health and social care providers and support;

(j) provide advice and support to people caring for themselves or for their families;

(k) allow certain persons to inspect the premises;

(l) participate in clinical governance.

Advanced Services

Advanced services can be provided by all contractors who have met the accreditation requirements.

Advanced services include:

- Medicines Use Review (MUR) and Prescription Intervention Service
- New Medicine Service (NMS)
- Appliance Use Review Service
- Stoma Appliance Customisation Service.

Enhanced Services

Enhanced services are commissioned by the Board according to their local needs.

These include:

- minor ailments service
- smoking cessation
- supervised administration of medication
- needle and syringe exchange schemes

- anticoagulant monitoring
- care home support
- Patient Group Direction (PGD) services
- clinical medication reviews
- palliative care services
- head lice management services
- gluten free food supply services
- services to schools
- out-of-hours services
- supplementary and independent prescribing by pharmacists
- medicines assessment and compliance support.

TERMS OF SERVICE

When a contractor applies to be entered on the list of NHS pharmacies, he or she agrees to the terms of service (TOS), which are contained in Schedule 4 of the NHS (Pharmaceutical and Local Pharmaceutical Services) Regulations 2013, SI No.349.

The TOS incorporate:

- the DT; and
- the parts of the Local Involvement Networks (LINks) (duty of service providers to allow entry) Regulations which concern entry and inspection of premises.

As a breach of any of these terms may result in disciplinary proceedings (see later), it is important that they be clearly understood. Each paragraph contains a number of requirements. Failure to comply with any one of them may give rise to a breach.

The requirements of these TOS are absolute. An error is just as much a breach as is a deliberate fraud. For instance, the supply of the wrong drug, in error, will constitute a breach.

However, the TOS are not all-embracing. For instance, they do not cover errors on dispensing labels, although such an error might give rise to criminal proceedings under the Medicines Act.

There may be specific requirements for any directed services.

Fundamental Requirements of the TOS

The fundamental requirement is to supply what is ordered.

Paragraph 4 states that: 'An NHS pharmacist must, to the extent that paragraphs 5 to 9 require and in the manner described in those paragraphs, provide proper and sufficient drugs and appliances to persons presenting prescriptions for drugs or appliances ordered by health care professionals in pursuance of their functions in the health service, the Scottish health service or the Northern Ireland health service'.

Paragraph 5(2) subject to the following provisions of this Part, where:

*(a)   any person presents to an NHS Pharmacist (P) a non-electronic prescription
        form which contains:*
  *(i)   an order for drugs, not being Scheduled drugs, or for appliances, not
          being restricted availability appliances, signed by a prescriber,*
  *(ii) an order for a drug specified in Schedule 2 to the Prescription of Drugs
          Regulations(1) (drugs, medicines and other substances that may be
          ordered only in certain circumstances), signed by a prescriber and
          including the reference "SLS", or*
  *(iii) an order for a restricted availability appliance, signed by a prescriber
          and including the reference "SLS"; or*
*(b)   subject to sub-paragraph (4), P receives from the Electronic Prescription
        Service an electronic prescription form which contains an order of a kind
        specified in paragraph (a)(i) to (iii) and:*
  *(i)   any person requests the provision of drugs or appliances in accordance
          with that prescription, or*
  *(ii) P has previously arranged with the patient that P will dispense that
          prescription on receipt.*
*P must, with reasonable promptness, provide the drugs so ordered, and such of the
appliances so ordered as P supplies in the normal course of business.*

Promptness

A pharmacy must supply 'with reasonable promptness'.   (Paragraph 5(2))

In the past, Discipline Committees have generally taken the view that most medicines should be supplied either from stock in the pharmacy or from the next reasonable wholesaler delivery. They have also taken into account the nature of the condition being treated and the rarity or scarcity of the medicine. The situation which frequently causes problems is where the patient is repeatedly asked to return to the pharmacy to collect an item alleged to be on order but which has not been delivered. This may have resulted from failure to provide an effective system for passing on messages between members of staff, or to 'progress chase' items on order. Breaches of the requirement to provide promptly have been found where a delay of several days occurred.

Paragraph 7(1) requires the pharmacy to give, on request, an estimate of the time when the completed prescription will be ready for collection. If the prescription is not ready at that estimated time, a revised estimate must then be given.

Refusal to Provide Drugs or Appliances Ordered

A pharmacy must supply any person who presents a valid form. However, Paragraph 9 sets out situations where the pharmacist may refuse supply. These are:

- the pharmacist believes the form is stolen or a forgery took place;
- there is an error on the form;
- supply would be contrary to the pharmacist's clinical judgement;

- there is a threat of violence;
- the person presenting the form, or someone accompanying him commits or threatens to commit a criminal offence;
- there are technical reasons not to supply a repeatable prescription (see later);
- a review is required of the treatment ordered on a repeatable prescription.

In the last case the pharmacist must inform the prescriber.

Such Drugs as May Be So Ordered

A pharmacy must supply any drugs ordered on a prescription form by a prescriber except those covered by the Selected List rules. The requirement is to supply the drugs ordered on the form, not any similar drugs. This provision therefore prohibits the supply of generic equivalents. It also prohibits the supply of parallel imports (PIs) where the name used on the product is different from that on the form. This provision has the somewhat unusual effect of occasionally requiring the pharmacist to supply an import where the prescriber's poor spelling has unwittingly produced the foreign name.

Where the wrong drug is supplied in error it will constitute a breach of Paragraph 5(1).

There are additional rules governing the prescribing and supply of Schedule 2 drugs. These are dealt with later.

Dentists may only prescribe from the Secretary of State's list which is in the DT. Although the list is in generic terms, it is accepted that proprietary products fitting those generic descriptions may be ordered and supplied.

Appliances

A pharmacist is only required to supply those appliances which he or she normally supplies in the course of business.

Prescription Forms

The expression 'prescription form' means a form supplied to enable persons to obtain PS as defined by the Act.[1]

A 'non-electronic prescription form' means a form for ordering a drug or appliance which is:

(a) provided by a Health Board, the Regional Health and Social Care Board, a Local Health Board, the NHS CB, NHS Trust or an NHS Foundation Trust (FT) for use by a prescriber;
(b) issued by a prescriber; and
(c) does not indicate that the drug or appliance ordered may be provided more than once.

Examples of images of prescription forms can be found here.[2]
Examples of current and out-of-date prescription forms can be found here.[3]

The term includes both 'electronic prescription form and a non-electronic prescription form'.   (Regulation 2(1) of the 2012 Regulations)

An 'electronic prescription form' means data created in an electronic form for the purpose of ordering a drug or appliance, which:

(a) is signed with a prescriber's advanced electronic signature;

(b) is transmitted as an electronic communication to a nominated dispensing contractor by the Electronic Prescription Service; and

(c) does not indicate that the drug or appliance ordered may be provided more than once.

An 'electronic repeatable prescription means data created in an electronic form, which:

(a) is signed with a repeatable prescriber's advanced electronic signature;

(b) is transmitted as an electronic communication to a nominated dispensing contractor by the Electronic Prescription Service;

(c) indicates that the drugs or appliances ordered may be provided more than once; and

(d) specifies the number of occasions on which they may be provided.

Signed

Paragraph 5(1) requires the prescriptions to be signed either actually or by means of an electronic signature.

An 'advanced electronic signature' means an electronic signature which is:

(a) uniquely linked to the signatory;

(b) capable of identifying the signatory;

(c) created using means that the signatory can maintain under his or her sole control; and

(d) linked to the data to which it relates in such a manner that any subsequent change of data is detectable.

Services may only be provided on receipt of a signed form, except in emergency. Accordingly unless the form is signed no drugs can be supplied. It also follows that an amendment agreed over the phone with the prescribing doctor does not take effect until either the doctor requests an emergency supply or he or she signs the original form again. In some circumstances, pharmacists will have to balance the possibility of a service case against the need for the patient to have the medicine.

The prescription forms education package is available here.[4]

Supervision of Dispensing

The dispensing of medicines must be by or under the direct supervision of a pharmacist. A company must undertake that all medicines supplied by them under the Act shall be dispensed by or under the direct supervision of a pharmacist (s.132 NHS Act 2006 as amended).

There are requirements with respect to supply in the Medicines Act and the Human Medicines Regulations 2012 – see Chapter 12

The Terms of Service state that:

8(2) Drugs or appliances so ordered shall be provided either by or under the direct supervision of a registered pharmacist.

That registered pharmacist must not be someone:

(a) who is disqualified from inclusion in a relevant list; or
(b) who is suspended from the General Pharmaceutical Council (GPhC) register.

Forgeries

Paragraph 9 states that a pharmacist may refuse to dispense a form which he or she believes is stolen or a forgery took place.

Exemption Declaration

Paragraph 7 requires the pharmacist to ask, in most cases, for evidence of entitlement to exemption.

Quality

Paragraph 8(5)of the TOS states that any drug which is provided as part of PS and included in the DT, the British National Formulary (BNF), the Dental Practitioner's Formulary (DPF), the European Pharmacopoeia (EP), or the British Pharmaceutical Codex (BPC) shall comply with the standard or formula specified in that publication.

The DT helpfully adds: Any drugs which are not included in the DT (or the publications listed in Paragraph 8(5) of the TOS) must be of a grade or quality not lower than that ordinarily used for medicinal purposes.

The DT contains a list of galenicals and generic medicines.

If he or she wishes the prescriber can specify a different standard, for example, by specifically referring to a foreign pharmacopoeia.

Where a prescription calls for a generic drug which is included in a monograph in one of the listed publications, the product supplied must comply with the relevant monograph and not just with the generic description.

Quantity

The quantity which is ordered should be supplied, unless the provisions of Paragraph 8(1) apply. This sub-paragraph was originally inserted into the TOS in 1965 in order to allow for the change-over from the old apothecary system of measures to metric measurements. An agreed system of conversion allowed apothecary measures to be converted into an approximate metric equivalent, for example, 12 fluid ounces into 300 ml.

In practice, flexibility is allowed for items which are supplied in special containers to protect the contents, and for creams supplied in tubes.

The DT allows payment to be made on the basis that the total amount in the special container has been ordered, but such a supply is strictly outside the requirements of the Medicines Act 1968.

Missing Details on Script

Paragraph 8(6) allows the pharmacist to fill in certain missing details of quantity, strength and dosage.

Where the prescription is for a drug other than a CD in Schedule 4 or 5, and the quantity, strength or dose is missing, the pharmacist may use his or her judgement to decide the missing information. He or she may give up to 5 days treatment at the appropriate dose. Where the product is a liquid antibiotic, an oral contraceptive or a combination pack he or she may give the smallest original pack even if that quantity is larger than a 5-day course.

Paragraph 8(6) states:

If the order is an order for a drug; but is not an order for a controlled drug within the meaning of the Misuse of Drugs Act 1971, other than a drug which is for the time being specified in Schedule 4 or 5 to the Misuse of Drugs Regulations 2001, and does not prescribe its quantity, strength or dosage, a pharmacist may provide the drug in such strength and dosage as in the exercise of his professional skill, knowledge and care he considers to be appropriate and subject to sub-paragraph (7), in such quantity as he considers to be appropriate for a course of treatment for a period not exceeding five days.

Where the strength or dosage is missing, the pharmacist has complete freedom to supply what is appropriate. Note that where the wrong strength is given the pharmacist is not authorised by the regulations to change it. NHS Prescription Services interprets the regulations as requiring the doctor to initial any alteration to the prescription which alters the strength ordered.

Professional practice requires that where an overdose is inadvertently ordered the pharmacist should reduce the dose to a safe one and discuss his or her action with the prescriber as soon as possible.

COURSE OF TREATMENT PACKS

Where an order to which sub-paragraph (6) of Paragraph 8 applies is for:

(a) an oral contraceptive substance,
(b) a drug, which is available for supply as part of PS only together with one or more drugs, or

(c) an antibiotic in a liquid form for oral administration in respect of which pharmaceutical considerations require its provision in an unopened package,

which is not available for supply as part of PS except in such packages that the minimum available package contains a quantity appropriate to a course of treatment for a patient for a period of more than 5 days, the chemist may provide that minimum available package.

DISPENSING FROM BULK

The TOS make special provision for dealing with products which are difficult to dispense from bulk.

Paragraph 8(8)

Where any drug to which this paragraph applies (i.e. a drug that is not one to which the Misuse of Drugs Act 1971 applies, unless it is a drug which is for the time being specified in Schedule 4 or 5 to the Misuse of Drugs Regulations 2001) ordered by a prescriber on a prescription form, is available for provision by a chemist in a pack in a quantity which is different to the quantity which has been so ordered, and that drug is:

    (a) sterile
    (b) effervescent or hygroscopic
    (c) a liquid preparation for addition to bath water
    (d) a coal tar preparation
    (e) a viscous preparation
    (f) packed at the time of its manufacture in a special container,

the pharmacist must provide the drug in the pack, whose quantity is nearest to the quantity which has been so ordered.

'Special container' means 'any container with an integral means of application or from which it is not practicable to dispense an exact quantity'.

Original Packs

Where a drug is ordered in a quantity that is readily available as an original pack (or in multiples of that quantity), the pharmacy must provide the drug in an original pack (or packs) of that size unless:

(a) it is not possible to obtain such a pack (or packs) with reasonable promptness in the normal course of business; or
(b) it is not practicable to provide such a pack (or packs) in response to the order (e.g., because of patient needs or the method of administration of the drug). (Paragraph 8(10))

Emergency NHS Supplies

Paragraph 6 deals with 'urgent supply without a prescription'. In an emergency a pharmacy may supply a drug, provided that it is not:

(a) a Scheduled drug, nor a controlled drug other than in Schedule 4 or 5, and
(b) the prescriber undertakes to give the pharmacy a prescription within 72 h of the request being made.

The pharmacist is enabled to supply before the form arrives. He or she is not obliged to do so.

Selected List

In 1985 the government introduced, by means of Regulations, the 'Selected List Scheme'. Doctors were prohibited from prescribing, and pharmacists from dispensing a number of medicines in various categories. The categories were:

indigestion remedies
laxatives
analgesics for mild to moderate pain
bitters and tonics
vitamins
benzodiazepine tranquillisers and sedatives.

Most of the medicines in these categories were put in Schedule 1 to the Regulations. Medicines listed on the Schedule may not be prescribed or dispensed under the NHS. Generic products were unaffected.

In December 1992 the department announced that the scheme would be extended to an additional 10 categories:

anti-diarrhoeal drugs
drugs for allergic disorders
hypnotics and anxiolytics
appetite suppressants
drugs for vaginal and vulval conditions
contraceptives
drugs used in anaemia
topical antirheumatics
drugs acting on the ear and nose
drugs acting on the skin

The current list is in Schedule 1 to the NHS (General Medical Services Contracts) (Prescription of Drugs) Regulations 2004, SI No. 629. References in the TOS to 'Scheduled drug' refer to medicines listed on that Schedule. The list of products is amended from time to time. An up-to-date list is included in the current DT.

Schedule 2 contains a list of medicines which can only be prescribed for certain listed conditions, and then only if the prescription form is endorsed by the prescriber with the initials 'SLS'.

Paragraph 8(11)

A pharmacy must only provide a Scheduled drug in response to an order by name, formula or other description on a prescription form or repeatable prescription if:

(a) it is ordered as specified in sub-paragraph (12); or
(b) in the case of a drug specified in Schedule 2 to the Prescription of Drugs Regulations (drugs, medicines and other substances that may be ordered only in certain circumstances), it is ordered in the circumstances prescribed in that Schedule.

Paragraph 8(12)

A Scheduled drug that is a drug with an appropriate non-proprietary name may be provided in response to an order on a prescription form or repeatable prescription for a drug ('the prescribed drug') that is not a Scheduled drug but which has the same non-proprietary name as the Scheduled drug if:

(a) the prescribed drug is ordered by that non-proprietary name or by its formula;
(b) the prescribed drug has the same specification as the Scheduled drug (so the Scheduled drug may be dispensed generically); and
(c) the Scheduled drug is not in a pack which consists of a drug in more than one strength, and providing it would involve the supply of part only of the pack.

Paragraph 8(13)

If a Scheduled drug is a combination of more than one drug, it can only be ordered as specified in sub-paragraph (12) if the combination has an appropriate non-proprietary name, whether or not the drugs in the combination each have such names.

Paragraph 8(13) is intended to catch certain products containing a number of constituent drugs.

Containers

Paragraph 8(14)

A pharmacist shall provide any drug which he or she is required to provide under Paragraph 5 in a suitable container. The DT expands this requirement:

- Capsules, tablets, pills, pulvules, etc., shall be supplied in airtight containers of glass, aluminium or rigid plastics.
- Card containers may be used only for foil/strip packed tablets, etc.

- Card containers shall not be used for ointments, creams or pastes.
- Eye, ear and nasal drops shall be supplied in dropper bottles or with a separate dropper where appropriate.

Doses Less than 5 ml

In 1992 the previous 'dilution convention' agreed between the Royal Pharmaceutical Society of Great Britain (RPSGB) and the British Medical Association (BMA), under which doses of less than 5 ml were diluted, was abandoned. Under the new agreement doses of less than 5 ml are to be measured by the patient using an oral syringe. The medicine is to be dispensed undiluted. The syringe must comply with the appropriate British or European standard. Patients requiring an oral syringe are to be supplied with one, without charge.

- When an oral liquid medicine is dispensed, a 5 ml plastic spoon or 1, 5 or 10 ml plastic oral syringe shall be supplied by the pharmacist unless the manufacturer's pack includes one.

Contraceptive Services

The supply of contraceptive substances and appliances forms part of the 'pharmaceutical services' to be provided. All contraceptive substances are available, but only those appliances included in the DT. For example, diaphragms are included in the DT, but condoms are not.

Under the provisions of SI 1975/719 a pharmacist could notify the Family Health Service Authority (FHSA) that he or she wished to be excluded from the arrangements for the supply of contraceptive substances. It was intended to take account of religious or moral objections to contraception. The provision disappeared from the Regulations in 1987, when an amendment (SI 1987/401) replaced the existing Regulation 26 with a new version which omitted the 'conscience clause'. It is also missing from the current Contract Regulations. When applying for a contract the pharmacist can specify the services he or she intends to provide. This would seem to be an opportunity to indicate any religious or moral restrictions on the service.

Contractors are only required to supply such appliances as they normally stock, so no problem arises with contraceptive appliances.

Opening Hours

Part 3 of Schedule 4 of the 2013 Regulations deals with opening hours.

Except where the pharmacist has agreed to open for not less than 100 h, PS shall be provided at the premises for not less than 40 h each week.

The NHS CB can direct a pharmacy to open for more than 40 h, or it can allow fewer hours. Where the NHS CB allows a variation from 40 h it may set the times and days of opening.

When doing this the NHS CB must seek to ensure that the hours of opening are such as to ensure that services are provided on such days and at such times as are necessary to meet the needs of people in the neighbourhood or other likely users of the pharmacy.

Each pharmacy must provide the NHS CB with opening hours and a list of services. Any change must also be notified to the NHS CB.

Notices

Each pharmacy, except a mail order or Internet pharmacy, must display:

(a) a notice which shows the opening hours;
(b) when the pharmacy is closed, a notice which indicates the addresses of other pharmacies nearby and their opening hours;
(c) when the pharmacy is closed, a notice which indicates the addresses of local pharmaceutical services (LPS) pharmacies nearby, their services and their opening hours.

Illness of Pharmacist

Where a chemist is prevented by illness or other reasonable cause from complying with his obligations under paragraph 23(1), he shall where practicable, make arrangements with one or more pharmacists or LPS pharmacists whose premises are situated in the neighbourhood for the provision of PS or LPS during that time.

The obligation to make alternative arrangements is with the affected pharmacy, but only when 'practicable'. The provision applies to illness or 'other reasonable cause'.

When alternative arrangements cannot be made, there is no breach of the TOS if there is a temporary suspension of services, provided:

- the NHS CB is notified as soon as practical;
- all reasonable endeavours are used to resume service as soon as possible. (Paragraph 22(9))

The TOS explicitly stated in Paragraph 23(11) that 'planned refurbishment' of a pharmacy is neither a 'reasonable cause' for the purposes of sub-paragraph (8) nor a 'reason beyond the control of the pharmacist' for the purposes of sub-paragraph (10).

CHANGES TO HOURS MADE BY THE NHS CB

Paragraph 24 deals with review of hours by the Board, in cases where it appears to them that the needs of the neighbourhood are not being met, and the Local Pharmaceutical Committees (LPC) must be consulted. The changes must be notified to the pharmacy. There is an appeal process.

Variation of Hours Instigated by the Pharmacy

Paragraph 26 deals with applications to vary the previous hours.

Provision of Advice to Patients

The pharmacist must provide appropriate advice to patients:

- about any drug or appliance provided to them
- about the safe keeping of the products
- about returning unwanted products to the pharmacy.

The advice is to enable patients to utilise the products appropriately and also to meet their 'reasonable needs' for general information.

The pharmacist must also:

- advise patients to only request repeats which are needed;
- provide owing slips and estimates when the product will be available;
- keep patient medication records, including in appropriate cases, of advice given and interventions made.   (Paragraph 10)

A pharmacist shall make all the necessary arrangements for measuring patients, and for fitting, when the appliance which is ordered requires this.   (Paragraph 8(4))

Disposal of Unwanted Drugs

Where the Board has made suitable arrangements the pharmacist must accept and dispose of unwanted drugs from:

- a private household
- a residential care home.

The pharmacist must carry out a risk assessment and train staff, on the handling of waste drugs, and have protective equipment available.   (Paragraph 13)

Healthy Lifestyle Messages

Where it appears to the pharmacist that a patient:

- has diabetes
- is at risk of coronary heart disease (CHD), especially with high blood pressure
- smokes or is overweight

then the pharmacist must, where appropriate, provide that person with advice aimed at increasing his or her knowledge and understanding of the relevant health issues. In addition to the advice the pharmacist may refer the patient elsewhere and/or give written material.   (Paragraph 16)

Where appropriate, records must be kept.

When requested by the Board, the pharmacy must participate in up to six public health campaigns each year. (Paragraph 18)

Signposting

Pharmacists must provide contact information to users of the pharmacy when it appears that they require advice, treatment or support that the pharmacist cannot provide, but which is available elsewhere in the health or social services. (Paragraphs 19, 20)

Records must be kept when appropriate.

Support for Self-Care

A pharmacist must provide advice and support to people caring for themselves or for their family:

- on treatment options and use of over-the-counter (OTC) medicines;
- on lifestyle changes. (Paragraph 21)

Records must be kept when appropriate.

Information to Be Provided to the NHS CB

Certain information about the pharmacist or the superintendent and directors of a company must be provided to the Board:

- information about criminal convictions, binding over, cautions, etc.;
- investigations into professional conduct by licensing, regulatory or other bodies;
- investigations by the NHS Counter Fraud and Security Management Service in relation to fraud;
- investigations by an equivalent body;
- removal or suspension on fitness to practise grounds from any equivalent list. (Paragraph 31)

A pharmacist shall tell the NHS CB of any change in the information recorded about him or her, including any change of private address, change in registered office of a company and any change affecting his inclusion in the Electronic Prescription Service (EPS) list.

Particulars of Qualified Staff

Paragraph 34

The NHS CB can require the name of any registered pharmacist employed in the dispensing of a particular prescription. (Paragraph 32)

Charges

Paragraph 36 states that subject to Regulations made under *Section 77* of the Act, all drugs, containers and appliances are to be supplied free.

The NHS (Charges for Drugs and Appliances) Regulations 2000, SI No. 620 are the ones made under *Section 77*. They are updated each year and contain the charges to be made for the supply of medicines and appliances.

Availability of Records

Paragraph 35 allows the NHS CB to inspect the pharmacy:

- to satisfy itself that the pharmacy is complying with the TOS
- to monitor and audit the provision for patient care
- to monitor and audit the management of the services.

There must be reasonable notice of entry, and the LPC should be invited to be present. Residential parts of the premises may only be inspected with permission.

Inducements

Paragraph 30

(1) An NHS pharmacist (including staff) must not give, promise or offer to any person any gift or reward (whether by way of a share of or dividend on the profits of the business or by way of discount or rebate or otherwise) as an inducement to or in consideration of:
   (a) presenting an order for drugs or appliances on a prescription form or repeatable prescription, non-electronic prescription form or non-electronic repeatable prescription;
   (b) nominating the pharmacy as the dispensing contractor (or one of them) in a patient's entry in the NHS Care Record; or
   (c) receiving from any directed services.
(2) Promising, offering or providing an auxiliary aid in relation to the supply of drugs or a home delivery service is not a gift or reward for the purposes of sub-paragraph (1).

This does not prohibit the supply of free controlled dosage systems to users of the pharmacy nor the availability of collection and delivery systems.

A gift which is not a medicine and which has a monetary value not exceeding £10 may be ignored for this purpose.

Professional Standards

Requirements as to professional standards were first inserted in 1996.
Paragraph 29 now reads:

An NHS pharmacist must provide pharmaceutical services and exercise any professional judgement in connection with the provision of such services in conformity with the standards generally accepted in the pharmaceutical profession.

The requirement refers to the 'generally accepted' standards. Although it does not specifically refer to the GPhC Standards, it is that document which will in most cases set out the generally accepted standards.

Complaints Procedure

NHS pharmacies are required to have in place a system for dealing with expressions of dissatisfaction by users of PS. The system should be essentially the same as that set out in the Local Authority Social Services and National Health Service Complaints (England) Regulations 2009. See also Chapter 9.

Self-Assessment Questions

1. Can the NHS CB provide PS?
   Answer: No.
2. Which patients can general practitioners (GPs) potentially provide with dispensed medicines?
   Answer: Patients living in a rural area, more than 1.6 km from a pharmacy, and patients who have satisfied the Board that they have serious difficulty in obtaining drugs or appliances from a pharmacy because of its distance or the poor communications. In both cases the correct procedures must be followed before supply can begin.
3. On what grounds can a community pharmacy refuse to supply the medicines on a prescription?
   Answer: If the pharmacist believes that the form is stolen or a forgery took place; if there is an error on the form; if the supply is contrary to the pharmacist's clinical judgement; if there is a threat of violence; if the person presenting the form, or someone accompanying him commits or threatens to commit a criminal offence; if there are technical reasons not to supply a repeatable prescription; if a review is required of the treatment ordered on a repeatable prescription.

ADDITIONAL RESOURCES

1. http://www.nhsbsa.nhs.uk/PrescriptionServices/Documents/prescription_form_types.pdf
2. http://www.google.co.uk/images?client=firefox-a&rls=org.mozilla%3Aen-GB%3Aofficial_s&hl=en-GB&q=prescription+forms+uk&gbv=2&gs
3. http://www.nhsbsa.nhs.uk/PrescriptionServices/Documents/PrescriptionServices/Current_and_Out_of_Date_Rx_Form_V3_Revised_Nov_2012.pdf
4. http://www.nhsbsa.nhs.uk/PrescriptionServices/1856.aspx

Chapter 4

The Drug Tariff

Reimbursement and Remuneration Structure for Community Pharmacy

Every month the NHS Prescription Services publishes the 'Drug Tariff' (DT). It contains:

- a list of drug prices;
- detailed information on appliances;
- rules to follow when dispensing NHS prescriptions, for example what can and cannot be prescribed on NHS prescriptions and by which class of practitioner;
- amount of fees and allowances to be paid.

Separate DTs are produced for England and Wales, Scotland and Northern Ireland.

NHS Prescription Services produces the DT on a monthly basis on behalf of the Department of Health (DH). It is supplied primarily to pharmacists and doctors surgeries.

Besides the list included in the Regulations (see below), the DT contains many other items of information useful to pharmacists and prescribers.[1]

LEGISLATIVE BASIS

Section 164 of the NHS Act 2006 as amended states:

(1) The remuneration to be paid to persons who provide pharmaceutical services under this Part must be determined by determining authorities.

(2) Determining authorities may also determine the remuneration to be paid to persons who provide those services in respect of the instruction of any person in matters relating to those services.

(3) For the purposes of this section and Section 165 determining authorities are:

    (a) the Secretary of State, and

    (b) so far as authorised by him to exercise the functions of determining authorities, the Board or other person appointed by him in an instrument.

(4) The instrument mentioned in 3(b) is called an 'instrument of appointment'.

Pharmacy Law and Practice. DOI: http://dx.doi.org/10.1016/B978-0-12-394289-0.00004-7

(5) An instrument of appointment:
*(a) may contain requirements with which a determining authority appointed
     by that instrument must comply in making determinations, and*
(b) may be contained in regulations.

Regulation 89 of the NHS (P & LPS) Regulations 2013 SI No. 349
states:

*(1) The DT referred to in Section 127(4) of the 2006 Act (arrangements for
     additional pharmaceutical services) is the aggregate of:*
*(a) the determinations of remuneration made by the Secretary of State,
     acting as a determining authority, under Section 164 of the 2006 Act(1)
     (remuneration for persons providing pharmaceutical services), but not
     the remuneration of dispensing doctors; and*
*(b) any other instruments that the Secretary of State is required by virtue of
     these Regulations or the 2006 Act to publish, or does publish, together
     with those determinations, in the publication known as the DT, which the
     Secretary of State shall publish in such format as the Secretary of State
     thinks fit.*
*(2) Determinations under Section 164 of the 2006 Act by the Secretary of State
     may be made by reference to:*
*(a) the drugs and appliances dispensed or expected to be dispensed in
     accordance with NHS prescriptions during a reference period determined
     by the Secretary of State;*
*(b) lists of published prices produced by suppliers of the drugs or appliances
     that are available from them on NHS prescription;*
*(c) scales, indices or other data that relate to volume and price that are
     produced by suppliers of the drugs or appliances that are available from
     them on NHS prescription; and*
*(d) any other scales, indices or other data (including formulae) by reference
     to which the Secretary of State considers it appropriate to make such
     a determination, and in these circumstances, the Secretary of State
     may provide that remuneration is to be determined by reference to data
     which is:*
(i)   in the form current at the time of the determination and
(ii) in any subsequent form taking effect after that time.
*(3) The DT is to include the arrangements for the claiming of payments by NHS
     chemists and the making of payments to NHS chemists under it, and:*
*(a) claims by NHS chemists for payments under the DT must be made in
     accordance with those arrangements; and*
(b) payments under the DT must be made:
(i)   by the Board and
*(ii) in accordance with those arrangements, subject as appropriate to
      any deduction that may or must be made in accordance either with
      those arrangements or with any provision of, or made under, the
      2006 Act (including the DT).*

DT FORMS PART OF PHARMACY CONTRACT

By virtue of Regulation 11 of the NHS (Pharmaceutical and Local Pharmaceutical Services) Regulations 2013, the DT lists of drugs and appliances are incorporated into the Terms Of Service (TOS). In other words, whatever is in the DT about prices to be paid for drugs and appliances is considered to be something which is agreed by the pharmacist on taking up the contract.

MONTHLY CHANGES

The DT is produced on a monthly basis and the amendments for the month are listed in the preface. The preface bears the words:

In accordance with Regulation 89(3) of the NHS (Pharmaceutical and Local Pharmaceutical Services) Regulations 2013 the Secretary of State for Health as respects England and in accordance with Regulation 18(e) of the National Health Service (PS) Regulations 1992, the Welsh Ministers have amended the Drug Tariff with effect from [date].

Amendments, including prices, come into effect on the date specified, regardless of whether the DT has been received by the pharmacist and regardless of whether the particular amendment has actually been printed in the DT.

BASIC PRINCIPLES OF PRESCRIBING AND DISPENSING IN NHS

The DT sets out much of the arrangement for prescribing and dispensing for NHS patients. The basic principles of prescribing under the NHS are that:

(1) Doctors may prescribe any medicine, unless its use at NHS expense is specifically prohibited by the Secretary of State or its use is restricted to specified circumstances.

(2) Doctors may prescribe an appliance or chemical reagent, only if its use at NHS expense is approved by the Secretary of State and only in the circumstances specified.

(3) Doctors may prescribe a 'borderline substance', only if its use at NHS expense is approved by the Secretary of State and only in the circumstances specified.

Pharmacists will be paid for any medicines (including over-the-counter (OTC) medicines, homoeopathic preparations and herbal products) provided the item does not appear in Schedule 1 of the NHS (General Medical Services (GMS) Contracts) (Prescription of Drugs, etc.) Regulations 2004, (the 'Black List'), which is reproduced in the DT as Part XVIIIA.

DT CLAUSES

Clause 1 requires that any drugs supplied must comply with the standard specified in the DT (if any such standard is included). Otherwise, the drug must comply with the relevant standard in the British National Formulary, Dental Practitioners' Formulary, European Pharmacopoeia, British Pharmacopoeia (BP) or British Pharmaceutical Codex (BPC). The prescriber may indicate that he requires some other standard. If the prescriber has not indicated the standard, and the drug does not appear in one of the relevant publications then the grade or quality must be no lower than that ordinarily used for medicinal purposes. There is no other requirement that the drugs or medicines supplied shall be licensed medicinal products (licensed under the Medicines Act 1968).

Clause 2 states that only the appliances listed in the DT may be supplied, and that they must comply with the specifications listed in the DT. Certain items in Part IXA are not prescribable on forms FP10 (CN) or FP10 (PN) and these are marked.

In practice, the 'Technical Specifications' of the DT were last issued as a separate document in 1981, although they are available on request from NHS Prescription Services. However, many of the individual entries contain details which in effect are specifications, for example the size of a bandage. Dressings are included in the category 'appliances'. Neither the NHS Act nor the Regulations refer to dressings as such except to define them as appliances.

Since June 1998, 'medical devices' (as defined in the Medical Devices Regulations 2002 (as amended)) which are supplied on prescription have been required to bear a CE mark.

Clause 3 states that only the chemical reagents listed may be supplied. According to *Section 275* of the NHS Act 2006, 'medicine' includes such chemical reagents as are included in a list approved by the Secretary of State for the purposes of *Section 126*.

Pharmacists are not required to ascertain the purpose for which prescribed items are to be used. All drugs may be supplied except those on Schedule 1. Pure chemical compounds, organic or inorganic may be supplied as drugs. Chemical reagents other than those listed could therefore be supplied, and the pharmacist would be paid for their supply.

Clause 4 states that the requirements for the Domiciliary Oxygen Theraphy Service (DOTS) are in Part X of the DT. However, the supply of oxygen by community pharmacies was discontinued by the DH in 2006. All oxygen therapy is supplied by designated contractors – there are four contractors that cover England and one of these also covers Wales.

NHS Boards and Health Facilities Scotland (HFS) (a division of NHS National Services Scotland) began introducing a centralised domiciliary oxygen supply system from May 2012 with an expectation that service rollout should be completed by November 2012.

Clause 5 deals with claims for payment. Forms must be endorsed, sorted and despatched as required by NHS Prescription Services or Health Solutions

Wales. The DT contains a number of rules about how prescription forms are to be handled in order for the correct payments to be made.

Failure to despatch the forms on time has previously been held to be a breach of the TOS. Occasional lateness is not considered to be a problem, but persistent and serious lateness is. The late submission of forms to the Pricing Authority causes extra costs and disrupts the system.

Clause 5A deals with the handling of forms for repeat dispensing services.

Clause 6 contains a brief description of the payment systems.

Clause 7 explains the way payments are calculated for drugs. Payment for the quantity supplied is calculated proportionately from the basic price. There is also a statement that if after being requested to properly endorse a form the contractor fails to do so, then the Secretary of State may decide the price.

Clause 8 states that the basic price for drugs, appliances and chemical reagents listed in Parts VIII and IX of the DT is the price in the DT. For other generic and branded drugs, it is the manufacturers' list price.

The Pricing Authority may, under specified circumstances, accept an endorsement that a price higher than the 'statutory maximum price' has been paid.

HOW MUST NHS PRESCRIPTION FORMS BE ENDORSED?

Rules for endorsing the forms are found in Clauses 9, 10 and 11, Part III and the Notes to Part VIII.

At the end of each calendar month, the contractor must sort the prescription forms in a manner directed by the NHS Commissioning Board. They must then be despatched, together with the appropriate claim form, not later than the fifth day of the next month.

The claim form is standard and also contains instructions for sorting.

The forms must be endorsed as required. The intention of endorsement is to ensure that the Pricing Authority has sufficient information to price accurately. The principle is that as far as possible the actual price paid by the pharmacist is paid by the NHS. Account is taken of the discounts obtained on purchases by averaging them and deducting an average discount from the totals of list prices.

Clause 9 contains the main endorsement requirements.

No endorsement is needed except for 'broken bulk' or where the quantity supplied differs from the order, for

(a) generic drugs listed in Part VIII;
(b) appliances listed in Part IX; and
(c) chemical reagents listed in Part IX.

The pack size and name of maker or wholesaler is needed for orders for generic drugs not in the DT.

Where no product is available to contractors at the Part VIII price, the prescription may be specially endorsed. This concession is only allowed when the Secretary of State has agreed that the product is not available. The contractor must have made all reasonable efforts to obtain the product at the DT price. The endorsement must include the brand name or manufacturer or wholesaler of the product, the pack size, the phrase 'no cheaper stock obtainable' (NCSO) and be signed and dated on behalf of the contractor.

The Prescription Pricing Authority (PPA) may request additional information in order to price the prescription.

Clause 10 details the provisions of Paragraph 8 of Schedule 4 of the 2013 Regulations. It allows the quantity supplied to deviate from the exact quantity ordered only in specified circumstances. These are instances where it is particularly difficult to open the container and dispense a part of its contents.

This applies to products which are:

* sterile;
* effervescent or hygroscopic;
* liquid products for addition to bath water;
* coal tar preparations;
* viscous external preparations;
* packed in a castor, collapsible tube, dropper bottle, pressurised aerosol, puffer pack, roll-on bottle, sachet, shaker, spray, squeeze pack, container with an integral means of application or any other container from which it is not practicable to dispense the exact quantity.

There is a list in Part II of products which are:

* liquid products for addition to bath water;
* coal tar preparations; or
* viscous external preparations.

Broken Bulk

Clause 11 sets out the rules whereby a contractor may be paid for the whole amount of a drug when less has been supplied. The rules appear to set out an objective test – that the remainder cannot readily be disposed of – whereas in practice a subjective test is used. The contractor may claim if he believes he will not readily dispose of the remainder. Subsequent supplies are deemed to have been made from the remainder for the next 6 months or until the remainder would in any event have been used up.

The Pricing Service interprets the 'broken bulk' facility by using a 'two-thirds' rule. If a contractor receives two or more prescriptions in the same calendar month, totalling more than two-thirds of a pack, the pricing authority assumes that this establishes usage and so considers the broken bulk claims as invalid.

In a service case where a contractor made a large number of broken bulk claims which were unjustified, the then FHSA decided that constituted a breach of the TOS and recommended a very large withholding. The conduct was also regarded as fraud by the Crown Court, resulting in a heavy fine.

Miscellaneous Matters

Clause 12. Out of pocket expenses over 50p may be claimed in certain circumstances.

Clause 13 extends the broken bulk rules in Clause 11 to allow for the payment of the full cost of using reconstituted products with a short life.

PRICES IN PART VIII

Part VIII contains a list of generic drugs which, if ordered on an NHS prescription, will be reimbursed to the pharmacy at the prices stated.

List Prices

Pharmacists are paid the DT basic price for dispensed medicines, less a discount as set out in Clause 6. If a drug is included in Part VIII, the price shown will be used for reimbursement regardless of what a pharmacist has dispensed to meet the order.

Exceptionally, when the DH has identified a shortage of a Part VIII generic, it may grant that product NCSO status. The pharmacist can endorse the form 'NCSO' and receive a payment based on what he has supplied.

For products ordered and supplied as a branded product, that DT basic price is the usual wholesale list price.

For generics, the price paid is usually set out in Part VIII. For products not listed, there the price will be the wholesale list price.

PART VIII CATEGORIES

Products in Part VIII are categorized according to the method used to determine the DT basic price. The category for each drug is shown in a column on the page.

Category A

The category contains drugs readily available as a generic. The reimbursement price is calculated from a weighted average of the list price from specific suppliers: AAH, Alliance Healthcare (Distribution) Ltd, Teva UK and Actavis.

Category B

This contains less common drugs. The reimbursement price is calculated from a weighted average of the list price from AAH, Alliance Healthcare (Distribution) Ltd, UCB Pharma and Thornton & Ross.

Category C

These drugs are not readily available as a generic. The price is based on the list price of a particular brand, manufacturer or supplier.

Category M

This category also contains drugs which are readily available as a generic. However, in this case the reimbursement price is calculated by the DH based on information submitted by manufacturers.[2]

Data collected for the latest quarter from manufacturers is analysed over the following quarter and is used to determine individual drug reimbursement for the quarter after that.

The Category M scheme is a voluntary (non-contractual) one made by the Secretary of State and the representative industry body within the meaning of *Section 261* of the NHS Act 2006. For the purpose of this agreement, the Secretary of State recognises the British Generic Manufacturers Association (BGMA) as the appropriate industry body as set out in *Section 266(6)* of the NHS Act 2006.

All companies supplying generic medicines are able to join the relevant scheme.

Those which do not join this Scheme or which are denied membership in accordance with the Scheme are subject to any statutory scheme setup under *Sections 262–264* of the NHS Act 2006. *Sections 262–264* of the NHS Act 2006 govern the price that may be charged for NHS medicines and the level of profit derived from their sale through statutory schemes.

Those sections do not apply to members of this Scheme.

The current scheme is intended to operate until 1 January 2014.

Details of the scheme may be found here.[3]

THE BLACKLIST AND THE SELECTED LIST

Any food, drug, toiletry or cosmetic may be prescribed on an NHS prescription unless the product is listed in Part XVIIIA of the DT. In 1984, the Government issued a list of preparations which would no longer be prescribable on NHS prescriptions. Initially, seven categories of medicine were examined and a selected range of drugs would be available on the NHS in seven categories: antacids, laxatives, analgesics for mild-to-moderate pain, cough and cold remedies, bitters and tonics, vitamins, and tranquillisers and sedatives.

The products excluded were mainly those which were ineffective, too expensive or with no medicinal use. Many were products which could be bought OTC. The DH estimated the change would mean a saving of £75–100 million.

The Blacklist

The 'Blacklist' is found in Schedule 1 to the NHS (GMS Contracts) (Prescription of Drugs, etc.) Regulations 2004 which is reproduced in Part XVIIIA of the DT.

According to Regulation 2 of NHS (GMS Contracts) (Prescription of Drugs, etc.) Regulations 2004:

A drug, medicine or other substance listed in Schedule 1 may not be ordered for patients in the provision of medical services under a GMS Contract.

The Selected List

The 'Selected List' is found in Schedule 2 to the NHS (GMS Contracts) (Prescription of Drugs, etc.) Regulations 2004 which is reproduced in Part XVIIIB of the DT.

According to Regulation 3 of NHS (GMS Contracts) (Prescription of Drugs, etc.) Regulations 2004:

A drug, medicine or other substance specified in an entry in column 1 of Schedule 2 may not be ordered for a patient in the provision of medical services under a GMS Contract unless:
that patient is a person of a description mentioned in column 2 of that entry and that drug, medicine or other substance is prescribed for that patient only for the purpose specified in column 3 of that entry.

The items included on the list may only be prescribed for the patient groups and for the purpose listed in the Tariff. The pharmacist is under no obligation to verify these.

Prescribers must endorse prescriptions for these products 'SLS'. If the 'SLS' endorsement is missing, the prescription should not be dispensed and will not be passed for payment by the NHS Prescription Services. Pharmacy staff cannot make the SLS endorsement.

Appliances

Only the appliances listed in Part IXA, B and C may be supplied.

For appliances, the quality will be determined either by an official standard referred to in the name, for example absorbent lint BPC or by a specification in the DT itself. DT Technical Specifications are obtainable on request from the PPA.

Part IX of the DT lists the appliances and dressings which may be supplied. The list is very specific, in some instances only certain sizes may be supplied although others are made. For example only 10 cm Non-Sterile Gauze Swabs packed in 100s may be supplied.

In some entries, where a general specification is given, any make which meets the specification may be supplied, for example Open Wove Bandage Type 1 BP 1988. In others, only the specified makes may be supplied. This is particularly noticeable where items for incontinence are concerned, where the detail extends to the model number.

Chemical and Diagnostic Reagents

The only chemical reagents which may be supplied are those listed in Part IXR. According to *Section 275* of the NHS Act 2006, 'medicine' includes such chemical reagents as are included in a list approved by the Secretary of State for the purposes of *Section 126*.

Some diagnostic reagents are regarded as drugs.

Regulation 2 of the 2012 Regulations states:

'drugs' includes medicines.

The effect is that the DT can make provision for diagnostic reagents only if they are drugs, chemical reagents, medicines or appliances. Since it is difficult to regard something used for determining whether an illness exists to be the means of treating that illness, diagnostic reagents might not be regarded as medicines.

The definition of a medicinal product in the Medicines Act 1968 specifically includes a substance used in 'diagnosing disease or ascertaining the existence, degree or extent of a physiological condition'.

The Human Medicines Regulations 2012 use a different wording. Regulation 2(1) states:

In these Regulations 'medicinal product' means:

(a) *any substance or combination of substances presented as having properties of preventing or treating disease in human beings or*

(b) *any substance or combination of substances that may be used by or administered to human beings with a view to:*

   (i) *restoring, correcting or modifying a physiological function by exerting a pharmacological, immunological or metabolic action or*

   (ii) *making a medical diagnosis.*

Non-dispensing GMS contractors may claim personal administration payments for the same diagnostic reagents.

HOW ARE PAYMENTS MADE?

The DT lays down the basic rules which will be followed by the PPA when calculating the payments to be made in respect of the drugs, etc., supplied on Forms FP10 and variants.

Basically, payment is made for the quantity supplied on the script. The price paid is calculated from the normal wholesale price of the product for supply to community pharmacists. This price is normally set out by the manufacturer in price lists.

A discount is deducted from the total due to each contractor for each months' dispensing. The discount is calculated according to the total amount due, on a sliding scale constructed to reflect the discounts generally achieved by contractors in their purchasing.

Zero Discount

The DT contains two 'Zero Discount' lists in Part II. These lists contain either descriptions of product groups (e.g., insulins for injection) or individual product names (e.g., Cystagon capsules; crystal violet powder BP 1980). No endorsement is necessary. The price for reimbursement will not have any discount taken off.

Containers

Part IV specifies that card containers may only be used to dispense foil or strip-packed tablets, capsules, etc. All other medicines, including creams and ointments, must be supplied in airtight containers of glass, aluminium or rigid plastic. Where appropriate, a dropper bottle or separate dropper shall be used.

Borderline Substances

Under the NHS, a general medical practitioner may prescribe (and the NHS may pay for) only drugs, medicines and certain appliances. Drugs and medicines are not clearly defined, but the category does not normally include food or cosmetics. Hospitals are not restricted in the same way and are able to provide anything needed for the care of the patient.

Part XV of the DT contains two lists providing information on borderline substances.

List A is an alphabetical index of the approved borderline products and the conditions they may be prescribed for.

List B is an alphabetical index of medical conditions and related approved products for managing those conditions.

The Advisory Committee on Borderline Substances advises on the classification and on whether or not they should be prescribed by GPs at NHS expense or prescribed only for patients with specified medical conditions.

PRICE CONTROL OF NHS MEDICINES

The prices of medicines supplied for NHS use are controlled in a number of ways.

Pharmaceutical Price Regulation Scheme

Firstly, the majority of branded medicine manufacturers belong to a voluntary price regulation scheme. The current scheme, called the Pharmaceutical Price Regulation Scheme (PPRS) was agreed between the DH and the Association of the British Pharmaceutical Industry (the trade organisation for the pharmaceutical industry). It came into effect on 1 January 2009 and is scheduled to run for 5 years. It covers those medicines which are manufactured by scheme members and which:

(a) have EC or UK marketing authorisations;
(b) are sold as branded products; and
(c) are supplied to the NHS.

The scheme includes branded medicines regardless of whether patent protection is in force, and medicines supplied on tender or on contract. OTC medicines dispensed against an NHS prescription are included. Generic medicines, 'standard' branded generics and OTC medicines sold directly to the public are not included. A 'standard' branded generic is defined as an out of patent product to which the manufacturer/supplier, who is not the originator company, has applied a brand name and that is directly comparable to a true generic that is readily available.

Under this scheme, prices are controlled indirectly. The control is exerted by limiting the profits made by manufacturers. Target profits are set as a percentage of capital invested. If the figure is exceeded the company is required to reduce its prices or to make a repayment to the DH. However, prices may only be raised with the approval of DH. A company has freedom to set the price for new products within the constraint of the profit target.

Proposed Changes to PPRS

As trailed in the White Paper Equity and Excellence: Liberating the NHS, value-based pricing of medicines will be introduced into the United Kingdom from January 2014. After that drug prices will be set according to the value medicines provided, with access likely to be no longer limited by NICE-set cost-effectiveness thresholds.

Value-based pricing will cover new medicines only and a successor scheme to the current PPRS agreement will be agreed to cover existing medicines.

The proposed new schemes represent the biggest reform to the pricing of medicines in the United Kingdom since the PPRS was set up more than 50 years ago.[4-6]

Statutory Control of Prices

Membership of the PPRS is voluntary. Companies that choose not to become members of the current PPRS are subject to the statutory price control under

Section 261 of the NHS Act 2006 (see below – Control of Branded Medicine Prices).

Legislation to Control the Prices of Branded Medicine

A company may choose not to join the PPRS scheme or may be excluded by the Secretary of State for Health if, for example, it has failed to comply with the requirements of the Scheme.

In such circumstances, a different, statutory scheme would prevail. The Health Service Medicines (Control of Prices of Branded Medicines) Regulations 2000, SI No 123, came into force on 14 February 2000 limiting the maximum price of prescription only, branded medicines supplied to the NHS and requiring manufacturers and suppliers of branded pharmaceutical companies to provide the DH with information on sales income and discounts.

Since then there have been periodic amendments and replacement regulations.

The current rules are found in the Health Service Branded Medicines (Control of Prices and Supply of Information) (No. 2) Regulations 2008, which are amended by the Health Service Branded Medicines (Control of Prices and Supply of Information) Amendment Regulations 2011.

The Regulations, which apply to the United Kingdom, control the price of branded medicines sold for NHS purposes. They apply only to medicines which:

(a) have EC or UK marketing authorisations;
(b) are sold as branded products;
(c) are supplied to the NHS; and
(d) are supplied by companies which are not scheme members within the meaning of *Section 262* of the NHS Act 2006.

Under the Regulations, the maximum price which may be charged for the supply for health service purposes of a branded health service medicine of a particular presentation shall not exceed:

(a) 94.5% of the 2008 price and for newer products the initial price.

Financial information must be provided to the DH.

There are penalties for failing to supply information and for supplying above the specified price.

Legislation to Control the Prices of Generic Medicines

The NHS reimbursement price for a generic medicine listed in Parts VIII and IX of the DT is the price stated in the DT.

However, maximum prices can be set by the DH.

The Health Service Medicines (Control of Prices of Specified Generic Medicines) Regulations 2000 SI No. 1763 came into effect on 3 August 2000.

These Regulations allow the DH to control the prices of generic medicines which are sold 'for the purposes of the NHSs in England and Wales, Scotland and Northern Ireland'.

Under the Regulations, the maximum price which is charged by a manufacturer or supplier for the supply of a specified generic medicine for health service use shall not exceed the 'specified price'.

'Supply' means supply by way of sale to a person lawfully conducting a retail pharmacy business or to a registered medical practitioner, in order to enable that person or practitioner (as the case may be) to provide pharmaceutical services.

The 'specified price' is the price specified in the list. Provision is made for the maximum price to be increased.

The Regulations apply only to the medicines specified in the list of controlled prices.

Printed copies of the list are available from the DH.

The Regulations apply only to medicines that have marketing authorisations.

The manufacturers and wholesalers must provide sales information to the Secretary of State. There are penalties for failing to supply information, and for supplying above the specified price.

Legislation to Require the Supply of Pricing Information

The Health Service Medicines (Information on the Prices of Specified Generic Medicines) Regulations 2001 No. 3798 require companies to provide information on the prices of specified generic medicines supplied to the health services in the United Kingdom. The Regulations apply only to information on medicines specified in the list of medicines published by the DH.

Appeals

A manufacturer or supplier affected by price controls made under the statutory provisions has a right of appeal in accordance with The Health Service Medicines (Price Control Appeals) Regulations 2000 SI No. 124.

Control of OTC Prices

Following a decision of the Restrictive Practices Court on 15 May 2001, there are no longer any controls on the prices of OTC medicines sold to the public.

Self-Assessment Questions

1. List the broad categories of information in the DT?
   Answer: The DT contains: a list of drug prices paid for dispensed prescriptions; the amount of fees and allowances to be paid for dispensing; detailed

information on appliances; rules to follow when dispensing NHS prescriptions, for example what can and cannot be prescribed on NHS prescriptions and by which class of practitioner, instructions on endorsements; and lists of products which are not allowed on NHS forms.

2. List the basic rules for prescribing by GPs?

   Answer: Doctors may prescribe any medicine, unless its use at NHS expense is specifically prohibited by the Secretary of State, or its use is restricted to specified circumstances. The list is not confined to the drugs listed in the DT, or to licensed products. Doctors may prescribe an appliance or chemical reagent, only if its use at NHS expense is approved by the Secretary of State, and only in the circumstances specified. Doctors may prescribe a 'borderline substance' only if its use at NHS expense is approved by the Secretary of State, and only in the circumstances specified.

3. Under what circumstances may a community pharmacist dispense a different quantity from that ordered?

   Answer: The quantity supplied may deviate from the exact quantity ordered only in specified circumstances as set out in Clause 10. These are where it is particularly difficult to open the container and dispense a part of its contents. This applies to products which are: sterile, effervescent or hygroscopic, liquid products for addition to bath water, coal tar preparations or viscous external preparations packed in a castor, collapsible tube, dropper bottle, pressurised aerosol, puffer pack, roll-on bottle, sachet, shaker, spray, squeeze pack, container with an integral means of application or any other container from which it is not practicable to dispense the exact quantity.

ADDITIONAL RESOURCES

1. http://www.nhsbsa.nhs.uk/924.aspx
2. http://www.nhsbsa.nhs.uk/PrescriptionServices/1821.aspx
3. http://www.dh.gov.uk/en/Publicationsandstatistics/Publications/PublicationsPolicyAndGuidance/DH_115260
4. http://www.abpi.org.uk/our-work/library/industry/Documents/Understanding%20the%20pprs%202009%20final.pdf
5. http://www.dh.gov.uk/en/Healthcare/Medicinespharmacyandindustry/Pharmaceuticalprice regulationscheme/PPRSlegislation/DH_092413
6. http://www.parliament.uk/briefing-papers/post-pn-364.pdf

Chapter 5

Applications to Dispense NHS Scripts

This chapter is concerned mainly with the provisions governing the opening of a pharmacy and the application for an NHS contract in an urban area. The rural dispensing arrangements are dealt with in Chapter 4.

Legislation places an obligation on the NHS Commissioning Board (NHS CB) to put arrangements in place so that drugs, medicines and listed appliances ordered via NHS prescriptions can be supplied to persons.

However, as noted below, pharmacies have no automatic right to supply prescriptions through the NHS. Applications to do so must be made according to the rules, and contracts are only granted when certain criteria are met.

Neither this chapter nor the one on rural dispensing arrangements is intended to give a step-by-step set of instructions on how applications should be made or how they are processed. Instead we aim only to outline the procedures.

The opening of a new pharmacy is subject to a number of controls. The law on the subject is complex and contained in Acts of Parliament, Regulations and case law from the courts.

PROFESSIONAL AND MEDICINES ACT CONTROLS

One set of controls relate to professional matters. They derive from the Medicines Act 1968 and from the law governing the profession of pharmacy. These are dealt with in Chapter 9.

NHS CONTRACT CONTROLS

The other set of controls relate to the granting of an NHS contract. A pharmacy may open without an NHS contract although such pharmacies are few in number.

HISTORY OF CONTROL OF ENTRY TO NHS PHARMACEUTICAL LISTS

Until 1983 an application to dispense NHS prescriptions in a pharmacy was automatically granted. Since 1983 there have been a number of restrictive measures.

Pharmacy Law and Practice. DOI: http://dx.doi.org/10.1016/B978-0-12-394289-0.00005-9

In 1987 amending regulations introduced a system of control to link the number of persons included in a pharmaceutical list as closely as possible to the need of the local population for reasonable access to the full range of NHS pharmaceutical services (PS). A new contract was only to be granted if it was 'necessary or desirable' to secure adequate provision in the neighbourhood.

In 2003 the Office of Fair Trading published a report 'The Control of entry regulations and retail pharmacy services in the UK' which recommended abolition of the statutory controls on entry in order to increase competition.

The government decided not to implement the proposals in full, but introduced a package of changes in the 2005 Regulations designed to increase competition whilst retaining controls on entry.

THE 2013 CHANGES

In 2012 the rules for entry and for making applications were changed again. The old test has been replaced by a new one based around needs or benefits identified in the relevant 'pharmaceutical needs assessment' (PNA).

The test is set out in s129 of the NHS Act 2006 (as amended) and the details of how this is to work are in the NHS (Pharmaceutical and Local Pharmaceutical Services) Regulations 2013SI No. 349. These Regulations replace both the 2005 Regulations and their amendments and the short-lived NHS (Pharmaceutical Services) Regulations 2012 which took no account of the passage of the NHS and Social Care Act 2012.

The new Regulations came into force on 1 April 2013. They run to 227 pages. Their predecessor Regulations had 15 sets of guidance to accompany them. New guidance was not available at the time of writing this section.

PROBLEMS WITH TERMINOLOGY

The 2012 Regulations were published after the Health and Social Care Act 2012 had been passed by Parliament. However, they came into force prior to most of that Act taking effect. The 2012 Act changes the structure of the NHS in a number of ways. As a consequence there will need to be legislation amending terms in several Regulations.

We have endeavoured to anticipate those changes to make it easier for this textbook to remain useful for some time. In particular an assumption has been made that the NHS CB will take over certain duties assigned to the Primary Care Trust (PCT). According to the Department of Health, from 1 April 2013, the NHS CB is expected to take over administration of the NHS (PS) Regulations 2012 as part of the implementation of the Health and Social Care Act 2012. The exception to this is that responsibility for the development and updating of PNAs transfers to local authority Health and Wellbeing Boards. With the passing of the 2013 Regulations we have attempted to correct the text to match the 2013 Regulations.

EXERCISE OF FUNCTIONS BY THE CB

By virtue of the new section 168A of the NHS Act 2006:

(1) The Secretary of State may direct the NHS CB to exercise any of the Secretary of State's functions relating to services that may be provided as PS, or as local pharmaceutical services (LPS), under this Part.

The amendments to *Subsection (2)(c)* provide that the NHS CB is to be responsible for determining applications for market entry in England (inclusion in the pharmaceutical list or additional premises) in line with the relevant PNA as prescribed in regulations.

THREE TYPES OF PROVIDER

There are three types of 'contractor' who may provide NHS PS.

• Firstly, and in the great majority of cases, these services are provided by 'pharmacy contractors'.
• Secondly, a more limited range of PS may be provided by 'appliance contractors' who may only supply appliances (e.g., incontinence aids, dressings, bandages) but not medicines.
• Thirdly, 'dispensing doctors' are authorised to dispense to patients who live in designated rural areas a distance away from pharmacies.

They have to be on a dispensing doctor list kept by the CB.

Most NHS community PS in England are provided by pharmacies on the basis set out in the 2012 Regulations and are referred to as PS.

'LPS' are now governed by the NHS (Pharmaceutical and Local Pharmaceutical Services) Regulations 2013 (the 2013 Regs).

THE PHARMACEUTICAL LIST

The NHS CB must keep 'pharmaceutical lists' of persons who undertake to provide PS. The lists are of:

(a) those who provide drugs (pharmacies)
(b) those who provide appliances.

Each list contains the name and address of the contractor and the hours at which the service is provided. The list of pharmacies must also indicate whether or not the pharmacy has undertaken to provide 'directed services'.

CONTROL OF ENTRY TO LISTS

The 2012 Regulations make new arrangements to control the entry of contractors or additional contractor premises onto pharmaceutical lists. The 'control of entry' test as set out in the 2005 Regulations, which was based on whether new premises were 'necessary or expedient' to provide services for a particular neighbourhood, has been replaced by a new market entry test. This is based around needs or benefits identified in the relevant PNA.

PHARMACEUTICAL NEEDS ASSESSMENT

A PNA is the statement of the assessment each Health and Wellbeing Board must make of the needs in its area for community PS provided as part of the NHS by all types of contractor. The PNA must describe the population profiles and local characteristics as well as providing an assessment of unmet needs for, and possible improvements and better access to, PS provision in the area.

This will enable the CB to determine applications for new entries (or certain other applications such as subsequent relocations) to the pharmaceutical list by reference to the relevant PNA.

Inevitably, it will not have been possible during the formulation of the PNA for every need and benefit to have been foreseen.

Therefore, the Regulations also allow for applications to be approved where applicants can demonstrate, in specified circumstances, that their application will bring 'unforeseen benefits'.

A successful applicant will need to show that the application will meet a gap in services identified in the PNA for the area.

Alternatively the applicant must demonstrate that its pharmacy would secure improvements or better access to services listed in the PNA or which were not foreseen when the PNA was drafted.

Detailed Information in the PNA

The detailed information which must be in the PNA is set out in Schedule 1 of the 2012 Regulations:

> It must relate to all the PS that may be provided under arrangements made by the NHS for:
>
> (a) the provision of PS (including directed services) by a person on a pharmaceutical list;
> (b) the provision of LPS under an LPS scheme; or
> (c) the dispensing of drugs and appliances by a person on a dispensing doctors list.
>
> The statement must:

- identify the current provision of services which are necessary to meet the need for PS in its area, and
- list the gaps in provision.

> It must also

- identify services which have secured improvements to or better access to PS in that area.

Such services may not have been necessary to meet the need for PS in the area. Such services may be provided inside or outside the area.

There must be an explanation of how the assessment has been carried out, and a map of the area must be included.

Each Health and Wellbeing Board must include a map in its PNA and, in so far as is practicable, keep it up to date.

New Market Entry Test

The market entry test describes the system whereby the NHS CB assesses an application that offers to:

- meet an identified current or future need or needs in the PNA;
- meet identified current or future improvements or better access to PS in the PNA; or
- provide unforeseen benefits, that is applications that offer to meet a need that is not identified in a PNA but which the Board is satisfied would lead to significant benefits to people living in the area.

Exceptions to the Market Entry Test

The main control of entry test is subject to exemptions in respect of new ownership of existing pharmacies and 'distance selling' pharmacies, referred to as 'excepted applications'.

APPLICATIONS TO NHS CB

Anyone who wishes to operate an NHS pharmacy, to open additional or new premises or to change the services which are provided must apply to the NHS CB.

Applications are divided into two categories:

(1) Routine applications
(2) Excepted applications.

Routine Applications

Routine applications are defined in Regulation 12. A 'routine application' is any application, other than an excepted application, by a person:

(a) for inclusion in a pharmaceutical list who is not already included in it; or
(b) who is included in a pharmaceutical list and who is seeking:

    (i) to open, within the area of the PCT whose list it is, additional premises from which to provide the same or different PS;
    (ii) to relocate to different premises, and at those premises to provide the same or different PS;
    (iii) to provide, from the person's listed chemist premises, services that are in addition to those already listed in relation to that person.

Information to Be Given in the Application

Any application must contain the information which is set out in Schedule 2 of the 2013 Regulations.

- PNA in whose area the proposed premises will be;
- the type of application being made;
- a statement of whether the application is a routine or an excepted application;
- the name and address of the applicant;
- GPhC registration number if the applicant is a sole trader;
- GPhC number of each partner if the applicant is in a partnership;
- GPhC registration number of the superintendent pharmacist for a body corporate applicant;
- the address of the premises or the best estimate of where the proposed premises will be;
- whether the applicant is currently in possession of the premises;
- the proposed core opening hours for the premises; and
- the total proposed opening hours for the premises (i.e., both core opening and supplementary opening hours);
- details of the directed services to be provided;
- confirmation that the applicant is accredited to provide the services, where the PCT requires such accreditation;
- confirmation that the premises are accredited in respect of the provision of services, where the PCT requires such accreditation;
- where relevant, a floor plan showing the consultation area where the applicant proposes to offer the directed services, unless one cannot be provided for reasons that the PCT accepts as good cause, for example the premises are not in the applicant's possession.

The applicant must confirm whether the application is a routine or an excepted application (paragraph 1(3) of Schedule 2). The applicant cannot switch between the two types of application once it has been made to the NHS CB. Should the applicant wish to change the type of application, the first application must be withdrawn and a second application submitted, along with the relevant fee.

Fitness to Practice Information

Applicants not already on the list are required to provide information to enable a decision on fitness to practice to be made. It includes information on:

- the individual making the application; or
- where it is a partnership, each partner; or
- where it is a body corporate, the director(s) and any superintendent pharmacist.

Specific Grounds for Refusal or Deferral of Routine Applications

(1) Fitness to practise grounds   (Regulation 33(i))
(2) Failure of European Economic Area (EEA) qualified pharmacist to meet required language ability   (Regulation 30)
(3) Where the relevant premises are designated under Regulation 4 of the LPS Regulations or are located within a designated area   (Regulation 32)
(4) Where the premises to which the application relates are already on the list   (Regulation 31)

Granting a Routine Application to Meet Current Need

A successful applicant will need to show that the application will meet a gap in services identified in the PNA for the area (current need).

Current Need

Routine applications to meet current need may only be granted if the NHS CB determines that granting it, or granting it in respect of only some of the services specified in it, would meet a current need:

(a) for PS, or PS of a specified type, in the area; and
(b) that has been included in its PNA in accordance with paragraph 2(a) of Schedule 1 of the 2013 Regulations.

Matters to Be Considered

Where the NHS CB receives a routine application to meet the current need identified within its PNA and:

- granting it would meet that current need for PS in general or specific PS in particular; or
- granting it in respect of some of the PS that the applicant is offering to provide in order to meet that current need for PS in general, or specific PS in particular.

Section 129 (2A) of the 2006 Act requires the Board to consider and be satisfied about certain matters set out in Regulation 13.

The NHS CB must have regard to whether it is satisfied that it would be desirable to:

(a) consider all current need applications together;   (Regulation 13(2)(a))
(b) consider another current need application at the same time;   (Regulation 13(2)(b))
(c) await the outcome of a pending appeal;   (Regulation 13(2)(c))

The NHS CB must also have regard to whether:

(d) there have been changes to the needs since the publication of the PNA such that refusing the application is essential in order to prevent significant detriment to the provision of PS in its area;   (Regulation 13(2)(d))

(e) granting the application would only meet the current need in part, and if the application were granted, it would be unlikely, in the reasonably foreseeable future, that the remainder of that need would be met;   (Regulation 13(2)(e))

(f) granting the application would only meet the current need in part; but it considers that, if the application were granted, it would not be unlikely, in the reasonably foreseeable future, that the remainder of that need would be met;   (Regulation 13(2)(f))

(g) the current need was for services other than essential services, and granting the application would result in an increased availability of essential services in the area;   (Regulation 13(2)(g))

(h) since the publication of the PNA, the current need has been met, or is due to be met, by another person providing services from listed chemist premises or LPS premises;   (Regulation 13(2)(h))

(i) the application needs to be deferred or refused by virtue of any provision of Parts 5–7.   (Regulation 13(2)(i))

Part 5 of the 2013 Regulations sets out specific grounds for refusal or deferral of applications under Parts 3 and 4 which are not linked to fitness grounds.

Part 6 sets out specific grounds for refusal, deferral and conditional inclusion in pharmaceutical lists of chemists on fitness grounds.

Part 7 sets out specific rules for governing areas that are controlled localities and reserved locations and for determining applications for new pharmacies within them.

When Is a Need Due to Be Met

A need is due to be met if:

(a) the person undertaking to meet that need is entitled to give a notice of commencement, as a consequence of which he or she will be able to commence the provision of services to meet that need, but has not yet given that notice; or

(b) the person has entered into an LPS scheme, as a consequence of which he or she will be able to commence the provision of services to meet that need, but has not yet done so.

Granting an Application to Meet Unforeseen Benefits

Inevitably, it will not have been possible during the formulation of the PNA for every need and benefit to have been foreseen.

The Regulations therefore allow for applications to be approved where applicants can demonstrate that their application will bring unforeseen benefits. The applicant must demonstrate that its pharmacy would secure improvements or better access to PS which were not foreseen when the PNA was drafted (unforeseen benefits).

The NHS CB may grant an application if it is satisfied, having regard to the PNA and to any matters prescribed by the Secretary of State in the regulations, it is satisfied that to grant the application would secure improvements or better access to PS in its area.

Refusal of Routine Applications That Are Based on Neither a PNA nor an Unforeseen Benefit

A routine application to which Regulation 19(6) does not apply can only be granted if that would:

(a) meet a current or future need for PS, or PS of a specified type, in its area that has been included in its PNA; or

(b) secure (including in the future) improvements, or better access, to PS, or PS of a specified type, in its area that have or has been included in its PNA.

The application may also be granted notwithstanding that the improvements or better access were or was not included in its PNA, provided the proposed service would confer significant benefits on persons in its area which were not foreseen when it published its PNA.

Notification of Application Which Has Not Been Summarily Refused

The Board must notify a list of persons (Schedule 2):

- the relevant LPC;
- the relevant Local Medical Committee (LMC);
- any person in the pharmaceutical list whose interests might be significantly affected if the application were granted;
- any person whose application has been granted but is not (yet) included, and whose interests might be significantly affected if the application were granted;
- any LPS chemist in the area whose interests might be significantly affected if the application were granted;
- any LINk for the area, and any other patient, consumer or community group in the area (e.g., Parish and Town Councils) which has a significant interest in the outcome of the application;
- any dispensing doctor in a controlled locality within 1.6 km of the premises who the PCT believes has a significant interest in the outcome of the application.

Excepted Applications

The main control of entry test is subject to exemptions, particularly in respect of existing pharmacies and 'distance selling' pharmacies. Excepted applications do not have to be assessed in the way that routine applications are:

- Applications from NHS chemists in respect of providing directed services   (Regulation 23)
- Relocations that do not result in significant change to PS provision   (Regulation 24)
- Distance selling premises applications   (Regulation 25)
- Change of ownership applications   (Regulation 26)
- Applications for temporary listings arising out of suspensions   (Regulation 27
- Applications from persons exercising a right of return to a pharmaceutical list   (Regulation 28)
- Applications relating to emergencies requiring the flexible provision of PS   (Regulation 29)

Sections 129(2A) and (2B) of the NHS Act 2006 do not apply to excepted applications. Such applications are therefore not required to meet a need, or to secure improvements or better access, to services.

Applications for Directed Services

An application by a person who is already in a pharmaceutical list is an excepted application if he is seeking to provide new directed services.

Applications to Relocate to New Premises

There are two different types of relocation applications:

(1) An application to relocate to new premises in order to meet a need identified within the PNA, and which would result in a significant change to PS provision in the area. This is treated as a routine application under Regulation 12(b)(ii).

(2) An excepted application to relocate to new premises does not result in a significant change to PS provision. If an application fails to meet any one of the criteria listed in Regulation 24, then it will be refused.

The exception set out in Regulation 24 only applies where the relocation to new premises would not result in a significant change to PS provision in the area.

Regulation 24 states:

> *(1) Sections 129(2A) and (2B) of the 2006 Act (regulations as to PS) do not apply to an application from a person already included in a pharmaceutical list to relocate to different premises in the area if:*
> > *(a) for the patient groups that are accustomed to accessing PS at the existing premises, the location of the new premises is not significantly less accessible;*
> > *(b) in the opinion of the NHS CB, granting the application would not result in a significant change to the arrangements that are in place for the*

*provision of LPS or of PS other than those provided by a person on a
dispensing doctor list:*

  (i) in any part of relevant area or

  *(ii) in a controlled locality of a neighbouring area, where that
       controlled locality is within 1.6 km of the premises to which the
       applicant is seeking to relocate;*

  *(c) the NHS CB is satisfied that granting the application would not cause
      significant detriment to proper planning in respect of the provision of PS
      in its area;*

  *(d) the services the applicant undertakes to provide at the new premises are
      the same as the services the applicant has been providing at the existing
      premises (whether or not, in the case of enhanced services, the NHS CB
      chooses to commission them); and*

  *(e) the provision of PS will not be interrupted (except for such period as the
      NHS CB may for good cause allow).*

The Regulations currently contain provisions to deal with relocations
across PCT borders. At the time of writing it is difficult to guess the future
wording of these provisions.

Applications for a Distance Selling Pharmacy

To qualify as an excepted application, a wholly mail order or internet-based
pharmacy must not provide NHS essential services direct to patients on the
premises. It may, however, sell or supply goods that are not NHS-related.

It may also provide advanced or enhanced services from its premises
where these services can be provided wholly separately from the provision of
essential services at the premises.

Applications for Change of Ownership

Applications for change of ownership occur where a person applies to provide
services at premises from which services are, at the time of the application,
provided by another person who is on the pharmaceutical list. (Regulation
26(1)(a))

The Board must be satisfied that the same PS will be provided by the new
owner as are provided by the person currently included in the pharmaceutical
list. (Regulation 26(1)(c))

Additionally, the applicant must show that the provision of PS will not be
interrupted, except for approved 'good cause'. The Board determines what is
and what is not 'good cause'. (Regulation 26(1)(d))

Oral Hearings

The Board is not required to hold oral hearings for every application decision. It may make a judgement on when it is necessary to do so. This is
based on the complexity of the application, previous applications in the area
and any appeals, particularly upheld appeals, to the FHSAU regarding those

applications, and the number and type of representations made in respect of the application from those notified of it.

If the PCT decides to hear oral representations prior to determining a routine application then it must:

- give the applicant and any additional presenters not less than 14 days' notice of the time and place for the oral hearing; and
- advise the applicant who has been invited to make representations at the hearing. This may include other applicants, where the PCT has decided to determine two or more applications together (paragraph 25(1) of Schedule 2).

Notification of Decisions on Routine and Excepted Applications

Notice of decisions must be given to:

(a) the applicant
(b) the LPC
(c) the LMC
(d) any other person whose interests might be significantly affected by the decision and is
  (i) included in its pharmaceutical list; or
  (ii) who is entitled to be included in its pharmaceutical list;
(e) any LPS chemist whose interests might be significantly affected by the decision;
(f) any relevant LINk, and any other patient, consumer or community group with a significant interest in the decision;
(g) if the applicant is seeking to locate premises in or within 1.6km of a controlled locality in its area:
  (i) any provider of primary medical services with a significant interest in the decision;
  (ii) any other person on its dispensing doctors list with a significant interest in the decision;
(h) any person:
  (i) notified under paragraph 19(2); and
  (ii) who made representations in writing about.

Appeals Against PCT Decisions on Pharmaceutical Applications

Under the Regulations, most decisions on market entry applications are appealable to the Secretary of State for Health who has delegated this responsibility to the NHS Litigation Authority (NHSLA). The appellate function is undertaken by the NHSLA's Family Health Services Appeal Unit (FHSAU).

Schedule 3 of the 2013 Regulations sets out the actions that the FHSAU may take.

In summary, the FHSAU may generally:

- confirm the decision or determination;
- quash the decision or determination and re-determine the application;

- substitute its decision or determination for any decision or determination the CB could have made; or
- quash the decision and remit the matter to CB for it to re-determine the application.

Where the FHSAU remits the matter back, this is generally where there have been procedural concerns of an administrative nature.

For the purposes of the 2013 Regulations, the FHSAU's decision becomes the CB decision on the matter. The FHSAU's decision may only be overruled by a court.

How to Appeal

An appeal must be made in writing to the NHSLA within 30 days from the date on which the decision letter is sent. The appeal must contain a concise and reasoned statement of the grounds for appeal.

An appeal under Schedule 3 can generally only be made by the applicant or by a contractor who has been formally notified of the decision.

Fees for Applications

Fees will continue to be paid for applications under the 2013 Regulations. Details are set out in the PS Fees for Applications Directions 2012. Guidance is in Annex F of the Guidance documents.

Commencing Service Provision

The applicant has a 6-month period from the date of grant of the application in which he or she may commence providing services. A valid notice of commencement must be sent, giving the Board 14 days' notice of the start of service provision.

European Diplomas

The Regulations place certain restrictions on pharmacists who hold diplomas in pharmacy granted by universities in other EEA countries. Such pharmacists are required to satisfy the NHS CB as to their knowledge of English before an application can be granted. (Regulation 30)

If the applicant is a pharmacist (or is in a partnership) who has qualified as a pharmacist in Switzerland or an EEA State other than the United Kingdom, he or she must satisfy the Board that the applicant has the level of knowledge of English which is necessary for the provision of services.

PLANNING LAW

The planning regulations which affect pharmacies are found in the Town and Country Planning (Use Classes) Order 1987. This lists the various classes of activity for which planning permission may be granted.

An explanatory note attached to the order says that 'dispensaries' will fall into Class A1. This is the class for shops. If the 'dispensary' is ancillary to a hospital then it may fall into Class C2 (residential institutions).

Under a previous order it was possible for pharmacies which were 'dispensing-only' to fall into a category of professional use of residential premises, thereby avoiding planning restrictions applicable to shops.

It is not necessary for the relevant planning permission to have been granted prior to the granting of an application for minor relocation or for a new contract.

Self-Assessment Questions

1. What is a PNA?

   Answer: The new test is based around needs or benefits for the local community identified in the relevant PNA. The PNA is the statement of the assessment each Health and Wellbeing Board must make of the needs in its area for community PS, provided as part of the NHS by all types of contractor. The PNA must describe the population profiles and local characteristics as well as providing an assessment of unmet needs for, and possible improvements and better access to, PS provision in the area. The detailed information which must be in the PNA is set out in Schedule 1 of the 2013 Regulations.

2. Can you sum up the new market entry test?

   Answer: The market entry test describes the system whereby the NHS CB assesses an application that offers to meet an identified current or future need or needs in the PNA; meet identified current or future improvements or better access to PS in the PNA or provide unforeseen benefits, that is applications that offer to meet a need that is not identified in a PNA but which the Board is satisfied would lead to significant benefits to people living in the area.

3. Which main categories of application are excepted from the normal rules?

   Answer: 'Excepted applications' are applications from NHS chemists in respect of providing directed services; relocations that do not result in significant change to PS provision; distance selling premises; change of ownership applications; applications for temporary listings arising out of suspensions; applications from persons exercising a right of return to a pharmaceutical list; applications relating to emergencies requiring the flexible provision of PS.

Chapter 6

Rural Dispensing

HISTORY

Doctors and pharmacists have argued over who should dispense for patients in rural areas since the advent of the NHS. In 1975 the two professions agreed a voluntary standstill on changes in dispensing arrangements while they engaged in discussions. Following these discussions a number of actions occurred:

1977 'Report of the National Joint Committee of the medical and pharmaceutical professions on the dispensing of NHS prescriptions in rural areas' – commonly known as the 'Clothier Report'.

1983 The Rural Dispensing Committee (RDC) was to determine applications for dispensing in rural areas and to determine the 'rurality' of an area.

1990 RDC abolished and decisions made by Family Health Service Authorities (FHSAs) (now Primary Care Trusts (PCTs)).

2001 The professions reach agreement on further reform.

2004 Advisory Group on Reform of the NHS Pharmaceutical Services (PS) Regulations 1992 propose introduction of more competition and choice.

2005 Proposals implemented in NHS (PS) Regulations 2005.

2012 The new Regulations basically repeat the provisions of the 2005 Regulations.

THE CURRENT RULES

The NHS Act 1977 made it clear that doctors would only be allowed to dispense drugs in exceptional circumstances and that the prime suppliers of medicines would be pharmacists.

The provisions to allow general practitioners (GPs) to dispense were introduced to provide access to dispensing services for patients in rural communities who do not have reasonable access to a community pharmacy.

The legislation provides that in certain rural areas classified as controlled localities the GPs may apply to dispense NHS prescriptions.

Permission is granted to GPs providing there is no 'prejudice' to the existing medical or PS. Prejudice is defined as being unable to comply with the medical or pharmaceutical terms of service (TOS).

Pharmacy Law and Practice. DOI: http://dx.doi.org/10.1016/B978-0-12-394289-0.00006-0

They may then dispense to patients who are residents in the controlled locality and living at a distance of more than 1.6 km from an NHS pharmacy. Distance selling pharmacies are excluded. The pharmacy itself does not have to be in the controlled locality.

According to the Dispensing Doctors Association, there are 1300 dispensing practices in the UK, with around 6500 doctors, supplying 4 million patients.

Pharmacy applications in rural areas are also required to satisfy the prejudice test and are subject to the additional control of entry test based on the relevant pharmaceutical needs assessment (PNA).

Serious Difficulty

An additional exception was made for patients who would otherwise have extreme difficulty in getting to a pharmacy. GPs may be directed to dispense for such patients. (Lord Justice Schieman in *R v. North Staffs HA, ex parte Worthington* 1996)

This occurs where a patient satisfies the Board that they would have serious difficulty in obtaining any necessary drugs or appliances from a pharmacy because of the distance or because of an inadequacy of means of communication (usually referred to as the 'serious difficulty test'). The patient may be resident anywhere in the country.

Current Legislation

The current legislation is mainly in Parts 7 and 8 of the NHS (P & LPS) Regulations 2013. Chapter 14 of the Department of Health (DH) Guidance deals with applications from pharmacists in rural areas.

Controlled Locality

The current rural dispensing rules apply to areas termed 'controlled localities'. A controlled locality is an area which has been determined to be 'rural in character'. PCTs were required to delineate the boundaries of the controlled areas on a map. Where a previous determination of rurality has been made under earlier regulations, then that area continues as a controlled locality.

Regulation 36(1) of the 2013 Regulations states:

Any area that was, or was part of, a controlled locality for the purposes of the 2005 Regulations immediately before these Regulations come into force continues to be, or to be part of, a controlled locality for the purposes of these Regulations (unless or until it is determined that the area is no longer, or no longer part of, a controlled locality).

The Board may at any time determine whether an area is rural. The Board must determine rurality if requested in writing by the Local Pharmaceutical Committees (LPC) or Local Medical Committee (LMC). (Regulation 31(3))

What Makes an Area 'Rural in Character'?

The DH issued guidance in the document 'Regulations under the Health Act 2009: Market entry by means of PNAs. Information for Primary Care Trusts Chapter 14 Provision of pharmaceutical services in controlled localities':

A controlled locality must be rural in character (Regulation 36(2)). There is, however, no prescribed way to define what is rural in character. Each case must be judged on individual circumstances and will depend on a variety of factors.

A rural area is normally characterised by a limited range of local services. There are a range of factors (as they pertain at the time of the determination) that might be considered by PCTs in determining whether an area is rural and these have been clarified over the years. They include, for example:

- *environmental – the balance between different types of land use;*
- *employment patterns (bearing in mind that those who live in rural areas may not work there);*
- *the size of the community and distance between settlements;*
- *the overall population density;*
- *transportation – the availability or otherwise of public transport and the frequency of such provision including access to services such as shopping facilities; and*
- *the provision of other facilities, such as recreational and entertainment facilities.*

In 2004 following a review in 2002 of the urban and rural area definitions used by government, the Department for Environment, Food and Rural Affairs (DEFRA) Rural Strategy described a definition of rurality which is available to download from the website:[1]

Areas which have not been classed as 'controlled' are not necessarily urban. According to the guidance document:

PCTs should be aware of misconceptions about rurality. The fact that an area is not classified as controlled or that a decision is taken to remove such a classification, does not necessarily mean that it is urban.

The 'Five-Year Rule'

Regulation 36(3) states that where a PCT has decided whether or not an area is rural, the question may not generally be considered again in the next 5 years. The exception is where the Board is satisfied that there has been a 'substantial change of circumstances' in relation to the area, or to a part of it, since the matter was last determined.

Meaning of 'Substantial Change'

No definition is given in the Regulations.

Appeals

Dispensing doctors and pharmacy contractors affected by the decision may appeal against a rurality decision, as may be relevant to the LMCs and LPCs.

Applications by Pharmacists to Dispense in Rural Areas

Pharmacists wishing to open in rural areas face a number of barriers and a complex application process.

There are five separate issues to be considered when a routine application is made for a pharmacy in an area that may be rural in character:

(1) whether the proposed premises are within a controlled locality
(2) whether or not the application needs to be refused on the basis of the 'five-year rule' as a preliminary matter
(3) whether or not the application relates to a reserved location
(4) the 'prejudice' test
(5) PNA tests.

Applications are made in a similar manner to those relating to non-controlled areas. They are subject to special procedures set down in Regulations. The Regulations lay down a timetable and indicate which other persons or bodies should be consulted before a decision is taken.

Stage 1 – Refusals Because of Preliminary Matters

The Board must first of all determine whether the application would be dismissed under Regulation 40.

This stage applies to all routine applications where the applicant is seeking the listing of pharmacy premises which are in a controlled locality and which are:

(a) for inclusion in a pharmaceutical list as an NHS pharmacist; or
(b) from an NHS pharmacist:
  (i) to relocate to different pharmacy premises in the area, or
  (ii) to open additional pharmacy premises within the area, from which to provide PS.

The application must be refused if the premises are at a location which is:

(a) in an area in relation to which outline consent has been granted under either the 2005 or 2013 Regulations within the 5-year period; or
(b) within 1.6 km of the location of proposed pharmacy premises, in respect of which:
  (i) a routine application under these Regulations, or
  (ii) an application to which Regulation 22(1) or (3) of the 2005 Regulations (relevant procedures for applications) applied, was

refused within the 5-year period. Distance selling premises are ignored for this decision.

The 5-Year Period

(i) starts on the date on which the proceedings relating to the grant of outline consent reached their final outcome, and

(ii) ends on the date on which the application is made.

Change of Circumstances

If the Board is satisfied that since the date on which the 5-year period started, there has been a 'substantial and relevant change of circumstances affecting the controlled locality' it may consider the application.

Stage 2 – Refusals Because Premises in a Reserved Location

The Board must determine whether to grant the application would be dismissed under Regulation 41.

Reserved Locations

The 2005 Contract Regulations introduced a new concept of 'reserved location'. A reserved location is an area within a controlled locality where the total of all patient lists for the area within a radius of 1.6 km (1 mile) of the proposed premises or location is fewer than 2750.

If a pharmacy opens in a reserved location, people living within a radius of 1.6 km may choose whether to use the doctor dispensing or pharmacy dispensing, or both.

The pharmacy does not have the usual 1.6 km radius where patients automatically cease to receive dispensing from the GP.

According to Regulation 41(3) of the 2013 Regulations the area within a 1.6 km radius of a relevant location is a 'reserved location' if:

(a) the number of individuals residing in that area who are on a patient list (which may be an aggregate number of patients on more than one patient list) is less than 2750; and

(b) the Board is not satisfied that if PS were provided at the relevant location, the use of those services would be similar to, or greater than, the use that might be expected if the number of individuals residing in that area who are on a patient list were 2750 or more.

The Board may not grant an application if a previous one relating to the same premises was refused, in the 5-year period, for the reasons relating to prejudice in:

Regulation 44(3) of the 2013 Regulations, or
Regulation 18ZA(2) of the 2005 Regulations.

Change of Circumstances

If the Board is satisfied that since the date on which the 5-year period started, there has been a substantial and relevant change of circumstances affecting the controlled locality it may consider the application.

Second and Subsequent Determinations of Reserved Location

The Board may make second and subsequent determinations of reserved location status under Regulation 42.

Stage 3 – the 'Prejudice Test'

A routine application for a contract in a controlled locality that is not also a reserved location is subject to the 'prejudice' test.

Regulation 44(3) states:

The Board must refuse the application if granting it would, in its opinion, prejudice the proper provision of relevant NHS services in the area or in a neighbouring area.

'Relevant NHS services' means PS, LPS and primary medical services.

What Is Meant by 'Proper Provision'

Proper provision means provision of the service to the standard which the contractor is obliged to provide in order to comply with the TOS.

What Is Meant by 'Prejudice'?

The services will be prejudiced if the contractor would be unable to comply with the TOS. A reduction in the standard of service will not, in itself, constitute prejudice to the proper provision. This interpretation has been approved by the Secretary of State in a number of decisions and it is also given in the Guidance document.

Location

At this stage an application is not required to give the exact address of the proposed pharmacy, but the location must be given sufficiently clearly for the test to be applied. In practice that seems to mean that it must be possible to look at the population within a 1.6 km radius of the proposed site, so as to determine how they are affected.

Appeals

The applicant or a person given notice of the determination who is mentioned in the regulations may appeal to the Secretary of State within 30 days of the decision. The appeal must include a concise and reasoned statement of the grounds of appeal.

The 'Serious Difficulty' Rule

Regulation 48 states:

Where a patient satisfies the Board that he would have serious difficulty in obtaining any necessary drugs or appliances from a pharmacy by reason of distance or inadequacy of means of communication he may at any time request in writing the doctor on whose list he is included to provide him with pharmaceutical service.

This provision applies to any patient, including any resident in urban areas.

In considering whether the patient has a serious difficulty, the PCT is expected to consider:

- personal circumstances of the patient
- local arrangements for medical and PS
- transport
- any collection and delivery services
- availability of telephones
- any other relevant factors.

There is no appeal procedure from a decision of the Board that the patient does not have any serious difficulty.

Temporary Residents

Doctors who provide PS to at least some of the patients on their list may also dispense to any temporary residents which they accept.   (Regulation 49)

APPLICATIONS BY DOCTORS

Existing dispensing practices were required to register their premises with the PCT by 30 April 2005.   (Regulation 68(2) of 2005 Regulations)

Additionally the Board must prepare and publish a dispensing doctor list. The dispensing doctor list includes:

- the premises where the doctor has premises approval;
- whether the premises approval is granted, temporary or residual;
- the date on which premises approval took effect or where it has not taken effect, the date when it was finally granted;
- the area where the doctor has outline consent and premises approval;
- premises, identified separately, where the doctor has outstanding applications for premises approval.   (Regulation 68(4) of 2012 Regulations)

The Board must refuse an application under Regulation 51(1) (but not under regulations 54, 55 or 58) for premises approval if the premises in respect of which approval is sought are within a radius of 1.6 km of pharmacy premises that are not distance selling premises.

Regulations 54, 55 and 58 apply to relocations and temporary arrangements.

Outline Consent

Otherwise doctors may apply for 'outline consent' to dispense for those of their patients who live more than 1 mile from a pharmacy. The same test is used – whether to grant the application would prejudice the proper provision of GMS or PS. (Regulation 51)

The application must specify the area for which the grant of 'outline consent' is sought. The application must be in writing, but no particular form is specified.

The effect of a grant is that the doctor may then dispense to any of his or her patients residing in the specified area, who request him or her to dispense, and who live more than 1.6 km of radius from an NHS pharmacy.

Relocations

A dispensing doctor who is providing PS from listed dispensing premises, and who wishes to relocate may apply in writing and that application must be granted if:

- the new location is not significantly less accessible for the existing patient groups;
- the change would not result in a significant change to the existing arrangements for the provision of PS;
- the change would not cause significant detriment to proper planning in respect of the provision of PS in its area.

Appeal Procedure

Appeals may be made within 30 days to the Secretary of State.

Self-Assessment Questions

1. What is a controlled locality?

   Answer: A controlled locality is an area which has been determined to be 'rural in character'. The former PCTs were required to delineate the boundaries of the controlled areas on a map. Where a previous determination of rurality has been made under those earlier regulations then that area continues as a controlled locality.

2. What is a reserved location?

   Answer: 'Reserved location' is a concept introduced by the 2005 Contract Regulations. A reserved location is an area within a controlled locality where the total of all patient lists for the area within a radius of 1.6 km (1 mile) of the proposed premises or location is fewer than 2750. If a pharmacy opens in a reserved location, people living within a radius of 1.6 km may choose whether to use the doctor dispensing or pharmacy dispensing, or both. The pharmacy does not have the usual 1.6 km radius where patients automatically cease to receive dispensing from the GP.

3. What is meant by 'prejudice'?

   Answer: The services will be prejudiced if the contractor would be unable to comply with the TOS. A simple reduction in the standard of service will not, in itself, constitute prejudice to the proper provision.

ADDITIONAL RESOURCE

1. http://www.defra.gov.uk/statistics/rural/what...rural/rural-urban-definition/

Chapter 7

Prescription Charges

The basic principle expressed in the NHS Act 2006, as amended by the 2012 Act, is that services are to be free unless there is some statement to the contrary.

Section 1(4) of the 2006 Act was amended by the 2012 Act. It now states:

The services provided as part of the health service in England must be free of charge except in so far as the making and recovery of charges is expressly provided for by or under any enactment, whenever passed.

Section 172 of the 2006 Act provides the power for making charges for pharmaceutical services (PS) in England and Wales:

(1) Regulations may provide for the making and recovery in such manner as may be prescribed of such charges as may be prescribed in respect of:
   (a) the supply under this Act (otherwise than under Chapter 1 of Part 7) of drugs, medicines or appliances (including the replacement and repair of those appliances); and
   (b) such of the pharmaceutical services referred to in that Chapter as may be prescribed.
(2) Regulations under this section may in particular make provision in relation to the supply of contraceptive substances and appliances under paragraph 8 of Schedule 1.
(3) This section does not apply in relation to the provision of any relevant dental service (within the meaning of section 176).

Section 173 lists the following exemptions:

(1) No charge may be made under regulations under section 172(1) in respect of:
   (a) the supply of any drug, medicine or appliance for a patient who is resident in hospital,
   (b) the supply of any drug or medicine for the treatment of sexually transmitted disease (otherwise than in the provision of primary medical services or in accordance with a pilot scheme established under section 134(1) of this Act or an LPS scheme),

Pharmacy Law and Practice. DOI: http://dx.doi.org/10.1016/B978-0-12-394289-0.00007-2

(c) *the supply of any appliance (otherwise than in pursuance of*
     paragraph 8(d) of Schedule 1) for a person who is under 16 years
     of age or is under 19 years of age and receiving qualifying full-time
     education; or
(d) *the replacement or repair of any appliance in consequence of a defect in*
     the appliance as supplied.

Wales abolished prescription charging on 1 April 2007.
Northern Ireland abolished prescription charging in 2010.
The Scottish Government abolished prescription charging on 1 April 2011.[1]

THE REGULATIONS

The current Regulations for England are the NHS (Charges for Drugs and
Appliances) Regulations 2000, SI No. 620. These substantive Regulations are
amended each year as new charges are announced.

Charges for Drugs in England

The regulations require that, subject to the exemptions, a pharmacist must
make and recover from a patient the specified charge in respect of the supply
of 'each quantity of a drug'. The term 'drug' includes 'medicine'. The inter-
pretations given in the Drug Tariff (DT), for example, are:

(1) The supply of water for injection with an antibiotic, or in accordance with
    the British National Formulary (BNF), is not charged.
(2) The supply of different strengths of the same tablet results in only one
    charge.
(3) The supply of both tablets and capsules of the same strength of the same
    drug would be two charges.

Definitions

The 2000 Regulations include a number of definitions which are specific
to the Charges Regulations and important to their meaning. In the 2000
Regulations:

(1) appliance – means a 'listed appliance', but excludes contraceptive
    appliances
(2) chemist – means any person who provides PS or local pharmaceutical ser-
    vices (LPS) (other than a doctor)
(3) drugs – includes medicines, but does not include contraceptive substances
(4) elastic hosiery – means anklet, legging, knee-cap, above-knee, below-
    knee or thigh stocking.

What is a Patient?

Patient means:

- any person for whose treatment a doctor is responsible under his or her terms of service (TOS); or
- any person who applies to a chemist for the provision of PS including a person who applies on behalf of another person; or
- a person who pays or undertakes to pay on behalf of another person a charge for which these regulations provide; or
- any person who seeks information or treatment from a walk-in-centre that is a centre at which information and treatment for minor conditions is provided to the public under arrangements made by or on behalf of the Secretary of State.

This last definition is added by the NHS (Charges for Drugs and Appliances) Amendment Regulations 2000, SI No. 122, which has the effect of making prescription charges applicable to supplies of drugs and appliances made from walk-in-centres.

When the regulations refer to a 'patient' the word also includes someone acting on behalf of the patient, such as a parent and also, say, someone collecting the prescription for a neighbour. That parent or neighbour must pay the charge on demand. Pharmacists are under no obligation to dispense a prescription until after the appropriate charges have been paid. They are entitled to collect the charge when the prescription is handed over for dispensing.

Out-of-Hours Providers

The introduction of new arrangements for out-of-hours provision of medical services has required a further amendment, in the NHS (Charges for Drugs and Appliances) and (Travel Expenses and Remission of Charges) Amendment Regulations 2005, SI No. 578, to cover the situation where an out-of-hours provider supplies medicine or appliances.

Thus a new Regulation 4A allows a provider of out-of-hours services to make and recover the usual charges from a patient, except for medicines for immediate treatment or where they are personally administered by the provider.

How Many Charges?

Provided the order is on one form, the supply of the same medicine in more than one container (whether ordered by the prescriber in that way or not) is treated as the supply of one quantity.

Guidance on what constitutes 'each quantity of a drug' is found in Part XVI of the DT.

Elastic Hosiery and Tights

Each piece of hosiery, for example, a stocking, is treated as one appliance and attracts a separate charge.

Appliances

There is only one charge payable for the supply of two or more appliances of the same type (excluding elastic hosiery).

The supply of two or more component parts of the same appliance also attracts only one charge.

Prescription Form

Prescription form means:

(a) a form provided by an NHS Trust or the NHS Commissioning Board (CB) and issued by a prescriber; or

(b) data that are created in an electronic form, signed with a prescribers advanced electronic signature and transmitted as an electronic communication to the electronic transmission of prescription (ETP) service, to enable a person to obtain PS or LPS and does not include a repeatable prescription.

This definition includes all variants of the forms including those issued by a hospital for dispensing at community pharmacies.

The 2005 Amendment Regulations also altered the definitions to reflect ETP.

A 'repeatable prescription' means a prescription which
  (a) either
      (i) is contained in a form provided by the NHS CB and issued by a repeatable prescriber which is in the format specified in Part I of Schedule 1 to the General Medical Services (GMS) Contract Regulations and which is generated by a computer and signed in ink by a repeatable prescriber; or
      (ii) is data that are created in an electronic form, signed with a repeatable prescriber's advanced electronic signature and transmitted as an electronic communication to the ETP service;
  (b) is issued or created to enable a person to obtain PS or LPS; and
  (c) indicates that the drugs or appliances ordered on that prescription may be provided more than once and specifies the number of occasions on which they may be provided.

Hospital Patients

The general rule is that treatment in hospital is free of charge. Hospitals can only charge for medicines which are provided to a patient for administration outside of the hospital. It means that medicines for the following patients are free:

- inpatients
- day patients whose medicines are administered to them whilst they are in the hospital
- patients attending accident and emergency (A&E) departments whose medicines are administered whilst they are in the hospital.

Charges are made for any medicines which are to be administered outside of the hospital.

Charges for medicines and appliances are the same as in community pharmacies, except for certain appliances which are only supplied under the NHS by hospitals. These appliances are surgical brassieres, abdominal or spinal supports and wigs.

Prisoners

No charges are payable by 'prisoners', that is, those detained in prisons. All prison-issued FP10 and FP10MDA prescriptions are exempt from the prescription charge arrangements where the letters 'HMP' along with the issuing prison address have been printed in the practice address box on the front of the prescription.

In 2008 there were amendments so that people living in England, who have just been released from prison, do not have to pay. This only applies to the prescription issued by the prison doctor, until the person can register with a general practitioner (GP).

To be exempt, their form must have 'HMP' printed in the prescriber address area on the front of the prescription form. In this instance a signature is not required on the back of the prescription form.

Instalment Prescribing

Where a medicine is ordered on a single prescription form, and it is supplied in instalments, the standard charge is payable when the first instalment is supplied. Only one charge is made, regardless of the number of instalments.

Receipts

Patients are entitled to a receipt if they ask for one. This must be on the form provided by the NHS.

Exemptions from Prescription Charges

The following persons are exempt:

(1) persons under 16 years
(2) persons under 19 years in full-time education

(3) persons aged 60 years or over
(4) a woman holding a maternity exemption certificate (expectant women and those who have given birth within the last 12 months)
(5) a person holding a medical exemption (MedEx) certificate
(6) a person holding a prescription prepayment certificate
(7) a person holding a War Pension exemption certificate (exemption only for prescriptions to treat their accepted disabilities)
(8) a person named on a current HC2 charges certificate (low income)
(9) a person receiving free of charge contraceptives
(10) a person who is themselves or whose partner is receiving various Social Security and similar allowances and payments.

These are:

Income Support
Income-based Jobseeker's Allowance
Income-related Employment and Support Allowance, or
Pension Credit Guarantee Credit.

Exemption Certificates

Exemption certificates are supplied to the patient by the Prescription Pricing Authority (PPA). They are valid for 5 years.
The following medical conditions entitle the person to exemption:

- a permanent fistula requiring continuous dressing or an appliance, fistula includes caecostomy, colostomy, laryngostomy and ileostoma
- epilepsy requiring continuous anti-convulsive therapy
- diabetes mellitus except where treatment is by diet alone
- myxodema or other conditions which require supplemental thyroid hormone
- hypoparathyroidism
- diabetes insipidus and other forms of hypopituitarism
- forms of hypoadrenalism (including Addison's disease) for which specific substitution therapy is essential
- myasthenia gravis
- a continuing physical disability which prevents the patient leaving his residence without the help of another person.

Cancer Patients

Prescription charges for cancer patients were abolished on 1 April 2009. Patients being treated for cancer, including the effects of cancer or the effects of cancer treatment, can apply for a MedEx certificate.
Guidance about the extension of the list of medical conditions has been issued by the NHS Business Services Authority (BSA). It includes guidance on which the new medical exemption is intended to cover.[2]

Prepayment Certificates

Prepayment certificates are available. The regulations state the amount to be paid for the 4- month and the 12-month certificate.

All exemptions, and the prepayment certificate, apply to all drugs and appliances provided to that patient. The exemption is not limited to treatment specifically for the condition for which exemption was granted.

NHS Low Income Scheme

A low income scheme (LIS) is available to those meeting certain income and capital limits. The scheme covers prescription costs,[3] dental costs,[4] eye care costs,[5] healthcare travel costs[6] and wigs and fabric supports.[7]

Accuracy of Exemption Statement

Paragraph 7(3) of the TOS requires the pharmacist to ask any person who fills in the exemption section on the back of the prescription form for evidence of entitlement to exemption. The question need not be asked if the exemption is claimed by virtue of Regulation 7(1) of the Charges Regulations and at the time the pharmacist had such evidence available to him.

The people covered are:

- persons under 16 years
- persons aged 60 years or over
- a woman holding a maternity exemption certificate (expectant women and those who have given birth within the last 12 months)
- persons holding a MedEx certificate
- persons holding a prescription prepayment certificate
- a person holding a War Pension exemption certificate (exemption only for prescriptions to treat their accepted disabilities).

If no satisfactory evidence is produced the pharmacist must endorse the form to that effect.

Under paragraph 7(3) before providing any drugs or appliances in accordance with a prescription form or a repeatable prescription, the pharmacist must ask any person who makes a declaration that the person named on the prescription form or the repeatable prescription does not have to pay the charges specified in Regulation 3(1) or (1A) of the Charges Regulations (4) (supply of drugs and appliances by chemists) by virtue of either:

> *(a)   entitlement to exemption under Regulation 7(1) of the Charges Regulations (5) (exemptions); or*
>
> *(b)   entitlement to remission of charges under Regulation 5 of the Remission of Charges Regulations (6) (entitlement to full remission and payment),*

to produce satisfactory evidence of such entitlement, unless the declaration is in respect of entitlement to exemption by virtue of sub-paragraph (a), (c), (d), (e), (f) or (g) of

Regulation 7(1) of the Charges Regulations or in respect of entitlement to remission by virtue of Regulation 5(1)(e) or (2) of the Remission of Charges Regulations, and at the time of the declaration P already has such evidence available to him. No exemption declaration need be made where the exemption is on age grounds and the age is computer generated on the prescription form.   (Regulation 11 of 2005 Amendment Regulations)

Declaration on Prescription Form

The declaration of entitlement to exemption or remission which appears on the prescription form must be duly completed, by or on behalf of the patient, in order for the exemption to be valid.

The amended Regulations require that where a person pays a prescription charge he or she shall sign the declaration on the prescription form that the relevant charge has been paid.

Penalty Charges

The NHS (Penalty Charge) Regulations 1999 came into force on 1 November 1999. They provide that a penalty notice may be served on any person who fails to pay a required prescription charge (or a charge for dental treatment and appliances, optical services, or any other appliances).

A penalty notice requires payment of the amount that the person has failed to pay plus an additional penalty charge calculated according to the Regulations.

Where the amount required to be paid under the penalty notice is not paid within 28 days, a further sum by way of penalty ('a surcharge' equal to 50% of the penalty charge) must be paid.

A person is not liable to a penalty charge, or a surcharge, if he or she shows that he or she did not act wrongfully, or with any lack of care, in respect of the original charge.

Additionally a person who fails to pay a charge when not exempt MAY be prosecuted for the new criminal offence of evading a prescription charge. (Guidance issued by the Department of Health (DH) restricts this to repeat offenders. The Guidance also indicates that either a penalty charge or a prosecution may be appropriate but not both.)

A patient's representative is jointly and severally liable with the patient for unpaid charges in a manner specific to this Act and MAY be issued with a penalty charge notice. The Guidance states that where a representative has signed the declaration of exemption, they are to be the initial recipient of any penalty notice and debt recovery action with the patient only being joined in that action if the representative enters a defence or otherwise fails to pay.

County Court judges should be asked to apportion liability between patients and representatives. (There is some debate as to how likely it is that a Judge will be prepared to do this.)

Bulk Scripts

No charges are payable for 'Bulk prescriptions'. A bulk script is defined in Part VIII (Notes) of the DT as:

(a) an order for two or more patients
(b) bearing the name of a school or institution in which:
  (i) at least 20 persons normally reside, and
  (ii) a particular doctor is responsible for the treatment of at least 10 of those persons.

The order must be for non-prescription only medicines (POMs) or for prescribable dressings which do not contain POM products.

Bulk prescribing is only allowed on NHS forms FP10NC and FP10C.

Contraceptives

There are no charges for contraceptive substances, or for those contraceptive appliances which are listed in the DT. *Section 77* gives Ministers power to charge for the supply of contraceptive substances and appliances, although the Regulations themselves specifically exclude contraceptive substances and appliances from charges.

Treatment of Sexually Transmitted Diseases

Prescriptions issued by NHS clinics for the treatment of sexually transmitted diseases are free of charge.

Dispensing Doctors

Dispensing doctors must charge patients for medicines and appliances in exactly the same way as pharmacists. They have similar obligations in respect of the evidence of exemption.

No charges are payable where the medicine or appliance is supplied for immediate treatment, and no order is written on a prescription form.

Similarly, no charge is payable for items administered or applied to the patient by the doctor personally. Although the Regulations state 'personally', it also applies when the nurse acts on behalf of the doctor.

Prescription Charge Refunds

The NHS (P & LPS) Regs 2013 states:

96.—(1) Where any person is entitled to repayment of a charge paid under the Charges Regulations presents an NHS pharmacist with a valid claim for the repayment within 3 months of the date on which the charge was paid, the NHS pharmacist must make the repayment.

(2) For the purposes of paragraph (1), a claim for repayment is only valid if duly made:

(a) in such form and manner as the Secretary of State has determined for an application for such a repayment under regulation 10(2)(b) of the Charges Regulations(1) (repayment of charges); or

(b) on the equivalent form issued in Scotland, Wales or Northern Ireland.

(Regulation 96)

Reward Scheme

A reward scheme, under Regulation 97 of the NHS (PS) Regulations 2013, allows pharmacists to claim a financial reward when they have identified fraudulent prescription forms and thereby prevented fraud. Participation is voluntary. It is not a requirement of the TOS.

The basic reward is £70. It is payable when a fraudulent prescription form is identified and reported, regardless of whether or not the items have been dispensed.

A Bonus Reward may be payable when the identification of a fraudulent form contributes to the detection and prevention of a fraud, or the recovery for the NHS of sums lost through fraud, regardless of whether items have been dispensed. It is 5% of the total savings resulting from the information provided, up to a maximum of £10,000. It is administered by the NHSBSA.

A similar scheme operates in Wales, though the details are different.

The NHS Counter Fraud and Security Management Service guide to 'Point of Dispensing Checks'[8] contains detailed guidance on the NHS prescription charge.

Self-Assessment Questions

1. How does the NHS Act deal with charging?

   Answer: *Section 1(4)* of the 2006 Act was amended by the 2012 Act. It now states: 'The services provided as part of the health service in England must be free of charge except in so far as the making and recovery of charges is expressly provided for by or under any enactment, whenever passed'.

2. How have the four countries of the United Kingdom dealt with charging for prescriptions?

   Answer: Charges remain in England except for certain categories of patient. Wales abolished prescription charging on 1 April 2007. Northern Ireland abolished prescription charging in 2010. The Scottish Government abolished prescription charging on 1 April 2011.

3. Under what circumstances may patients receive free medicines even when not covered by the specific exemptions?

Answer: No charges are payable where the medicine or appliance is supplied for immediate treatment, and no order is written on a prescription form. Similarly, no charge is payable for items administered or applied to the patient by the doctor personally. Although the Regulations state 'personally', this exception also applies when the nurse acts on behalf of the doctor.

ADDITIONAL RESOURCES

1. http://www.onmedica.com/NewsArticle.aspx?id=ec448c85-fb1c-4486-b430-dc0e8f9b257a
2. http://www.nhsbsa.nhs.uk/HealthCosts/Documents/HealthCosts/Guidance_issued_to_GPs_and_oncology_departments_regarding_cancer.pdf
3. http://www.nhs.uk/NHSEngland/Healthcosts/Pages/Prescriptioncosts.aspx
4. http://www.nhs.uk/NHSEngland/Healthcosts/Pages/Dentalcosts.aspx
5. http://www.nhs.uk/NHSEngland/Healthcosts/Pages/Eyecarecosts.aspx
6. http://www.nhs.uk/NHSEngland/Healthcosts/Pages/Travelcosts.aspx
7. http://www.nhs.uk/NHSEngland/Healthcosts/Pages/Wigsandfabricsupports.aspx
8. http://www.nhsbsa.nhs.uk/CounterFraud/Documents/pod_guide.pdf

Chapter 8

The Interests of the Public

THE NHS CONSTITUTION

The NHS was created out of the ideal that good health care should be available to all, regardless of wealth. When it was launched in 1948, it was based on three core principles:

(1) that it meet the needs of everyone
(2) that it be free at the point of delivery
(3) that it be based on clinical need, not ability to pay.

The NHS Constitution was first published on 21 January 2009, with a revised version in 2012. It was again altered from April 2013 by the National Health Service (Revision of NHS Constitution—Principles) Regulations 2013 SI No. 317. It applies to NHS services in England. The Constitution will be renewed every 10 years.

The Constitution contains the following elements:

- a short overview outlining the purpose of the NHS and of the Constitution;
- the principles of the NHS;
- NHS values developed by patients, public and staff;
- rights and pledges for patients and the public, as well as their responsibilities;
- rights and pledges for staff, as well as their responsibilities.

The rights and responsibilities in the Constitution generally apply to everyone who is entitled to receive NHS services and to NHS staff.

Seven key principles are set out in the Constitution:

(1) The NHS provides a comprehensive service, available to all irrespective of gender, race, disability, age, sexual orientation, religion or belief, gender reassignment, pregnancy and maternity or marital or civil partnership status.
(2) Access to NHS services is based on clinical need, not an individual's ability to pay.
(3) The NHS aspires to the highest standards of excellence and professionalism.
(4) The NHS aspires to put patients at the heart of everything it does.
(5) The NHS works across organisational boundaries and in partnership with other organisations in the interest of patients, local communities and the wider population.

Pharmacy Law and Practice. DOI: http://dx.doi.org/10.1016/B978-0-12-394289-0.00008-4

(6) The NHS is committed to providing best value for taxpayers' money and the most effective, fair and sustainable use of finite resources.

(7) The NHS is accountable to the public, communities and patients that it serves.

DUTY OF THE SECRETARY OF STATE AS TO THE NHS CONSTITUTION

According to a new *Section 1B* of the NHS Act 2006:

(1) In exercising functions in relation to the health service, the Secretary of State must have regard to the NHS Constitution.

(2) In this Act, 'NHS Constitution' has the same meaning as in Chapter 1 of Part 1 of the Health Act 2009 (see *Section 1* of that Act).

HEALTH AND WELLBEING BOARDS

Health and Wellbeing Boards are expected to be formally established when the relevant provisions of the Health and Social Care Act are brought into force from April 2013.

However, in many areas local authorities have established shadow Health and Wellbeing Boards to prepare for establishment.

From April 2013, the boards will be committees of the local authority. Their role is to:

• prepare the joint strategic needs assessment;
• prepare the Joint Health and Wellbeing Strategy; and
• to promote integrated working between NHS, public health and social care commissioners.

Establishment of Health and Wellbeing Boards

According to *Section 194* of the 2012 Act:

(1) *A local authority must establish a Health and Wellbeing Board for its area.*

(2) *The Health and Wellbeing Board is to consist of:*

　(a) *subject to* Subsection (4), *at least one councillor of the local authority, nominated in accordance with* Subsection (3);

　(b) *the director of adult social services for the local authority;*

　(c) *the director of children's services for the local authority;*

　(d) *the director of public health for the local authority;*

　(e) *a representative of the Local Healthwatch organisation for the area of the local authority;*

　(f) *a representative of each relevant clinical commissioning group (CCG); and*

(g)   *such other persons, or representatives of such other persons, as the local authority thinks appropriate.*

From April 2013, boards will be under a statutory duty to involve local people in the preparation of Joint Strategic Needs Assessments (JSNAs) and the development of joint health and wellbeing strategies.

Boards will also be accountable to local people through the membership of local councillors and Local Healthwatch.

Health and Wellbeing Boards will have a duty to encourage integrated working between decision makers and service providers in health and social care.

The Government envisages that Health and Wellbeing Boards will be the 'focal point for decision-making about local health and wellbeing', facilitating joint working between CCGs, local authorities and community stakeholders.

A core role of Health and Wellbeing Boards is to facilitate communication between local authorities and CCGs. This focus extends to scrutinising the CCG commissioning process, leading on joint commissioning where appropriate and bringing together representatives from health and social care and public health to encourage a cohesive approach across these three domains.

Health and Wellbeing Boards will be responsible for leading on the production of the JSNA, an assessment of local health and wellbeing needs across health care, social care and public health.

Health and Wellbeing Boards will be responsible for producing a 'Joint Health and Wellbeing Strategy' in response to the JSNA. The Joint Health and Wellbeing Strategy will provide a strategic framework for local commissioning plans.

CCG Duty to Consult

CCGs are required to consult the views of the Health and Wellbeing Board throughout the commissioning process to ensure that commissioning plans follow the Joint Health and Wellbeing Strategy.

The NHS Commissioning Board (NHS CB) will seek the views of the Health and Wellbeing Board when compiling their annual assessment of CCGs, in particular with relation to whether the CCG has aided the delivery of the Joint Health and Wellbeing Strategy.

Board in Every Upper Tier Local Authority

In the 2012 Act, 'local authority' means:

(a)   a county council in England;
(b)   a district council in England, other than a council for a district in a county for which there is a county council;
(c)   a London borough council;
(d)   the Council of the Isles of Scilly;
(e)   the Common Council of the City of London in its capacity as a local authority.

HEALTHWATCH

A new organisation called 'Healthwatch' is the new consumer champion for health and social care in England, and answerable to the Care Quality Commission (CQC).

It is divided into two bodies:

(1) Healthwatch England: a national organisation that enables the collective views of the people who use NHS and social care services to influence national policy. Healthwatch England was established in October 2012.

(2) Local Healthwatch: it represents the views of people who use services, carers and the public. It also acts as a channel for complaints about services.

Healthwatch England

Healthwatch England is a statutory committee of the CQC. It has three main functions:

(1) It provides leadership, guidance and support to Local Healthwatch organisations.

(2) It has the power to recommend that action is taken by the CQC when there are concerns about health and social care services.

(3) It provides advice to the Secretary of State, NHS CB, Monitor and the English local authorities, and they are required to respond to that advice.

The Secretary of State for Health must consult Healthwatch England on the mandate for the NHS CB.

Healthwatch England is required to make an annual report and lay a copy before Parliament.

The Chair of Healthwatch is a non-executive director of the CQC.

Healthwatch England has its own identity within CQC, but it is supported by CQC's infrastructure and has access to CQC's expertise.

Local Healthwatch

Local Healthwatch committees are statutory organisations that are funded through and remain accountable to local authorities.

Each Local Healthwatch has a direct relationship and ongoing dialogue with Healthwatch England for advice and support and is able to raise serious concerns with the CQC.

From April 2013, Local Healthwatch committees take over the statutory functions of the Local Involvement Network (LINk) together with additional duties including:

- reposition from influencing policy to participating in decision-making through a seat on Health and Wellbeing Board representing the patient
- public and carer's voice

- understand and present community views
- disseminating information to the public to enable patient choice.

Additionally Healthwatch will provide signposting to advocacy services commissioned by the local authority.

Current Statutory Roles of LINks

- Promoting involvement of local people in the commissioning, development and assessment of local health and social care services.
- Monitoring health and care services through 'enter and view visits', listening to users and carers and surveys to assess the effectiveness of services.
- Obtaining the views of users of health and social care services on the effectiveness of these services – access-quality-meeting local need.
- Issuing reports and recommendations on the local services to the commissioners and providers of services in order to create better services.
- Influencing commissioners of health and social care (adult) so that their plans meet our needs.

What Will Be New or Different?

Local Healthwatch will have the same powers as LINks but will also carry out some additional activities, including:

- Local Healthwatch will either provide or signpost the public to NHS complaints advocacy to support people with complaints.
- Local Healthwatch will provide advice, information and will support patients to choose the services which best meet their needs. The Patient Advocacy and Liaison Services (PALS) currently provided by Primary Care Trusts (PCTs) will transfer, with its funding, to the Local Healthwatch. It will be important for data and information about services and clients and ongoing 'live' cases also to be transferred to the new Local Healthwatch.
- Under the Local Authorities (Public Health Functions and Entry to Premises by Local Healthwatch Representatives) Regulations 2013 SI No. 351, local Health Watch has a right of entry to service providers (including pharmacies) to
  - enter and view those premises; and
  - observe the carrying-on of activities on those premises.

INDEPENDENT COMPLAINTS ADVOCACY SERVICES

Section 12 of the Health and Social Care Act 2001 placed a statutory responsibility on the Secretary of State for Health to make appropriate arrangements for the delivery of independent advocacy services to support people in making complaints about the NHS.

The Department of Health set up the Independent Complaints Advocacy Services (ICAS) on 1 September 2003.

The requirement was continued in the NHS Act 2006.

Section 248(1) states:

The Secretary of State must arrange, to such extent as he considers necessary to meet all reasonable requirements, for the provision of independent advocacy services.

What Does ICAS Do?

ICAS provides information, support and guidance to help people wishing to complain about the treatment or care they receive under the NHS. Trained advocates (case workers) with the knowledge of the NHS complaints procedure help people to understand whether they wish to pursue a complaint. Where required advocates provide support to people in making and progressing a complaint.

Arrangements from 2013

From April 2013 the local authority will be required to commission advocacy services which will be accessed through Local Healthwatch (but not necessarily provided by them).

ICAS services can be commissioned in the following ways:

(a) a contract with an ICAS provider for the NHS advocacy service;

(b) a number of local authorities contracting with a single ICAS provider for the NHS advocacy service;

(c) the contracted Local Healthwatch also contracted to provide the NHS advocacy service for the area;

(d) the Local Healthwatch contractor subcontracting for the NHS advocacy service for the area;

(e) local authorities contracting with an advocacy provider for both NHS and social care advocacy using a single contract.

PATIENT ADVOCACY AND LIAISON SERVICES

PALS are trust-based services able to assist and support patients. They provide information and resolve problems and difficulties. They act on behalf of their service users when handling patient and family concerns.

The PALS will also advise patients on how to access independent advocacy to support their complaints.

The service provides:

● confidential advice and support to patients, families and their carers;
● information on the NHS and health-related matters;
● confidential assistance in resolving problems and concerns quickly;
● explanations of NHS complaints procedures and contact details;
● information on the NHS locally;

- a focal point for feedback from patients to inform service developments;
- an early warning system for NHS Trusts, PCTs and Patient and Public Involvement Forums by monitoring trends and gaps in services and reporting these to the trust management for action.

CARE QUALITY COMMISSION

The CQC is a non-departmental public body of the United Kingdom. It was established by the Health and Social Care Act 2008 to replace three bodies:

(1) Healthcare Commission
(2) Commission for Social Care Inspection
(3) Mental Health Act Commission.

The CQC[1] regulates most health and adult social care services in England, including those provided by the NHS, local authorities, private companies or voluntary organisation.

It also protects the interests of people detained under the Mental Health Act. It is governed by four sets of Regulations:

(1) Health and Social Care Act 2008 (Regulated Activities) Regulations 2010, (SI 2010/781)
(2) CQC (Registration) Regulations 2009 No. 3119 ("the Registration Regulations")
(3) CQC (Membership) Regulations 2008 No.2252 ("the Membership Regulations")
(4) CQC (Registration and Membership) (Amendment) Regulations 2012 No. 1186.

All providers of regulated activities are required to register with the Commission.

The Regulated Activities Regulations set out essential levels of safety and quality in the provision of health and adult social care in England. Further registration requirements are set out in the Registration Regulations.

Providers of regulated activities are required to meet these registration requirements in order to become and remain registered with the Commission.

The Commission has a range of enforcement powers that it can use in order to protect patients and service users from the risk of harm. These include fines and public warnings.

The CQC can apply specific conditions in response to serious risks. For example, it can demand that a hospital ward or service is closed until the provider meets safety requirements or is suspended. It can take a service off the register if absolutely necessary. Under Regulations 16 and 18 of the Registration Regulations, a registered health service provider of regulated activities is required to notify deaths of service users or serious incidents to the Commission.

The CQC also carries out periodic and special reviews in order to improve health and social care in the United Kingdom.

What Are Regulated Activities?

Regulated activities are listed in Schedule 1 of the Health and Social Care Act 2008 (Regulated Activities) Regulations 2010. They are:

- Personal care
- Accommodation for persons who require nursing or personal care
- Accommodation for persons who require treatment for substance misuse
- Accommodation and nursing or personal care in the further education sector
- Treatment of disease, disorder or injury
- Assessment or medical treatment for persons detained under the Mental Health Act 1983
- Surgical procedures
- Diagnostic and screening procedures
- Management of supply of blood and blood-derived products
- Transport services, triage and medical advice provided remotely
- Maternity and midwifery services
- Termination of pregnancies
- Services in slimming clinics
- Nursing care
- Family planning services.

All NHS primary medical services working under one of the following contracts or agreements must register.

- General Medical Services
- Personal Medical Services
- Alternative Provider Medical Services
- NHS Act 2006 *Section 3* (contracts with the Secretary of State).

Providers of the following are included:

- out-of-hours services
- primary medical services
- urgent care centres
- minor injury units
- general practitioner-led health centres
- walk-in centres
- health and adult social care.

Regulated activities are listed in Schedule 1 of the Health and Social Care Act 2008 (Regulated Activities) Regulations 2010.

The Regulations contain a definition of 'health care professionals'. The term means a person who is a:

- medical practitioner
- dental practitioner
- dental hygienist

- dental therapist
- dental nurse
- dental technician
- orthodontic therapist
- nurse
- midwife
- biomedical scientist
- clinical scientist
- operating department practitioner
- radiographer.

Pharmacy

Pharmacists are excluded from this list. Stand-alone treatment services run by pharmacists are not required to register.

Para 13 of Schedule 2 excludes them from the operation of the Act:

Pharmaceutical services and local pharmaceutical services provided under Part 7 of the 2006 Act and services of a kind which, if provided in pursuance of that Act, would be provided as pharmaceutical services or local pharmaceutical services under that Part.

Exemptions Currently Without a Time Limit

- Doctors in independent practice.
- An individual medical practitioner who practises privately in a surgery or consulting room is exempt if they (as individuals) also provide services under NHS arrangements there or elsewhere.
- Independent midwives are exempt if they meet all of the following criteria:
  - they provide services independently (not in the NHS);
  - they work on their own (not as part of an organisation or a partnership); and
  - they only provide services on an individual basis to people in their own homes.
- Pharmacy services.
- Primary ophthalmic services.

THE HEALTH SERVICE COMMISSIONER FOR ENGLAND

The 1973 Act provided for the creation of the post of Health Service Commissioner. The function is to investigate and report and make recommendations on complaints about the activities of health authorities and those for whom they are responsible.

Separate Commissioners were created for England and Wales. The NHS (Scotland) Act 1972 similarly created the post for Scotland. The provisions of the 1973 Act were repeated in the consolidating act of 1977. The Health

Service Commissioners Act 1993 consolidated the legislation relating to the Health Service Commissioners for England, Wales and Scotland.

In practice the Parliamentary and Health Service Ombudsman (the Ombudsman) combines the two statutory roles of Parliamentary Commissioner for Administration (the Parliamentary Ombudsman) and Health Service Commissioner for England (Health Service Ombudsman). The post is currently held by Dame Julie Mellor DBE.

How to Complain

The Commissioner acts only on a written complaint, received within a year of the event. The complaint must be made by the person who has suffered the injustice (unless he or she is unable to act for oneself).

Jurisdiction

The commissioner investigates complaints that a person has suffered injustice or hardship because of a failure by a health authority to provide services properly or as a result of maladministration.

From 1 April 1996, Health Service Commissioner (Amendment) Act 1996 extended the jurisdiction of the commissioner.

Section 1 adds family health service providers and independent providers to the list of those about whom the commissioner may investigate complaints.

Section 6 removes a statutory bar on the commissioner investigating matters of clinical judgement.

Section 7 allows the commissioner to investigate complaints about family health services.

PUBLIC HEALTH ENGLAND

Public Health England is an executive agency of the Department of Health. The Chief Executive is accountable to both the Permanent Secretary and the Secretary of State for Health.

The role of Public Health England is to provide expert evidence and intelligence, together with cost–benefit analyses to enable government, the NHS and others to:

- invest effectively in prevention and health promotion
- enable people to live healthier lives
- reduce demand on health and social care services
- protect the public by providing a comprehensive range of health protection services
- commission and deliver safe and effective health care services and public health programmes.

THE HEALTH PROTECTION AGENCY

The Health Protection Agency (HPA) was created on 1 April 2003 as a Special Health Authority to cover England and Wales.

On 1 April 2005, the Agency was established as a non-departmental public body, replacing the HPA (Strategic Health Authority) and the National Radiological Protection Board and with radiation protection as part of health protection incorporated in its remit.

On 1 April 2009 the Agency merged with the National Institute of Biological Standards and Control.

The structure from 2013 onwards is unclear at the time of writing but it is likely to become an executive agency of the Department of Health.

From 1 April 2013 the HPA became a directorate of Public Health England.

It provides an integrated approach to health protection in order to reduce the impact of infectious diseases, poisons, chemicals, biological and radiation hazards.

It provides:

- information and advice to professionals and the public; and
- independent advice to the Government on public health protection policies and programmes.

It integrates expertise that was previously distributed between a number of organisations, including:

- The Public Health Laboratory Service, including the Communicable Disease Surveillance Centre and Central Public Health Laboratory
- The Centre for Applied Microbiology and Research
- The national focus for chemical incidents
- The regional service provider units that support the management of chemical incidents
- The National Poisons Information Service
- NHS public health staff responsible for infectious disease control, emergency planning and other protection support
- National Institute of Biological Standards and Control.

The HPA operates from four major centres:

(1) HPA Colindale
(2) HPA Porton
(3) The Centre for Radiation, Chemical and Environmental Hazards in Chilton
(4) The National Institute for Biological Standards and Control in Potters Bar.

There are also local and regional offices across England.

The HPA Act requires the Agency to be accountable for the standards of the health care services it provides as if it were an NHS authority. This means that the Agency is subject to registration by the CQC.

PUBLIC HEALTH OBSERVATORIES

There are 12 regional Public Health Observatories (PHOs) across the five nations of England, Scotland, Wales, Northern Ireland and the Republic of Ireland. There are nine in England.

They were established as part of the implementation of the White Paper 'Saving Lives: Our Healthier Nation'.

They produce information, data and intelligence on people's health and health care for practitioners, policy makers and the wider community.

Their role is to:

- monitor the health of the population and the underlying causes
- highlight future health problems
- assess the health impact of potential and past policies
- work in partnership with regional and local health policy makers, the NHS and the public health community and those interested in the health of the population.

'ScotPHO' is a collaboration of key national organisations involved in public health intelligence and is led by the Information and Statistics Division Scotland and NHS Health Scotland.

In Wales 'Public Health Wales Observatory' is an NHS organisation providing professionally independent public health advice and services to protect and improve the health and wellbeing of the population of Wales.

'Ireland and Northern Ireland's Population Health Observatory' is housed within the Institute of Public Health in Ireland. It covers both the Republic of Ireland and Northern Ireland.

MONITOR

Monitor is a non-departmental public body established under the Health and Social Care (Community Health and Standards) Act 2003. The Health and Social Care Act 2012 makes changes to the way NHS service providers will be regulated.

Under the Act Monitor has a role in assessing NHS trusts for foundation trust status and for ensuring that foundation trusts are financially viable and well-led, in terms of both quality and finances.

In carrying out that role, Monitor will license providers of NHS services in England and exercise functions in three areas:

(1) regulating prices;
(2) enabling integrated care and preventing anti-competitive behaviour; and
(3) supporting service continuity.

The licences will set out a range of conditions that providers must meet.

Monitor has powers to intervene in the running of a foundation trust in the event of failings in its health care standards or other aspects of its activities, which amount to a significant breach in the terms of its authorisation.

AUDIT COMMISSION

The Audit Commission covers NHS bodies. The Audit Commission is an independent body responsible for ensuring that public money is used economically, efficiently and effectively. Its function is the audit of local authority and NHS bodies. It is responsible for appointing external auditors to audit financial statements and to carry out reviews of governance arrangements and performance in all local authorities, strategic health authorities, trusts and other public bodies such as the police and fire authorities. In the course of producing its national studies, it may send out questionnaires to collect data and visit a sample of NHS trusts.

The Health Act 1999 established that the Audit Commission may work with the Commission for Health Improvement to support it to undertake a number of its functions.

FREEDOM OF INFORMATION ACT 2000

The Freedom of Information Act 2000, which came fully into effect on 1 January 2005, replaced the previous NHS Guidance on Openness.

The Act gives a general right of access to all types of recorded information held by public authorities. The Information Commissioner oversees the operation of the Act (see later).

ACCESS TO MEETINGS

NHS trusts and authorities are subject to the Public Bodies (Admission to Meetings) Act 1960. This states that generally the public have access to many formal meetings of health care bodies. An exception may be made where the body resolves to exclude the public because of the confidential nature of the business to be discussed.

Public bodies to which the public have access include:

- Council for the Regulation of Health Care Professionals
- CQC
- Monitor
- Local Healthwatch organisations
- Professional Standards Authority for Health and Social Care
- Office of the Health Professions Adjudicator
- NHS CB
- Special Health Authority (if the establishment order allows)
- NHS trusts in Wales
- Wales Centre for Health
- National Institute for Health and Care Excellence
- Health and Social Care Information Centre.

Similar bodies are specified for Scotland.

The Department of Health has issued guidance indicating that trusts are expected to conduct their business in as open a manner as possible.

Non-executive members are appointed for their personal skills and experience and not as representatives of any particular professional group. They are expected to have links with the local community. The Department of Health advises that those working in provider units managed by the trust or in units which have a contract with the trust should not be appointed. This is to avoid a conflict of interest.

Schedule 7 of the NHS Act 2006 requires the meetings of the council of governors of an NHS foundation trust to be open to the public. However, a trust's constitution can allow for members of the public to be excluded for special reasons.

There is currently no legal requirement for NHS foundation trusts to hold meetings of their board of directors in public; it is at the discretion of the individual foundation trust to decide whether to allow public access to meetings.

The amended Schedule 7 also requires a public benefit corporation to hold an annual meeting of its members which must be open to the public.

NATIONAL PATIENT SAFETY AGENCY

The Health and Social Care Act 2012 abolished the National Patient Safety Agency. Its functions have been taken on by the NHS CB.

The NHS Constitution Handbook[2]

The NHS Constitution[3]

Self-Assessment Questions

1. What are the main elements in the NHS Constitution which protect the patient?

   Answer: The Constitution contains the following elements which protect the patient:
   - a short overview outlining the purpose of the NHS and of the Constitution
   - the principles of the NHS
   - NHS values developed by patients, public and staff
   - rights and pledges for patients and the public, as well as their responsibilities
   - rights and pledges for staff, as well as their responsibilities.

2. What are the main ways in which local NHS services will be accountable to local people?

   Answer: The main ways in which local NHS services will be accountable to local people are likely to involve Health and Wellbeing Boards, which must be established by each upper tier local authority, and Local Healthwatch, which represents the views of people who use services, carers and the public. Local Healthwatch also acts as a channel for complaints about services. CCGs are required to consult the views of the Health and Wellbeing Board throughout the commissioning process to ensure that commissioning plans follow the Joint Health and Wellbeing Strategy.

3. What are the main functions of the CQC?

Answer: The CQC[4] regulates most health and adult social care services in England, including those provided by the NHS, local authorities, private companies or voluntary organisation. It also protects the interests of people detained under the Mental Health Act.

ADDITIONAL RESOURCES

1. http://en.wikipedia.org/wiki/Care_Quality_Commission
2. http://www.dh.gov.uk/en/Publicationsandstatistics/Publications/PublicationsPolicyAnd Guidance/DH_132960
3. http://www.dh.gov.uk/prod_consum_dh/groups/dh_digitalassets/@dh/@en/documents/digitalasset/dh_132958.pdf; What will Local Healthwatch and Healthwatch England look like? http://www.pifonline.org.uk/what-will-local-healthwatch-and-healthwatch-england-look-like/; NALM Healthwatch Briefing No. 1 http://www.nalm2010.org.uk/uploads/6/6/0/6/6606397/nalm_healthwatch_briefing_no_1_-_april20-2012.pdf
4. http://www.cqc.org.uk/

Chapter 9

Complaints and Breaches of the Terms of Service

CARE QUALITY COMMISSION

The Care Quality Commission (CQC) regulates and inspects health and social care services in England. It has a range of enforcement powers that can be used to protect patients and service users from the risk of harm. However, the CQC does not investigate complaints for the purpose of resolving them (except for those regarding the Mental Health Act). The providers are legally responsible for investigating complaints about their service.

Complaints by the Public About NHS Services

The NHS complaints procedure covers complaints made by a person about any matter connected with the provision of NHS services by NHS organisations or primary care practitioners: general practitioners (GPs), dentists, opticians and pharmacists. The procedure also covers services provided overseas or by the private sector where the NHS has paid for them.

If the complainant is not satisfied with the response the matter can be taken to the Parliamentary and Health Service Ombudsman or the Local Government Ombudsman.

Pharmacy Contract Requirement

Under the provisions of the NHS (Pharmaceutical and Local Pharmaceutical Services) Regulations 2013[1] pharmacy contractors are required to have in place arrangements for dealing with complaints about any matter connected with its provision of pharmaceutical services.

According to paragraph 34 of Schedule 4 to the 2013 Regulations:

a pharmacist shall have in place arrangements which comply with the requirements of the Local Authority Social Services and National Health Service Complaints (England) Regulations 2009(c), for the handling and consideration of any complaints made on or after 1st April 2009.

Pharmacy Law and Practice. DOI: http://dx.doi.org/10.1016/B978-0-12-394289-0.00009-6

There is a similar requirement in Schedule 2 to the NHS (Local Pharmaceutical Services (LPS) etc.) Regulations 2006.[2]

The regulations also impose a duty on the NHS Commissioning Board (CB) to ensure that pharmacy contractors have those arrangements in place.

There is a similar requirement for each of the NHS primary care professions.

Power to Make Regulations

Section 113 of the NHS (Community Health and Standards) Act 2003 now states:

> *(1)   The Secretary of State may by regulations make provision about the handling and consideration of complaints made under the regulations about:*
>
> (a)   *the exercise of any of the functions of an English NHS body or a cross-border SHA;*
>
> (b)   *the provision of health care by or for such a body;*
>
> (c)   *the provision of services by such a body or any other person in pursuance of arrangements made by the body under section 75 of the National Health Service Act 2006 or section 33 of the National Health Service (Wales) Act 2006 in relation to the exercise of the health-related functions of a local authority.*
>
> (d)   *anything done by the National Health Service Commissioning Board or a clinical commissioning group in pursuance of arrangements made under section 7A of the National Health Service Act 2006.*

The Complaints Regulations

The actual arrangements are set out in the Local Authority Social Services and NHS Complaints (England) Regulations 2009, SI No. 309 (the 'Complaints Regulations').[3] They apply to England and Wales.

Regulation 3 of the Complaints Regulations requires 'responsible bodies' to make arrangements for the handling and consideration of complaints.

Definitions

'Responsible bodies' are defined (in Regulation 2) to mean local authorities, NHS bodies and certain other providers who provide services under arrangements with NHS bodies.

Pharmacies are included by the definitions in Regulation 2, which states:

> *"independent provider" means a person or body who:*
>
> (a)   *provides health care in England under arrangements made with an NHS body; and*
>
> (b)   *is not an NHS body or primary care provider;*

"responsible body" means a local authority, NHS body, primary care provider or independent provider;
"primary care provider" means a person or body who:
  (f) *provides pharmaceutical services in accordance with arrangements made under section 126 of the 2006 Act;*
  (g) *provides additional pharmaceutical services in accordance with arrangements made under section 127 of the 2006 Act; or*
  (h) *provides local pharmaceutical services in accordance with an LPS scheme established under paragraph 1 of Schedule 12 to the 2006 Act.*

Purpose of the Arrangements

The arrangements ensure:

- complaints are properly and efficiently dealt with
- complainants are treated with respect and courtesy
- complainants receive, so far as is reasonably practical:
  - assistance in understanding the process
  - advice on where they may obtain assistance
  - a timely and appropriate response
- complainants are informed about the outcome and
- further action is taken if necessary.   (Regulation 3 Complaints Regulations 2009)

Responsible Person

The pharmacy contractor is required to designate a responsible person, to be responsible for ensuring compliance with the arrangements and in particular ensuring that action is taken, if necessary, in the light of the outcome of a complaint.

The responsible person is required to be the chief executive officer of the company, or, if the pharmacy contractor is a partnership firm, must be one of the partners. In the case of a pharmacy business operated by a sole proprietor, the responsible person must be that sole proprietor.

The functions of the responsible person may be performed by any person authorised by the pharmacy contractor to act on behalf of the responsible person – but ultimately, the responsibility for ensuring compliance remains with the chief executive, partner or sole proprietor as appropriate.   (Regulation 4 Complaints Regulations 2009)

Complaints Manager

The pharmacy contractor is also required to designate a complaints manager, to be responsible for managing the procedures for handling and considering complaints in accordance with the arrangements.

The complaints manager need not be an employee. He could be the same person as the responsible person or could even be a complaints manager designated by another pharmacy contractor.

The functions of the complaints manager may be performed by any person authorised by the responsible body to act on behalf of the complaints manager. (Regulation 4 Complaints Regulations 2009)

The complaints procedure is intended only to resolve complaints. It does not investigate disciplinary matters or apportion blame.

The arrangements for handling complaints must be in writing and a copy must be given, free of charge, to any person who makes a request for one.

The pharmacy contractor is responsible for compliance with the regulations and must designate a 'complaints manager', to manage the procedures for handling and considering complaints. A deputy complaints manager may also be authorised, to act in the absence of the complaints manager.

Who Can Make a Complaint

A complaint may be made by:

(a) a person who receives or has received services from a responsible body; or
(b) a person who is affected, or likely to be affected, by the action, omission or decision of the pharmacy concerned.

A complaint can also be made by a representative of a person who:

- has died
- is a child under the age of 18 years
- is unable to make a complaint because of a physical incapacity or lack of mental capacity
- has requested the representative to act on their behalf.

Where the complaint is made on behalf of a child or a person lacking capacity, the pharmacy contractor must not consider the complaint unless satisfied that there are reasonable grounds for the complaint being made by the representative instead of the child or person lacking capacity.

The pharmacy contractor must also be satisfied that the representative is conducting the complaint in the best interests of the person affected.

If the pharmacy contractor does not believe there are reasonable grounds for the representative making the complaint, or that the complaint is in the best interests of the person, the pharmacy must notify the representative in writing, with reasons. (Regulation 5 Complaints Regulations 2009)

Duty to Handle Complaints

A pharmacy contractor has a duty to handle complaints under the regulations only about the pharmaceutical services provided under arrangements with an NHS body.

Complaints that Are Not Required to Be Dealt Formally

Some complaints are not required to be dealt with under the NHS arrangements:

- A complaint which is made orally and is resolved to the complainant's satisfaction on the next working day.
- A complaint involving the same subject matter as that of a previously resolved oral complaint.
- A complaint by a 'responsible body' (e.g., another pharmacy contractor) although where the complaint has simply been forwarded by one of these bodies, the pharmacy contractor is under a duty to deal with the complaint.
- A complaint which has previously been investigated under the current regulations.
- A complaint which is being or has been investigated by a Health Service Commissioner under the Health Service Commissioners Act 1993.
- A complaint arising out of the alleged failure by the pharmacy contractor to comply with a request for information under the Freedom of Information Act 2000.   (Regulation 8 Complaints Regulations 2009)

Time Limits for Making a Complaint

A complaint must be made no later than 12 months after the date on which the matter occurred, or if later, the date on which the matter came to the notice of the complainant.

A complaint may be made orally, in writing or electronically. The pharmacy contractor must make a written record of an oral complaint and provide a copy of this record to the complainant.

The pharmacy contractor must acknowledge the complaint not later than 3 working days after the date on which the complaint is received. The acknowledgement may be made orally or in writing.

Working days under these regulations means Mondays to Fridays which are not Christmas Day, Good Friday or a bank holiday.   (Regulation 13 Complaints Regulations 2009)

At the time it acknowledges the complaint, the pharmacy must offer to discuss with the complainant, at an agreed time:

(a) the manner in which the complaint is to be handled; and
(b) the period ('the response period') within which:
  (i) the investigation of the complaint is likely to be completed; and
  (ii) the response is likely to be sent to the complainant.

If the complainant does not accept the offer of a discussion, the responsible body must itself:

(a) determine the response period; and
(b) notify the complainant in writing of that period.

The pharmacy contractor has up to 6 months in which to make the response to the complainant.

Complaints Made to the NHS Commissioning Board

Complaints may be made to the Board about the provision of services by a primary care provider under arrangements made between it and the Board. (Regulation 7 Complaints Regulations 2009)

EXTRACT FROM COMPLAINTS REGULATIONS

Responsibility for Complaints Arrangements

4.—*(1) Each responsible body must designate:*

(a) a person, in these Regulations referred to as a responsible person, to be responsible for ensuring compliance with the arrangements made under these Regulations, and in particular ensuring that action is taken if necessary in the light of the outcome of a complaint; and

(b) a person, in these Regulations referred to as a complaints manager, to be responsible for managing the procedures for handling and considering complaints in accordance with the arrangements made under these Regulations.

(4) The responsible person is to be:

(a) in the case of a local authority or NHS body, the person who acts as the chief executive officer of the authority or body;

(b) in the case of any other responsible body, the person who acts as the chief executive officer of the body or, if none:

    (i) the person who is the sole proprietor of the responsible body;

    (ii) where the responsible body is a partnership, a partner; or

    (iii) in any other case, a director of the responsible body, or a person who is responsible for managing the responsible body.

(5) The complaints manager may be:

(a) a person who is not an employee of the responsible body;

(b) the same person as the responsible person;

(c) a complaints manager designated by another responsible body under paragraph (1)(b).

Persons who May Make Complaints

5.—*(1) A complaint may be made by:*

(a) a person who receives or has received services from a responsible body; or

(b) a person who is affected, or likely to be affected, by the action, omission or decision of the responsible body which is the subject of the complaint.

(2) A complaint may be made by a person (in this regulation referred to as a representative) acting on behalf of a person mentioned in paragraph (1) who:

(a) has died;

(b) is a child;

(c) is unable to make the complaint themselves because of:

    (i) physical incapacity; or

    (ii) lack of capacity within the meaning of the Mental Capacity Act 2005(a); or

(d) has requested the representative to act on their behalf.

(3) Where a representative makes a complaint on behalf of a child, the responsible body to which the complaint is made:

    (a) must not consider the complaint unless it is satisfied that there are reasonable grounds for the complaint being made by a representative instead of the child; and

    (b) if it is not so satisfied, must notify the representative in writing, and state the reason for its decision.

(4) This paragraph applies where:

    (a) a representative makes a complaint on behalf of:

        (i) a child; or

        (ii) a person who lacks capacity within the meaning of the Mental Capacity Act 2005; and

    (b) the responsible body to which the complaint is made is satisfied that the representative is not conducting the complaint in the best interests of the person on whose behalf the complaint is made.

(5) Where paragraph (4) applies:

    (a) the complaint must not be considered or further considered under these Regulations; and

    (b) the responsible body must notify the representative in writing, and state the reason for its decision.

(6) In these Regulations any reference to a complainant includes a reference to a representative.

Duty to Handle Complaints

6.—*(1) This regulation applies to a complaint made on or after 1st April 2009 in accordance with these Regulations to:*

    (b) an NHS body about:

        (i) the exercise of its functions; or

        (ii) the exercise of any function discharged or to be discharged by it under arrangements made between it and a local authority under section 75 of the 2006 Act in relation to the exercise of the health-related functions of a local authority;

    (c) a primary care provider about the provision of services by it under arrangements with an NHS body; or

    (d) an independent provider about the provision of services by it under arrangements with an NHS body.

(4) Where this regulation applies to a complaint, the responsible body to which the complaint is made must handle the complaint in accordance with these Regulations.

Complaints about the Provision of Health Services

7.—*(1) This regulation applies to a complaint which is:*

　(a) made to the NHS CB in accordance with these Regulations on or after 1st April 2009;

　(b) about the services provided by a provider under arrangements with the Board; and

　(c) not specified in regulation 8(1).

(2) In this regulation, "provider" means an NHS body, primary care provider or independent provider.

(3) Where a Primary Care Trust receives a complaint to which this regulation applies:

　(a) the Primary Care Trust must ask the complainant whether the complainant consents to details of the complaint being sent to the provider; and

　(b) if the complainant so consents, the Primary Care Trust must as soon as reasonably practicable send details of the complaint to the provider.

(4) If the Primary Care Trust considers that it is appropriate for the Primary Care Trust to deal with the complaint:

　(a) it must so notify the complainant and the provider; and

　(b) it must continue to handle the complaint in accordance with these Regulations.

(5) If the Primary Care Trust considers that it is more appropriate for the complaint to be dealt with by the provider, and the complainant consents:

　(a) the Primary Care Trust must so notify the complainant and the provider;

　(b) when the provider receives the notification given to it under sub-paragraph (a):

　　(i) the provider must handle the complaint in accordance with these Regulations; and

　　(ii) the complainant is deemed to have made the complaint to the provider under these Regulations.

SANCTIONS FOR BREACH OF TERMS OF SERVICE

The 2013 Regulations set out various procedures which are available to the NHS CB should it find that a pharmacy contractor has breached the terms of service (TOS).

Regulation 70(1) *Where an NHS chemist (C) breaches a term of service and the breach is capable of remedy, the NHS CB may by a notice ('a remedial notice') require C to remedy the breach.*

The NHS CB may also make a withholding of remuneration.

Regulation 71(1) *Where an NHS chemist (C) breaches a term of service and the breach is not capable of remedy, the Primary Care Trust (PCT1) with which C has the arrangements to provide the pharmaceutical services to which the breach relates may by a notice ('a breach notice') require C not to repeat the breach.*

Again the NHS CB may make a withholding of remuneration. Any withholding is subject to the following:

(a) the NHS CB is satisfied that the breach is, or was, without good cause;
(b) the amount withheld is justifiable and proportionate, having regard to the nature and seriousness of the breach and the reasons for it;
(c) the NHS CB includes in the notice its reasons for both the decision to withhold remuneration and the amounts.

Removal from the Pharmaceutical List

The NHS CB may remove a contractor from the pharmaceutical list if the contractor:

(a) fails to take the steps set out in a remedial notice and the Board is satisfied that it is necessary to remove the contractor from the pharmaceutical list, or remove the listing of particular listed chemist premises:
   (i) to protect the safety of any persons to whom the contractor may provide pharmaceutical services; or
   (ii) to protect the NHS CB from material financial loss; or
(b) has breached the TOS, and:
   (i) the contractor has repeatedly been issued with remedial notices or breach notices;
   (ii) previously been issued with a remedial notice or breach notice and the Board is satisfied that the contractor is likely to persist in breaching the TOS without good cause.

The NHS CB may only remove:

(a) particular chemist premises from the listing if the relevant breaches all relate to those particular chemist premises; or
(b) the contractor from its pharmaceutical list if the relevant breaches all relate to listed chemist premises which are that contractor's only listed premises.

The NHS CB may only remove the contractor, or chemist premises listed in relation to that contractor, from its pharmaceutical list under paragraph (1) if:

(a) the removal is justifiable and proportionate, having regard to the nature and seriousness of the breaches (or likely breaches) and the reasons for the same; and
(b) The NHS CB, when it notifies the contractor of the decision, includes in the notice its duly justified reasons for the decision.

NHS Fitness to Practice Procedures

The Department of Health issued guidance to Primary Care Trusts (PCTs) on the Fitness to Practise procedures in July 2005. (Delivering quality in primary care: PCT management of primary care practitioners' lists – community chemist contractors/bodies corporate.) This Guidance has not been updated since the 2012 Regulations came into law.

The Fitness to Practice provisions in the 2013 Regulations permit the NHS CB to defer or reject an application for inclusion in the pharmaceutical list and also provide the power to remove a pharmacy contractor from the pharmaceutical list.

Mandatory Refusal of Application for Contract

Regulation 33 of the 2013 Regulations sets out circumstances where the NHS CB must refuse to grant an application on fitness grounds.

These are:

(a) where the applicant, a director or a superintendent:
- has been convicted in the United Kingdom of murder
- has been sentenced to a term of imprisonment of over 6 months for an offence committed after 1 April 2005.

(b) where the applicant:
- is subject to national disqualification
- has not updated his application following an investigation or hearing set out in Regulation 26(4).

Discretionary Refusal

The NHS CB has discretion to refuse applications on grounds of suitability, fraud or efficiency.

The Board should take into account issues such as:

- nature of offence or incident
- timescale
- number of offences or incidents
- any action taken or penalties imposed
- relevance to provision of NHS pharmaceutical services
- whether any offence was a 'sexual offence'
- decisions of other PCTs.

REMOVAL OR SUSPENSION OF PRACTITIONERS

The Board may and in some cases must suspend and remove practitioners from the relevant lists on the grounds of inefficiency, fraud or unsuitability. They may also impose conditions on continued presence on the list.

The criteria are similar to those relevant to decisions on applications.

Where a director or superintendent of a limited company has been convicted of murder or has been sentenced to more than 6 months imprisonment, the limited company has 28 days to remove that person from office or the entire limited company will be removed from the list.

Contingent Removals

The Board may impose conditions on persons on the list to prevent:

- any prejudice to the efficiency of the service
- any continuation of fraud.

If the conditions are not agreed then the Board may remove that person from the list. Conditions must be reviewed on receipt of a written request.

Conditions cannot be imposed in 'suitability' cases. The guidance states that: 'a chemist is either suitable or unsuitable. There are no degrees of suitability'. Therefore, the Board must remove the contractor from the list if it decides he or she is unsuitable.

Suspension

The Board may suspend a contractor if the action is necessary to protect the public. (*Section 154* of the NHS Act 2006)

A suspended contractor may appoint a 'temporary chemist' to provide services on his or her behalf.

Suspension may only be for 6 months unless:

- the Family Health Services Appeals Authority (FHSAA) agrees otherwise
- the Board is awaiting the outcome of regulatory body or criminal investigations
- the Board has decided to remove or contingently remove a contractor from the list and it has imposed a suspension until the appeal process has been completed.

Suspended contractors are paid according to Directions from the Department of Health, which take account of previous levels of payment.

NATIONAL DISQUALIFICATION

The Board may apply to the FHSAA for the national disqualification of a practitioner that it has removed from one of its lists.

Performers' Lists

The Health and Social Care Act 2012 adds new sections to the NHS Act 2006 to create the legislative framework for the NHS CB to establish and maintain a list of people approved to perform pharmaceutical services.

Future regulations are expected to specify how pharmacists and pharmacy assistants may apply for inclusion in order to provide pharmaceutical services such as dispensing of medicines and the provision of minor ailments and smoking cessation services.

Pharmacy assistants will also be included on a performers' list.

EXTRACT FROM NHS ACT 2006 AS AMENDED

Section 147A Performers of Pharmaceutical Services and Assistants

(1) Regulations may make provision for the preparation, maintenance and publication by the Board of one or more lists of:

> *(a) persons approved by the Board for the purpose of assisting in the provision of pharmaceutical services which the Board arranges;*
>
> *(b) persons approved by the Board for the purpose of performing local pharmaceutical services.*

(2) The regulations may, in particular, provide that:

> *(a) a person of a prescribed description may not assist in the provision of pharmaceutical services which the Board arranges unless the person is included in a list prepared by virtue of subsection (1)(a);*
>
> *(b) a person of a prescribed description may not perform local pharmaceutical services unless the person is included in a list prepared by virtue of subsection (1)(b).*

Formal Complaints to the General Pharmaceutical Council

Complaints may be made to the General Pharmaceutical Council (GPhC) where a pharmacist or technician's fitness to practise is called into question. The GPhC also deals with complaints involving registered pharmacy premises. Complaints may be made by a member of the public or another health professional.

Examples of Fitness to Practice Issues

The GPhC investigates a range of matters including:

- dispensing errors
- dishonesty, for example, fraud or theft
- working under the influence of alcohol or drugs
- sexual misconduct.

Issues Not Usually Investigated by the GPhC

The GPhC will not normally investigate matters such as:

- claims for compensation
- customer service issues (such as impolite pharmacy staff)
- contract issues (e.g., hours of opening or charges for private prescriptions).

GPhC Fitness to Practise

The GPhC describes 'fitness to practise' as 'a person's suitability to be on the register without restrictions'.

According to the GPhC this means:

maintaining appropriate standards of proficiency, ensuring good health and good character, and adherance to the principles of good practice set out in our various, standards, guidance and advice.

Sanctions

If a pharmacy professional's fitness to practise is found to be impaired, the GPhC can:

- issue the individual with a warning
- impose conditions on their practice
- suspend them from practising
- remove them from the register.

Pharmacy Student Code of Conduct

All students studying on an MPharm degree, Overseas Pharmacists' Assessment Programme (OSPAP), or foundation degree in pharmacy must at all times abide by the GPhC Student Code of Conduct based on the GPhC's 'Standards of conduct, ethics and performance'.[4] Students must demonstrate professional conduct in the same way as they will be expected to once they qualify as a registered pharmacist.

Pharmacy Student Fitness to Practice

Applicants for registration as a pharmacist must demonstrate their fitness to practise. The GPhC has issued guidance to all schools of pharmacy offering accredited MPharm degrees, foundation degrees and OSPAP courses to provide them with advice on how to develop and apply consistent fitness to practise procedures for students.[5]

The code and fitness to practice will be implemented on a local level within pharmacy schools, which have a duty to report issues to the GPhC of any unresolved issues upon graduation.

Self-Assessment Questions

1. What services are covered by the NHS complaints procedures?

    Answer: The NHS complaints procedure covers complaints made by a person about any matter connected with the provision of NHS services by NHS organisations or primary care practitioners: GPs, dentists, opticians and pharmacists. The procedure also covers services provided overseas or by the private sector where the NHS has paid for them.

2. What is the purpose of the procedure?

   Answer: The arrangements ensure that complaints are properly and efficiently dealt with and that complainants are treated with respect and courtesy. Complainants receive, so far as is reasonably practical, assistance in understanding the process, advice on where they may obtain assistance and a timely and appropriate response. They are informed about the outcome and further action is taken if necessary. (Regulation 3 Complaints Regulations 2009)

3. Who may be a complaints manager in a pharmacy?

   Answer: The pharmacy contractor is required to designate a complaints manager who is responsible for managing the procedures for handling and considering complaints in accordance with the arrangements. He need not be an employee. He could be the same person as the responsible person, or could even be a complaints manager designated by another pharmacy contractor.

ADDITIONAL RESOURCES

1. http://www.legislation.gov.uk/uksi/2012/1909/contents/made
2. http://www.legislation.gov.uk/uksi/2006/552/contents/made
3. www.legislation.gov.uk/uksi/2009/309/contents/made
4. http://www.pharmacyregulation.com/sites/default/files/Code%20of%20conduct%20for%20phamacy%20students%20s.pdf
5. http://www.pharmacyregulation.com/sites/default/files/Guidance%20on%20student%20fitness%20to%20practise%20procedures%20s.pdf

Chapter 10

Retail Pharmacy

THE NATURE OF THE CONTROL

The operation of a pharmacy is subject to a number of laws, which deal with ownership and with the activities carried on in the premises. In excess of 200 different pieces of legislation exist. This chapter deals only with those directly relevant to the establishment and running of the professional practice.

HISTORY

The Pharmacy Act 1852 established a system of control over the practice of pharmacy by requiring registration as a 'chemist and druggist' or a 'pharmaceutical chemist'. Passing an exam entitled the person to registration and to the right to sell poisons.

The Pharmacy and Poisons Act 1933 compelled all pharmacists to become members of the then Pharmaceutical Society of Great Britain (PSGB). The Statutory Committee system was established to disqualify persons from membership and hence from being an 'authorised seller of poisons'.

The Pharmacy Act 1954 removed the connection between poisons and pharmacy (which had been present since the Arsenic Act 1851) and dealt only with the profession of pharmacy.

In 2006 the Department of Health published a report, The Regulation of Non-medical Healthcare Professionals, which recommended considerable change to the regulation of the profession. This report became known as the 'Foster Report'.

In 2007 the Pharmacists and Pharmacy Technicians Order SI 2007 No. 289, made under powers in *Section 60* of the Health Act 1999, made changes to the Royal Pharmaceutical Society of Great Britain (RPSGB) which reflected the Foster Report.

The Order made changes to the registers, introduced new statutory committees, brought in new 'fitness to practise' powers and procedures and extended regulation to pharmacy technicians.

In the same year a government White Paper announced further changes, in particular splitting the regulatory function from the professional one.

Pharmacy Law and Practice. DOI: http://dx.doi.org/10.1016/B978-0-12-394289-0.00010-2

The Pharmacy Order 2010, SI No. 231, established a new regulator for pharmacy, the General Pharmaceutical Council (GPhC), and set out the arrangements, in Great Britain, for the professional regulation of pharmacists, pharmacy technicians and registered pharmacy premises. Details of processes for registering pharmacists, pharmacy technicians and pharmacy premises are set out in accompanying rules. The change took effect on 27 September 2010.

Part IV of the Medicines Act 1968, which deals with pharmacies, has been extensively amended.

Section 9 of the Poisons Act 1972 (c.66), in respect of the regulation and inspection of registered pharmacies in Great Britain, is amended.

The Pharmacists and Pharmacy Technicians Order 2007 was repealed by the Pharmacy Order 2010.

REGISTERED PHARMACY

The GPhC (Registration) Rules Order of Council 2010 SI No. 1617 came into force on 27 September 2010. These 'Registration Rules' set out the rules for registration of premises and professionals.

Section 74(1) of the Medicines Act 1968 defines a 'registered pharmacy' as:

(a) *in relation to Great Britain, premises entered in the register required to be kept under Article 19 of the Pharmacy Order 2010 for the purposes of Sections 74A and 74J of the Medicines Act 1968; and*
(b) *in relation to Northern Ireland, premises entered in the register required to be kept under Section 75(34) of the Medicines Act 1968.*

The Registrar of the GPhC is required to keep a register of premises in Great Britain where the business meets the requirements of *Section 74B*.

According to the GPhC website, 'The GPhC will only register pharmacy premises if the principal activity at the premises is the retail sale or supply of pharmacy (P) medicines and/or prescription only medicines (POMs).'

The Registrar of the Pharmaceutical Society of Northern Ireland (PSNI) is required to keep a similar register for premises in Northern Ireland.

Applications to enter premises in the register of premises are made in writing to the Registrar.

For registered pharmacies the Register will include:

- address of the premises;
- name and address of the person carrying on a retail pharmacy business (RPB) at the premises;
- name under which the business trades;
- date of first and any subsequent entry in the Register;
- period for which the entry is valid;
- any conditions which attach to the entry;
- any annotations in respect of specialisations;

- where the owner of the business is a body corporate, the name and home address of the superintendent pharmacist;
- details of any improvement notices issued under Article 13 of the Pharmacy Order 2010;
- recording information in the Welsh language, where appropriate;
- marking the Register to distinguish those premises which have temporary registration under emergency registration provisions (*Section 74J* of the Medicines Act 1968).

RETAIL PHARMACY BUSINESS (RPB)

The Medicines Act and the Human Medicines Regulations 2012 use the term 'RPB'. This is defined as:

a business (other than a professional practice carried on by a doctor or dentist) which consists of or includes the retail sale of medicinal products that are not subject to general sale.

In other words, a business is an 'RPB' if it is:

- a business which consists of the retail sale of POM or P medicine, or
- a business which includes the retail sale of POM or P medicine, and
- it is not part of the professional practice of a doctor or dentist.

The phrase 'registered pharmacy' refers to the premises, and the term 'RPB' refers to the professional practice of a pharmacist who sells medicines and dispenses prescriptions.

Who May Own a Pharmacy?

Section 69 of the MA 1968 lists the persons who can operate a pharmacy.
An RPB may be lawfully carried on by:

(a) a pharmacist
(b) a partnership of pharmacists
(c) a 'body corporate'
(d) a 'representative' of a pharmacist.

There are a number of additional conditions for each circumstance outlined above.

Partnerships

In England, Wales and Northern Ireland, partnerships can only carry on a pharmacy if all the partners are registered pharmacists. In Scotland, the partnership running the pharmacy must have one partner who is a pharmacist, but the rest need not be qualified as pharmacists.

One of the partners who is a pharmacist or another pharmacist must be the 'responsible pharmacist' at those premises.

The Limited Liability Partnership Act 2000 came into force on 6 April 2001. The limited liability partnership is a hybrid of partnerships and companies. Limited liability partnerships are treated by the Medicines Act as companies rather than partnerships and therefore they may include non-pharmacist members. They need to appoint a superintendent pharmacist.

The general law relating to partnerships is discussed in Chapter 29.

Body Corporate

This is a term applied to any association of individuals which is so constituted as to acquire a collective legal personality. The law recognises that some groups of people ought to be treated as a single individual, which is a separate 'legal entity' from those who make up the group.

There are two types of 'body corporate':

(1) A 'corporation sole'. The Crown, Ministers and an archbishop are examples. The idea of a 'body corporate' enables the post to be sued instead of the person who holds the post for the time being.
(2) A 'corporation aggregate'. There are various types, including:
    (i)   public corporations such as the BBC
    (ii) cooperative societies
    (iii) mutual building societies
    (iv) private limited companies
    (v)   public limited companies.

The most important and numerous are private limited companies. Generally speaking, where the term 'body corporate' is used the term 'company' can replace it.

The business of keeping, preparing and dispensing P medicines and POMs must be under the management of a superintendent pharmacist.

Superintendent

(1) The superintendent must be a pharmacist.
(2) He or she must not act in a similar capacity for any other body corporate.
(3) He or she must send a statement to the Registrar stating whether or not he or she is a member of the board of the body corporate.
(4) The statement must be in writing, signed by the superintendent and signed on behalf of the body corporate.

Representative

A representative of a pharmacist may carry on the pharmacy in certain circumstances (*Section 72*). These are:

(a) Where the pharmacist has died
(b) Where he or she has become bankrupt

(c) He or she becomes a person who lacks capacity (within the meaning of the Mental Capacity Act 2005) to carry on the business, or in Scotland, a guardian or judicial factor is appointed for the representative on the ground that he or she suffers from mental disorder, or in Northern Ireland, a committee, receiver or guardian is appointed in the case under the Lunacy Regulation (Ireland) Act 1871.

The representative is:

(a) The executor or administrator of a deceased pharmacist. For the first 3 months after the death any person beneficially interested in the estate may carry on the business.
(b) The trustee in bankruptcy (or similar).
(c) The donee of an enduring or a lasting power of attorney (or similar) of a mentally incapacitated pharmacist.

The representative may carry on business for a period of 5 years after the death of a pharmacist or for 3 years in any other case.

The name and address must be notified to the Registrar of the GPhC. There must be a 'responsible pharmacist' at all premises where the retail sale or supply of P medicine and POM occurs.

RESPONSIBLE PHARMACIST

The Medicines (Pharmacies) (Responsible Pharmacist) Regulations 2008[1] came into force on 1 October 2009.

A 'responsible pharmacist' must be in charge of the sale or supply of P medicine and POM by retail or as dispensed medicines at each of the premises. The responsible pharmacist must be:

(a) the superintendent mentioned in *Subsection (1)(a)* of this section, or
(b) a pharmacist subject to the directions of the superintendent.

A 'responsible pharmacist' must be in charge of the part of the business at those premises which concerns:

(a) the retail sale at those premises of medicinal products (whether they are on a general sale list or not), and
(b) the supply at those premises of such products in circumstances corresponding to retail sale.

A notice must be conspicuously displayed at those premises stating:

(a) the name of the responsible pharmacist for the time being,
(b) the number of the registration under Part 4 of the Pharmacy Order 2010 or in relation to Northern Ireland, under the Pharmacy (Northern Ireland) Order 1976, and

(c) the fact that he or she is for the time being in charge of the business at those premises.

The responsible pharmacist must be:

(a) the person carrying on the business, or
(b) if the business is carried on by a partnership, one of the partners or, in Scotland, one of the partners who is a person registered in Part 1 of the register maintained under Article 19 of the Pharmacy Order 2010 (pharmacists other than visiting practitioners), or
(c) another pharmacist.

Guidance for owners and superintendent pharmacists who employ responsible pharmacists can be found here.[2]

Retail Sale

Regulation 8(3) of the Human Medicines Regulations 2012 defines 'retail sale' as the sale of a substance or an article to a person who buys it other than to sell it, supply it, administer it or cause it to be administered in the course of business.

Regulation 8(3) states:

In these Regulations, references to selling by retail, or to retail sale, are references to selling a product to a person who buys it otherwise than for a purpose specified in Regulation 18(8).

The purposes in Regulation 18(8) are:

(a) selling or supplying the product; or
(b) administering it or causing it to be administered to one or more human beings, in the course of a business carried on by that person.

Wholesale Dealing

Wholesale dealing means selling or supplying a product (or procuring or holding or exporting) to another European Economic Area (EEA) state for someone else to sell or supply or administer it to a human being in the course of business.

Regulation 8(2) states:

In these Regulations references to distribution of a product by way of wholesale dealing are to be construed in accordance with Regulation 18(7) and (8).

Regulation 18(7): In these Regulations a reference to distributing a product by way of wholesale dealing is a reference to:

(a) selling or supplying it; or
(b) procuring or holding it or exporting it to another EEA State for the purposes of sale or supply, to a person who receives it for a purpose within paragraph (8).

(8) Those purposes are
  (a) selling or supplying the product; or
  (b) administering it or causing it to be administered to one or more human
       beings, in the course of a business carried on by that person.

Supply in Circumstances Corresponding to Retail Sale

Regulation 8(4) defines this 'as a supply *otherwise than a sale* of a substance or article to a person who buys it other than to sell it, supply it, administer it or cause it to be administered in the course of business.'

Regulation 8(4) states:

In these Regulations, references to supplying anything in circumstances corresponding to retail sale are references to supplying it, otherwise than by way of sale, to a person who receives it otherwise than for a purpose specified in regulation 18(8).

Supply of NHS Medicines

Legally, the supply of medicines on an NHS script is not a sale.

This has been considered by the courts on two occasions. In 1965, the House of Lords considered whether the Minister of Health could import medicines for which Pfizer Corp. held patents in this country. In dealing with this, they decided that there was no sale of medicines by a hospital to a patient (Pfizer Corporation v. Minister of Health, 1965, 1 AER, 450).

In 1968 a court had to deal with contaminated medicine supplied to a patient. The case was brought under the Food and Drugs Act, which required that the medicine had been sold to the complainant. The court decided that the pharmacy had a contract with the then Executive Council for the supply of services. The pharmacy was paid remuneration for the services, and there was not a sale of medicine to the Executive Council (Appleby v. Sleep, 1968, 2 AER, 265).

Dispensing Only Pharmacies

The definition of an RPB, taken originally from *Section 132* of the Medicines Act and repeated in the Human Medicines Regulations, suggests that a business where no retail sales took place (that is which only dispensed NHS scripts) would not be an RPB.

But Regulation 220 also restricts the supply of P medicine and POM to an RPB in a registered pharmacy.

The phrase 'supply in circumstances corresponding to retail sale' covers the supply of dispensed medicines in the NHS. Therefore, even dispensing-only pharmacies have to be registered, because the operation of such pharmacies can only be as part of an 'RPB'. The legislation does not envisage a pharmacy where no retail sales occur.

Sale or supply of medicinal products not subject to general sale.

220—(1) Unless paragraph (2) applies, a person ("P") may not sell or supply, or offer for sale or supply, a medicinal product that is not subject to general sale.

(2) This paragraph applies if:

> *(a) P is a person lawfully conducting a retail pharmacy business;*
>
> *(b) the product is sold, supplied, or offered for sale or supply, on premises that are a registered pharmacy; and*
>
> *(c) P or, if the transaction is carried out on P's behalf by another person, that other person is, or acts under the supervision of, a pharmacist.*

(3) This regulation is subject to Chapter 3.

Register of Pharmacists

A pharmacist is a person whose name is entered in the Register of Pharmacists. This was established originally by the Pharmacy Act 1852, but now exists, in Great Britain, as a result of the Pharmacy Order 2010.

For Northern Ireland, the Register is maintained under a requirement in *Section 9* of the Pharmacy and Poisons Act (Northern Ireland) 1925.

Restricted Titles

The use of some professional titles is restricted by Article 38 of the Pharmacy Order 2012.

Only pharmacists entered in the GPhC Register may 'take or use' the title Pharmacist or fferyllydd (its equivalent in the Welsh language).

Similarly, the title 'pharmacy technician' or 'technegydd fferylliaeth' (its equivalent in the Welsh language) is restricted to persons whose name is entered as a pharmacy technician in Part 2 or 5 of the Register.

The use of 'prescribed specialist titles' is also restricted. A prescribed specialist title, in the case of a pharmacist, is a title which the Council prescribes by rules as being one that is only to be used by a registrant with a particular annotation.

The abbreviations MRPharmS and FRPharmS are the approved abbreviations indicating membership and fellowship of the Royal Pharmaceutical Society.

The GPhC does not specify any post-nominals to indicate registration as a pharmacist, although the title 'pharmacist' is itself restricted.

Additionally, *Section78* of the MA 1968 specifies that no one may use any of these titles in connection with a retail business (or a business which consists of or includes a supply in circumstances corresponding to retail sale) unless the premises are a registered pharmacy or a hospital:

> Chemist, chemist and druggist, druggist, dispensing chemist, and dispensing druggist

In Northern Ireland the titles Member of the PSNI and Fellow of the PSNI are restricted.

The Department of Health had stated that there will be no restriction on individuals who have left the register from referring to themselves as 'former' or 'retired' pharmacists.

Pharmacy

The use of the term 'pharmacy' is restricted to a registered pharmacy or the pharmacy department of a hospital or health centre. (*Section 78(4)* of the MA 1968)

Its use in circumstances which cannot be confused with the operation of a pharmacy is still unclear. In 1998 the Society considered whether or not to instigate proceedings against a restaurant called 'Pharmacy', but it did not take any action in court. The restaurant subsequently closed.

Use of Title by Companies

Companies operating an RPB may use the title 'pharmacy' in connection with the premises.

Companies may also use the following titles:

- chemist and druggist
- druggist
- dispensing chemist
- dispensing druggist.

A body corporate may only use the title 'chemist' if the superintendent is a member of the board. It may use 'pharmacy' even though the superintendent is not on the board.

Representatives may use any title which the pharmacist was entitled to use.

European Union Nationals

Article 7 of the European Commission (EC) Directive 85/433 (which deals with the mutual recognition of the qualifications of EC pharmacists) allows nationals of Member States of the EC to use the lawful academic titles of their home state. They may do this if they are registered with the GPhC.

Evidence of Registration

The name and registration number of the responsible pharmacist at each of the premises must be 'conspicuously displayed' together with the fact that he or she is for the time being in charge of the business at those premises. (*Sections 70, 71, 72* MA 68 as amended)

Pharmacy Staff

The GPhC document 'Standards for pharmacy owners and superintendent pharmacists of retail pharmacy businesses'[3] states:

Employees must be supported when carrying out their professional and legal duties. They must be provided with training and development opportunities to strengthen and improve their knowledge, skills and competencies. You must make sure that staff are employed, managed and trained appropriately.

You must when employing, managing or leading others:
• Make sure your staff have or will undertake appropriate training to attain the skills, knowledge and competency, including sufficient language competence for their role;
• Be satisfied that staff understand their individual roles and responsibilities, including the activities and decisions which have and have not been delegated to them;
• Be satisfied that there are appropriate policies setting out the number of staff and their required experience and that they are made known to relevant staff.

Pharmacy Technicians

The GPhC regulates pharmacy technicians by:

• approving qualifications for pharmacists and pharmacy technicians;
• accrediting education and training providers;
• maintaining a register of properly qualified pharmacists and pharmacy technicians and pharmacy premises;
• setting standards for professional, fitness to practise and ethical standards;
• setting and promoting standards for the safe and effective practice of pharmacy at registered pharmacies, ensuring all registrants maintain their knowledge by completing continuing professional development;
• monitoring pharmacy professionals' fitness to practice.

From 1 July 2011, all pharmacy technicians must be registered with the GPhC. This is a legal requirement to practise as a pharmacy technician in the United Kingdom.

The definition of practising set out in the Pharmacy Order 2010 reflects a broad interpretation of pharmacy practice.

For the purposes of this Order, a person practises as a pharmacist or a pharmacy technician if, whilst acting in the capacity of or purporting to be a pharmacist or a pharmacy technician, that person undertakes any work or gives any advice in relation to the preparation, assembly, dispensing, sale, supply or use of medicines, the science of medicines, the practice of pharmacy or the provision of health care.

Standard Operating Procedures

In January 2005 the RPSGB made it a requirement for pharmacies to have standard operating procedures in place for the dispensing process, including the transfer of prescribed items to patients.

The requirement is now found in the GPhC standards.

The GPhC document 'Standards for pharmacy owners and superintendent pharmacists of retail pharmacy businesses' states that the superintendent or owner must:

Make sure there are standard operating procedures for all aspects of the safe and effective provision of pharmacy services, and these are maintained and regularly reviewed

Be satisfied that procedures respect and protect confidential information about patents and employees in accordance with current legislation, relevant codes of practice and professional guidelines.

Self-Assessment Questions

1. What is an RPB?
    Answer: A business is an 'RPB' if it is:
    *   a business which consists of the retail sale of POM or P medicine, or
    *   a business which includes the retail sale of POM or P medicine, and
    *   it is not part of the professional practice of a doctor or dentist.
    The legislation, for example the Human Medicines Regulations, frequently uses this term to refer to the professional practice of a pharmacist who sells medicines and dispenses prescriptions.
2. What is the difference between pharmacy ownership in England and Scotland?
    Answer: In England, Wales and Northern Ireland partnerships can only carry on a pharmacy if all the partners are registered pharmacists. In Scotland the partnership running the pharmacy must have one partner who is a pharmacist, but the rest need not be qualified as pharmacists. One of the partners who is a pharmacist or another pharmacist must be the 'responsible pharmacist' at those premises.
3. What are the main responsibilities of a 'responsible pharmacist'?
    Answer: A 'responsible pharmacist' must be in charge of the part of the business at those premises which concerns the retail sale and supply at those premises of medicinal products (whether they are on a general sale list or not).

ADDITIONAL RESOURCES

1. http://www.legislation.gov.uk/uksi/2008/2789/made
2. http://www.pharmacyregulation.org/sites/default/files/GPhC%20RP%20Owners%201%20 3%20FINAL.pdf
3. http://www.pharmacyregulation.org/sites/default/files/Standards%20for%20owners%20 and%20superintendent%20pharmacist%20of%20retail%20pharmacy%20businesses%20s.pdf

Chapter 11

The Manufacture and Licensing of Medicinal Products

THE MEDICINES ACT 1968 AND OTHER CONTROLS

In this chapter we deal with the licensing of the product, its manufacture and distribution.

Although there were some controls on poisons in the nineteenth century, and on biological products in the early twentieth century, the current legislative framework for medicines production and supply dates from the Medicines Act 1968.

EUROPEAN DIRECTIVES

Since 1968 the European Union has issued several Directives which establish a Community wide system of control on medicines. The guiding principle of European and UK medicines legislation is to ensure the quality, safety and efficacy of medicinal products, with the overall aim of safeguarding public health.

A number of Directives cover the licensing of medicines.

The main European medicines legislation is Directive 2001/83/EC on the Community code relating to medicinal products for human use, which repealed and re-enacted the original Directive 65/65/EEC and many subsequent directives on related subjects, with the aim of simplifying the European regulatory structure.

It requires that medicines placed on the market must have a licence (known as a marketing authorisation, MA). This is based on showing that the product meets standards of safety, quality and efficacy.

Since 1 January 1994 the licensing system has a centralised system and a decentralised or national (European Member State) system. The centralised licensing system is administered by the European Medicines Agency (EMA) and enables the granting of an EC wide MA.

The decentralised system is under the control of member states and provides for the granting of MAs which may be recognised in other member states. In the United Kingdom this system is administered by the Medicines and Healthcare products Regulatory Agency (MHRA) on behalf of the government.

Pharmacy Law and Practice. DOI: http://dx.doi.org/10.1016/B978-0-12-394289-0.00011-4

THE MEDICINES ACT 1968

The Medicines Act 1968 laid down the general framework for controlling dealings in medicinal products by way of a licensing system. It was produced in response to two main factors: the Thalidomide tragedy in the early 1960s and the Directives issued by the European Economic Community (as it was then called). Although the United Kingdom did not join until 1973, the intention to do so was well known. In many ways the MA 1968 was a consumer safety act, concerned with protecting the public from faulty products by introducing a licensing system.

The opportunity was taken to include controls on the operation of pharmacies.

The MA 1968 was written in a difficult style. It starts off by prohibiting almost all dealings with medicines – referred to as 'medicinal products'. It continues by setting out a number of exemptions to the general rules, thereby allowing, for instance, the sale and manufacture of medicines. The first set of exemptions relate to licences. The second set refers to various activities done by professionals – practitioners. The third set removes some types of products from some controls, e.g., GSL.

In order to discover the rules governing an activity it was usually necessary to read a number of inter-related sections of the Act. Also the MA 1968 often set out very general law with the detail being found in regulations.

The basic framework of medicines control was set out in the Medicines Act 1968. Subsequently EC legislation has become dominant in this area. The Act allows for secondary legislation (Orders or Regulations), which can (and do) very considerably modify the provisions of the Act itself. In this way the later requirements of the EU Directives have been incorporated into the existing framework, first by the Medicines for Human Use (Marketing Authorisations, etc.) Regulations 1994 and now by the Human Medicines Regulations 2012.

The UK legislation requires persons responsible for the composition of a product to hold a licence. Licences are also required by wholesale dealers and by manufacturers. It is unlawful for the products concerned to be manufactured, sold or supplied in, or imported into, the United Kingdom (and certain biological products may not be exported) except with the appropriate licences, certificates or exemptions.

The 1968 Act was altered considerably by the Medicines for Human Use (Marketing Authorisations, etc.) Regulations 1994, SI 1994 No. 3144 which implemented later Directives. The 1994 Regulations were the main legislation until 2012.

HUMAN MEDICINES REGULATIONS 2012

These almost entirely replace the provisions of the Medicines Act 1968 which deal with the licensing of medicines and their labelling. The whole of the 1994 Regulations has been repealed.

The Human Medicines Regulations 2012 also replace about 200 other statutory instruments which previously covered the same areas.

Not all of the Medicines Act 1968 has been repealed. In particular, *Sections 69–84* of Part IV of the Act, which deals with the registration and conduct of pharmacies, remain in force. Certain powers to make secondary legislation are also retained. Most of *Section 10*, which deals with exemptions for pharmacies, remains in force.

Legislation concerning clinical trials, the administration of radioactive medicinal products and fees charged by the MHRA for the administration of procedures under the provisions being consolidated has also been left in place.

The Medicines Regulations 2012 implement for the first time Directive 2010/84/EU. This Directive introduces a stronger, clearer and more proportionate regime for pharmacovigilance in the European Union.

The Regulations are in 17 parts, with 35 schedules. They are ordered in a much more logical way, with each part or each chapter generally dealing with one topic.

The UK Licensing Authority

Authorisations and licences are issued by the 'Licensing Authority' which for human medicines consists of the Health Ministers of the United Kingdom.

In practice, the licensing of human medicines is handled by the MHRA of the Department of Health.

The licensing of veterinary products is generally dealt with by the Veterinary Medicines Agency, an Executive Agency of the Department for Environment, Food and Rural Affairs (DEFRA).

MEDICINAL PRODUCTS

A medicinal product is defined by the Human Medicines Regulations as:

(i) *Any substance or combination of substances presented as having properties for treating or preventing disease in human beings; or*

(ii) *Any substance or combination of substances which may be used in or administered to human beings either with a view to restoring, correcting or modifying physiological functions by exerting a pharmacological, immunological or metabolic action, or to making a medical diagnosis.*

Certain products used outside the human body, such as preservation agents for transplant organs, are also included.

The definition in the Regulations is taken from the amended Article 10 of Directive 2001/83/EC as amended by Directive 2004/27/EC.

The Regulations do not apply to:

(a) whole human blood; or

(b) any human blood component, other than plasma prepared by a method involving an industrial process.

In practice, most medicines which are sold or supplied in the United Kingdom are covered by the EC Directive definition.

Persons who are responsible for the composition of a product must hold a licence, termed a 'marketing authorisation'. In order to get an MA a company must demonstrate the efficacy, safety and quality of its proposed medicine.

MARKETING AUTHORISATION

All new medicines are required by law to meet standards for quality, safety and effectiveness. Persons who are responsible for the composition of a product must hold a licence, termed a 'marketing authorisation'. In order to get an MA a company must demonstrate the efficacy, safety and quality of its proposed medicine.

The Regulations prohibit the placing on the market of most medicinal products unless they have an EU or UK MA:

46.—(1) A person may not sell or supply, or offer to sell or supply, an unauthorised medicinal product.

(2) A person may not sell or supply, or offer to sell or supply, a medicinal product otherwise than in accordance with the terms of:

(a) marketing authorisation;

(b) certificate of registration;

(c) traditional herbal registration; or

(d) Article 126a authorisation.

There are a number of different types of application, depending on the nature of the active ingredient of the product.

There are different types of applications, including:

- for products containing new active substances;
- for products whose active ingredients have previously been evaluated known as abridged applications;
- for biological and biotechnology products manufactured by recombinant DNA technology;
- for products where genetic manipulation of cells is required, or a monoclonal antibodies.

MAs are available to 'relevant medicinal products' which are medicinal products other than:

(a) a registrable homoeopathic medicinal product; or

(b) a traditional herbal medicinal product.   (Regulation 48)

In effect an MA is required by the person responsible for the composition of the product, i.e., either the manufacturer or the person to whose order the product is manufactured.

Prior to 1994 the MA was termed a 'product licence'. These were designated on the product label with the initials PL and a number. This 'PL' designation is still used for MAs.

Quality, Safety and Efficacy in Clinical Trials

The MHRA acts as the government's licensing body. Medicines are considered for approval after laboratory screening, animal testing and closely monitored trials on healthy volunteers and patients. Data is needed from two separate species of animal before a medicine can be used in clinical trials involving humans.

The potential new medicine then goes through four phases of clinical assessment in humans.

Clinical Assessment of New Medicines

The potential new medicine goes through four phases of clinical assessment in humans. They are as follows:

- In phase one a small number (up to 100 people) of healthy volunteers receive it. The medicine is tested to find out how it works in the body and whether side effects increase at higher doses.
- In phase two 2–400 patients receive it. It is tested with a particular condition or disease to see how effective it is and to identify common, short-term side effects.
- In phase three 3000 patients receive it. If the results are satisfactory, the data (which will consist of many thousands of pages) are presented to the MHRA, which will refer the evidence to an advisory committee – the Commission on Human Medicines (CHM). The CHM may then recommend that the MHRA should grant an MA.
- After the drug has gone into general use, phase four studies are done on many thousands of patients. Phase four studies monitor the medicine on an ongoing basis to see if there are any unexpected side effects or if the medicine causes problems in certain categories of people.
- Doctors assist companies in post-marketing surveillance by reporting back on new products and any adverse reactions are reported to the CHM using the Yellow Card System.

Applications for a 'MA'

Applications must be in writing, comply with relevant EU provisions and be accompanied by the correct fee. Details of the necessary accompanying material are set out in EC Directive 2001/83/EC.

Grant of MA

The licensing authority has to be satisfied as to the safety, quality and efficacy of a product before it may grant an MA. The appropriate committee (CHM or ABRHP) must be consulted where the authority intends to refuse a licence.

The licensing authority may grant an application only if, having considered the application and the accompanying material, the authority thinks that:

(a) The applicant has established the therapeutic efficacy.
(b) The positive therapeutic effects of the product outweigh the risks to the health of patients or of the public.
(c) The application and accompanying material complies with Regulations 49–55.
(d) The product's qualitative and quantitative composition is as described in the application and the accompanying material.

26 copies of the application and accompanying material are required for a new application.

What Information Does an MA Include?

The authorisation for a medicine includes information such as:

- What health condition the medicine should be used to treat?
- What dose of the medicine should be used?
- What form the medicine takes – such as a tablet or liquid?
- Who can use the medicine, e.g., only people above a certain age?
- How long treatment with that medicine should last?
- Warnings about known safety issues, such as side effects and interactions with other medicines.
- How the medicine should be stored?
- When the medicine expires?

There must be a Summary of Product Characteristics (SPC) which contains certain required information about the therapeutic indications, contra-indications and side effects of the product. Other information includes dosage, method and route of administration, shelf life, storage precautions and the results of clinical trials and tests.

Revocation of MA

Regulation 68 sets out the grounds for suspending, revoking or varying an MA. The most important is the availability of new factual information relevant to the licence. Other reasons include failure to keep to conditions in the authorisation, e.g., standards of quality.

The licensing authority may revoke, vary or suspend a UK MA in any of the following circumstances where the licensing authority thinks:

(1) that the product is harmful
(2) the risk/benefit balance is unsatisfactory
(3) the product lacks therapeutic efficacy
(4) the composition is not as described in the application
(5) the application or the material supplied with it is incorrect.
(6) there has been a breach of the authorisation

(7) there has been a breach of the packaging and leaflets requirements

(8) other conditions have not been fulfilled

(9) the holder has not provided required information

(10) the holder has ceased to be established in the European Union

(11) the product is manufactured in the United Kingdom; and the manufacturer has not complied with requirements

(12) the product is manufactured in a Member State and the licensee under the manufacturer's licence (ML) has not met requirements of that state

(13) urgent action to protect public health is necessary

(14) the holder applies to vary the authorisation by consent.

Provision of Safety Information

Article 8 of Directive 2001/83/EC introduced an obligation on applicants for authorisation to provide all information relevant to the evaluation of quality, safety and efficacy of a product.

This obligation is set out in the Human Medicines Regulations.

95. A person is guilty of an offence if, in the course of an application for the grant, renewal or variation of a marketing authorisation for a relevant medicinal product, the person:

(a) fails to provide the licensing authority with any information that is relevant to the evaluation of the safety, quality or efficacy of the product;

(b) provides to the licensing authority any information that is relevant to the evaluation of the safety, quality or efficacy of the product but that is false or misleading in a material particular;

(c) fails to provide the EMA with any information that is relevant to the evaluation of the safety, quality or efficacy of the product as required by paragraph (7) or (11) in the "Introduction and general principles" of Annex 1 to the 2001 Directive as applied by Article 6(1) of Regulation (EC) No 726/2004; or

(d) provides to the EMA any information of the kind described in sub-paragraph (c) that is false or misleading in a material particular.

There are criminal offences for failures to provide information relevant to the evaluation of safety, quality or efficacy of a medicinal product for human use and for the provision of information to the licensing authority which is relevant to an evaluation of the safety, quality or efficacy of medicinal products for human use but which is false or misleading in a material particular.

96.—(1) The holder of a marketing authorisation is guilty of an offence if the holder provides any information to which paragraph (2) applies that is relevant to the evaluation of the safety, quality or efficacy of a medicinal product but that is false or misleading in a material particular to:

(a) the licensing authority;

(b) the EMA; or

(c) the competent authorities of other EEA States.

(2) This paragraph applies to information about the product that is supplied
pursuant to the obligations in:
    (a) these Regulations; or
    (b) Regulation (EC) No 726/2004.
(3) This regulation is without prejudice to the operation of regulation 95.

Generic Products

An abridged application may be made for a generic medicinal product
which meets the requirements of Article 10 (2)b of the Directive 2001/83/EC.
Article 10 was amended by Directive 2004/27/EC.

According to the Directive a 'generic medicinal product' is defined as a
product which

has the same qualitative and quantitative composition in active substances and
the same pharmaceutical form as the reference medicinal product, and whose
bio-equivalence with the reference medicinal product has been demonstrated by
appropriate bioavailability studies.

Abridged applications do not require full preclinical or clinical dossiers for
the products. Instead applicants are required to identify a 'reference medicinal product' from which the MHRA can determine the preclinical and clinical
data.

Regulation 51 of the Human Medicines Regulations deals with generics.

The applicant must demonstrate:

  (i) that the product is a generic of a reference medicinal product authorised
     in the United Kingdom and that the MA holder has consented to the toxi-
     cological, pharmacological and/or clinical references being used for the
     application;
 (ii) that the constituents of the product have a well-established medicinal use,
     with recognised efficacy and an acceptable level of safety;
(iii) that the product is a generic of a reference medicinal product which has
     been authorised within the Community for not less than 8 years.

If a UK MA is granted in accordance with this procedure, it is a term of the
authorisation that the generic product must not be sold or supplied, or offered
for sale or supply, in the United Kingdom before the patent expiry date until
10 years from the initial authorisation of the reference product.

The 10-year period is extended to 11 years if the original holder of the MA
obtains a new therapeutic indication which brings a significant clinical benefit
in comparison with existing therapies.

Applicants within the first 8 years must do their own safety and toxicology
work, and their own clinical trials.

Medicinal Claims

The MHRA will generally regard a product as a medicinal product if medicinal claims are made for it. Medicinal claims are claims to treat or prevent disease, or to interfere with normal operation of a physiological function of the human body.

The definition of a medicinal product in Article 1 of Directive 2001/83/EC was amended by Directive 2004/27/EC. The new definition states that a medicinal product is:

(i) *Any substance or combination of substances presented as having properties for treating or preventing disease in human beings; or*

(ii) *Any substance or combination of substances which may be used in or administered to human beings either with a view to restoring, correcting or modifying physiological functions by exerting a pharmacological, immunological or metabolic action, or to making a medical diagnosis.*

LEGAL CLASSIFICATION

The legal classification of a medicine, e.g., P, POM or GSL, is written into the authorisation. A new product will be POM if it is an injection, or may be misused, or presents a danger to health if used without the supervision of a doctor or dentist.

Classification of Medicine as GSL, P or POM

62.—*(1) A UK marketing authorisation must include a term that the product to which the authorisation relates is to be available:*

(a) *only on prescription;*

(b) *only from a pharmacy; or*

(c) *on general sale.*

(2) In making a determination under paragraph (1), the licensing authority must have regard to the following in relation to the product:

(a) *the maximum single dose;*

(b) *the maximum daily dose;*

(c) *the strength of the product;*

(d) *its pharmaceutical form;*

(e) *its packaging; and*

(f) *such other circumstances relating to its use as the licensing authority considers relevant.*

(3) A UK marketing authorisation must be granted subject to a condition that the product to which the authorisation relates is to be available only on prescription if the licensing authority considers that the product:

(a) *is likely to present a direct or indirect danger to human health, even when used correctly, if used without the supervision of a doctor or dentist;*

(b) is frequently and to a very wide extent used incorrectly, and as a result is likely to present a direct or indirect danger to human health;
(c) contains substances, or preparations of substances, of which the activity requires, or the side effects require, further investigation; or
(d) is normally prescribed by a doctor or dentist for parenteral administration.

Manufacturer's Licence

It is illegal to manufacture, assemble or import from a state other than an EEA State any medicinal product except in accordance with a 'manufacturer's licence'.

It is also illegal to possess a medicinal product for the purpose of manufacture, assembly or import without a licence. (Regulation 17)

Regulations 37–41 set out conditions in relation to an ML.

The licence holder must:

(a) comply with the Good Manufacturing Practice Directive;
(b) generally only use active substances as starting materials which comply with the Good Manufacturing Practice Directive;
(c) maintain such staff, premises and equipment as are necessary for processes undertaken by the licence holder in accordance with:
  (a) the ML; and
  (b) the relevant MAs, Article 126a authorisations, certificates of registration or traditional herbal registrations;
(d) not manufacture or assemble medicinal products, or classes of medicinal products, other than those specified in the licence;
(e) not manufacture or assemble medicinal products on premises other than those specified in the licence;
(f) ensure that blood, or blood components, imported into the United Kingdom and used as a starting material or raw material in the manufacture of a medicinal product meet:
  (a) the standards in Directive 2004/33/EC; or
  (b) equivalent standards.

The requirement about only using as starting materials active substances which comply with the Good Manufacturing Practice Directive does not apply to the manufacture or assembly of special medicinal products.

Qualified Person

No batch of medicinal product can be released for sale or supply without certification by a QP that the batch is in accordance with the relevant requirements.

Schedule 7 of the Human Medicines Regulations deals with the requirements and responsibilities of the QP in detail.

It is the legal responsibility of the Qualified Person (QP) to certify batches of medicinal products prior to release for sale or supply. The QP must ensure that the requirements of the MA, Article 126a authorisation, certificate of registration or traditional herbal registration have been met.

The QP must have a degree, diploma or other formal qualification in one of the following subjects:

(a) pharmacy
(b) medicine
(c) veterinary medicine
(d) chemistry
(e) pharmaceutical chemistry and technology
(f) biology.

In addition some level of practical experience is required.

Wholesaling

It is illegal to distribute a medicinal product by way of wholesale dealing or to possess a medicinal product for the purpose of such distribution except in accordance with a wholesale dealer's licence (WDL).

Persons holding an ML do not need a separate licence for the wholesale supply of the products they manufacture.

The holder of a WDL may only legally obtain medicinal products from licensed manufacturers or licensed wholesale dealers in the United Kingdom or other EEA Member States.

The 2012 Regulations also require that a WDL holder shall ensure, within the limits of his/her responsibility as a distributor, the appropriate and continued supply of products to pharmacies and persons who may lawfully sell such products by retail or who may lawfully supply them in circumstances corresponding to retail sale so that the needs of patients in the United Kingdom are covered.

A WDL is not required if the activity is solely:

(a) transporting an imported product; or
(b) acting as an import agent, where the product is imported solely to the order of another person who intends to sell the product or offer it for sale by way of wholesale dealing or to distribute it in any other way.
(c) distribution of a medicinal product by way of wholesale dealing, or to the possession of a medicinal product for the purpose of such distribution, if the distribution or possession is solely for the purpose of exporting the product to states other than EEA States.   (Regulation 19)

Responsible Person

The licence holder must have a Responsible Person (RP) who is legally responsible for safeguarding products against potential hazards arising from poor distribution practice. He/She must ensure that the conditions of the WDL are met, and the guidelines of Good Distribution Practice are complied with. He/She must ensure that the quality of medicinal products handled by the licence holder is being maintained in accordance with the requirements of the MAs, Article 126a authorisations, certificates of registration or traditional herbal registrations.

The RP must satisfy the licensing authority that he/she has adequate knowledge and experience of the relevant activities and procedures to be carried out.

WHOLESALING BY PHARMACIES

The Human Medicines Regulations repeal *Section 10(7)* of the Medicines Act because it was not compatible with the EU Falsified Medicines Directive 2011/62/EU. The Section previously allowed pharmacies to wholesale medicines in some circumstances without a WDL.

The repeal of *Section 10(7)* means that pharmacies trading commercially will need a wholesaler dealer licence. Small scale supplies from one pharmacy to another to meet individual patient needs will still be permitted, as will supplies to other health care providers.

The MHRA has issued a statement which says that it will not take action against a pharmacy that supplies medicines to other UK pharmacies and healthcare providers if they are for supply to patients (e.g., if the recipient pharmacy has run out of stock).

If pharmacies without a licence make a supply, they will technically be breaking the law. However the MHRA statement means that if they act within the scope of the guidance they will not be prosecuted.

From now on, anyone without a licence can only trade where it is occasional, not-for-profit and intended to meet the needs of individual patients. The MHRA will not be concerned with pharmacists that conduct non-commercial trade.

However, pharmacists should be aware that whilst this may be the approach the MHRA has decided to adopt, it is not actually what the law says.

Revocation of a WDL or ML

Regulations 26 and 27 deal with the procedure for suspending, revoking or varying a licence. The most important is the availability of new factual information relevant to the licence. Other reasons include failure to keep to conditions in the licence, e.g., standards of quality.

Appeal Process

An aggrieved applicant for a licence may first take his/her case to the CSM, VPC or ACRHP. He/She may then appeal to the Medicines Commission. The final appeal is to an independent person appointed by the licensing authority.

THE EUROPEAN MEDICINES AGENCY

The EMA (formerly the European Medicines Evaluation Agency) is a part of the EU bureaucracy. It is established by Article 55 of the EC Regulation No. 726/2004. Its function is to handle the EC centralised procedure, which is used for new active substances and certain high-technology and biotechnology products. The EMA is advised by the Committee for Proprietary Medicinal Products (CPMP) whose members are drawn from the Member States of the European Union. Where the centralised procedure is used, companies submit one single MA application to the EMA. A single evaluation is carried out through CHMP. If the relevant Committee concludes that quality, safety and efficacy of the medicinal product is sufficiently proven, it adopts a positive opinion. This is sent to the Commission to be transformed into a single market authorisation valid for the whole of the European Union, as well as in Iceland, Liechtenstein and Norway.

The centralised procedure is compulsory for:

- human medicines for the treatment of HIV/AIDS, cancer, diabetes, neuro-degenerative diseases, auto-immune and other immune dysfunctions, and viral diseases;
- veterinary medicines for use as growth or yield enhancers;
- medicines derived from biotechnology processes, such as genetic engineering;
- advanced-therapy medicines, such as gene therapy, somatic cell therapy or tissue-engineered medicines;
- officially designated 'orphan medicines' (medicines used for rare human diseases).

For medicines that do not fall within these categories, companies have the option of submitting an application for a centralised MA to the Agency, as long as the medicine concerned is a significant therapeutic, scientific or technical innovation, or if its authorisation would be in the interest of public or animal health.

THE ADVISORY MACHINERY

A number of committees of experts are established by the Human Medicines Regulations. The Medicines Act 1968 Advisory Bodies Annual Reports 2011 published by MHRA listed 28 advisory committees.

The Commission on Human Medicines

The CHM replaced both the former Medicines Commission and the former Committee on Safety of Medicines in 2005.

The functions of the CHM are set out in Regulation 10 of the Human Medicines Regulations.

(1) The Commission must give advice to either or both of the Ministers in relation to the matters listed in Paragraph (2) if:
(a) the Minister, or Ministers, request it; or
(b) the Commission considers it appropriate to give it.
(2) The matters mentioned in Paragraph (1) are matters:
(a) relating to the execution of any duty imposed by these Regulations or the Clinical Trials Regulations;
(b) relating to the exercise of any power conferred by these Regulations or the Clinical Trials Regulations; or
(c) otherwise relating to medicinal products.
(3) Without prejudice to Paragraphs (1) and (2), or to any other functions conferred on the Commission by or under these Regulations, the Commission must:
(a) give advice with respect to the safety, quality and efficacy of medicinal products; and
(b) promote the collection and investigation of information relating to adverse reactions, for the purposes of enabling such advice to be given.
(4) The Commission must also advise the licensing authority if:
(a) the licensing authority is required under Schedule 11 (advice and representations) or the Clinical Trials Regulations to consult the Commission about any matter arising under those provisions; or
(b) the licensing authority consults the Commission about any matter arising under those provisions.

Composition

The Commission has at least eight members, who are appointed by Ministers. (Regulation 9)

British Pharmacopoeia Commission

The British Pharmacopoeia Commission (BPC) is responsible for preparing the BP, which contains standards for human medicines. It is also responsible for selecting non-proprietary names for medicinal substances. Regulation 11 sets up the BPC.

Expert Advisory Groups

The Medicines Commission and the BPC are known as 'advisory bodies'.

An advisory body may, with the approval of the licensing authority, appoint one or more sub-committees, to be known as expert advisory groups.

Further, Regulation 15 allows an advisory body to delegate any of its functions, other than the functions specified in Paragraph (2), to an expert advisory group.

The functions which may not be delegated are functions of providing advice to the licensing authority in any case where the licensing authority is required to consult the advisory body under:

(a) Schedule 11 (advice and representations); and
(b) the Clinical Trials Regulations.

The Expert Advisory Groups include:

- Biologicals Expert Advisory Group, to advise on the safety, quality and efficacy of medicinal products of biological or bio-technological origin, including vaccines;
- Chemistry, Pharmacy and Standards Expert Advisory Group, to advise on the quality, and quality in relation to safety and efficacy, of medicinal products which are the subject of an application for an MA, or a request for authorisation pursuant to Regulation 17 of the Clinical Trials Regulations;
- Pharmacovigilance Expert Advisory Group, to advise on pharmacovigilance and other issues relating to the safety of medicinal products.

Chairmen of the Expert Advisory Groups are automatically appointed as members of the CHM.

Advisory Board on the Registration of Homoeopathic Products

The Advisory Board on the Registration of Homoeopathic Products (ABRHP) was established in 1994 to give advice on the safety and quality of a homoeopathic product for human and veterinary use, for which a certificate of registration could be granted. It is an Expert Committee which provides advice to the MHRA.

It is governed by the Human Medicines Regulations 2012. Its terms of reference are:

To give advice on safety and quality in relation to any homeopathic medicinal product for human use in respect of which a certificate of registration has been granted, or which is the subject of an application for such a certificate; and the safety, quality and efficacy of any homeopathic medicinal product in respect of which a marketing authorisation has been granted, which is the subject of an application for such an authorisation, or in respect of which a licence of right has been granted

According to Regulation 8 of the Human Medicines Regulations:

'Homoeopathic medicinal product' means a medicinal product prepared from homoeopathic stocks in accordance with a homoeopathic manufacturing procedure described by:

(a) the European Pharmacopoeia; or
(b) in the absence of such a description in the European Pharmacopoeia, in any pharmacopoeia used officially in an EEA State;

According to Regulation 103(1):

The licensing authority may, subject to regulation 104, grant an application for a certificate of registration for a registrable homoeopathic medicinal product in response to an application made in accordance with this Part

Herbal Medicines Advisory Committee

The Herbal Medicines Advisory Committee advises Ministers directly on issues relating to the registration of traditional herbal medicinal products under the Traditional Herbal Medicines Registration Scheme and to the safety and quality of unlicensed herbal remedies sold under Part 7 of the Human Medicines Regulations.

Statutory Procedure for Classifying Borderline Substances

The MHRA will generally regard a product as a medicinal product if medicinal claims are made for it. Medicinal claims are claims to treat or prevent disease or to interfere with normal operation of a physiological function of the human body.

The Human Medicines Regulations give power to stop a company selling a product, which the licensing authority believes is a medicine, without a marketing approval. That approval may be an MA, traditional herbal registration, certificate of registration or Article 126a authorisation. The licensing authority must explain why they consider the product to be a medicine.

Exemptions from the Need to Hold Licences

Pharmacists

According to the Human Medicines Regulations:

4.—(1) Regulations 17(1) (manufacturing of medicinal products: requirement for licence) and 46 (requirement for authorisation) do not apply where any provision of section 10 of the Medicines Act 1968(1) so provides.

Section 10 provides that no licence is required for the normal activities of a pharmacist.

Some activities are covered simply because they are done by a pharmacist, whereas others are covered only if the activities take place in a registered pharmacy.

Section 10 of the Medicines Act 168 has been heavily amended and now reads:

(1) The restrictions imposed by regulations 17(1) (manufacturing of medicinal products) and 46 (requirement for authorisation) of the 2012 Regulations do not apply to anything which is done in a registered pharmacy, a hospital, a care

home service or a health centre and is done there by or under the supervision of a pharmacist and consists of:

(a) preparing or dispensing a medicinal product in accordance with a prescription given by an appropriate practitioner, or

(b) assembling a medicinal product provided that where the assembling takes place in a registered pharmacy:

(i) it shall be in a registered pharmacy at which the business in medicinal products carried on is restricted to retail sale or to supply in circumstances corresponding to retail sale and the assembling is done with a view to such sale or supply either at that registered pharmacy or at any other such registered pharmacy forming part of the same retail pharmacy business, and

(ii) the medicinal product has not been the subject of an advertisement]; and those restrictions do not apply to anything done by or under the supervision of a pharmacist which consists of procuring the preparation or dispensing of a medicinal product in accordance with a prescription given by a practitioner, or of procuring the assembly of a medicinal product.

(2) Those restrictions do not apply to the preparation or dispensing in a registered pharmacy of a medicinal product by or under the supervision of a pharmacist in accordance with a specification furnished by the person to whom the product is or is to be sold or supplied, where the product is prepared or dispensed for administration to that person or to a person under his care,

(3) Without prejudice to the preceding subsections, the restrictions imposed by regulations 17(1) (manufacturing of medicinal products) and 46 (requirement for authorisation) of the 2012 Regulations do not apply to anything which is done in a registered pharmacy by or under the supervision of a pharmacist and consists of:

(a) preparing or dispensing a medicinal product for administration to a person where the pharmacist is requested by or on behalf of that person to do so in accordance with the pharmacist's own judgment as to the treatment required, and that person is present in the pharmacy at the time of the request in pursuance of which that product is prepared or dispensed, or

(b) preparing a stock of medicinal products with a view to dispensing them as mentioned in subsection (1)(a) or subsection (3) of this section or in paragraph (a) of this subsection provided that such stock is prepared with a view to retail sale or to supply in circumstances corresponding to retail sale and the preparation is done with a view to such sale or supply either at that registered pharmacy or at any other registered pharmacy forming part of the same retail pharmacy business;

and those restrictions do not apply to anything which is done in a hospital or a health centre by or under the supervision of a pharmacist and consists of preparing a stock of medicinal products with a view to dispensing them as mentioned in subsection (1)(a) of this section.

(4) Without prejudice to the preceding subsections, the restrictions imposed by Regulation 46 of the 2012 Regulations do not apply to the preparation or dispensing in a registered pharmacy of a medicinal product by or under the supervision of a pharmacist where:

> *(a) the medicinal product is prepared or dispensed otherwise than in pursuance of an order from any other person, and*
> *(b) the medicinal product is prepared with a view to retail sale or supply in circumstances corresponding to retail sale at the registered pharmacy at which it is prepared, and*
> *(c) the medicinal product has not been the subject of an advertisement.*

(5) Without prejudice to the preceding subsections, the restrictions imposed by regulation 17(1) of the 2012 Regulations do not apply to anything which is done in a registered pharmacy by or under the supervision of a pharmacist and consists of preparing a medicinal product with a view to retail sale or to supply in circumstances corresponding to retail sale at that registered pharmacy.

(6A) The Ministers may make regulations prescribing conditions which must be complied with if a thing is to be considered for the purposes of this section as done under the supervision of a pharmacist.

(6B) Conditions prescribed under subsection (7A) may relate to supervision in the case where the pharmacist is not at the place where the thing is being done, and in that case the thing is not to be so considered if no such conditions are prescribed.

(6C) In any case, compliance with any applicable conditions is sufficient for the thing to be so considered.

(7) For the purposes of this section "advertisement" shall have the meaning assigned to it by regulation 7 (advertisements relating to medicinal products) of the 2012 Regulations.

(8) In subsection (1) of this section, "care home service" has the meaning given by paragraph 2 of schedule 12 to the Public Services Reform (Scotland) Act 2010.

Mixing of Medicines

It is specifically stated that the mixing of medicines by a nurse, pharmacist or supplementary prescriber does not count as manufacture if that mixing is needed for the clinical management of the patient or is in accordance with the written directions of a prescriber.

Regulation 20(1) Regulation 17(1) (manufacturing of medicinal products) does not apply to the mixing of medicines by:

> *(a) a nurse independent prescriber;*
> *(b) a pharmacist independent prescriber;*
> *(c) a supplementary prescriber, if the mixing of medicines forms part of the clinical management plan for an individual patient;*
> *(d) a person acting in accordance with the written directions of a:*
> > *(i) doctor,*
> > *(ii) dentist,*

(iii) nurse independent prescriber, or

(iv) pharmacist independent prescriber; or

(e) a person acting in accordance with the written directions of a
supplementary prescriber, if the mixing of medicines forms part of the clinical
management plan for an individual patient.

(2) In this regulation "mixing of medicines" means the combining of two or more
medicinal products together for the purposes of administering them to meet the
needs of an individual patient.

Administration

Administer means to give to someone as a medicine. This may be:

orally, by injection, by introduction into the body in any other way, by external
application

There may be direct contact with the body, e.g., a cream, or indirect, e.g., inhalation.

Any reference in the Regulations to administering anything is to administering it in its existing state or after it has been dissolved or dispersed in, or diluted or mixed with, a substance used as a vehicle.   (Regulation 8)

Assembly

According to Regulation 8 of the Human Medicines Regulations:

'assemble' in relation to a medicinal product includes the various processes of dividing
up, packaging and presentation of the product, and 'assembly' has a corresponding
meaning;

This term is used to include various packaging activities:

- enclosing the product in a container, which is then labelled before sale or supply;
- labelling the container of medicine.

A container is the box, bottle or carton in which the product is contained. It does not mean the capsule in which the product is to be administered.

The assembly of a medicine is an activity which requires an ML or an exemption.

SUMMARY OF PRODUCT CHARACTERISTICS

It is a requirement of the licensing process that there must be a SPC which contains certain required information about the therapeutic indications, contra-indications and side effects of the product. Other information includes dosage, method and route of administration, shelf life, storage precautions and the results of clinical trials and tests.

Regulation 8 Human Medicines Regulations

'the summary of the product characteristics' in relation to a medicinal product means:
  (a) where the product has a UK marketing authorisation or traditional herbal registration, the summary of the product characteristics:
    (i) as approved by the licensing authority in granting the authorisation or registration, or
    (ii) where the summary has been varied since that approval, as so amended; or
  (b) where the product has an EU marketing authorisation, the summary of the product characteristics:
    (i) as approved by the European Commission in granting the authorisation, or
    (ii) where the summary has been varied since that approval, as so amended;
After granting a marketing authorisation, the licensing authority must make publicly available:
  (a)   the marketing authorisation;
  (b)   the package leaflet;
  (c)   the summary of the product characteristics.

PATIENT INFORMATION LEAFLET

EC Directive 2001/82//EC required all medicines to be supplied with a 'patient information leaflet' (PIL). The information is directed at patients and the leaflet must be understandable. The contents are approved by the MRHA.

According to Regulation 260:

(1) A package leaflet for a medicinal product must:
  (a) be drawn up in accordance with the summary of the product characteristics; and
  (b) contain all the information specified in Schedule 27 in the order specified in that Schedule.
(2) A package leaflet relating to a medicinal product must be legible, clear and easy to use, and the applicant for, or holder of, an MA, Article 126a authorisation or traditional herbal registration relating to the product must ensure that target patient groups are consulted in order to achieve this.

PRODUCT INFORMATION

The SCP, the package leaflet and the immediate and outer packaging are referred to as the 'product information'.

Placed on the Market

A product is placed on the market when it is first made available in return for payment or charge with a view to distribution, use or both on the Community market.

The term 'made available' means the transfer of the ownership of the product, or the passing of the product to the final consumer or user in a commercial transaction. It may be for payment or free of charge. The legal instrument by which the transfer is achieved, e.g., sale, loan, lease, gift, is irrelevant.

A product is not placed on the market if it is made in a hospital pharmacy and then used elsewhere in the same hospital to treat patients.

Specials Licence

A pharmacist or a doctor may ask a pharmaceutical manufacturer to prepare a medicinal product for him/her. No product licence is necessary provided the manufacturer holds an ML specifically authorising him/her to produce 'specials' [see later].

MEDICAL DEVICES

Prior to 1994 many medical devices were controlled under the MA 1968. They are now controlled under consumer safety legislation, specifically the Medical Devices Regulations 2002 (SI 2002/618) as amended.

Medical devices are subject to the controls of Directives 93/42/EEC, 98/79/EC and 90/385/EEC, implemented in the United Kingdom by the Medical Devices Regulations.

A medical device is 'an instrument, apparatus, appliance, material or other article, whether used alone or in combination, together with any software necessary for its proper application which:

(1) is intended by the manufacturer to be used for human beings for the purpose of:
   (a) diagnosis, prevention, monitoring, treatment or alleviation of disease;
   (b) diagnosis, prevention, monitoring, treatment or alleviation of or compensation for an injury or handicap;
   (c) investigation, replacement or modification of the anatomy or of any physiological process; or
   (d) control of contraception; and
(2) does not achieve its principal intended action in or on the human body by pharmacological, immunological or metabolic means, even if it is assisted in its function by such means.'

The definition includes devices which are intended to administer a medicinal product or which incorporate a substance which would be a medicinal product if used on its own.

Such devices include intra-uterine devices, diaphragms, dental fillings, contact lens care products, non-medicated dressings, sutures and ligatures.

Medical devices must comply with the regulations and with the 'essential requirements' set out in Directive 93/42/EEC. There are specific labelling requirements.

The MHRA administers the legislation.

Further information on the "**Medicines** and **Medical Devices Regulation**: What you need to know" can be found here.[1]

NEW RULES

The European Union has adopted new rules which will gradually come into effect from 2015 to 2019. All medical devices will have to undergo a thorough, independent assessment of safety and performance before they can be sold on the European market. There will be better information on the benefits for patients and health professionals. The residual risks and the overall risk/benefit ratio will be clearer to help make the best use of medical equipment. Updated classification rules will divide medical devices into four different risk categories and health and safety requirements to keep pace with technological and scientific progress.

Self-Assessment Questions

1. Which bodies are responsible for licensing medicines on sale in the United Kingdom?

   Answer: Authorisations and Licences are issued by the Licensing Authority which for human medicines consists of the Health Ministers of the United Kingdom. In practice, the licensing of human medicines is handled by the MHRA of the Department of Health. The licensing of veterinary products is generally dealt with by the Veterinary Medicines Agency, an Executive Agency of the Department for Environment, Food and Rural Affairs. The centralised licensing system is administered by the EMA and enables the granting of an EC wide MA.

2. What is a medicinal product?

   Answer: A medicinal product is defined by the Human Medicines Regulations as:

   (i) any substance or combination of substances presented as having properties for treating or preventing disease in human beings; or

   (ii) any substance or combination of substances which may be used in or administered to human beings either with a view to restoring, correcting or modifying physiological functions by exerting a pharmacological, immunological or metabolic action, or to making a medical diagnosis.

3. What are phase four studies of medicines?

   Answer: After the drug has gone into general use, phase four studies are done on many thousands of patients. Phase four studies monitor the medicine on an ongoing basis to see if there are any unexpected side effects or if the medicine causes problems in certain categories of people.

ADDITIONAL RESOURCE

1. http://www.mhra.gov.uk/home/groups/comms-ic/documents/websiteresources/con2031677 .pdf

Chapter 12

Control on Sales of Medicines

Various parts of the Medicines Act 1968 and the Human Medicines Regulations 2012 place restrictions on the supply of medicines by restricting who may sell medicines and where they may be sold.

CONTROL OF RETAIL SALES

The underlying principle of the control on the retail sales of medicines is that they should normally be supplied through pharmacies.

There are three main exceptions to that.

First, certain medicines are designated as ones which may be sold to the public by an ordinary shop.

Secondly, medicines may be sold by a hospital or health centre even where there is no pharmacy if the products are sold or supplied:

- in the course of the business of the hospital or health centre, and
- they are for the purpose of being administered in accordance with the directions of a doctor or dentist.

It does not matter whether they are to be administered in the hospital or health centre or elsewhere. The doctor or dentist is not required to be an employee of the hospital or to be associated with it in any way.

The 'directions of a doctor' need not comply with the requirements for a prescription set out in the prescription only medicine (POM) Order (as amended).

Thirdly, Patient Group Directions may empower certain health professionals to supply medicines to the public in accordance with protocols. This supply may take place anywhere.

In addition to the principle that the retail sales of medicines should be through pharmacies, the Medicines (Pharmacies) (Responsible Pharmacist) Regulations 2008, SI No. 2789 require that a 'Responsible Pharmacist' is 'in charge of the business at the premises' where this relates to the retail sale and supply (i.e., in circumstances corresponding to retail sale) of all medicinal products, including General Sale List (GSL) medicines.

Pharmacy Law and Practice. DOI: http://dx.doi.org/10.1016/B978-0-12-394289-0.00012-6

Legal Categories of Medicines

The European Community (EC) Directive on Legal Classification (2001/82/EC) consolidated a number of earlier directives. This Directive requires Member States to classify medicines into those which may only be sold or supplied on prescription, and those which may be obtained without a prescription. The Directive is amended by Directive 2004/27/EC.

The Directive lays down the criteria which must be used to determine whether a product should be subject to prescription control. These criteria have been incorporated into law by the Human Medicines Regulations 2012.

Classification of UK Marketing Authorisation

Regulation 62 of the Human Medicines Regulations requires each application for the grant of a marketing authorisation (MA) to indicate whether the product is one that could be available:

(a) only on prescription
(b) only from a pharmacy
(c) on general sale.

The application must also indicate whether the authorisation should include any other restrictions on the sale or supply of the product, for example, a restriction on promotion.

Where the community marketing authorisation contains such restrictions, Ministers are required to include the product in the POM Order.

Regulation 62(2) also lists criteria to which the licensing authority must have regard when determining the classification:

(a) the maximum single dose
(b) the maximum daily dose
(c) the strength of the product
(d) its pharmaceutical form
(e) its packaging and
(f) such other circumstances relating to its use as the licensing authority considers relevant.

Regulation 62(3) requires that a product must be available only on prescription if it is:

(a) is likely to present a direct or indirect danger to human health, even when used correctly, if used without the supervision of a doctor or dentist;
(b) is frequently and to a very wide extent used incorrectly, and as a result is likely to present a direct or indirect danger to human health;
(c) contains substances, or preparations of substances, of which the activity requires, or the side effects require, further investigation; or
(d) is normally prescribed by a doctor or dentist for parenteral administration.

Schedule 1 of the Human Medicines Regulations contains descriptions of certain medicinal products which are made available only on prescription, or only from pharmacies.

General Sale List

This is a list of medicines which can be sold, with reasonable safety, without the supervision of a pharmacist. The sales have to take place from proper shops, that is ones which can be closed so as to exclude the public. This prohibits sales being made from vans or other vehicles, or from open market stalls.

There is a separate list of products which may be sold from automatic vending machines.

The legislation is Regulation 221 of the Human Medicines Regulations 2012.

To sum up, GSL medicines may be sold:

- without the supervision of a pharmacist
- from any ordinary shop (not a pharmacy)
- shop must be one which can be closed up
- not from a vehicle or market stall.

Pharmacy Medicines (P)

Pharmacy medicines may be sold only in a registered pharmacy by or under the supervision of a pharmacist. This is the default category, into which all medicines fall unless placed by legislation into either of the other two categories.

Pharmacy medicines may only be sold:

- in a registered pharmacy
- by or under the supervision of a pharmacist.

Regulation 220 states:

(1)   Unless paragraph (2) applies, a person ("P") may not sell or supply, or offer for sale or supply, a medicinal product that is not subject to general sale.

(2)   This paragraph applies if:

    (a)   P is a person lawfully conducting a retail pharmacy business;

    (b)   the product is sold, supplied, or offered for sale or supply, on premises that are a registered pharmacy; and

    (c)   P or, if the transaction is carried out on P's behalf by another person, that other person is, or acts under the supervision of, a pharmacist.

(3)   This regulation is subject to Chapter 3.

Chapter 3 sets out exemptions relating to supply in specific circumstances (e.g., via a Patient Group Direction).

Prescription Only Medicines

POM may only be sold or supplied:

- in a registered pharmacy
- by or under the supervision of a pharmacist
- in accordance with the prescription of a doctor, dentist or veterinary practitioner.

Regulation 49 of the Human Medicines Regulations requires each application for the grant of an MA to indicate whether the product is one that could be available:

(a) only on prescription
(b) only from a pharmacy
(c) on general sale.

Regulation 214 of the Human Medicines Regulations requires that a person may not sell or supply a POM except in accordance with a prescription given by an appropriate practitioner.

A product is to be designated as a POM if:

(a) it needs medical supervision in use to prevent a direct or indirect danger to human health;
(b) it is widely and frequently misused, and so presents a danger to health;
(c) it is a new active substance;
(d) it is for parenteral administration.

RECLASSIFICATION OF MEDICINES

New medicines are usually authorised for use as POMs. Additional safety data may become available after use which allows a change. If there is sufficient evidence of safety, a medicine may be reclassified for sale or supply under the supervision of a pharmacist (P).

Before a medicine can be reclassified from POM to P, Ministers must be satisfied that it would be safe to allow it to be supplied without a prescription. It must be a medicine which no longer meets any of the criteria in Regulation 62(3).

Reclassifying from P to GSL

Similarly, a medicine can be reclassified from P to GSL if Ministers are be satisfied that it 'can with reasonable safety be sold or supplied otherwise than by or under the supervision of a pharmacist'.

'Reasonable safety' may be usefully defined as: 'Where the hazard to health and the risk of misuse and the need for special precautions in handling are small, and where wider sale would be a convenience to the purchaser'.

The POM Order

Although most of the POM (Human Use) Order 1997 No. 1830 has been repealed by the Human Medicines Regulations, some provisions remain in effect.

Schedule 1 of the POM Order contains a list of substances. Medicinal products containing any of them are usually classed as POM.

Articles 1(1)–1(5) of the Order remain – containing a list of definitions.

Article 5 sets out certain exemptions for specified products or ingredients.

Article 10 sets out provisions, which exempt from the POM rules, some homeopathic products which are highly diluted. Regulation 242 of the Human Medicines Regulations expands this.

Medicinal Products on Prescription Only

Generally the following medicinal products are POM:

(a) medicinal products consisting of or containing a substance listed in column 1 of Schedule 1 of the POM Order
(b) controlled drugs (CDs)
(c) medicinal products that are for parenteral administration
(d) cyanogenetic substances other than preparations for external use
(e) radiopharmaceuticals and generators
(f) medicinal products for human use which are licensed by the EC and classed as prescription only.

There are a number of exceptions.

Schedule 1 sets out a list of medicines together with the conditions which make a product exempt from POM.

Four categories are set out in Schedule 1. They are based on:

(a) maximum strength
(b) route of administration, use or pharmaceutical form
(c) treatment limitations
(d) maximum quantity.

Schedule 2 excludes some <u>CDs</u> from POM when the preparation complies with the conditions.

Administration of POMs

The Regulations state that no one can administer a POM, except to himself, unless he or she is either:

- a prescriber, or
- a person acting in accordance with the directions of a prescriber.

Regulation 214(2) reads:

A person may not parenterally administer (otherwise than to himself or herself) a prescription only medicine unless the person is:

    (a) an appropriate practitioner other than an EEA health professional; or

    (b) acting in accordance with the directions of such an appropriate practitioner.

INJECTIONS

All parenteral products are POM.

Water for Injection

Sterile water for injection is a POM. Water for injection may be supplied without prescription 'in the course of provision of lawful drug treatment services' in 2 ml vials. (Schedule 17 Part 2 of the Human Medicines Regulations)

Pharmacies may supply water for injection without a prescription if the sale or supply is to a person:

    (a) for a purpose other than parenteral administration; or

    (b) who has been prescribed dry powder for parenteral administration but has not been prescribed the water for injection that is needed as a diluent. (Schedule 17 Part 1of the Human Medicines Regulations)

Administration of Certain Medicines in an Emergency

Some injections are specifically exempted from the blanket prohibition. They are the ones which might be needed in an emergency.

Regulation 238 states:

Regulation 214(2) does not apply to the administration of a prescription only medicine specified in Schedule 19 where this is for the purpose of saving life in an emergency.

The medicines specified in Schedule 19 are:

Adrenaline 1:1000 up to 1 mg for intramuscular use in anaphylaxis
Atropine sulphate and obidoxime chloride injection
Atropine sulphate and pralidoxime chloride injection
Atropine sulphate injection
Atropine sulphate, pralidoxime mesilate and avizafone injection
Chlorphenamine injection
Dicobalt edetate injection
Glucagon injection
Glucose injection
Hydrocortisone injection
Naloxone hydrochloride

Pralidoxime chloride injection
Pralidoxime mesilate injection
Promethazine hydrochloride injection
Snake venom antiserum
Sodium nitrite injection
Sodium thiosulphate injection
Sterile pralidoxime

Ambulance paramedics may administer a range of injections only for the immediate, necessary treatment of sick or injured persons.   (Schedule 17 Part 3 of the Human Medicines Regulations)

A number of other exceptions are made to allow the supply and use of POMs for research, business or in various unusual circumstances.

Prescription Requirements

POMs may generally only be supplied on prescription. A prescription for POMs must meet the conditions set out in the Regulation 217 of the Human Medicines Regulations.

(1) All prescriptions must be signed in ink by the practitioner.

(2) Private prescriptions must be written in ink, or otherwise be indelible.

(3) NHS prescriptions, other than for a CD, may be written by means of carbon paper or similar material.

(4) No prescription may be dispensed more than 6 months after the appropriate date, except:

　(a) scripts may bear a date before which they may not be dispensed. The 6 months runs from that date if it is later than the date of signing.

　(b) where a script contains a direction that it may be dispensed more than once, then the first dispensing must be within the 6-month period.

(5) Where a script contains directions that it may be dispensed more than once, those directions must be followed. If the number of repeats is not specified, only one repeat is allowed, except:

　(a) oral contraceptives may be dispensed six times in total before the end of the 6-month period.

(6) All scripts shall contain the following particulars:

　(a) address of the practitioner giving it

　(b) the appropriate date

　(c) an indication of the kind of prescriber, for example, doctor, dentist, pharmacist, etc.

　(d) name and address of patient

　(e) age of patient (if under 12 years).

(7) For vet scripts:

　(a) name and address of person in charge of the animal

　(b) declaration by vet that the medicine is for an animal or herd under his care.

EUROPEAN ECONOMIC AREA HEALTH PROFESSIONALS

A prescription from an appropriate practitioner who is an European Economic Area (EEA) health professional must meet the following conditions:

(1) it is an EEA prescription
(2) signed in ink by the EEA health professional giving it
(3) written in ink or be indelible
(4) indicate whether the EEA health professional is a doctor or dentist
(5) give the name of the patient
(6) may not be dispensed more than 6 months after the date it was signed or if a repeatable script not be dispensed for the first time after that period
(7) where a script contains directions that it may be dispensed more than once, those directions must be followed. If the number of repeats is not specified, only one repeat is allowed, except:
oral contraceptives that may be dispensed six times in total before the end of the 6-month period.

Due Diligence Clause

Regulation 214(1) states that a person may not sell or supply a POM except in accordance with a prescription given by an appropriate practitioner.

However, Regulation 246 states that if the person making the sale or supply has exercised due diligence and accordingly believes on reasonable grounds that the conditions are fulfilled, he or she will not commit an offence if it turns out that the practitioner did not in fact fulfil the conditions.

246. Regulation 214(1) does not apply to the sale or supply of a prescription only medicine otherwise than in accordance with a prescription given by an appropriate practitioner if:

(a) the sale or supply is otherwise than in accordance with such a prescription because a condition in regulation 217, 218 or 219 is not met; and

(b) the person selling or supplying the prescription only medicine, having exercised all due diligence, believes on reasonable grounds that the condition is met.

(Regulation 246)

Records of Transactions

Records must be kept of the retail sale or supply of POMs. Entries must be made in a written or computerised record kept for that purpose. The entry must be made on the day of the transaction, or on the next day. The record must contain the details set out in Schedule 23 of the Human Medicines Regulations.

Regulation 253.—(1) A person lawfully conducting a retail pharmacy business must, in respect of every sale or supply of a prescription only medicine, make or cause to be made an entry in a written or computerised record kept for that purpose.

(Human Medicines Regulations)

Records are not required for:

(1) the sale or supply on an NHS prescription
(2) the sale or supply of oral contraceptives
(3) where records are made in the CD Register
(4) sale or supply to persons in respect of a drug testing scheme
(5) sale or supply in Scotland, to a doctor under the Stock Order scheme
(6) sale or supply in Northern Ireland to a doctor for NHS use by way of immediate administration
(7) sale by way of wholesale dealing when a copy order or invoice is retained.

What Details of Scripts Must Be Recorded

For sale or supply of POMs on a script:

(1) date of transaction
(2) name and quantity of medicine
(3) form and strength of medicine (unless obvious)
(4) date of script
(5) name and address of prescriber
(6) name and address of patient (or of owner of animal).

Repeat Scripts

When second or third, etc., supplies are made on repeat scripts, a shortened record may be made. The date of supply must be recorded together with a reference to the original entry.

Emergency Supplies at Request of Prescriber

Where the sale or supply is made under Regulation 224 (emergency sale, etc., by a pharmacist where the prescriber is unable to provide a prescription), the date on the prescription and the date on which the prescription relating to that sale or supply is received may be entered on the day that the prescription is received.

Emergency Supplies at Request of Patient

Where the sale or supply is made under Regulation 225 (emergency sale, etc., by a pharmacist at the patient's request), the details below must be recorded:

(1) the date on which the POM was sold or supplied;
(2) the name, quantity and, except where it is apparent from the name, the pharmaceutical form and strength of the POM sold or supplied;
(3) the name and address of the person requiring the POM; and
(4) the nature of the emergency.

Schedule 18 contains a list of substances that may not be sold or supplied at the request of a patient in the absence of a prescription.

Ammonium bromide
Calcium bromide
Calcium bromidolactobionate
Embutramide
Fencamfamine hydrochloride
Fluanisone
Hexobarbitone
Hexobarbitone sodium
Hydrobromic acid
Meclofenoxate hydrochloride
Methohexitone sodium
Pemoline
Piracetam
Potassium bromide
Prolintane hydrochloride
Sodium bromide
Strychnine hydrochloride
Tacrine hydrochloride
Thiopentone sodium

ELECTRONIC PRESCRIPTIONS

Electronic prescriptions may be signed with an 'advanced electronic signature', provided the prescription is transferred as an electronic communication to the person who dispenses it.
Electronic prescriptions are not valid for CDs in Schedules 1, 2 and 3 of the Misuse of Drugs Regulations 2001.

Regulation 219—(1) This regulation applies to a prescription that is not a health prescription for a controlled drug.
Electronic prescriptions for POMs must meet the following conditions:
If given by an appropriate practitioner who is not an EEA health professional, then the script must be:

    (a) created in electronic form;
    (b) signed with an advanced electronic signature; and
    (c) sent to the person by whom it is dispensed as an electronic communication (whether or not through one or more intermediaries);
must contain
    (a) the address of the appropriate practitioner giving it;
    (b) the appropriate date;
    (c) an indication of the kind of appropriate practitioner giving it;

(d)   the name and address of the person for whose treatment it is given; and
(e)   if that person is under 12, that person's age.
    (a)   is not dispensed after the end of the period of six months beginning with the appropriate date; or
    (b)   in the case of a repeatable prescription:
        (i)   it is not dispensed for the first time after the end of that period, and
        (ii)   it is dispensed in accordance with the directions contained in the prescription.
(6)   Condition E is that, in the case of a repeatable prescription that does not specify the number of times it may be dispensed:
    (a)   it is not dispensed on more than two occasions, or
    (b)   in the case of a prescription for an oral contraceptive, it is not dispensed on more than six occasions or after the end of the period of six months beginning with the appropriate date.

'Advanced Electronic Signature'

'Advanced electronic signature' means an electronic signature that is:

(a) uniquely linked to the person ('P') giving the prescription;
(b) capable of identifying P;
(c) created using means that P can maintain under P's sole control; and
(d) linked to the data to which it relates in such a manner that any subsequent change of data is detectable.

Supervision of Sales

In addition to the principle that the retail sales of medicines should be through pharmacies, the Medicines Act also requires the involvement of the pharmacist in the process.

Prior to the introduction of the Responsible Pharmacist, *Sections 70–72* of the Medicines Act required each pharmacy business to be under the personal control of a pharmacist. The Medicines Act did not define 'personal control' nor how the pharmacist was to comply with the requirement. There was little case law.

Personal Control Changes to Responsible Pharmacist

Sections 27–29 of the Health Act 2006 amend *Sections 70–72* of the Medicines Act 1968 to remove the 'personal control' requirement and to provide for the new requirement for a 'Responsible Pharmacist' to be in charge of each registered pharmacy.

Like 'personal control', the new requirement relates to all registered pharmacies in the community and in hospitals. If a pharmacy does not have a responsible pharmacist, it is operating illegally in relation to the retail sale and supply of all medicines.

The New Responsible Pharmacist Requirement

Section 30 of the Health Act inserted a new *Section 72A* into the Medicines Act. It requires each registered pharmacy premises to have a responsible pharmacist in charge in order to operate lawfully. The Act puts a legal duty on the responsible pharmacist to secure the safe and effective running of the pharmacy in relation to the retail sale and supply of all medicines.

The new requirement makes clear that the responsible pharmacist is 'in charge of the business at the premises' where this relates to the retail sale and supply (i.e., in circumstances corresponding to retail sale) of all medicinal products, including GSL medicines.

This is a Medicines Act requirement that relates to the sale and supply of medicines. It does not concern the provision of NHS pharmaceutical services that do not involve the sale or supply of medicinal products (e.g., screening or diagnostic testing) – which is a matter for separate NHS law.

Display of Notice

The Health Act 2006 amended the Medicines Act to require the responsible pharmacist to display a notice in the pharmacy stating that he or she is the pharmacist in charge of the pharmacy on that date and at that time. The registration number must be on the notice.

Compliance with Duty

Section 72A sets out how the responsible pharmacist is to comply with the duty. He or She must:

• Establish (where not already in place), maintain and review pharmacy procedures designed to secure the safe and effective running of the pharmacy – *Section 72A(3)*.
• Make a record (which must be available at the pharmacy premises) of the pharmacist responsible for the pharmacy on any date and at any time – *Section 72A(4)*.

Legal Duty on the Pharmacy Owner

Section 72A also places a legal duty on the pharmacy owner. The owner must:

• Ensure that for each registered pharmacy, the responsible pharmacist maintains the pharmacy record as required – *Section 72A(5)(a)*.
• Preserve the pharmacy record for the required period set out in the regulations – *Section 72A(5)(b)*.

Sanctions for Breach of Duty

Section 30 of the Health Act also inserts a new *Section 72B* into the Medicines Act.

Failure by the responsible pharmacist to comply with the requirements of *Section 72A* and the Regulations is a matter of professional misconduct to be considered by the General Pharmaceutical Council (GPhC).

A failure to keep the pharmacy record as required is a criminal offence, subject on conviction to the payment of a fine.

The pharmacy owner will also be guilty of an offence where there is a failure to ensure the responsible pharmacist keeps the pharmacy record, or where the owner fails to preserve the record for at least the period set out in the Regulations – *Section 72A(5)*.

Responsible Pharmacist Regulations

Section 72A gives the Health Ministers powers to make further regulations concerning the 'Responsible Pharmacist'.

The Medicines (Pharmacies) (Responsible Pharmacist) Regulations 2008, SI No. 2789[1,2] came into force on 1 October 2009. They set out in detail how the responsible pharmacist is to comply with the legal duty in relation to:

- the pharmacy procedures,
- the pharmacy record, and
- absence from the pharmacy.

Medicines Counter Assistants

The GPhC requires pharmacy owners and superintendent pharmacists of retail pharmacy businesses to ensure that staff are trained appropriately to attain the skills, knowledge and competency, including sufficient language competence for their role.

Dispensing Staff

From 1 July 2011, all pharmacy technicians must have received suitable training and be registered with the GPhC.

WHOLESALING OF MEDICINES

A wholesale dealer's licence (MDL) is required by any person who distributes a 'medicinal product' by way of wholesale dealing. The person may be a real person, a body of persons or a limited company.

What Is Wholesaling?

According to Regulation 18 of the Human Medicine Regulations, wholesaling a product means:

(a) selling or supplying it or
(b) procuring or holding it or exporting it to another EEA State for the purposes of sale or supply,

to a person who receives it for the purpose of

(a) selling or supplying the product or
(b) administering it or causing it to be administered to one or more human beings,

in the course of a business carried on by that person.

The term 'business' includes a professional practice, such as that of a medical practitioner. Thus sales to a medical or dental practitioner 'for use in his practice' will be wholesale sales.

Moreover, the provision of services under the NHS is considered to be the carrying on of a business by the appropriate Minister. (*Section 131* Medicines Act 1968)

Veterinary medicinal products are subject to separate specific legislation.

The Legislation

Wholesale dealing is controlled by the Human Medicines Regulations.

Who May Wholesale Medicinal Products?

Wholesaling of medicinal products may be carried out by:

(a) the holder of a WDL, or
(b) the holder of an MA.

Pharmacies Which Wholesale Small Amounts of Medicinal Products

Section 10(7) of the Medicines Act 1968 was repealed with effect from July 2012. It allowed wholesale sales by pharmacies, provided the wholesale sales constituted 'no more than an inconsiderable part' of the business.

The Medicines and Healthcare Products Regulatory Agency (MHRA) now takes the view that the supply of medicines by community and hospital pharmacies to other health care providers in the United Kingdom who need to hold medicines for treatment of or onward supply to their patients represents an important and appropriate part of the professional practice of both community and hospital pharmacy and falls within the definition of provision of health care services. In such circumstances, the MHRA will not deem such transactions as commercial dealing and pharmacies will not be required to hold a WDL.

Pharmacists needing to obtain small quantities of a medicine from another pharmacist to meet a patient's individual needs may do so without the need for the supplying pharmacy to hold a WDL only if the transaction meets all of the following criteria:

- It takes place on an occasional basis.
- The quantity of medicines supplied is small and intended to meet the needs of an individual patient.
- The supply is made on a not-for-profit basis.

This restriction does not apply to exchange of stock between pharmacies that are part of the same legal entity.

No licence is required where a person merely acts as a carrier.

No licence is required where an import agent imports a product to the order of another person who intends to distribute it.

No licence is required for export from the United Kingdom direct to companies outside the EC.

Who May Buy?

POM and P medicine may only be sold by way of wholesale dealing to persons listed in Schedule 22 of the Human Medicines Regulations:

(1) Doctors and dentists.

(2) Persons lawfully conducting a retail pharmacy business within the meaning of *Section 69* of the Medicines Act 1968.

(3) Authorities or persons carrying on the business of:
   (a) an independent hospital, independent clinic or independent medical agency;
   (b) a hospital or health centre which is not an independent hospital or independent clinic; or
   (c) in Northern Ireland, a nursing home.

(4) Ministers of the Crown and Government departments:
   - Scottish Ministers
   - Welsh Ministers
   - Northern Ireland Ministers.

(5) An NHS Trust:
   - An NHS foundation trust
   - The Common Services Agency
   - A health authority or a special health authority.

(6) A person other than an excepted person who carries on a business consisting (wholly or partly) of supplying medicinal products in circumstances corresponding to retail sale, or of administering such products, pursuant to an arrangement made with:
   (a) an NHS Trust or an NHS foundation trust;
   (b) the Common Services Agency;
   (c) a health authority or a special health authority.

(7) A person other than an excepted person who carries on a business consisting (wholly or partly) of the supply or administration of medicinal products for the purpose of assisting the provision of health care by or on behalf of, or under arrangements made by:
(a) a police force in England, Wales or Scotland;
(b) the Police Service of Northern Ireland;
(c) a prison service; or
(d) Her Majesty's Forces.

'Excepted person' means:

(a) a doctor or dentist; or
(b) a person lawfully conducting a retail pharmacy business within the meaning of *Section 69* of the Medicines Act 1968.

Licence Types

(a) Manufacture and assembly
Allows the holder to manufacture and assemble (package) medicinal products.
(b) Assembly only
Allows the holder to assemble (package) medicinal products.
(c) Manufacturer 'specials' (MS)
Allows the holder to manufacture unlicensed medicinal products (commonly referred to as 'Specials').
(d) Full wholesale dealerAllows the holder to wholesale deal pharmacy (P), POM and GSL medicines.
(e) Wholesale dealer (GSL)
Allows the holder to wholesale deal GSL medicines only.
(f) Wholesale dealer's import
Allows the holder to wholesale deal medicines imported from countries outside the EEA.

Requirements for Wholesalers

Schedule 3 of the Human Medicines Regulations sets out the information to be given on the applications for a WDL.

Applicants must specify the classes of products, give the address of each site of business, a description of the facilities available, details of record keeping, details of plans for recalling defective products and the name of a 'Responsible Person'.

Schedule 4 of the Human Medicines Regulations sets out the Standard Provisions for wholesalers.

The wholesaler must maintain suitable staff, premises and facilities; provide information as required; record transactions; have an emergency recall plan; only buy from licensed manufacturers and wholesalers or exempt persons and only sell to those who may lawfully handle the products.

When supplied for retail sale or supply the wholesaler must provide an invoice detailing the date of transaction, the name and pharmaceutical form of the product, the quantity supplied and the name and address of the supplier.

Records of Wholesale Transactions

(1) where a POM is sold by wholesale dealing and no order or invoice or copy of the order or invoice has been retained, or

(2) the sale or supply is one to which Regulation 214(1) does not apply by reason of an exemption other than that it is an emergency supply the particulars to be recorded are:

(a) the date on which the POM is sold or supplied;

(b) the name, quantity and, except where it is apparent from the name, the pharmaceutical form and strength of the POM sold or supplied;

(c) the name and address and trade, business or profession of the person to whom the POM is sold or supplied; and

(d) the purpose for which the POM is sold or supplied.

How Long Must the Records Be Kept

The record must be kept for 2 years from the date of the last entry. Private prescriptions must be retained for 2 years from the date of last dispensing. The owner of the retain pharmacy business (RPB) is responsible for preserving the records.

The Responsible Person

The responsible person (RP) is responsible for ensuring good distribution practice. The RP must ensure that the licence conditions of the Guidelines on Good Distribution Practice are complied with.

The RP does not have to be an employee of the wholesaler and need not be a pharmacist. If not a pharmacist then he or she must have relevant knowledge and experience.

RECORDS

WDL and product licence (PL) holders must keep sufficient records to enable the recall of defective medicines.

Pharmacies which wholesale POMs must retain for 2 years the order or invoice relating to the transaction.

'PSEUDO' - WHOLESALE TRANSACTIONS

Some transactions appear on the surface to be wholesale, but on closer examination are seen not to be.

(a) The supply by one hospital to another hospital in a unit owned by the same trust.

There is no sale or supply, because although a nominal book charge may be made for accounting purposes, the units belong to the same body. One cannot sell or supply to oneself.

(b) Supply by a hospital pharmacy to wards, for administration to patients in that ward by nursing staff or doctor.

Again there is no sale, even though the condition of supply for the purpose of administration is fulfilled. The hospital pharmacy and the ward are part of the same entity.

(c) Co-operatives. Sometimes groups of pharmacists are formed for the purpose of buying goods for subsequent retail sale by the individual members. Where the orders are simply bulked together the group will not normally require a WDL. However, if the group has a separate legal identity, for example, as a limited company then a licence may be required. If the group sells its purchases to persons who buy in order to sell on (whether those persons are members of the group or not) then a licence will be required.

Importers

Regulation 19(4) states that there is no need for a WDL where the only activity in relation to the product is:

(a) the provision of transport facilities
(b) the business of an import agent who imports for another person who intends to deal with it by wholesale or to otherwise distribute it.

Regulation 19(5) states that a WDL is not required for the wholesale distribution of a medicinal product, or for the possession of a medicinal product for the purpose of such distribution, if the distribution or possession is solely for the purpose of exporting the product to states other than EEA States.

Parallel Imports

Parallel imports (PIs) are medicines imported from another member state of the EC. They may have been manufactured in this country, or elsewhere. They are sold 'in parallel' to the brands marketed in this country by the manufacturers. The PIs may bear the same English brand name, a foreign language version or a completely different name.

Market prices for pharmaceuticals differ considerably between the countries in the EU. The price differences are mainly due to the following factors:

• The degree of price control exerted in some form by the government.

- The pricing policies adopted by manufacturers to meet the competition from similar products.
- Different margins at wholesale and retail level.

Legal Basis for the Trade

The Treaty of Rome promotes free trade between EC countries. Articles 30-34 generally prohibit restrictions on imports. The Treaty does not allow either direct restrictions, such as a complete ban, or indirect restrictions such as laws which favour the sale of home produced products rather than imported ones.

Article 36 allows import restrictions if they are justified on grounds of protection of health and life of humans, animals and plants.

In 1976 the European Court of Justice (ECJ) ruled that 'national restrictions on parallel imports within the Community would be against community rules on freedom of trade'.   (Case 104/75, De Peijper/Centrapharm)

The ECJ has considered PIs on a number of occasions since then. PIs must be allowed if:

- the imported product is therapeutically equivalent to the domestic product;
- it is manufactured in accordance with correct quality control standards;
- it is manufactured within the same company or group of companies; or
- subject to some conditions, it is manufactured under licence from the original manufacturer.

The medicines regulatory agency in the importing country is responsible for verifying that the imports satisfy the criteria. This is done in the United Kingdom by the MHRA.

Parallel Import Licences

Regulation 46(1) states 'A person may not sell or supply, or offer to sell or supply, an unauthorised medicinal product'.

As only products for which a PL has been issued may be marketed in the United Kingdom, the MHRA issues a version for PIs known as the PI licence. This is issued subject to the following conditions:

(1) The product must be imported from an EEA state.
(2) It must be a product which is already the subject of a standard marketing authorisation issued by an European Union (EU) member state.
(3) The imported product must be a 'proprietary medicinal product' which is not a vaccine, toxin, serum, human blood product, radio-active isotope or homoeopathic product.
(4) It must have the same therapeutic effect as the UK product.
(5) It must be made by or under licence from the manufacturer of the UK product.

(6) The importer must prove that the import conforms with the specifications for the product.

Regulation 172(1) states:

The prohibitions in regulation 46 (requirement for authorisation) do not prevent:
(a) the holder of a parallel import licence from placing the medicinal product to which the licence relates on the market; or
(b) the sale or supply, or offer for sale or supply, of a medicinal product to which a parallel import licence relates, in accordance with the terms of that licence.
(2) In this regulation "parallel import licence" means a licence that:
(a) is granted by the licensing authority in compliance with the rules of European Union law relating to parallel imports; and
(b) authorises the holder to place on the market a medicinal product imported into the United Kingdom from another EEA State.

Other Requirements for the Importer

If the product is repacked the importer will need a Manufacturer's Licence for assembly.

A WDL is required to distribute the product.

Sufficient records to enable batch recalls must be kept.

Labelling

The Human Medicines Regulations require all medicinal products to be labelled in English.   (Regulation 266)

Products with Different Name

In 1986 both the Department of Health and the Royal Pharmaceutical Society of Great Britain (RPSGB) stated that pharmacists must not dispense a PI bearing a different brand name from that which the doctor had prescribed. The rule was challenged and the ECJ decided in 1989 that the rule was justified on public health grounds.   (Cases 266 and 267/87 Association of Parallel Importers)

The rule applies even where the difference in name is small and due to language problems. The rule applies to the written names. Names which are spelt differently but which sound the same are treated as different names. It makes no difference that the therapeutic effect and quality of the products are identical.

Self-Assessment Questions

1. Where medicines may be sold or supplied?
   Answer: The default situation is that medicines may be sold only in a registered pharmacy by or under the supervision of a pharmacist. This category – P Medicines – is the one into which medicines fall unless placed by legislation into either of the other two categories. Medicines which can be sold, with reasonable safety, without the supervision of a pharmacist may be designated as GSL medicines. The sales have to take place from proper shops, that is, ones which can be closed so as to exclude the public. POM may only be sold or supplied in a registered pharmacy, by or under the supervision of a pharmacist and only in accordance with the prescription of a doctor, dentist or veterinary practitioner.

2. What notice must be displayed in a pharmacy?
   Answer: The Health Act 2006 amended the Medicines Act to require the responsible pharmacist to display a notice in the pharmacy stating that he or she is the pharmacist in charge of the pharmacy on that date and at that time. The registration number must be on the notice.

3. What are PIs?
   Answer: PIs are medicines imported from another member state of the EC. They may have been manufactured in this country, or elsewhere. They are sold 'in parallel' to the brands marketed in this country by the manufacturers. The PIs may bear the same English brand name, a foreign language version or a completely different name.

ADDITIONAL RESOURCES

1. http://www.legislation.gov.uk/uksi/2008/2789/made
2. http://www.pharmacyregulation.org/standards/guidance

Chapter 13

Emergency Supplies, Deliveries and Faxed Prescriptions

SUPPLY OF MEDICINES IN AN EMERGENCY

In an emergency a pharmacist can lawfully sell or supply most prescription only medicines (POMs), provided certain conditions are satisfied.

Regulation 214 of the Human Medicines Regulations generally requires that a person may not sell or supply a POM except in accordance with a prescription given by an appropriate practitioner.

Regulations 224 and 225 set out exemptions from this requirement in certain circumstances. The supply must be made by a person lawfully conducting a retail pharmacy business.

Two situations are envisaged:

- a request made by a relevant prescriber,
- a request made by a patient.

Which Prescribers Are Covered?

Regulation 213 defines 'relevant prescriber' as any of the following:

(a) a doctor,
(b) a dentist,
(c) a supplementary prescriber,
(d) a nurse-independent prescriber,
(e) a pharmacist-independent prescriber,
(f) a community practitioner nurse prescriber,
(g) an optometrist-independent prescriber, and
(h) a European Economic Area (EEA) health professional.

Supply Made at the Request of a Prescriber

Regulation 224 allows a pharmacy to sell or supply a POM if certain conditions are met.

Pharmacy Law and Practice. DOI: http://dx.doi.org/10.1016/B978-0-12-394289-0.00013-8

The conditions are:

(a) the pharmacist must be satisfied that the sale or supply has been requested by a prescriber who by reason of an emergency is unable to furnish a prescription immediately,

(b) the prescriber has undertaken to furnish the pharmacy with a prescription within 72 h,

(c) the POM is sold or supplied in accordance with the directions of the prescriber requesting it,

(d) the POM is not a controlled drug in Schedule 1, 2 or 3 of the Misuse of Drugs Regulations 1985,

(e) a record must be made of:

   (i) name and address of the patient,

   (ii) date on the prescription,

   (iii) the date on which the prescription is received.

The date on the prescription and the date on which the prescription relating to that sale or supply is received may be entered in the record on the day that the prescription is received.

Emergency Supplies at Request of Patient

Regulation 224 allows a pharmacy to sell or supply a POM at the request of the patient if certain conditions are met:

(1) The pharmacist by or under whose supervision the POM is to be sold or supplied has interviewed the person requesting it and is satisfied:

   (a) that there is an immediate need for the POM to be sold or supplied and that it is impracticable in the circumstances to obtain a prescription without undue delay;

   (b) that treatment with the POM has on a previous occasion been prescribed by a relevant prescriber for the person requesting it; and

   (c) as to the dose which in the circumstances it would be appropriate for that person to take.

(2) The quantity of the product that is sold or supplied does not exceed set limits.

(3) The POM:

   (a) does not consist of or contain a substance specified in Schedule 18; and

   (b) is not a controlled drug, other than a POM that:

      (i) consists of or contains phenobarbital or phenobarbital sodium, and

      (ii) is sold or supplied for use in the treatment of epilepsy.

(4) A record must be made within the specified time, stating:

   (a) the date on which the POM was sold or supplied;

   (b) the name, quantity and, except where it is apparent from the name, the pharmaceutical form and strength of the POM sold or supplied;

   (c) the name and address of the person requiring the POM; and

   (d) the nature of the emergency.

(5) The inner or outer packaging of the POM is labelled to show:
   (a) the date on which the POM is sold or supplied;
   (b) the name, quantity and (unless apparent from the name) the pharmaceutical strength of the POM;
   (c) the name of the person requesting the POM;
   (d) the name and address of the registered pharmacy from which the POM is sold or supplied; and
   (e) the words 'Emergency Supply'.

Substances that May Not Be Supplied at the Request of a Patient

Schedule 18 contains a list of substances that may not be sold or supplied at the request of a patient in the absence of a prescription.

Ammonium bromide
Calcium bromide
Calcium bromidolactobionate
Embutramide
Fencamfamin hydrochloride
Fluanisone
Hexobarbitone
Hexobarbitone sodium
Hydrobromic acid
Meclofenoxate hydrochloride
Methohexitone sodium
Pemoline
Piracetam
Potassium bromide
Prolintane hydrochloride
Sodium bromide
Strychnine hydrochloride
Tacrine hydrochloride
Thiopentone sodium

Maximum Quantities

A POM that:

(a) is a preparation of insulin, an aerosol for the relief of asthma, an ointment or cream, and	The smallest pack that the pharmacist has available for sale or supply.
(b) has been made up for sale in a package elsewhere than at the place of sale or supply.	
An oral contraceptive.	A quantity sufficient for a full treatment cycle.

An antibiotic for oral administration in liquid form.	The smallest quantity that will provide a full course of treatment.
A controlled drug within the meaning of Schedule 4 or 5 of the Misuse of Drugs Regulations 2001 or Schedule 4 or 5 of the Misuse of Drugs Regulations (Northern Ireland) 2002.	Five days' treatment.
Any other POM.	Thirty days' treatment.

In this regulation 'aerosol' means a product that is dispersed from its container by a propellant gas or liquid.

Controlled Drugs

Schedule 1, 2 or 3 controlled drugs cannot be supplied in an emergency – except for Phenobarbital for epilepsy.

Doctors and dentists from EEA or Switzerland cannot request emergency supplies of controlled drugs, including Phenobarbital.

In an emergency a practitioner can personally obtain a Schedule 2 or 3 drug if he cannot immediately supply a signed requisition. This does not authorise supply direct to the patient. The practitioner must undertake to deliver a signed requisition within 24 h of receiving the drug.

Royal Pharmaceutical Society Guidance

You should be mindful of patients abusing emergency supplies, for example where the patient medication record shows the patient has on a number of occasions requested a medicine as an emergency supply on several occasions.

It is possible to make an emergency supply even when the surgery is open. Trying to obtain a prescription may sometimes cause undue delay in treatment and potentially cause harm to the patient.

If patients are away from home and have run out of their medicines, referring them to the nearest surgery to register as a temporary patient may not always be appropriate. You could make an emergency supply if you were satisfied conditions in this guidance were met.

Urgent Supply Without a Prescription Under the NHS

Paragraph 6 of Schedule 4 of the 2012 Pharmaceutical Services Regulations applies where, in a case of urgency, a prescriber requests an NHS pharmacist to provide a drug or appliance.

A pharmacist may provide the drug or appliance requested before receiving a prescription form or repeatable prescription in respect of that drug or appliance, provided that:

(a) in the case of a request for a drug, the drug is neither:
    (i) a Scheduled drug, nor

    (ii) a controlled drug within the meaning of the Misuse of Drugs Act 1971, other than a drug which is for the time being specified in Schedule 4 or 5 to the Misuse of Drugs Regulations 2001 (which relate to controlled drugs excepted from certain prohibitions under the Regulations); and

(b) in the case of a request for a drug or an appliance, the prescriber undertakes to:

    (i) give the pharmacist a non-electronic prescription form or non-electronic repeatable prescription in respect of the drug or appliance within 72 h of the request being made, or

    (ii) transmit an electronic prescription to the Electronic Prescription Service within 72 h of the request being made.

There is no procedure in England and Wales for a patient to request an emergency NHS supply.

Scotland

In Scotland a national Patients Group Direction (PGD) has been in place since 2006. This enables pharmacists in Scotland located in premises with an NHS Pharmaceutical Care Service Contract to provide patients with up to one cycle of their repeat medicines (or appliances) when they cannot obtain a prescription during out-of-hours periods, for example, at weekends or on public holidays.

The PGD can only be used when the patient's most recent prescription for the particular medicine requested was issued by the patient's prescriber, that is two successive supplies of the same medicine is not permissive under this PGD.

The request may come direct from the patient, the patient's representative, the patient's prescriber, an out-of-hours collaborative, NHS 24 or hospital A & E departments.

The pharmacist must satisfy themselves that the situation is appropriate for a PGD. The patient must be registered with a NHS GP in Scotland or have temporary registration in Scotland

EEA Practitioners

The Human Medicines Regulations 2012 permit a UK pharmacist to make an emergency supply at the request of a doctor or dentist from an EEA country or Switzerland, and also at the request of a patient who has previously been prescribed a particular medicine by an EEA or Swiss doctor or dentist.

Emergency supplies of Schedules 1, 2, and 3 controlled drugs cannot be made on the basis of a non-UK EEA prescription. The Royal Pharmaceutical Society (RPS) advises that pharmacists should be mindful of patients abusing emergency supplies.

Supply of Emergency Hormonal Contraception

The POM (Human Use) Amendment (No. 3) Order 2000 SI No. 3231 came into force on 1 January 2001.

This enables emergency hormonal contraception (EHC) consisting of or containing Levonorgestrel to be sold by pharmacists without a prescription. The maximum strength allowed is 0.75 mg. The tablets may only be sold or supplied exclusively for use as an emergency contraceptive in women aged 16 and over.

PGDs may allow for supply of EHC to women aged under 16 who are Gillick competent.

Pharmacists Who Choose Not to Supply EHC

The GPhC Code states:

If you do not supply Emergency Hormonal Contraception (EHC) (either over the counter or against a prescription), women should be referred to an alternative appropriate source of supply available within the time limits for EHC to be effective.

Administration by Ambulance Paramedics for Immediate, Necessary Treatment of Sick or Injured Persons

A list of medicines which may only be administered by ambulance paramedics on their own initiative for immediate, necessary treatment of sick or injured persons

Diazepam 5 mg/ml emulsion for injection,
Succinylated modified fluid gelatin 4% intravenous infusion.

POMs containing one or more of the following substances but no other active ingredient:

Adrenaline acid tartrate
Adrenaline hydrochloride
Amiodarone
Anhydrous glucose
Benzylpenicillin
Compound sodium lactate intravenous infusion (Hartmann's solution)
Ergometrine maleate
Frusemide
Glucose
Heparin sodium (NB: Administration is only allowed for the purpose of cannula flushing.)
Lignocaine hydrochloride
Metoclopramide
Morphine sulphate

Nalbuphine hydrochloride
Naloxone hydrochloride
Ondansetron
Paracetamol
Reteplase
Sodium chloride
Streptokinase
Syntometrine
Tenecteplase

Registered paramedics may obtain stocks of these medicines from a pharmacy (or from a wholesaler) as well as pharmacy medicines for administration in the course of a business operated by them.

COLLECTION AND DELIVERY SCHEMES

Certain types of collection and delivery schemes are given special exemption from the general Medicines Act requirement that the supply of medicines must be from a pharmacy.

Section 248 of the Human Medicines Regulations disapplies Regulations 220 and 221 where the medicine:

- is for human use,
- is supplied in accordance with a prescription from a doctor, dentist, nurse-independent prescriber, pharmacist-independent prescriber or optometrist-independent prescriber,

and where the supply is as part of a collection and delivery arrangement used by a pharmacy.

Regulation 220 restricts supply of POM and pharmacy medicine to pharmacy premises.

Regulation 221 normally imposes conditions on the sale of general sales list (GSL) products so that:

(a) the supply is only from premises which can 'be closed so as to exclude the public',
(b) products are made up for sale elsewhere,
(c) the immediate and outer packaging has not been opened since the product was made up for sale in it.

A 'collection and delivery arrangement' means any arrangement whereby a person takes or sends a prescription to premises other than a pharmacy, and later collects or has collected the dispensed medicine from those premises.

A common example is where a grocery shop in an isolated village acts as a collecting point for scripts written by visiting GPs. After dispensing they are held in the shop until the patient collects them.

The script must have been dispensed at a registered pharmacy, by or under the supervision of a pharmacist. The premises used must be capable of being closed so as to exclude the public.

The arrangements are not limited to the NHS. There are no other formal legal requirements.

Delivery Direct from the Pharmacy

Many pharmacists have a service where they collect prescriptions from a doctor, dispense them and deliver the medicines to the patient's home. These arrangements are not covered by the restrictions outlined above. They are subject to normal legal requirements.

The RPS offers the following guidance:

DELIVERY SERVICES STANDARDS

A delivery service is where the medicine is handed to the patient, their carer or other designated person other than on registered pharmacy premises. When providing medicines via a delivery service you still have a professional responsibility to ensure that patients or their carers know how to use the medication safely, effectively and appropriately and check that they are not experiencing adverse effects or compliance difficulties. You must ensure that:

    6.1. on each occasion a delivery service is provided you use your professional judgement to determine whether direct face-to-face contact with the patient or their carer is necessary.

    6.2. you obtain consent from the patient or their carer to provide the delivery service on a single occasion or for a set period of time.

    6.3. delivery to a person other than the patient or carer is undertaken only where they have been specifically designated by the patient or their carer.

    6.4. you maintain appropriate records of requests for the service.

    6.5. the delivery mechanism used:

        ⦿ *enables the medicine to be delivered securely and promptly to the intended recipient with any necessary information to enable safe and effective use of their medicine;*

        ⦿ *caters for any special security/storage requirements of the medicine;*

        ⦿ *incorporates a verifiable audit trail for the medicine from the point at which it leaves the pharmacy to the point at which it is handed to the patient, their carer or other designated person, or returned to the pharmacy in the event of a delivery failure;*

        ⦿ *safeguards confidential information about the medication that a patient is taking.*

GOOD PRACTICE GUIDANCE

    • *Wherever possible a signature should be obtained to indicate safe receipt of the medicines.*

    • *Systems should be in place to inform a patient who is not at home that delivery was attempted.*

Faxed Prescriptions

The Human Medicines Regulations require that 'prescriptions' be signed by the prescriber. A fax received in a pharmacy does not meet that requirement and is therefore not itself a valid prescription. However, views differ on what this means in practice.

According to advice given by the RPS in 2010

A faxed prescription is not a legally valid prescription and a supply against a faxed prescription is therefore not a legal supply.

The RPS suggests a similar result can usually be achieved by the use of emergency supply legislation:

Emergency supply exists as a legal mechanism and can achieve a similar outcome in most scenarios. It is the legal and recommended route for providing urgent prescription only medicines in the absence of a prescription. For example, a doctor may fax a prescription to you for a POM, requesting you to dispense from it and the prescription will be posted to you the next day. In this instance there is a legal alternative mechanism in place (i.e., emergency supply at the request of a prescriber) for you to supply the POM without having the original legally valid prescription to hand, provided the conditions of emergency supply discussed in this guidance are met.

The Society acknowledges that in some 'secure environments' the use of faxed prescriptions has become routine.

An alternative view is that the legislation does not specifically require a prescription to be in the hand of the pharmacist at the time of dispensing – merely that it be in existence. The fax is good evidence of the existence of the prescription and can therefore be dispensed.

Controlled drug legislation contains more stringent requirements for prescriptions for Schedule 2 and 3 medicines, in particular that the prescription must be in the handwriting of the prescriber. Accordingly such medicines cannot be dispensed against a fax.

Emergency Sale by Pharmacist During a Pandemic

Regulation 226 sets out arrangements to allow pharmacists to sell POMs without a prescription during a pandemic:

(1) Regulation 214(1) does not apply to the sale or supply of a POM by a person lawfully conducting a retail pharmacy business if conditions A and B are met.
(2) Condition A is that the supply is made whilst a disease is, or in anticipation of a disease being imminently:
   (a) pandemic; and
   (b) a serious risk, or potentially a serious risk, to human health.

(3) Condition B is that the pharmacist by or under whose supervision the POM is to be sold or supplied is satisfied:

    (a) that treatment with the POM has on a previous occasion been prescribed by a relevant prescriber for the person to be treated with it; and

    (b) as to the dose which in the circumstances it would be appropriate for that person to take.

Regulation 247 allows for a protocol to specify the treatment:

(1) Regulations 214(1), 220 and 221 do not apply to the supply of a medicinal product that meets the following conditions.

(2) Condition A is that the supply is made whilst a disease is, or in anticipation of a disease being imminently:

    (a) pandemic; and

    (b) a serious risk, or potentially a serious risk, to human health.

(3) Condition B is that the supply is in accordance with a protocol that:

    (a) is approved by the Ministers, an NHS body or the Health Protection Agency;

    (b) specifies the symptoms of and treatment for the disease; and

    (c) contains requirements as to the recording of:

        (i) the name of the person who supplies the product to the person to be treated ('the patient') or to a person acting on the patient's behalf, and

        (ii) evidence that the product was supplied to the patient or to a person acting on the patient's behalf.

Supply in Response to Spread of Pathogenic Agents, etc.

174. The prohibitions in regulation 46 (requirement for authorisation) do not apply where the sale or supply of a medicinal product is authorised by the licensing authority on a temporary basis in response to the suspected or confirmed spread of:

    (a) pathogenic agents;

    (b) toxins;

    (c) chemical agents; or

    (d) nuclear radiation,

which may cause harm to human beings.

Sale of Medicinal Products from Automatic Machines

Only GSL medicines may be sold from automatic vending machines.

222. A person may not sell or offer for sale a medicinal product by means of an automatic machine if the product is not subject to general sale.

(Human Medicines Regulations)

Self-Assessment Questions

1. What are the conditions to a successful request by a prescriber for an emergency supply of medicines?

Answers:
   a. The pharmacist must be satisfied that the sale or supply has been requested by a prescriber who by reason of an emergency is unable to furnish a prescription immediately.
   b. The prescriber has undertaken to furnish the pharmacy with a prescription within 72 h.
   c. The POM is sold or supplied in accordance with the directions of the prescriber requesting it.
   d. The POM is not a controlled drug in Schedule 1, 2 or 3 of the Misuse of Drugs Regulations 1985.
   e. A record must be made of:
      i. name and address of the patient,
      ii. date on the prescription,
      iii. the date on which the prescription is received.

2. What conditions govern the supply of EHC by a pharmacist?
   Answers: The only product which may be sold by a pharmacist without a prescription is Levonorgestrel. The maximum strength allowed is 0.75 mg. The tablets may only be sold or supplied exclusively for use as an emergency contraceptive in women aged 16 and over.

3. Describe how a collection and delivery arrangement works?
   Answers: Section 248 of the Human Medicines Regulations disapplies Regulations 220 and 221 where a medicine is supplied on a prescription as part of a collection and delivery arrangement used by a pharmacy. A 'collection and delivery arrangement' means any arrangement whereby a person takes or sends a prescription to premises other than a pharmacy, and later collects or has collected the dispensed medicine from those premises. A common example is where a grocery shop in an isolated village acts as a collecting point for scripts written by visiting GPs. After dispensing they are held in the shop until the patient collects them. The script must have been dispensed at a registered pharmacy, by or under the supervision of a pharmacist. The premises used must be capable of being closed so as to exclude the public.

Chapter 14

Unlicensed Products

Under the Human Medicines Regulations a company may only market, that is advertise and sell, their product in the United Kingdom if they hold a marketing authorisation for that product. Furthermore the therapeutic or diagnostic purposes for which the product can be marketed are limited by the terms of the authorisation. Thus a product licensed only for the treatment of gastric ulcers may not be marketed for the treatment of indigestion.

However, this legislation does not affect the clinical freedom of doctors to prescribe what they believe is best for their patient. They may use or recommend medicines which do not have a licence (unlicensed) or use medicines in ways different to those specified in the marketing authorisation (off-label).

UNLICENSED PRODUCTS

Doctors may prescribe several categories of unlicensed products. Some substances, for example raw chemicals may on occasions be prescribed as medicines, although they are not normally thought of as medicines, and are not marketed as such. Other medicines may be available in another country but not licensed in the United Kingdom.

OFF-LABEL USE

'Off-label' medicine describes the use of licensed medicines in a dose, age group or by a route not in the product licence specification. The product cannot be marketed for any use outside the licence conditions, but doctors are free to prescribe outside those conditions. Such use is now generally referred to by the US term 'off-label use'. Many medicines used in children are prescribed and used off-label. Clinical trials are rarely carried out on children, especially very young children, so the licensed use is restricted to those groups of patients where clinical trials have been carried out.

Pharmacy Law and Practice. DOI: http://dx.doi.org/10.1016/B978-0-12-394289-0.00014-X
195

REASONS FOR USING UNLICENSED PRODUCTS

They may be used because:

- The medicine is prepared by the original manufacturer, but is not on sale in United Kingdom.
- It is the prescriber's own formula for a specific patient.
- It is an unusual form, for example liquid preparation of a medicine normally available only as capsules.
- It is an unusual strength.
- It is an unusual combination of active ingredients.
- It is an unusual formulation, for example no preservative eye drops, lactose free tablets.
- It is a discontinued product.
- The normal product is temporarily unavailable.

EXEMPTIONS FOR UNLICENSED MEDICINES

Most of the relevant legislation is to be found in the Human Medicines Regulations. These provide exemptions from the normal licensing requirements, so as to allow pharmacists to order Specials and to hold stock ready for dispensing.

OBTAINING UNLICENSED PRODUCTS

Unlicensed medicines may be obtained in three ways:

(1) Prepared extemporaneously in the pharmacy
(2) Obtained from a 'Specials' manufacturer
(3) Imported from another country via a wholesaler.

EXTEMPORANEOUS PREPARATION IN THE PHARMACY

Pharmacists may carry out the preparation of an unlicensed medicine in the pharmacy.

The exemptions allow a pharmacist to:

- prepare or dispense a product against a prescription;
- prepare a stock in anticipation of dispensing;
- prepare or dispense a medicinal product against a specification given by the intended purchaser, where the product is to be administered to that purchaser or to someone under his care;
- prepare a product for counter-prescribing.

Dispensing Against a Prescription

A pharmacist can prepare a product or assemble a product against a prescription given by a prescriber.

PREPARATION OF STOCK

Regulations 17 and 46 of the Human Medicines Regulations prohibit the placing on the market or the wholesale distribution of a relevant medicinal product unless it has a marketing authorisation. Products specially made for a particular patient will not have a marketing authorisation.

A pharmacist can prepare a stock of medicinal products in a registered pharmacy:

- *with a view to dispensing them in accordance with a prescription given by a practitioner OR*
- *with a view to dispensing them in accordance with a specification from a person who is going to administer them to himself or to someone under his care.*

((s10)(4)(b) Medicines Act 1968)

The product must be prepared under the supervision of a pharmacist, and in a pharmacy, hospital or a health centre.

Dispensing to a Formula

A pharmacist may prepare or dispense a medicinal product in a registered pharmacy:

- by or under the supervision of a pharmacist, and
- in accordance with a specification furnished by the person to whom the product is or is to be sold or supplied, and
- if the person is going to administer the product to himself or to someone under his care.

Counter-prescribing

A pharmacist may prepare or dispense a medicinal product in a registered pharmacy, if the following conditions are satisfied:

- *the product is for administration to a person*
- *the pharmacist was requested by or on behalf of that person to exercise his judgement as to the treatment required*
- *the person was present in the pharmacy at the time of the request.*

((s10)(4)(a) Medicines Act 1968)

Chemist's Nostrums

The pharmacist may prepare a medicinal product (or a stock of such products) with a view to retail sale rather than to supply against an order. The sale must be from the registered pharmacy where the product was prepared. The product may not be advertised.

GUIDANCE ON THE EXEMPTION FOR PHARMACISTS

The Medicines and Healthcare products Regulatory Agency (MHRA) Guidance Note No.14 'The supply of unlicensed relevant medicinal products for individual patients' indicates how in practice MHRA will determine whether an activity is 'preparation' or 'manufacture'. Criteria include location of the process, nature of the activity, and scale of the activity.

Following a case where a mixture was wrongly dispensed, resulting in the death of a child, the pharmacist and post-graduate trainee involved were both found guilty of a breach of *Section 64* of the MA 1968.

At the time the Royal Pharmaceutical Society of Great Britain (RPSGB) issued guidance:

Pharmacists are advised to check carefully all calculations, paying particular attention to the decimal points, and to either carry out the preparation themselves or to delegate to suitably trained staff. In all cases the pharmacist should verify the formula used, the weightings or other measurements, and the calculations. Where possible an independent check is advisable. The pharmacist should always undertake a final review before the product is supplied to the patient.

The RPS issued a separate guidance document entitled 'Dealing with Specials' in June 2010.[1]

SPECIALS

The terms 'named–patient medicine' and 'Specials' are used interchangeably to refer to an unlicensed medicine specially ordered from a manufacturer. It is usually a medicine available ready-made from the manufacturer, not made up to a recipe supplied by the pharmacy or the doctor.

According to the Human Medicines Regulations, medicinal products which have no marketing authorisation may be marketed in the following circumstances:

- The company must hold a special manufacturers licence
- The manufacture must be under adequate conditions and supervision
- Records must be kept
- The product must be formulated in accordance with the specification of a prescriber
- The product is supplied for use by a prescriber, or by his individual patients, on his direct responsibility
- The supply must be to the prescriber or for use under the supervision of a pharmacist in a pharmacy, hospital or health centre
- The product must be distributed by a licensed wholesaler.

RECORD KEEPING

The 'Specials' manufacturer, the pharmacist and any practitioner who sells or supplies a 'special' must keep records for at least 5 years, which show:

- the source of the product
- the name of the person who obtained the product
- the date of the transaction
- the quantity of each sale or supply
- the batch number
- details of any adverse reaction to the product which he knows about.

Advertising of Specials

- Unlicensed medicines cannot be advertised to the public.
- Orders must be unsolicited – no advertisements are allowed. Catalogues and circular letters may only be sent to health care professionals on receipt of a bona fide unsolicited order.
- However, a Specials manufacturer, distributor or importer can issue a price list to health care professionals without first having received a bona fide unsolicited order. Regulation 7(3) excludes 'trade catalogues' and 'price lists' from the definition of 'advertisement'.

The MHRA advise that any price list should consist only of a basic line listing providing the following information:

- reference number
- drug name (BAN or equivalent)
- dosage form
- strength
- pack size
- price

No product claims may be included.

IMPORTS

A further exemption allows importation of unlicensed products. Regulation 167 of the Human Medicines Regulations[2] allows for the importation and supply of unlicensed relevant medicinal products for the special needs of individual patients, commonly, but incorrectly called 'named patients'.

These regulations allow a licensed wholesaler to import an unlicensed product in response to a bona fide unsolicited order to fulfil special needs, formulated in accordance with the specification of a doctor or dentist and for use by his individual patients on his direct personal responsibility.

There are conditions laid down in the regulations:

(1) The importer must give written notice to the MHRA before importing and allow MHRA 28 days to object.
(2) The quantity imported must not exceed 25 single doses or 25 therapeutic courses (each not to exceed 3 months).
(3) The product must not be promoted.
(4) Records must be kept, and the MHRA notified of any adverse reactions.

EXEMPTION FOR DOCTORS

Doctors may prepare products themselves for use on patients. They may order the products from a registered pharmacy, which may make them without any further licensing. Doctors may order products themselves from licensed Specials manufacturers.

Regulation 3 of the Human Medicines Regulations 2012 states that the restrictions imposed by Regulations 17 and 46 (which generally require licenses) do not apply, where:

(1) a medicinal product is manufactured or assembled by a doctor or dentist; and
(2) the medicinal product is supplied:
   (a) to a patient in the course of the treatment of that patient; or
   (b) to a patient of another doctor or dentist who is a member of the same medical or dental practice.
(3) the product is not manufactured or assembled:
   (a) on a large scale; or
   (b) by an industrial process.

This allows a doctor to make or order an unlicensed product.

There are restrictions on the amount of stock held by a doctor – 5 l of fluid and 2.5 kg of solids.

Records must be kept for 5 years of the supplier, the recipient, the date of supply, batch details and details of any suspected reaction of which the supplier is aware.

Mixing of Medicines Prior to Administration

Until recently the view was that mixing of two medicines in a syringe prior to administration produced a new unlicensed medicine and was therefore an illegal act.

The matter has now been clarified by Regulation 20 of the Human Medicines Regulations.

(1) Regulation 17(1) (manufacturing of medicinal products) does not apply to the mixing of medicines by:

(a) a nurse independent prescriber;

(b) a pharmacist independent prescriber;

(c) a supplementary prescriber, if the mixing of medicines forms part of the clinical management plan for an individual patient;

(d) a person acting in accordance with the written directions of a:

(i) doctor,

(ii) dentist,

(iii) nurse independent prescriber or

(iv) pharmacist independent prescriber; or

(e) a person acting in accordance with the written directions of a supplementary prescriber, if the mixing of medicines forms part of the clinical management plan for an individual patient.

(2) In this regulation 'mixing of medicines' means the combining of two or more medicinal products together for the purposes of administering them to meet the needs of an individual patient.

Mixing of Controlled Drugs

Similarly the Misuse of Drugs (Amendment No. 2) (England, Wales and Scotland) Regulations 2012,[3] which came into force on 23 April 2012, allows for the compounding or mixing of controlled drugs (CDs) for administration.

The regulations provide that:

a nurse independent prescriber acting in her capacity as such, or a supplementary prescriber acting under and in accordance with the terms of a clinical management plan, may compound any drug specified in Schedule 3 or 4 for the purposes of administration in accordance with regulation 7;

And similarly:

any person acting in accordance with the written directions of a doctor, a dentist, a nurse independent prescriber, a pharmacist independent prescriber, or a supplementary prescriber acting under and in accordance with the terms of a clinical management plan, may compound any drug specified in Schedule 3 or 4 for the purposes of administration in accordance with regulation 7.

Liability Issues with Use of Specials

Special consideration should be given to issues of liability when unlicensed products are used, or when products are used off-licence. The summary of product characteristics gives some information about the use of any particular medicine, and prescribing within its limitations is unlikely to give rise to claims of negligence on the part of either doctor or pharmacist. Other information may be obtainable from specialist units.

The prescriber assumes legal liability when he or she prescribes unlicensed or off-label products. If a patient is harmed by the prescribing of an unlicensed or off-label product, then it may be alleged that the prescriber and/or the pharmacist has been negligent. The test of whether a doctor or pharmacist is negligent is referred to as the 'Bolam test'. This broadly states that a professional person will not be negligent if what he does would be approved of by a responsible body of opinion in his profession. See Chapter 23.

The liability of the manufacturer for any harm caused by off-label use remains untested in court, although theoretically there could be liability under the Consumer Safety Act 1987.

Similarly there may be a possibility that the pharmacist might be liable in circumstances where he was aware of the use, where he knew about the possibility of harm and where he could have taken action.

Advice Given to Doctors

The Medical Defence Union has advised doctors using off-label products for child patients that they must explain to those with parental responsibility that the drug is not appropriately licensed for paediatric use. Several studies recently have indicated that many doctors are unaware of the limitations for use set out in the data sheets for a product, and they may be grateful for a reminder.

Article 126a Authorisation

In order to increase the availability of some medicinal products, in particular on smaller markets, Article 126a of Directive 2001/83/EC provides that, even in the absence of a marketing authorisation a medicinal product, which has already been authorised in another Member State, may be placed on the market.

In such cases, the competent authority of the Member State has to inform the marketing authorisation holder where the medicinal product concerned is authorised.

The Member State must ensure that the following requirements are complied with:

- the labelling and package leaflet
- the classification of the medicinal product
- advertising
- pharmacovigilance and
- supervision.

The publicly available register of the medicinal products authorised to be placed on the market under Article 126a is available at the Commission web site.[4]

Article 126a authorisations are dealt with by Regulation 156 of the Human Medicines Regulations:

(1) The licensing authority may grant an Article 126a authorisation for a medicinal product if the following conditions are met.

(2) Condition A is that no United Kingdom marketing authorisation, certificate of registration or traditional herbal registration is in force for the product.

(3) Condition B is that no application is pending in the United Kingdom for a marketing authorisation, certificate of registration or traditional herbal registration for the product.

(4) Condition C is that the licensing authority considers that the placing of the product on the market in the United Kingdom is justified for public health reasons.

(5) Condition D is that the product is imported from another Member State that has, in accordance with the 2001 Directive, authorised the placing on the market of the product in that Member State.

(6) Condition E is that the person to whom the authorisation is granted is established in the European Union.

(7) Before granting an Article 126a authorisation, the licensing authority must notify the authorisation holder in the Member State mentioned in paragraph (5) of the proposal to grant the Article 126a authorisation.

(8) Before granting an Article 126a authorisation, the licensing authority may request the competent authority in the Member State mentioned in paragraph (5) to provide in accordance with Article 126a(3)(b) of the 2001 Directive a copy of:

(a) the assessment report for that product as mentioned in Article 21(4) of the 2001 Directive; and

(b) the authorisation in force for that product.

(9) An Article 126a authorisation remains in force for the period specified in it unless revoked before the end of that period.

(10) That period may be specified by reference to the occurrence or non-occurrence of a particular event or events.

EXTRACTS FROM THE HUMAN MEDICINES REGULATIONS 2012

Special Provisions for Pharmacies, etc.

4.—(1) Regulations 17(1) (manufacturing of medicinal products: requirement for licence) and 46 (requirement for authorisation) do not apply where any provision of section 10 of the Medicines Act 1968(1) so provides.

(2) Chapter 1 of Part 13 (requirements for packaging and package leaflets relating to medicinal products) does not apply to a medicinal product that is sold or supplied in circumstances where paragraph (3) or (4) applies in relation to the product, except to the extent set out in paragraph (6), but the requirements of paragraph (5) shall apply.

(3) This paragraph applies in a case where a medicinal product is the result of a process of manufacture to which regulation 17(1) does not apply by virtue of any provision of section 10 of the Medicines Act 1968.

(4) This paragraph applies in the case of a medicinal product where:

> *(a) the product is the result of a process of assembly of a medicinal product that is an authorised medicinal product within the meaning of regulation 3(15);*
>
> *(b) regulation 17(1) does not apply to the process of assembly by virtue of any provision of section 10 of the Medicines Act 1968;*
>
> *(c) the process of assembly results in a change in the presentation of the authorised medicinal product; and*
>
> *(d) by reason of that change the product so assembled is not sold or supplied in accordance with the terms of:*
>
> > *(i) the marketing authorisation,*
> >
> > *(ii) the certificate of registration,*
> >
> > *(iii) the traditional herbal registration, or*
> >
> > *(iv) the Article 126a authorisation,*

that relates to the authorised medicinal product.

(5) The information specified in Part 2 of Schedule 26 must appear on the outer packaging, or, if there is no outer packaging, on the immediate packaging of a medicinal product that is sold or supplied in circumstances where paragraph (3) or (4) applies in relation to the product.

(6) Regulations 269 (offences relating to packaging and package leaflets: other persons) and 271 (offences: penalties) shall have effect in relation to paragraph (5) as if that paragraph were a requirement of Part 13.

Regulation 167 Supply to Fulfil Special Patient Needs

(1)   The prohibitions in regulation 46 (requirement for authorisation) do not apply in relation to a medicinal product (a "special medicinal product") if:

> *(a)   the medicinal product is supplied in response to an unsolicited order;*
>
> *(b)   the medicinal product is manufactured and assembled in accordance with the specification of a person who is a doctor, dentist, nurse independent prescriber, pharmacist independent prescriber or supplementary prescriber;*
>
> *(c)   the medicinal product is for use by a patient for whose treatment that person is directly responsible in order to fulfil the special needs of that patient; and*
>
> *(d)   the following conditions are met*

(2)   Condition A is that the medicinal product is supplied:

> *(a)   to a doctor, dentist, nurse independent prescriber, pharmacist independent prescriber or supplementary prescriber; or*
>
> *(b)   for use under the supervision of a pharmacist in a registered pharmacy, a hospital or a health centre.*

(3)   Condition B is that no advertisement relating to the medicinal product is published by any person.

(4) Condition C is that:

   (a) the manufacture and assembly of the medicinal product are carried out under such supervision; and

   (b) such precautions are taken, as are adequate to ensure that the medicinal product meets the specification of the doctor, dentist, nurse independent prescriber, pharmacist independent prescriber or supplementary prescriber who requires it.

(5) Condition D is that written records of the manufacture or assembly of the medicinal product in accordance with condition C are maintained and are available to the licensing authority or to the enforcement authority on request.

(6) Condition E is that if the medicinal product is manufactured or assembled in the United Kingdom or imported into the United Kingdom from a country other than an EEA State:

   (a) it is manufactured, assembled or imported by the holder of a manufacturer's licence that relates specifically to the manufacture, assembly or importation of special medicinal products; or

   (b) it is manufactured, assembled or imported as an investigational medicinal product by the holder of a manufacturing authorisation granted by the licensing authority for the purposes of regulation 36 of the Clinical Trials Regulations.

(7) Condition F is that if the product is imported from an EEA State:

   (a) it is manufactured or assembled in that State by a person who is the holder of an authorisation in relation to its manufacture or assembly in accordance with the provisions of the 2001 Directive as implemented in that State; or

   (b) it is manufactured or assembled as an investigational medicinal product in that State by the holder of an authorisation in relation to its manufacture or assembly in accordance with Article 13 of the Clinical Trials Directive as implemented in that State.

(8) Condition G is that if the product is distributed by way of wholesale dealing by a person who has not, as the case may be, manufactured, assembled or imported the product in accordance with paragraph (6)(a) or (7)(a),then that person must be the holder of a wholesale dealer's licence in relation to the product in question.

(9) In this regulation "publish" has the meaning given in regulation 277(1) (interpretation: Part 14 advertising).

Regulation 168 Use of Non-Prescription Medicines in the Course of a Business

Regulation 168 allows the use of unlicensed non-prescription only medicines (POM) by health care professionals in the course of business:

   (1) The prohibitions in regulation 46 (requirement for authorisation) do not apply to anything done in relation to a medicinal product if the following conditions are met.

   (2) Condition A is that the medicinal product is not a POM.

(3) *Condition B is that the medicinal product is sold or supplied to a person who is a health care professional exclusively for use by that person:*
  (a) *in the course of a business carried on by that person, and*
  (b) *for the purposes of administering it or causing it to be administered otherwise than by selling it.*

(4) *Condition C is that the medicinal product is:*
  (a) *manufactured and assembled in accordance with the specification; and*
  (b) *for use by a patient, for whose treatment that person is directly responsible, in order to fulfil the special needs of that patient.*

(5) *Condition D is that if sold or supplied through the holder of a wholesale dealer's licence the medicinal product is sold or supplied to such a person and for such use as mentioned in condition B.*

(6) *Condition E is that no advertisement relating to the medicinal product is published by any person.*

(7) *Condition F is that the sale or supply of the medicinal product is in response to an unsolicited order.*

(8) *Condition G is that if the medicinal product is:*
  (a) *manufactured or assembled in the United Kingdom or imported into the United Kingdom from a country other than an EEA State, it is manufactured, assembled or imported by the holder of a manufacturer's licence that relates specifically to the manufacture, assembly or importation of special medicinal products; or*
  (b) *imported from an EEA State, it is manufactured or assembled in that State by a person who is the holder of an authorisation in relation to its manufacture or assembly in accordance with the provisions of the 2001 Directive as implemented in that State.*

(9) *In this regulation "publish" has the meaning given in regulation 277(1) (interpretation: Part 14 advertising).*

Advertisements Relating to Medicinal Products

Regulation 7

(1) *In these regulations "advertisement", in relation to a medicinal product, includes anything designed to promote the prescription, supply, sale or use of that product.*

(2) *This includes, in particular, the following activities:*
  (a) *door-to-door canvassing;*
  (b) *visits by medical sales representatives to persons qualified to prescribe or supply medicinal products;*
  (c) *the supply of samples;*
  (d) *the provision of inducements to prescribe or supply medicinal products by the gift, offer or promise of any benefit or bonus, whether in money or in kind, except where the intrinsic value of such inducements is minimal;*
  (e) *the sponsorship of promotional meetings attended by persons qualified to prescribe or supply medicinal products; and*
  (f) *the sponsorship of scientific congresses attended by persons qualified to prescribe or supply medicinal products, including the payment of their travelling and accommodation expenses in that connection.*

*(3)   But references in these Regulations to an "advertisement" do not include any
of the following:*

(a)   a medicinal product's package or package leaflet;

*(b)   reference material and announcements of a factual and informative
nature, including:*

    *(i)   material relating to changes to a medicinal product's package or
package leaflet,*

    (ii)   adverse reaction warnings,

    (iii)   trade catalogues, and

    (iv)   price lists,

provided that no product claim is made; or

*(c)   correspondence, which may be accompanied by material of a non-
promotional nature, answering a specific question about a medicinal
product.*

*(d)   In this regulation "person qualified to prescribe or supply medicinal
products" has the meaning given in regulation 277(1) (interpretation:
Part 14 advertising).*

Mixing of General Sale Medicinal Products

*169.—(1) The prohibitions in regulation 46 (requirement for authorisation) do not
apply to a medicinal product ("the product") in respect of which the following
conditions are met.*

*(2) Condition A is that the product is manufactured by the mixing of authorised
medicinal products with other authorised medicinal products, or with substances
that are not medicinal products.*

*(3) Condition B is that any authorised medicinal product that is so mixed is subject
to general sale.*

*(4) Condition C is that the product is manufactured by a person ("H") who is the
holder of a manufacturer's licence that:*

*(a) relates specifically to the manufacture of medicinal products in accordance
with this regulation; and*

*(b) was granted or renewed not more than five years before the date on
which the product is sold or supplied in accordance with paragraphs (5)
and (6),*

and that the product is manufactured in accordance with the terms of that licence.

*(5) Condition D is that the product is sold or supplied by H to a person ("P") for
administration to P or to a member of P's household.*

*(6) Condition E is that P is present and asks H to use H's judgment as to the
treatment required.*

*(7) Condition F is that no advertisement relating to the product is published by any
person.*

*(8) Condition G is that written records of the manufacture of the product and of
the sale or supply of the product are maintained and are made available to the
licensing authority or to the enforcement authority on request.*

(9) In this regulation, "authorised medicinal product" means a medicinal product that is the subject of:
(a) a marketing authorisation;
(b) a certificate of registration; or
(c) a traditional herbal registration.

RECORD-KEEPING REQUIREMENTS

170.—(1) Where the sale or supply of a medicinal product relies on the exemptions under regulations 167, 168 or, subject to paragraph (4), 169, the person who sells or supplies the product must maintain for at least five years a record showing:
(a) the source from which and the date on which the person obtained the product;
(b) the person to whom and the date on which the sale or supply was made;
(c) the quantity of the sale or supply;
(d) the batch number of the batch of that product from which the sale or supply was made; and
(e) details of any suspected adverse reaction to the product so sold or supplied of which the person is aware or subsequently becomes aware.
(2) The person must make the records available for inspection by the licensing authority on request.
(3) The person must notify the licensing authority of any suspected adverse reaction to the medicinal product which is a serious adverse reaction.
(4) In the case of a medicinal product that is sold or supplied in reliance on the exemption in regulation 169:
(a) the reference in paragraph (1)(a) to "the product" means all the medicinal products that were mixed in the course of the manufacture of the product; and
(b) paragraph (1)(d) shall not apply.

Exempt Advanced Therapy Medicinal Products

An 'advanced therapy medicinal product' is a medicinal product described in Article 2(1)(a) of Regulation (EC) No. 1394/2007. An ATMP is:

(a) a gene therapy 'medicinal product'
(b) a somatic cell therapy 'medicinal product'
(c) a tissue engineered product – a product that contains or consists of cells or tissues that either have been subject to 'substantial manipulation' or are not intended to be used for the same essential function(s) in the recipient as in the donor and is presented as having properties for treating or preventing disease in patients.

171.—(1) The prohibitions in regulation 46 (requirement for authorisation) do not apply in relation to an advanced therapy medicinal product (an "exempt advanced therapy medicinal product") if the following conditions are met.

(2) Condition A is that the product is prepared:
(a) on a non-routine basis;
(b) in the United Kingdom; and
(c) according to specific quality standards equivalent to those provided for advanced therapy medicinal products authorised under Regulation (EC) No 726/2004.
(3) Condition B is that the product is used:
(a) in a hospital in the United Kingdom;
(b) under the exclusive professional responsibility of a doctor; and
(c) in order to comply with an individual medical prescription for a product made to order for an individual patient.
(4) Condition C is that no advertisement relating to the medicinal product is published by any person.
(5) Condition D is that the sale or supply of the medicinal product is in response to an unsolicited order.
(6) In this regulation "publish" has the meaning given in regulation 277(1) (interpretation Part 14 advertising).

Section 10 of the Medicines Act 1968 has been extensively modified over the years and now reads:
10 Exemptions for pharmacists. E + W+S + N.I.

(1)   The restrictions imposed by regulations 17(1) (manufacturing of medicinal products) and 46 (requirement for authorisation) of the 2012 Regulations do not apply to anything which is done in a registered pharmacy, a hospital, a care home service or a health centre and is done there by or under the supervision of a pharmacist and consists of:
(a)   preparing or dispensing a medicinal product in accordance with a prescription given by an appropriate practitioner, or
(b)   assembling a medicinal product provided that where the assembling takes place in a registered pharmacy:
(i)   it shall be in a registered pharmacy at which the business in medicinal products carried on is restricted to retail sale or to supply in circumstances corresponding to retail sale and the assembling is done with a view to such sale or supply either at that registered pharmacy or at any other such registered pharmacy forming part of the same retail pharmacy business, and
(ii)   the medicinal product has not been the subject of an advertisement]; and those restrictions do not apply to anything done by or under the supervision of a pharmacist which consists of procuring the preparation or dispensing of a medicinal product in accordance with a prescription given by a practitioner, or of procuring the assembly of a medicinal product.
(2)   Those restrictions do not apply to the preparation or dispensing in a registered pharmacy of a medicinal product by or under the supervision of a pharmacist

in accordance with a specification furnished by the person to whom the product is or is to be sold or supplied, where:

(a)   *the product is prepared or dispensed for administration to that person or to a person under his care.*

(3)   *Without prejudice to the preceding subsections, the restrictions imposed by regulations 17(1) (manufacturing of medicinal products) and 46 (requirement for authorisation) of the 2012 Regulations do not apply to anything which is done in a registered pharmacy by or under the supervision of a pharmacist and consists of:*

(a)   *preparing or dispensing a medicinal product for administration to a person where the pharmacist is requested by or on behalf of that person to do so in accordance with the pharmacist's own judgment as to the treatment required, and that person is present in the pharmacy at the time of the request in pursuance of which that product is prepared or dispensed, or*

(b)   *preparing a stock of medicinal products with a view to dispensing them as mentioned in subsection (1)(a) or subsection (3) of this section or in paragraph (a) of this subsection provided that such stock is prepared with a view to retail sale or to supply in circumstances corresponding to retail sale and the preparation is done with a view to such sale or supply either at that registered pharmacy or at any other registered pharmacy forming part of the same retail pharmacy business];*

and those restrictions do not apply to anything which is done in a hospital or a health centre by or under the supervision of a pharmacist and consists of preparing a stock of medicinal products with a view to dispensing them as mentioned in subsection (1)(a) of this section.

(4)   *Without prejudice to the preceding subsections, the restrictions imposed by Regulation 46 of the 2012 Regulations do not apply to the preparation or dispensing in a registered pharmacy of a medicinal product by or under the supervision of a pharmacist where:*

(a)   *the medicinal product is prepared or dispensed otherwise than in pursuance of an order from any other person, and*

(b)   *the medicinal product is prepared with a view to retail sale or supply in circumstances corresponding to retail sale at the registered pharmacy at which it is prepared, and*

(c)   *the medicinal product has not been the subject of an advertisement.*

(5)   *Without prejudice to the preceding subsections, the restrictions imposed by regulation 17(1) of the 2012 Regulations do not apply to anything which is done in a registered pharmacy by or under the supervision of a pharmacist and consists of preparing a medicinal product with a view to retail sale or to supply in circumstances corresponding to retail sale at that registered pharmacy.*

(6A) *The Ministers may make regulations prescribing conditions which must be complied with if a thing is to be considered for the purposes of this section as done under the supervision of a pharmacist.*

(6B) *Conditions prescribed under subsection (7A) may relate to supervision in the case where the pharmacist is not at the place where the thing is being done, and in that case the thing is not to be so considered if no such conditions are prescribed.*

(6C) In any case, compliance with any applicable conditions is sufficient for the thing to be so considered.

(7) For the purposes of this section "advertisement" shall have the meaning assigned to it by regulation 7 (advertisements relating to medicinal products) of the 2012 Regulations.

(8) In subsection (1) of this section, "care home service" has the meaning given by paragraph 2 of schedule 12 to the Public Services Reform (Scotland) Act 2010 (asp 8) (3).

Self-Assessment Questions

1. What do the specific exemptions allow for pharmacists to supply unlicensed products?

   Answer: The exemptions allow a pharmacist to:
   - prepare or dispense a product against a prescription
   - prepare a stock in anticipation of dispensing
   - prepare or dispense a medicinal product against a specification given by the intended purchaser, where the product is to be administered to that purchaser or to someone under his care
   - prepare a product for counter-prescribing.

2. What records must be kept by a Specials manufacturer?

   Answer: The 'Specials' manufacturer, the pharmacist and any practitioner who sells or supplies a 'special' must keep records for at least 5 years, which show:
   - the source of the product
   - the name of the person who obtained the product
   - the date of the transaction
   - the quantity of each sale or supply
   - the batch number
   - details of any adverse reaction to the product which he knows about.

3. What exemptions in relation to Specials apply to doctors?

   Answer: Doctors may prepare products themselves for use on patients or they may order the products from a registered pharmacy or licensed Specials manufacturer.

   Doctors may prepare products themselves where the medicinal product is supplied:
   a. to a patient in the course of the treatment of that patient; or
   b. to a patient of another doctor or dentist who is a member of the same medical or dental practice; and
   c. the product is not manufactured or assembled on a large scale; or by an industrial process.

ADDITIONAL RESOURCES

1. http://www.rpharms.com/best-practice/specials.asp
2. http://www.mhra.gov.uk/Howweregulate/Medicines/Importingandexportingmedicines/ Importing unlicensedmedicines/index.htm
3. http://www.legislation.gov.uk/uksi/2012/973/made
4. http://pharmacos.eudra.org/

Chapter 15

Traditional and Alternative Medicines

The Human Medicines Regulations 2102 make special provision for two difficult areas: homeopathy and herbal medicines. Both present problems for the licensing system. Both represent traditional forms of treatment which have numbers of practitioners who are unable to use the exemptions from control provided for doctors and pharmacists.

HERBAL PRODUCTS

Herbal products which make no medicinal claims (even if they may have a medicinal use) can be sold as foods, e.g., parsley, as food supplements or as cosmetics. Where an ingredient has no use other than a medicinal use the product will fall within the medicines controls.

Special arrangements have been made to enable herbal practitioners to continue to practice and to enable the sale of simple herbs to continue. Due to numbers it would be impracticable to list all herbs.

Specified groups of herbal medicines to be sold or supplied only by practitioners who do so after using their own judgement as to the treatment required for persons who are physically present in the premises where the supply takes place.

HERBAL REMEDIES

A herbal remedy is a medicinal product consisting of:

- a substance produced by subjecting a plant or plants to drying, crushing or any other process, or
- a mixture whose sole ingredients are two or more substances so produced, or
- a mixture of one or more such substances and water or some other inert substance. (*Section 132(1)* of the Medicines Act 1968)

Pharmacy Law and Practice. DOI: http://dx.doi.org/10.1016/B978-0-12-394289-0.00015-1
213

Controls on Supply of Herbal Remedies

Previous controls on the supply of herbal medicines were substantially altered by the Medicines (Traditional Herbal Medicinal Products for Human Use) Regulations 2005 which only became fully operational in 2011. For the first time, the regulations allowed only long-established and quality-controlled medicines to be sold.

These regulations have been repealed by the Human Medicines Regulations. Only Paragraph 8(a)(i) and (b) of Schedule 7, and Regulation 12 remain. However, the general principles have been carried forward in the new regulations.

There are now three different systems for controlling the supply of herbal products (referred to by Medicines and Healthcare products Regulatory Agency (MHRA) as 'herbal medicines'.

Unlicensed Herbal Remedies

Where herbal remedies meet the conditions set out in Regulation 3 of the Human Medicines Regulations 2012 they are exempt from licensing requirements.

Regulation 3 allows a person to make, sell and supply a herbal remedy during the course of their business provided the remedy is manufactured or assembled on the premises and that it is supplied as a consequence of a consultation between the herbal practitioner and the patient.

The product must not contain a substance specified in Part 1 of Schedule 20.

The product must comply with the maximum doses and percentages set out in Part 2 of Schedule 20.

Licensed Herbal Medicinal Products

Herbal remedies which meet the safety, quality and efficacy criteria in a similar manner to any other licensed medicines may have a marketing authorisation (product licence) in the same way as conventional products.

Registered Traditional Herbal Medicines

The Traditional Herbal Medicines Registration Scheme was set up by the European Directive on Traditional Herbal Medicinal Products (2004/24/EC) but did not come into effect until 30 April 2011 because of a long transitional period.

The Directive required Member States to enact specific regulatory arrangements for those traditional herbal medicinal products which are suitable for use without medical supervision and for which there was evidence of traditional use but insufficient evidence of efficacy to meet the requirements for a marketing authorisation.

The purpose of the Directive was to establish within the Community a harmonised legislative framework for authorising the marketing of traditional herbal medicinal products, involving a simplified registration procedure. Previously there were no specific safeguards on quality and safety for unlicensed herbal remedies. It is difficult for herbal products to meet the conventional requirements of efficacy and safety needed for a marketing authorisation.

The UK Legislation

The Human Medicines Regulations 2012 now implements the Traditional Herbal Medicines Registration Scheme.

Regulations 17 and 46 prohibit the manufacture or distribution of a medicinal product unless it has a marketing authorization, Article 126a authorisation, certificate of registration or traditional herbal registration or is otherwise exempt.

127.—(1) The licensing authority may, subject to regulation 130, grant an application for a traditional herbal registration for a traditional herbal medicinal product in response to an application made in accordance with this Part.

Regulation 125 of the Human Medicines Regulations sets out how a Traditional Herbal Medicinal Product may meet the conditions for registration by the licensing authority:

(1) the product must be appropriate for use without the need for a medical practitioner to:
   (a) diagnose the condition to be treated by the product;
   (b) prescribe the product; or
   (c) monitor the product's use.
(2) the product must be intended to be administered at a particular strength and in accordance with a particular posology.
(3) the product is intended to be administered externally, orally or by inhalation.
(4) the product has been in medicinal use for a continuous period
   (a) of at least 30 years, and
   (b) of at least 15 years in the European Union
(5) there is sufficient information about the traditional use of the product so that (in particular):
   (a) it has been established that the traditional use of the product is not harmful; and
   (b) the pharmacological effects or efficacy of the product are plausible on the basis of long-standing use and experience.

There is no requirement to present data on tests and trials relating to efficacy. The evidence of the medicine's use for at least 30 years will indicate the efficacy of the medicine.

Classification of Product with Traditional Herbal Registration

131.—(1) A traditional herbal registration must include a term that the product to which the registration relates is to be available:
   (a) only from a pharmacy; or
   (b) on general sale.

(2) A traditional herbal registration may include a term that the product to which the registration relates is to be available on general sale only if the licensing authority considers that the product can with reasonable safety be sold or supplied otherwise than by, or under the supervision of, a pharmacist.

Labelling and Packaging

Schedule 29 of the Human Medicines Regulations deals with the labelling of traditional herbal medicinal products.

All products must carry the following:

(1) A statement to the effect that the product is a traditional herbal medicinal product, for use for specific purposes by reason of long-standing use.
(2) A statement that the user should consult a doctor or other health care practitioner if symptoms persist during use of the medicinal product, or if adverse effects not mentioned on the package or package leaflet occur.

The outer packaging and the immediate packaging of traditional herbal medicinal products which are P medicines must be labelled to show the capital letter 'P' within a rectangle if they are:

(a) sold by retail;
(b) supplied in circumstances corresponding to retail sale;
(c) in the possession of a person for the purpose of sale or supply as mentioned in Paragraph (a) or (b); or
(d) distributed by way of wholesale dealing.

The rectangle enclosing the 'P' must contain no other matter of any kind.

Regulation 265 relaxes the requirements to allow for transparent packaging, products for export and ampoules.

(1) Schedule 29 imposes additional requirements in relation to traditional herbal medicinal products.
(2) Nothing in this regulation or Schedule 29 requires information to appear on:
   (a) a package containing a traditional herbal medicinal product where part of the package is transparent or open, provided that the information required by this regulation and that Schedule is clearly visible through the transparent or open part of the package;
   (b) a paper bag or similar wrapping in which a package that contains a traditional herbal medicinal product and bears information in accordance with the requirements of this regulation and that Schedule is placed at the time of sale or supply;
   (c) a package enclosing a package of a traditional herbal medicinal product for export;
   (d) an ampoule or other container of not more than 10 millilitres' nominal capacity which is enclosed in a package on which information appears in accordance with the requirements of this regulation and that Schedule; or
   (e) a blister pack or similar packaging, enclosed in a package labelled in accordance with the requirements of this regulation and that Schedule.

Labelling and the user package leaflet must be in English. They must fully meet the requirements of Article 54–65 of Directive 2001/83/EC (as amended by Directive 2004/27/EC).

Labelling and leaflets must include information and instructions about the safe use of the product, as with any licensed medicine.

Advertising of Traditional Herbal Medicinal Products

All adverts for traditional herbal medicinal products must contain the words:

(a) *"Traditional herbal medicinal product for use in"; followed by*
(b) *a statement of one or more therapeutic indications for the product consistent with the terms of the registration; followed by*
(c) *the words "exclusively based on long standing use".*

(Regulation 302 Human Medicines Regulations)

Manufacturing

Manufacturers will need to meet approved standards of Good Manufacturing Practice (GMP) and have a manufacturer's licence (ML). Manufacturers require a qualified person.

Good Manufacturing Practice

The principles and guidelines of GMP are specified in Directive 2003/94/EC. This requires suitable premises, technical equipment and quality control facilities.

Requirements for Wholesale Dealers

All UK wholesale dealers of traditional herbal medicinal products require an appropriate wholesale dealer's licence (WDL), from the MHRA. They need a responsible person.

Restriction of Sale to Pharmacies

Regulation 231 allows the licensing authority to specify whether the product may be sold:

(a) only from a pharmacy; or
(b) on general sale.

Nature and Quality

Section 64 of the Medicines Act 1968 provides that no person shall, to the prejudice of the purchaser, sell any medicinal product which is not of the nature or quality demanded by the purchaser.

Thus although there are often no applicable official standards for herbal medicines, poor quality or unsafe medicines are illegal.

Herbal Medicines Advisory Committee

The Herbal Medicines Advisory Committee advises Ministers directly on issues relating to the registration of traditional herbal medicinal products under the Traditional Herbal Medicines Registration Scheme and to the safety and quality of unlicensed herbal remedies. Members are appointed by the MHRA.

Herbal Practitioners

The Medicines Act 1968 generally requires the manufacture of and dealing in medicinal products to be licensed.

Regulation 3 of the Human Medicines Regulations exempts herbal remedies from some of these requirements.

It allows a person to make, sell and supply a herbal remedy

> *during the course of their business*
> *provided the remedy is manufactured or assembled on the premises and that it is supplied as a consequence of a consultation between the herbal practitioner and the patient*
> *The person being treated must be present on the premises, but another person may make the request on his behalf.*

Future Regulation of Herbal Practitioners

At present there is no system of registration for herbal practitioners.

The House of Lords' Select Committee on Science and Technology had called for UK herbalists to be statutory regulated in its report on Complementary Medicine in 2000.

There was a consultation paper in 2009 entitled 'A Joint Consultation on the Report to Ministers from the DH Steering Group on the Statutory Regulation of Practitioners of Acupuncture, Herbal Medicine, Traditional Chinese Medicine and Other Traditional Medicine Systems Practised in the UK'.

On 16 February 2011 the Secretary of State for Health announced that all UK practitioners prescribing herbal medicines are to be statutorily regulated via the Health and Care Professions Council. This is to ensure that practitioners meet specified registration standards, giving practitioners and consumers continuing access to unlicensed manufactured herbal medicines to meet individual patient needs via the exemption.

The legislation has not yet appeared.

HOMEOPATHIC MEDICINES

Homeopathy is a system of treatment elaborated by Samuel Hahnemann (1755–1843), a German physician. Its basis is treatment with minute quantities of the drugs capable of producing the symptoms of the disease treated. Conventional medicine is referred to as 'allopathy'.

Homeopathic medicines are the preparations used in homeopathy. The high dilutions are prepared from 'unit preparations' which are defined as:

A preparation, including a mother tincture, prepared by a process of solution, extraction or trituration with a view to being further diluted tenfold, or serially in multiple powers of ten, in an inert diluent, and then used either in this diluted form or where applicable, by impregnating tablets, granules, powders, or other inert substances for the purpose of being administered to human beings.

A preparation prepared by a process of solution, extraction or trituration with a view to being further diluted tenfold, or serially in multiple powers of ten, in an inert diluent and then used either in this diluted form or where applicable, by impregnating tablets, granules, powders, or other inert substances for the purpose of being administered to human beings.

Homeopathic medicines are generally included in the General Sale List, although parenteral homeopathic medicines and certain strengths of some substances are restricted to prescription only medicine (POM).

Licensing

When the Medicines Act 1968 came into force, existing homoeopathic products were issued with product licences of right. These were given without any evidence of quality, safety or efficacy.

A new scheme was set up when Directive 92/73/EEC (The Homoeopathic Directive) was implemented. A codified text, including homoeopathic provisions, is now in Directive 2001/83/EEC.

Under this scheme a homoeopathic product may be given a 'certificate of registration' if it meets quality and safety standards. It is not necessary to show efficacy. Because there are no demonstrations of efficacy, medical claims may not be made for the products. Certificates of registration last for 5 years. Registration under the scheme is compulsory only in respect of homoeopathic products new to the UK market.

The Directive defines a homoeopathic medicine as:

Any medicinal product prepared from products, substances or composition called homoeopathic stocks in accordance with a homoeopathic manufacturing procedure described by the European Pharmacopoeia or, in the absence thereof, by the pharmacopoeias currently used officially in the Member States.

Advisory Board on the Registration of Homoeopathic Products

The Medicines (Advisory Board on the Registration of Homoeopathic Products) Order 1995, SI No. 309 established the Board in 1995. It is now an Expert Committee of the MHRA. The function of the Advisory Board is to give advice to the licensing authority on the safety and quality of homoeopathic products.

Registration of Homoeopathic Products

Part 6 of the Human Medicines Regulations applies to homoeopathic products. It applies to all homoeopathic products except those which are made to a magistral or officinal formula as defined in the Directive 2001/83/EEC. Products which fall into this system are:

- for oral or external use;
- contain not more than 1 part in 10,000 of the mother tincture; or
- if the active ingredient is POM contain not more than 1 part in 100 of the smallest allopathic dose;
- are prepared in accordance with a homoeopathic manufacturing procedure described in the European Pharmacopoeia or an official pharmacopoeia of a Member State.

Products may not use a brand name or be labelled with a specific therapeutic indication.

The licensing authority may, subject to Regulation 104, grant an application for a certificate of registration for a registrable homoeopathic medicinal product in response to an application made in accordance with this part.

The applicant must provide each of the following for each product:

(a) a statement of the scientific or other name of the homoeopathic stock or stocks from which the product is derived;

(b) a statement of the routes of administration, pharmaceutical forms and degree of dilution of the product;

(c) a dossier describing how the homoeopathic stock or stocks are obtained and controlled and justifying their homoeopathic use on the basis of an adequate bibliography;

(d) a manufacturing and control file for each pharmaceutical form and a description of the method of dilution and potentisation of the product;

(e) details of the ML or (as the case may be) its equivalent in an EEA State);

(f) if appropriate an authorisation to place the product on the market by another Member State;

(g) a mock-up of the outer and immediate packaging of the product; and

(h) data concerning the stability of the product.

This material, taken as a whole, must be such as to demonstrate the pharmaceutical quality and batch-to-batch homogeneity of each product to which the application relates.

Legal Classification

(1) The certificate of registration must include a term that the product to which the certificate relates is to be available:
  (a) only from a pharmacy; or
  (b) on general sale.

(2) A certificate of registration may include a term that the product to which the certificate relates is to be available on general sale only if the licensing authority considers that the product can with reasonable safety be sold or supplied otherwise than by, or under the supervision of, a pharmacist.

(Regulation 106 Human Medicines Regulations)

Sale, Supply or Administration of Homeopathic Medicines

Many of the drugs used in homeopathy are restricted to POM or P when used at conventional strengths. Regulation 242 of the Human Medicines Regulations allows diluted products to be on general sale provided they meet the requirements in Schedule 21 which contains lists of dilutions,

It should be remembered that although homeopathic practitioners claim that the more highly diluted products have greater potency, these are subject to restrictions based on conventional thinking, i.e., the lower restriction applies to the more dilute.

Labelling Requirements for Homoeopathic Products

Containers and packages of homoeopathic must be labelled in clear and legible form to show a reference to their homoeopathic nature, in particular by clear mention of the words 'homoeopathic medicinal product'. This is in addition to any other particulars required by regulations. (Regulation 264)

The outer packaging and immediate packaging and, where a package leaflet is included, the package leaflet of a registrable homoeopathic medicinal product must also include the information specified in Part 1 of Schedule 28. No other information is allowed.

(1) The scientific name of the stock or stocks followed by the degree of dilution, making use of the symbols of the pharmacopoeia used in relation to the homoeopathic manufacturing procedure described therein for that stock or stocks.

(2) The name and address of the holder of the certificate of registration and, where different, the name and address of the manufacturer.

(3) The method of administration and, if necessary, route.

(4) The expiry date of the product in clear terms, stating the month and year.

(5) The pharmaceutical form.

(6) The contents of the sales presentation.

(7) Any special storage precautions.

(8) Any special warning necessary for the product concerned.

(9) The manufacturer's batch number.

(10) The registration number allocated by the licensing authority preceded by the letters 'HR' in capital letters.

(11) The words 'homoeopathic medicinal product without approved therapeutic indications'.

(12) A warning advising the user to consult a doctor if the symptoms persist during the use of the product.

ADVERTISING OF REGISTERED HOMOEOPATHIC PRODUCTS

Advertisements for registered homoeopathic medicinal products must:

(a) not mention any specific therapeutic indications
(b) only contain the details mentioned in Schedule 28.

(Regulation 301 Human Medicines Regulations)

Vitamins and Food Supplements

The Food Supplements Directive 2002/46/EC came into force in July 2002 and was implemented in England by the Food Supplements (England) Regulations 2003 SI No. 1387.

Separate, equivalent legislation has been made in Scotland, Wales and Northern Ireland. The Directive and these regulations apply from 1 August 2005.

The Regulations apply to food supplements sold as food and presented as such. They do not apply to medicinal products as defined by Directive 2001/83/EC.

The regulations define a 'food supplement' as:

any food the purpose of which is to supplement the normal diet and which

(a) is a concentrated source of a vitamin or mineral or other substance with a nutritional or physiological effect, alone or in combination; and

(b) is sold in dose form.

Under Regulation 4, 'no person shall sell any food supplement to the ultimate consumer unless it is prepacked'.

A food supplement shall be regarded as prepacked for the purposes of these Regulations if:

(a) it is ready for sale to the ultimate consumer or to a catering establishment; and

(b) it is put into packaging before being offered for sale in such a way that the food supplement cannot be altered without opening or changing the packaging.

Prohibitions on Sale Relating to Composition of Food Supplements

Under Regulation 5

(1) Subject to Paragraph (3), no person shall sell a food supplement in the manufacture of which a vitamin or mineral has been used unless that vitamin or mineral:

(a) is listed in column 1 of Schedule 1; and

(b) is in a form which:

(i) is listed in Schedule 2, and

(ii) meets the relevant purity criteria.

If the vitamin or mineral is not listed then it can only be used if:

3 (a) the substance in question was used in the manufacture of a food supplement which was on sale in the European Community on 12th July 2002;

(b) a dossier supporting use of the substance in question was submitted to the Commission by the Food Standards Agency or a member State other than the United Kingdom by 12th July 2005; and

(c) the European Food Safety Authority has not given an unfavourable opinion in respect of the use of that substance, or its use in that form in the manufacture of food supplements.

The Regulations also provide a framework which can be used, if needed, to restrict the maximum and minimum levels of vitamins in food supplements.

Article 6(2) of the Directive (labelling, presentation and advertising must not attribute to food supplements the property of preventing, treating or curing a human disease, or refer to such properties) is already implemented in the Food Labelling Regulations 1996 (Regulation 40(1) and Schedule 6, Part I, Paragraph 2).

Legal Challenges

In October 2003 the National Association of Health Stores and the Health Food Manufacturers Association brought proceedings in the High Court challenging the validity of the Food Supplements Regulations.

The claimants argued that the legislation was restrictive to trade in goods and was made on the wrong legal basis.

The judge referred the case to the European Court of Justice (ECJ) requesting it to give a preliminary ruling on the validity of the underlying Directive. In 2005 the ECJ confirmed the validity of the Directive.

In March 2011, the Alliance for Natural Health announced that it intends to launch a legal challenge to the Directive in the High Court, on the grounds that it is 'disproportionate, non-transparent and discriminatory'. ANH then hopes to have the case referred to the European Court of Justice in Luxembourg.

The European Court judgement can be accessed here.[1]

Medical Foods Regulations

The Medical Food Regulations (England) 2000 SI No. 845 implement European Commission Directive 99/21/EC, which was developed to meet the Commission's requirement under framework Directive 89/398/EC to introduce specific rules for dietary foods for special medical purposes.

Corresponding regulations have been introduced in Wales, Northern Ireland and Scotland.

Medical foods are a unique group of foods used in the dietary management of specific diseases or medical conditions. The government considered that the population group for whom these products are intended is particularly vulnerable, and therefore specific controls, in addition to the general provisions of the Food Safety Act, are appropriate.

The Regulations define foodstuffs which may be sold as 'Food(s) for Special Medical Purposes' (FSMPs); lay down specific compositional and labelling requirements for them; and introduce a notification system to facilitate efficient monitoring of new products.

Maximum and minimum vitamin, mineral and trace element levels for specific categories of FSMPs are set by the Regulations.

The labeling requirements supplement those required by the Food Labeling Regulations 1996 (as amended) and are intended to provide sufficient nutritional and other information to health professionals and consumers to ensure the appropriate and effective use of these products under medical supervision.

The Regulations introduce a formal obligation to notify new products when first placed on the market.

Self-Assessment Questions

1. Under what circumstances can a non-medically qualified herbal practitioner supply unlicensed herbal medicines?

   Answer: The Human Medicines Regulations allow a person to make, sell and supply a herbal remedy during the course of their business provided the remedy is manufactured or assembled on the premises AND that it is supplied as a consequence of a consultation between the herbal practitioner and the patient. The person being treated must be present on the premises, but another person may make the request on his behalf.

2. In what ways are adverts for traditional herbal products different from other medicines?

   Answer: All adverts for traditional herbal medicinal products must contain the words 'Traditional herbal medicinal product for use in'; followed by a statement of one or more therapeutic indications for the product consistent with the terms of the registration; followed by the words 'exclusively based on long standing use'.

3. In what ways are adverts for homoeopathic products different from other medicines?

   Answer: Advertisements for registered homoeopathic medicinal products must: not mention any specific therapeutic indications and can only contain the details mentioned in Schedule 28.

ADDITIONAL RESOURCE

1. http://curia.eu.int

Chapter 16

Controlled Drugs

The Misuse of Drugs Act 1971 controls activities concerned with certain dangerous and harmful drugs. It covers the import, export, production, supply and possession of 'Controlled Drugs (CDs)'.

The Act achieves control by means of extensive and detailed Regulations. It prohibits all activities with 'CDs' except where the Regulations provide exceptions.

The Misuse of Drugs Act 1971 extends to Northern Ireland, although there are separate Regulations for Northern Ireland.

GENERAL PROHIBITIONS IN THE MISUSE OF DRUGS ACT 1971

It is illegal to manufacture, produce, possess, supply, import or export CDs unless any of the following apply:

- there is a specific exemption in the 1971 Act
- there is a specific exemption in the Misuse of Drugs Regulations 2001
- you possess a Home Office licence to do so.

The administrative burden is eased for certain organizations regularly handling CDs, for example:

- Private hospitals and care homes – only require licences for Schedule 1 and 2 drugs.
- University research departments – do not require licences to possess and supply drugs in Schedules 2–4 – Part I and Part II – and Schedule 5.

However, they do require licences to:

- possess and/or supply drugs in Schedule 1
- produce any of the drugs in Schedules 2–5.

Pharmacy Law and Practice. DOI: http://dx.doi.org/10.1016/B978-0-12-394289-0.00016-3

The Act prohibits the possession, supply, manufacture, import or export of CDs except as allowed in the Regulations or by a licence from the Secretary of State:

(1) *Sections 7, 10* and *22* enable and require the Home Secretary to make Regulations affecting the way health professionals and others deal with CDs.

(2) *Section 12* enables the Home Secretary to give directions to a doctor, dentist or pharmacist who has been convicted of an offence under the Act (or a related offence under the Customs and Excise Management Act). The directions can prohibit the person concerned from dealing in CDs or in authorising their administration.

(3) *Section 13* enables similar directions to be given where a doctor contravenes the Misuse of Drugs (Supply to Addicts) Regulations 1997 SI No. 1001.

(4) *Section 13* also allows for directions to be given after a tribunal has found a doctor or dentist to have prescribed CDs in an irresponsible manner.

(5) *Section 23* empowers the police or other authorised persons to enter business premises to inspect stock of CDs and related documents.

CLASSES OF CDs

The drugs subject to control are listed in Schedule 2 of the Act.[1] The Schedule is divided into three classes depending on the degree of danger the drugs present. The three classes – Class A, Class B and Class C – are used when determining penalties for offences under the Act. (*Section 25*)

Class A are the most harmful drugs and attract the severest penalties.

Class A includes cocaine, diamorphine, morphine, opium, pethidine LSD, methylenedioxymethamfetamine, methamphetamine (crystal meth), magic mushrooms containing ester of psilocin and Class B substances when prepared for injection.

Class B includes oral amphetamines, barbiturates, codeine, cannabis, pentazocine and pholcodine. All cathinone derivatives, including mephedrone, methylone, methedrone and MDPV were brought under control as Class B substances in 2010.

Class C includes benzfetamine, buprenorphine, mebrobamate, most benzodioazepines, androgenic and anabolic steroids, somatropin, GBL and GHB, and ketamine.

The list of CDs may be altered by an Order in Council approved by an affirmative resolution of both Houses of Parliament. The Advisory Council on the Misuse of Drugs must be consulted before any change.

The original list contained in the Act has been changed by the following Orders: SIs 1973/771, 1975/421, 1977/1243, 1979/299, 1985/1995, 1986/2230, 1989/1340, 1990/2589, 1995/1966, 1996/1300, 1998/750, 2001/3932, 2003/1243 and 2003/3201, 2005/3178, 2006/3331, 2008/3130, 2009/3209, 2010/1207, 2010/1833, 2011/744 and 2012/1390.

A list of all drugs controlled under the Misuse of Drugs legislation together with their class and schedule is available from the Home Office.[2]

RECLASSIFICATION OF CANNABIS

Cannabis has been reclassified twice. The current position is that from 26 January 2009 the Misuse of Drugs Act 1971 (Amendment) Order 2008 reclassified cannabis, cannabis resin, cannabinol and its derivatives from Class C to Class B drugs.

This includes any preparation or other product containing these substances.

In addition, any substance which is an ester or ether either of cannabinol or of a cannabinol derivative is reclassified as a Class B drug.

As a result of these changes, it should be noted that cannabis oil is also subject to control as a Class B drug.

CULTIVATION OF CANNABIS PLANT

The cultivation of any plant of the genus *Cannabis* is illegal without a Home Office licence. The maximum penalty for conviction in the Crown Court is 14 years plus a possible fine. Merely positioning a plant in the window to secure the best light, with the objective of growing the plant, is sufficient (*Tudhope v. Robertson 1980*). It is a defence for the accused to show that he neither knew nor suspected nor had reason to suspect that the plant was a CD.

INTERNATIONAL CONVENTION

Many of the changes to both the Act and the Regulations are made because of the United Kingdom's obligations under the United Nations Single Convention on Narcotic Drugs 1961 and the United Nations Convention on Psychotropic Substances 1971. These conventions seek to regulate the worldwide traffic in drugs of abuse. The Government is advised on any communication relating to the conventions by the Advisory Council.

The Advisory Council on Misuse of Drugs

The Advisory Council was established by the Act in 1972. Its purpose is to advise the relevant Ministers on various matters concerned with drug misuse.

The relevant Ministers are:

(1) In England:
   The Home Secretary
   Secretary of State for Health
   Secretary of State for Education

(2) In Scotland, Wales and Northern Ireland:
Ministers responsible for Health
Ministers responsible for Education.

Composition of the Advisory Council

There are at least 20 members, who are appointed by the Secretary of State after consultation with appropriate organisations. Members are required to have wide and recent experience of each of the following:

- practice of medicine
- practice of dentistry
- practice of veterinary medicine
- practice of pharmacy
- the pharmaceutical industry
- chemistry
- the social problems connected with the misuse of drugs.   (Schedule 1 of the Act)

Duties of the Advisory Council

The Advisory Council on Misuse of Drugs (ACMD) is required to keep under review the situation in the United Kingdom with respect to drugs which are being, or appear likely to be, misused.   (*Section 1*) If it considers that misuse could cause harmful effects which might then constitute a social problem, it must advise on the action to be taken. It must advise on measures:

- to restrict the availability of such drugs or to supervise the arrangements for their supply;
- to enable persons affected by the misuse of such drugs to obtain proper advice;
- to secure the provision of proper facilities and services for the treatment, rehabilitation and aftercare of such persons;
- to promote co-operation between the various professional and community services which it believes have a part to play in dealing with the social problems of drug misuse;
- to educate the public (particularly the young) in the dangers of drug misuse and to publicise those dangers;
- to promote research into, or obtain information about, any matter relevant to drug misuse prevention or the social problems of drug misuse.

The Secretary of State is empowered to conduct such research, or to assist it.   (*Section 32*)

Additionally the ACMD must advise on any matter relating to drug dependence or drug misuse if asked to do so by a relevant Minister.

The ACMD must be consulted before any Regulations are made under the Misuse of Drugs Act.

The ACMD discharges these duties by holding meetings either of the full Council or of committees established by it and by issuing reports.

REGULATIONS CONCERNED WITH MISUSE OF DRUGS

Four sets of Regulations have been made under the Act: They are broadly concerned with four separate topics:

(1) Rules for handling CDs

The Misuse of Drugs Regulations 2001 No. 3998, amended by Statutory Instruments 2003 No. 1432, 2003 No. 1482, 2003 No. 1653, 2003 No. 2429, 2004 No. 1771, 2005 No. 271, 2005 No. 1653, 2005 No. 2864, 2005 No. 3372, 2006 No. 986, 2006 No. 1450, 2006 No. 2178, 2007 No. 2154, 2009 No. 3136, 2010 No. 448, 2010 No. 1144, 2010 No. 1799, 2011 No. 448, 2012 No. 973 and 2012 No. 1311.

(2) Addiction

The Misuse of Drugs (Notification of and Supply to Addicts) Regulations 1997 SI No. 1001.

(3) Safe custody

The Misuse of Drugs (Safe Custody) Regulations 1973 as amended by the Misuse of Drugs (Safe Custody) (Amendment) Regulations 1974 No. 1449, 1975 No. 294, 1984/1146, 1985/2067 and 1986/2332, 1999/1403, 2001 No. 1149, 2007 No. 2154 and 2011 No. 2085.

(4) System of administrative control

The CDs (Supervision of Management and Use) Regulations 2006.

Proposed Consolidations

The Home Office is planning to update, consolidate and clarify the Misuse of Drugs Regulations 2001 to ensure that they work effectively and reflect current policies and professional practice about CDs.

At present, there are 18 amendments to the original statutory instrument that introduced the regulations, so the government is proposing both that all 19 are consolidated into a single piece of legislation that will be less complex to follow and that changes are made at the same time to update the regulations in line with current policy on CDs where appropriate.

A consultation period on the changes has finished but at the time of writing no new draft regulations have been produced by the Home Office.

The Health Act 2006 and its associated regulations – currently the CDs (Supervision of Management and Use) Regulations 2006, which set out the requirements for the governance and monitoring of CDs is the responsibility of the Department of Health.

The Health and Social Care Act 2012 makes significant structural changes for the National Health Service (NHS) in England, including the abolition of Primary Care Trusts (PCTs) from April 2013.

As a result of these changes, the current Regulations (the 2006 Regulations) require revision. Without revision the 2006 Regulations will make little sense after April 2013.

In preparation for the changes, the Department of Health set up a working group of interested stakeholders from England and Scotland to make recommendations as future legislation. The group reported in July 2012. Ministers from England and Scotland have accepted the Group's recommendations for a similar but improved regulatory regime and structure.

Draft CDs (Supervision of Management and Use) Regulations 2013 regulations have been published but were not passed by parliament at the time of writing. We have assumed that they will be passed without change and have written the sections accordingly.

Designation Orders

Section 7(3) of the Misuse of Drugs Act 1971 requires regulations to be made so that some of the drugs which are subject to control under the Act may be used for legitimate medical purposes.

The current legislation is the Misuse of Drugs (Designation) Order 2001 No. 3997. The drugs in Part I of the Schedule to this Order are designated as drugs to which *Section 7(4)* of the Misuse of Drugs Act 1971 applies.

Section 7(3) allows the legitimate medicinal activities to take place. *Section 7(4)* prevents any unauthorized activity without licence.

> *Section 7(4) If in the case of any controlled drug the Secretary of State is of the opinion that it is in the public interest:*
>
> > *(a) for production, supply and possession of that drug to be either wholly unlawful or unlawful except for purposes of research or other special purposes; or*
> >
> > *(b) for it to be unlawful for practitioners, pharmacists and persons lawfully conducting retail pharmacy businesses to do in relation to that drug any of the things mentioned in subsection (3) above except under a licence or other authority issued by the Secretary of State,*
>
> *he may by order designate that drug as a drug to which this subsection applies; and while there is in force an order under this subsection designating a controlled drug as one to which this subsection applies, subsection (3) above shall not apply as regards that drug.*

No activities can take place in relation to drugs subject to *Section 7(4)* without a licence from the Home Office. This is usually restricted to research purposes.

The Misuse of Drugs (Designation) Order 2001 has been amended a number of times as the legislation has been extended to include the so-called designer drugs for recreational use. The original Order has been amended by 2005 No. 1652, 2009 No. 3135, 2010 No. 1143, 2010 No. 1800, 2011 NO 447, 2012 No. 1310 and 2013 No. 177.

THE MISUSE OF DRUGS REGULATIONS 2001

The Misuse of Drugs Regulations 2001 provide exceptions to the blanket restrictions of the Act so that certain classes of people can produce, supply, prescribe or administer CDs in the practice of their profession.

The Regulations contain Schedules of drugs. It is these Schedules which are of most importance to practice, as they affect the degree of control to be applied to various drugs and medicines when they are used for lawful purposes.

CDs are listed in five schedules, according to the degree of control required.

The Classes of drugs in the Misuse of Drugs Act, for example Class A, B or C, define the penalties for each group of drugs.

The rules for possession, production and supply, etc., of a drug vary according to the Schedule of the Misuse of Drugs Regulations in which the drug is placed.

Schedule 1

This Schedule contains drugs subject to the strictest controls. The drugs have little or no medical value but cause social problems through misuse. A licence from the Home Secretary is necessary to possess, produce, supply, offer to supply, administer or cause to be administered these drugs. They include LSD, mescaline, psilocin (when extracted from magic mushrooms), cannabis, raw opium and coca leaf.

Schedule 2

This Schedule contains most of the drugs with medical use, including the opiates (such as heroin, morphine and methadone) and the stimulants such as amphetamines, cocaine and methylphenidate. It is illegal for people to be in possession of these drugs without having been prescribed them by a doctor. The drugs in this schedule are subject to the full controls relating to prescriptions, safe custody and record-keeping. Licences are needed for import or export. They may be manufactured or compounded by a pharmacist, doctor, dentist or vet, or by a person who holds a licence.

Schedule 3

This Schedule includes the barbiturates, diethylpropion, meprobamate, pentazocine temazepam and flunitrazepam. It is illegal for people to be in possession of these drugs without having been prescribed them by a doctor. Transactions do not need to be entered in the CD Register, although invoices must be retained. The requirements concerning destruction do not apply. Safe custody rules apply to temazepam, diethylpropion, buprenorphine and flunitrazepam. Other drugs in Schedule 3 are exempt from safe custody requirements.

Schedule 4

This Schedule is split into two parts.

Part I contains most of the benzodiazepines other than temazepam and flunitrazeam, plus eight other drugs. They are subject to full import and export control. Unauthorised possession is an offence.

Part II contains anabolic steroids. Drugs in Part II require a Home Office licence for import or export unless the substance is in the form of a medicinal product for personal use. There is no restriction on the possession of a drug from this Schedule when it is part of a medicinal product but it is illegal to supply to other people.

Records need not be kept by retailers. There are no safe custody requirements.

Schedule 5

This Schedule contains dilute preparations of drugs in Schedule 2, which are not likely to produce dependence or to cause harm if they are misused. Examples are tablets and oral mixtures containing small amounts of codeine or morphine. Controls are minimal, consisting mainly of a requirement to keep invoices for 2 years. For this reason this schedule is sometimes referred to as 'CD Inv'.

Exempt Products

Certain products, used for scientific or diagnostic purposes, which contain an extremely small amount and proportion of CDs are exempted from the prohibitions on production, supply and possession.

The Misuse of Drugs Regulations 2001 sets out the definition:

An exempt product is a preparation or other product consisting of one or more components parts, any of which contains a controlled drug, where

    (a) the preparation or other product is not designed for administration of the controlled drug to a human being or animal;

    (b) the controlled drug in any component part is packaged in such a form, or in combination with other active or inert substances in such a manner, that it cannot be recovered by readily applicable means or in a yield which constitutes a risk to health; and

    (c) no one component part of the product or preparation contains more than one milligram of the controlled drug or one microgram in the case of lysergide or any other N-alkyl derivative of lysergamide.

Production

Production is generally prohibited by *Section 4* of the Act. 'Production' means producing the drug by manufacture, cultivation or by any other method.

The Regulations provide that the following persons may lawfully produce, manufacture or compound a CD:

(a) A practitioner acting in his capacity as such.
(b) A pharmacist acting in his capacity as such.
(c) A person lawfully conducting a retail pharmacy business (RPB) at his registered pharmacy.   (Regulation 8)
(d) A person authorised in writing by the Secretary of State may produce drugs in Schedules 3 and 4. The authority specifies the premises and may specify other conditions.
(e) Persons holding a licence issued by the Secretary of State.

Import

The import of a CD is prohibited except in accordance with a licence granted by the Home Office or where the drug is exempted by Regulations.

The Regulations exempt Schedule 4 Part II and Schedule 5 drugs from import controls. In addition, patients arriving in the United Kingdom with no more than a 15-day supply of a prescribed drug may do so without a licence.

POSSESSION OF CDS

Various categories of persons are allowed by the Regulations to possess CDs.

It is unlawful for any person to be in possession of CDs unless:

(1) they are drugs in Schedule 5;
(2) they are medicinal products containing drugs in Schedule 4 Part II;
(3) that person holds an appropriate Home Office licence;
(4) that person is specified in the Misuse of Drugs Regulations 2001;
(5) the drugs have been lawfully prescribed for that person (or for that person's animal).

In any case, possession or supply is not lawful unless the person concerned is acting in his capacity as a member of his class, for example as a pharmacist; or in accordance with the terms of his licence or group authority.

Wholesaler dealers, importers and exporters must obtain Home Office licences. 'Wholesale dealer' in this context means a person who carries on the business of selling drugs to persons who buy to sell or supply again.

Practitioners and pharmacists are amongst those who have a general authority to possess, supply and procure all CDs, except those in Schedule 1.

Any person who is lawfully in possession of a CD may supply that drug to the person from whom he lawfully obtained it.

Possession as a Patient

A person may possess a CD for his own use or for administration to another, in accordance with the directions of a doctor.

This authority is negated where a patient lied in order to obtain the prescribed drug or failed to notify the doctor that he was already being supplied with that drug by another doctor.

These provisions are intended to prevent drug misusers and dealers from obtaining several prescriptions from different practitioners.

The Regulations allow different groups of persons to possess drugs in different Schedules.

Possession of Schedule 1 CDs

Schedule 1 drugs have no medical use, so generally only people with a Home Office licence may possess these.

There are exceptions:

(1) The medicinal product Sativex™ is in Schedule 1 as it is a cannabinoid extract product. The Home Office has exempted it from requiring a licence.
(2) A pharmacist may take possession of any CD for the purpose of destroying it.
(3) A pharmacist may take possession of any CD for the purpose of handing it over to a police officer.

The Home Office has granted a general licence to enable (2) and (3) above.

Possession of Schedule 2–4 CDs

The following persons may possess CDs in Schedules 2–4:

Health professionals
- a practitioner
- a pharmacist
- a person lawfully conducting an RPB
- midwives acting in their capacity as such (only those CDs that she or he may administer in accordance with Medicines Act)
- the person or acting person in charge of a publicly maintained hospital or care home
- the senior registered nurse or acting senior registered nurse of a ward, theatre or other department of a publicly maintained hospital or care home providing nursing care (but only for drugs supplied to her by the person responsible for supply of medicines there)
- paramedics when working (only those CDs which are the subject of the Home Office Group Authority)
- health care professionals supplying or administering certain categories of CDs under a Patient Group Direction (PGD)
- a supplementary prescriber acting in accordance with a clinical management plan

Analysts, laboratories, etc.
- a person engaged in a forensic laboratory
- a person in charge of a laboratory
- a public analyst appointed under *Section 27* of the Food Safety Act 1990
- a sampling officer under Schedule 31 to the Human Medicines Regulations 2012
- a person in connection with the NHS Drug Testing Scheme in Scotland

Carriers
- a carrier
- a person engaged in the business of a postal operator
- a person engaged in conveying the drug to a person who may lawfully have it in his possession

Various officials
- a constable in the course of his duty
- a Revenue & Excise officer in the course of his duty
- an MHRA Inspector

Persons authorised by the Home Office
- a person authorised under a Home Office group authority (Schedules 2 and 3)
- a person holding a Home Office written authorization. (Schedules 3–5 only)

Ships and Oilrigs

The master of a foreign ship in a port in Great Britain may possess any Schedule 2 or 3 drug so far as necessary for the equipment of the ship.

Any person may possess Schedule 2 or 3 in order to comply with statutory requirements.

Doctors Treating Themselves

Doctors and dentists are allowed to possess and supply CDs when they are 'acting in their capacity as practitioners'. It has been held by the courts (*R v. Dunbar [1982] 1 AER 188*) that a doctor bona fide treating himself is 'acting in his capacity as a doctor' for these purposes.

Confiscated Illicit CDs

Illicitly obtained drugs are sometimes handed over to teachers, social workers, etc., by those who no longer require them. The Act states that in certain circumstances the person who receives them will not himself be committing an offence. The circumstances are that:

(1) he knew or suspected the substance to be a CD
(2) he took possession for the purpose of:
     preventing another person from committing an offence, or
     continuing to commit an offence in connection with that drug OR

delivering it into the custody of a person lawfully entitled to take custody of it

(3) as soon as possible after taking possession he took all steps reasonably open to him to either:

destroy the drug, or

deliver it into the custody of a person lawfully entitled to take custody.

Midwives

Special arrangements are made for midwives, who routinely use CDs in their professional practice.

A midwife may possess and administer any CD which she may lawfully administer under the provisions of the Regulations. The Human Medicines Regulations contain a list of drugs which a midwife may give by parenteral administration. This list includes pethidine, pentazocine, morphine and diamorphine. The MDA Regulations impose further conditions:

she is a registered midwife
the local supervising authority has been notified of her intention to practise
the authority is given only so far as is necessary to her professional practice
excess stocks must be surrendered to the appropriate medical officer
the drugs must have been obtained on a midwives supply order signed by the
appropriate medical officer.

A 'midwife's supply order' means an order in writing specifying the name and occupation of the midwife obtaining the drug, the purpose for which it is required and the total quantity to be obtained. It must be signed by a doctor who is for the time being authorised in writing for the purpose of the Regulations by the local supervising authority for the region or area in which the drug is or was to be obtained.

Student midwives may not administer diamorphine, morphine or pethidine hydrochloride.

Supply

Section 4 of the Act prohibits the supply of (or an offer to supply) CDs except where Regulations permit. 'Supply' includes distribution.

A person who is authorised by the Regulations to supply a CD may only do so:

- to another person authorised to possess, and
- subject to any provisions of the Human Medicines Regulations 2012 (e.g., the prescription only medicine (POM) requirements).

Various categories of persons are allowed by the Regulations to supply or distribute CDs in Schedules 2–5.

Health Professionals

A practitioner.

A pharmacist.

A person lawfully conducting an RPB:

- the person or acting person in charge of a hospital or care home providing nursing care
- the senior registered nurse or acting senior registered nurse of a ward, theatre or other department of a hospital or care home
- a supplementary practitioner acting under a CMP.

Analysts, Laboratories, etc.

A person in charge of a laboratory.

A public analyst appointed under *Section 27* of the Food Safety Act 1990.

A sampling officer within the meaning of Schedule 3 to the Medicines Act 1968.

A person employed or engaged in connection with an NHS Drug Testing Scheme.

Person in Charge of a Hospital or Care Home Providing Nursing Care

The Regulations recognise that some institutions do not have a pharmacist available and provision is made for other persons to possess and supply.

The Regulations allow the person in charge of a publicly maintained hospital or care home to possess and supply CDs in Schedules 2–5 if no pharmacist is responsible for dispensing.

'Publicly maintained' means wholly or mainly maintained:

- *by a public authority out of public funds or*
- *by a charity or*
- *by voluntary subscriptions.*

Thus 'publicly maintained' includes NHS Trusts but excludes private care homes and hospitals which are operated for profit.

The person in charge of a private hospital, care home or hospice without a pharmacist needs a Home Office licence to supply Schedule 2 CDs.

Senior Registered Nurse in Charge of Ward or Department

The senior registered nurse or acting senior registered nurse in charge of a ward or department may only supply drugs for administration to a patient in that ward or department in accordance with the directions of a doctor, dentist, supplementary prescriber acting under and in accordance with the terms of a clinical management plan or subject to paragraph 3A a nurse independent prescriber or a pharmacist independent prescriber The authority only applies to drugs supplied by the person responsible for dispensing at the hospital or nursing home.

A Person in Charge of a Laboratory

The laboratory must be recognised as one whose activities include the conduct of scientific education or research, and which is attached to a university, university college or hospital which is publicly maintained. The Secretary of State may approve any other institution for the purpose.

Ships and Oilrigs

Special arrangements are made for the unusual situations encountered on ships and oilrigs.

The master of a foreign ship in a port in Great Britain may possess any Schedule 2 or 3 drug which is necessary for the equipment of the ship.

The following persons are authorised to supply any drugs in Schedules 2–5 to anyone on the ship or rig as set out below:

- the owner or master of a ship which does not carry a doctor among the seamen employed in it
- the installation manager of an offshore installation.

The CDs may be supplied as follows:

- in order to comply with certain statutory requirements
- to return drugs to the person who lawfully supplied them
- to supply drugs to a constable for destruction.

The statutory obligations are found in:

(a) the Merchant Shipping Acts
(b) the Mineral Workings (Offshore Installations) Act 1971
(c) the Health and Safety at Work etc. Act 1974.

REQUIREMENTS FOR WRITING PRESCRIPTIONS

Regulation 15 lays out the requirements for prescriptions for CDs other than those in Schedule 4 or 5, or for temazepam.

Prescriptions for Schedule 2 and 3 CDs must meet the following requirements:

(a) be written so as to be indelible
(b) be signed by the prescriber with his usual signature
(c) be dated by the prescriber
(d) specify the address of the prescriber (except for FP10 and variants)
(e) if a private prescription for human beings, be written on a form provided by a relevant body specially for the purpose
(f) state 'for dental treatment only' if issued by a dentist
(g) if issued by a vet, state that the CD is prescribed for an animal or herd under his care

(h) where instalment dispensing is intended the script must contain a direction specifying the interval between instalments, and the amount to be given on each occasion

(i) specify:

(i) the name and address of the patient

(ii) the dose to be taken

(iii) the pharmaceutical form and (where appropriate) the strength of the preparation of the CD

(iv) the total quantity (in both words and figures) OR

(v) the number (in words and figures) of dosage units of the preparation

(vi) where the prescription is not for a preparation, then the total quantity (in words and figures) of the CD.

Although most of the prescription must be handwritten by the prescriber, the date may be inserted by a rubber stamp. The requirement in the Regulations is that the prescription be 'dated' by the prescriber. The Home Office takes the view that computer generated dates are not acceptable as these could have been added by someone other than the prescriber.

The requirement to specify the 'form' is interpreted by the Home Office as requiring the pharmaceutical form, for example tablets to be specified even if only one form of the product is available. It should also be specified where the brand name gives an indication of the form, for example MST.

There are no special CD requirements for temazepam prescriptions, which have to comply with the POM regulations.

There are no specific requirements for Schedule 4 and 5 CDs other than the POM regulations.

The NPC gave advice on the use of pre-printed adhesive labels on prescriptions in 2009. Technically the new legislative requirements for computer-generated prescriptions for CDs do not prevent the use of pre-printed adhesive labels on prescriptions. Where they are used, they should be tamper-evident (i.e., it is obvious if an attempt has been made to remove them). If an adhesive label is used, prescribers should also sign the sticky label or at least start their signature on the sticky label. This is a further safeguard to ensure sticky labels are not tampered with or that another adhesive label is not placed on top of the one the prescriber signed for.

Handwriting Exemptions

The Home Office is allowed to waive the requirement that the body of a prescription for CDs must be in writing. In practice it does so only for specific named doctors, who either are working in drug dependency units or are physically unable to write. The prescription must be signed by the doctor and he must date the prescription. The current view of the Home Office and the Royal Pharmaceutical Society of Great Britain (RPSGB) is that a computer-dated script is not legal, but one dated by the prescriber with a rubber stamp or a typewriter is legal.

(If the date is generated by the computer without intervention by the prescriber, it is arguable that the prescriber has not dated the script. But conversely if the computer program requires the doctor operating the computer to type in the date, which is printed out in the appropriate space, it arguably IS dated by the prescriber.)

'Signed' means signed by the prescriber with his usual signature. This may be only a set of initials or presumably a symbol such as a cross.

What the Pharmacist Must Do

A pharmacist may only dispense a script for a Schedule 2 and 3 CDs if:

- the script complies with the requirements set out above;
- the prescriber's address is in the United Kingdom;
- the pharmacist knows the prescriber's signature, and he has no reason to suppose it is a forgery; or
- the pharmacist has taken 'reasonably sufficient' steps to satisfy himself that it is genuine;
- it is not before the appropriate date;
- it is not later than 28 days after the appropriate date;
- the script is marked, at the time of supply, with the date on which the drug is supplied;
- the prescription is for a Schedule 2 drug when the pharmacist must ascertain whether the person collecting it is the patient, a health professional or a representative:
  - if the patient, he must be satisfied as to that person's identity before making the supply;
  - if the medicine is being collected by a health professional acting in his professional capacity on behalf of the patient, then he must record that person's name and address.

The 'appropriate date' is either the date on which it was signed or a later date indicated by the prescriber as being the date before which it shall not be supplied.

With instalment prescriptions the first supply must be made not later than 28 days after the date in the script. The script must be marked with the date of each dispensing. It must be retained for 2 years after the last instalment is supplied.

Prescribing CDs Under PGDs

The Misuse of Drugs (Amendment No. 2) (England, Wales and Scotland) Regulations 2012 SI No. 973 came into force on 23 April 2012.

Those amendments mean that nurses and pharmacists registered as independent prescribers are able to prescribe CDs in Schedules 2–5 where it is clinically appropriate and within their professional competence.

They are able to supply or administer morphine and diamorphine under PGDs, for urgent treatment of very sick or critically injured groups of patients for 'the immediate, necessary treatment of sick or injured persons (excluding the treatment of addiction)'.

However, they cannot prescribe cocaine, diamorphine and dipipanone for the treatment of addiction.

Nurse independent prescribers who work in substance misuse can now supply articles for administering or preparing CDs.

Emergency Supply

Supplies may be made to a practitioner in an emergency. He must represent that he urgently requires a CD for professional purposes. The supplier must be satisfied:

- *that the statement is true*
- *that because of some emergency the practitioner is unable to furnish a requisition before the supply is made*
- *obtain an undertaking from the practitioner to furnish a requisition in 24 hours.*

It is an offence for the practitioner not to produce the requisition as promised.

Emergency supplies to the patient of Schedule 2 or 3 CDs are not allowed, except for phenobarbital for the treatment of epilepsy.   (Regulation 14)

Supplies Within the Hospital or Care Home Providing Nursing Care

The assumption is that the normal supply is by pharmacists or doctors, who are authorised to supply drugs in Schedules 2–5. The Regulations recognise that some institutions do not have a pharmacist available and provision is made for other persons to possess and supply.

Supplies within the hospital or care home are governed by Regulation 14(6) of the Misuse of Drugs Regulations 1985.

Where a person responsible for the dispensing and supply of medicines at any hospital or care home providing nursing care supplies a CD to the sister or acting sister for the time being in charge of any ward, theatre, or other department, he shall:

(1) obtain a requisition in writing, signed by the recipient, which specifies the total quantity off the drug to be supplied, AND
(2) mark the requisition in such manner as to show that it has been complied with, AND
(3) retain the requisition in the dispensary for 2 years.

A copy of the requisition or a note of it shall be retained by the recipient for 2 years.

Hospital Prescriptions

The general requirements for writing CD prescriptions apply to all hospital and care home situations, with an exception. The requirement to put on the name and address of the patient is relaxed where the prescription is written in the patient's bed card or case sheet.

Prescription requirements do not apply when medicines are administered to patients from ward stocks. This procedure is considered to be 'administration in accordance with the directions of a doctor'.

How Are Supplies Made Commercially?

Supplies may be made by pharmacies, practitioners or wholesalers. Wholesalers handling CDs require Home Office authority. A separate licence is required for each Schedule 2 CD. The Misuse of Drugs Act defines a 'wholesale dealer' as someone who 'carries on the business of selling drugs to persons who buy to sell again'. Retail pharmacies who undertake a small amount of wholesaling to other health professionals and hospitals, etc., are not usually required by the Home Office to be separately licensed. Where the amount of wholesaling is substantial, as is the case with some NHS hospital pharmacies which are registered with RPSGB, then the Home Office will require a licence to be held.

Requisitions

A wholesaler does not need a requisition in order to supply a pharmacy. The list of persons from whom a requisition is required is in Regulation 14(4).

A requisition is required where a supply is made to:

- a practitioner
- the person in charge of a hospital or care home providing nursing care
- the person in charge of a laboratory
- the owner of a ship, or the master of a ship which has no doctor on the crew
- the installation manager of an offshore installation
- the master of a foreign ship in a port in Great Britain
- a supplementary prescriber
- a nurse independent prescriber
- a pharmacist independent prescriber.

Hospital Requisitions

A requisition is required before a supplier can make a supply to a hospital or care home providing nursing care. In this case 'supplier' means any person other than a doctor, dentist or vet.

The requisition must:

- be signed by the recipient
- state the name and address of the recipient
- state the occupation of the recipient
- state the purpose for which the drug is required
- specify the total quantity of drug to be supplied

The supplier must be reasonably satisfied that the signature is authentic and that the person is engaged in the profession or occupation specified.

Residential Homes

Residential homes cannot themselves possess or supply CDs. CDs may be prescribed for individual patients resident in the homes. Residential homes are not subject to the Safe Custody requirements.

Messengers

When a person supplies a CD on requisition, he may not give that CD to a person who claims to be a messenger unless:

- he has a written statement, which the supplier reasonably believes is genuine, from the person giving the requisition, stating that he is empowered to collect the drug.
- the messenger is otherwise authorised by Regulations.

Supplementary Prescribers

The Misuse of Drugs (Amendment) Regulations 2005 No. 271 alter the main Regulations to allow nurse and pharmacist supplementary prescribers to prescribe CDs in Schedules 2–5 in accordance with the terms of a clinical management plan.

Export

The export of a CD is prohibited except in accordance with a licence granted by the Home Office or where the drug is exempted by Regulations. The regulations exempt CDs in Schedules 4 and 5.

Doctors who wish to take emergency supplies of CDs out of the country may require a licence from the Home Office, which is usually granted only when there is a real need, such as a hazardous expedition. Special arrangements are made where doctors wish to accompany pilgrims to Lourdes. Form MD50A is available from the Home Office and should be used to make the application.

Import licences may be required for the country being visited.

Patients Requiring CDs When Abroad

An 'Open General Licence' (OGL) was introduced by the Home Office in 1987. It provides a general authority for the export of small quantities of CDs which are in medicinal products, for medical reasons. The licence is made under *Section 3(2)(b)* of the Misuse of Drugs Act.

It applies to:

- a traveller carrying CDs for administration to himself
- a member of his household who is unable to administer the medicine himself
- a doctor accompanying a patient who requires treatment during a journey to or from the United Kingdom.

Generally this will apply if less than 3 months supply is being carried.

Records

The Regulations contain a number of requirements relating to the keeping of records for CDs.

CD REGISTER

Particulars of Schedule 1 (excluding Sativex™) and 2 drugs purchased or supplied must be entered in a register. The register must be a bound book or an electronic record. The regulations specifically prohibit a loose leaf or record card system. Either a different register or a separate part of the same register must be used for each class of drugs. Basically a class consists of a different drug together with its stereo-isomers, its salts and any preparations containing them. The words of Regulation 19(1)b are:

he shall use a separate register or separate part of the register for entries made in respect of each class of drugs, and each of the drugs specified in paragraphs 1 and 3 of Schedule 1 and paragraphs 1, 3 and 6 of Schedule 2 together with its salts and any preparation or other product containing it or any of its salts shall be treated as a separate class, so however that any stereo-isomeric form of a drug or its salts shall be classed with that drug.

It is permissible to use separate parts of a register for different drugs or strengths within the class.

A register must not be used for any other purpose. It must be kept at the premises to which it relates. Only one register for each class must be in use at one time. Where the premises consist of several departments the Home Office may approve the keeping of separate registers in each department. Registers must be preserved for 2 years from the date of the last entry.

Electronic Registers

Computerised records must be:

- attributable
- capable of being audited
- compliant with best practice
- accessible from the premises
- capable of being printed out.

The software must be designed so that once made entries cannot be altered.

Entries in the Register

- All entries must be made in chronological order.
- Entries must be made on the day of the transaction or on the next day.
- Entries must not be cancelled, obliterated or altered. Corrections should be made by dated notes on the page.
- All entries and corrections must be in ink, or otherwise indelible.

Who Must Keep a Register

Any person authorised to supply Schedule 1 or 2 drugs must keep a register except that a senior registered nurse or acting senior registered nurse in charge of a ward, theatre or register is not required to keep a register. The person who dispenses the drugs to the ward, whether a pharmacist or a person in charge of the hospital, must keep a register.

Preservation of Prescriptions, etc.

Requisitions, orders or prescriptions for CDs in Schedules 1–3 must be retained for 2 years. NHS prescriptions are used for payment purposes and are not required to be retained.

Invoices

Pharmacists must keep the invoices or copies when they receive and supply drugs and medicines in Schedules 3 and 5. There are similar rules for producers, wholesalers, hospitals and laboratories for the drugs they may handle. The invoices must bear the date of the transaction and the identity of the parties involved.

The invoices must be kept for 2 years.

Requests for Information

Certain people are authorised by the Secretary of State to request details about stocks, supplies and receipts of CDs. They may also inspect the stock, registers, requisitions and invoices. Confidential personal records, for example patient medication records need not be produced.

The authorised persons are:

MHRA Inspectors
Home Office Drugs Branch Inspectors
Authorised Medical and Dental Officers of the Health Departments of England, Scotland and Wales.

The people required to produce the information are:

producers
persons authorised to import and export CDs
wholesalers
pharmacists
practitioners
persons in charge of hospitals or nursing homes
persons in charge of laboratories
persons authorised to supply Schedule 3 and 4 drugs.

Destruction of CDs

(1) By patients

Patients may destroy any CDs in their possession, which are left over from their treatment. No records are required.

(2) By pharmacists

Pharmacists may destroy CDs which are returned by a patient or patient's representative. There is no need to make any records or have the destruction witnessed.

Medicines used for animal treatment may be similarly dealt with by vets as well as pharmacists.

Other than above, pharmacists may only destroy CDs in the presence of a witness authorised by the Secretary of State. In particular the destruction of expired stock of Schedule 2 drugs must be witnessed.

(3) Ships and offshore oilrigs

Excess Schedule 2 drugs in the possession of a master or owner of a ship, or the installation manager of an offshore installation may not be destroyed. They should be handed to a constable or to a pharmacist or licensed dealer.

Schedules 3–5

Schedule 3, 4 and 5 CDs may be destroyed without an authorized witness. It is not necessary to keep records of the destruction.

Denaturing CDs

The Home Office has advised that CDs should be denatured before disposal.

SAFE CUSTODY

The Misuse of Drugs (Safe Custody) Regulations 1973 (as amended) require Schedule 1–3 CDs (with some exceptions) to be kept in a locked receptacle. Where CDs are kept in a 'retail pharmacy' or in a nursing home or private hospital, the receptacle must be a safe, cabinet or room which meets certain standards. These Regulations have not been amended to reflect the collective term 'care home' which now includes both nursing and residential homes. Thus at present residential care homes are not legally required to use locked receptacles, though this would be good practice.

Schedule 2 drugs (except quinalbarbitone) and the Schedule 3 drugs buprenorphine, diethylpropion and temazepam must be kept in a CD cupboard in nursing care homes and private hospitals.

The General Requirement

A person in possession of CDs must store them in a locked receptacle to which only he (and persons authorised by him) has the key.

The courts have held that a car does not constitute a locked receptacle for this regulation. However, it would appear that a doctor's locked bag may be a suitable 'locked receptacle' (*Rao v. Wyles 1949*).

Exceptions to the General Requirement

This requirement does not apply to:

- a carrier in the course of his business
- a person engaged in the business of the Post Office
- a person who has been supplied with the CD on prescription, for his own use or for the treatment of another person or an animal.

In addition, a CD can remain out of the cabinet as long as it is under the pharmacist's direct personal supervision.

The safe custody requirements apply to all CDs in Schedules 1 and 2 (except quinalbarbitone) and to diethylpropion, temazepam and buprenorphine.

Locked Safe, Cabinet or Room

The Regulations specify that when CDs are kept on any premises occupied by a person lawfully conducting an RPB, they must be stored in a locked safe, cabinet or room which complies with the structural standards laid down in the Regulations. It is with these standards that the 'CD cabinet' complies.

The requirement also applies when CDs are kept in:

(a) any premises occupied by a pharmacist engaged in supplying drugs to the public at a NHS health centre
(b) any care home registered with the Care Quality Commission (CQC).

Hospitals

Regulation 3 does not apply to hospitals unless the pharmacy department is registered as an RPB with the RPSGB. Hospital wards are required to keep CDs in a locked receptacle.

Standards

The standards specify that cabinets must be made of steel sheet or welded mesh. It must be designed with a close-fitting door fitted with a dead-bolt, and a five lever lock or equivalent. The cabinet must be rigidly attached to a wall or floor with at least two rag-bolts which pass through an internal anchor plate.

Nothing shall be displayed outside a safe or cabinet to indicate that drugs are kept inside it.

There are detailed standards for secure rooms which contain CDs. The room is an alternative to the use of a cabinet or safe.

Where the CDs are kept in a 'retail pharmacy' the local police can issue a certificate stating that a room, safe or cabinet provides an adequate degree of security even though it does not comply with the specific standards laid down. This procedure enables the use of 'money' safes which may be constructed in a different way. The certificate lasts for a year after the inspection visit and may be renewed.

ADDICTS

The Misuse of Drugs (Notification of and Supply to Addicts) Regulations 1997 No. 1001 deals with the treatment of addicts by doctors.

The National Treatment Agency for Substance Misuse produced a report on addiction in 2011.[3]

What Is an 'Addict'?

A person is to be regarded as an addict 'if, and only if, he has as a result of repeated administration become so dependent upon the drug that he has an overpowering desire for the administration of it to be continued'.

Which Drugs Are Affected

The Regulations apply to the following drugs:

cocaine, dextromoramide, diamorphine, dipipanone, hydrocodone, hydromorphone, levorphanol, methadone, morphine, opium, oxycodone, pethidine, phenazocine and piritramide. Also included is any salt, ester or ether or stereoisomer (except dextrorphan) of the above drugs.

Supply to Addicts

If a doctor considers or has reasonable grounds to suspect that a person is addicted to any drug listed in the Supply to Addicts Regulations, then he may not prescribe cocaine, diamorphine or dipipanone (or their salts or preparations) to that person unless:

(a) he is treating an organic disease or injury, or
(b) he holds a Home Office licence.

Notification

The National Drug Treatment Monitoring System (NDTMS) was set up in 2001. Doctors are expected to report to the national or regional centres when a patient starts treatment for drug misuse. All types of problems should be reported.

In Northern Ireland the Regulations require notification to the Chief Medical Officer.

NHS Prescriptions for Addicts

Two types of NHS prescription forms are provided in E&W for doctors to use when prescribing for addicts. The forms enable addicts to receive supplies of drugs in daily instalments.

FP10NC

This form is used by doctors in drug addiction clinics. There are no regulations specifically covering this form, but the form itself bears the information that it may only be used for prescribing the following drugs:

cocaine, diamorphine hydrochloride, dextromoramide, dipipanone, methadone hydrochloride, morphine, and pethidine hydrochloride.

The prescription must state the amount to be dispensed on each instalment and the interval between instalments. Other drugs and appliances may be ordered on the same form, but the supply may be made on one occasion only.

FP10MDA

Use of this form is governed by the NHS (General Medical Services Contracts) Regulations 2004.

The form is issued to any general practitioner on request. The form may be used for the instalment prescribing of any Schedule 2 CD being used in the treatment of addiction in the patient. Only Home Office licensed doctors may prescribe diamorphine, cocaine or dipipanone (or their salts) to addicts for their addiction.

Some preparations of Schedule 2 drugs appear in Schedule 5 (e.g., tablets of dihydrocodeine) and the Home Office interpretation is that those preparations are consequently not in Schedule 2. It appears that Schedule 2 consists of a list of drugs, and Schedule 5 a list of preparations of some of the drugs in Schedule 2. An alternative interpretation would be that the word 'drug' in the Instalment Prescribing Regulations refers to entries in Schedule 2, and that an additional entry in Schedule 5 is irrelevant. There has been no case law on the issue to date.

The prescription must state the amount per instalment and the interval between instalments. The Regulations restrict the supply to a maximum of 14 days per form. The number of instalments must be stated.

The form may not be used for any purpose except instalment prescribing for addicts. It may, however, be used to order a single supply of a quantity of Water for Injection.

Failure to comply with the conditions for use of the form would make a doctor liable to disciplinary committee action. A pharmacist would seem to be in a slightly different position. The question remains open whether a form which does not meet the conditions of use may still be dispensed by the pharmacist without breach of his Terms of Service.

NHS Repeatable Prescriptions

The legislation does not allow Schedule 2 or 3 CDs to be prescribed on NHS repeat prescriptions.

Helping Addicts to Inject

It is not a supply to inject a person with that persons own CD. Thus where Charlie injects Snow with heroin at Snow's request, Charlie has not unlawfully supplied it – at least not by injecting it. (*R v. Harris 1968*)

Controls on Specific Drugs

In recent years the Misuse of Drugs Act and its regulations have been used to impose new controls on certain products which are subject to abuse and illicit use.

Temazepam, Flunitrazepam and Midazolam

Although most benzodiazepines remain in Schedule 4, temazepam, flunitrazepam and midazolam have been moved to Schedule 3. However, they are not subject to the normal prescription writing and records-keeping rules which apply to Schedule 2 and 3 drugs:

- Prescriptions do not need to be in the prescriber's own handwriting.
- The date does not need to be written by the prescriber.
- No CD register entry is required.

Midazolam is the only Schedule 3 CD that, in certain circumstances, can be included in a PGD.

All temazepam and flunitrazepam products, including liquids, are subject to safe custody requirements.

Magic Mushrooms

Section 21 of the Drugs Act 2005 added 'Fungus (of any kind) which contains psilocin or an ester of psilocin' to Class A.

This together with the Misuse of Drugs (Designation) (Amendment) Order 2005 SI No. 1652 and the Misuse of Drugs (Amendment) (No. 2) Regulations 2005 SI No. 1653 make it an offence to have any dealings with (containing psilocin or an ester of psilocin) except where they are growing wild or being picked for destruction.

Dealing includes import, export, produce, supply, possess or possess with intent to supply magic mushrooms, including in the form of grow kits.

Exceptions will be made for people who unknowingly pick the mushrooms in the wild or find them growing in their garden.

Mephedrone, etc.

The government has steadily included 'designer drugs' and synthetic stimulants such as mephedrone in the Misuse of Drugs legislation, generally by use of Designation Amendment Orders.

Steroids

Anabolic and androgenic steroids, polypeptide growth hormones and the adrenoceptor stimulant Clenbuterol are in Class C of the MDA. They are also in Schedule 4 Part 1 of the Regulations.

Steroids are subject to the usual Schedule 4 requirements. In addition they require a Home Office licence for import or export unless the substance is in the form of a medicinal product for personal use. Possession of listed steroids is an offence unless they are formulated as a medicine.

Supply of Paraphernalia to Drug Misusers

Section 34 of the Drug Trafficking Offences Act 1986 added a new *Section 9A* to the MDA 1971, making it an offence for anyone to knowingly sell items to drug addicts which could help them prepare or administer illicit CDs.

The Section States

It is an offence for a person to supply or offer to supply any article which may be used or adapted for use in the administration of a CD to himself or another, believing that the article is to be so used, or to supply or offer to supply any article which may be used to prepare a CD for administration to himself or another, believing that the article is to be so used in circumstances where the administration is unlawful.

Any administration of a CD which is not in accordance with the instructions of a practitioner will be unlawful.

Syringes and needles are exempt from this, by virtue of *Section A(2)*.

The Misuse of Drugs (Amendment) (No. 2) Regulations 2003 No. 1653 provides that practitioners, pharmacists and persons lawfully providing drug treatment services may supply:

(a) a swab
(b) utensils for the preparation of a CD
(c) citric acid
(d) a filter
(e) ampoules of water for injection,

where the articles are believed to be used for the purposes of administering or preparing CDs.

Water for Injection

The Human Medicines Regulations 2012 allow Water for Injection in ampoules up to 5 ml to be supplied in the course of a lawful drug treatment service.

The CDs (Supervision of Management and Use) Regulations 2006

The CDs (Supervision of Management and Use) Regulations 2006 came into effect in England on the 1 January 2007. These Regulations set out the requirements for certain NHS bodies and independent health care bodies to appoint an accountable officer and describe the duties and responsibilities of accountable officers to improve the safe management and use of CDs. The regulations also require bodies to co-operate with each other, including with regard to sharing information, about concerns about use and management of CDs and set out arrangements relating to powers of entry and inspection.

The 2006 Regulations were revoked by and replaced by the Controlled Drugs (Supervision of Management and Use) Regulations 2013 SI No.373 which take account of the changes in the NHS from April 2013.

Firstly the 2103 Regulations require the appointment of CD Accounting Officers (CDAO).

Regulation 3 lists the bodies that must appoint a CDAO in England. These are:

- NHS trusts and foundation trusts,
- independent hospitals (subject to the exemptions described below),
- the NHS Commissioning Board (NHS CB), and
- the armed forces.

Clinical Commissioning Groups (CCGs) and local authorities (LAs) are not required to appoint a CDAO – only the NHS CB.

The CDAO must be:

- a person of sufficient seniority,
- an officer or employee of the designated body (or bodies if acting jointly), and
- have little or no contact with CDs within that body.

The principal functions of CDAOs are:

- CDAOs in provider bodies must establish and operate, or ensure that the bodies do, appropriate arrangements for securing the safe management and use of CDs in their own organisations, and
- review them as appropriate.
- CDAOs in commissioning bodies must ensure that those from who they commission services do the same.

These arrangements include:

- compliance with relevant Misuse of Drugs legislation;
- systems for recording and reporting, as appropriate, concerns or incidents, and up-to-date standard operating procedures (SOPs) relating to the pre-scribing, supply and administration of CDs and clinical monitoring of patients using CDs.

Finally, CDAOs must ensure relevant people receive information, educa-tion or training on CD SOPs.

Inspections

In England, local CDAOs will not inspect premises which are subject to inspection by the CQC, General Pharmaceutical Council or the armed forces

Exemptions for Small Independent Hospitals

'English independent hospital' is a body that runs a hospital in England at or from which health care is provided to individuals but which is not a health service hospital or a hospital with fewer than 11 individuals (including volunteers) which provide health care in England.

'Scottish independent hospital' is similarly a body that runs a hospital in Scotland which is an independent hospital or a 'private psychiatric hospital' within the meaning of the NHS (Scotland) Act 1978.

Neither of the above will be required to appoint a CDAO if the CQC is satisfied that it would place disproportionate difficulties on the organisation concerned.

Relevant Persons

'Relevant persons' may be subject to investigations, etc. by CDAOs in relation to their management or use of CDs in the environment in which they work.

Relevant persons are:

- all health care professionals who provide health care to NHS and private patients other than at independent hospitals, or
- who provide care on behalf of an LA in England,
- relevant support staff.

MISCELLANEOUS LEGISLATION AFFECTING CDs

The Drugs Act 2005

This amends the Misuse of Drugs Act 1971, principally to strengthen police powers in relations to drug misuse.

Road Traffic Act 1972

It is an offence to be in charge of a motor vehicle while 'unfit to drive through drink or drugs'. The drugs can include illegal drugs, prescribed medicines or solvents.

Drug Trafficking Act 1994

It is an offence generally to sell articles for the preparation or administration of CDs – such as cocaine snorting kits. The Act also allows for the seizure of assets and income of someone who is found guilty of drug trafficking, even if the assets and income cannot be shown to have come from the proceeds of drug trafficking.

Crime and Disorder Act 1998

This Act introduces, for the first time, enforceable drug treatment and testing orders, for people convicted of crimes committed in order to maintain their drug use.

Self-Assessment Questions

1. What is the difference between Class A and Schedule 1?

   Answer: The three classes – Class A, Class B and Class C – are used when determining penalties for offences under the Misuse of Drugs Act. Class A is the most harmful drug and attracts the severest penalties. Class A includes cocaine, diamorphine, morphine, opium, pethidine LSD, methylenedioxymethamfetamine, methamphetamine (crystal meth), magic mushrooms containing ester of psilocin and Class B substances when prepared for injection. Under the Misuse of Drugs Regulations, CDs are listed in five schedules, according to the degree of control required for reasons of public safety. Schedule 1 contains drugs subject to the strictest controls. The drugs have little or no medical value, but cause social problems through misuse. A licence from the Home Secretary is necessary to possess, produce, supply, offer to supply, administer or cause to be administered these drugs. They include LSD, mescaline, psilocin (when extracted from magic mushrooms), cannabis, raw opium and coca leaf.

2. What controls are applicable to Schedule 5?

   Answer: This Schedule contains dilute preparations of drugs in Schedule 2, which are not likely to produce dependence or to cause harm if they are misused. Examples are tablets and oral mixtures containing small amounts of codeine or morphine. Controls are minimal, consisting mainly of a requirement to keep invoices for 2 years. For this reason the schedule is sometimes referred to as 'CD Inv'.

3. Which institutions may be exempted from the need to appoint CDs Accountable Officers?

   Answer: In both England and Scotland, 'independent hospitals' with less than 11 staff, including volunteers, may be exempted if the CQC is satisfied that it would place disproportionate difficulties on the organisation concerned.

ADDITIONAL RESOURCES

1. http://www.homeoffice.gov.uk/drugs/drug-law/
2. http://www.homeoffice.gov.uk/publications/alcohol-drugs/drugs/drug-licences/controlled-drugs-list?view = Binary
3. http://www.nta.nhs.uk/uploads/addictiontomedicinesmay2011a.pdf

Chapter 17

Labelling, Leaflets, Packaging and Advertising

Most legislation dealing with the labeling and packaging of medicinal products is now in Part 13 of the Human Medicines Regulations 2012 and its associated schedules.

The legislation regulates labelling in order to ensure descriptions are correct, to ensure that suitable instructions are given and to promote safety. Regulation provides that it is an offence not to comply.

They apply to 'relevant medicinal products' which constitute the vast majority of products. Relevant medicinal products constitute all products for human use except those prepared on the basis of a magistral or official formula, products intended for research or development trials and intermediate products intended for further processing.

GENERAL PROVISIONS FOR LABELLING

(1) All labelling of containers and packages of relevant medicinal products shall be:

   (a) easily legible and indelible; and

   (b) comprehensible;

   (c) either in the English language only or in English and in one or more other languages provided that the same particulars appear in all the languages used.

Symbols, diagrams, pictures or additional information may be used to clarify the standard labelling requirements. However they must not include any element of a promotional nature. Additional information useful for health education may appear on the label so long as it is not of a promotional nature.

The information specified in Part 1 of Schedule 24 must appear:

(a) on the outer packaging of a medicinal product; and

(b) on the immediate packaging of the product, unless it is a blister pack or is otherwise too small to display the information.

If the product is a blister pack and is placed in outer packaging, then the information may be on the outer packaging alone.

Pharmacy Law and Practice. DOI: http://dx.doi.org/10.1016/B978-0-12-394289-0.00017-5

Schedule 24 Part 1 requires:

(1) The name of the medicinal product.

(2) The strength and pharmaceutical form of the product.

(3) Where appropriate, whether the product is intended for babies, children or adults.

(4) Where the product contains up to three active substances, the common name of each active substance.

(5) A statement of the active substances in the product, expressed qualitatively and quantitatively per dosage unit or according to the form of administration for a given volume or weight, using their common names.

(6) The pharmaceutical form and the contents by weight, by volume or by number of doses of the product.

(7) A list of:
   (a) where the product is injectable or is a topical or eye preparation, all excipients; or
   (b) in any other case, those excipients known to have a recognized action or effect and included in the guidance published pursuant to Article 65 of the 2001 Directive.

(8) The method of administration of the product and if necessary the route of administration.

(9) Where appropriate, space for the prescribed dose to be indicated.

(10) A warning that the product must be stored out of the reach and sight of children.

(11) Any special warning applicable to the product.

(12) The product's expiry date (month and year), in clear terms.

(13) Any special storage precautions relating to the product.

(14) Any special precautions relating to the disposal of an unused product or part of a product, or waste derived from the product, and reference to any appropriate collection system in place.

(15) The name and address of the holder of the marketing authorisation, Article 126a authorisation or traditional herbal registration relating to the product and, where applicable, the name of the holder's representative.

(16) The number of the marketing authorisation, Article 126a authorisation or traditional herbal registration for placing the medicinal product on the market.

(17) The manufacturer's batch number.

(18) In the case of a product that is not a prescription only medicine (POM), instructions for use.

Immediate packaging: blister packs Schedule 24 Part 2:

(1) The name of the medicinal product.

(2) The strength and pharmaceutical form of the product.

(3) Where appropriate, whether the product is intended for babies, children or adults.

(4) Where the product contains up to three active substances, the common name of each active substance.

(5) The name of the holder of the marketing authorisation, Article 126a authorisation or traditional herbal registration relating to the product.

(6) The product's expiry date (month and year), in clear terms.

(7) The manufacturer's batch number.

What Is the 'Immediate Packaging?'

The immediate packaging is the container or receptacle which actually contains the tablets, capsules, syrup, etc.

What Is the Packaging?

The outer packaging is the box, packet, etc., in which the container is enclosed.

Small Packages

Small packages must contain the above information plus the method of administration of the product and if necessary the route of administration.

Ampoules and other containers of 10 ml capacity or less are not required to have all of the standard particulars on the ampoule itself. The outer package must bear the full standard particulars.

PARACETAMOL WARNINGS

Products containing paracetamol must have additional warnings:

(1) Except where the name of the product includes the word 'paracetamol' on the outer and immediate packaging, the words 'Contains paracetamol'.

(2) The words 'Do not take more medicine than the label tells you to. If you do not get better, talk to your doctor', must appear adjacent to either the directions for use or the recommended dosage.

(3) Adult preparations must carry the warning 'do not take anything else containing paracetamol while taking this medicine' and

    (a) if the package leaflet includes the words, 'Talk to a doctor at once if you take too much of this medicine even if you feel well. This is because too much paracetamol can cause delayed, serious liver damage', then the package must state 'Talk to a doctor at once if you take too much of this medicine, even if you feel well'.

    (b) if there is no package leaflet or it does not include the words, 'Talk to a doctor at once if you take too much of this medicine even if you feel well. This is because too much paracetamol can cause delayed, serious liver damage', then instead the package must include that warning.

(4) Children's preparations must carry the warning: 'Do not give anything else containing paracetamol while giving this medicine' and

(a) if the package leaflet includes the words, 'Talk to a doctor at once if your child takes too much of this medicine, even if they seem well', then instead the package must include that warning.

(b) if there is no package leaflet or it does not include the words, 'Talk to a doctor at once if your child takes too much of this medicine, even if they seem well. This is because too much paracetamol can cause delayed, serious liver damage', then instead the package must include that warning.

P AND POM PRODUCTS

The packaging of Pharmacy only products must bear the capital letter 'P' within a rectangle within which there is to be no other matter of any kind.

The packaging of POM must bear the capital letters 'POM' within a rectangle within which there is to be no other matter of any kind.

PACKAGING REQUIREMENTS: INFORMATION FOR BLIND AND PARTIALLY SIGHTED PATIENTS

259.—(1) The name of a medicinal product must also be expressed in Braille format on the outer packaging of the product (or, if there is no outer packaging, on the immediate packaging of the product).

(2) The holder of a marketing authorisation, Article 126a authorisation or traditional herbal registration for a medicinal product must ensure that the package leaflet is made available on request in formats suitable for blind and partially-sighted persons.

LABELLING OF DISPENSED MEDICINAL PRODUCTS

A dispensed medicinal product is a medicinal product prepared or dispensed in accordance with a prescription given by a practitioner.

The container shall be labelled with:

(1) the name of the patient
(2) the name and address of the person who sells or supplies the product
(3) the date of dispensing
(4) the following details if requested by the practitioner:
  (a) the name of the medicinal product or its common name
  (b) the directions for use
  (c) the precautions relating to its use
(5) the words 'keep out of reach of children' or similar
(6) the words 'for external use only' if the product:
  (a) is a P or POM medicine which is a liquid or gel
  (b) consists of an embrocation, liniment, lotion, antiseptic or other preparation and
  (c) is for external use.

Where the pharmacist believes that any of the particulars in (4) as requested by the practitioner are inappropriate, he may substitute those he believes to be appropriate.

(Schedule 25 Human Medicines Regulations)

SUPPLY BY DOCTORS, DENTISTS, NURSES AND MIDWIVES

Products supplied by dentists, nurses and midwives should bear the following information:

(1) Where the product is to be administered to a particular individual, the name of that individual.

(2) The name and address of the person who sells or supplies the product.

(3) The date on which the product is sold or supplied.

(4) Such of the following particulars as the person under whose responsibility the product is sold or supplied considers appropriate:

    (a) the name of the product or its common name;

    (b) directions for use of the product; and

    (c) precautions relating to the use of the product.

Name

'Name' in relation to a medicinal product means:

(a) where the product has a UK marketing authorisation or traditional herbal registration, the name:

    (i) as approved by the licensing authority in granting the authorisation or registration, or

    (ii) where that name has been varied since that approval, as so amended;

(b) where the product has an EU marketing authorisation, the name:

    (i) as approved by the European Commission in granting the authorisation, or

    (ii) where that name has been varied since that approval, as so amended; and

(c) where the product has an Article 126a authorisation, the name:

    (i) as approved by the licensing authority to appear on the packaging and any package leaflet of the product under the authorisation, or

    (ii) where that name has been varied since that approval, as so amended.

In any case where there is more than one pharmaceutical form or more than one strength of a product, a statement of the pharmaceutical form or strength of that product must appear on the label. This can be as part of the name of that product, but otherwise must be added immediately after the name, in the same style and size of letters as the name. 'Strength' means the suitability of the product for a baby, child or adult.

The requirement for a container or package of a relevant medicinal product to be labelled to show its name is not met by the container or package being labelled to show an invented name which is liable to be confused with the common name.

Additional information useful for health education may appear on the label so long as it is not of a promotional nature.

Labelling details must be approved by the licensing authority and any changes notified to them. The licensing authority has a 90-day period during which it may object to any changes.

Standard Labelling Requirements for Homoeopathic Products

Containers and packages of homoeopathic must be labelled in clear and legible form to show a reference to their homoeopathic nature, in particular by clear mention of the words 'homoeopathic medicinal product'. This is in addition to any other particulars required by regulations (see Chapter 14).

PHARMACISTS' OWN REMEDIES

Products prepared in a pharmacy for retail sale from that pharmacy, and which are not advertised are sometimes known as 'nostrums'. They must be labelled with the following:

(1) Name of product
(2) Pharmaceutical form on the package
(3) Appropriate quantitative details
(4) Quantity
(5) Directions for use
(6) Special handling and storage requirements
(7) Expiry date
(8) Name and address of seller
(9) 'Keep out of reach of children'
(10) Where appropriate, the warnings for 'P' medicines.

DISPENSED MEDICINES IN CRCs

There is no law requiring the general use of CRCs for dispensed medicines. However in 1981 the pharmaceutical and medical professions agreed that all solid-dose oral preparations should be dispensed in CRCs or in strip or blister packs. Exceptions are allowed for:

(a) original packs
(b) patients who experience difficulty in opening CRCs
(c) specific requests from patients.

The voluntary scheme became a professional requirement from 1 January 1989 and appears as a requirement in the RPSGB Code of Ethics.

This was extended by a Council Statement in February 1994, which stated that from 1 January 1995 it would be a professional requirement for CRCs to be used for all liquid medicines dispensed from bulk.

Legislation

Regulation 272 defines 'regulated medicinal product' as a medicinal product containing aspirin, paracetamol or more than 24 mg of elemental iron, in the form of tablets, capsules, pills, lozenges, pastilles, suppositories or oral liquids, but does not include:

(a) effervescent tablets containing not more than 25% of aspirin or paracetamol by weight;
(b) medicinal products in sachets or other sealed containers which hold only one dose;
(c) medicinal products which are not intended for retail sale or for supply in circumstances corresponding to retail sale; or
(d) medicinal products which are for export only.

Regulation 273 of the Human Medicines Regulations requires that 'Regulated medicinal products' may be sold or supplied only in containers which are:

(a) opaque or dark tinted; and
(b) child resistant.

Thus only those medicines containing aspirin, paracetamol or more than 24 mg of elemental iron must legally be placed on the market in packaging which has been shown to be child resistant.

The requirement does not apply to medicines dispensed on a prescription where

(a) it is not reasonably practicable to provide the regulated medicinal products in containers that are both opaque or dark tinted and child resistant; or
(b) a person who is aged 16 or over specifically requests that the regulated medicinal products not be contained in a child-resistant container.

Regulation 273 also does not apply to the sale or supply of regulated medicinal products:

(a) by a doctor or dentist to a patient, or the patient's carer, for the patient's use;
(b) by a doctor or dentist to a person who is an appropriate practitioner, at the request of that person, for administration to a patient of that person; or
(c) in the course of the business of a hospital or health centre, where the sale or supply is for the purposes of administration, whether in the hospital or health centre or elsewhere, in accordance with the directions of an appropriate practitioner.

Child Resistance

Containers which are not reclosable are child resistant if they have been evaluated in accordance with, and comply with the requirements of the British Standards Institution or meet any equivalent or higher technical specification for non-reclosable child-resistant packaging recognised for use in the European Economic Area.

Limit on Amounts in Containers for Sale

Products that contain aloxiprin, aspirin, paracetamol or ibuprofen are GSL products when they are packed in quantities less than those set out in Schedule 15.

Use of Ribbed or Fluted Bottles

The Medicines (Fluted Bottles) Regulations 1978, SI No. 40 were repealed by the Human Medicines Regulations 2012. There is no longer a requirement for any medicines to be dispensed in fluted or ribbed bottles.

STANDARD REQUIREMENTS FOR PATIENT INFORMATION LEAFLETS

Regulation 260 requires 'medicinal products' to have a 'patient information leaflet' included in the packaging of a medicinal product.

The package leaflet must be legible, clear and easy to use, and the applicant or holder of a marketing authorisation, etc., must ensure that target patient groups are consulted in order to achieve this.

Directive 2004/27/EC now states:

The package leaflet shall reflect the results of consultations with target patient groups to ensure that it is legible clear and easy to use.

The package leaflet must:

(a) be drawn up in accordance with the Summary of Product Characteristics (SPC); and
(b) contain all the information specified in Schedule 27:
    (1) The name of the medicinal product.
    (2) The strength and pharmaceutical form of the product.
    (3) Where appropriate, whether the product is intended for babies, children or adults.
    (4) Where the product contains up to three active substances, the common name of each active substance.
    (5) The pharmaco-therapeutic group, or type of activity, of the product, in terms easily comprehensible for the patient.
    (6) The product's therapeutic indications.
    (7) A list of:
        (a) contra-indications;
        (b) appropriate precautions for use;
        (c) interactions with other medicinal products which may affect the action of the product;

(d) interactions with other substances, including alcohol, tobacco and foodstuffs, which may affect the action of the product; and

(e) special warnings, if any, relating to the product.

(8) The list mentioned in Paragraph 7 must:

    (a) take into account the special requirements of particular categories of users (including, in particular, children, pregnant or breastfeeding women, the elderly and persons with specific pathological conditions);

    (b) mention, if appropriate, possible effects on the ability to drive vehicles or to operate machinery; and

    (c) list any excipients:

        (i) if knowledge of the excipients is important for the safe and effective use of the product, and

        (ii) the excipients are included in the guidance published pursuant to Article 65 of the 2001 Directive.

(9) Instructions for proper use of the product including in particular:

    (a) the dosage;

    (b) the method and, if necessary, route of administration;

    (c) the frequency of administration (including, if necessary, specifying times at which the product may or must be administered);

    (d) the duration of treatment if this is to be limited;

    (e) symptoms of an overdose and the action, if any, to be taken in case of an overdose;

    (f) what to do if one or more doses have not been taken;

    (g) an indication, if necessary, of the risk of withdrawal effects; and

    (h) a specific recommendation to consult a doctor or pharmacist, as appropriate, for further explanation of the use of the product.

(10) A description of the adverse reactions which may occur in normal use of the medicinal product and, if necessary, the action to be taken in such a case.

(11) A reference to the expiry date printed on the packaging of the product with:

    (a) a warning against using the product after that date;

    (b) if appropriate, details of special storage precautions to be taken;

    (c) if necessary, a warning concerning visible signs of deterioration;

    (d) the full qualitative composition (in active substances and excipients), and the quantitative composition in active substances, using common names, of each presentation of the medicinal product;

    (e) for each presentation of the product, the pharmaceutical form and content in weight, volume or units of dosage;

    (f) the name and address of the holder of the marketing authorisation, Article 126a authorisation or traditional herbal registration relating to the product and, if applicable, the name of the holder's appointed representative; and

    (g) the name and address of the manufacturer of the product.

(12) Where the product is authorised under different names in different Member States in accordance with Articles 28–39 of the 2001 Directive, a list of the names authorised in each Member State.

(13) For medicinal products included in the list referred to in Article 23 of Regulation (EC) No 726/2004, the statement: 'This medicinal product is subject to additional safety monitoring'.

(14) The statement: 'Also you can help to make sure that medicines remain as safe as possible by reporting any unwanted side effects via the internet at yellow card.[1] Alternatively you can call Freephone 0808 100 3352 (available from 10 a.m. to 2 p.m. Monday to Friday) or fill in a paper form available from your local pharmacy'.

(15) The date on which the package leaflet was last revised

See – Best Practice Guidance on Patient Information Leaflets 2012.[2]

Offences

It is an offence for any person in the course of business carried on by him/her to sell, supply or possess for sale any medicine which does not comply with the requirements. It is also an offence to have any leaflet which does not comply.

Medicinal products must be sold in containers. Containers, packages and leaflets must properly describe the product and must not mislead as to the nature or quality of the product.

Contravention is punishable by a fine or up to £2000 and up to 2 years imprisonment.

Hospital Practice

Where medicines are given to patients in hospitals as individual doses, for example on a ward, the leaflet need not be included in the packaging but must be provided to the patient on request.

RADIOPHARMACEUTICALS

The regulations also impose special requirements for the leaflets supplied with radiopharmaceuticals and with radiopharmaceutical-associated products (Regulation 4).

Labelling Requirements for Radionuclides

(1) Where a medicinal product contains radionuclides:

(a) the carton and the container of the product must be labelled in accordance with the regulations for the safe transport of radioactive materials laid down by the International Atomic Energy Agency; and

(b) *the labelling on the shielding and the vial must comply with the remaining provisions of this regulation.*

(2) *The label on the shielding must:*

(a) *include the information specified in Part 1 of Schedule 24;*

(b) *explain in full the codings used on the vial;*

(c) *indicate, where necessary, for a given time and date, the amount of radioactivity per dose or per vial; and*

(d) *indicate the number of capsules or, for liquids, the number of millilitres per container.*

(3) *The label on the vial must include:*

(a) *the name or code of the medicinal product, including the name or chemical symbol of the radionuclide;*

(b) *the batch identification and expiry date of the product;*

(c) *the international symbol for radioactivity;*

(d) *the name and address of the manufacturer; and*

(e) *the amount of radioactivity;*

(4) *The vial shall be labelled to show:*

(a) *the name or code of the medicinal product, including the name or chemical symbol of the radionuclide;*

(b) *the international symbol for radioactivity;*

(c) *the name of the manufacturer; and*

(d) *the amount of radioactivity as specified in paragraph 2 above.*

(Human Medicines Regulations 262)

Leaflets Relating to Radionuclides

(1) *A detailed instruction leaflet must be enclosed with:*

(a) *radiopharmaceuticals;*

(b) *radionuclide generators;*

(c) *radionuclide kits; or*

(d) *radionuclide precursors.*

(2) *The leaflet must include the information specified in Schedule 27.*

(3) *The leaflet must also include:*

(a) *any precautions to be taken by the user and the patient during the preparation and administration of the medicinal product; and*

(b) *special precautions for the disposal of the packaging and its unused contents.*

(Human Medicines Regulations 262)

ADVERTISING AND SALES PROMOTION

The advertising of medicines is controlled by Part 14 of the Human Medicines Regulations. There are specific prohibitions on the advertising of treatments for various diseases. The GPhC Standards Document deals with advertising by pharmacists. It states that the pharmacist must be satisfied that any advertising and promotional activity for professional services or medicines is legal, decent and truthful and complies with appropriate advertising codes of practice.

The use of certain titles, for example pharmacist, is also restricted by law. Some consumer law carries restrictions which are applicable to pharmacy.

The regulations implement the European Community Directive 2001/83/EC on the advertising of medicinal products.

279. A person may not publish an advertisement for a medicinal product unless one of the following is in force for the product:

(a) a marketing authorisation;
(b) a certificate of registration;
(c) a traditional herbal registration; or
(d) an Article 126a authorisation.

(1) Regulation 280 prohibits adverts:
 * *which do not comply with the SPC for the products*
 * *which do not encourage rational use of the product by presenting it objectively and without exaggerating its properties and*
 * *which are misleading.*

(2) Regulation 281 sets out certain duties which holders of marketing authorisations have:
 * *to monitor information received about their product*
 * *to provide information about adverts to regulatory authorities on request*
 * *to comply with directions given by regulatory authorities about advertisements and*
 * *to provide adequate training for sales representatives.*

What Is an 'Advertisement'?

For the purposes of the Medicines Act, an advertisement includes every form of advertising:

* in a publication
* by display of a notice
* by means of a catalogue or price list
* circular letters
* letters addressed to particular people
* in any other document
* words inscribed on an article
* photographs
* cinema film
* sound recording
* radio and television
* or in any other way.

It does not include spoken words which are not part of a recording or broadcast on radio or television, or the supply of a medicine in a labelled container.

Under the regulations, price lists, trade catalogues, reference materials and factual informative statements or announcements are not advertisements unless they make a product claim.

Consent of Marketing Authorisation Holder

Advertisements may only be issued by marketing authorisation holders or with their consent.

ADVERTS TO THE PUBLIC

The regulations differentiate between advertising directed to the public and advertising aimed at health professionals.

POM medicines may not be advertised directly to the public. Where the retail sale of products has been restricted by a 'safety order' under *Section 62*, then those products may not be advertised either. Products subject to the Narcotics Drugs Convention cannot be advertised.

All advertisements must clearly be such and the product must clearly be identified as a medicine. The advertisement must include:

- The name of the product.
- The common name of the ingredient of a single active ingredient product.
- How to use it.
- An invitation to read the instructions.

Prohibitions

Some claims and statements in adverts are prohibited by regulations:

(a) any advert which offers a diagnosis
(b) comparative advertising
(c) suggestions that health care is improved by not taking a product
(d) adverts directed at children
(e) scientific or celebrity endorsements
(f) suggestions that a medicine is a foodstuff or cosmetic
(g) suggestions that the efficacy or safety is due to the fact that the product is natural
(h) any advert which might lead to erroneous self-diagnosis
(i) any advert which refers in improper, alarming or misleading terms to claims of recovery
(j) any advert which uses pictures in an improper, alarming or misleading manner
(k) any advert which mentions that the product has been granted a marketing authorisation.

Abortion

Products for abortion cannot be advertised to the public.   (Regulation 283)

Contraceptive Products

Oral contraceptive products are POM and hence cannot be advertised to the public. (Regulation 284)

Narcotics

The advertising to the public of medicines containing psychotropic or narcotic substances controlled under the Narcotics Drugs Convention 1961 or the Psychotropic Substances Convention 1971 is prohibited (except for those products containing very small amounts). (Regulation 285)

Promotional Sales to the Public

Manufacturers, wholesalers and marketing authorisation holders are prohibited from selling or supplying medicinal products for promotional purposes to the public. (Regulation 293)

Small-sized packs may be sold on normal business terms through normal trade outlets.

ADVERTISEMENTS TO HEALTH PROFESSIONALS

The regulations lay down certain specified particulars to be included in adverts which are intended to induce practitioners to prescribe or supply the products. The advertisements must comply with Schedule 30.

The regulations cover advertising to 'persons qualified to prescribe or supply'. This phrase is defined so as to include the employees of those who 'in the course of their profession or in the course of a business may lawfully prescribe, sell by retail or supply in circumstances corresponding to retail sale, relevant medicinal products.'

The adverts must include the PL number and details of the marketing authorisation holder, the legal classification of the product, lists of active ingredients, one or more of the licenced indications for use, the side effects, cautions and contra-indications from the SPC, warnings and cost.

Small, abbreviated adverts in professional publications are allowed which contain only name of product, legal classification, name of PL holder, ingredients and an indication of where further information may be found.

Free Samples

Regulation 298 limits supply of free samples to people qualified to prescribe. It does not allow supply to persons qualified only to supply. There are a number of conditions laid down. Failure to comply may be punished by a fine.

- Samples may only be supplied in limited numbers.
- There must be a signed dated written request.

- There must be a system of control and accountability.
- Only small size packs are allowed.
- Each pack must be marked 'free medical sample – not for resale'.
- Each sample must be accompanied by a copy of the SPC.

Samples of medicines containing psychotropic or narcotic substances controlled under the Narcotics Drugs Convention 1961 or the Psychotropic Substances Convention 1971 are prohibited (except for those products containing very small amounts).

Promotional Aids

The regulations allow for 'promotional aids' such as pens and mugs to carry the name of the product and the company without any other information. "Promotional aid" means a non-monetary gift made for a promotional purpose by a commercially interested party. It should be relevant to the practice of medicine or pharmacy.

Inducements

Regulation 300 states that it is an offence to solicit or accept any prohibited 'gift, pecuniary advantage, benefit in kind, hospitality or sponsorship'.

All gifts, pecuniary advantages and benefits in kind are prohibited in relation to the promotion of medicine unless they are 'inexpensive and relevant to the practice of medicine or pharmacy'.

Any hospitality payments must be reasonable in level, subordinate to the main purpose of the meeting and offered only to health professionals. Hospitality may include the payment of travelling or accommodation expenses at events 'for purely professional or scientific purposes' or 'held for the promotion of relevant medicinal products'.

Regulation 300(6) allows 'measures or trade practices relating to prices, margins or discounts which were in existence on 1 January 1993, thus allowing most business purchase discount schemes to continue'.

It is an offence both to offer prohibited inducements and to accept them. Offering or supplying inducements is punishable with a fine and/or imprisonment and soliciting or accepting them may be punished with a fine.

Association of the British Pharmaceutical Industry Code of Practice

The Code covers the promotion of medicines for prescribing to both health professionals and appropriate administrative staff. It also includes requirements for interactions with health professionals. In addition it sets standards for the provision of information about POM to the public and patients, including patient organisations. The Code incorporates principles set out in relevant international industry and professional codes and in the Directive 2001/83/EC on the Community Code relating to medicinal products for human use.

NHS Prescribing Incentives

In 2010 decision, the European Court of Justice held that the prohibition on incentives to prescribe did not apply to national public health authorities that control public funds, despite the fact that individual doctors can profit from these incentives.

The Bribery Act 2010

Under this Act it is a criminal offence:

- to offer or give a reward, or
- to request or accept a reward

for not performing a public function in an impartial way.It is also an offence for a commercial organization to fail to prevent bribery unless the business has adequate procedures in place to stop such conduct.

Medical Representatives

Medical representatives must receive adequate training. They must provide information which is as precise and complete as possible about the products. On each visit, medical representatives must give a copy of the SPC for the product they are promoting.

Summary of Product Characteristics

An SPC is a document prepared by the holder of the marketing authorisation. It must contain the information laid down in the Human Medicines Regulations. Details of type, size and layout are also specified.

The SPC may be distributed in the form of a compendium. The Association of the British Pharmaceutical Industry (ABPI) produces an annual compendium of SPC for products on the UK market.

Advertisements for Registered Homoeopathic Medicinal Products

Advertisements relating to a registered homoeopathic medicinal product must contain only the details in Schedule 5 and must not mention any specific therapeutic indications.

Complaints

Complaints about the content of advertisements may be referred by the Medicines Control Agency to a suitable self-regulatory body for investigation and action. The three most important self-regulatory bodies are the Advertising Standards Authority, the Prescription Medicines Code of Practice Authority and the Proprietary Association of Great Britain. The Monitoring Regulations also set out formal procedures which allow the MHRA to take enforcement action in both civil and criminal courts.

Advertising of NHS Pharmaceutical Services

Prior to 1992 the Terms of Service contained a restrictive clause prohibiting the advertising of NHS services. This no longer exists. Any advertising which is done is subject to the GPhC Standards.

Self-Assessment Questions

1. What are the broad rules governing labeling of medicines?
   Answer: All labelling of containers and packages of relevant medicinal products shall be:
   a. easily legible and indelible; and
   b. comprehensible;
   c. either in the English language only or in English and in one or more other languages provided that the same particulars appear in all the languages used.
   Symbols, diagrams, pictures or additional information may be used to clarify the standard labelling requirements. However they must not include any element of a promotional nature. Additional information useful for health education may appear on the label so long as it is not of a promotional nature.
   The information specified in Part 1 of Schedule 24 must appear:
   a. on the outer packaging of a medicinal product; and
   b. on the immediate packaging of the product, unless it is a blister pack or is otherwise too small to display the information.
   If the product is a blister pack and is placed in outer packaging, then the information may be on the outer packaging alone.
2. How is the legal classification of a medicine indicated on the box?
   Answer: The packaging of Pharmacy only products must bear the capital letter 'P' within a rectangle within which there is to be no other matter of any kind. The packaging of POM must bear the capital letters 'POM' within a rectangle within which there is to be no other matter of any kind.
3. How may POM medicines be advertised?
   Answer: The regulations differentiate between advertising directed to the public and advertising aimed at health professionals. POM medicines may not be advertised directly to the public. This restriction includes products for abortion and oral contraceptive products.
   Where the retail sale of products has been restricted by a 'safety order' under *Section 62*, then those products may not be advertised either. Products subject to the Narcotics Drugs Convention cannot be advertised.

ADDITIONAL RESOURCES

1. http://www.mhra.gov.uk/yellowcard
2. http://www.mhra.gov.uk/home/groups/pla/documents/websiteresources/con157151.pdf

Chapter 18

Poisons and Dangerous Substances

There are a number of controls on the sale, storage, labelling and other dealings with those poisons which are not medicines.

The Poisons Act 1972 sets up a mechanism to designate substances as poisons, and to lay down rules on how they are to be treated.

THE POISONS BOARD

Section 1 of the Poisons Act creates an advisory committee (in reality a continuation of one established by earlier legislation, the Pharmacy and Poisons Act 1933).

The Board consists of at least 16 members. Five of them must be appointed by Royal Pharmaceutical Society of Great Britain, and one of these must be engaged in the manufacture of pharmaceuticals. Members hold office for 3 years. The Chairman is appointed by the Secretary of State.

POISONS LIST

The main task of the Board is to recommend to the Secretary of State which substances should be listed as poisons. *Section 2* of the Act creates a Poisons List, which is set out from time to time in a Poisons List Order. The list consists of two parts:

Part I is a list of poisons which can only be retailed from a pharmacy.

Part II is a list of poisons which can be sold from either a pharmacy or by a 'listed seller'.

LISTED SELLERS

A 'listed seller' is a person allowed by the local county or borough council to sell Part II poisons. The local authority can refuse permission if it believes the person is unfit. Names may also be removed from the list for non-payment of the retention fee. A court may remove a name from the list following a conviction which would make the person unfit to sell poisons.

Pharmacy Law and Practice. DOI: http://dx.doi.org/10.1016/B978-0-12-394289-0.00018-7
© 2013 Elsevier BV. All rights reserved.

The local authority list must include particulars of the premises and the names of the persons listed. The permission is specific to the person. Up to two deputies may be named. The list is open to public inspection without charge.

The local authority is entitled to charge reasonable fees for inclusion and for retention.

Listed sellers may not use any title, emblem or description which might suggest he or she is entitled to sell poisons other than those in Part II.

Enforcement

Enforcement is shared between the GPhC and the local authorities, with the GPhC dealing with pharmacies.

Penalties

A person who fails to comply with the law relating to poisons is liable on conviction to a fine of up to £1000. Offences involving the misuse of titles or the obstruction of an inspector may incur a fine of £100.

When the offences are related to the sale or supply of a poison the employer remains liable even though an employee acted without his authority (*Section 8*).

Substances on the List

Only substances which appear on the Poisons List are legally poisons. Other substances, despite their toxicity, are not legally poisons.

Some poisons may only be sold by listed sellers when the poison is in a specified form. Some poisons may only be sold to certain categories of purchaser.

THE POISONS RULES

The detail of the law is found in the Poisons Rules, which categorise poisons into a number of Schedules. There are different rules governing each of the Schedules. The current law is found in the Poisons Rules 1982, SI No. 218, as amended by the Poisons Rules Amendment Order 1985. The rules also contain a number of general provisions which apply to all poisons.

General Requirements

Generally, poisons in Part I must be sold:

(1) by a pharmacist or person lawfully conducting a retail pharmacy business (RPB),

(2) at the pharmacy,
(3) by or under the supervision of the pharmacist.

Poisons in Part II must be sold:

(1) from a pharmacy, or
(2) by a listed seller from his premises.

Listed sellers may not sell any Part II poisons which they have altered or processed in such a way as to expose the poison.

Schedule I

Extra conditions are specified for the sale, storage and record-keeping of poisons in Schedule I.

Supervision

All Schedule I poisons, even those on Part II of the List, must be sold under the supervision of the pharmacist when sold from a pharmacy. When sold from 'listed premises' the sale must be effected by the listed seller or one of his deputies.

Storage

Schedule I poisons must be stored separately from other items. They must be in:

(a) a cupboard or drawer used solely for poisons, or
(b) a part of the premises separated from the rest so as to exclude the public, or
(c) on a shelf used only for storing poisons, and which has no food below it.

Schedule I poisons which are used in agriculture, horticulture or forestry must be kept separate from food products. If stored in a drawer or cupboard no other products may be kept with them.

When poisons are transported in vehicles, adequate steps must be taken to avoid contamination of any food carried in the same vehicle.

Knowledge of the Purchaser

Purchasers of Schedule I poisons must be known to the seller, or to a responsible person on his staff, as being 'of good character'. The person on the staff may be a pharmacist, or in the case of listed sellers, the person in charge of the premises or of the department.

Where the purchaser is not known, they must present a certificate stating that they are of good character. This must be in the prescribed form, and given by a householder. If the householder is not known to the seller then the certificate must be endorsed by a police officer in charge of a police station. The endorsement certifies that the householder is known to the police as a person of good character. It does not itself certify the purchaser.

Records

Sellers of Schedule 1 poisons are required to keep a 'Poisons Book', and enter in it:

(1) date of sale
(2) name and address of purchaser
(3) name and address of person giving the certificate
(4) date of the certificate
(5) name and quantity of poison
(6) purpose for which the poison is stated to be required.

The format is laid down in Schedule 11 of the Poisons Rules.

The entry must be signed by the purchaser. Purchasers who require a poison for trade or professional purposes may present a signed order instead of signing the Poisons Book.

A Poisons Book must be retained for 2 years after the last entry.

Signed Order

A signed order must contain the following:

(1) name and address of purchaser
(2) trade, business or profession
(3) purpose for which the poison is required
(4) total quantity to be bought.

The seller must be reasonably satisfied that the signature is genuine, and that the person does indeed carry on the trade or profession stated.

The seller must retain the certificate, giving it a reference number for identification.

In an emergency a Schedule I poison may be supplied on an undertaking to supply a signed order in 24 h.

Relaxations

The requirements relating to knowledge of the purchaser and entries in the Poisons Book do not apply to the sale of poisons:

(1) for export
(2) by wholesale.

There are specific relaxations for the sale of nicotine dusts (less than 4%) and rat poisons containing barium carbonate or zinc phosphide.

SCHEDULE I POISONS SUBJECT TO EXTRA CONTROLS

The following Schedule 1 poisons are subject to extra controls:

Sodium and potassium arsenites
Strychnine
Fluoroacetic acid, its salts or fluoroacetamide
Thallium salts
Zinc phosphide.

They may only be sold or supplied:

(a) by wholesale
(b) for export
(c) for education, research or analysis.

These poisons may also be sold or supplied in the circumstances outlined below.

In September 2006, a new EU law regulated a wide range of poisons, including strychnine, to ensure they were safe and had no harmful effect on the environment.

Strychnine and strychnine hydrochloride is no longer authorised for supply or use for mole control.

Fluoroacetic acid, its salts or fluoroacetamide may be sold to a person with a certificate authorising the use as a rodenticide. The certificate must state the quantity and identify the place where it is to be used.

It may only be used in ships, sewers, drains and dock warehouses. Certificates are issued by local authorities or port health authorities or by DEFRA.

Thallium salts may also be sold to:

(a) local authorities or port health authorities,
(b) government departments,
(c) persons with a written authority issued by MAFF authorising the use of thallium sulphate for killing rats, mice or moles for pest control,
(d) manufacturers who regularly use them in the manufacture of articles in the business (except thallium sulphate),
(e) persons as an ingredient in any article not intended for consumption by persons or animals (except thallium sulphate).

Zinc phosphide may be sold:

(a) to a local authority,
(b) to a government department,
(c) to a person for his trade or business.

Calcium, potassium and sodium cyanides may only be sold under the so-called *Section 4* exemptions. Sales are not allowed for private purposes.

Section 4 Exemptions

Exempted transactions of Part 1 poisons may be made without pharmacist supervision, provided the sales are not made on retail premises:

- wholesale dealing,
- export,
- to doctor, dentist, vet for professional purposes,
- for use in hospital or similar public institution,
- sale by wholesale to:
    - government department,
    - for education or research,
    - enable employers to meet any statutory obligation with respect to medical treatment of employees,
    - a person requiring the substance for trade or business.

THE CHIP4 REGULATIONS 2009

All poisons must be labelled and packaged in accordance with the Chemicals (Hazard Information and Packaging for Supply) Regulations 2009 SI No. 716.

The regulations require the manufacturer or distributor of a 'chemical' to decide if it is 'hazardous' and then to label it appropriately and to supply a safety data sheet.

Background

Two European Directives establish a single market for the supply of chemicals in the EU by harmonising rules on how to classify, label and package hazardous chemicals. They are:

- Dangerous Substances Directive (No. 67/548/EEC), and
- Dangerous Preparations Directive (No. 1999/45/EC).

The Directives are implemented in Great Britain by the 'CHIP4' Regulations. There are similar regulations in Northern Ireland.

Classification

'Chemical' includes solids, liquids and gases and includes pure chemical substances such as ethanol as well as preparations of chemicals such as cleaning fluid. They are classified as follows:

(1) Chemicals which are dangerous because of their physical or chemical properties: explosive, oxidising, extremely flammable, highly flammable, flammable.
(2) Chemicals which are toxic, very toxic, harmful, corrosive, irritant or carcinogenic, mutagenic or toxic to reproduction.
(3) Chemicals which are dangerous for the environment.

Information

When classified chemicals are supplied in connection with work they must be accompanied by a 'safety data sheet'. Should any new safety information become available, the data sheet must be revised and copies given to anyone who obtained the chemical during the previous 12 months. There is thus an implicit requirement to keep records of sales for use in connection with work.

The information in the data sheets must be given under standard headings.

Labelling

The regulations set out details of labelling which include:

- the name and address of supplier
- name of the chemical
- the type of danger
- warnings about use
- EU number
- warning pictograms.

Packaging

Chemicals must be packaged safely. Toxic, very toxic and corrosive chemicals which are sold to the public must be in containers with child-resistant closures. This applies regardless of the quantity. It also applies to solid products. Tactile danger warnings must be on containers sold to the public of chemicals which are harmful, highly flammable, extremely flammable, toxic, very toxic or corrosive.

Advertisements

Adverts must mention the type of hazard that is mentioned on the label.

Exemptions

Some products are exempt from the CHIP Regulations because they are controlled in other ways, for example radioactive substances. The CHIP Regulations do not apply to preparations intended for use as cosmetics or medicinal products.

Future Legislation

On 1 June 2015, the European Regulation (EC) No. 1272/2008 on the Classification, Labelling and Packaging of Substance and Mixtures (CLP Regulation) comes into full effect. It will replace and fully repeal the Dangerous Substances Directive and the Dangerous Preparations Directive.

The CLP Regulation is directly acting in all EU Member States and does not require separate implementation into national law. The CHIP4 Regulations will remain in force throughout the transitional period of the CLP Regulation but, with the exception of Regulation 14 (enforcement), will also be repealed on 1 June 2015.

THE ENVIRONMENTAL PROTECTION ACT 1990

This Act places a duty of care on 'waste producers' to dispose of 'controlled waste' legally.

Waste producers are persons in business, but not householders where their own waste is concerned.

The Hazardous Waste (England and Wales) Regulations 2005 SI No. 894 came into effect on 16 July 2005.

Every person who produces or stores hazardous waste must notify the Environment Agency, except where the premises are 'shop premises' and the waste arises as a result of the activity of the shop. Thus a pharmacy which dispenses prescriptions, and accepts waste from individuals and households, will be exempt from notification requirements.

Different types of hazardous waste may not be mixed. Hazardous waste may not be mixed with non-hazardous waste.

The Controlled Waste (England and Wales) Regulations 2012 classify waste as household, industrial or commercial waste, and list the types of waste for which local authorities may make a charge for collection and disposal.

'Clinical waste' means waste from a healthcare activity (including veterinary healthcare) that:

(a) contains viable micro-organisms or their toxins which are known or reliably believed to cause disease in humans or other living organisms,
(b) contains or is contaminated with a medicine that contains a biologically active pharmaceutical agent, or
(c) is a sharp, or a body fluid or other biological material (including human and animal tissue) containing or contaminated with a dangerous substance within the meaning of Council Directive 67/548/EEC,

and waste of a similar nature from a non-healthcare activity.

Clinical waste is classed as 'industrial' unless the premises that produce the waste are domestic properties. The clinical waste from a care home (nursing) is industrial waste. Residential homes are included in an exemption and their waste is classed as 'household' even though the name has changed to 'care home'.

'Hazardous waste':

(a) in relation to England, has the meaning given in Regulation 6 of the Hazardous Waste (England and Wales) Regulations 2005(7);

(b) in relation to Wales, has the meaning given in Regulation 6 of the Hazardous Waste (Wales) Regulations 2005(8).

'Offensive waste' means waste that:

(a) is not clinical waste,
(b) contains body fluids, secretions or excretions, and
(c) falls within code 18 01 04, 18 02 03 or 20 01 99 in Schedule 1 to:
   (i) the List of Wastes (England) Regulations 2005, in relation to England, or
   (ii) the List of Wastes (Wales) Regulations 2005 in relation to Wales.

A community pharmacy may legally act as an intermediary in the process of medication disposal only for care homes offering personal care.

Cytotoxic and Cytostatic Medicines

The Hazardous Waste Regulations classify cytotoxic and cytostatic medicines as clinical hazardous waste and include any medicine that has one or more of the hazardous properties toxic, carcinogenic, mutagenic and toxic for reproduction. This wide definition includes many hormone-based preparations, antimicrobial substances such as chloramphenicol as well as chemotherapy.

Pharmacies must therefore segregate their waste medicines into:

- cytotoxic and cytostatic medicines, and
- other medicines.

The regulations require that pharmacies:

(1) keep hazardous waste separate, and
(2) place a duty on a pharmacy to separate mixed waste, provided it is safe and practical to do so.

MEDICINES RETURNED FROM DOMESTIC PREMISES

The DH guidance 'Safe management of healthcare waste 2011'[1] is that domestic households (which are not subject to the prohibition on mixing) may return mixed waste medicines to the pharmacy.

All reasonable steps should be taken to segregate the medicines, bearing in mind the health and safety implications.

Where possible, the returned medicines should be either examined in the container or emptied temporarily onto a tray (which will contain the waste and avoid spillage onto other surfaces).

This may be necessary to identify if controlled drugs are present.

Identifying individual loose tablets is often impracticable and is not required.

The provision of a disposal service in respect of unwanted drugs is an Essential Service set out in *Paragraphs 13* and *14* of Schedule 4 to the NHS (Pharmaceutical and Local Pharmaceutical Services) Regulations 2013:

An NHS pharmacist must, to the extent paragraph 14 requires and in the manner described in that paragraph, accept and dispose of unwanted drugs presented to the NHS pharmacist for disposal.

Controlled Drugs

Since 1 January 2007, the Controlled Drugs (Supervision of Management and Use) Regulations 2006 have required pharmacies in England to have SOPs that include arrangements for recording the return of Schedule 2 controlled drugs from patients, and recording the denaturing of such drugs.

COSHH

The Control of Substances Hazardous to Health Regulations 2002 SI No. 2677 affects the use of hazardous substances in a work situation, by laying down measures which an employer must take to control hazardous substances and to protect people who are exposed to such substances.

Regulation 6 requires that an employer may not carry on any work that is liable to expose any person to any substance hazardous to health, unless a suitable and sufficient assessment of the risks has been made.

What Is a Substance Hazardous to Health?

A substance hazardous to health is defined as:

> *any natural or artificial substance: solid, liquid, gas, vapour or hazardous micro-organism and certain dust levels.*

Substances hazardous to health can include:

(1) any substance classed as:
    toxic, very toxic, harmful, corrosive or irritant.
(2) any micro-organism,
(3) any dust,
(4) any substance which has a prescribed maximum exposure limit, e.g., formaldehyde,
(5) any other substance which can adversely affect the health.

Helpfully, the regulations state that a substance is NOT hazardous when it is at a level that nearly all the population can be exposed to it, repeatedly, without ill effect.

Certain situations are specifically excluded from COSHH:

(a) those covered by the Control of Lead at Work Regulations 1980,
(b) those covered by the Control of Asbestos at Work Regulations 2002,

(c) when the hazard is radioactivity,

(d) when the hazard is the explosive or flammable properties of the substance,

(e) underground mines,

(f) medicines administered to patients.

What Must the Employer Do?

The employer must first of all decide whether or not any substance is potentially hazardous. This must be done by a competent person.

The employer must then:

(1) assess the risk to health from the use of the substance in the workplace,

(2) decide what precautions are needed,

(3) introduce appropriate measures to control the risk,

(4) tell employees about the risk, and about what precautions must be taken,

(5) ensure that precautions are taken,

(6) if appropriate, monitor the exposure and carry out health surveillance.

Assessment

The assessment must be carried out by a competent person. The results of the assessment must be made available to staff.

If the assessment indicates a risk, then the employer must take steps to prevent exposure. If prevention is impossible then the exposure must be reasonably controlled.   (Regulation 7)

PACKAGING WASTE

The Producer Responsibility Obligations (Packaging Waste) Regulations 1997 SI No. 648 implement the European Directive 94/62/EEC on the recycling of waste. The regulations are made under the Environment Act 1995.

The regulations place a 'producer responsibility' on businesses involved in the packaging chain to recover and recycle certain percentages of packaging waste. The obligation applies to businesses with a turnover of more than £5 million a year and which handle more than 50 tonnes of packaging a year. Packaging which contained 'special waste' is partially exempted from the regulations. Smaller businesses are subject to a requirement to keep records of the tonnage of waste handled each year and of any steps taken to promote the recovery of this packaging.

DANGEROUS SUBSTANCES AND EXPLOSIVE ATMOSPHERES REGULATIONS 2002

These regulations require businesses to carry out risk assessments when using potentially dangerous substances. They must provide measures to eliminate or reduce as far as possible the identified explosion or fire risks.

FOOD SAFETY ACT 1990

The Food Premises (Registration) Regulations 1991 require all premises which sell food to be registered with the local authority. It is an offence to use unregistered premises for a food business. Food includes packed baby foods, confectionery, etc.

The General Food Regulations 2004 require food retailers to keep records of the source of food items. Details of the purchaser must be kept if the supply is a wholesale one. Food includes baby foods, baby milks and dietary supplements which are not medicinal products.

THE OFFENSIVE WEAPONS ACT 1996

Section 6 of the Act prohibits the sale of knives and similar objects to people under 16 years old. The prohibited items include 'any knife blade or razor blade' and 'any other article which has a blade or is sharply pointed and which is made or adapted for causing injury to the person'. Items in pharmacies which might fall within these wide definitions include corn knives, metal nail files, scissors and the like.

Self-Assessment Questions

1. What are the general requirements for the sale of poisons in a pharmacy?
   Answer: Generally, poisons in Part I must be sold at the pharmacy by a pharmacist or person lawfully conducting an RPB or under the supervision of the pharmacist. All Schedule I poisons, even those on Part II of the list, must be sold under the supervision of the pharmacist when sold from a pharmacy.
2. How might the COSHH rules apply to pharmacies?
   Answer: The Control of Substances Hazardous to Health Regulations 2002 SI No. 2677 affect the use of hazardous substances in a work situation, by laying down measures which an employer must take to control hazardous substances and to protect people who are exposed to such substances. The regulations require that an employer may not carry on any work that is liable to expose any person to any substance hazardous to health, unless a suitable and sufficient assessment of the risks has been made. A substance hazardous to health includes any substance classed as toxic, very toxic, harmful, corrosive or irritant. This can also include cytotoxic drugs. Thus the COSHH regulations apply when staff is sorting returned medicines for disposal. In such a situation the employer must then:
   1. assess the risk to health from the use of the substance in the workplace,
   2. decide what precautions are needed,
   3. introduce appropriate measures to control the risk,
   4. tell employees about the risk, and about what precautions must be taken,
   5. ensure that precautions are taken,
   6. if appropriate, monitor the exposure and carry out health surveillance.

3. How does the Offensive Weapons Act 1996 apply to pharmacies?
   Answer: *Section 6* of the Act prohibits the sale of knives and similar objects to people under 16 years old. The prohibited items include 'any knife blade or razor blade' and 'any other article which has a blade or is sharply pointed and which is made or adapted for causing injury to the person'. Items in pharmacies which might fall within these wide definitions include corn knives, metal nail files, scissors and the like.

ADDITIONAL RESOURCE

1. http://www.spaceforhealth.nhs.uk/England/topics/health-technical-memorandum-07-01-%E2%80%93-safe-management-healthcare-waste

Chapter 19

Patient Group Directions

WHAT ARE PATIENT GROUP DIRECTIONS

Patient Group Directions (PGDs) (formerly termed as 'group protocols') are written instructions for the supply or administration of named medicines to groups of patients who are not individually identified before they present for treatment.

They are documents which make it legal for medicines to be given to groups of patients – for example in a mass casualty situation – without individual prescriptions having to be written for each patient.

They can also be used to authorise persons who are not 'prescribers', for example paramedics, to legally supply and to administer the medicine in question.

BACKGROUND

The legal framework for medicines control was traditionally based on the principle that doctors prescribe for individual patients. Over time the definition of prescriber has been widened. Some health professionals (e.g., paramedics) are authorised to use medicines in defined circumstances.

In some cases, the legal necessity to have a prescription signed by a doctor and dispensed by a pharmacist restricted the development of new services that were both safe and effective.

To facilitate the development of patient-focused services, organisations within the NHS began to use 'group protocols' under the previous Article 12. Group protocols enabled nurses and other health care professionals to supply or administer medicines directly to certain groups of patients.

In 1998 a report on the Supply and Administration of Medicines under Group Protocols was published. The report recommended that the legal position about protocols for supply should be clarified, and in August 2000 the relevant medicines legislation was amended in respect of the NHS and those services funded by the NHS that were provided by the private, voluntary or charitable sector.

Subsequently, the legislation was further amended to permit the sale, supply or administration of medicines under PGDs in specified health care

Pharmacy Law and Practice. DOI: http://dx.doi.org/10.1016/B978-0-12-394289-0.00019-9

289

establishments throughout the United Kingdom, provided through the private, charitable or voluntary sector, and in certain UK Crown establishments.

PGDs do not extend to independent and public sector care homes or to those independent sector schools that provide health care entirely outside the NHS. They cannot produce PGDs for use within their individual institutions. However, health care professionals who visit patients in nursing and care homes in their routine practice can use PGDs authorised by their own organisations for domiciliary visits.

The Law

Part 12 Chapter 3 of the Human Medicines Regulations contains the current rules. Schedule 16 contains lists of what must be in the PGD and who must sign it.

DEFINITION

The Human Medicines Regulations 2012 contains the following definition in Regulation 213:

"Patient Group Direction" or "PGD" means:
a written direction that relates to the sale or supply and to the administration of a description or class of medicinal product and that:
 (a) is signed:
   (i) by a doctor or dentist and by a pharmacist, and
   (ii) by any other person who may be required to sign it in the circumstances specified for its use in any provision of this Part; and
 (b) relates to sale or supply and to administration to persons generally (subject to any exclusions that may be specified in the PGD).

The legislation applies mainly to the NHS. It includes activity in the private and voluntary sectors which is funded by the NHS. It covers treatment provided by NHS trusts, health authorities, group practitioner (GP) practices, dental practices, walk-in centres, NHS funded family planning clinics and police and prison services.

Apart from those situations where services are funded by the NHS it does not apply to private hospitals or other private or voluntary services. PGDs do not extend to independent and public sector care homes or to those independent sector schools that provide health care entirely outside the NHS.

DIFFERENCES BETWEEN PGDs AND WRITTEN DIRECTIONS

Regulation 229 of the Human Medicines Regulations authorises the supply of a POM by:

(a) the Common Services Agency;

(b) a health authority or special health authority;

(c) an NHS trust;

(d) an NHS foundation trust;

(e) a Primary Care Trust (PCT); or

(f) where the person supplies the product pursuant to an arrangement with one of the persons specified in paragraphs (a)–(e);

provided the supply meets either of the two conditions:

Condition A is that the product is supplied for the purpose of being administered to a person in accordance with the 'written directions' of a doctor, dentist, nurse independent prescriber, optometrist independent prescriber or pharmacist independent prescriber relating to that person, regardless of whether the directions comply with Regulation 217 (requirements for prescriptions). Such directions are patient specific.

Condition B refers to PGDs.

PGDs allow a range of specified health care professionals to supply or administer a medicine directly to a patient with an identified clinical condition without them necessarily seeing a prescriber.

The health care professional working within the PGD is responsible for assessing that the patient fits the criteria set out in the PGD.

A patient-specific direction is used once a patient has been assessed by a prescriber. The prescriber (doctor, dentist or independent nurse prescriber) then instructs another health care professional in writing to supply or administer a medicine directly to that named patient or patients.

Generally speaking, patient-specific directions are a direct instruction and do not require an assessment of the patient by the health care professional instructed to supply or administer the medicine.

TYPES OF PGD

At present there are six main situations for use of a PGD, each with a specific relevant regulation:

(1) Use of a PGD by NHS bodies   (Regulation 229)

(2) Use of a PGD for supply to assist doctors or dentists   (Regulation 230)

(3) Use of a PGD for supply by independent hospitals, etc.   (Regulation 231)

(4) Use of a PGD for supply by dental practices and clinics: England and Wales   (Regulation 232)

(5) Use of a PGD for supply by a pharmacy   (Regulation 233)

(6) Use of a PGD for supply to assist the police, etc.   (Regulation 234)

INFORMATION IN THE PGD ITSELF

The legislation specifies that each PGD must contain the following information:

• the name of the business to which the direction applies;

• the date the direction comes into force and the date it expires;

- a description of the medicine(s) to which the direction applies;
- class of health professional who may supply or administer the medicine;
- signature of a doctor or dentist, as appropriate, and a pharmacist;
- signature by an appropriate organisation;
- the clinical condition or situation to which the direction applies;
- a description of those patients excluded from treatment under the direction;
- a description of the circumstances in which further advice should be sought from a doctor (or dentist, as appropriate) and arrangements for referral;
- details of appropriate dosage and maximum total dosage, quantity, pharmaceutical form and strength, route and frequency of administration and minimum or maximum period over which the medicine should be administered;
- relevant warnings, including potential adverse reactions;
- details of any necessary follow-up action and the circumstances;
- a statement of the records to be kept for audit purposes.

THE GROUPS WHO MAY SUPPLY OR ADMINISTER

The qualified health professionals who may supply or administer medicines under a PGD are:

- nurses
- midwives
- health visitors
- optometrists
- pharmacists
- chiropodists
- radiographers
- orthoptists
- physiotherapists
- ambulance paramedics
- dental hygienists and dental therapists.

They must be named individuals, either in the PGD or in a separate document.

They must be registered members of their profession and act within their own council's code of professional conduct and as described in the PGD.

THE SIGNATURES REQUIRED

The PGD must be signed by a senior doctor (or, if appropriate, a dentist) and a pharmacist, both of whom should have been involved in developing the direction.

Additionally, the PGD must be signed on behalf of the appropriate body as set out in the legislation.

Who Signs for the Appropriate Body

Health care provider
Person by whom or on whose behalf the Direction must be signed.
An independent hospital, clinic or medical agency (England, Wales and Scotland only)
The registered provider and if there is a relevant manager for the hospital, clinic or agency that manager.
A nursing home (Northern Ireland only)
The registered provider and if there is a relevant manager for the home that manager.
A police force in England or Wales
The chief officer of police for that police force and a doctor who is not employed/engaged or providing services to any police force.
A police force in Scotland
The chief constable of that police force and a doctor who is not employed/engaged or providing services to any police force.
The Police Service of Northern Ireland
The Chief Constable of the Police Service of Northern Ireland and a doctor who is not employed/engaged or providing services to any police force.
The prison service in England and Wales
The governor of the prison in relation to which the health care in question is being provided.
The prison service in Scotland
The Scottish Prison Service Management Board.
The prison service in Northern Ireland
The Northern Ireland Prison Service Management Board
Her Majesty's Forces
(i) the Surgeon General,
(ii) a Medical Director General, or
(iii) a chief executive of an executive agency of the Ministry of Defence.

Organisations Where PGDs May Be Used

- A Special Health Authority
- An NHS trust
- A doctor's or dentist's practice, in the provision of NHS services
- A body not run by an NHS body, but providing treatment under an arrangement made with one of the NHS bodies in 1 or 2 above (e.g., a family planning clinic, health centre or walk-in centre)
- Health care services provided by the Prison Services in the United Kingdom
- Health care services provided by police forces in the United Kingdom
- Health care services provided by the Defence Medical Services

- Health care services provided by independent hospitals, clinics and medical agencies as defined in the Care Standards Act 2000, the Regulation of Care Act (Scotland) 2001 and equivalent arrangements in Northern Ireland.

PGDs can be used by all NHS organisations. In addition, those services funded by the NHS but provided by the private, voluntary or charitable sector can also use PGDs.

Providers of specified regulated activities in England are required to register with the Care Quality Commission (CQC).

INDEPENDENT HOSPITALS, CLINICS AND MEDICAL AGENCIES

The Human Medicines Regulations 2012 allow independent hospitals, clinics and medical agencies to authorise their own PGDs if they are registered with the CQC for one of the following activities:

- treatment of disease, disorder or injury;
- assessment or medical treatment of persons detained under the Mental Health Act 1983;
- surgical procedures;
- diagnostic and screening procedures;
- maternity and midwifery services;
- family planning.

The Regulations also allow dental practices and clinics which are registered with the CQC for the treatment of disease, disorder or injury and/or diagnostic and screening procedures to authorise PGDs.

Registered providers are also able to enter into arrangements with an NHS body to supply and administer medicines under a PGD as part of an NHS funded service.

ARRANGEMENTS FOR SCOTLAND

Currently, in Scotland only independent hospitals and hospices are registered under the Regulation of Care (Scotland) Act 2001. No commencement order for independent clinics and independent medical agencies has been made at this time.

PGDs can only be set up for use in independent hospitals and hospices. This will be the case until the Scottish legislative regime governing the regulation of care services is extended to include independent clinics and medical agencies.

Also a PGD signed by a provider of an independent health care service registered in England and Wales cannot be used to authorise the supply or administration of medicines by its own staff in Scotland.

However, a provider registered in England and Wales can enter into an arrangement with a pharmacist based in a Scottish community pharmacy to operate under a PGD. The same applies to the use of PGDs in England and Wales by a provider registered in Scotland.

Labelling of Supplied Products

The labelling and packaging regulations apply to all supplies of medicines, including those supplied under PGDs, for example a patient information leaflet should be made available to patients treated under PGDs.

Medicines Without a Marketing Authorisation

The Human Medicines Regulations require that only licensed medicines may be supplied under a PGD – for example '... when the product is supplied, a marketing authorisation, Article 126a authorisation, certificate of registration or traditional herbal registration is in force in relation to it'.

Exceptional Products

Black triangle drugs (i.e., those recently licensed and subject to special reporting arrangements for adverse reactions) and medicines used outside the terms of the Summary of Product Characteristics (SPC) (e.g., as used in some areas of specialist paediatric care) may be included in PGDs provided such use is exceptional, justified by current best clinical practice and that a direction clearly describes the status of the product. Where the medicine is for children, particular attention will be needed to specify any restrictions on the age, size and maturity of the child. Each PGD should clearly state when the product is being used outside the terms of the SPC and the documentation should include the reasons why, exceptionally, such use is necessary.

CONTROLLED DRUGS

The Misuse of Drugs (Amendment No. 2) (England, Wales and Scotland) Regulations 2012 (SI No. 2012/973), which came into force on 23 April 2012,

(a) authorises the supply of morphine and diamorphine by registered nurses and pharmacists under PGDs in any setting, where administration of such drugs is required for the immediate, necessary treatment of sick or injured persons (excluding the treatment of addiction)

(b) authorises the possession of specific controlled drugs – such as ketamine and midazolam – by health care professionals, including paramedics, under PGDs.

RADIOPHARMACEUTICALS

The administration of radiopharmaceuticals continues to be regulated by the Medicines (Administration of Radioactive Substances) Regulations 1978 and should not be included in PGDs.

EXTRACTS FROM THE HUMAN MEDICINES REGULATIONS

The relevant parts of the Human Medicines Regulations now read as follows:

Regulation 229 Exemption for Supply by NHS Bodies

(1) Regulations 214(1), 220 and 221 do not apply to the supply of a medicinal product in accordance with Condition A or B by:

   (a) the Common Services Agency;

   (b) a health authority or special health authority;

   (c) an NHS trust;

   (d) an NHS foundation trust;

   (e) a PCT; (subject to amendment)

   (f) a person who is not a doctor, dentist or person lawfully conducting a retail pharmacy business (RPB), where the person supplies the product pursuant to an arrangement with one of the persons specified in paragraphs (a)–(e).

(2) Condition A is that the product is supplied for the purpose of being administered to a person in accordance with the written directions of a doctor, dentist, nurse independent prescriber, optometrist independent prescriber or pharmacist independent prescriber relating to that person, regardless of whether the directions comply with Regulation 217 (requirements for prescriptions).

(3) Condition B is that:

   (a) the product is supplied for the purpose of being administered to a person in accordance with a PGD;

   (b) the PGD relates to the supply of a description or class of medicinal product by the person by whom the medicinal product is supplied and has effect at the time at which it is supplied;

   (c) the PGD contains the particulars specified in Part 1 of Schedule 16;

   (d) the PGD is signed on behalf of the person specified in column 2 of the table in Part 2 of that Schedule ('the authorising person') against the entry in column 1 of that table for the class of person by whom the product is supplied;

   (e) the individual who supplies the product:

     (i) belongs to one of the classes of individual specified in Part 4 of that Schedule, and

     (ii) is designated in writing, on behalf of the authorising person, for the purpose of the supply or administration of products under the PGD; and

   (f) when the product is supplied, a marketing authorisation, Article 126a authorisation, certificate of registration or traditional herbal registration is in force in relation to it.

Exemption for Supply, etc. Under a PGD to Assist Doctors or Dentists Regulation 230

(1) *Regulations 214, 220 and 221 do not apply to the supply or administration of a medicinal product by an individual belonging to one of the classes specified in Part 4 of Schedule 16 where:*

    (a) *the individual supplies or (as the case may be) administers the product to assist a doctor in the provision of NHS primary medical services or a dentist in the provision of NHS primary dental services;*

    (b) *the product is supplied for the purpose of being administered to a person in accordance with a PGD; and*

    (c) *the following conditions are met.*

(2) *Condition A is that the PGD relates to the supply or (as the case may be) administration of a description or class of medicinal product in order to assist the doctor or dentist in providing the services (whether or not it relates to such supply in order to assist any other doctor or dentist).*

(3) *Condition B is that the PGD has effect at the time at which the product is supplied or (as the case may be) administered.*

(4) *Condition C is that the PGD contains the particulars specified in Part 1 of Schedule 16 (but with the omission of paragraph 4 in the case of a PGD relating to administration only).*

(5) *Condition D is that the PGD is signed:*

    (a) *by the doctor or dentist; or*

    (b) *where it also relates to supply or administration to assist one or more other doctors or dentists, by one of those doctors or dentists.*

(6) *Condition E is that the PGD is signed:*

    (a) *in the case of:*

        (i) *NHS primary medical services, or*

        (ii) *NHS primary dental services in England or Wales,on behalf of the health authority or PCT with which a contract or agreement for the provision of those services has been made or which provides those services;*

    (b) *in the case of dental services in Scotland under the National Health Service (Scotland) Act 1978(1), or general dental services in Northern Ireland, on behalf of the health authority with which an arrangement for the provision of those services has been made; and*

    (c) *in the case of personal dental services provided under a pilot scheme in Scotland or Northern Ireland, on behalf of the health authority which is a party to the pilot scheme.*

(7) *Condition F is that the individual supplying the product is designated in writing for the purpose of the supply or (as the case may be) administration of medicinal products under the PGD:*

    (a) *by the doctor or dentist; or*

    (b) *where it also relates to supply to assist one or more other doctors or dentists, by one of those doctors or dentists.*

(8) *Condition G is that when the product is supplied or (as the case may be) administered, a marketing authorisation, Article 126a authorisation, certificate of registration or traditional herbal registration is in force in relation to it.*

Exemption for Supply, etc. Under a PGD by Independent Hospitals, etc. Regulation 231

(1) Regulations 214, 220 and 221 do not apply to the sale or supply, or administration, of a medicinal product in accordance with the following conditions by:

(a) an independent hospital;

(b) an independent clinic;

(c) an independent medical agency; or

(d) a nursing home (in Northern Ireland).

(2) Condition A, which applies only to England, is that the registered provider at the hospital, clinic or agency is registered in compliance with Section 10 of the Health and Social Care Act 2008(1) in respect of one or more of the following regulated activities(2):

(a) treatment of disease, disorder or injury;

(b) assessment or medical treatment of persons detained under the Mental Health Act 1983;

(c) surgical procedures;

(d) diagnostic and screening procedures;

(e) maternity and midwifery services; and

(f) family planning.

(3) Condition B is that the product is sold or supplied for the purpose of being administered to a person in accordance with a PGD.

(4) Condition C is that the PGD:

(a) relates to the sale or supply or (as the case may be) administration of a description or class of medicinal product by the person by whom the medicinal product is sold or supplied or administered; and

(b) has effect at the time at which it is sold or supplied.

(5) Condition D is that the PGD contains the particulars specified in Part 1 of Schedule 16 (but with the omission of paragraph 4 in the case of a PGD relating to administration only).

(6) Condition E is that the PGD is signed:

(a) by or on behalf of the registered provider; and

(b) if there is a relevant manager for the independent hospital, clinic or medical agency, or nursing home, by that manager.

(7) Condition F is that the individual who sells or supplies or (as the case may be) administers the product:

(a) belongs to one of the classes of individual specified in Part 4 of Schedule 16; and

(b) is designated in writing for the purpose of the sale or supply or (as the case may be) administration of products under the PGD:

(i) by or on behalf of the registered provider, or

(ii) if there is a relevant manager for the independent hospital, clinic or medical agency, or nursing home, by that manager.

(8) Condition G is that when the product is supplied, a marketing authorisation, Article 126a authorisation, certificate of registration or traditional herbal registration is in force in relation to it.

Exemption for Supply, etc. Under a PGD by Dental Practices and Clinics: England and Wales Regulation 232

(1)   Regulations 214, 220 and 221 do not apply to the sale or supply, or administration, of a medicinal product in accordance with the following conditions by:

   (a)   a dental practice in England and Wales to which paragraph (2) applies; or

   (b)   a dental clinic in England and Wales to which paragraph (2) applies.

(2)   This paragraph applies to a dental practice or dental clinic:

   (a)   in England, in respect of which the registered provider is registered in compliance with Section 10 of the Health and Social Care Act 2008 in respect of one or both of the following regulated activities:

      (i)   treatment of disease, disorder or injury, or

      (ii)   diagnostic and screening procedures;

   (b)   in Wales, in which dental services are provided by private dentists and those dentists are registered with Healthcare Inspectorate Wales in accordance with the Private Dentistry (Wales) Regulations 2008(1), in relation to the services provided by those dentists.

(3)   Condition A is that the product is sold or supplied for the purpose of being administered to a person in accordance with a PGD.

(4)   Condition B is that the PGD:

   (a)   relates to the sale or supply or (as the case may be) administration of a description or class of medicinal product by the person by whom the medicinal product is sold or supplied or administered; and

   (b)   has effect at the time at which it is sold or supplied.

(5)   Condition C is that the PGD contains the particulars specified in Part 1 of Schedule 16 (but with the omission of paragraph 4 in the case of a PGD relating to administration only).

(6)   Condition D is that the PGD is signed:

   (a)   in England:

      (i)   by or on behalf of the registered provider, and

      (ii)   if there is a relevant manager for the practice or clinic, by that manager;

   (b)   in Wales:

      (i)   by the private dentist who is treating the person, and

      (ii)   if there is a manager for the practice or clinic, by that manager.

(7)   Condition E is that the individual who sells or supplies or (as the case may be) administers the product:

   (a)   belongs to one of the classes of individual specified in Part 4 of Schedule 16; and

   (b)   is designated in writing for the purpose of the sale or supply or (as the case may be) administration of products under the PGD:

      (i)   in England:

         by or on behalf of the registered provider, or

         if there is a relevant manager for the practice or clinic, by that manager, or

      (ii)   in Wales, by the private dentist who is treating the person.

(8)   Condition F is that when the product is supplied, a marketing authorisation, Article 126a authorisation, certificate of registration or traditional herbal registration is in force in relation to it.

(9)   In relation to Wales, in this regulation 'manager' means:

　　(a)   a person who carries on the dental practice or dental clinic; or

　　(b)   if there is no such person, a person who manages the practice or clinic.

Exemption for Supply, etc. Under a PGD by a Pharmacy Regulation 233

(1)   Regulation 214 does not apply to the sale or supply, or administration, of a prescription only medicine (POM) by a person lawfully conducting an RPB where:

　　(a)   the person sells, supplies or (as the case may be) administers the POM pursuant to an arrangement for the supply or administration of POMs with:

　　　　(i)   the Common Services Agency,

　　　　(ii)   a health authority or special health authority,

　　　　(iii)   an NHS trust,

　　　　(iv)   an NHS foundation trust,

　　　　(v)   a PCT,

　　　　(vi)   a police force in England, Wales or Scotland,

　　　　(vii)   the Police Service of Northern Ireland,

　　　　(viii)   a prison service,

　　　　(ix)   Her Majesty's Forces, or

　　　　(x)   an authority or a person carrying on the business of an independent hospital, an independent clinic, an independent medical agency or, in Northern Ireland, a nursing home;

　　(b)   the POM is sold or supplied for the purpose of being supplied or (as the case may be) is administered to a person in accordance with a PGD; and

　　(c)   the following conditions are met.

(2)   Condition A is that the PGD relates to the sale or supply or (as the case may be) administration of a description or class of medicinal product by the person lawfully conducting an RPB who sells or supplies or (as the case may be) administers the POM.

(3)   Condition B is that the PGD has effect at the time at which the POM is sold or supplied or (as the case may be) administered.

(4)   Condition C is that the PGD contains the particulars specified in Part 1 of Schedule 16 (but with the omission of paragraph 4 in the case of a PGD relating to administration only).

(5)   Condition D is that the PGD is signed:

　　(a)   in the case of an arrangement with a body referred to in paragraph (1)(a) (i)–(v) (health bodies), on behalf of that body;

　　(b)   in the case of an arrangement with a police force in England, Wales or Scotland or with the Police Service of Northern Ireland:

　　　　(i)   by or on behalf of a person specified in column 2 of Part 3 of Schedule 16 against the entry in column 1 for that body, and

     (ii) *by a doctor who is not employed or engaged by, and does not provide services under arrangements made with, any police force or the Police Service of Northern Ireland;*

  (c) *in the case of an arrangement with a prison service, by or on behalf of a person specified in column 2 of Part 3 of Schedule 16 against the entry in column 1 for that body;*

  (d) *in the case of an arrangement with Her Majesty's Forces, by or on behalf of a person specified in column 2 of Part 3 of Schedule 16 against the entry in column 1 for Her Majesty's Forces;*

  (e) *in the case of an arrangement with an authority or person referred to in paragraph (1)(a)(x) (independent hospitals, etc.):*

     (i) *by or on behalf of the registered provider, and*

     (ii) *if there is a relevant manager for the establishment or agency in question, by that manager.*

(6) *Condition E is that, where the POM is administered by the person lawfully conducting an RPB, the person belongs to one of the classes of individual specified in Part 4 of Schedule 16 and is designated in writing for the purpose of the administration of medicinal products under the PGD:*

  (a) *in the case of an arrangement with a body referred to in paragraph (1)(a)(i)–(v) (health bodies), on behalf of that body;*

  (b) *in the case of an arrangement with a body referred to in paragraph (1)(a)(vi)–(ix) (a police force, the Police Service of Northern Ireland, a prison service and Her Majesty's Forces), by or on behalf of a person specified in column 2 of Part 3 of Schedule 16 against the entry in column 1 for that body; and*

  (c) *in the case of an arrangement with an authority or a person referred to in paragraph (1)(a)(x) (independent hospitals, etc.):*

     (i) *by or on behalf of the registered provider, or*

     (ii) *if there is a relevant manager for the establishment or agency in question, by that manager.*

(7) *Condition F is that when the POM is supplied or (as the case may be) administered, a marketing authorisation, Article 126a authorisation, certificate of registration or traditional herbal registration is in force in relation to it.*

Exemption for Supply, etc. of Products Under a PGD to Assist the Police, etc. Regulation 234

(1) *Regulations 214, 220 and 221 do not apply to the supply or administration of a medicinal product by an individual belonging to one of the classes specified in Part 4 of Schedule 16 in accordance with the following conditions.*

(2) *Condition A is that the individual supplies or (as the case may be) administers the product to assist the provision of health care by, on behalf of, or under arrangements made by, one of the following bodies ('the relevant body'):*

  (a) *a police force in England and Wales or in Scotland;*

  (b) *the Police Service of Northern Ireland;*

  (c) *a prison service; or*

  (d) *Her Majesty's Forces.*

(3) *Condition B is that the product is supplied for the purpose of being administered to a person in accordance with a PGD.*

(4) *Condition C is that the PGD relates to the supply or (as the case may be) administration of a description or class of medicinal product to assist the provision of health care by, on behalf of, or under arrangements made by, the relevant body.*

(5) *Condition D is that the PGD has effect at the time at which the product is supplied or (as the case may be) administered.*

(6) *Condition E is that the PGD contains the particulars specified in Part 1 of Schedule 16 (but with the omission of paragraph 4 in the case of a PGD relating to administration only).*

(7) *Condition F is that the PGD is signed:*
   (a) *by or on behalf of a person specified in column 2 of Part 3 of Schedule 16 against the entry in column 1 for the relevant body; and*
   (b) *where the relevant body is a police force or the Police Service of Northern Ireland, by a doctor who is not employed or engaged by, and does not provide services under arrangements made with, any police force or the Police Service of Northern Ireland.*

(8) *Condition G is that the individual who supplies the product is designated in writing by or on behalf of the relevant body for the purpose of the supply or (as the case may be) administration of medicinal products under the PGD.*

(9) *Condition H is that when the product is supplied, a marketing authorisation, Article 126a authorisation, certificate of registration or traditional herbal registration is in force in relation to it.*

Self-Assessment Questions

1. What is a PGD?

   Answer: A 'PGD' is a written direction that relates to the sale or supply and to the administration of a description or class of medicinal product. It must be signed by a doctor or dentist and by a pharmacist, and by another person who is defined in the relevant regulation. The direction relates to sale or supply and to administration to persons generally (subject to any exclusions that may be specified in the PGD).

2. How may PGDs be used in private clinics?

   Answer: The legislation applies mainly to the NHS. It includes activity in the private and voluntary sectors which is funded by the NHS. It covers treatment provided by NHS trusts, health authorities, GP practices, dental practices, walk-in centres, NHS funded family planning clinics and police and prison services. Apart from those situations where services are funded by the NHS it does not apply to private hospitals or clinics or other private or voluntary services. PGDs do not extend to independent and public sector care homes or to those independent sector schools that provide health care entirely outside the NHS.

3. What is a patient-specific direction?

   Answer: A patient-specific direction is used once a patient has been assessed by a prescriber. The prescriber (doctor, dentist or independent nurse prescriber) then instructs another health care professional in writing to supply or administer a medicine directly to that named patient or patients. Generally speaking, patient-specific directions are a direct instruction and do not require an assessment of the patient by the health care professional instructed to supply or administer the medicine.

Chapter 20

Non-Medical Prescribing

BACKGROUND

The final report of the Review of Prescribing, Supply and Administration of Medicines (1999)[1] recommended that two types of prescriber should be recognised:

(a) An independent prescriber who would be responsible for the assessment of patients with undiagnosed conditions and for decisions about the clinical management required, including prescribing.

(b) A dependent prescriber who would be responsible for the continuing care of patients who have been clinically assessed by an independent prescriber. The term 'Dependent Prescriber' used in the Report has been replaced by the term 'Supplementary Prescriber'.

Continuing Care

The Report envisaged that this continuing care might include prescribing, which would be informed by clinical guidelines and be consistent with individual treatment plans or might consist of continuing an established treatment by issuing repeat prescriptions, with the authority to adjust the dose or dosage form according to the patients' needs.

The Review recommended that there should be provision for regular clinical review by the assessing clinician.

WHAT IS NON-MEDICAL PRESCRIBING?

Non-medical prescribing is prescribing by specially trained pharmacists and other health professionals, working within their clinical competence as either independent or supplementary prescribers.

Pharmacy Law and Practice. DOI: http://dx.doi.org/10.1016/B978-0-12-394289-0.00020-5

LEGISLATION

Section 63 of the Health and Social Care Act 2001 enabled the Government to extend prescribing responsibilities to other health professions.

It also enabled the introduction of new types of prescriber, including the concept of a supplementary prescriber, by allowing Ministers to make regulations which attach conditions to their prescribing.

Section 42 (for England and Wales) and *Section 44* (Scotland) of the Act relate to the dispensing by community pharmacists of prescriptions written by these new prescribers.

Amendments to the Prescription Only Medicines Order and to National Health Service (NHS) regulations enabled the introduction of supplementary prescribing for first level registered nurses, registered midwives and registered pharmacists from April 2003.

Amendments in April 2005 enabled chiropodists/podiatrists, physiotherapists and radiographers to become supplementary prescribers.

Further amendments in July 2005 enabled optometrists to become supplementary prescribers.

More recent amendments have added to the range of professions and extended the drugs which may be prescribed.

The current legislation is the Human Medicines Regulations 2012.

What Is Independent Prescribing?

Independent prescribing is

prescribing by a practitioner (e.g., doctor, dentist, nurse, pharmacist or optometrist) who is responsible and accountable for the assessment of patients and for decisions about the clinical management required, including prescribing.

What Is Supplementary Prescribing?

The working definition of supplementary prescribing is

a voluntary partnership between an independent prescriber (a doctor or dentist) and a supplementary prescriber to implement an agreed patient-specific Clinical Management Plan with the patient's agreement.

INDEPENDENT PRESCRIBING

In practice, there are TWO distinct forms of non-medical independent prescriber.

(i) An independent prescriber may currently be a specially trained pharmacist, nurse, midwife or optometrist who can prescribe any licensed medicine within their clinical competence. Nurse and pharmacist independent prescribers can also prescribe unlicensed medicines.

(ii) A community practitioner nurse prescriber (CPNP) can independently prescribe from a limited formulary called the Nurse Prescribers' Formulary for Community Practitioners (NPFCP), which can be found in the British National Formulary. This formulary includes the majority of dressings and appliances, and a limited range of prescription only medicines (POMs), such as some treatments for head lice, thrush and pain relief.

Legislation limits the prescribing of POMs to 'appropriate prescribers'. Chapter 3 of the regulations then sets out certain circumstances which are exceptions to this rule.

Regulation 214 of the Human Medicines Regulations requires that POM medicines may only be sold or supplied on a prescription from 'an appropriate prescriber' which is a doctor, a dentist, a supplementary prescriber, a nurse independent prescriber, and a pharmacist independent prescriber.

A CPNP may be an appropriate practitioner in relation to a POM which is specified in Schedule 13.

An optometrist independent prescriber may be an appropriate practitioner in relation to any POM other than a CD or an injection.

An European Economic Area (EEA) health professional may be an appropriate practitioner in relation to any POM which is not a CD.

214.—(1) A person may not sell or supply a prescription only medicine except in accordance with a prescription given by an appropriate practitioner.

(2) A person may not parenterally administer (otherwise than to himself or herself) a prescription only medicine unless the person is:

(a) an appropriate practitioner other than an EEA health professional; or

(b) acting in accordance with the directions of such an appropriate practitioner.

(3) The following are appropriate practitioners in relation to any prescription only medicine:

(a) a doctor;

(b) a dentist;

(c) a supplementary prescriber;

(d) a nurse independent prescriber; and

(e) a pharmacist independent prescriber.

(4) A community practitioner nurse prescriber is an appropriate practitioner in relation to a prescription only medicine specified in Schedule 13.

(5) An optometrist independent prescriber is an appropriate practitioner in relation to any prescription only medicine other than:

(a) a medicinal product that is a controlled drug; or

(b) a medicinal product that is for parenteral administration.

(6) An EEA health professional is an appropriate practitioner in relation to any prescription only medicine other than a controlled drug.

(7) This regulation is subject to Chapter 3 (exemptions)

SUPPLEMENTARY PRESCRIBING

According to the Department of Health the supplementary prescribing program is designed 'to ease the burden on doctors and improve access to medicines'. Supplementary Prescribing has two tiers:

(a) Doctors or dentists ('independent prescribers') are responsible for the diagnosis of the patient and for determining the class or description of medicines that may be prescribed by the supplementary prescriber under a Clinical Management Plan (CMP) for the patient.

(b) Other health professionals ('supplementary prescribers') who are responsible for the continuing care of the patient in accordance with a CMP. They have authority to prescribe specific medicines for particular medical conditions in accordance with the Plan.

215.—(1) A supplementary prescriber ("S") may not give a prescription for a prescription only medicine unless S meets conditions A and C.

(2) A supplementary prescriber ("S") may not:

    (a) parenterally administer a POM; or

    (b) give directions for the parenteral administration of a POM,

unless S meets conditions B and C.(3) Condition A is that S is acting in accordance with the terms of a clinical management plan that:

    (a) relates to the patient to whom the product is prescribed;

    (b) has effect when the prescription is given; and

    (c) includes the particulars specified in Schedule 14.

(4) Condition B is that S is acting in accordance with the terms of a clinical management plan that:

    (a) relates to the patient to whom the product is, or is to be, administered;

    (b) has effect when the product is administered or (as the case may be) the direction is given; and

    (c) includes the particulars specified in Schedule 14.

(5) Condition C is that S has access to health records that:

    (a) are the health records of the patient to whom the plan relates; and

    (b) are used by any doctor or dentist who is a party to the plan.

(6) This regulation is subject to regulation 216.

(7) In this regulation:

    "clinical management plan" means a written plan (which may be amended from time to time) relating to the treatment of an individual patient agreed by:

        (a) the patient to whom the plan relates;

        (b) the doctor or dentist who is a party to the plan; and

        (c) any supplementary prescriber who is to prescribe, give directions for administration or administer under the plan;

    "health record" has the meaning given by section 68(2) of the Data Protection Act 1998(1).

Definition of 'Supplementary Prescriber'

The definition of 'supplementary prescriber' is in Regulation 8 of the Human Medicines Regulations

"supplementary prescriber" means a person who is noted in the relevant register as qualified to order drugs, medicines and appliances as a supplementary prescriber (or, in the case of a registered nurse or registered midwife, as a nurse independent/ supplementary prescriber) and is:

  (a) a pharmacist;
  (b) a registered midwife;
  (c) a registered nurse;
  (d) a chiropodist, podiatrist, physiotherapist or radiographer; or
  (e) a registered optometrist.

The 'Relevant Register'

The 'relevant register' means:

  (a) in relation to a pharmacist:
      (i) in Great Britain, Part 1 of the Register of pharmacists and pharmacy technicians maintained under Article 19(2) of the Pharmacy Order 2010, or
      (ii) in Northern Ireland, the register maintained in pursuance of Articles 6 and 9 of the Pharmacy (Northern Ireland) Order 1976;
  (b) in relation to a registered nurse or registered midwife, the professional register;
  (c) in relation to a registered optometrist, the register of optometrists maintained under Section 7(a) of the Opticians Act 1989 or the register of visiting optometrists from relevant European States maintained under Section 8B(1)(a) of that Act; and
  (d) in relation to a chiropodist or podiatrist, a physiotherapist or a radiographer, the part of the Health and Care Professions Council register relating to:
      (i) chiropodists and podiatrists,
      (ii) physiotherapists, or
      (iii) radiographers.

THE CLINICAL MANAGEMENT PLAN

Regulation 215 of the Human Medicines Regulations defines a 'Clinical Management Plan (see above).

Before supplementary prescribing can take place, it is obligatory for an agreed CMP to be in place (written or electronic) relating to a named patient and to that patient's specific condition(s) to be managed by the supplementary prescriber. This should be included in the patient record.

Schedule 14 of the Human Medicines Regulations specifies that the CMP must include the following:

- The name of the patient to whom the plan relates.
- The illness or conditions which may be treated by the supplementary prescriber.
- The date on which the plan is to take effect, and when it is to be reviewed by the doctor or dentist who is party to the plan.
- Reference to the class or description of medicines or types of appliances which may be prescribed or administered under the plan.
- Any restrictions or limitations of strength or dose of any medicine which may be prescribed or administered under the plan, and any period of administration or use of any medicine or appliance which may be prescribed or administered under the plan.
- Relevant warnings about known sensitivities of the patient to or known difficulties that the patient may have with particular medicines or appliances.
- The arrangements for notification of:
  (a) Suspected or known reactions of clinical significance to any medicine which may be prescribed or administered under the plan and suspected or known clinically significant adverse reactions to any other medicine taken at the same time as any medicine prescribed or administered under the plan.
  (b) Incidents occurring with the appliance which might lead, might have led or has led to the death or serious deterioration of state of health of the patient.
- The circumstances in which the supplementary prescriber should refer to, or seek the advice of, the doctor or dentist who is party to the plan.

What May Be Prescribed by Supplementary Prescribers?

Nurse and pharmacist supplementary prescribers are able to prescribe any medicines that are listed in an agreed CMP.

These may include any:

- General Sales List, Pharmacy, or POM prescribable at NHS expense
- Antimicrobials
- 'Black triangle' drugs and those products suggested by the British National Formulary to be 'less suitable' for prescribing Controlled Drugs (except those listed in Schedule 1 of 'The Misuse of Drugs Regulations 2001' that are not intended for medicinal use)
- Products used outside their UK licensed indications (i.e., 'off-label' use). Such use must have the joint agreement of both prescribers and the status of the drug should be recorded in the CMP
- Unlicensed drugs (i.e., a product that is not licensed in the United Kingdom).

There are no legal restrictions on the clinical conditions that may be dealt with by a supplementary prescriber.

The Department of Health advises that supplementary prescribing is primarily intended for use in managing specific long-term medical conditions or health needs affecting the patient. However, acute episodes occurring within long-term conditions may be included in these arrangements, provided they are included in the CMP.

PARENTERAL ADMINISTRATION BY SUPPLEMENTARY PRESCRIBERS

In order to legally

(a) parenterally administer a POM or
(b) give directions for the parenteral administration of a POM
  - a supplementary prescriber must act accordance with the plan and have access to health records, or
  - the supplementary prescriber must act in accordance with the directions of another person who is an appropriate practitioner (other than a supplementary prescriber or an EEA health professional) in relation to the POM in question

Community Practitioner Nurse Prescriber

'Community practitioner nurse prescriber" means a person:

(a) *who is a registered nurse or a registered midwife; and*
(b) *against whose name is recorded in the professional register an annotation signifying that the person is qualified to order drugs, medicines and appliances from the Nurse Prescribers' Formulary for Community Practitioners in the current edition of the British National Formulary.*

Schedule 13 enables the prescribing by CPNPs of the limited range of POMs referred to above

CPNPs are treated as 'appropriate practitioners' when prescribing the following medicines POM listed in Schedule 13. They do not have to meet the conditions in Regulation 215 but must comply with Regulation 214.

Co-danthramer Capsules NPF
Co-danthramer Capsules Strong NPF
Co-danthramer Oral Suspension NPF
Co-danthramer Oral Suspension Strong NPF
Co-danthrusate Capsules
Co-danthrusate Oral Suspension NPF
Mebendazole Tablets NPF

Mebendazole Oral Suspension NPF
Miconazole Oral Gel NPF
Nystatin Oral Suspension
Nystatin Pastilles NPF
Streptokinase and Streptodornase Topical Powder NPF
Water for injections

In this Schedule 'NPF' means the Nurse Prescribers' Formulary Appendix in the British National Formulary.

Controlled Drugs

The Misuse of Drugs Regulations 2001 were amended by the Misuse of Drugs (Amendment) Regulations 2005 No. 271 to enable nurse and pharmacist supplementary prescribers to prescribe some controlled drugs.

Further amendment by the Misuse of Drugs (Amendment 2) (England, Wales, and Scotland) Regulations 2012 SI No 973 came into effect from 23 April 2012. As a result:

- Independent pharmacist prescribers and independent nurse prescribers are now enabled to prescribe, administer and give directions for the administration of Schedules 2, 3, 4 and 5 controlled drugs.
- Neither independent pharmacist nor nurse prescribers will be able to prescribe diamorphine, dipipanone or cocaine for treating addiction but may prescribe these items for treating organic disease or injury.

The GMS/PMS regulations which came into effect on 14 April 2005 enabled supplementary prescribers to prescribe CDs in NHS primary care situations.

AHPs supplementary prescribers may not prescribe Controlled Drugs.

Nurse independent prescribers who work in substance misuse can now supply articles for administering or preparing controlled drugs.

Registration Conditions to Undertake Independent Non-Medical Prescribing

Nurses and Midwives

The Nursing and Midwifery Council (NMC) keeps a register of all nurses and midwives that are qualified to prescribe.

Undertaking a nurse/midwife independent and supplementary prescribing programme is a mandatory requirement for those practitioners who wish to prescribe. This leads to recognition by the NMC as possessing a licence as a prescriber.

Course Eligibility

To be eligible for the course applicants must meet the following NMC requirements:

- Have been qualified at least 3 years with the last year in the clinical area in which they intend to prescribe.
- Have been deemed competent to assess and diagnose within their proposed area of prescribing practice.
- Have the required numeracy and literacy skills.
- If employed by the NHS, must ensure that they have the written support of the designated non medical prescribing lead within their trust.
- The applicant must have had a successful CRB check within the previous 3 years.
- Before enrolling on the course applicants need to have secured the agreement of a designated medical practitioner to supervise them during the practice placement days.

Successful completion of the training course enables a nurse to qualify as both a nurse independent prescriber and a supplementary prescriber.

Pharmacists

Pharmacists in England have been able to train as independent prescribers since autumn 2006.

All pharmacists must meet the following requirements:

- Current registration with GPhC and/or PSNI as a practising pharmacist.
- Have at least 2 years appropriate patient-orientated experience practising in a hospital, community or primary care setting following their pre-registration year.
- Identify an area of clinical practice and need in which to develop their prescribing skills.
- Have up-to-date clinical, pharmacological and pharmaceutical knowledge relevant to their intended area of prescribing practice.
- Demonstrate how they reflect on their own performance and take responsibility for their own CPD.
- Demonstrate how they will develop their own networks for support, reflection and learning, including prescribers from other professions.

Pharmacists qualify as both independent and supplementary prescribers on successful completion of the prescribing course.

Registration Conditions to Undertake Supplementary Prescribing

A nurse supplementary prescriber must be a first level Registered Nurse or Registered Midwife whose name in each case is held on the NMC professional register, with an annotation signifying that the nurse has successfully completed an approved programme of preparation and training for supplementary prescribing.

All newly qualified district nurses and health visitors are able to prescribe from the NPFCP, as training is built into their specialist practitioner programme.

They are not able to prescribe as nurse independent prescribers from a full formulary without undergoing the specific training programme.

A pharmacist supplementary prescriber must be a registered pharmacist whose name is held on the GPhC register with an annotation signifying that the pharmacist has successfully completed an approved programme of training for supplementary prescribing.

A supplementary prescriber who is a chiropodist/podiatrist, physiotherapist or radiographer must be a registered professional whose name is held on the relevant part of the Health Professions Council membership register with an annotation signifying that the individual registrant has successfully completed an approved programme of training for supplementary prescribing.

A supplementary prescriber who is an optometrist must be a registered optometrist whose name is entered in the register of optometrists maintained under *Section 7(a)* of the Opticians Act 1989.

NUMBERS OF NON-MEDICAL PRESCRIBERS

According to the NMC, nurse and midwife prescribing is now widespread practice across the United Kingdom with approximately 54,000 nurse and midwife prescribers across the four UK countries (NMC March 2010).

Over 1 million items were prescribed each month by non-medical prescribers in primary care on FP10 prescription in England in 2009.

It was estimated in 2011 that a total of 47,725 prescribers were made up of

Community Practitioner Nurse Prescribers   26,023
Nurse Independent/Supplementary Prescribers   19,357
Pharmacist Independent/Supplementary Prescribers   1,531
Pharmacist Supplementary Prescribers   336
Optometrist Independent Prescribers   87
Physiotherapist Supplementary Prescribers   219
Podiatrist Supplementary Prescribers   143
Radiographer Supplementary Prescribers   29

The Future

A Department of Health report in 2009 'Allied health professions prescribing and medicines supply mechanisms scoping project report' recommended that several other members of the Allied Health Profession be given prescribing rights.

Self-Assessment Questions

1. What is the difference between independent and supplementary prescribing?
   Answer: Independent prescribing is prescribing by a practitioner (e.g., doctor, dentist, nurse, pharmacist or optometrist) who is responsible and accountable for the assessment of patients and for decisions about the clinical management required, including prescribing.

   Supplementary prescribing is a voluntary partnership between an independent prescriber (a doctor or dentist) and a supplementary prescriber to implement an agreed patient-specific CMP with the patient's agreement.

2. How can independent nurse prescribers write prescriptions for CDs?
   Answer: Independent pharmacist prescribers and independent nurse prescribers are enabled by the legislation to prescribe, administer and give directions for the administration of Schedules 2, 3, 4 and 5 controlled drugs. Neither independent pharmacist nor nurse prescribers will be able to prescribe diamorphine, dipipanone or cocaine for treating addiction but may prescribe these items for treating organic disease or injury.

ADDITIONAL RESOURCE

1. http://www.dh.gov.uk/assetRoot/04/07/71/53/04077153.pdf

Chapter 21

Rights of Access

ACCESS TO PHARMACIES

Because of the complex nature of community pharmacy, as a business, a profession and as retailers, many organisations have statutory rights of access to pharmacies.

As well as entry to premises some persons are able to access records and information stored there.

GPhC INSPECTORS

Articles 10–12 of the Pharmacy Order 2010 give a General Pharmaceutical Council (GPhC) Inspector the power to enter any registered pharmacy premises at any reasonable hour in order to conduct an inspection. The Inspector must provide evidence of identity and that they are an authorised GPhC Inspector. Advance notification is not required; however the GPhC will normally give advance notice and also ask the pharmacist to complete a self-assessment form.

The GPhC website contains a checklist indicating what an inspector is looking for,[1] and the Controlled Drug self-assessment form.[2]

The inspectors are divided into three regional groups: the Northern, Central and South-Eastern region, each of which is managed by a Regional Lead Inspector.

Section 8 of the Pharmacy Order sets out the functions of inspectors:

- Inspection visits – to registered pharmacy premises to monitor and secure compliance with relevant legal requirements and professional standards.
- Investigations – following complaints and allegations involving registered pharmacists or registered pharmacy technicians.

The inspector may also formally interview pharmacists, their employees or owners of pharmacies in accordance with the provisions of the Police and Criminal Evidence Act 1984 and the relevant Codes of Practice made under that Act and may seize evidence as part of the investigation.

Pharmacy Law and Practice. DOI: http://dx.doi.org/10.1016/B978-0-12-394289-0.00021-7

It is an offence to intentionally obstruct an inspector exercising the functions under Article 10 or 11, or to fail to give any assistance or information that the inspector may reasonably require for the performance of those functions.

Inspectors also provide advice on compliance issues and liaise with other regulatory and enforcement agencies such as the police, the Care Quality Commission and the Medicines and Healthcare Products Regulatory Agency.

REGULATION OF INVESTIGATORY POWERS ACT 2000

This Act sets out a legal framework for the interception of communications, surveillance in the course of authorised investigations and related matters. It provides exemptions from the general human rights set out in the Human Rights Act 1998, which make it unlawful for a public authority to act in a way, which is incompatible with any of the Convention rights, including the right to privacy.

Any organisation listed in Schedule 1 of Regulation of Investigatory Powers (RIPA) as a public authority can authorise directed covert surveillance under *Section 28*, as part of investigations to detect or prevent crime, or in the interests of public safety or public health, among other purposes.

The GPhC is listed under Part 11 of Schedule 1 as a relevant authority. The change from the Royal Pharmaceutical Society of Great Britain (RPSGB) was made in Schedule 1 of the Pharmacy Order 2010. At the time of writing no corresponding change has yet been made to the RIPA (Directed Surveillance and Covert Human Intelligence Sources) Order 2010, which prescribes who (at the relevant public authority) is lawfully entitled to grant directed surveillance authorisations. Currently, the Order still lists the RPSGB (the former regulator) in schedule 1 part 2.

Therefore, the current position is that the GPhC is unable to undertake directed surveillance until this position is changed.

DIRECTED SURVEILLANCE

Under the Act, directed surveillance is defined under *Section 26(2)* as covert surveillance which does not entail the presence of individuals or use of monitoring devices on residential premises or in private vehicles. The surveillance must also be proportionate and be carried out for the purposes of a specific investigation. It may only be authorised by the Society for one of these three reasons:

(i) for the purpose of preventing or detecting crime or for preventing disorder
(ii) in the interests of public safety
(iii) for the purpose of protecting public health.

Authorisations have to be given in writing, other than in urgent cases, and must specify the nature of the surveillance, the circumstances in which it is to be carried out and the nature of the investigation being undertaken. Oral authorisations expire after 72 h, unless renewed; written authorisations are valid for 3 months, unless renewed.

Authorisation is necessary for investigations which might lead to either criminal action or fitness to practice proceedings.

The Act is in force in England and Wales, but by virtue of the RIPA (Authorisations Extending to Scotland) Order SI 2000/2418 (as amended) the GPhC's authority extends to Scotland.

Covert Human Intelligence Sources (CHIS)

The GPhC is not permitted to authorise the use of a CHIS, that is person who establishes or maintains a personal or other relationship for the purpose of (i) covertly using the relationship to obtain information or provide access to information about another person or (ii) covertly disclosing information obtained by the use of such a relationship.

Intrusive Surveillance

The GPhC is not permitted to authorise 'intrusive surveillance'. This is defined in the Act as covert surveillance carried out in relation to anything taking place on any residential premises or in any private vehicle and involves the presence of an individual on the premises or in the vehicle or is carried out by means of a surveillance device.

This does not preclude inspectors carrying out directed covert surveillance on a person and noting vehicle registration plates and movements in and out of residential properties.

Test purchases

Test purchases do not require authorisation under RIPA.

These are usually undertaken when an inspector has received allegations that sales of restricted medicines (e.g., pharmacy only and prescription only medicines) are being made in the absence of a pharmacist. Test purchases involve a member of the inspectorate entering a pharmacy in an area where they are unknown in order to purchase a restricted medicine and make a request to speak to the pharmacist on duty. Test purchases may also be used as a means to test a pharmacist's competence.

NHS COMMISSIONING BOARD

The Terms of Service for Chemists provides that a person authorised by the NHSCB, may at any reasonable time on request, inspect the premises of pharmacies providing NHS pharmaceutical services (NHS PS). This is for the purpose of (a) ascertaining compliance with the TOS and (b) auditing, monitoring and analysing the provision and management of patient care and treatment.

A pharmacy undertaking NHS PS must also, on request, make available to the NHS CB any information required to audit, monitor and analyse the provision for patient care and the management of the services provided.

Inspections and Review

Schedule 4 of the NHS(P & LPS) Regulations 2013 Paragraph 28(2) (a) (vi)

An NHS pharmacist must, in connection with the PS, participate in the manner reasonably required by the NHS CB in an acceptable system of clinical governance which comprises the following components—(inter alia)

a requirement that P co-operates appropriately with any reasonable inspection or review that the NHS CB or any relevant statutory authority wishes to undertake.

Paragraph 35 Inspections and Access to Information

(1) An NHS pharmacist must allow persons authorised in writing by the NHS CB to enter and inspect the pharmacy premises at any reasonable time, for the purposes of:

  (a) ascertaining whether or not the pharmacist is complying with the requirements of this Schedule;

  (b) auditing, monitoring and analysing:

  (i) the provision made by the pharmacist, in the course of providing PS, for patient care and treatment, including any arrangement made with a person in respect of provision of appliances, and

  (ii) the management by the pharmacist of the PS provided, where the conditions in sub-paragraph (2) are satisfied.

(2) The conditions are that:

  (a) reasonable notice of the intended entry has been given;

  (b) the Local Pharmaceutical Committee for the area where the pharmacy premises are situated have been invited to be present at the inspection, where this is requested by the pharmacist;

  (c) the person authorised in writing carries written evidence of authorisation, which he or she produces on request; and

  (d) the person does not enter any part of the premises used solely as residential accommodation without the consent of the resident.

(3) the pharmacist must, at the request of the NHS CB or of the authorised person, allow or access to any information which the Board or the authorised person reasonably requires:

  (a) for the purposes mentioned in sub-paragraph (1); or

  (b) in the case of the NHS CB, in connection with its functions that relate to PS.

LOCAL HEALTHWATCH

Section 225 of the Local Government and Public Involvement in Health Act 2007 and The Local Authorities (Public Health Functions and Entry to Premises by Local Healthwatch Representatives) Regulations 2013 impose a duty on pharmacy contractors (and other specified NHS providers) requiring them to allow authorised representatives of a Local Healthwatch organisation or a Local Healthwatch contractor to enter and view premises owned or controlled by the pharmacy contractor and to allow authorised representatives to observe the carrying on of certain activities on such premises. The Regulations confirm that a person providing services which are pharmaceutical services or local pharmaceutical services is a service provider for the purposes of the Act.

The duty does not apply if the presence of an authorised representative would compromise the effective provision of care services or the privacy or dignity of any person; or to premises or any parts of premises when care services are not being provided on those premises or parts of premises; or if in the opinion of the pharmacy contractor the authorised representative in seeking to enter and view the premises and observe the carrying on of activities is not acting reasonably and proportionately.

Pharmacists have been advised to avoid any breach of the rights of privacy of patients and public who use the pharmacy.

For example, authorised representatives should not sit in on an Medicines Use Review consultation or be in a position to read details in the patient medication record or on the computer screen.

The Regulations require the authorised representative not to compromise the provision of care services or the privacy or dignity of any person.

The authorised representative must produce written evidence that he or she is authorised by a local authority under the Local Government and Public Involvement in Health Act 2007.

NHS COUNTER FRAUD SERVICE

The Counter Fraud Service was established in September 1998 and is now part of the NHS Business Services Authority which is a Special Health Authority. Its role is to reduce all losses to fraud and corruption in the NHS.

The Pharmaceutical Fraud team carry out most of their investigations from their offices and by contacting patients and other health professionals.

The counter fraud specialists can enter pharmacies, with police officers on a Magistrates' warrant, provided they have been included on the warrant. If they are not mentioned on the warrant, they can enter the premises only with the consent of the pharmacist (or other person in charge).

POLICE CONTROLLED DRUGS INSPECTORS

These officers are sometimes referred to as Chemist Inspection Officers.

The Misuse of Drugs Act 1971 authorises a police officer (or any other person authorised by the Secretary of State) to enter pharmacy premises and to demand production of any books or documents relating to dealing in controlled drugs. The police officer may inspect books, documents and stocks of controlled drugs. This applies to all controlled drugs, not just those in Schedule 2 to the Misuse of Drugs Regulations 2001.

In addition, the Misuse of Drugs Regulations requires the pharmacy to produce any register, book or document required to be kept under the Regulations. The position of the private prescription register is peculiar. It is not required to be kept under the Regulations and there is no automatic right to examine it under these Regulations. However the officer can demand production under the general rights of enforcement given by the Act.

The Controlled Drugs Inspectors are also charged with the task of alerting the Home Office of any trends involving the misuse of other products which ought to be scheduled under the Misuse of Drugs Act 1971.

Section 23 of the Misuse of Drugs Act 1971 (the '1971 Act') is limited to entering the premises of a person carrying on business as a producer or supplier of any controlled drugs.

The Health Act 2006 extended the powers. *Section 20* creates a power for police constables or other authorised persons to enter the premises of health care providers and to inspect the arrangements for the safe management of controlled drugs in 'any relevant premises'.

Under *Section 20*:

(1) A constable or an authorised person may, for the purpose of securing the safe, appropriate and effective management and use of controlled drugs:
   (a) enter any relevant premises;
   (b) inspect any precautions taken on the premises for the safe custody of controlled drugs;
   (c) inspect any stocks of controlled drugs kept on the premises;
   (d) require any relevant records kept on the premises to be produced for his inspection.
(2) The powers conferred by *subsection (1)* may be exercised only:
   (a) at a reasonable hour, and
   (b) on production (if required) of the written authority of the person exercising them.

The intention is that the inspections would generally be carried out by police constables or by accountable officers appointed under *Section 17* and their staff, or by the regulatory bodies with inspection rights such as the GPhC or the Care Quality Commission (CQC). The section allows for other persons to be authorised by the relevant authority.

THE CQC

The CQC is the independent inspection body for the NHS and for social services. It was established under the Health and Social Care Act 2008, replacing three separate bodies. Part of the Commission's remit is protecting the interests of people whose rights have been restricted under the Mental Health Act.

The Act sets out the CQC's functions:

- assuring safety and quality,
- assessing the performance of commissioners and providers,
- monitoring the operation of the Mental Health Act, and
- ensuring that regulation and inspection activity across health and adult social care is coordinated and managed.

Health and social care providers – including, for the first time, NHS providers – are required to register with the new regulator in order to provide services.

From April 2012, legislation requires other providers whose sole or main purpose is NHS primary medical services to register with the CQC. There are already a number of regulations including:

- The CQC (Registration) Regulations 2009 SI No. 3112
- The Health and Social Care Act 2008 (Registration of Regulated Activities) Regulations 2009 SI No. 660
- The Health and Social Care Act 2008 (Commencement No. 13, Transitory and Transitional Provisions and Electronic Communications) Order 2009 SI No. 3023.

This includes NHS trusts and local authorities, general practitioners (GPs) and dentists but not community pharmacies, which are currently exempt.

CQC Inspectors visit health and adult social care services across England to check that they are meeting the standards. They make unannounced inspections of services on a regular basis and at any time in response to concerns.

The inspectors have extensive powers to exercise the Commission's functions, including:

- Entering and inspecting premises that are, or are reasonably believed to be, 'regulated premises'. Regulated premises are premises or vehicles that are used to 'carry on' a regulated care activity, or are owned or controlled by an NHS body or local authority, or are used – or proposed to be used – to provide NHS care or adult social services.
- Accessing or obtaining documents or records (including those held on computer) in the course of an inspection.
- Requiring any information, documents or records necessary for the exercise of regulatory functions from:
    - Any English NHS body.
    - Any person providing health care commissioned (purchased or arranged) by the NHS.
    - Any English local authority.
    - Any person providing adult social care services commissioned by an English local authority.
    - Any person who 'carries on' or manages a health or social care activity of a type regulated by CQC.

Inspectors also have powers derived from *Section 20* of the Health and Safety at Work Act (H&SWA) 1974 allowing reasonable access to premises in relation to medical exposure to radiation.

Persons authorised in writing by the Commission may at any reasonable time, enter and inspect premises owned or controlled by a service provider and used for purposes connected with the services provided.

HER MAJESTY'S REVENUE AND CUSTOMS

This department resulted from the 2005 merger of the Inland Revenue and Customs & Excise. Customs officers continue responsibility for VAT, but are also concerned with the legislation relating to excise duties (e.g., spirits, including IMS and ethanol use in medicines).

For the purpose of exercising any powers under the Finance Acts an authorised person may at any reasonable time enter premises used in connection with the carrying on of a business and inspect any goods found on them. An authorised person can also demand to see, and can seize, any documents relating to the goods or services provided.

An authorised person can apply to a Magistrate for a warrant, which will allow entry at any time stated within the warrant and using force if necessary. During entry under a warrant, the officer can seize and remove any documents or other things which he has reasonable cause to believe may be required as evidence. The officer may also search persons on the premises that he has reasonable cause to believe may be in possession of any such documents or other things.

HEALTH AND SAFETY INSPECTORS

Health and safety is enforced by inspectors both from the Health and Safety Executive and from the local authority.

Inspectors have the right to enter any workplace without giving notice. They can inspect the workplace, the work activities, the management of health and safety and check that the owner is complying with health and safety law.

They have a right to speak to employees, take photographs and make copies of documents. They can also take away equipment for examination or as evidence.

They must, on request, produce their identification, before being allowed entry to the premises.

The inspector may provide employees with information where necessary for the purpose of keeping them informed about matters affecting their health, safety and welfare.

Some matters of health and safety, for example fire precautions in the workplace, are enforced by other enforcement bodies. In the case of fire precautions, the fire service can appoint inspectors, to enforce the Fire Precautions Act 1971 and in particular the Fire Precautions (Workplace) Regulations 1997. As well as giving advice, these inspectors can issue enforcement notices requiring immediate attention.

TRADING STANDARDS (WEIGHTS AND MEASURES)

Trading Standards Officers, formerly known as 'weights and measures' inspectors, enforce legislation relating to foodstuffs, consumer protection and fair trading. this legislation includes:

- Consumer Protection Act 1987
- Health and Safety at Work Act 1974
- Trade Descriptions Act 1968
- Food Safety Act 1990
- Business Names Act 1985
- Supply of Goods and Services Act 1982
- Sale and Supply of Goods Act 1994
- The Sale and Supply of Goods to Consumers Regulations 2002
- Unfair Contract Terms Act 1977
- Unfair Terms in Consumer Contracts Regulations 1999
- Sunday Trading Act 1994
- Weights and Measures Act 1985
- Others not so relevant to pharmacy.

The inspectors are appointed locally and are restricted to working within their geographical area.

Because the officers enforce a wide range of provisions, they have powers under the different legislative regimes. For example, under the Food Safety Act 1990, an authorised officer on producing, if required, an authenticated document showing the authority, has a right at all reasonable hours to enter any premises within the authority's area for the purpose of ascertaining whether there is or has been any contravention of the provisions of the Food Safety Act or its regulations.

Admission to any private dwelling house requires 24 h notice of the intended entry to be given to the occupier. A Magistrates' warrant will authorise entry without notice, and by force if necessary.

An authorised officer may inspect any records relating to a food business and, where kept by means of a computer, may require the records to be produced in a form in which they may be taken away.

Similar provisions apply to the other Acts.

Trading standards officers enforce some parts of the Medicines Act 1968 and the Poisons Act 1972 in non-pharmacy premises.

DISCLOSURE OF CONFIDENTIAL INFORMATION

Disclosure of confidential information is usually a breach of confidence. It is authorised in certain circumstances by the following laws:

Police and Criminal Evidence Act 1984

PACE allows police to access medical records for the purpose of a criminal investigation, provided they make an application to a circuit judge.

Road Traffic Act 1988

The police are entitled on request any person to provide information, e.g., name and address, which might identify a driver alleged to have committed a traffic offence. However, clinical information should not normally be disclosed without the patient's consent or a court order.

NHS (Venereal Diseases) Regulations 1974

It allows limited disclosure of information for contact tracing in the case of sexually transmitted diseases. Such disclosure can only be made to a doctor, or to someone working on a doctor's instruction in connection with treatment or prevention. It forbids those working in a genito-urinary clinic to inform an insurance company of a patient's sexually transmitted disease – even with the patient's consent. GP's are not routinely informed of the patient's attendance at such clinics, although the patient may request that the GP be informed.

Children Act 1989

Regulates many aspects of childcare including professionals' duties when there is suspicion of child abuse.

Prevention of Terrorism (Temporary Provisions) Act 2000

All citizens must inform the police, as soon as possible, of any information that may help to prevent an act of terrorism or help in apprehending or prosecuting a terrorist.

NORTHERN IRELAND PHARMACY INSPECTORS

The routine inspection of pharmacies is carried out by the Northern Ireland Department of Health and Social Services's pharmacy inspectors.

Inspections are conducted according to relevant legislation and the professional standards and ethics of the Pharmaceutical Society of Northern Ireland.[3]

The Pharmaceutical Society of Northern Ireland's 'Standards for registered pharmacy premises' is used by their inspectors as a guide to the 'essential' and 'desirable' standards for all registered pharmacy premises during inspections.

Self-Assessment Questions

1. Will the GPhC give the notice of when they are inspecting?
   Answer: Advance notification is not required by the legislation. The GPhC will normally give advance notice of routine inspections. They may also ask the pharmacist to complete a self-assessment form.
2. Does the NHS CB have the right to inspect the flat above the pharmacy?
   Answer: The authorised person does not enter any part of the premises used solely as residential accommodation without the consent of the resident.
3. Can the authorised person from Local Healthwatch look at the computer records?
   Answer: *Section 225* of the Local Government and Public Involvement in Health Act 2007 puts a duty on pharmacy contractors to allow authorised representatives of a Local Healthwatch to enter and view premises and to observe the carrying on of certain activities on such premises. The duty does not apply if the presence of an authorised representative would compromise the effective provision of care services or the privacy or dignity of any person.

ADDITIONAL RESOURCES

1. http://www.pharmacyregulation.org/sites/default/files/Inspector%20checklist%20website%20version%20Sep12.pdf
2. http://www.pharmacyregulation.org/sites/default/files/CD%20Self%20Assessment%20Form%20website%20version%20Sep12.pdf
3. http://www.psni.org.uk/

Chapter 22

Confidentiality

The professional relationship between a patient and the pharmacist depends in part on trust. The confidentiality of information held by pharmacists is a matter both of law and of ethics.

THE DATA PROTECTION ACT 1998

The Data Protection Act (DPA) 1998 controls the use of 'personal data', which is data relating to an identifiable living person. The Act came into effect in March 2000. All systems have been required to comply since October 2001. The DPA 1998 implements an EC Directive 95/46/EEC, which requires Member States 'to protect the fundamental rights and freedoms of natural persons, in particular their right to privacy with respect the processing of personal data'.

Personal data covers both facts and opinions about the individual. It also includes information regarding the intentions of the data controller towards the individual, although in some limited circumstances exemptions will apply.

'Data' is information which is being processed by equipment operating automatically in response to instructions given for that purpose:

- is recorded with the above intention,
- is recorded as part of a structured filing system, or
- forms part of an accessible record, for example a health record.

The DPA 1998 applies both to computerised data and to paper records and filing systems. All computer records come within the terms of the DPA 1998 if they can be used to identify the individual the record refers to, no matter how they are filed. Manual records will be covered if specific information relating to particular individuals is readily accessible.

Data Controller

The data controller is the person responsible for determining how any personal data is processed. The data controller is responsible for ensuring that the terms of the DPA 1998 are followed.

Pharmacy Law and Practice. DOI: http://dx.doi.org/10.1016/B978-0-12-394289-0.00022-9

The Data Processor

The data processor is any person (other than an employee of the data controller) who processes the data.

Processing

Processing includes obtaining, recording or holding information and the organisation, alteration, retrieval, accessing, disclosure or erasure of the data, whether in a manual or electronic form.

Information Commissioner

The DPA 1998 is administered by the 'Information Commissioner', created by the Act to maintain a register of data users (those who hold or process the information).

Registration

All businesses that process personal data (such as prescription data) must notify the Information Commissioner of their processing activity. Notification can be undertaken at online.[1]

It is an offence to hold or process personal data unless registered with the Commissioner.

The use of computers for labelling medicines or for stock control does not require registration. However, the keeping of patient medication records (PMRs) on computer must be registered. The data controller must notify the Commissioner of:

- The name and address of the data controller (and a representative if one is nominated)
- The description of the data being processed
- The purposes of the processing
- Other parties who may have access to the data.

Offences

Failure to comply with the notification requirements of the Act is a criminal offence and a conviction can result in a maximum fine of £5000 in the Magistrates Courts and unlimited fines in Crown Courts.

THE PRINCIPLES

Section 2 of the Act requires data users to comply with a set of 'Principles' which are found in Schedule 1 of the Act. These state that personal data shall be:

- fairly and lawfully processed;
- processed for limited purposes;

- adequate, relevant and not excessive;
- accurate;
- not kept longer than necessary;
- processed in accordance with the data subject's rights;
- secure;
- not transferred to countries without adequate protection.

These principles apply to the handling of all data. The general effect is that data may not be processed at all unless either the subject has given permission, or a series of other conditions are met.

SENSITIVE PERSONAL DATA

The Act imposes extra requirements for 'sensitive personal data'.

'Sensitive personal data' means personal data consisting of information as to:

(a) the racial or ethnic origin of the data subject,

(b) his or her political opinions,

(c) his or her religious beliefs or other beliefs of a similar nature,

(d) whether he or she is a member of a trade union (within the meaning of the Trade Union and Labour Relations (Consolidation) Act 1992),

(e) his or her physical or mental health or condition,

(f) his or her sexual life,

(g) the commission or alleged commission by him or her of any offence, or

(h) any proceedings for any offence committed or alleged to have been committed by him or her, the disposal of such proceedings or the sentence of any court in such proceedings.

Health data is classified by the Act as 'sensitive personal data'. This includes information about the subject's racial or ethnic origin, physical or mental health or condition and sexual life.

Where sensitive personal data are health data, including health records, the subject must give explicit consent to the processing of his or her health data, unless it is necessary for medical purposes and is undertaken either by a health professional or by a person with a similar duty of confidentiality.

What Is a 'Health Record'?

A 'Health record' is a record which consists of information relating to the physical or mental health or condition of an individual which has been made by or on behalf of a health professional in connection with the care of that individual.

The individual must be identifiable from that information or from that together with other details held by the record holder.

It is clear, therefore, that many of the records being held by pharmacies, surgeries, NHS trusts and other health care institutions will constitute 'health records' and will therefore fall within the scope of the 1998 Act's subject access provisions. The definition of a 'health record' could apply to material held on an X-ray, an MRI scan or a blood pressure monitor printout, for example.

What Are 'Medical Purposes'?

'Medical purposes' include the purposes of preventative medicine, medical diagnosis, medical research, the provision of care and treatment and the management of health care services.

Generally sensitive personal data requires that the subject give explicit consent, but this is not required when the data is processed for a health professional and is for medical purposes.

THE SUBJECT'S RIGHTS

The DPA 1998 gives seven main rights to the data subject.

Right of Access

Section 7 of the DPA 1998 gives a right of access to all information held about a person. A copy may be obtained by applying in writing to the data user. A period of 40 days is allowed for the copy to be supplied. A fee of up to £10 may be charged.

Unauthorised disclosure may entitle the person to compensation.

There are various exemptions to the right of access, for example where data is held for taxation purposes.

Right to Prevent Processing Likely to Cause Damage or Distress

An individual can serve written notice prohibiting a controller from processing data that can cause substantial damage or distress. The controller has 21 days to either comply or to give reasons why the request is unreasonable.

Right to Prevent Processing for Direct Marketing

Individuals can prevent their data being used for marketing purposes.

The Act also gives individuals rights to compensation when they have suffered damage as a result of a contravention of the Act; and rights to rectification of incorrect records. Individuals can also ensure that decisions which affect them are not based solely on automated processing. They can ask the Commissioner to assess compliance with the Act.

USE OF PERSONAL DATA FOR RESEARCH OR ANALYSIS

Personal data may be used for research without explicit permission where:

- The data is used exclusively for that purpose
- The analysis does not identify individuals
- The analysis is not in support of decisions relating to particular individuals
- No damage or distress is caused to any individual.

NON-COMPUTERISED RECORDS

The DPA covers many types of manual records and files. A manual record is subject to the Act if:

- There is a 'set' of information about individuals, with a common theme or an element. The set need not all be kept in one place.
- There is a 'structure' to the set. This may either be by reference to individual's name or a code number or other identifier or by reference to criteria such as age, purchases, illness, etc.
- The structure allows specific information to be 'readily accessible'.

The Act also covers personal data which is recorded with the intention that it should be processed by means of a computer. Thus information obtained by for example customer survey forms will be subject to the Act even before it has been inputted.

Two earlier Acts deal with specific circumstances where a patient may wish to access medical records held about them.

ACCESS TO HEALTH RECORDS ACT 1990

The DPA 1998 only covers the records of living patients. If a person has a claim arising from the death of an individual, he or she has a right of access to information in the deceased's records necessary to fulfil that claim. These rights are set out in the Access to Health Records Act 1990 or Access to Health Records (Northern Ireland) Order 1993.

ACCESS TO MEDICAL REPORTS ACT 1988

The Access to Medical Reports Act 1988 gives a patient a right to view the clinical information contained in his or her own medical history when released by the general practitioner (GP) as a medical report for insurance or employment purposes. A medical report is a 'report relating to the physical or mental health of the individual prepared by a medical practitioner who is or has been responsible for the clinical care of the patient'.

The GP may charge a 'reasonable fee' if a copy is provided. The rights given under this Act relate solely to records prepared by a GP. There is no direct effect on pharmacists and the information is included to give a complete picture.

USE OF ANONYMISED DATA FOR RESEARCH

In the case of *R v Department of Health, Ex Parte Source Informatics Limited 1999*, the Court of Appeal held that the disclosure by pharmacists of anonymised prescription data does not amount to a breach of confidentiality.

Source Informatics, a division of IMS, obtained information from pharmacies on doctors' prescribing habits in order to sell the data on to pharmaceutical companies so that the companies might market their products more effectively. Source was interested in the doctors' names and the products they prescribed but not the names or identities of the patients concerned. They marketed this data from NHS patients in an aggregated and anonymised form.

A Department of Health policy document issued in July 1997 stated that the sale of such data breached patient confidentiality. Source Informatics challenged that view and sought a declaration that it was wrong in law. They initially lost the case and appealed. The Court of Appeal held that participation in Source's scheme by doctors and pharmacists would not expose them to any serious risk of successful breach of confidence proceedings by a patient. Therefore pharmacists could sell anonymised information if they wished. The court said if the Department of Health viewed such schemes as operating against the public interest then it should make laws to control the situation.

The Department of Health later indicated that their original position had not been fully thought through in regard to its consequences for the collection of research information. However they promptly introduced new law for this area.

CONTROL OF PATIENT INFORMATION UNDER THE NHS ACT 2006

Under *Section 251* of the NHS Act 2006, the Secretary of State may make regulations which require or regulate the processing of patient information in prescribed circumstances. This, for instance, makes it possible for patients to receive more information about their clinical care and for confidential patient information to be lawfully processed without informed consent to support prescribed activities such as cancer registries.

Safeguards

The NHS Act 2006 built in a number of safeguards over the use of this power, to protect patients' interests.

Firstly, regulations can only provide for the processing of patient information for medical purposes, where there is a benefit to patient care or where this is in the public interest. Medical purposes means:

(a) preventative medicine, medical diagnosis, medical research, the provision of care and treatment and the management of health and social care services;

(b) informing individuals about their physical or mental health or condition, the diagnosis of their condition or their care and treatment.

Secondly, regulations can only require the processing of confidential patient information, where there is no reasonably practicable alternative.

Thirdly, any such regulations can only be made under the affirmative resolution procedure, requiring the consent of both Houses of Parliament.

Fourthly, all the controls of the DPA remain in place.

The Confidentiality Advisory Group (CAG) of the Health Research Authority advises on whether applications to access patient information without consent should or should not be approved. There must be sufficient justification to access the requested confidential patient information.

THE HEALTH SERVICE (CONTROL OF INFORMATION) REGULATIONS 2002

The Health Service (Control of Patient Information) Regulations 2002 SI No. 1438 allow the Department of Health to collect certain information for specified purposes, but do not otherwise alter the Source Informatics judgement.

THE NHS ACT 2006

Section 251 of the NHS Act 2006 provides the power to ensure that patient-identifiable information needed to support essential NHS activity can be used without the consent of patients.

It can only be used to support medical purposes that are in the interests of patients or the public in situations where consent is not practicable and where anonymised information will not suffice.

Section 252 provides that the Secretary of State for Health is required to consult with the PIAG before making any regulations under *Section 251*.

Researchers are required to seek permission from PIAG to enable the lawful processing of patient information where it is not possible to obtain consent.

Permission is not automatically granted. The applicant must show that their application will improve patient care or is in the public interest, and must explain why they are unable to either gain consent or use anonymised information.

CONFIDENTIALITY AND CHILDREN

A child's right to confidentiality is as important as the adult's right, even in the face of parental enquiries.

The Royal Pharmaceutical Society of Great Britain (RPSGB) advises that when the patient is a child, the pharmacist may have to decide whether to release information to parents or guardians without the consent of the child, but in the child's best interests. Much will depend on the maturity of the child concerned and his or her relationship with parents or guardians.

Such decisions are particularly difficult when the issue concerns contraception. The courts have laid out some helpful guidance in this area, following the Gillick case in 1985 (see later).

Confidentiality is not normally breached if parents seek advice in relation to their children who are under 16 years of age. If the young person is the client, the visit and discussions are confidential, even in the face of parental enquiries.

Medical Records

Young people under 16 have the right of access to personal information (including medical records) stored on computers, and to their written medical records providing that the holder of the records considers them capable of understanding the nature of the request. A parent or guardian will not be given access unless the young person consents or is incapable of understanding the nature of the request and the granting of access would be in their best interests. (DPA 1998)

Human Rights Act 1998

Article 8 of the Human Rights Act sets out a 'right to respect for private and family life'. This reinforces the duty to preserve confidentiality.

THE CALDICOTT REVIEW 1997

This Review was commissioned by the Chief Medical Officer of England owing to increasing concern about the ways in which patient information is used in the NHS in England and Wales and the need to ensure that confidentiality is not undermined.

The review set out a list of principles for handling patient information.

Caldicott Principles

Principle 1 – Justify the purpose(s). Every proposed use or transfer of patient-identifiable information within or from an organisation should be clearly defined and scrutinised, with continuing uses regularly reviewed by an appropriate guardian.

Principle 2 – Do not use patient-identifiable information unless it is absolutely necessary. Patient-identifiable information items should not be used unless there is no alternative.

Principle 3 – Use the minimum necessary patient-identifiable information. Where use of patient-identifiable information is considered to be essential, each individual item of information should be justified with the aim of reducing identifiability.

Principle 4 – Access to patient-identifiable information should be on a strict need to know basis. Only those individuals who need access to patient-identifiable information should have access to it, and they should only have access to the information items that they need to see.

Principle 5 – Everyone should be aware of their responsibilities. Action should be taken to ensure that those handling patient-identifiable information – both clinical and non-clinical staff – are aware of their responsibilities and obligations to respect patient confidentiality.

Principle 6 – Understand and comply with the law. Every use of patient-identifiable information must be lawful. Someone in each organisation should be responsible for ensuring that the organisation complies with legal requirements.

Caldicott Guardian

Recommendation 3 of the Review was that a senior person, preferably a health professional, should be nominated in each health organisation to act as a guardian, responsible for safeguarding the confidentiality of patient information. This person has become known as the 'Caldicott Guardian'.

The RPSGB has stated that all NHS pharmacies should appoint a Caldicott Guardian and comply with the recommendations of the report.

DEPARTMENT OF HEALTH CODE OF PRACTICE

The DH issued a Code of Practice on Confidentiality in 2003. The Code was amended in 2010.

The Code can be accessed here.[2]

The 2010 supplementary guidance is here.[3]

ETHICAL OBLIGATIONS PLACED ON PHARMACISTS

The General Pharmaceutical Council (GPhC) issued a guidance booklet 'Guidance on patient confidentiality' in April 2012.

It states that a pharmacist has a professional and legal duty to keep confidential the information obtained during the course of professional practice.

It sets out how pharmacists should take 'all reasonable steps to protect the confidentiality of information'.

A pharmacist must:

take all reasonable steps to keep information confidential;
store documents and records, etc. safely;
not allow the public access to confidential information;
ensure discussions are not overheard;
not allow patients to be identified on websites, etc.;
ensure staff follow similar procedures;
raise any issues with data controllers;
continue to protect confidentiality after a patient's death.

The GPhC guidance is here.[4]

Persons with Legal Rights to Access Confidential Information

Some persons are given legal rights to access data that would otherwise be confidential. A pertinent pharmacy example is the right of inspection of controlled drugs (CDs) registers, which is given to people appointed by the Home Office, for example policemen. The right is specific to information recorded in the CD Register or in the private prescription register, and does not extend to other information about that patient contained, for example in the PMR.

Disclosure may be ordered by a coroner, a court, or by the Crown Prosecution Office or by the Procurator Fiscal in Scotland.

Sharing Data within the NHS Family

It is often considered that sharing information between health professionals who are each bound by professional rules of confidentiality does not require consent. The Health Service Commissioner has stated that this is too wide. In the Commissioner's view a patient's record could not be made generally available to a patient's previous doctor, who has ceased to have care of that patient.

The British Medical Association (BMA) accepts that the exchange of identifiable information between health professionals caring for a patient is essential, unless the patient has expressly prohibited it. However the BMA does not accept that such data can be routinely circulated to others simply because they are health professionals or are members of the NHS family. A need to know justification applies to the sharing of information necessary to provide care or treatment for an individual patient.

Patients should be made aware that health teams need to share essential relevant information in order to ensure that the safety and effectiveness of treatment are maximised.

RECORDS

Pharmacies keep various records which include personal details of patients. Some records are kept because of a legal requirement, e.g. CD Register, some by a contractual requirement, e.g., PMRs for the elderly, and some for professional reasons only, e.g., PMRs for children.

The following are likely to be encountered:

CD Register
NHS PMRs (written)
NHS PMRs (on computer)
Private PMRs (written)
Private PMRs (computer)
Prescription book.

Various legal issues arise in relation to the different types of record.

CD Register

The legal requirements are dealt with in Chapter 16.

NHS PMRs

Paragraph 10 of the NHS Terms of Service requires the pharmacy to keep PMRs.

Prescription Book

The following details must be recorded about the sale or supply of prescription only medicines (POMs):

(1) date of sale or supply
(2) name and quantity of medicine, where it is not apparent from the name, the strength and pharmaceutical form must also be included
(3) date of the script
(4) name and address of prescriber
(5) name and address of patient (or owner of animal).

Repeat Scripts

It is sufficient to record the date of supply, together with a reference to the original entry.

Keeping the Prescription Book

The book used to record POM supplies must be kept for 2 years after the last entry.

Keeping the Prescriptions

The prescriptions must be retained for 2 years after they were dispensed.

Computer Records

The Human Medicines Regulations 2013 permit records of private prescriptions and emergency supplies to be held on computer.

The same details are required as for paper records. The computer records must be kept for 2 years. The RPSGB has advised that the computer records should contain an accurate audit trail of entries.

DISCLOSURES REQUIRED BY LAW

Some disclosures are required by law, for example:

- The notification of certain diseases under the Public Health (Control of Disease) Act 1984 or under the Public Health (Infectious Disease) Regulations 1988. (This list of notifiable diseases varies between the countries of the United Kingdom.)
- Road Traffic Act 1988.
- Terrorism Act 2000.

Guidance

See additional resources.[5-7]

Self-Assessment Questions

1. According to the DPA, what is 'data'?
   Answer: 'Data' is information which is being processed by equipment operating automatically in response to instructions given for that purpose; is recorded with the above intention; is recorded as part of a structured filing system; or forms part of an accessible record, for example a health record. The DPA 1998 applies both to computerised data and to paper records and filing systems. All computer records come within the terms of the DPA 1998 if they can be used to identify the individual the record refers to, no matter how they are filed. Manual records will be covered if specific information relating to particular individuals is readily accessible.

2. What is a 'health record'?
   Answer: A 'Health record' is a record which consists of information relating to the physical or mental health or condition of an individual which has been made by or on behalf of a health professional in connection with the care of that individual. The individual must be identifiable from that information or from that together with other details held by the record holder. It is clear, therefore, that many of the records being held by pharmacies, surgeries, NHS trusts and other health care institutions will constitute 'health records' and will therefore fall within the scope of the 1998 Act's subject access provisions. The definition of a 'health record' could apply to material held on an X-ray, an MRI scan or a blood pressure monitor printout, for example.

3. When can information about children be given to their parents?
   Answer: A parent or guardian will not be given access unless the young person consents or is incapable of understanding the nature of the request and the granting of access would be in their best interests. (DPA 1998)

ADDITIONAL RESOURCES

1. http://www.ico.gov.uk/
2. http://www.dh.gov.uk/en/Publicationsandstatistics/Publications/PublicationsPolicy AndGuidance/DH_4069253
3. http://www.dh.gov.uk/prod_consum_dh/groups/dh_digitalassets/@dh/@en/@ps/documents/ digitalasset/dh_122031.pdf
4. http://www.pharmacyregulation.org/guidance-patient-confidentiality
5. http://www.gmc-uk.org/guidance/ethical_guidance/confidentiality.asp
6. http://www.connectingforhealth.nhs.uk/systemsandservices/infogov/links/ GPelectronicrecords2011.pdf
7. http://www.dh.gov.uk/en/Publicationsandstatistics/Publications/PublicationsPolicyAndGuidance/ DH_112916

Chapter 23

Consent

It is sometimes wrongly assumed that informed consent is necessary only for surgery or invasive procedures. Consent is necessary in any professional relationship between a patient and a health care provider. For major procedures or treatments involving risk to the patient, such as surgical procedures, it is usual for informed consent to be obtained in writing.

Consent is necessary for all treatment, but it is often is implied in the interaction, for example in the normal pharmacist–patient where the patient seeks and accepts the advice of the pharmacist on treatment. Examples would be buying an over the counter (OTC) or having a prescription dispensed.

For some services now being provided by pharmacists, explicit consent is required. It is especially important where touching is concerned, as for instance when a blood sample is taken.

DEFINITION OF CONSENT

The Department of Health's Mental Health Act 1983: Code of Practice (1999) gives the following definition of consent (15.13):

'Consent' is the voluntary and continuing permission of the patient to receive a particular treatment, based on an adequate knowledge of the purpose, nature, likely effects and risks of that treatment including the likelihood of its success and any alternatives to it. Permission given under and unfair undue pressure is not 'consent'.

The Department of Health publication 'Reference guide to consent for examination or treatment, second edition 2009'[1] updates earlier versions. It provides a guide to obtaining valid consent for any examination, treatment or care.

The GPhC issued its guidance on consent in 2012.[2]

Explicit Consent

Explicit consent can be verbal or written. When explicit consent is obtained the patient should have the procedure adequately explained. The attendant risks should also be explained. In order to give valid consent the patient must have understood and must have the legal capacity to consent.

Pharmacy Law and Practice. DOI: http://dx.doi.org/10.1016/B978-0-12-394289-0.00023-0

Implicit Consent

Implied consent occurs when the patient agrees to the procedure simply by being a patient and by not objecting to therapeutic procedures about which they have received general information, for instance by holding out an arm for an injection.

BASIS FOR THE CONSENT CONCEPT

The bases for the concept of informed consent lie in civil and criminal law and in the ethical concept of autonomy.

Criminal Law

Strictly, it is unlawful to touch or even threaten to touch a person without their permission. Such a touch would constitute 'battery', and there are remedies in both civil and criminal courts. It is not necessary to prove that there was any damage. Therefore treatments or investigations performed without consent constitute 'battery'.

There are exceptions, such as emergency life saving procedures.

Civil Law – Negligence

Consent is part of the agreement between the patient and the professional. Without consent there can be no agreement. Indeed the first case brought by a patient claiming that he or she did not consent to the procedure took place in 1767.

Consent must be based on adequate information especially about the risks. If inadequate information is given a patient may win a negligence claim. A court may regard any consent as invalid if it is based on inadequate information. (*Chatterton v Gerson 1981*)

How Much Information Must Be Given to the Patient

The professional standard with regard to the provision of information was dealt with in two legal cases:

- *Bolam v Friern Hospital Management Committee*,
- *Sidaway v Board of Governors of the Bethlem Royal and the Maudsley Hospital*.

Generally the amount of information to be given is at the discretion of the doctor, provided he or she follows recognised good practice.

To make an informed and valid consent a patient must be given the information relevant to the decision he or she is going to make. The case law indicates that this should be the information that a responsible body of professional opinion would consider necessary.

The courts have said that patients should be told of risks which are 'obviously necessary to an informed choice on the part of the patient that no reasonably prudent medical man would fail to make it'.

Questions asked by the patient must be truthfully answered.

In Bolam a patient was given ECT without relaxant drugs. The patient was not given any warning of any risk by the treating physician. An unusual fracture occurred during treatment. The judgement sets out the 'Bolam' test which is applied to conduct alleged to be negligent. A professional person should act in accordance with a responsible body of professional opinion. (*Bolam v Friern Hospital Management Committee (1957) 2 All ER 118*) Read more here.[3]

In Sidaway a spinal operation was properly performed but the nerve root was damaged – a known risk. Unfortunately the surgeon had only informed the patient of possible damage to the spinal cord itself, and further the surgeon had not told the patient that the operation was one of choice. It was not a necessary operation. The patient's claim for negligence was upheld. (*Sidaway v Board of Governors of the Bethlem Royal Hospital (1985) AC 871*) Read more here.[4]

Since Sidaway, judgments in a number of negligence cases (relating both to the provision of information and to the standard of treatment given) have shown that courts are willing to be critical of a 'responsible body' of medical opinion. It is now clear that the courts will be the final arbiter of what constitutes responsible practice, although the standards set by the health care professions for their members will still be influential.

In Chester v Afshar (2004) UKHL 41, a neurosurgeon failed to warn a patient that there was a small risk of injury even if the surgery was properly performed. The House of Lords held that the neurosurgeon was liable to the patient when that risk materialised. This was so even though the risk was not increased by the failure to warn and the patient had not shown that she would never have had an operation carrying the same risk. The failure to warn of the risk denied the patient the ability to make an informed decision.

The fundamental principle underlying the decision was the right of a patient to make an informed choice as to whether to have an operation. The traditional test of causation is to ask what would have happened 'but for' the accident. Here the HL departed from that on the basis that policy and justice required a modification to causation principles.

The judgment held that it is advisable that health practitioners give information about all significant possible adverse outcomes and make a record of the information given. Read more here.[5]

Qualifications of the Person Seeking the Consent

Consent is often given because the patient recognises the qualifications of the person seeking the consent. For instance hairdressers are allowed to touch clients in situations where other people might not get consent.

The patient may make assumptions about the status of the other person that affects consent. Some patients may be confused about supplementary prescribing. They may assume that anyone who 'prescribes' is a doctor, and therefore they consent to accepting the prescription on that basis. They may feel differently about accepting a prescription from a pharmacist. Any pharmacist undertaking prescribing in such a situation should make his or her profession clear to the patient at the outset.

Touching a Patient

In the course of a determination made on 1 December 2011 about the fitness to practise of a pharmacist, the Chairman of the Disciplinary Committee of the General pharmaceutical Council made the following statement:

A pharmacist is not competent to undertake a physical examination which includes the touching of a patient's body as part of a diagnostic procedure.

This statement was made in the context of an unproved allegation of sexual touching by the pharmacist. The pharmacist did, however, admit that he pressed the patient's back in the kidney area in order to ascertain whether the pain she complained of related to a kidney infection.

The Chairman also said in the determination that the examination was carried out without the clear express consent of the patient.

The GPhC has issued guidance on maintaining sexual boundaries here.[6]

Is the Patient Capable of Making an Informed Decision?

Consent is based on the assumption that the patient is capable of making an informed and voluntary decision. There are two aspects to this:

- the information given about what is to happen, and
- the patient's ability to make a decision.

Adult patients are normally presumed to be competent to make decisions about their health, and therefore to accept or refuse treatment. However this presumption can be challenged in court, especially where the patient does not have the mental capacity to make reasoned decisions.

How to Determine Whether a Person Can Validly Consent

The courts have suggested three tests to determine capacity:

(1) Did the patient understand what was said to him or her?
(2) Did the patient believe it?
(3) Did the patient consider the information, and balance needs and risks before reaching his or her decision?

In Re C 1994, an elderly paranoid schizophrenic had delusions that he was a doctor. The courts held that nevertheless he was capable of refusing consent for an amputation to treat gangrene, because he understood the information about treatment.

Generally speaking a mentally competent patient has right to refuse medical treatment, regardless of consequences and how beneficial or necessary treatment may be. As the judge in Sidaway put it ' a competent adult has a right to refuse treatment ...for reasons which are rational or irrational, or for no reason'.

Re C can be contrasted with Re T 1992 where the courts found that a woman had been influenced by her Jehovah's Witness mother into refusing a necessary blood transfusion. The court declared that she had not been fully rational when she refused, due to the influence of her mother, and partly due to the medications received.

CONSENT BY CHILDREN

The above cases concerned adults. Children may also be considered competent to take decisions about their health.

The Family Reform Act 1969 lowered the age of majority to 18 years and gave 16- and 17-year-olds the same right to consent to treatment as adults. *Section 8(1)* says:

...the consent of a minor who has attained the age of sixteen...shall be as effective as it would be if he were of full age; and where a minor has...given an effective consent to any treatment it shall not be necessary to obtain any consent for it from his parent or guardian.

Children Under 16

The parental right to determine whether a child below the age of 16 has medical treatment ends if, and when, the child achieves sufficient understanding and intelligence to comprehend fully what is proposed.

It is for the doctor to use his or her clinical judgement to decide whether the child has reached such a level of understanding and intelligence.

The Gillick case established broad principles on the capacity of children aged under 16. (*Gillick v West Norfolk and Wisbech Area Health Authority (1985) 3 All ER 402*)

The Gillick Case

The Department of Health and Social Security issued a circular stating that in exceptional circumstances doctors could give contraceptive advice and prescriptions to girls under 16 without the consent of the parents.

Mrs Gillick sought an assurance from her local health authority that her daughters would not be given advice or contraception without her prior consent. When this was refused, she challenged the legality of the circular. The House of Lords gave judgement in 1985. Read more here.[7]

This case established the following broad principles:

- Parental rights exist for the benefit of the child not the parent.
- The parental right to determine whether a child below the age of 16 has medical treatment ends if, and when, the child achieves sufficient understanding and intelligence to comprehend fully what is proposed.
- It is for the doctor to use his or her clinical judgement to decide whether the child has reached such a level of understanding and intelligence.

The Gillick decision is reinforced by the Children Act 1989, under which parental rights yield to children's rights to make their own decisions, once children have enough understanding and intelligence to make up their own minds.

Consent to Contraception

A girl under 16 can consent to contraceptive advice and treatment, and the doctor can proceed without her parent's knowledge or consent if satisfied:

(1) she understands the advice;
(2) she cannot be persuaded to inform her parents, or to allow the doctor to do so;
(3) she is likely to have sexual intercourse with or without contraceptive treatment;
(4) unless she has contraceptive advice or treatment her health (physical or mental) will suffer;
(5) her best interests require that she receive contraceptive advice and treatment without the knowledge or consent of her parents.

These are the guidelines sometimes referred to as Fraser Guidelines, after one of the judges in the House of Lords in the Gillick case.

Strictly speaking the criteria in the judgement are different from the guidelines given by Lord Fraser, one of the judges. For many years the criteria that have been referred to as the test for Gillick competence have provided clinicians with an objective test of competence. This identifies children aged under 16 have the legal capacity to consent to medical examination and treatment, provided they can demonstrate sufficient maturity and intelligence to understand and appraise the nature and implications of the proposed treatment, including the risks and alternative courses of actions.

Lord Fraser's guidance is narrower and relates only to contraception.

Application to Pharmacists

The phrases used in the judgement are directed at doctors. Similar conditions will apply to the supply of OTC products by pharmacists. It may be more difficult for pharmacists to satisfy the criteria, especially No. (4).

Refusal of Consent by the Child

The Gillick case concerns the giving of consent. It does not apply where a Gillick competent child refuses to give consent. There may be a more limited right to refuse to give consent. Under the Children Act 1989, the 'child's welfare shall be the court's paramount consideration'. The Act itself gives young people who understand what is happening a limited right to refuse certain treatments in circumstances connected to care proceedings. The right to refuse treatment is also limited by two judgements Regulation R and Regulation W. In both cases the child's refusal to accept treatment was overruled and the parents' wishes for treatment prevailed.

Both in the United States and in the United Kingdom, courts have ordered necessary blood transfusions for a child whose parents objected because they were practising Jehovah's Witnesses. UK courts have also overridden the wishes of the parent in order to facilitate a procedure of benefit to the child, but which was refused by the parents.

Clinical Trials and Children

In clinical trials the Clinical Trials Regulations supercede the Gillick judgement and require that written informed consent from a parent or guardian is always required.

THE LAW IN SCOTLAND

Gillick is English law and does not apply in Scotland, which is covered by the Age of Legal Capacity (Scotland) Act 1991.

Self-Assessment Questions

1. What are the essential elements of consent?
   Answer: 'Consent' is the voluntary and continuing permission of the patient to receive a particular treatment, based on an adequate knowledge of the purpose, nature, likely effects and risks of that treatment including the likelihood of its success and any alternatives to it. Permission given under and unfair undue pressure is not 'consent'.

2. How can one tell if a patient has validly consented?

   Answer: The courts suggest that one should consider three things: Did the patient understand what was said to him or her? Did the patient believe it? Did the patient consider the information and balance needs and risks before reaching his or her decision?

3. When can a young person be given contraception?

   Answer: A girl under 16 can consent to contraceptive advice and treatment, and the health professional concerned can proceed without her parent's knowledge or consent if satisfied:

   * she understands the advice;
   * she cannot be persuaded to inform her parents, or to allow the doctor to do so;
   * she is likely to have sexual intercourse with or without contraceptive treatment;
   * unless she has contraceptive advice or treatment her health (physical or mental) will suffer;
   * her best interests require that she receive contraceptive advice and treatment without the knowledge or consent of her parents.

ADDITIONAL RESOURCES

1. http://www.dh.gov.uk/en/Publicationsandstatistics/Publications/PublicationsPolicy AndGuidance/DH_103643
2. http://www.pharmacyregulation.org/sites/default/files/GPHC%20Guidance%20on% 20consent.pdf
3. http://en.wikipedia.org/wiki/Bolam_v_Friern_Hospital_Management_Committee
4. http://judgmental.org.uk/judgments/UKHL/1985/[1985]_UKHL_1.html
5. http://www.publications.parliament.uk/pa/ld200304/ldjudgmt/jd041014/cheste-1.htm
6. http://www.pharmacyregulation.org/sites/default/files/GPHC%20Guidance%20on%20 sexual%20boundaries.pdf
7. http://www.cirp.org/library/legal/UKlaw/gillickvwestnorfolk1985/

Chapter 24

The European Union

The law of the European Union (EU), commonly referred to as European Community (EC) law, is automatically part of UK law, and consequently it is necessary for pharmacists to have some knowledge of the EU and the way it works. Community law overrides national laws of the Member States.

The European Communities Act 1972 was the instrument whereby the United Kingdom was able to accede to the European Communities.

It also enables government ministers to lay regulations before Parliament to implement changes to UK law that are required by the EU (e.g., EU Directives; Decisions of the European Court of Justice (ECJ)).

It also provides, in *Section 2(4)*, that all UK legislation, including primary legislation (Acts of Parliament), shall have effect 'subject to' directly applicable EC law.

All EU decisions and procedures are based on the Treaties which constitute its legal basis and which are agreed by all Member States.

THE BEGINNINGS

The Treaty of Paris in 1951 established the forerunner of the EU – the European Coal and Steel Community (ECSC).

The European Economic Community (EEC) was established by the Treaty of Rome in 1957. The original members were Belgium, France, Germany, Italy, Luxembourg and the Netherlands.

The United Kingdom joined the EEC in 1973, along with Denmark and the Republic of Ireland, by the Treaty of Accession of 1972.

There were further enlargements in 1981, 1986, 1995, 2004 and 2007.

Membership now stands at 27 states with a total population of around 500 million. There are 23 official languages.

In 1995 the European Free Trade Area countries of Austria, Finland and Sweden joined to form the European Economic Area (EEA).

Croatia[1] is expected to become the 28th member state of the EU on 1 July 2013. Iceland, the Former Yugoslav Republic of Macedonia, Serbia, Montenegro and Turkey are in the process of negotiating their accession to the EU.

Pharmacy Law and Practice. DOI: http://dx.doi.org/10.1016/B978-0-12-394289-0.00024-2

KEY DATES AND TREATIES

The first major revision was in February 1986.

The Single European Act

The Single European Act (SEA) introduced measures to shorten the legislative process in order to facilitate an internal European market. The SEA introduced qualified majority voting in the Council and gave the European Parliament more powers in the legislative process. The SEA intended to remove barriers and to increase harmonisation and competitiveness among its countries.

A core element of the SEA was to create a 'single market' within the EC by 1992 with free movement of goods, services, people and money.

The Maastricht Treaty

The original treaty was modified in 1992 by the 'Maastricht Treaty on EU' which gave new powers and responsibilities to the Community institutions.

The 12 nations of the EC began calling themselves the EU. The Maastricht Treaty established the EU by forming what are known as the three pillars of the EU.

The three pillars are:

(1) the European Communities, consisting of the EC, the ECSC and Euratom;
(2) a Common Foreign and Security Policy (CFSP) allowing Member States to take joint action in the field of foreign policy and;
(3) Police and Judicial Cooperation in Criminal Matters.

The first pillar is managed by the institutions of the EU, while the second and third work through intergovernmental cooperation. The Treaty defined the function of the Council as providing the general political guidelines for the EU's development.

The Maastricht Treaty[2] also introduced the euro.

European Economic Area

The EEA was established on 1 January 1994 following an agreement between the Member States of the European Free Trade Association and the EC, later the EU. It allows Iceland, Liechtenstein and Norway to participate in the EU's Internal Market without the conventional EU membership.

The Treaty of Amsterdam

The Treaty of Amsterdam in 1997 amended some pre-existing European Treaties. It dealt with a number of issues in preparation for EU enlargement. The United Kingdom agreed to the Social Chapter.

The Treaty of Nice

In 2003 the Treaty of Nice made provision for membership of the EU to be increased to up to 27 Member States:

- the size and composition of the European Commission was changed,
- the number of votes each member state had in the European Council was adjusted, and
- qualified majority voting was extended to more policy areas.

The Treaty of Lisbon

In December 2007 the EU countries signed the Treaty of Lisbon. It was ratified by all the EU countries and came into force on 1 December 2009.

The Treaty of Lisbon creates:

- a single legal personality for the EU;
- a President of the European Council;
- a High Representative of the Union for Foreign Affairs and Security Policy.
- it empowers European citizen's through the 'right of initiative';
- it empowers national parliaments in European political affairs, and
- it underpins the Charter of Fundamental Rights.

THE SCHENGEN AGREEMENT

The Schengen Agreement in 1985 abolished internal borders, eventually enabling passport-free movement between 26 EU Member States, excluding the United Kingdom.

THE INTRODUCTION OF THE EURO

The Maastricht Treaty[2] also introduced the concept of the EU and the single currency – the euro.

Member States set strict criteria for participation in the currency:

- the budget deficit was to be less than 3% of Gross Domestic Product (GDP)
- the debt ratio was to be less than 60% of GDP
- the country had to have low inflation
- the prevailing interest rates were to be close to the EU average.

In the event these criteria were widely ignored.

The currency was introduced in book form as electronic transfers, banking, etc., at midnight on 1 January 1999.

On 1 January 2002 the new euro notes and coins were introduced in 12 of the countries. Since then another five countries have adopted the euro.

LAW-MAKING INSTITUTIONS

The Treaty of Rome established several institutions to deal with the law-making and administrative processes of the Community.

The European Parliament

The Parliament is composed of directly elected representatives of the citizens of the Member States. It has three main roles:

(1) It is a legislative body.
(2) It controls the Commission's budget.
(3) It exercises democratic supervision over the other EU institutions.

There are 752 members (MEPs) (reducing to 736 at the next election in 2014), with the numbers reflecting the size of each country's population. MEPs are elected by proportional representation and every citizen has the right to vote at 18. Every EU citizen of a member state living in another country of the EU may vote or stand for election in their country of residence.

The European Parliament enjoys co-legislative powers with the European Council in a number of important EU law-making areas; including health, education and the completion of the internal market.

The Council of the EU

This was formerly called the Council of Ministers. It is the legislative and decision-making body of the EC. It is composed of ministers from each of the member governments, normally the Foreign Ministers but it may be any appropriate minister. One minister attends from each state. Most decisions are taken on a majority basis. The Presidency rotates between the states, in alphabetical order, at 6-month intervals.

The Committee of Permanent Representatives (known by the French acronym COREPER) consists of senior civil servants from each state, and it acts as the administrative arm of the Council. The members are the heads of the permanent delegations in Brussels. Disputes are often sorted out here.

The European Council is the name given to the regular meetings of heads of governments, which discuss broad policy. It is the institution through which EU intergovernmental activities are channelled. It establishes policy guidelines which are then translated into legislative suggestions to be considered during meetings of the Council of the EU.

The Council:

- passes European laws, often jointly with the European Parliament;
- coordinates the broad economic and social policies of the Member States;
- concludes international agreements between the EU and other countries;
- approves the EU's budget, jointly with the European Parliament;

- develops the EU's Common Foreign and Security Policy (CFSP), based on guidelines set by the European Council;
- coordinates cooperation between the national courts and the police forces in criminal matters.

The European Commission

The Commission is charged with seeing that the treaties are implemented. There are 27 Commissioners with a large supporting staff. Commissioners are appointed for a 5-year term, serve the EC as a whole, and can only be removed from office by the ECJ or by the European Parliament (which can only dismiss the entire Commission on a two-third majority vote). Each Commissioner is responsible for an area of policy. The staff are organised into Directorates-General.

The Commission has four main roles:

(1) promoting new legislation
(2) managing and implementing EU policies and the budget
(3) enforcing EU law (jointly with the ECJ)
(4) representing the EU on the international stage.

The ECJ

The Court is based in Luxembourg. It is responsible for ensuring that Community legislation is correctly interpreted and applied.

- Cases may be brought by a member state, a community institution or an individual.
- The court responds to requests from national courts for an interpretation of Community law.
- It has the power to impose fines.
- Member States in breach of Community law are required to comply with the orders of the court.
- Judges are appointed from each country.
- There is no system of precedent and judgements of the ECJ are decided by majority. Dissenting opinions are not given.

There is a Court of First Instance which has jurisdiction relating to competition policy and to cases brought by individuals, companies and some organisations.

The European Civil Service Tribunal gives rulings on employment disputes of the Commission staff.

Economic and Social Committee

This influential committee, known as 'Ecosoc', advises the Commission and the Council on economic matters. It is made up of representatives of the employers, workers and other interest groups in the Member States. The representatives are proposed by the governments, and appointments are made by the Council.

The European Court of Auditors checks that expenditure is received and lawfully spent.

The European Central Bank is responsible for managing the euro.

The Committee of the Regions represents regional and local authorities.

The European Investment Bank finances certain investments to promote the objectives of the EU.

The European Ombudsman acts as an intermediary between EU citizens and EU authorities.

COMMUNITY LAW

EU law consists of:

- EU primary legislation, represented by the treaties. The treaties are the first source of EU law and contain the founding legal acts. They contain the basic provisions and the majority of EU economic law. The treaties also create the decision-making and legal rule-making powers of the EU institutions;
- EU secondary legislation, in the form of regulations, directives, decisions, and recommendations;
- rulings on cases brought before the ECJ.

The law created by EU institutions is binding on all EU Member States. Article 10 of the Treaty requires all states to: 'take all appropriate measures, whether general or particular, to ensure fulfilment of the obligations arising out of this Treaty ...'

There are four categories of Community secondary law:

- Regulations are laws issued by the Community which have effect throughout the Community as they stand. There is no need for the EC law to be 'transposed' into national law.
- Directives are binding on the Member States. They lay down the result to be achieved but leave to the national authorities the task of enacting the necessary national legislation. This may be done by creating new primary legislation, for example Acts of Parliament or secondary legislation, for example Regulations or Orders.
- Decisions are binding on the individuals or institutions to whom they are addressed.
- Recommendations are merely advisory statements.

DIRECTIVES AFFECTING PHARMACY

A number of Directives have been issued concerning medicines. They are based on Articles 100 and 100A of the Treaty of Rome. The majority of the medicines directives are concerned with the licensing process, laying down the procedures to be adopted, the types of data to be required and giving definitions.

Laws about the quality, safety and efficacy of medicines have mainly been codified in Directive 2001/83/EC and in Regulation (EEC) 726/2004.

Directive 2001/83/EC

The main Directive replaced Directive 65/65/E. It was itself amended by Directive 2004/27/EC. It sets out the most important aspects of the marketing of medicines. These include the common principles which should be adhered to by each Member State with regard to the conditions for granting a marketing authorisation, manufacture and quality control procedures, labelling and information leaflets and detailed guidance on data requirements.

The Directive requires that a marketing authorisation (product licence) is granted on grounds of safety, efficacy and quality – the same grounds as are laid down in the Medicines Act 1968.

The Directive 2001/83/EC applies to 'medicinal products' which are defined as

any substance or combination of substances presented for treating or preventing disease in human beings. Any substance or combination of substances which may be administered to human beings with a view to making a medical diagnosis or to restoring, correcting or modifying physiological functions in human beings.

Directive 2001/83/EC and Directive 2004/27/EC are put into UK law ('transposed') by the Human Medicines Regulations 2012 SI No. 1916.

Regulation EC 726/2004

Regulation EC 726/2004 lays down Community procedures for the authorisation and supervision of medicinal products. It also established the European Medicines Agency. The Regulation covers much the same topics as the Directive, but covers medicines based on new active substances for treatment of certain major diseases, and certain advanced or biological medicines.

The Human Medicines Regulations 2012 also provide for the enforcement in the Regulation EC 726/2004 in the United Kingdom.

The 'Transparency' Directive

Directive 89/105/EEC is known as the 'Transparency Directive'. It requires Member States which impose controls on the prices of medicinal products, or on the profits of the pharmaceutical industry to publish their criteria, and the reasons for the decisions. The intention is to ensure that all procedures are operated in accordance with the Treaty, that is they are fair and are not discriminatory.

Article 1 states:

Member States shall ensure that any national measure, whether laid down by law, regulation or administrative action, to control the prices of medicinal products for human use or to restrict the range of medicinal products covered by their national health insurance systems complies with the requirements of this Directive.

Later articles lay down a timetable of 90 days for the authorities to make a decision about a product.

The Directive applies to the Selected List scheme, the ACBS approval scheme, and by virtue of Article 5, to the PPRS scheme.

Directive 2004/24/EC

The European Directive on Traditional Herbal Medicinal Products requires all herbal medicinal products to have prior authorisation before they can be marketed in the EU. Unlicensed remedies that are made up for a patient following a consultation with a herbalist are exempt.

Directive 2010/84/EU

Together with Regulation (EU) No 1235/2010, this directive tightens the requirements for pharmacovigilance. The EU legislation has been transposed by the Human Medicines Regulations 2012.

Directive 2011/62/EU

The European Directive on Falsified Medicines (FMD) introduces measures to prevent the entry of counterfeit medicines into the legal supply chain.

FREE MOVEMENT OF PROFESSIONALS

The right to free movement of pharmacists across the EU is established by Directive 2005/36/EC[3] on the recognition of professional qualifications.

UK Law

The Free Movement Directive was transposed into UK law by two Regulations:

European Communities (Recognition of Professional Qualifications) Regulations 2007 SI No. 2781

European Qualifications (Health and Social Care Professions) Regulations 2007[4] SI No. 3101

Finally, the Pharmacy Order 2010 SI No.231 sets out how the General Pharmaceutical Council (GPhC) is to handle applications from pharmacists and technicians.

The Directive establishes a system for the recognition of professional qualifications, in order to help make labour markets more flexible. It encourages automatic recognition of qualifications and simplifies administrative procedures.

The Directive applies to all EU Member State nationals who wish to practise a 'regulated profession', on either a self-employed or an employed basis, in a Member State other than that in which they obtained their professional qualifications.

A 'regulated profession' is:

a professional activity which is subject to the possession of specific professional qualifications; in particular, the use of a professional title limited to holders of a given professional qualification.

The automatic recognition of training qualifications based on the coordination of minimum training conditions covers the following professions: doctors, nurses responsible for general care, dental practitioners, veterinary surgeons, midwives, pharmacists and architects.

The Directive lays down minimum training conditions for each of these professions, including the minimum duration of studies. The formal qualifications conforming to the Directive issued by Member States are listed in Annex V. These qualifications enable holders to practise their profession in any Member State.

The basic criteria are:

- training of at least 5 years, including 4 years full-time theoretical and practical study and a 6-month traineeship in a pharmacy;
- coverage of the knowledge and skills listed in Article 44 and Annex V.5.6.1 of the Directive on recognition of professional qualifications.

Where a qualification is not listed in Annex V.5.6.2 because it does not meet the basic criteria, it may still be recognised under an acquired rights regime. To take advantage of this provision a pharmacist must demonstrate at least 3 years of professional experience within the last 5 years.   (Article 23)

The Directive makes a distinction between 'freedom to provide services' and 'freedom of establishment' on the basis of criteria identified by the ECJ, that is duration, frequency, regularity and continuity of the provision of services.

Registration of a Pharmacist

The Directive allows a person to register as a pharmacist in any state (provided that the standard requirements for registration are fulfilled) if they are:

 (i) a national of a Member State of the EEA
 (ii) in good standing with their professional authority in their Member State
(iii) entitled to practise as a pharmacist in the EEA.

An applicant must provide evidence that he/she complies with the above.

There are time limits on the process. The competent authority has 1 month to acknowledge receipt of an application and to draw attention to any missing documents. Generally a decision has to be taken within 3 months of the date of the application. However, this deadline may be extended by 1 month in cases falling under the general system for the recognition of qualifications.

Reasons have to be given for any rejection. A rejection or a failure to take a decision by the deadline can be contested in national courts.

Temporary or Occasional Basis

Any EU national who is legally established in a Member State may provide services on a temporary and occasional basis in another Member State under his/her original professional title without having to apply for recognition of his/her qualifications.

If the host Member State requires *pro forma* registration with the competent professional association, this must be automatic. The competent authority must forward the applicant's file to the professional organisation or body on receipt of the prior declaration. For professions that have public health or safety implications and do not benefit from automatic recognition, the host Member State may carry out a prior check of the service provider's professional qualifications within the limits of the principle of proportionality.

LANGUAGE ABILITY

Member States may require applicants to have the language knowledge necessary for practising the profession. This provision must be applied proportionately, which rules out the systematic imposition of language tests before a professional activity can be practised.

The 2005 European directive on the recognition of professional qualifications prevents health care regulatory bodies across Europe from testing the language competence of applicants for membership who have achieved their professional qualification within the EEA. This is set out in the Pharmacy Order 2010.

The GPhC cannot ask for evidence of English language competency from EEA nationals who simply want to register with the GPhC as a pharmacy professional.

However, once on the GPhC register, pharmacists are required to practise pharmacy in Great Britain according to the GPhC's standards of conduct, ethics and performance.

Principle 7 of the GPhC's standards of conduct, ethics and performance, paragraph 7.2 states:

Make sure that you and everyone you are responsible for have the language skills to communicate and work effectively with colleagues

Failing to meet the GPhC's standards of conduct, ethics and performance can result in allegations of misconduct before the GPhC's Fitness to Practise committees.

Linguistic ability for pharmacists on a pharmaceutical list is now covered by Regulation 30 of the NHS (PS) Regulations 2013.

Refusal: language requirement for some NHS pharmacists
An application for inclusion in a pharmaceutical list by a person not already included must be refused if the applicant is an individual (X) who qualified as a pharmacist in Switzerland or an EEA state other than the United Kingdom, unless X satisfies the NHS Commissioning Board that X has the level of knowledge of English which, in the interests of X and the persons making use of the services to which the application relates, is necessary for the provision of those services in the relevant area.

Personal Control of 'New' Pharmacies

When mutual recognition of EU pharmacists was first implemented the government took advantage of a derogation which prohibited EU pharmacists from becoming the pharmacist 'in personal control' (now replaced by the Responsible Pharmacist), of a pharmacy which had been established for less than 3 years.

This prohibition was removed in 2011 by the Medicines Act 1968 (Pharmacy) Order 2011 SI No. 2647, which amended the Medicines Act.

TITLES

Pharmacists from other EC states can qualify for temporary registration with the GPhC and are then entitled to use the titles by which they are known in their own state, provided this does not cause confusion.

If they are permanently registered with the GPhC they may use the UK protected title of 'Pharmacist'.

Directive 2005/36/EC states:

If, in a host Member State, the use of a professional title relating to one of the activities of the profession in question is regulated, nationals of the other Member States who are authorised to practise a regulated profession ... shall use the professional titles of the host Member State, which corresponds to that profession in that Member State, and make use of any associated initials.

Information from the GPhC

The GPhC has information on registering as a EU qualified pharmacist here.[5]

Self-Assessment Questions

1. In what way can pharmacies be affected by EU law without there being any law passed in the United Kingdom?

   Answer: Regulations are laws issued by the Community which have effect throughout the Community as they stand. There is no need for the EC law to be 'transposed' into national law. More usually the EU issues a Directive, which each member state must put into law.

2. In which areas of law is the EU likely to affect pharmacy?

   Answer: Pharmacy is mostly affected by Directives concerned with the running of a free market in Europe. Such Directives set common standards for goods. They also create rules for free movement of professionals, whereby pharmacists with similar standards of education may practice throughout the EU.

ADDITIONAL RESOURCES

1. http://en.wikipedia.org/wiki/Croatia
2. http://www.eurotreaties.com/maastrichtext.html
3. http://eur-lex.europa.eu/LexUriServ/LexUriServ.do?uri=CELEX:32005L0036:EN:NOT
4. http://www.gmc-uk.org/European_Quals__Health_and_Social_Care_Professions__Regs_2007.pdf_25407547.pdf
5. http://www.pharmacyregulation.org/node/119

Chapter 25

The Pharmacy Profession

HISTORY

Chemists and Druggists

The history of pharmacy as a profession distinct from the practice of medicine begins in 1794. Until then medicines had been dispensed by physicians and apothecaries as part of an ancillary service, but the compounding of prescriptions became more complex and expensive as new avenues of supply were explored. Chemists and druggists had started to appear, with the primary purpose of dispensing the prescriptions of medical men.

An Association

In response to the commercial threat posed by this new breed of merchant, the apothecaries formed a pharmaceutical association to restrain chemists and druggists from dispensing prescriptions and interfering with what was perceived as the legitimate business of apothecaries. The association was formed in 1794. When the association failed to stem the chemists and druggists, the apothecaries tried to enlist help at Westminster. In the original draft of the Apothecaries Act 1815 the apothecaries sought to prohibit the dispensing of medicines other than by apothecaries licensed under the provisions of the Act. After much intense lobbying by the chemists and druggists the proposal was abandoned. *Section 28* of the Apothecaries Act expressly preserved 'the trade or business of a chemist and druggist in the buying, preparing, compounding, dispensing, and vending drugs, medicines, and medicinal compounds, wholesale and retail'. This was the first recognition of the pharmacy profession in an Act of Parliament.

Training

There was nevertheless a problem. Whereas the apothecaries could practise only after passing examinations required by the Apothecaries Act 1814, there was no equivalent requirement for chemists and druggists. Yet the measuring and compounding of medicines was a skilled and exact science. Compulsory

Pharmacy Law and Practice. DOI: http://dx.doi.org/10.1016/B978-0-12-394289-0.00025-4

pharmaceutical training was required in other European countries such as France, Germany and Sweden, and there was genuine concern that chemists and druggists in this country were neither licensed nor trained. On a number of occasions enterprising individuals tried to introduce an improved system, but few chemists and druggists supported ideas for reform.

The Hawes Bill

The introduction of a medical bill by Mr. Hawes provided the necessary catalyst for reform in 1841. The Hawes Bill sought to give supervision of chemists and druggists to medical practitioners, who would set up a system of education and licensing along European lines. In order to oppose the Bill leading chemists in London formed a Society, the Pharmaceutical Society; the object of the Society being to improve the education of pharmaceutical chemists.

Royal Charter

The Hawes Bill failed, but the legislative attempt achieved its purpose. Following discussions with London University, the College of Physicians and the College of Surgeons, the Pharmaceutical Society established an educational programme and founded its own Board of Examiners. The Pharmaceutical Society's membership grew from 668 members (not including associates and apprentices) in 1841 to 1640 in 1843 when a Royal Charter was granted. The Royal Charter declared that existing chemists and druggists could be admitted as members, but assistants, apprentices and students would be admitted only after being examined and certified as qualified for admission. After a few years, the Pharmaceutical Society obtained the introduction of a Bill in order to place the education and certification of pharmaceutical chemists on a statutory footing. The Society of Apothecaries did not oppose the Bill.

Statutory Regulation

The Pharmacy Act 1852 confirmed the Royal Charter, empowering examiners appointed by the Pharmaceutical Society to grant or refuse certificates of competent skill and knowledge to exercise the business of pharmaceutical chemist. It became a criminal offence fraudulently to exhibit a certificate purporting to be a certificate of membership.

In the 150 years which have followed, the Pharmaceutical Society has grown from strength to strength. The Royal Charter was superseded by a second Charter in 1953 and then on 7 December 2004 a third new Royal Charter came into force.

The Pharmacy Act 1852 was repealed and replaced by the Pharmacy Act 1954, and together these provisions governed the education and organization of the modern profession. The Pharmacy Act 1954 was repealed in 2007 by the

Pharmacists and Pharmacy Technicians Order 2007/28. Prior to this abolition, members of the Pharmaceutical Society were divided into pharmaceutical chemists, and chemists and druggists, but the latter class was abolished in 1953. In 1988 the Queen permitted the Society to be known as the Royal Pharmaceutical Society of Great Britain (RPSGB). In 2004, a supplementary charter was granted and in 2009, amendments to this charter were permitted by the Queen. The RPSGB was subsequently split in 2010, with the Royal Pharmaceutical Society ('RPS') taking over the representative function and the General Pharmaceutical Council (GPhC) overseeing the regulatory function. The RPS estimated in its Annual Review (2010) that it now had some 32,000 members.

THE RPS

Objects

The main objects of the RPS under the amended 2004 Charter are as follows:

- To advance knowledge of, and education in, pharmacy and its application, thereby fostering good science and practice.
- To safeguard, maintain the honour and promote the interests of pharmacists in their exercise of the profession of pharmacy.
- To promote and protect the health and well-being of the public through the regulation and professional leadership and development of the pharmacy profession and regulation of other persons engaged in related activities.
- To maintain and develop the science and practice of pharmacy in its contribution to the health and well-being of the public.

These objects were defined to similar effect, albeit with less emphasis on the promotion of well-being of the public, in the 1953 Royal Charter and have been considered in detail by the courts on two occasions.

Not a Trade Association

In the first case, *Jenkin v. Pharmaceutical Society (1921)*, the court decided that the objectives of the predecessor to the RPS, the RPSGB, were not intended to cover activities normally associated with a trading association. It followed that the RPSGB was unable:

(1) to regulate the terms of employment (hours, wages and conditions) between employer and employee members of the RPSGB;
(2) to expend its funds in the formation of an industrial council committee to further these purposes;
(3) to insure its members against insurable risks.

A distinction had to be drawn between activities which promoted the interests of those engaged in the exercise of the profession of pharmacy as a whole and the promotion of the interest of an individual or individuals. The formation of an industrial council committee was an activity which fell into the latter category and therefore could not be said to promote the exercise of the profession of pharmacy within the meaning of the Charter. Although decided under the 1843 Royal Charter, the same decision would almost certainly be reached today.

No Power to Restrain Trade

In the second case, *Pharmaceutical Society v. Dickson (1970)*, the RPSGB had sought to include in the Code of Ethics a rule which amongst other things would have confined the trading activities of new pharmacies to pharmaceutical and 'traditional' goods. The sale of 'non-traditional' goods, such as jewellery, beach wear, handbags, Thermos flasks, etc., was, in the Society's opinion, degrading the quality and status of the profession. As in *Jenkins*, the House of Lords held that the proposed restrictions went outside the expressed objects of the Society. In the absence of evidence to show that professional standards had been eroded by reason of the trade in 'non-traditional' goods, the proposed restraint could not be said to be necessary to maintain and safeguard the honour of the profession or to promote the interests of members in the exercise of the profession.

Governance of the RPS

The governing bodies of the RPS comprise three national boards in England, Scotland and Wales, respectively. These boards are overseen by the Assembly, whose membership is comprised of 11 members of the national pharmacy board and three other members. These three other members include a pharmaceutical scientist, an academic and a lay member.

The GPhC

This body was established pursuant to *Section 4(1)* of the Pharmacy Order 2010. It is now responsible for the regulation of the profession, once undertaken by the RPSGB.

The objects of the council are:

(1) to establish and maintain a register of pharmacists, pharmacy technicians and premises at which a retail pharmacy business (RPB) is, or is to be, carried on;

(2) to set and promote standards for the safe and effective practice of pharmacy at registered pharmacies;

(3) to set requirements by reference to which registrants must demonstrate that their fitness to practise is not impaired;

(4) to promote the safe and effective practice of pharmacy by registrants (including, for example, by reference to any code of conduct for, and ethics relating to, pharmacy);

(5) to set standards and requirements in respect of the education, training, acquisition of experience and continuing professional development (CPD) that it is necessary for pharmacists and pharmacy technicians to achieve in order to be entered in the Register or to receive an annotation in the Register and to maintain competence; and

(6) to ensure the continued fitness to practise of registrants.

The GPhC is the statutory regulator for the pharmacy professions in Great Britain. The GPhC was established by the Pharmacy Order 2010 as permitted under the auspices of the Health and Social Care Act 2008. The GPhC is an independent statutory body which is also responsible for the registration of pharmacy premises and for the enforcement of provisions of the Medicines Act 1968 and the Poisons Act 1972.

Register of Pharmaceutical Chemists

In order to practise within the United Kingdom as a pharmacist, it is necessary to be registered with the GPhC. Registration is renewable each year and it involves demonstrating that professional, ethical and fitness to practise standards are satisfied.

Under Part 4 of the Pharmacy Order 2010, the GPhC is obliged to appoint a registrar. The registrar's principal duty is to maintain a register of pharmaceutical chemists. The register must contain the names and addresses of all persons who are entitled to have their names registered, and the registrar must publish a list known as the 'annual register of pharmaceutical chemists' every year. Registration is essential to a practising pharmacist. Only a registered pharmacist is entitled to buy and sell drugs and to compound and dispense medicines. Similarly, only a registered pharmacist can run an RPB.

Every registered pharmaceutical chemist must pay an annual fee to the GPhC. A person is entitled to have his name included in the register if he satisfies the registrar that he is qualified, whether by examination or under bye laws made by the GPhC, to receive a certificate of competence to practise.

Certificate of Registration

A pharmacist should display his certificate of registration at each premise along with a notice carrying the pharmacist's name and number. It is a criminal offence fraudulently to exhibit a certificate purporting to be a certificate of registration of the GPhC. It is further a criminal offence to forge a certificate or allow it to be used by any other person.

Removal of Name from the Register

The GPhC may direct the registrar to remove the name of a pharmaceutical chemist from the register if he has failed to pay the annual fee within 2 months of the date of demand. The GPhC may also direct the removal of the name of a pharmaceutical chemist from the register if he has been guilty of a crime or professional misconduct.

Registration of Premises

The registrar is obliged to keep a register in which he enters any premises in respect of which an application for registration is made. The registrar must be satisfied that at the time of the application the applicant is a person lawfully conducting an RPB or entitled to conduct an RPB lawfully from the premises. The meaning of these terms is explained earlier in Chapter 9.

Since 27 September 2010, the GPhC has been empowered to conduct covert surveillance under the Regulation of Investigatory Powers Act 2000. The GPhC is included in a list of public authorities allowed to authorise directed surveillance as part of an investigation into the detection or prevention of crime. Directed surveillance is defined as covert surveillance which does not entail the presence of individuals or use of monitoring devices on residential premises or in private vehicles. The surveillance must be proportionate and be carried out for the purposes of a specific investigation.

THE STATUTORY COMMITTEES OF THE GPHC

Introduction

The Pharmacy Order 2010 makes statutory provision for three committees to aid the GPhC in its functions. These are the Investigating Committee, the Fitness to Practise Committee and the Appeals Committee.

Under *Section 80* of the Medicines Act 1968, the relevant committee additionally considers cases against companies carrying on an RPB, where:

- the company has committed an offence under medicines legislation;
- a director, officer or employee of the company has been convicted of an offence, or is alleged to have committed misconduct.

The Investigating Committee

The Investigating Committee is a screening committee; it meets in private and does not hear oral evidence. It is required to consider all cases referred to it and decide whether the allegation ought to be considered by the Fitness to Practise Committee.

It must assess all documents and recommendations placed before it by the Registrar and also have regard to its own published referral criteria. The Committee will also consider any written submissions made by the registrant involved in the allegation.

This committee may also recommend that further investigations should be undertaken, obtain advice from a legal, clinical or other specialist adviser and adjourn consideration of the allegation until any further information has been obtained, any comments from the informant, if any are received, or any reports where the person concerned has undergone a medical examination.

Possible Sanctions of the Investigating Committee

If a fitness to practise allegation is referred by the Registrar to the Investigating Committee, the committee must decide whether the case needs to be considered by the Fitness to Practise Committee.

If the Investigating Committee determines that the case does not need to be referred, it may:

- dismiss the case
- give a warning to the registrant and decide that details of the warning should be recorded in the register
- give advice to the registrant, or any other person or organisation involved in the investigation
- agree undertakings with the registrant
- decide that a criminal prosecution should be initiated.

The Investigating Committee can also, in a health case, request a registrant to undergo a medical examination.

However, if the Investigating Committee believes that the Fitness to Practise Committee will consider that the registrant's fitness to practise is impaired, it will refer the case to the committee. The Registrar may also refer a case directly to the Fitness to Practise Committee. For example, this may occur in the event the Registrar considers that the Committee should make an interim suspension order or needs to urgently consider a case (because it is in the public interest to do so).

Referral Procedures

Once the Registrar has taken a decision to refer a fitness to practise allegation or a disqualification allegation to the Investigating Committee, a number of procedures must be followed. Initially, a notice of referral to the Investigating Committee must be served, along with copies of all documentation, summaries and any relevant information that is to be used by the Investigating Committee. The subject of the complaint must also be provided with a copy of the threshold criteria.

The notice of referral must also specify the allegation and any recommendations made by the Registrar that may expedite the resolution of the case. The notice must also indicate the date on which the Investigating Committee will consider the allegation. This date must be no less than 28 days after the date of service of the notice of referral. The notice of referral must also:

- Inform the recipient of the Investigating Committee's powers.
- Indicate that the recipient has 21 days after the date of service of the notice to confirm or deny the particulars of the allegation in question.
- Indicate that the recipient has 21 days in which to furnish the Committee with written representations and that any such responses may be shown to the informant for comment.
- Inform the recipient that the Investigating Committee may seek further information from any source for the purposes of carrying out its functions, including from the registrant's employer.

Once the Investigating Committee has considered an allegation, the subject of the allegation in question will be informed of its decisions no later than 10 days thereafter. The notice must include the reasons for the decision and be accompanied by any legal advice considered by the Investigating Committee.

In the event that the Investigating Committee has decided not to refer an allegation to the Fitness to Practise Committee the notice should clarify for the subject of the allegation that the Investigating Committee may nevertheless reconsider the allegation afresh in certain circumstances.

Procedure at the Hearing of the Fitness to Practise Committee

Once an allegation or matter is referred to the Fitness to Practise Committee, it must assess the fitness to practise of the person in respect of whom the allegation is made.

Part 6 of the General Pharmaceutical Council Fitness to Practise Rules Order of Council 2010 provides for the procedures of this committee with regard to oral hearings. Hearings must be held in public apart from those hearings relating to either a health allegation or an interim order hearing which must both be held in private. This may be dispensed with in the event that the Committee is satisfied that the public interest in holding a public hearing outweighs the interest of the registrant concerned or the third party in maintaining their privacy. All evidence adduced is subject to the requirements of relevance and fairness. The civil standard of proof is applicable and in considering whether the person before the Committee is fit to practise, a breach of the standards of conduct, ethics and performance may be considered.

The Decision of the Fitness to Practise Committee

Once the Fitness to Practise Committee determines that the fitness to practise of the person concerned is impaired, there are a number of measures available, namely:

- Giving warning to the person concerned in connection with any matter arising out of, or related to, the allegation and give a direction that details of the warning be recorded in the Register;

- Providing recommendations to any other person or other body involved in the investigation of the allegation or any issue arising out of, or related to, the allegation;
- Removal from the pharmaceutical register;
- Suspension from the register for a period not more than 12 months; or
- Entry in the pharmaceutical register is conditional on compliance with any order, for a period of time not exceeding 3 years.

The subject of the allegation must be informed of the decision, the reasons underpinning the decision and the right of appeal. This is usually done by the Committee Secretariat the next working day after any decision has been reached.

Section 80 of the MA 1968 gives the power to direct removal from the register of a limited company which carries on an RPB and any member of the company's board or any officer employed by the company.

Application for Restoration

A person whose name has been removed from the register as a result of criminal conviction or misconduct may apply to have his name restored to the register. Article 57 of the Pharmacy Order 2010 stipulates that, in considering applications for restoration, the GPhC may make provision for:

- *the form and manner in which applications are to be made (including rules to the effect that applicants must apply using application forms that are in such form as the Council may determine from time to time);*
- *the information to be provided by the applicant; and*
- *in the case of applications for restoration made in respect of individuals:*
  - *fitness to practise matters;*
  - *whether any, and if so what, additional education, training or experience is required before restoration, and the rules may make provision for these issues to be determined in individual cases by the Registrar,*
  - *whether, and if so what, continuing professional development is required after restoration, and the rules may make provision:*
    - *for these issues to be determined in individual cases by the Registrar, and*
    - *enabling the Registrar to determine that the application for restoration is to be granted subject to the applicant agreeing to comply with such undertakings with regard to continuing professional development as the Registrar considers appropriate.*

An application for restoration cannot occur before the expiration of 5 years from the date of removal or within 12 months of the date of an earlier application.

Purpose of Sanction Imposed by the GPhC

When considering an application for restoration, the purpose of the original sanction of removal from the register must be borne in mind. The purpose of the sanction is threefold, namely:

(1) The protection of the public
(2) The maintenance of public confidence in the profession
(3) The maintenance of proper standards of behaviour.

Principles to Be Applied When Considering a Restoration Application

Removal from the register is the most serious sanction available to the GPhC. Once removed from the register, a former practitioner is considered no longer fit to be a member of the profession. In ordinary circumstances, the GPhC will not entertain an application for restoration within any period shorter than 5 years from the date that the removal from the register took effect.

Guidance on the approach to be adopted is provided in the following cases. The Master of the Rolls in *Bolton v. Law Society, 1994* stated:

It often happens that a former solicitor appearing before the tribunal can adduce a wealth of glowing tributes from his professional brethren. He can often show that for him and his family the consequences of striking off or suspension would be little short of tragic. Often he will say, convincingly, that he has learned his lesson and will not offend again. On applying for restoration after striking off, all these points may be made, and the former solicitor may also be able to point to real efforts made to re-establish himself and redeem his reputation. All of these matters are relevant and should be considered. But none of them touches the essential issue, which is the need to maintain among members of the public a well founded confidence that any solicitor whom they instruct will be a person of unquestionable integrity, probity and trustworthiness. [...] The reputation of the profession is more important than then fortunes of any individual member. Membership of a profession brings many benefits, but that is a part of the price.

In *Gosai v. General Medical Council, 2003*, these points were reiterated by the Privy Council:

The Professional Conduct Committee accepted that the appellant was making real efforts to demonstrate his fitness to practise. However, the Professional Conduct Committee was entitled to conclude, in relation to ... the refusal of restoration ... that the efforts he had made were outweighed by other factors. These included the seriousness of the original offence when the Professional Conduct Committee stated that the appellant had "fallen lamentably below the professional standards to which patients were entitled," "demonstrated clinical incompetence of the most basic kind", and [had] "not been truthful."

The committee will give careful consideration to all the circumstances of an individual case and the representations made by the applicant. However, the applicant will need to present a strong argument and will be required to demonstrate his suitability to be restored to the register.

Case Study

Facts: Y appeals against the decision of a disciplinary committee of the RPSBG that he is unfit to have his name on the register of pharmacists because he has been convicted of falsifying NHS prescriptions. It is also alleged that Y had altered a number of prescriptions forms and forged a doctor's signature. Two days prior to the disciplinary hearing, Y asks for an adjournment on the grounds of ill-health. He fails to supply medical evidence and the application is ultimately refused. Y is absent at the hearing but it proceeds anyway because he has voluntarily chosen not to attend. The committee holds that Y's name should be removed from the pharmaceutical register because of his conviction and the other allegations of falsifying prescriptions that the committee find to be true.

Question: Was the committee incorrect in refusing to adjourn the hearing even though Y was too ill to attend? Was the decision to remove Y's name from the register a disproportionate response?

Answer: The committee had been correct to proceed and had been entitled to remove Y from the register. The application for adjournment had been made very late and did not have corroborating evidence to support it. The committee had also provided compelling reasons for the decision to sanction Y in such a way. Y's actions were instances of serious misconduct in a professional context and it is unsurprising that the committee had concluded that this was the most appropriate response.

This case study is based on *Yusuf v. Royal Pharmaceutical Society of Great Britain, 2009*, EWHC 867 (Admin).

The Appeals Committee

A person or a limited company affected by an 'appealable decision' of the Fitness to Practise Committee may, within 28 days from the date of the decision, lodge an appeal with the Appeals Committee. The appellant must file a notice of appeal with the Registrar.

Once the Appeals Committee makes a decision, it must inform the person bringing the appeal of the outcome, the reasons for it and of any right of appeal.

An appeal against such a decision has to be filed with the High Court and served on the GPhC within 28 days from the date that the written notice was sent (or within such longer period as the relevant court may allow). It is open to the court to dismiss the appeal; allow the appeal; substitute the sanction for another sanction that the Fitness to Practise Committee could have imposed or finally, remit the case to the Registrar or the Fitness to Practise Committee for disposal in accordance with the court's directions.

The function of the High Court is not to impose its own view in substitution for a view taken by the GPhC unless it came to the conclusion that it was plainly wrong or the committee had misdirected itself in reaching its conclusion – see *Thobani v. Pharmaceutical Society of Great Britain, 1990,* and *Singh v. General Medical Council, 2001.*

Fitness to Practise

The Pharmacy Order 2010 repealed the Pharmacists and Pharmacy Technicians Order 2007 and introduced, in Part 6, new requirements of fitness to practise. Article 48 provides that the GPhC must:

(a) set standards relating to the conduct, ethics and performance expected of registrants;

(b) make provision in rules regarding the criteria to which the Fitness to Practise Committee is to have regard when deciding, in the case of any registrant, whether or not the requirements as to fitness to practise are met in relation to that registrant.

In order to be admitted to the register, a pharmacist or pharmacy technician must satisfy the GPhC that they have the skills, knowledge, character and health required to do their job safely and effectively.

'Fitness to practise' is defined by the GPhC as a person's suitability to be on the register, without any limitations or restrictions. In practice, this means a pharmacist should maintain an appropriate standard of proficiency, maintain good health and good character, and comply to the principles of good practice set out in the various standards issued by the GPhC.

Fitness to practise can be deemed to be impaired on grounds such as misconduct, lack of competence, ill-health or through having been convicted of a criminal offence.

Case Study

Facts: Z is found guilty of serious professional misconduct on the grounds that his fitness to practise was impaired. A patient had been under the joint care of Z and another individual (S). Scans indicated that the patient's illness was due to brain tumour as opposed to an abscess. Z was on holiday and during this time, the patient was sent home before surgery. However, the patient later died at home from an infected abscess. Z was found unfit to practise because he excluded the alternative diagnosis and had failed to take a number of precautionary measures.

Question: Can Z appeal on the grounds that he had suggested that a number of precautionary measures to S? Even if Z did make these recommendations, would this make any difference to the finding of serious professional misconduct?

Answer: Yes, Z was allowed to appeal against the decision of the professional regulator. In making its decisions, the regulator failed to consider a previous finding that Z had made the recommendations in question. Also, the regulator could not demonstrate that sending the patient home had been an act of misconduct.

Also, evidence that Z, in the past, was a good and safe doctor was important factor in determining whether Z was currently unfit to practise and this evidence had not been considered by the regulator until the third and final stage of the inquiry, that of mitigation. This evidence ought to have been considered by the regulator at an earlier stage in the proceedings.

Reason: When assessing whether an individual's serious professional misconduct or deficient performance resulted in an impaired ability to practise, it is necessary to determine whether any impairment was still current.

This case study is based on R *(on the application of Zgymunt) v. General Medical Council, 2008,* EWHC 2643 (Admin).

Continuing Professional Development

Pursuant to Article 43 of the Pharmacy Order 2010, the GPhC implemented a framework through which the CPD requirements and conditions of the members of the register could be monitored and assessed. Members are required to complete an annual declaration of compliance and must submit records in support of this declaration. The GPhC has issued Standards for Continuing Professional Development (September 2010) which recommends that a pharmacist keep a record of CPD activities undertaken in a manner that is legible, either in written or electronic form. Further, members are advised to make a minimum of nine CPD entries annually. These activities should be representative of the scope and context of the work undertaken by the pharmacist or pharmacy technician.

The standards also advise that the pharmacists conduct will be judged by reference to these standards and failure to comply could jeopardise a member's registration.

THE STANDARDS OF PROFESSIONAL CONDUCT

Code of Ethics

The GPhC maintains a code of conduct, ethics and performance for its members with the aim of safeguarding and promoting the interests of the public and the profession. The public places great trust in the knowledge, skills and professional judgement of pharmacists. This trust requires pharmacists to ensure and maintain, throughout their career, high standards of personal and professional conduct and performance, up-to-date knowledge and continuing competence relevant to their sphere of practice whether or not they work in direct contact with the public. The Standards of Conduct, Ethics and Performance are reproduced on the GPhC's web site.[1]

Key Responsibilities

The Standard identifies the key responsibilities of a pharmacist in the following terms:

(1) Make patients your first concern
(2) Use your professional judgement in the interests of patients and the public
(3) Show respect for others
(4) Encourage patients and the public to participate in decisions about their care
(5) Develop your professional knowledge and competence
(6) Be honest and trustworthy
(7) Take responsibility for your working practices.

Obligations

The GPhC formed the view that it was necessary to elaborate on the seven core principles so as to form a brief summary of the pharmacist's obligations in each area. Any complaint of misconduct would be based upon an alleged breach of these obligations and, by inference, of the principle which governs them.

Guidance

In order to assist pharmacists in the practical discharge of their professional obligations, the GPhC has set out some guidance which is intended to reflect the standards which pharmacists should meet in their daily lives. For example, the first principle enumerated obliges a pharmacist to 'Make patients your first concern'. The GPHC elaborates on this and what compliance with this standard entails:

The care, well-being and safety of patients are at the heart of professional practice. They must always be your first concern. Even if you do not have direct contact with patients your decisions or behaviour can still affect their care or safety.

The Standards indicate that this obligation is satisfied once the following directions are complied with:

(1.1) Make sure the services you provide are safe and of acceptable quality
(2.1) Take action to protect the well-being of patients and the public
(3.1) Promote the health of patients and the public
(4.1) Get all the information you require to assess a person's needs in order to give the appropriate treatment and care
(5.1) If you need to, refer patients to other health or social care professionals, or to other relevant organisations
(6.1) Do your best to provide medicines and other professional services safely and when patients need them
(7.1) Be satisfied that patients or their carers know how to use their medicines
(8.1) Keep full and accurate records of the professional services you provide in a clear and legible form

(9.1) Make sure you have access to the facilities, equipment and resources you need to provide your professional services safely and effectively

(10.1) Organise regular reviews, audits and risk assessments to protect patient and public safety and to improve your professional services.

Within the specific recommendations pertaining to compliance with each of the seven principles, the GPhC has published further guidance on individual recommendations. An example of this is 7.7 of the standards of the conduct, ethics and performance which states:

Make sure that you keep to your legal and professional responsibilities and that your workload or working conditions do not present a risk to patient care or public safety.

According to the guidance provided, in order to lawfully run an RPB, a registered pharmacist must be in charge of the registered pharmacy and be aware of the scope of the role and responsibilities that this entails. Any ambiguities should be clarified as soon as possible. A pharmacist can only be the registered pharmacist of one business at any given time. It is also crucial that the pharmacy record be maintained accurately, in either written or electronic form.

Under the Medicines (Pharmacies) (Responsible Pharmacist) Regulations 2008, a responsible pharmacist cannot be away from the premises for any longer than 2h during the pharmacy's business hours. These regulations also require that an RPB implement and document precisely pharmacy procedures relating to how medicinal products are ordered, stored, prepared and sold by retail, and this should be done in a safe and effective manner. Pharmacy procedures should also anticipate and provide guidance on the circumstances in which a member of staff who is not the pharmacist can provide advice about medicinal products. Certain members of staff who are deemed competent to perform certain tasks relating to the business should be identified, pursuant to these regulations. Finally, all pharmacy procedures should be in written and/or electronic form and should be available at the premises for inspection by either the person carrying on the pharmacy business, the registered pharmacist or members of staff. These procedures should also be subject to periodic review.

Similar guidance is also provided in relation to standard 3.4 which obliges a pharmacist to:

… make sure that if your religious or moral beliefs prevent you from providing a service, you tell the relevant people or authorities and refer patients and the public to other providers.

The GPhC recommends that, prior to accepting employment, a pharmacist should think about the area in which he will be working and the type of services he will be providing. A further consideration is whether the pharmacist will be working alone or alongside others who could provide alternative service. Employers, relevant authorities and colleagues should all be informed of the pharmacist's religious or moral conviction where they may prevent the pharmacist from providing certain services.

The Guidance refers particularly to the dispensing of Emergency Hormonal Contraception (EHC) and Routine Hormonal Contraception (RHC). With regard to EHC, it is recommended that if a pharmacist does not supply EHC, women should be referred to an alternative appropriate supply within the appropriate time limits. If a pharmacist does not supply RHC then he should refer patients to another appropriate supplier within a time period which will not compromise the women's contraceptive protection.

A pharmacist who refers a patient to a doctor's surgery or hospital should consider whether the patient will be seen within the necessary time frame so as to ensure that the treatment is effective.

Breach of the Code

In law, the arbiter of what constitutes misconduct is the relevant committee. Misconduct does not necessarily involve some sort of moral censure; rather, misconduct may be defined as 'incorrect or erroneous conduct of any kind provided that it is of a serious nature', that is judged according to the rules written or unwritten of the pharmaceutical profession, see *R v. Statutory Committee of the Pharmaceutical Society of Great Britain, ex parte Sokoh, 1986*. Moreover, in that case the High Court held that it was possible that just one error may constitute misconduct, if the error was sufficiently serious.

The incorrect or erroneous conduct must, however, be regarded as so serious as to justify a finding of misconduct. Where a member of the pharmaceutical register is alleged to have failed to comply with the standards of conduct, ethics and performance set by the GPhC, this failure will not in itself constitute misconduct but may be considered in any subsequent proceedings against that member (Pharmacy Order 2010, Article 48). Deliberate breach of the policy made by the GPhC will not automatically amount to misconduct; in such a case the Committee has to satisfy itself that the deliberate breach of policy was of such a quality as to constitute serious misconduct, see *R v. Statutory Committee of the Royal Pharmaceutical Society ex parte Boots the Chemists PLC, 1997*. In that case Boots deliberately flouted policy made by the Council in June 1993 to prohibit the introduction of collection and delivery services in areas where a community pharmacy already exists. The chairman of the Statutory Committee advised that Boots' conduct did not amount to misconduct in law. The High Court agreed and said that the legally unqualified majority of the committee should have followed the chairman's advice.

The Inspectorate

The GPhC, as a professional regulatory body, is unusual because it has its own inspectorate, charged primarily with investigations and inspection visits.

Inspectors visit all registered pharmacy premises in Great Britain to ensure sufficient compliance with all legal requirements and regulatory standards. The pharmacy will be assessed in light of the objective of providing safe and effective service to the public. In the event that the pharmacy being assessed is not compliant with legal or regulatory requirements, the inspector will advise on the steps necessary to secure compliance. In the event of persistent non-compliance, an inspector may initiate disciplinary proceedings. Most pharmacies will be inspected at least once in every 5-year period. However, depending on the pharmacy (if for example the services provided are high risk or there is a real concern for patient safety), inspection may occur more frequently.

The inspectorate is also responsible for investigating complaints made against registered pharmacists, registered pharmacy technicians and pharmacy owners. Further, an investigation may also be initiated after an inspection during which the inspector found evidence of persistent non-compliance with legal or regulatory standards or there is a significant risk to public safety. An investigation will usually entail speaking to the complainant and any relevant witnesses as well as discussing the complaint with the relevant registered pharmacist or technician. By virtue of the Police and Criminal Evidence Act 1984 and the codes of practice published there under, an inspector is empowered to formally interview the pharmacist, any employees or owners of the pharmacy.

In order to ensure that the GPhC effectively regulates professional pharmacists and pharmacy technicians, inspectors are conferred with a number of powers under the Pharmacy Order 2010. Inspectors are entitled to investigate allegations that an individual is unfit to practise, enforce the standards set by the GPhC, secure compliance with the Poisons legislation, secure compliance with the relevant parts of the Medicines Act 1968 legislation, enforce provisions within the Order relating to offences relating to the register, enforce the relevant provisions of the Veterinary Medicines Regulations.

INTERNET PHARMACY

The internet offers an unprecedented medium unhindered by geographical barriers, and the opportunities to utilise its power for delivering and receiving information are almost boundless. However, in providing such freedom the internet has created difficulties. In the medical context one major difficulty faced concerns the regulation of online prescribing.

The popularity of the drug Viagra (sildenafil citrate) provides a key example. Within days of the United States Food and Drug Administration's approval of Viagra the internet was flooded with web sites dedicated to the selling of the 'lifestyle drug'.

The internet's exponential growth and the potential to accumulate major profits fuelled this expansion. Such sites sell everything, from licensed drugs to 'miracle cures' with astounding claims of efficacy.

Doctors from the United States were the first to grasp the opportunity, launching sites such as Confirmed.com.[2] They were quickly followed by online pharmacies, both licensed and unlicensed including those purveying antidepressants and infertility pills.

Although many sites are convincing the internet is not discriminating in whom it allows to view them. A US case in which a child bought Viagra with the use of his parent's credit card has highlighted the ease of which purchases can be made and the lack of regulatory control surrounding drug prescribing on the internet. Further problems of the internet include the ease with which patients can fail to provide a full clinical history or disguise their true intent, whilst it is difficult for a doctor to effectively evaluate the risks and benefits of prescription.

Internet Prescribing of Drugs Online in the United Kingdom

The British Medical Association (BMA) has also maintained a call for a ban on doctors prescribing medicinal products online. The main concern is that doctors cannot ascertain sufficient detail about a patient's condition simply by an exchange of email. Furthermore, there are concerns that patients may use the internet to obtain medicinal products they do not need or that the medicines that are obtained may be counterfeit. The World Health Organization estimates that 50% of medicines supplied from online pharmacies, which conceal their physical address, are counterfeit.

Buying medicines online from a pharmacy that does not have a registered address could potentially pose a number of problems. For example, the medicines may not meet UK safety standards or if they are past their 'sell by date', the effectiveness of the drug may be substantially reduced.

The GPhC acknowledges that indications suggest that the general public is confused about the regulation of internet pharmacies and to that end, it has produced an internet pharmacy logo which can be displayed only by pharmacies who offer professional services registered in the United Kingdom. This logo has a unique registration for each online pharmacy and by clicking on the logo, a prospective online purchaser is redirected to the GPhC online register webpage where the details of the pharmacy can be confirmed.

Guidance published by the GPhC on the 'Standards for Pharmacy Owners and Superintendent Pharmacists of Retails Pharmacy Businesses' makes provision for standards applicable to online pharmacies.

Pharmacists and Legality of Selling Prescription Drugs Over the Internet

A ruling by the European Court of Justice (ECJ) in the case of *Deutsche Apothekerverband v. 0800 DocMorris NV, 2005*, has provided some clear guidance to all EC pharmacists as to the legality of prescription drug sales online. The ECJ held that whilst European pharmacies are free to sell over-the-counter medicines on the internet they cannot do the same for prescription drugs. The case was raised by a German court who had queried whether a national ban on all sales breached EU rules on the free movement of goods.

A German pharmacy trade body, the Deutsche Apothekerverband, had complained that Dutch online pharmacy 0800 DocMorris.com[3] was selling prescription and non-prescription medicines, in languages including German, for consumers in Germany. The ECJ stated that where the ban related to medicinal products that had been authorised for sale on the German market, there was breach of the EU laws on the free movement of goods.

However, such a breach is only acceptable if it is justified by circumstances specified in EU law. In this case, said the Court, the breach could be justified by reason of being necessary for the 'health and life of humans'. Thus the ban could be justified with regard to authorised medicines only available on prescription, because 'there may be risks attaching to the use of these medicinal products'. Accordingly, 'the need to be able to check effectively and responsibly the authenticity of doctors' prescriptions and to ensure that the medicine is handed over either to the customer himself or to a person to whom its collection has been entrusted by the customer is such as to justify a prohibition on mail-order sales'. In addition the Court considered the provisions of the advertising law that prohibits the advertising of mail order. The Court ruled that where a prohibition of that kind applies to medicinal products that require authorisation but have not been authorised, or to medicinal products available only on prescription, the prohibition is in keeping with an existing prohibition in EU law.

NHS PRESCRIPTION FRAUD

Prescription fraud has proved a highly controversial topic within the NHS – it was reported that in 1998, prescription fraud was costing the NHS in excess of £150 million a year. A concerted effort by the NHS Counter Fraud and Security Management Service has significantly reduced this figure following the introduction of fines and greater rigour in eligibility.

Pharmacists are required to ask people who get free prescriptions for proof. People entitled to free prescriptions include those who are 60 or over, those under the age of 16 or 16–18 and in full-time education, people who are pregnant or have had a baby in the previous 12 months and have a valid maternity exemption certificate (MatEx) or have a specified medical condition and have a valid medical exemption certificate (MedEx), people who have a continuing physical disability that makes them dependent on third parties and have a valid MedEx or people who hold a valid war pension exemption certificate and the prescription is for an accepted disability, or a person who is an NHS inpatient.

Thus between 1999 and 2004, counter-fraud work cut pharmaceutical patient fraud by 60%, dental patient fraud by 25%, optical patient fraud by

23% and, in some areas, fraud by NHS professionals by 31–46%. Fraud detection rates have improved by more than 1400% and there is a 96% successful prosecution rate.

Pharmacists are offered a reward of £70 for every time they spot and report a false or fraudulent claim. Anyone caught making a false claim, or trying to make a false claim, face going to court and receiving a £100 fine. However, as with many other counter-fraud regimes it has been suggested that this greater rigour has discouraged genuinely eligible people from getting what they are entitled to, through excessive bureaucracy.

Both patients and professionals can perpetrate fraud. An example provided by the NHS Counter Fraud is a patient who obtained three prescriptions by giving false names and addresses and by stealing a number of prescriptions from a doctor's surgery. The patient then used these to obtain drugs including dihydrocodeine and temazepan, both of which are commonly abused. This offence resulted in 6–8 months imprisonment.

Professional fraud can be committed by altering prescriptions, falsely claiming for work and the use of fictional patient identities to make fraudulent claims. In one example cited by the NHS Counter Fraud, one pharmacist claimed the difference between the medicine prescribed and the cheaper generic drug he supplied. To do this, the pharmacist withheld the genuine prescriptions and produced falsified prescriptions. This scheme resulted in a financial gain of £21,000. The pharmacist was ultimately sentenced to 9 months imprisonment.

Forged Prescriptions

It can be extremely difficult to detect a forged prescription, but every pharmacist should be alert to the possibility that any prescription calling for a misused product could be a forgery.

In many instances, the forger may make a fundamental error in writing the prescription or the pharmacist may get an instinctive feeling that the prescription is not genuine because of the way the patient behaves.

If the prescriber's signature is known, or the patient is not known to be suffering from a condition which requires the medicinal product prescribed, the signature should be scrutinised and, if possible, checked against an example on another prescription known to be genuine. Large doses or quantities should be checked with the prescriber in order to detect alterations to previously valid prescriptions.

If the prescriber's signature is not known, the prescriber must be contacted and asked to confirm that the prescription is genuine. The prescriber's telephone number must be obtained from the telephone directory, or from directory inquiries, not from the headed notepaper, as forgers may use false letter headings.

A list of matters should alert a pharmacist and cause him to check further. These include the following:

- An unknown prescriber
- A new patient
- Excessive quantities
- Uncharacteristic prescribing or method of writing prescription by a known doctor
- The prescriber's signature.

These precautions should be applied to all prescriptions for medicinal products liable to abuse and not only for controlled drugs.

Self-Assessment Questions

1. Since the implementation of the Pharmacy Order 2010, how is the pharmacy profession regulated and how does a pharmacist comply with these obligations?

   Answer: Regulation is now overseen by the GPhC which has produced a number of standards and guides to enable a pharmacist to understand the obligations with which he must comply. A pharmacist should also be aware of the Medicines (Pharmacies) (Responsible Pharmacist) Regulations 2008 that a registered pharmacist be on the premises for a certain period of time during retail hours and require the implementation of responsible, effective pharmacy procedures. A pharmacist is also obliged to undertake activities to further his CPD and must also keep a detailed account of these activities.

2. How is the regulatory regime enforced?

   Answer: The GPhC investigates complaints from the general public but it also has its own inspectorate which conducts both investigations and inspection visits. The inspectorate has a number of statutory powers and is entitled to interview the pharmacist, the complainant if there is one and any members of staff. Further, there are three statutory bodies within the GPhC that handle disciplinary issues within the profession. These are the Investigations Committee, the Fitness to Practise Committee and the Appeals Committee. A pharmacist can face a number of sanctions including removal from the pharmaceutical register, temporary suspension from the register or conditional entry in the register, depending on compliance with conditions set by the relevant committee.

ADDITIONAL RESOURCES

1. http://www.pharmacyregulation.org/standards/conduct-ethics-and-performance
2. http://www.Confirmed.com
3. http://www.Docmorris.com

Chapter 26

Liability in Negligence

DISPENSING MISTAKES

A pharmacist, like any other professional person, can make a mistake and, like doctors, the consequences of a pharmacist's mistake can be most serious. The customer may suffer serious personal injuries as a result of the mistake.

The Centre for Medication Safety and Service Quality (CMSSQ) is a joint initiative between the Pharmacy Department at Imperial College Healthcare NHS Trust and The School of Pharmacy (SOP), University of London. It has conducted extensive research into medication safety and in 2007, a study conducted by the Centre which compared items awaiting collection with the original prescription found a content error in 49 (1.7%) of 2859 dispensed items and a labelling error in 46 (1.6%).

The law concerning a pharmacist's civil liability for mistakes is considered in this section of the book. With the increase in professional negligence litigation, it is an area of law with which the contemporary community pharmacist needs to have some familiarity.

BREACH OF CONTRACT

Where a customer obtains medicinal products on the strength of an NHS prescription, even though the customer pays a prescription charge, the courts have held that the products are not supplied under a contract of sale but rather by virtue of the pharmacist's statutory duty to supply of the medicinal products (*Pfizer Corp v. Ministry of Health (1965)*). Accordingly, if the customer is to recover any damages for a mistake in the dispensing process, he or she has to establish a case in negligence against the pharmacist at common law.

NEGLIGENCE

A customer who wishes to recover damages for personal injuries has to prove four things:

(1) That the defendant owed him a duty of care.
(2) That the defendant was in breach of that duty.

Pharmacy Law and Practice. DOI: http://dx.doi.org/10.1016/B978-0-12-394289-0.00026-6

(3) That he or she has suffered damages as a result of that breach.
(4) That the damage was reasonably foreseeable in all the circumstances.

Duty of Care

A duty to take reasonable care arises when the defendant can reasonably foresee that the claimant (the one who complains) is likely to be injured by his or her conduct. As Lord Atkin said in *Donoghue v. Stephenson (1932)*:

You must take reasonable care to avoid acts or omissions which you can reasonably foresee would be likely to injure your neighbour. Who, then, in law, is my neighbour? The answer seems to be … persons who are so closely and directly affected by my act that I ought reasonably to have them in contemplation as being so affected when I am directing my mind to the acts or omissions which are called in question.

Breach of Duty

It is always a question of fact whether the defendant has failed to show reasonable care in the particular circumstances of a case. The law lays down the general rules which determine the standard of care which has to be attained, and it is for the court to apply that legal standard of care to its findings of fact so as to find whether the defendant has attained that standard. The legal standard is not the standard of the defendant himself but that of a person of ordinary prudence or a person using ordinary skill. In cases where a person has a particular skill, such as a pharmacist, the person is required to show the skill normally possessed by persons undertaking work of a similar nature. Thus in the case of a pharmacist, the pharmacist must exercise the standard of skill which is usual in his or her profession, and he or she must exercise the same degree of care which a reasonably competent pharmacist would exercise in performing the same task.

Occasionally, situations arise where the claimant is not able to establish exactly how the accident occurred. Nevertheless, the mere fact of the happening of the accident in certain circumstances may justify the inference that the defendant has probably been negligent and his negligence caused the injury. The maxim, known as *res ipsa loquitur* (i.e., 'the thing speaks for itself'), is an evidentiary rule to the effect that the fact of the injury and the circumstances in which it was sustained establish a *prima facie* case of negligence against the defendant, which the defendant must then rebut in order to avoid a finding of liability.

Damage as a Result of the Breach

The claimant must show that the defendant's wrongdoing was a cause, though it need not necessarily be the sole or dominant cause, of the claimant's injuries. In general, a defendant who commits a wrong takes his or her victim as he or she finds him. It is no answer to a claim for damages to say that the victim would have sustained no or less injury if he or she had not suffered from some pre-existing condition.

Foreseeable Damage

There is a final hurdle which a claimant must surmount before he or she can recover damages for negligence. The type of injury which the claimant has suffered must be reasonably foreseeable, in the sense that a reasonable man would have foreseen the type of injury as being likely to flow from the defendant's breach of duty.

Negligence Causing Death

All causes of action which accrue to the benefit of a claimant will survive for the benefit of his or her estate after his or her death under the provisions of the Law Reform (Miscellaneous Provisions) Act 1934. Additionally, where the breach of duty has caused death, the deceased's dependants may maintain an action and recover damages against the person liable in respect of the death under the Fatal Accidents Act 1976. The action must be brought by the deceased's personal representatives, and since only one action may be brought, claims must be included for all the dependants. In assessing damages under the Fatal Accidents Act, other than damages of £11,800 for bereavement, the court seeks to compensate the dependants for the loss which they have sustained as a result of the death.

Choice of Defendant

In some cases the claimant may be faced with a choice of defendants. A typical situation arises where the claimant was a passenger in a motor car, which was in collision with another. If there is evidence to show that both drivers are to blame, it is normal practice to commence legal proceedings against both drivers. The same principles will apply where a patient has suffered injury caused by the breach of duty of a doctor and a pharmacist. Both may be sued together in one action. The basic rule is that each of the two tortfeasors will be liable for the whole damage resulting from their tortious act. However, where tortfeasors are jointly liable, the tortfeasors can ask the court to assess their respective liability in respect of the accident. This is done by one of the tortfeasors commencing proceedings against the other for contribution under the Civil Liability (Contribution) Act 1978.

Defences

The obvious defence, raised in most negligence actions, is the basic denial that the defendant has been guilty of any negligence and the further denial that, in the event of the claimant establishing any breach of duty against him or her, the injury resulted from accident. The following specific defences tend to arise in practice in cases where pharmacists are involved.

Contributory Negligence

Where the injury suffered is partly the result of the fault of the claimant, the recoverable damages are reduced by the court to the extent it thinks fit, having regard to the plaintiff's responsibility for the injuries: the Law Reform (Contributory Negligence) Act 1945. Under this Act the court determines the percentage of contributory negligence. It will not deal in minute percentages, so the normal practice is to disregard responsibility evaluated at less than 10%.

Novus Actus Interveniens (A New Act Intervening)

Situations sometimes arise where the sequence of events following on from the defendant's act or omission is interrupted. Once it is established that, in the ordinary course of events, the defendant's act or omission would not have resulted in the damage but for the intervening act (whether of some third party or of the claimant), the chain of causation is broken. In such an event the defendant will not be liable.

Volenti Non Fit Injuria (That to Which a Man Consents Cannot Be Considered an Injury)

To raise this defence it is necessary to show that the claimant agreed to run the risk involved; mere silence on the subject is not normally sufficient.

Limitation

In personal injury cases the claimant must normally commence his or her action within 3 years of the date when the cause of action accrued. The date when the cause of action accrued will be the date when the injury was sustained. There are, however, special cases. After sustaining personal injury a claimant may not have discovered the effects of the injury or the identity of the defendant until after the limitation period has expired. In this case a special period of limitation is prescribed. The period of limitation will be deemed to run for 3 years from the date when the claimant became possessed of full information about his or her case. The period begins to run when the claimant has knowledge of all of the following matters:

(1) That claimant's injury was significant.
(2) That the injury was attributable in whole or in part to the acts or omissions of which the claimant complains.
(3) The identity of the defendant.

However, it is right to add that a party who has sustained injuries will be imputed with knowledge which he or she might reasonably have been expected to acquire either by his or her own observation or enquiry or by expert advice, which it might have been reasonable for him to seek. Finally, a court may direct that the limitation provisions should be disregarded in a personal injury case if in the view of the court it would be equitable for action to proceed, having regard to the degree of prejudice suffered by the claimant on account of the rules of limitation as well as the prejudice the defendant would suffer if the limitation period were disregarded.

Application of the Law to Pharmacists

Amongst other duties it is clear that a pharmacist is obliged as a supplier of medicinal products to take reasonable care to:

(1) Ensure that the correct medicinal products are supplied.
(2) Warn customers of the potential dangers or adverse effects of the medicinal products.
(3) Ensure that customers are instructed as to the correct dosage.

Failure to take reasonable care in the discharge of any of these tasks will render the pharmacist liable to legal proceedings for breach of professional duty. The application of these principles is demonstrated by a consideration of the following reported cases.

Dispensing the Wrong Medicine

Collins v. Hertfordshire County Council (1947)

The pharmacist at a pre-NHS hospital was asked to dispense '100 ml of 1% cocaine with adrenaline, for injection'. The pharmacist did not question the order for an unheard-of dosage of a dangerous drug. He made up the cocaine and adrenaline as an injection and supplied it to the operating theatre. During the operation the cocaine preparation was injected and the patient died. In fact the final-year student doctor who had ordered cocaine had herself misheard the consultant surgeon who had actually ordered procaine. The hospital's standing instructions on ordering dangerous drugs had not been complied with by either the doctor or the pharmacist. The hospital authority was held liable for the pharmacist's failure to question the order and for the student doctor's mistake.

Prendergast v. Sam and Dee Ltd, Kozary and Miller (1989)

A pharmacist misread a doctor's writing on a prescription. The doctor had prescribed Amoxil but the pharmacist read it as Daonil. He dispensed Daonil, and the patient, who was not a diabetic, suffered hypoglycemia and irreversible brain damage. The patient (Prendergast) sued the pharmacy company (Sam and Dee Ltd), the pharmacist (Kozary) and the doctor (Miller). The court found all the three defendants liable. The doctor's writing was adjudged to fall below the standard of legibility required of him in the exercise of his duty to the patient. The court also held that although the writing was bad, the word could have been read as Daonil, and that certain aspects of the prescription should have alerted the pharmacist. On appeal the court specifically held that the chain of causation starting with the poor handwriting was not broken.

The court held that the pharmacist had a duty to give some thought to the prescription he was dispensing and he should not dispense it mechanically. If there is any doubt the pharmacist must contact the doctor for clarification. In this case, if the pharmacist had been paying attention he would have realised that there was something wrong with the prescription, since the dosage and the small number of tablets were unusual for Daonil. Additionally, the claimant had paid for the prescription, yet drugs for diabetes (such as Daonil) were free under the NHS. The court apportioned damages between the defendants: 25% to the doctor and 75% shared between the company and the pharmacist.

Case Study

Facts: W is prescribed an oral contraceptive, Microgynon, by her general practitioner. She continues to be prescribed and take this contraceptive for 2 years. D dispenses her prescription but instead dispenses another oral contraceptive pill, Logynon, rather than Microgynon. W takes the incorrect prescription for 2 consecutive days before noticing the dispensing mistake. She resumes taking the correct prescription but falls pregnant soon after and gives birth. She suffers from post-natal depression after giving birth. W alleges that D was negligent and breached the duty of care owed to W.

Question: Is W entitled to damages for care, expenses and loss of earnings flowing from the pregnancy and the period of post-natal depression?

Answer: No. The pharmacist, D, had been negligent in dispensing the wrong medication, but that error had neither caused nor materially contributed to the failure of the contraception and the resulting pregnancy.

Reason: The court's conclusion was based on the factual issue of whether the temporary change in the oral contraceptive resulted in the failure of the contraception and the resulting pregnancy. Ultimately, the court rejected the medical evidence advanced for W on level of increased risk of contraceptive failure.

This case study is based on the decision of *Wootton v. J Docter Ltd and Another (2008) All ER (D) 256 Dec.*

Dispensing the Wrong Dosage

Dwyer v. Roderick (1983)

This case is usually referred to as the *Migril* case. The facts can be summed up in three sentences.

(1) A doctor negligently directed the patient to take an overdose in the prescription.

(2) The pharmacist failed to spot the error.

(3) The pharmacist was held liable in negligence.

These facts illustrate the difficulties for pharmacists.

The owner of the pharmacy admitted negligence, and the court held that he was 45% liable for the damages of £100,000.

The judge emphasised that the pharmacist:

(1) Should have owed a duty to the patient to ensure that drugs were correctly prescribed.

(2) Should have spotted the error.

(3) Should have queried the prescription with the doctor.

As a result of this case the Royal Pharmaceutical Society of Great Britain (RPSGB) issued this Council Statement:

Pharmacists are reminded that patients who are prescribed Migril tablets should take no more than four tablets for any single migraine attack and no more than six in any one week. Because there have been occasional reports of severe toxic effects from overdosage, the Council advises pharmacists to ensure that patients are aware of the maximum dosage

---

Case Study

Facts: H had taken one 0.5 mg of dexamethasone daily for a number of years. E, a doctor, provided H with previous prescriptions for the correct dosage of the drug but in this instance, E provided a prescription with a dosage that was eight times higher in strength and omitted to specify the dosage.

Both prescriptions had been processed by the same pharmacist (G) and the computerised system of the pharmacy chain for which G worked indicated that the same branch had dispensed the drug to H on several previous occasions. G noticed that the strength of the dosage was much increased and looked up the accepted dosage range for therapeutic use, only to find that the increased strength was within a normal range.

Consequently, G did not question the prescription with E, the doctor. The initial prescription of an incorrect dosage resulted in H being prescribed an even greater dosage while abroad and this resulted in a severe deterioration of H's physical and mental health.

Question: Should G have consulted either H or E once he noticed that the most recent prescription was eight times the strength of all previous prescriptions that the pharmacy branch had dispensed on previous occasions?

Answer: Yes. A pharmacist is required by the RPSGB's Code of Medicines, Ethics and Practice to consider whether the medication prescribed is suitable for the patient. In this case, this obligation was reproduced in the pharmacy chain's branch procedures manual.

Also, considering that H had obtained a number of repeat prescriptions from the same branch, the significant increase in the strength of the dosage should have alerted G to the possibility that the prescription might be inaccurate. G should have asked whether the prescription represented what E, the doctor, had intended to prescribe or whether the increase in strength was a mistake.

> **Reasons:** By failing to follow branch procedure and by failing to discuss whether the prescription was correct with either the patient or the prescribing doctor, the pharmacist had breached the duty of care that could have been expected of a reasonably careful and competent pharmacist.
>
> This case study is based on the case of *Horton v. Evans (2006) EWHC 2808 (QB)*.

Taking Precautions

High prescription volumes, pharmacist fatigue, pharmacist overwork, interruptions to dispensing and similar or confusing drug names can be the principal contributing factors to dispensing errors.

In its 2001 report to the Committee on Safety of Medicines, the Working Group on Labelling and Packaging of Medicines conducted a review of dispensing errors and near misses and concluded that the similarity in drug names and packaging were contributory factors.

Further, a report by the Council of Europe Expert Group on Safe Medication Practices (2006) states that 6.3–12.9% of hospitalised patients in the United States suffered at least one adverse drug reaction during their admission and that between 10.8% and 38.7% of these reactions were caused by medicines. The reports also indicate that between 30.3% and 47% of these reactions were attributable to medication errors and were, therefore, preventable.

The Future

As with medical negligence cases, the incidence of negligence claims against pharmacists will undoubtedly increase in future years. For example, a pharmacist will be liable if he or she dispenses medicinal products that are obsolete or damaged in such a way as to be dangerous, or where he or she fails to supply product leaflets intended by the manufacturer to be passed to the user.

For example, in the recent case of *Shah v. General Pharmaceutical Council (2011)*, a pharmacist appealed against the decision to remove him from the pharmacy register after a customer complained of having received an out-of-date prescription and subsequently, an unlabelled prescription. An inspection revealed that the pharmacy stocked out-of-date medicines in the dispensary, medicines where dates of expiry and batch numbers were absent or had been removed, mixed batches of medicines, medicines from other pharmacies, labelled several years previously, which were stored alphabetically with current stock in the dispensary drawers. A further five medicines in the dispensary had been removed from the manufacturer's packaging and were unlabelled or only partially labelled and European products on the first floor of the pharmacy did not bear a product licence number.

The disciplinary committee found that these offences constituted serious misconduct and went beyond mere negligence and the appeal judge agreed, ultimately dismissing the appeal. Recent research into the administration of carbamazepine (prescribed to epilepsy sufferers) has disclosed that dispensing errors occur, most often where the pharmacist confuses 200 and 400 mg modified release tablets. On occasions these errors led to profound medical, social and psychological consequences. The research concludes that inadvertent intoxication of epilepsy sufferers with carbamazepine is widespread as a result of dispensing errors, but that these errors could be avoided by changing the appearance of both the packaging and the tablets for different product strengths (see Research paper by Mack, Kuc, Grunewald, published in the *Pharmaceutical Journal*, 18 November 2000). The RPSGB has given guidance in a fact sheet on how to deal with dispensing errors. Insurers prefer to settle these cases quietly, rather than run the risks of an adverse result with unwanted media attention and significantly increased legal costs.

LIABILITY AS AN OCCUPIER OF PREMISES

The Occupiers' Liability Act

A community pharmacist may also find himself or herself liable as an occupier if an accident occurs on his or her premises. The provisions of the Occupiers' Liability Act 1957 regulate the duty which an occupier of premises owes to his or her visitors in respect of dangers due to the state of the premises, or to things done, or omitted to be done on them. Where an act or omission creates a dangerous condition that later causes harm to a visitor, the Act applies. Typical examples would be where a chair for customers waiting for prescriptions collapses because it was in need of repair, or where the floor covering has become raised, thus constituting a danger to all customers who might enter the pharmacy.

An Occupier

In order to be an occupier of premises, exclusive occupation is not needed. The test is whether a person has some degree of control associated with, or arising from his presence in, and use of, or activity in the premises.

A Visitor

A visitor includes all persons to whom the occupier has given an invitation or permission to enter the premises.

The Duty

The duty of the occupier is to take such care as in all the circumstances of the case is reasonable to see that the visitor will be reasonably safe in using the premises for the purposes for which he or she is invited or permitted by the occupier to be there.

Warning and Knowledge of Danger

In determining whether an occupier of premises has discharged the common duty of care, regard will be had to all the circumstances. For example, where the occupier warns a visitor of danger and despite the warning damage is caused to the visitor, the warning itself does not absolve the occupier from liability, unless in all the circumstances it was enough to enable the visitor to be reasonably safe.

Access for Disabled People

Section 20(1) of the Equality Act 2010 imposes a duty to make reasonable adjustments in respect of disabled people. One of these duties includes taking such steps as are reasonable to ensure that people with a disability are not at a substantial disadvantage in terms of 'physical features'. A physical feature for the purposes of the Act is defined as:

(a) a feature arising from the design or construction of a building;
(b) a feature of an approach to, exit from or access to a building;
(c) a fixture or fitting, or furniture, furnishings, materials, equipment or other chattels; in
(d) or on premises; or
(e) any other physical element or quality.

Minimising the disadvantage that a disabled person may face can involve removing the physical feature, altering it or providing a reasonable alternative.

With these considerations in mind, it is important for a community pharmacist to ensure that he or she does not have any practices or procedures which would make it difficult for a disabled person to make use of the services, that the pharmacist provides auxiliary aids or services to enable disabled people to make use of the services and that the pharmacist provides a reasonable alternative method of making a service available where the physical features of the premises impede a disabled person in the use of the service.

Some community pharmacies operate from narrow retail units, where wheelchair access is often difficult if not impossible. Consideration must be given to constructing a ramp, or if this is not possible, to installing a bell at wheelchair height outside the pharmacy so that a disabled person could call for assistance. The layout of the pharmacy must also facilitate wheelchair access to the prescription dispensing area.

Before making any changes to the premises, a community pharmacist should contact the local disablement officer at the nearest Job Centre. In addition to advising on changes which could be made to comply with the provisions of the Act, the officer will know if there are any local funds available to assist with alterations made for this purpose.

The definition of a disabled person for the purposes of the Act is very wide. It embraces any person who has either 'a physical or mental impairment' or 'a physical or medical impairment which has substantial and long-term adverse affects on his or her ability to carry out day-to-day activities'.

Criminal Liability for Negligent Conduct

In most situations, the malpractice action brought against a pharmacist, like all other health professionals, is unlikely to also give rise to liability in criminal law. Nevertheless, there is the possibility that a criminal prosecution may be brought in certain situations. An example is the case of *R v. Ziad Khatab (2000)* in which a pharmacist was charged for manslaughter as a result of a grossly negligent dispensing error.

In the case of *R v. Seymour (1983)*, the court required it to be established that the conduct of the defendant amounted to an 'obvious and serious' risk of death. This approach was confirmed again in the House of Lords judgment in *R v. Adomoko (1994)* where an anaesthetist in the course of an eye operation failed to notice that the endotracheal tube used to assist the patient's breathing had become disconnected. After 9 min, the patient suffered a heart attack and died. It was confirmed in the judgment of *R v. Misra (Amit) (2004)* that to establish manslaughter by gross negligence, the negligence in question had to be so gross that if all other constituent elements of the offence were proven, it amounted to a crime and had to be punished accordingly. In determining whether an act constitutes the offence of gross negligence manslaughter, the prosecution must establish the following:

- There was a duty of care owed by the accused to the deceased.
- There was a breach of that duty of care by the accused.
- The death of the accused was caused by breach of the duty of care owed by the accused and was not too 'remote' from the breach.
- The breach of the duty of care by the accused was so great as to be characterised as gross negligence and therefore a crime.

If no duty of care has been imposed by law, the prosecution has to consider whether the defendant accepted such a duty towards the deceased. Such considerations that need to be addressed concern:

- Nature and duration of relationship between accused and deceased; the longer and more involved the relationship, the greater the likelihood of a duty of care having been accepted.
- Action by the accused to prevent any other person from helping the deceased, where such assistance could have prevented death. This amounts to acceptance by the accused of a duty of care which must be performed to a reasonable standard.

- Whether the accused has claimed that they possess the skills necessary to perform an action competently, thereby leading others to allow them to carry it out.

The Law Commission has suggested various reforms in this area. It proposed that there should be a new offence of reckless killing. This would be committed if:

- A person by his or her conduct causes the death of another.
- He or she is aware of a risk that his or her conduct will cause death or serious injury.
- It is unreasonable for him or her to take that risk, having regard to all the circumstances as he or she knows or believes them to be.

CORPORATE MANSLAUGHTER

In addition to the pharmacist in person, it is possible for his or her company to be prosecuted for gross negligence manslaughter. However, there are a number of difficulties that need to be addressed if a company is to be prosecuted successfully.

Identification of a Controlling Mind

For a company to be guilty of manslaughter, it is necessary to identify a 'controlling mind', which is also personally guilty of manslaughter. This person must have acted 'as the company', to the extent that his or hers 'is the mind of the company'. He or she will therefore hold a senior position in the company. The individual or individuals will usually be prosecuted as well, but there may be particular circumstances whereby they are not. Even when the individuals are not prosecuted, the prosecution must still be able to demonstrate that the named individual is guilty of the offence.

It is not possible to add up the negligence of several individuals to show that a company is grossly negligent. Even if a number of people, including directors, have acted negligently, the company is not guilty of manslaughter. A specific individual must be identified as the 'controlling mind' for corporate manslaughter to be proven.

Once an individual controlling mind is established, all the other elements of gross negligence must be established. The prosecution must prove that the individual officer of the company had a duty of care towards the deceased; that there was a breach of that duty; that the breach directly caused the death; and that the breach was so great as to be classified as gross negligence.

CORPORATE MANSLAUGHTER AND CORPORATE HOMICIDE ACT 2007

The Corporate Manslaughter and Corporate Homicide Act introduced a new offence of corporate killing, broadly corresponding to the individual offence of killing by gross carelessness. A company will be guilty of the new offence of corporate manslaughter where the way in which any of its activities are managed or organised by its senior managers causes a person's death through a gross breach of a duty of care.

The maximum penalty for a corporate manslaughter conviction will be an unlimited fine. There are no sentences of imprisonment. Although this is the same maximum penalty as under the common law, it is thought that the stigma attached to a corporate manslaughter conviction will be considerably greater. In addition, where a company is convicted of corporate manslaughter the court may also impose an order requiring it to remedy the breaches that led to the death. Failure to comply with a remedial order is punishable by a further fine.

This is intended to make it easier for prosecutions to succeed against companies. This is primarily owing to the fact that under the new law the prosecution will no longer have to identify the controlling mind behind the organisation's activities. Instead, the prosecution will focus on the conduct of the senior management, both individually and collectively. In these circumstances, companies and their employees must do everything reasonably practicable to ensure the health, safety and welfare of everyone affected by their activities. In particular, appropriate safety management systems must be set up and followed, with adequate training, supervision, monitoring and auditing.

Although community pharmacists will already have proper systems and safeguards in place, there is some potential for the Corporate Manslaughter Act to have an impact on hospital and community pharmacists. It is probably only a matter of time before a hospital or community pharmacist is prosecuted for gross negligence, together with his company or hospital under the Corporate Manslaughter Act, following a dispensing error. The courts appear to be adopting an increasingly hard line with regard to the imposition of fines upon conviction of corporate manslaughter. In the case of *R v. Cotswold Geotechnical Holdings Ltd (2011)*, it was held that a fine which had the effect of putting a company out of business was acceptable.

Self-Assessment Questions

1. What satisfies the standard of the duty of care that a pharmacist owes to a customer?

   Answer: The standard of care required is that which a reasonably competent pharmacist would provide and this is applied objectively, regardless of an individual's particular circumstance or characteristics. A pharmacist must take reasonable care in ensuring that the correct medications are supplied and that he or she has advised the customers of the potential adverse effects of the prescribed medications.

In the event of any uncertainty as regards the name of the drugs prescribed or the dosage, a pharmacist should raise a query with the customer or with the prescribing physician.

2. What are the potential sanctions a pharmacist may face if he or she is found to have acted negligently?

Answer: There are a number of sanctions depending on the gravity of the effect of the negligence in question. If a pharmacist's negligent actions contribute to the death of any individual, the corporate body may be liable under the Corporate Manslaughter and Corporate Homicide Act 2007. Alternatively, if the negligent actions of the pharmacist in either dispensing the wrong dosage or type of medication cause harm to the customer, the pharmacist will have provided a substandard duty of care and will be responsible for any harm accruing as a result, subject to any defence. Ultimately, the pharmacist will be obliged to provide damages to the customer.

Chapter 27

Business Premises

When setting up a pharmacy, a pharmacist has to decide whether to buy shop premises or rent shop premises from a landlord. The purpose of this part of the book is to assist a pharmacist in making this decision, by explaining the basic difference between owning and renting business premises and by describing the principal rights and obligations of leasehold ownership. Business premises, like residential dwellings, are either freehold or leasehold.

FREEHOLD PREMISES

The owner of freehold premises owns them absolutely. In other words, the owner has freedom to make such use of them as he wishes. He may lease the premises to a tenant, and he may raise a mortgage or loan against the equity in the property. The only qualification to this freedom will be in the form of easements or restrictive covenants.

Easements

An easement is a continuing right or privilege enjoyed by someone other than the freeholder over the freeholder's land. For example, where A and B own adjacent premises, B may enjoy a right of way over A's land.

Restrictive Covenants

A restrictive covenant is a restriction attaching to the premises which prevents the owner from carrying out specified activities. Such covenants are of particular importance to the purchaser of business premises as one of the most common forms prevents the carrying out of specified trades or activities on the premises. For example, if A owns two shop premises in the same road and sells one of those to B, a covenant may be included whereby B undertakes not to pursue a similar trade to A in the newly purchased premises. When B subsequently sells to C, the burden of the covenant will continue to attach to the premises.

Pharmacy Law and Practice. DOI: http://dx.doi.org/10.1016/B978-0-12-394289-0.00027-8

In the normal course of events such covenants will become apparent before purchase during the normal searches carried out by the purchaser's solicitors. Failure to detect and warn about easements or covenants may render the solicitor liable to the purchaser in damages for negligence.

Pre-Contractual Enquiries

There are significant pitfalls to be avoided when a community pharmacist buys an existing retail pharmacy business (RPB), particularly where there are unresolved applications for a new contract, minor relocation and/or doctor dispensing rights. Unexpected changes in the way in which general medical services or pharmaceutical services are provided can impact significantly on the profitability of an RPB which is the subject of the purchase.

It is, therefore, imperative for the purchaser to discover the existence of any unresolved applications which might adversely affect the economic viability of the RPB. This is not as easy as it sounds because a seller, whether a freehold seller or an assignor of leasehold premises, is under no legal obligation to disclose the existence of an unresolved application. Primary Care Trusts (PCTs) are not obliged to do any more than make available for inspection a copy of the pharmaceutical list – see National Health Service (Pharmaceutical Services) Regulations 2005, Regulation 70(1)(a). The Health and Social Care Bill 2011 contains proposals for the abolition of PCTs. At the time of writing, the second reading of the Bill in the House of Lords was scheduled to begin in early October 2011.

In these circumstances, it is absolutely vital for an intending purchaser and his solicitor to ask the right questions of the vendor/assignor. As well as asking both orally and in writing (by pre-contractual enquiries) about planning permission, the profitability of the RPB and other matters of commercial interest which form the usual subjects of enquiry, an intending purchaser and his solicitor must ask the vendor/assignor whether there are any unresolved applications for a new pharmacy, minor relocation or doctor dispensing; whether any such applications have been made within the last 5 years and whether the vendor/assignor has received notice (either formally or informally) that any such application is likely to be made. The intending purchaser must also probe the extent of the vendor/assignor's knowledge of any plans by a nearby doctor's surgery to move premises. If the answer to any of these questions is 'yes', the vendor/assignor must explore full details of the application or plans and obtain details of any determination which was reached. Any incorrect answer may give rise to an action in damages as a breach of warranty and/or as a negligent misrepresentation under *Section 2* of the Misrepresentation Act 1967.

The importance of making careful pre-contractual enquiries was demonstrated in the case of *Banks v. Cox (2000)* where during the sale of a nursing home, the purchaser asked the vendor whether there had been any material change in the nature or conduct of the business. The Court held that the vendor was guilty of fraudulent misrepresentation when he failed to bring to the purchaser's attention a change in social services policy which seriously affected the profitability of the business.

LEASEHOLD PREMISES

Instead of purchasing a freehold interest, a pharmacist may acquire a leasehold interest in business premises. A lease is, like a freehold, an interest in land. The leaseholder is in effect the owner of the leasehold premises for the duration of the lease. A business lease should be negotiated by a solicitor and contained in written form; however, more informal agreements do sometimes occur. Whether the lease is contained in a formal document or not, there are certain preconditions which must exist to create a lease, as opposed to a mere licence, which is no more than permission, revocable at will, to be present on the premises. For a lease to exist, the agreement must be for a fixed term at a rent and grant exclusive possession of the premises.

Fixed Term

A lease does not have to be for a term of years, but must be expressed for a fixed, ascertainable duration. Usually the lease will be for a definite period of time terminating on a specific date. A periodic tenancy may also be created where the lease is renewable at short intervals, e.g., monthly, quarterly or yearly. As long as the intervals are expressly specified, a lease is capable of being created.

Exclusive Possession

Exclusive possession means that the tenant has the sole right to occupy the premises. A possible qualification to this may be a clause in the lease which confers on the landlord a right to re-enter the premises from time to time in order to inspect them or to carry out repairs. A grant of anything less than exclusive possession is incapable of creating a tenancy.

Rent

The term 'rent' is more or less self-explanatory. Most leases will contain specific clauses dealing with the amount of rent payable and the dates upon which it should be paid. It is very unusual for rent to take a form other than money, but it is possible for it to take the form of the provision of services. If rent is not payable, it is highly unlikely that anything other than a mere licence has been created.

Formalities

In order to create a legal lease which exceeds 3 years in duration, it is necessary for the lease agreement to be contained in a deed (*Section 52* of the Law of Property Act 1925). A lease agreement for a term exceeding 7 years also needs to be contained in a deed and needs to be registered (Land Registration Act 2002, *Section 4*). The document creating the lease will set out the names of the parties and the period for which the lease is to run. A rent will be specified and each party will undertake in various clauses to abide by certain obligations. For example, the tenant may undertake to keep the premises in a good state of repair. There will usually be a clause by which the landlord is permitted to re-enter the premises should the tenant fail to pay the rent, or if he is in breach of certain of his obligations. If for some reason a lease has not been created by deed, it may be recognised by a court if it can be ascertained that the parties intended to create a lease and that acts consistent with that intention have been carried out by the parties.

Terms of a Business Lease

A lease will, by its clauses, impose obligations on both parties. It will create rights for the benefit of one party in the event of a breach of an obligation by the other. A distinction exists between terms which are known as conditions and those which are known as covenants.

Conditions

Conditions are terms which have to be fulfilled for the lease to come into existence or for it to continue. For example, it may be a condition of the lease that the premises are to be used exclusively for the purposes of carrying on business as a pharmacy. Should the tenant cease to comply with this condition, the landlord will have the right to re-enter the premises whether or not that right is expressly reserved in the lease.

Covenants

A covenant is an agreement between the parties whereby one party promises to fulfil certain obligations. Examples include covenants:

- to pay rent
- to maintain the premises in a certain condition
- to insure the premises
- not to sublet.

A breach of covenant may give rise to certain legal remedies such as damages or an injunction. A breach on the part of the tenant will not automatically entitle the landlord to re-enter unless this has been expressly provided for.

If an enforceable lease has been entered into which does not contain covenants, a court will imply the usual covenants. These may include covenants on the part of the tenant:

- to pay rent
- to repair the premises at the end of the term

- to pay rates
- to deliver the premises up to the landlord at the end of the term.

The landlord will be obliged to grant quiet enjoyment of the premises to the tenant and will be entitled to re-enter the premises for non-payment of rent.

Specific Covenants

The covenants which commonly give rise to the greatest potential for difficulty or dispute during the currency of the lease are specific covenants:

- not to assign or sublet
- not to change the use made of the premises
- not to alter or improve the premises
- to repair and to insure the premises.

Each of these merits some closer attention.

Covenants Limiting the Right to Assign or Sublet

If the landlord wishes to restrict the tenant's right to sublet or assign premises (i.e., to prevent the tenant from creating a sub-lease or vesting the benefit of a lease in a third party), he must do so by express words in the lease. Such a covenant will not be implied. If the words of the covenant are unconditional and prevent any subletting or assignment whatsoever, then the tenant is bound by the covenant absolutely. Assignment without consent is permissible under building leases granted for a term exceeding 40 years of which more than 7 years remain unexpired (*Landlord and Tenant Act 1927, Section 19(1)(b)*).

However, it is common for a clause to be inserted whereby assigning or subletting is permitted subject to the landlord's consent. Where this is the case, *Section 19(1)* of the Landlord and Tenant Act 1927 then inserts into the covenant a proviso that such consent will not be withheld unreasonably. The question of when it is reasonable for a landlord to refuse consent is discussed below, but the effect of an unreasonable refusal is the removal of the covenant, so that assignment or subletting can take place without consent. The usual course for the tenant to take when faced with an unreasonable refusal is to seek a declaration in the county court (under *Section 53* of the Landlord and Tenant Act 1954) that the landlord's refusal was unreasonable. The tenant formerly bore the burden of proving unreasonableness but this has now been reversed by the Landlord and Tenant Act 1988 *Section 1* (*Midland Bank PLC v. Chart Enterprises Inc. (1990)*). The standard of proof remains the same.

Under the Landlord and Tenant Act 1988, *Section 1*, a landlord who is asked to give the consent to assignment or subletting must give his consent or justify his refusal as reasonable. Failure to do so may render the landlord liable in damages or to an injunction.

A landlord can circumvent the application of *Section 19* of the Landlord and Tenant Act 1927 by either including an express prohibition on any subletting or assigning or by including a condition that if the tenant wishes to assign or sublet, he must first offer to surrender the lease to the landlord. The landlord may then take possession of the premises if he does not wish to allow the assignment or subletting.

Unreasonable Refusal

Where a tenant makes a written application for consent to assign or sublet the landlord must within a reasonable time give written notice of the reasons for refusing consent (Landlord and Tenant Act 1988 *Section 1(3)(b)(ii)*). The landlord does not have to justify as fact the matters he relied upon if he has acted as a reasonable person might do in the same circumstances (*Air India v. Balabel (1993)*). A refusal of consent will be unreasonable if the grounds for refusal do not relate to the personality or credit-worthiness of the proposed assignee or sub-tenant, or to the effect of the proposed assignment or sub-lease on the use or occupation of the premises (*Houlder Bros & Co. v. Gibbs (1925), Bromley Park Garden Estates Ltd v. Moss (1982)*).

Motives

The landlord is entitled to be selfish in his reasons, except where the reason for his refusal is to achieve some purpose totally unconnected with the lease, or where there is such disproportion between the benefit to the landlord and the detriment to the tenant brought about by the refusal, that it would be unreasonable for the landlord to withhold his consent. Where the assignee has an ulterior motive in obtaining the benefit of the lease, e.g., in using the nuisance value of the lease to force his way into a new development, refusal may be reasonable.

It is unreasonable for a landlord to refuse consent on the grounds of race, sex or disability. Under the Equality Act 2010, which came into force on 1 October 2010, a person whose permission is required for the disposal of premises must not discriminate against another by not giving permission for the disposal of the premises. Disposal includes assignment, subletting, granting a right to occupy or parting with possession (Equality Act 2010, *Section 38*). There a number of characteristics that this legislation identifies as 'protected' – these include age, disability, gender reassignment, marriage and civil partnership, pregnancy and maternity, race, religion and belief, sex and sexual orientation (Equality Act 2010, *Section 4*). However, age and marriage or civil partnership are not characteristics protected under the section of this legislation applicable to the disposal and management of premises (Equality Act 2010, *Section 32(1)(a) and (b)*). Also in the case of a private disposal (where the landlord does not use a letting agent or an advertisement), the prohibition against discrimination does not extend to include discrimination on the basis of religion or belief or sexual orientation (Equality Act 2010, Schedule 5, *Section 1(4)*).

Where the covenant provides that the landlord's consent is required for subletting or assigning, money may not be requested as a condition of consent being granted (unless the lease expressly provides for such a payment), but a reasonable amount may be requested to cover expenses.

In some cases, the covenant restricting assignment and subletting will clearly evidence the purpose for which the covenant was made. In such a case the words of the covenant will be strictly construed. An assignment or subletting will not be permitted where to do so would defeat the original purpose of the covenant. Finally, assignment of a lease must be made by deed, regardless of the term (*Crago v. Julien (1992)*).

Covenants Concerning Change of Use

Many legal documents substitute the term 'user' for 'use'. The above heading would appear as 'Covenants Concerning Change of User'.

Many business leases contain a covenant preventing the tenant from changing the use made of the premises during the period of the tenancy. Such a covenant will either be absolute or conditional upon the consent of the landlord. Where the landlord's consent is required for a change of use, *Section 19(3)* of the Landlord and Tenant Act 1927 prevents the granting of consent from being conditional upon the payment of money by the tenant. The landlord may, however, be entitled to compensation for any loss as a result of the change of use.

Unlike *Section 19(1)* which imposes a requirement of reasonableness on the landlord's granting of consent, *Section 19(3)* makes no such provision. Often the covenant may include words to the effect that the landlord may not refuse his consent unreasonably. In determining whether consent has been unreasonably withheld, similar considerations apply as to the requirement of reasonableness in consenting to subletting or assignment (see above). An example of unreasonable refusal can be found in the case of *Anglia Building Society v. Sheffield County Council (1983)* in which the refusal was held to be unreasonable where it was used merely as an attempt to secure an advantage for the landlord wholly unconnected with the lease and wholly outside the intention of the parties. Refusal to consent may be deemed reasonable where the landlord believes that the assignment could lead to a breach of the user covenant in the lease. It is always a question of fact to be determined by the tribunal of fact (*Ashworth Frazer Ltd v. Gloucester City Council (2001)*). The correct procedure for challenging the reasonableness of the landlord's decision is to seek a declaration in the county court under *Section 53* of the Landlord and Tenant Act 1954. If the refusal is declared unreasonable, the covenant becomes ineffective, and the tenant can change the use he makes of the premises as desired. The burden of establishing unreasonableness falls on the tenant. Finally, the tenant has no statutory right to damages under the Landlord and Tenant Act 1988 in the case of the unreasonable refusal of the landlord to consent to a change of use.

Case Study

Facts: The drafting of a lease agreement is very important and covenants in a lease can affect the ability of a lessee to deal freely with their premises. For example, Y enters into a lease agreement with Z. The lease contains a covenant obliging Y, upon the determination of the lease, to do his best to procure the transfer of the necessary licence to a person nominated by the landlord to ensure the continued operation of the premises as a pharmacy. This prevents Y from relocating his business to nearby premises at the end of the leasehold term because the relevant authority will not allow both the relocation of the pharmacy business by Y and the opening of a new pharmacy in the current leased premises. Expert evidence indicates that the relevant authority will only give permission for Y to relocate. But since he has covenanted not to do this, his hands are tied and he will not be able to relocate to nearby premises.

Question: This covenant amounts to an unreasonable restraint in trade and Y claims that this is unreasonable.

Answer: No, while the covenant does amount to a restraint in trade, it is reasonable both in the public interest and the interest of the parties.

Reason: The Court of Appeal decided that Y had the option of either renegotiating a renewal of the lease on satisfactory terms or the option of assigning the lease on terms that reflected the goodwill generated by the business. Consent to the assignment could not be unreasonably withheld by the partnership and in light of this, the validity of the clause was upheld.

For the Court of Appeal a determining factor in coming to this decision was the limitations imposed by the National Health Service (Pharmaceutical Services) Regulations 1992, Regulation 4 which regulates the operation of pharmacies. The Court recognised that these regulations were designed to ensure greater stability in the provision of pharmaceutical services, which had been threatened by the indiscriminate opening and relocation of pharmacies.

Ultimately the Court supported the imposition of anti-competitive restrictions on the pharmacy trade that Parliament believed to be in the public interest.

This case study is based on *Young v. Evans-Jones (2001)*.

Landlord's Remedies for Tenant's Breach of User Covenant

Where the tenant breaches the change of user covenant, the landlord has a remedy in damages; and where the covenant contains a proviso for re-entry, the lease may be forfeited. The court may also grant an interlocutory injunction preventing the change of use pending a full trial of the issue. It should be remembered that the change of use will be subject to any restrictive covenants attaching to the freehold of the premises and to planning regulations. Any change of use should therefore always be carried out in consultation with the landlord.

Covenants Against Alterations or Improvements

A lease may contain covenants not to carry out any alterations or improvements to the premises. These may be either absolute prohibitions or qualified by the requirement of the landlord's consent. If the covenant is absolute, the tenant's hands are tied. Where the landlord's consent is required, *Section 19(2)* of the Landlord and Tenant Act 1927 provides that any refusal must be reasonable if the alterations amount to improvements. This section also provides that the landlord may require a sum of money for any diminution in the value of the premises, or of any neighbouring premises belonging to the landlord, or may require the tenant to reinstate the premises to its original state at the conclusion of the tenancy.

The court will decide whether an alteration amounts to an improvement from the tenant's point of view (*Lambert v. F.W. Woolworth and Co. Ltd (1938)*). It was also said in that case that many considerations, aesthetic, historic or even personal, may be relied upon as yielding reasonable grounds for refusing consent.

A tenant who breaches a covenant against alteration or improvement may be liable in damages and to forfeiture should the landlord succeed in proving that his consent was not unreasonably withheld. Therefore, as with activities encroaching on all types of covenants, the tenant should negotiate with the landlord and as a last resort seek a declaration from the county court.

Repairing Covenants

Covenants obliging either party to repair the premises will either be express or implied. In commercial leases such covenants will usually be expressed in the lease. Should no such covenants be contained in the lease, obligations may be implied by common law.

The only obligation imposed on the tenant at common law is to occupy the premises in a tenant-like manner, i.e., to take reasonable care of the premises and to make good any damage which is caused by the tenant or his employees or visitors. This does not extend to making good minor damage caused by fair wear and tear. A landlord is obliged to maintain his own premises ancillary to the leased premises where maintenance of his premises is necessary for the enjoyment of the leased premises. For example, where the tenant has leased a shop on the ground floor of premises, the remainder of which is owned by the landlord, the landlord will be obliged to maintain the roof and common parts of the building unless the lease expressly provides otherwise.

The landlord may also be obliged to carry out such repairs as are necessary to give business efficacy to the agreement. For example, where the tenant has covenanted to maintain and repair the interior, the landlord may be required to ensure the good repair of the exterior.

Express Covenants to Repair

Express covenants to repair are usually expressed as obligations to keep the premises in good, habitable or tenantable repair. The old case of *Proudfoot v. Hart (1890)* provides general guidance that this means:

such repair as, having regard to the age, character and locality of the premises, would make it reasonably fit for the occupation of a reasonably minded tenant of the class who would be likely to take it at the time when the lease was granted.

Covenants to Repair Do Not Create an Obligation to Renew or Improve the Premises

The line between repair and improvement is a difficult one to draw, but as a rule of thumb, the duty can be no higher than restoring the premises to the condition in which they were originally found. The question of what amounts to simple repair is a question to be decided in the specific circumstances. For example, repair will not normally include the duty to cure inherent defects in the premises, e.g., replacing defective guttering. However, in some circumstances the secondary damage can only be repaired by repairing the primary cause. The repair of the primary cause may be construed as an improvement, but may nevertheless be covered by the repairing covenant. The tenant is not obliged to repair a structural defect in the building which pre-dates the commencement of the lease (*Quick v. Taff Ely Borough Council (1985)*). If, however, a pre-existing defect causes secondary damage, e.g., a leaking roof causing damp penetration, secondary damage caused during the period of the lease will have to be repaired by the tenant.

Special care should be taken prior to the signing of the lease to ensure that the tenant is not to be held liable for the rebuilding of premises destroyed by fire or flood, etc. It is common for the liability for rebuilding to be expressly attached to the landlord in the lease.

Landlord's Remedies for Breach of Repairing Covenant

If a tenant is in breach of his covenant to repair, the landlord has the remedies of damages and forfeiture. The measure of damages is the difference between the value of the unrepaired premises, and the value of the premises had the repairs been executed. However, if it is the landlord's intention to demolish the premises at the end of the tenancy, there will be no justification for such an award of damages.

Forfeiture

If a landlord seeks to obtain forfeiture of the premises consequent upon a breach of a repairing covenant, he must serve a notice under *Section 146* of the Law of Property Act 1925 containing details of the breach, requiring the breach to be remedied and requiring the payment of compensation. In the case of premises leased for at least 7 years with at least 3 years left to run, special procedures are provided by the Leasehold Property (Repairs) Act 1938. When the landlord serves a notice under *Section 146* of the Law of Property Act 1925, he must inform the tenant of his right to serve a counter-notice under the 1938 Act. If a counter-notice is served within 28 days, the landlord's action cannot proceed without the leave of the court. Leave will only be granted if one of the following five circumstances exists:

(1) The value of the landlord's interest in the premises has been, or is likely to be, substantially diminished if the repairs are not carried out.

(2) The repair is necessary to comply with an order of any authority or local bye-law.

(3) Where the tenant does not occupy the premises, the repair is necessary in the interests of another occupier.

(4) An immediate repair will avoid further deterioration leading to more expensive repairs.

(5) There are special circumstances making leave to proceed just and equitable.

(6) The landlord must prove both the breach of covenant and the ground or grounds relied on, on the balance of probabilities (*Associated British Ports v. C. H. Bailey (1990)*).

Case Study

Facts: C demises a site to D. D covenants, under the terms of the lease, to erect a medical practitioner's surgery, at its own cost and within a defined timetable. The lease contains a negative covenant not to use or permit the use of the premises otherwise than as a surgery for use in connection with National Health Service patients together with a retail pharmacy.

Two years later, C serves notice on D under the Law of Property Act 1925, *Section 146*, alleging breach of covenant because no surgery has been built and the premises was not used for that purpose.

Question: D sought relief against forfeiture.

Answer: The Court denies relief against forfeiture to D on the grounds that it had been in continuous breach of a covenant in the lease to build the surgery. D was having financial difficulties and the Court concluded that even if relief against forfeiture was granted, it would not be in a position to comply with the covenant.

Reason: The Court recognised its ability to exercise 'fresh' discretion under *Section 146(2)* of the Law of Property Act 1945 but in doing so, it distinguished between a change of heart and a change of circumstance. This was an appeal against a refusal to grant relief against forfeiture and the Court of Appeal upheld the decision to deny relief. D claimed there had been a change of circumstance to justify granting relief but the Court of Appeal did not accept this and stated that it was necessary to look at all the circumstances and the conduct of D in the past. D maintained that its financial position had changed and it was now able to comply with the covenant to build the medical surgery but it had only relied on this change of circumstance at the last minute.

This case study is based on *Darlington Borough Council v. Denmark Chemists (1993)*.

Finally, the legislation in this area strives to maintain a balance between protecting the rights of the tenant *vis-à-vis* the power of the landlord. The Leasehold Property (Repairs) Act 1938 is an example of this balancing of interests. It was introduced to prevent individuals who bought the reversion on a long lease from forcing an early surrender by harassing the tenant with minor repairs. The 1938 Act reflects a conscious policy decision to strengthen the position of tenants by limiting the availability of certain remedies in the event of a breach of a tenant's covenant to repair.

Right of Entry to Repair

Under some leases the landlord may have a right to enter the premises to carry out repairs and to recover the cost of repairs as a debt. It was traditionally thought that a landlord could not force the tenant to carry out repairs (i.e., that the contractual remedy of specific performance is not available). It has now been held that specific performance may in principle be available where damages are not adequate compensation for the landlord (*Rainbow Estates v. Tokenhold (1998)*).

Tenant's Remedies for Breach of Repairing Covenant

The tenant of business premises may sue the landlord for damages if the landlord is in breach of a repairing covenant. In the past, damages have been awarded for discomfort, loss of enjoyment of the premises and bouts of ill-health caused by the poor state of repair. There have also been some indications in the decided cases that the cost of alternative accommodation is recoverable. The landlord of business premises cannot be forced to repair, i.e. the remedy of specific performance is not available to the tenant.

Cost of Repairs Set Off Against Rent

The case of *Lee Parker v. Izzet (1971)* decided that a tenant may deduct the cost of repairs from future rent. However, to avoid complications over whether the amounts spent on repair are reasonable, it is advisable for a tenant to obtain a county court declaration that the landlord is in breach of his covenant.

Insurance Covenants

A commercial lease will make express provision for the insurance of the building. Often the tenant will be required to pay the insurance premiums and to refrain from acts which will suspend the cover.

Destruction of a Building

A clause will usually be inserted to oblige the landlord to use insurance moneys to rebuild the premises should they be destroyed during the period of the lease. In the absence of such a covenant, the landlord will not be obliged to rebuild the premises. Where a building has been destroyed and the landlord does not intend to rebuild, a dispute may arise as to which of the parties is entitled to the insurance moneys and in what proportions. Following the case of *Beacon Carpets Limited v. Kirkby (1984)* the most likely outcome is that the moneys will be divided between the parties in proportion to their interest in the building.

Rent

Commercial leases will invariably contain express terms setting out:

- the amount of rent to be paid
- the times at which it is to be paid
- the consequences of non-payment (usually forfeiture)
- provision for a review of the amount of rent payable at a set date or dates during the tenancy.

The rent is payable for the land upon which the premises stand and not for the premises themselves. Therefore, should the building be destroyed during the period of the lease, rent continues to be payable.

Rent on Assignment or Subletting

Until the Landlord and Tenant (Covenants) Act 1995, an original tenant used to be liable to the landlord for rent under the terms of the lease, even where he had assigned or sublet the lease with the landlord's permission. The 1995 Act was passed to alleviate the considerable hardship which this rule imposed on original tenants, requiring them in effect to guarantee payment of rent for the duration of the term of the lease, even after their interest in the lease had been assigned to a third party. The 1995 Act distinguishes between 'old' and 'new' tenancies. For the purposes of the 1995 Act, a 'new' tenancy is one granted on or after 1 January 1996. This definition does not include a tenancy granted in pursuance of an agreement entered into before that date or of an order of a court made before that date (Landlord and Tenant (Covenants) Act 1995, *Section 1(3)*). The 1995 Act provides that, on assigning the whole demised premises under a 'new' tenancy, the original tenant is released from the tenant covenants and prevented from enjoying any landlord covenants (Landlord and Tenant (Covenants) Act 1995, *Section 5*).

The effect of the 1995 Act in easing the position of the tenant is to some extent mitigated by allowing the landlord to require the original tenant to enter into an 'authorised guarantee agreement' (AGA) which guarantees payment by the immediate person to whom the tenant may in future assign the lease, a transaction over which the tenant does, after all, have some control. The use of an 'AGA' is confined to tightly worded leases in which, due to a 'lawfully imposed' condition, the tenant is required to agree to an AGA to obtain the landlord's consent to the assignment of the lease (Landlord and Tenant

(Covenants) Act 1995, *Section 16(3)(b)*). The requirement that this condition be 'lawfully imposed' effectively introduces a requirement of reasonableness. In the event of a dispute about the imposition of such a condition in the lease, the tenant would have to demonstrate that 'no reasonable landlord could, in the circumstances, require entry into an AGA' (*Wallis Fashion Group Ltd v. CGU Life Assurance (2000)*) (*See Gray, 'Elements of Land Law', (2009) Oxford University Press, 5th ed., pp. 526–556*).

In the 1980s and early 1990s, the landlord of an insolvent assignee easily had recourse to the ultimate contractual liability of the original tenant. This was often wholly unanticipated and devastating in its effect. For example, in the case of *RPH v. Mirror Group Newspapers (1992)*, the original tenant was liable for rent arrears of almost £2 million unpaid by the assignee under the lease. The scope of liability of the original tenant also included rent arrears in respect of an upward rent review negotiated between the landlord and the assignee (*Selous Street Properties Ltd v. Oronel Fabrics Ltd (1984)*). Although this decision was overturned on appeal, the Landlord and Tenant (Covenants) Act 1995 had already received royal assent.

The implementation of the 1995 Act was the result of a concerted effort to prohibit continuing liability against the original tenant and to strike a balance between the legislative protection of the landlord on the one hand and the tenant on the other. The inclusion of AGAs undermines this balance and undercuts the protection available to the tenant; an unfortunate parliamentary compromise between two competing interests.

A landlord can assign his interest (the 'reversion') in the premises to a third party. The rent then becomes payable to the assignee, but only if the landlord has issued a notice to the tenant complying with *Section 151(1)* of the Law of Property Act 1925.

Guarantors

If payment of rent is secured by guarantors under the terms of the lease, they will be fully liable for payment of unpaid rent should the tenant fall into arrears. The guarantors are then left to pursue the tenant for the sums in which they have been held liable. Where the tenant is a small private company it is common for landlords to require the directors or main shareholders (who are usually the same) to give guarantees in their personal capacity. This is to protect the landlord in the event of the company going into liquidation but means the directors/shareholders carry considerable personal risk. Under an AGA, the original tenant may become the sole or principal debtor (Landlord and Tenant (Covenants) Act 1995, *Section 16(5)(a)*). However, where the original tenant acts as a guarantor the normal rules relating to guarantors apply and thus, any material variation of the lease agreement between the landlord and the assignee will discharge the liability of the original tenant as a guarantor (Landlord and Tenant (Covenants) Act 1995, *Section 16(8)*).

Rent Review

A commercial lease will usually contain a clause stating that at a fixed date or dates during the lease the rent will be revised by an independent third party, usually a surveyor. The lease may provide that the landlord and tenant should agree on the appointment of a surveyor jointly, or it may provide that a third party, e.g., the President of the Royal Institution of Chartered Surveyors, should make the appointment.

The review clause will specify that the rent is to be revised according to the current market rent. The decision of the surveyor is usually expressed to be final, and a clause is often inserted whereby even if the surveyor determines that a reasonable market rent would be less than that already being paid, rent will nevertheless continue to be paid at the existing rate.

The surveyor is under a duty to carry out the rent review according to his professional standards. All relevant factors will be taken into account such as the rent being paid for similar premises in the same area, the condition of the premises and the effect of, for example, the existence of a covenant restricting change of user. For obvious reasons, it is vitally important that the tenant makes himself aware of the rent review procedure at the outset.

Consequences of Non-Payment of Rent

The usual remedy for non-payment of rent is forfeiture. All formal leases will inevitably include a clause providing for the surrender of the premises if the rent should cease to be paid for a specified period after the due date. The usual procedure is for the landlord to make a formal demand for unpaid rent before commencing forfeiture proceedings, although many leases will dispense with this requirement.

Once he has commenced forfeiture proceedings, if the landlord then does any act which indicates that he accepts the continuation of the tenancy, he loses the right to forfeiture. Accepting payment of arrears would constitute such an act. However, the landlord still has the right to receive rent for the continuing occupation. Such sums are known as 'mesne profits' (pronounced 'meen') and are assessed at current market rates.

Relief Against Forfeiture

In High Court proceedings the tenant has a right to relief against forfeiture of the lease where he is no more than 6 months in arrears and if he pays all outstanding sums and costs into court before judgment is given. Thereafter there is a mere equitable right to relief upon payment of all arrears and costs at any time up to 6 months from the date of the landlord's re-entry. As the right is only equitable, it will be granted only where the High Court considers it fair to do so in all the circumstances. In county court proceedings, the tenant has the automatic right to relief against forfeiture if all arrears and costs are paid up to 5 days before the date set for the possession hearing. Under *Section 138* of the County Courts Act 1984, the county court has discretion to order relief against forfeiture if all costs and arrears are paid within 4 weeks after the granting of the order for possession. Once the landlord has recovered possession, the court still retains discretion to grant relief to the tenant if an application is made within 6 months of the landlord's recovery (Country Court Act 1984, *Section 138(9a)*). The 6-month period is strictly enforced (*United Dominions Trust Ltd v. Shellpoint Trustees Ltd (1993)*).

The court is generous in respect of granting relief against forfeiture in respect of rent arrears. Relief is generally withheld only in the most egregious of cases.

Renewal of Tenancies

The procedure for the renewal of business tenancies and compensation for improvements carried out by a tenant during the currency of the lease is governed by Part II of the Landlord and Tenant Act 1954 and by Part I of the Landlord and Tenant Act 1927. These statutes create mechanisms which come into play at the end of a tenancy, and which have as their object the resolution of matters between landlord and tenant by means of mutual agreement rather than resort to the courts.

The legislation creates a framework of procedural steps which must be complied with if a business tenancy is to be terminated and provides for the continuation of the tenancy on its existing terms should these steps not have been taken. The legislation also creates a right to request a renewal of the tenancy for a period of up to 14 years.

Tenancies Covered by the Legislation

Section 23 of the 1954 Act states that the Act covers:

any tenancy where the property comprised in the tenancy is or includes premises which are occupied by the tenant and are so occupied for the purposes of a business carried on by him or for those and other purposes.

These words are to a large extent self-evident. Formally agreed business leases in documentary form will invariably be covered if the business is not being carried out in breach of a user clause.

Under *Section 43(3)(a)*, the Act does not normally apply to tenancies granted for a period of less than 6 months where there is no provision for renewing the term. However, if in that case the tenant has been in occupation for over 12 months he is deemed to have an established business which will be protected by the Act. The only other notable exceptions are leases where the landlord is a government department, local authority, a statutory undertaking or a development corporation, or where the landlord has specified that the use of the premises will change on a specified date.

Contracting Out of the 1954 Act

The parties to the lease may contract out of the 1954 Act, and thereby avoid the protection afforded by it, by following the procedures set out in *Section 38A* of the Landlord and Tenant Act 1954. This procedure was altered by the Regulatory Reform (Business Tenancies) (England and Wales) Order 2003 and requires that the tenant be served with notice, alerting him to the consequences of entering into an agreement to exclude the protection offered by the 1954 Act. The tenant must confirm by way of written declaration that he has received the notice, read it and accepts the consequences. Finally, a reference to the notice or declaration must be contained in or endorsed in the instrument creating the tenancy.

The Procedure for Renewal

Section 24(1) of the 1954 Act provides that the lease will continue after its expiry upon the same terms as during the currency of the lease, until either party issues a notice to renew the tenancy.

The renewal procedure may be initiated by either the landlord or the tenant issuing a notice in the prescribed form. A tenant may make a request for a new tenancy under *Section 26*. In order to issue such a notice, the tenant must have held the lease for at least 1 year and must request a starting date for a new tenancy between 6 and 12 months from the date of service of the notice. The notice must also refer to the property to be comprised in the new lease and to the terms and rent proposed.

The tenant cannot serve a notice under *Section 26*:

(1) if the landlord has already served a notice under *Section 25* (see below); or

(2) if the tenant has already given notice to quit; or

(3) if he has given notice under *Section 27* that he will be surrendering the lease at the end of the fixed term.

Under *Section 25* the landlord may serve a notice to propose a new tenancy (usually with modified rent), or to state grounds of objection to a new tenancy under *Section 30*. The landlord's notice cannot take effect until a specified date between 6 and 12 months from the date of service, and in any event, not before the expiry date of a fixed term lease. The notice must contain the proposed terms of the new lease, or if continuation is objected to, the grounds of objection must be set out. The tenant must serve a counter-notice within 2 months of the service of the landlord's notice stating whether he intends to give up possession.

In theory, the notice procedure is intended to stimulate negotiations between the landlord and the tenant and to encourage settlement between the parties. Failure of either side to respond to a notice issued by the other within the prescribed 2-month period will result in an agreement being presumed in the terms of the notice. Following the Regulatory Reform (Business Tenancies) (England and Wales) Order 2003 SI 2003/3096 either party may now apply to the court for renewal of the tenancy (provided the other has not already done so). The tenant can apply any time after the service of a *Section 25* notice, but neither party can apply until 2 months has elapsed since the serving of a *Section 26* notice.

Within 6 months of the issue of a *Section 25* notice, either party may apply under *Section 24A* of the Act for an interim rent to be determined by the court. If the renewal of the lease is unopposed the interim rent is likely to be based on market rent, if the renewal is opposed the interim rent is based on what it would be reasonable for the tenant to pay.

The Landlord's Grounds of Opposition

Under *Section 30* the landlord has seven grounds of opposition to the grant of a renewed tenancy:

(1) The failure of the tenant to comply with repairing obligations under the lease resulting in the property being in a state of disrepair. The extent of the disrepair and the requirements of the repairing covenant will be the major factors the court will have to consider in exercising its discretion under this head.

(2) Persistent delay by the tenant in paying rent when it has become due.

(3) Other substantial breaches of covenant by the tenant, or 'any other reason connected with the tenant's use or management of the holding'. There is considerable room for judicial discretion under this head, but substantial and/or frequent breaches of covenant will have to be proved by the landlord.

(4) The offer by the landlord of suitable alternative premises on terms which are reasonable having regard to the terms of the current tenancy and to all other relevant circumstances, e.g., the suitability of the proposed new premises for the tenant's business including the tenant's need to preserve goodwill.

(5) Where the current tenancy is a subletting of part of premises in which the landlord has an interest in the freehold reversion at the conclusion of the superior tenancy, and the landlord could get a much better return by letting the premises as a whole.

(6) Where on the termination of the tenancy the landlord intends to demolish or reconstruct the whole or a substantial part of the premises, and the proposed works can only be carried out by obtaining possession. In order for

the landlord to succeed under this head he must be able to prove his intent at the date of the hearing. This is usually done by pointing to some actual steps which have been taken towards carrying out the intention. In order for the requirement of reconstruction to be proved, it must be proved that the demolition of at least part of the premises will be necessitated (*Cadle v. Jacmarch (1957)*).

(7) That the landlord intends to use the premises or part of them for his own business or residence at the end of the tenancy. This ground of objection requires the landlord to prove his intent and to show that he is the one who will occupy the premises. It is not sufficient for him to intend to let it to others.

The tenant has two defences, provided by *Section 31A*, to the assertion that possession is required to execute the work:

- That a new lease could be granted, but containing a clause permitting the landlord to enter to execute the works. This will only succeed if it can be shown that the tenant's business will not be substantially interfered with and that the works can be carried out with the tenant remaining; or
- That the tenant could be granted a new lease in an economically severable part of the premises and that the granting of such a lease would not prevent the landlord from carrying out the works.

Where the landlord succeeds in proving one of the grounds for objection, he will be awarded possession after the expiry of a minimum period of 3 months.

Under *Section 31(2)*, if the court decides that one of the grounds (4), (5) or (6) above are not proved at the date of the hearing, but would be in up to 12 months time, the grant of a new tenancy may nevertheless be refused and an order made specifying the date on which the court would have been satisfied of the grounds. In this event the existing tenancy subsists until that date and the tenant can apply to the court within 14 days under *Section 31(2)* to amend the date.

The Grant of a New Tenancy

Where no objection is raised by the landlord or where his objection fails, the tenant may be granted a new tenancy. Under *Section 32*, the tenant has a *prima facie* right to a tenancy only of the premises to which the original lease applied. If this raises matters of dispute, they can be resolved by the court.

The court is in theory entitled to award a new tenancy of anything up to 15 years' duration, but in practice tends only to grant leases of similar length to that which previously subsisted.

Rent under the new tenancy may be fixed by the court where the landlord and tenant fail to agree. It will be fixed at a level at which 'having regard to the terms of the tenancy, the holding might be expected to be let on the open market by a willing lessor'. However, the court will not take into account the following:

- The tenant's previous occupation.
- Any goodwill attaching to the premises generated by the tenant's business.
- Improvements carried out by the tenant other than those required by covenant, provided that the tenancy has always been protected by the Act, that the improvements were carried out within 21 years of the renewal and provided that the tenant did not surrender the premises at the end of the tenancy in which the improvements were carried out.
- The value attributable to a liquor licence on licensed premises.

Under *Section 35*, the court has a very wide discretion to determine other terms of a new lease which the landlord and tenant have failed to agree, but there will be a strong presumption in favour of the terms of the original lease. This presumption can be rebutted if there is good reason, but such reasons would have to be very strong, e.g., certain terms will need to be included in order to give commercial efficacy to the agreement.

Tenant's Compensation at the End of a Tenancy

At the conclusion of a tenancy, whether by surrender or by court order, the tenant may be able to recover compensation for improvements made during the lease. Under *Section 37* of the 1954 Act the right to compensation arises where the tenant has been unsuccessful in obtaining a renewed tenancy due to a successful objection by the landlord on one of the grounds numbered (4), (5) and (6) in the list in the section above entitled 'The Landlord's Grounds of Opposition' (i.e., the grounds in *Section 30*), providing that the landlord has not offered suitable alternative accommodation.

The right to compensation cannot be excluded where the tenant has been in occupation for at least 5 years (*Section 38*). However, if the tenant is a successor to a business which has been carried on at the premises for at least 5 years, the right will remain even if the successor has been in occupation for less than 5 years.

The parties may contract out of the compensation provisions at any time before the commencement or during the currency of the lease, or as part of an application to the court to contract out of the protection afforded by the Act generally.

The amount of compensation payable is dependent upon the length of time the tenant has been in occupation. *Section 37* provides that tenants who have been in occupation for more than 14 years will receive a sum of twice the rateable value of the premises times the 'multiplier' (which in most cases is currently one). Tenants who have been in occupation for less than 14 years will receive the rateable value times the multiplier.

Compensation for Improvements

At the conclusion of a tenancy the tenant is able to claim compensation for loss of authorised improvements carried out by the tenant under *Section 1* of the Landlord and Tenant Act 1927.

The availability of compensation will not be affected by the reason for the termination of the tenancy. An application to the court for compensation must be made within 3 months of the service of the landlord's counter-notice if the tenant has terminated the tenancy by applying for a renewal; between 3 and 6 months before the termination of the tenancy if it is to terminate by effluxion of time or within 3 months of a court order for forfeiture or re-entry.

In order to claim compensation the following requirements must all be met.

(1) The premises must have been used for business purposes.

(2) The improvements must have been executed by the tenant.

(3) The improvements must not have been executed pursuant to an obligation under the lease.

(4) The landlord must agree, or the court must have issued a certificate stating that the improvements add to the value of the premises without devaluing neighbouring property of the landlord.

(5) A formal claim for compensation must be made to the court.

Level of Compensation

Section 1 of the 1927 Act provides that the level of compensation will be calculated either on the basis of the additional value to the premises by the improvements, or on the basis of the cost of carrying out the improvements at the end of the tenancy, minus an appropriate sum representing the cost of putting the improvements into a good state of repair. The court has a discretion to settle any differences arising and finally to settle the compensation sums.

Misrepresentation

Where the tenant can show that the court's refusal to grant a new tenancy was based on a misrepresentation by the landlord, 'the court may order the landlord to pay to the tenant such a sum as appears sufficient as compensation for damage or loss sustained by the tenant as the result of the order or refusal' (*Section 37A* of the 1954 Act, as inserted by the Regulatory Reform (Business Tenancies) (England and Wales) Order 2003/3096, Schedule 5, paragraph 2). For example, where the landlord has successfully opposed an application for a renewed tenancy on the basis that he intends to use the premises for his own business, if he subsequently lets the premises to another party, the former tenant may apply for compensation to the court which ordered possession.

Compulsory Acquisition

If the premises are acquired compulsorily, in assessing the compensation payable, the local authority is obliged, by *Section 47* of the Land Compensation Act 1973, to assess the potential loss that may be suffered by the tenant as a result of his loss of rights to renew the tenancy of the lease.

PLANNING LAW

Changes of Use and Alterations of Premises

A change in the use of a business premises may arise by a simple alteration in the nature of the use, or through alterations and additions which modify the use. A change of use may also arise through a material intensification in the present use, or by subtly altering the present use to a point where the changes amount to development.

Planning permission will be required for the construction of new business premises with the exception of some minor extensions, repairs and maintenance, internal alterations, small works outside the building (such as installing an alarm box) and putting up walls, fences, etc. within height limits. Unlike domestic properties the range of permitted development rights available to commercial properties are more limited.

A change of use is not always a clear-cut issue and should be treated with care. Certain types of change do not require planning permission. For example, a change of use from one type of shop to another does not (normally) require planning permission. These are set out in the Town and Country Planning (Use Classes) Order 1987.

Certain changes are permissible without the need for planning permission, subject to satisfying the appropriate criteria. Shops can alter their use to another type of shop without planning permission. Therefore a newsagent could be changed to a chemist shop without permission.

Other uses are considered *sui generis*; that is, they are uses on their own which are not allocated any particular class under the 1987 Order. Examples include a theatre, a laundrette, an amusement arcade or a scrapyard.

There may be circumstances where the intention is to make a minor alteration to the use of land or premises and this opens up the question of whether the change is so substantial as to require planning permission.

Any change of use must be a 'material change of use' in order to require consent. Defining what is and what is not a material change is often difficult and open to interpretation. Inevitably the courts have provided guidance over the years in deciding cases, but given the diversity of potential uses the issue remains open to debate.

Additional or supplementary uses may also create a situation where planning permission is required. A builders yard used for the storage only of building materials, which then becomes used for the parking of vehicles may require planning permission, depending upon the circumstances of the case.

The limitations on use imposed by the planning permission over the land or buildings and any conditions that may be attached should not be overlooked. The wording of planning permissions is often critical. For example, 'use of building for B8 storage' is substantially different from 'use of building for the storage of farm implements only'.

Extensions

Extensions to shops and offices will require planning permission. Planning permission will be required if:

- The allowable increase in volume has already been used for previous extensions.
- The extension will affect the external appearance of the building.
- The extension is to be within 5 m of the property boundary.
- The extension will be on land required for parking or vehicle turning.

Self-Assessment Questions

1. If a tenant wants to assign the lease, in what circumstances can a landlord withhold consent if the proposed assignee wants to use the premises for a purpose other than a pharmacy?

   Answer: It depends on the wording of the covenant in the lease. There are two possibilities. Either the covenant is absolute, in which case a change of use is not permissible or alternatively, the covenant will require the consent of the landlord. In this case, the applicable legislation is the Landlord and Tenant Act 1927, *Section 19(3)*, which makes no provision for reasonableness in consenting to a change of user. If the covenant in the lease does not stipulate that the consent of the landlord is not to be unreasonably withheld, then it is possible for the landlord to refuse consent. If the covenant contains words to the effect that consent is not to be unreasonably withheld, then the landlord is bound to act reasonably. The tenant can challenge this decision under the Landlord and Tenant Act 1954 but the burden of proving the decision of the landlord was unreasonable falls on the tenant.

2. In what circumstances will a tenant be liable to the landlord where the tenant has assigned the lease and the assignee acts in breach of covenant?

   Answer: The applicable legislation is the Landlord and Tenant (Covenants) Act 1995. The effect of its application varies depending on whether the tenant has a tenancy pre-dating the legislation ('old tenancies') or whether the tenancy was created after the implementation of the legislation. These tenancies, which are post-1995, are called 'new tenancies'.

If a tenant assigns the whole of the premises demised to him under a 'new tenancy', then he will no longer be liable for any tenant covenants and will not benefit from any landlord covenants (Landlord and Tenant (Covenants) Act 1995, *Section 5(2)*). This does not prevent a tenant from being liable for a breach of any tenant covenants that happened prior to assigning the lease.

If a tenant has an 'old tenancy' there is no automatic statutory release from liability for breach of tenant covenants under the lease. While in theory a tenant remains responsible for the default of his assignee, the scope of liability has been reduced by the 1995 Act. The original tenant will remain liable to the landlord for any 'fixed charge' payable under the covenants of the lease where the landlord serves the tenant with statutory notice, within 6 months of these charges falling due, indicating that the charge is due and that the landlord intends to recover from the former tenant such amount as is specified in the notice (Landlord and Tenant (Covenants) Act 1995, *Section 17(2)*). A fixed charge includes rent, service charge or 'any amount payable under a tenant covenant of the tenancy providing for the payment of a liquidated sum in the event of a failure to comply with any such covenant' (Landlord and Tenant (Covenants) Act 1995, *Section 17(6)(a), (b), (c)*).

Finally, the statutory notice served by the landlord must be in the statutorily prescribed form or in a form that has substantially the same effect. Otherwise it will be ineffective under this provision (Landlord and Tenant (Covenants) Act 1995, *Section 27(4)*).

Chapter 28

Business Associations

When setting up in business there are several different ways in which a pharmacist may operate. A pharmacist may set up either as a sole trader, in partnership with some other party, as a limited liability partnership or as a corporate body. Each manner of operation has certain advantages and disadvantages. These are considered in this section of the book, with particular reference being made to the limited company.

THE SOLE TRADER

The sole trader carries on business either in his or her own name or one created for the business. The sole trader bears the burden of full personal responsibility for the business and all its liabilities. Unlike a limited company, in which the company and its managing director are separate legal entities, the sole trader and his or her business are one and the same thing: the sole trader is liable for all the debts of the business, and his or her personal property is therefore put at risk.

Trading as a sole trader is therefore advisable only for those who do not expect to incur business debts or liabilities on any large scale. In setting up a pharmacy, a sizeable outlay will be made in the purchase of business premises and stock, and the potential personal liability will be considerable.

PARTNERSHIP

Partnerships are comparatively common and so require considerably more explanation. A partnership arises where two or more persons carry on a business in common with a view to making a profit. A partnership is called a firm, but the partnership has no legal entity of its own and the liability of the partners is personal.

The law relating to partnerships is to be found mostly in the Partnership Act 1890. This statute lays down the rules for determining the existence of a partnership, the relationship between partners and third parties, the relationship between partners and the rules governing termination of partnerships. All references to statutory sections below are to the Partnership Act unless otherwise indicated.

Pharmacy Law and Practice. DOI: http://dx.doi.org/10.1016/B978-0-12-394289-0.00028-X

Partners and Third Parties

Every partner is an agent of the firm and accordingly any acts done as a partner, including the incurring of extensive liabilities, will bind all the other partners. The relationship between partners therefore has to be based upon a high degree of trust. The exception to this rule is where a partner pledges the credit of the firm for his or her own personal debts. In this event the firm will not be bound. The partners' liabilities for the firm are joint and several. Thus each partner is potentially liable for the whole of the firm's liabilities, subject to the partners' rights of indemnity against each other. However, the right of indemnity may be of little use where only one of the partners in a firm has sufficient funds to pay a judgement debt to a creditor, the partner will have to pay the creditor and take his or her chance against the other partners.

By *Sections 10–12* of the Act, partners are rendered liable for wrongful acts and omissions of other partners acting in the ordinary course of business or with the consent of the other partners, and for misapplication of money or property received for the firm or in the firm's custody. However, a partner is not liable for any liabilities incurred by the firm while he or she is not a partner. Furthermore, by *Section 14*, any person who is not a partner of the firm, but who holds himself out as being a partner, is liable to the representee as if he or she were a partner.

Relations Between Partners

Formally created partnerships are usually governed by a partnership deed which will set out the rights and obligations of the partners in the firm. There is no express requirement for a partnership deed, but it lends certainty. By *Section 19* of the Act, partners may vary the terms of their partnership by mutual consent, or such variation may be implied from a course of dealing.

Fiduciary Duty

The basic duty of a partner towards the others is one of good faith, that is to act honestly and for the benefit of the partnership as a whole. In modern times this is known as a fiduciary duty. There are three statutory aspects to this duty:

(1) *Section 28* provides that 'partners are bound to render a true account of all things affecting the partnership to any partner or his legal representative'. This means that partners are bound to inform each other of all material facts in relation to partnership business.

(2) *Section 29* provides that 'every partner must account to the firm for any benefit derived by him without the consent of the other partners from any transaction concerning the partnership, or from any use made by him of the partnership name or business connection'. An example of the operation of this section is where a partner makes a secret profit which he or she fails to disclose to the others. When it is discovered, the others may

take out an action for account which may result in the secret profit being redistributed amongst the partners.

(3) *Section 30* provides that 'if a partner, without the consent of the other partners, carries on any business of the same nature as and competing with that of the firm, he must account for and pay over to the firm all profits made by him in that business'. This section is quite clear; the key question is whether the other business is in competition with the firm. If competition is established, liability is established.

Partnership Property

Additionally, *Section 20* provides that all property originally brought into the partnership or acquired on account of the firm for the purposes and in the course of partnership business, constitutes partnership property and must be held and applied as such in accordance with the partnership agreement. Thus all partnership property is held jointly by all the partners for their mutual benefit. Unless the contrary intention appears in the partnership agreement, the following provisions, created by the Act, apply.

Section 21 provides simply that unless it has been agreed otherwise, property bought with the firm's money is deemed to have been bought on behalf of the firm and will therefore be held for the benefit of all the partners.

Section 24 provides that:

(1) Partners are entitled to take part in the management of the business, but are not entitled to remuneration for so doing. The idea is that each partner will receive his reward by a straightforward share of the profits, and possibly interest on his original capital investment.

(2) Partners are entitled to indemnity from the firm in respect of liabilities incurred in the proper conduct of the business or in its preservation. Partners are therefore entitled to reimbursement for expenses, etc., incurred whilst carrying out partnership business.

(3) Partners are entitled to equal shares in the capital and profits of the firm, and are liable to contribute equally towards losses.

(4) Partners are entitled to interest on money advanced to the firm, but not on capital until the profits have been ascertained. In practice this provision makes little difference, as interest is frequently payable on capital, but it creates the automatic right to interest on money lent to the firm, subject to contrary agreement.

Termination of Partnership

Where the partnership is for an indefinite duration, it may be dissolved by one partner giving notice to the others (*Section 32* of the Partnership Act 1890). A partnership may also be dissolved by the court on the application of a partner:

(1) Where one of the partners becomes permanently incapable of performing his or her part of the partnership contract.

(2) Where one of the partners has been guilty of conduct calculated to prejudice the carrying on of the business.

(3) Where the business of the partnership can only be carried on at a loss.

(4) Where circumstances arise which make it just and equitable that the partnership is dissolved.

A partnership may also be rescinded like any other contract for fraud or misrepresentation. In this eventuality, *Section 41* gives the partner who has been the victim of the misrepresentation or fraud at the hands of another partner, the right to indemnity for his or her loss and the rights over partnership property to cover his or her loss.

On dissolution, the property of the partnership is applied first in the payment of the firm's debts and liabilities, then in the payment of what is due to each partner, first for advances and then for capital. Any surplus is divided among the partners in the proportion in which profits are divisible (according to the terms of the partnership agreement). Losses are paid out of profits if there are any, and if not, out of capital. If the residual capital is insufficient, losses are paid personally by the partners in the proportion in which they were entitled to profits.

Limited Partnership

The limited partnership is a hybrid form where the firm has at least one general partner with unlimited liability, and one or more limited partners who contribute money or property to the partnership and are liable only to the extent of their contribution. This form of partnership is governed by the Limited Partnership Act 1907.

The main reason for instituting a limited partnership is to attract capital into the business. Hence the provisions in the Limited Partnership Act that the limited partner is prohibited on pain of unlimited liability from taking part in the management of the business and cannot bind the firm; the partner's death or bankruptcy does not dissolve the partnership; the partner's consent to the introduction of a new partner is not necessary; the partner has no power to dissolve the partnership; the charging of his or her share (i.e., the raising of money against it) is not a ground for dissolution; and the partner can take no part in the winding-up of partnership affairs unless the court directs. Furthermore, the limited partner is unable to withdraw any part of his or her contribution during the continuance of the partnership. Precisely because the position of the limited partner is so precarious, that is, he or she has no right to determine what use is made of his or her investment in the partnership, there are very few limited partnerships in existence. The modern simplification of the process of creating a limited company has almost entirely replaced the limited partnership.

Disadvantages of Partnerships

The major disadvantage of partnership is the unlimited liability of members. The creation of a limited company avoids this problem and is far more attractive to those wishing to set up in a business which is going to incur any level of indebtedness or in which extensive commercial risks will be taken. The many small businesses which make the transition to company status enjoy comparative security and have a prescribed structure within which to conduct the firm's affairs.

Limited Liability Partnership

From 6 April 2001 pharmacists have been able to utilise a new trading entity introduced by the Limited Liability Partnerships Act 2000. This new entity may be formed by two or more persons 'associated for carrying on a lawful business with a view to profit', and unlike a partnership, the entity will have a legal personality in its own right. The partners in a limited liability partnership may be individuals or companies, and since the entity will have its own legal identity the partners will not have any contractual liability to the partnership's creditors. It is unclear at the present time whether circumstances may arise where the corporate veil will be lifted in a case where an individual acts negligently.

The internal arrangements between the partners will closely resemble the position in a conventional partnership. Relations between the partners will be regulated by agreement, and where there is no agreement the provisions in the Partnership Act 1890 will apply. However, the limited liability partnership will have to file an annual return, with audited accounts, and many of the provisions of the Companies Acts will apply. Partners will be taxed individually, and the creation of a limited liability partnership will be taxed neutral.

There is no restriction on the type of business that can trade as a limited liability partnership. It is expected that the main users of limited liability partnerships will be firms of accountants and solicitors, but there is no reason why others, such as pharmacists, should not conduct their professional activities using this entity.

At the present time it is difficult to tell whether this new entity will prove popular with pharmacists as a vehicle for professional practice. It is quite possible that the more familiar limited company will continue to be, a more attractive proposition when the competing advantages and disadvantages are taken into account.

THE LIMITED COMPANY

There are three types of limited company, the most significant of which for present purposes is the private limited company. The others are the public limited company and the company limited by guarantee.

Public limited companies (plcs) are quite large in operations. They must have an allotted share capital of at least £50,000 (one-quarter of which must be paid-up capital), and the company may offer their shares or debentures (explained below) for sale to the public. Many public limited companies are quoted on the Stock Exchange, and their shares may be bought and sold through stockbrokers. Their basic structure, however, is similar to that of the private limited company (explained below).

Companies limited by guarantee are usually non-profit-making companies formed for purposes ranging from the charitable, religious or educational, to the merely administrative, such as companies set up to manage a block of flats on behalf of the residents. This form of company is used chiefly as a method of incorporating groups of persons with common interest who do not have profit as the main motive.

Advantages of Creating a Limited Company

There are a number of advantages in trading as a private limited company which can be summarised as follows:

(1) The liability of the members is limited to the value of their shares.
(2) The company has a legal personality of its own separate from its members.
(3) The name of the company is prevented from being used by other companies.
(4) There are certain advantages in borrowing money (see below).
(5) The interests and responsibilities of the persons engaged in the business are clearly defined, including the management responsibilities of the firm.
(6) The company has a continuing existence of its own, independent of its members.
(7) In some circumstances there are taxation advantages.
(8) The appointment, retirement or removal of directors is carried out in the prescribed manner.
(9) Employees may gain the opportunity of acquiring shares in the company, and outside investors may become shareholders.

The Company's Legal Personality

An incorporated company has a separate legal personality which enables it to carry transactions and other functions in its own right. For example, the company may enter into contracts, purchase or lease property and sue or be sued in the company name.

A company is the beneficial owner of its own property, that is, it does not hold it as trustee for its members, and they have no legal or equitable interest in it. A company's transactions are carried out solely in the company name. A shareholder cannot enforce a contract made by the company, and neither he nor she is a party to the contract nor is he or she entitled to the benefits out of it. Likewise, a shareholder cannot be sued on contracts made by the company, nor can a court compel a shareholder to vote at a company's general meeting in such a way as to ensure that the company fulfils its contractual obligations, or prohibit the shareholder from voting in any other way.

A member of a company cannot sue in respect of civil wrongs (known technically as 'torts') committed against the company and cannot be sued for such wrongs committed by it. Even where it is proved that the company has committed a tort, the directors will only be liable where it can be shown that they actually participated in its commission.

Exceptions to the Rule of Separate Legal Identity

There are several statutory exceptions to the rule that companies have a separate legal personality.

First, under the Companies Act 2006, the directors of a public limited company will be liable where the company begins to trade and borrow money prior to obtaining a trading certificate.

Secondly, group accounts can be prepared where the company is subject to the small companies regime (where, for example, there is a holding company and subsidiaries). In order to determine whether this provision is applicable, it is necessary to lift the corporate veil and determine whether there is a holding company–subsidiary relationship. (Companies Act 2006, *Sections 398–408*)

Thirdly, in the event that a member of a company petitions the court on the grounds that the company's affairs are being conducted in a manner that is prejudicial to the interests of the shareholders or that an action or omission is or could be prejudicial, it may be necessary to lift the corporate veil to assess, for example, the basis on which the company was formed. (*Re London School of Electronics* (1986) (Companies Act 2006, *Section 994*))

Fourthly, if after having been disqualified, a director continues in that role, he or she will be held personally liable for the debts and obligations of the company. (Company Directors Disqualification Act 1986, *Section 15*).

Fifthly, if an individual petitions the court for the winding-up of a company on the grounds that it would be just and equitable to do so, the court may lift the corporate veil in order to assess the factual basis of these grounds. (Insolvency Act 1986, *Section 122(1)(g)*).

Sixthly, an individual will be liable to make contributions to the company's assets where, upon the winding-up of the company, it appears that the company was used with the intent to defraud creditors of the company or has been used for fraudulent purposes (Insolvency Act 1986, *Section 213*). This is also a criminal offence under the Companies Act 2006.

Finally, where a company has entered into insolvent liquidation and at some point prior to this, a director of the company knew or should have known that there was no reasonable prospect that the company would avoid insolvency, that person may be held liable to make a contribution to the company's assets. (Insolvency Act 1986, *Section 214*)

There are also a number of judicial exceptions to the rule that a company has a separate legal personality. For example, the courts have consistently lifted the corporate veil in an effort to combat fraud (*Jones v. Lipman (1962)*) or where an agency relationship is found to exist. (*Smith, Stone and Knight Ltd v. Birmingham Corp (1939)*).

Limited Liability

The concept of limited liability means that the liability of a company's shareholders is limited to the value of their shares (including any amount unpaid towards the value of the shares). In most private companies shares are fully paid up, so investors stand only to lose their investment plus any loan made to the company. Other potential liabilities may be personal guarantees for company borrowings or liabilities, for example, bank overdrafts or guarantees of rent payments under business leases. In practice, banks lending money to a small private company and landlords of business leases will inevitably require such personal guarantees, so for these debts the concept of limited liability is a fiction.

If a company is unable to pay its debts, its creditors may petition the court to wind it up under the provisions of the Insolvency Act 1986. If the court orders the company to be wound up, a liquidator is appointed to realise the company's assets. If the liquidator fails to realise sufficient assets to meet liabilities, then the value of the shares in the company will be called up.

As a shareholder is not liable to pay the company's debts himself or herself, a creditor of the company cannot sue him or her. A creditor can only obtain unpaid capital by petitioning the court to wind the company up, and await such payment as can be met by the liquidator. The liquidator discharges the company's debts rateably, thereby ensuring that one creditor does not get preferred treatment merely by being the first to sue. (The protection afforded by limited liability is of course subject to the exceptions to the principle of separate legal identity discussed above.)

The Protection of Company Names

Protection is given to company names by Part V of the Companies Act 2006. Under the Act there is a prohibition on using any name the use of which would constitute an offence or be offensive. The Secretary of State is also entitled to oblige a company to seek the comments of government departments where the proposed company name contains some connection with government or public bodies or contains sensitive words or expressions. Further, under *Section 66*, a company cannot use the same name as another company already appearing in the registrar of company names. If a name is too similar to an already existing name, the Secretary of State can require the company to change its name within 12 months of registration. (Companies Act 2006, *Section 77*)

There are also a number of provisions relating to the required indications for limited companies. The name of public limited companies must end with the words 'public limited company' (Companies Act 2006, *Section 58*), whereas the name of a private company, limited by shares or by guarantee, must end with 'limited' or with the recognised abbreviation 'ltd'. (Companies Act 2006, *Section 59*)

Financing the Company – Shares and Loan Capital

Shares

Most small companies have only one type of share known as ordinary shares. They are issued in order to provide permanent capital for the company and will normally carry with them the voting rights and an entitlement to a share of the company's profits or dividends.

Larger companies usually have a greater number of shareholders. In companies where there are many shareholders, there may be different classes of shares. The most common form of shares other than ordinary shares are preference shares. The holder of preference shares is entitled to a dividend of a fixed amount before any dividend is paid to the holders of ordinary shares. The terms of issue of preference shares often provide that the holder is also entitled to a priority in the repayment of share capital in the event of a winding-up.

The preference shareholder is in a more secure position than the ordinary shareholder as he or she is entitled to fixed dividends, usually calculated as a percentage of the value of the shares. The ordinary shareholder, however, has the opportunity of greater return as the level of dividend is not restricted to a fixed amount and will fluctuate in accordance with the company's profitability. Furthermore, in a winding-up, when preference shareholders have been repaid the nominal value of their shares, unless they have an express entitlement to a share in any surplus, the whole of the remaining assets of the company will be distributed among the ordinary shareholders in proportion to their holding. Ordinary shareholders hold most of the power at general meetings, and it will be they who will control company affairs and appoint directors. Thus the ordinary shareholder has more rights in determining the way in which a company conducts itself, but the nature of the investment carries a greater risk.

Loan Capital

Loan capital is an expression used to describe the long-term indebtedness of the company secured by mortgages, debenture stock and loan stock. All companies have an implied power to borrow and to give security for loans made to them. Unless the company's Memorandum of Association (explained below) provides otherwise, the amount a company may borrow is unlimited.

One way in which a company may raise capital is to issue debentures. Debentures are similar to shares in that they have a nominal value. They are usually redeemable at a fixed future date, and their nominal value is the amount payable to the holder on redemption (unless by the terms of issue a premium is also payable on redemption). Debentures usually carry a fixed rate of interest on the amount invested in the company and are usually secured by a fixed or floating charge over the company's assets. Thus in theory they represent a relatively safe form of investment. The debenture is therefore akin to an I owe you ('IOU') issued by a company to an investor, with prearranged terms concerning interest and repayment. As with preference shares, debentures enjoy priority in the repayment of interest and repayment of capital in the event of the company being wound up. However, they do not carry voting rights, and holders do not participate in the running of the company.

Bank Loans and Overdrafts

Loans by banks are usually secured by a fixed or floating charge over company assets and by personal guarantees given by directors. Even if assets are subject to a floating charge they may be dealt with freely, as the charge is not fixed to any asset or assets in particular until it becomes operational, that is, until repayments are not made and the bank seeks to realise company assets to meet the debt. Loans subject to a fixed charge are secured against specific company assets, usually business premises and/or stock.

The Creation and Structure of a Private Limited Company

Formalities

To incorporate a company, various documents must be completed and lodged at Companies House.

(1) Memorandum of Association (discussed below).
(2) Articles of Association (discussed below).
(3) Statement of the particulars of the first director(s) and company secretary, together with their signed consents to acting in these capacities, and the address of the registered office.
(4) Statement of particulars of shares to be issued on incorporation signed by a director or by the secretary.
(5) Declaration of compliance with the Companies Act. This statement does not need to be witnessed and may be made in paper or electronic form. It is open to the registrar to determine who may make this statement and the form that it should take.

The Memorandum and Articles of Association must state that the subscribers wish to form a company under the Companies Act 2006 and that they agree to become members and, in the event that a company is to have a share capital, to take at least one share each. The memorandum must be in the prescribed form and must be authenticated by each subscriber. The Registrar examines the documents, and if they are correct a certificate of incorporation is issued. The issuing of the certificate may take several weeks, but once it is issued the company's subscribers may begin to act as a body corporate.

Memorandum and Articles of Association

The company's constitution is set out in two documents known as the Memorandum and Articles of Association. The Memorandum lays down the company's powers and its relationship with the outside world, and the Articles regulate dealings between the company and its members, directors and other officers.

The Memorandum

The Memorandum of Association consists of clauses containing the following information:

(1) The name of the company.

(2) The location of the registered office, that is, whether it is in England, England and Wales, Wales or Scotland. It need not be more specific. Documents of companies whose registered office is to be situated in Scotland must be lodged at the Companies Registration Office in Edinburgh. These will be classified as Scottish companies. A company must at all times have a registered office at a particular address to which all communications and notices may be addressed.

(3) The objects of the company. It is invariably the longest clause and requires careful thought. The objects will set out the company's purpose and will set out the kind of activities in which the company seeks to be engaged. The clause will be subdivided as follows:

(a) The first subclause will set out the nature of the company's main business. It must be comprehensive and must detail all potential areas of business. If required, it can be amended at a later date by means of specific resolution.

(b) The second subclause usually covers any other business which in the opinion of the directors may be advantageously or conveniently carried on in conjunction with the main business of the company.

(c) The subsequent subclauses will cover general objects common to most businesses. These may include, for example, powers to lease, sell and purchase property; to purchase/lease equipment or machinery; to mortgage, charge or let out loans against company property; to issue and purchase shares; to issue debentures; to purchase shares in other companies; to sell the company; to draw bills of exchange and negotiable instruments; to distribute property amongst members; and to do all such things as may be necessary towards the attainment of the company's main objective. This list is by no means exhaustive, and will vary considerably between undertakings.

(4) The limited liability of the members.

(5) The amount of share capital with which the company proposes to be registered and the nominal value of each of the shares into which the share capital is to be divided. The division of shares into different classes, the

proportion of shares in each class and the rights conferred on the holders of each class of shares are sometimes stated, but this is very rarely done in practice as it is then more difficult to vary the rights at a later date. These matters are usually dealt with in the Articles so that any alteration can be effected by passing a special resolution.

(6) Further additional clauses may be included, usually of a kind found in the Articles of Association. The advantage of inserting additional matters in the Memorandum is that they can be protected against subsequent alteration, whereas if they are in the Articles of Association, they can be altered by a special resolution passed by a general meeting of the company.

(7) The Memorandum of Association concludes with an association clause by which two or more subscribers state that they are desirous of being formed into a company in pursuance of the Memorandum, and if the company has share capital, that they agree to take the number of shares set opposite their names.

The Articles

The Articles of Association regulate the internal affairs of the company and are, essentially, the constitution of the company. These regulations govern the relationship between the company and its shareholders and the relationship of the shareholders between themselves. It is unnecessary to register Articles of Association of a public limited company or a private limited company if the model Articles of Association promoted by the Secretary of State have been used. These model articles are contained in statutory instruments. The following is a non-exhaustive list of categories of provisions usually found in Articles of Association:

(a) Classes of shares. Where there is more than one type of share, the rights attaching to the owners of each class will be set out. For example, the priority of preference shareholders in the payment of dividends, the rules governing the apportionment of capital and the voting rights attaching to the holders of different classes will be set out. The Articles may also state the way in which these rights may be altered or the classes of shares created.

(b) Share transfer. The Articles will often give the directors the discretion not to register a transfer of shares. In a small business with only a few shareholders, the right of pre-emption is usually given to existing shareholders when one member decides to sell his or her shares. The Articles will contain detailed procedural provisions regulating this process.

(c) Company's purchase of its own shares. In a private limited company, the Articles may provide that a company has authority to purchase its own shares. However, advice should always be taken as to the taxation implications of such a course. Often the Articles of a small company name directors as permanent directors. This is achieved either through private agreement within the company (which can be overturned by a resolution at a company meeting) or more securely by attaching enhanced voting rights to the directors' shares, thus enabling them to vote out any resolution tabled for their removal.

(d) Power of directors and remuneration. The power to run a company is normally vested in the directors who will exercise this function through resolutions passed at duly convened board meetings. In practice, in small firms, however, decisions are taken on a daily basis by all directors.

The Articles usually contain a provision to vest in the directors the power to deal in company property, to mortgage company property and to issue securities. It is possible, if required, to limit the total amount of debt the directors may incur on behalf of the company at any one time without the prior consent of the shareholders. Provision for directors' remuneration and expenses is made in the Articles, however, a contract of employment is usually drawn up separately to cover the directors' entitlements to salary, share of profits and expenses.

(e) Miscellaneous provisions. Further provisions in the Articles will deal variously with matters such as allocation of shares following the death of a shareholder; the procedures for calling and conducting general meetings; voting rights at company meetings; appointment and removal of directors and the company secretary; use of the company seal; payment of dividends on shares and provisions governing the winding-up of the company.

The Companies Act 2006 has altered the common law position regarding the capacity of the company to enter into contracts. Prior to the 2006 Act, this capacity was limited to contracts which were connected with the stated object of the company. For example, the main object of a pharmacy operating as a company would be the sale and supply of legal and medically prescribed medications. Contracts entered into in pursuance of this object would therefore be within the power of the company. However, entering into another contract which is totally unconnected with the object of the sale and supply of prescription drugs would be outside the power of the company.

However, this position has changed and now, unless a specific limitation is included in the objects of the company, its objects are presumed to be unrestricted.

FORMAL REQUIREMENTS FOR RUNNING A COMPANY

Every company must have a registered office, the location of which determines the tax office which will deal with the company's tax matters. The company must display its company name outside its registered office and every other office or place of business. The registered office does not have to be the company's place of business, sometimes a company will nominate its solicitors or accountants to act in this capacity and give their address.

Company Stationery

The company name must appear on all stationery including letters, cheques, invoices (which must also state the company value added tax (VAT) number) and receipts. Business letters must also show the address of the registered office, the place of registration and the registered number of the company.

Accounts

A company must decide a date on which all its accounts for the preceding year will be presented (the accounting reference period). In respect of a private company, the period for filing is 9 months from the end of the relevant accounting reference period, whereas for a public company it is 6 months after the end of the relevant accounting reference period. The applicable time frames for a public and private limited company respectively are dependent upon the status of the company prior to the end of the relevant accounting reference period.

The Companies Act 2006 imposes the requirement that accounts must be kept which are capable of showing with reasonable accuracy the financial position of the company at any given time. Accounts must show:

(1) All moneys paid and received by the company and the details of the transactions.
(2) The current assets and liabilities of the company.
(3) The level of stock held at the end of each financial year.
(4) Details of creditors and debtors.

Accounts must be laid before a general meeting of members within 6 months of the accounting reference period. The company auditor should be appointed before the first Annual General Meeting (AGM) and must be a chartered or certified accountant, or a person authorised as an auditor by the Department of Trade and Industry. The auditor of a small company is often its accountant, but the liability to prepare accounts and make tax returns vests in the directors. The duty of the auditor is to inform the members of the accuracy of the company's accounts.

Company Seal and Statutory Books

A formal register must be kept giving details of shares and shareholders, directors and the company secretary, directors' interests, and mortgages and charges. All share issues and transfers must be documented in the register. A numbered share certificate will then be issued by the company secretary and pressed with the company seal. A minute book and a book of share certificates must also be maintained. A company must have a seal with its name engraved upon it. The seal must be used on formal company documents which would be made by deed if executed by an individual, for example, mortgage documents, share certificates and debentures.

Meetings

The conduct of the business of the company is determined in meetings of directors and company members. The procedure for calling and conducting meetings is contained in the Articles of Association.

The meetings held by directors or 'board meetings' deal with the day-to-day conduct of the company's affairs. At the very first board meeting the directors should ensure that the formalities outlined above have been complied with or are under way.

At general meetings the members of the company exercise their power over the company affairs by passing resolutions. Private companies are not required to hold AGMs, but public companies must hold AGMs which correspond to the reporting cycle in order to facilitate shareholder participation. A public company must hold an AGM within the 6 months following its accounting reference date.

Members must have 21 days' notice of an AGM. The main functions carried out at AGMs are:

(1) The receipt of the company accounts and chairman's report.
(2) The proposal of a dividend on shares.
(3) The re-election of directors and other officers and the re-election of auditors.

Extraordinary general meetings (EGMs) may be called at 14 days' notice to deal with urgent business that cannot wait until the AGM. The procedure for proposing and voting on resolutions is similar to that used in AGMs.

Mortgages, Debentures and Charges

Every charge or mortgage created or debenture issued must be registered with the Registrar of Companies within 21 days of its commencement. If a company fails to register a charge, the company and any officer of it in default could be liable upon conviction on indictment to a fine or upon summary conviction, to a fine not exceeding the statutory maximum.

The Registrar will issue a certificate of registration for every debenture issued, which must be endorsed. When a charge has been satisfied a memorandum of satisfaction should be lodged with the Registrar.

Annual Return

Every company must deliver to the Registrar of Companies successive annual returns each of which is made up to a date not later than the date which is from time to time the company's 'return date', that is either the anniversary of the company's incorporation, or if the company's last return was made up to a different date, the anniversary of that date. This document states the address of the registered office, details of the company's shares and shareholders, details of the company's debts, a list of all members and changes in members since the last return and details of the directors and secretary. The return must be signed by a director and the company secretary and be submitted together with the correct registration fee. If a company fails to deliver an annual return before the end of the period of 28 days after a return date, the company is guilty of an offence and liable on summary conviction to a fine not exceeding the statutory maximum and, on conviction after continued contravention, to a daily default fine not exceeding one-tenth of the statutory maximum. (Companies Act 2006, *Section 858*)

Taxation

Corporation tax is charged on the profits of a company's accounting period and is payable 9 months after the expiration of that period (1 April–31 March). The corporation tax accounting period is normally 12 months long and usually corresponds with the company's 12-month financial year. The company's financial year begins and ends with the dates covered by the company's annual report and accounts (financial accounts) which are submitted to Companies House. These accounts are sometimes called statutory accounts or audited accounts.

Corporation tax should be paid within 12 months after the end of corporation tax accounting period. If a company's accounting period straddles financial years for which different rates of corporation tax have been fixed, profits will be apportioned to the period falling either side of the end of the year. Tax returns are made quarterly and additionally on the annual accounting date if that does not coincide with a quarterly accounting date. By careful consideration of the first accounting reference period, the first payment of tax can be considerably lessened and cash flow improved for the first year. Professional advice should be taken in this respect.

VAT is dealt with separately and collected by Her Majesty's Revenue and Customs. VAT returns must be made quarterly on prescribed dates. Strict rules govern the keeping of VAT accounts and hefty fines are levied for late payment. VAT matters are invariably dealt with by the company accountant.

NOTIFICATION OF CHANGES AFTER INCORPORATION

The Registrar of Companies must be notified of any of the following changes taking place after incorporation:

(1) Change of directors or secretary
(2) Change of registered office
(3) Increase in company capital
(4) Change in allotment of shares
(5) Change of company name together with a copy of the special resolution authorising the change

(6) Changes in the Memorandum or Articles of Association together with the authorising of special resolution within 15 days.

Winding-Up

A company can be wound up or dissolved by the members themselves or by the court. There are three routes to winding-up or liquidation:

(1) voluntary winding-up by the members
(2) voluntary winding-up by the creditors
(3) compulsory winding-up by the court.

The first two forms do not involve the intervention of the court. They are so named because it is either the members or the creditors who take the initiative in winding-up. This will either be done because the purposes for which the company was formed have been completed or exhausted, or because the company has run into financial trouble from which it cannot reasonably be expected to recover.

Upon liquidation the powers of the directors cease and the management of the company is taken over by a liquidator. The liquidator may be appointed by the members, creditors or court. The liquidator must use his or her best endeavours to satisfy as much of the company's indebtedness as possible and must draw up accounts demonstrating what funds and/or assets are available for the satisfaction of the creditors.

The liquidator owes fiduciary duties to the company whose agent he or she is, that is, the liquidator owes a duty to the company to do the best financially for it as he or she can. In a compulsory liquidation, the liquidator may be empowered to engage in litigation in the company's name, carry on such of the company's business as may be necessary and pay the company's debts or enter into such compromises or arrangements with creditors as are necessary. If there are sufficient funds within the company to satisfy all the creditors, the remainder will be divided among the shareholders according to their entitlements as laid out in the Articles of Association.

Prejudicial Conduct of the Company's Affairs

The Companies Act 2006 provides the court with a number of wide ranging powers to protect members of the company against unfair prejudice. Minority shareholders frequently rely on these provisions where the actions of the majority shareholders are thought to be inimical to the minority shareholders. The remedy most often sought is an order that the majority shareholders must purchase the shares of the minority at a price that represents their proportional value of the company. A petition may be brought by a member of the company in relation to actions which unfairly prejudice the interests of the members of the company generally or in relation to actions which prejudice the interests of a group of shareholders of which the petitioner is a member.

Case Study

Facts: K is a minority shareholder in a family owned company and petitions the court to compel a share buyout because it is alleged that the company is being run in a manner that is prejudicial to his interests. K argues that he had a legitimate expectation that, on his request, a property that comprised the company's sole asset, would be sold to enable him realise the value of his investment. K says that at the time of purchase, it was agreed that he would have final say on matters relating to the property and because the sale of it had not been approved by the other shareholders, his legitimate expectation was frustrated.

Question: Have K's interests been prejudiced by the actions of the other shareholders?

Answer: No. There was no unfairness in the way in which the affairs of the company had been conducted and there had been no agreement that K would be the deciding voice on matters relating to the property.

Reason: The management of the business had not been conducted in an unfair manner and consequently, there was no right to request winding-up because the criteria for the exercise of discretion under each jurisdiction were coextensive.

This case study is based on the case of *Kaneria v. Patel (2001) BCC 692*.

Striking-off the Register

A company may be struck off the register where it appears to the Registrar that it has ceased trading. This inference will be raised where no annual return is filed. However, striking-off of a company is only applicable to a private company if, in the past 3 months, it has not:

- traded or otherwise carried on business;
- changed its name;
- disposed of value of property or rights that immediately before ceasing to be in business or trade, it held for disposal or gain in the normal course of that business or trade; or
- engaged in any other activity except one necessary or expedient for making a striking-off application, settling the company's affairs or meeting a statutory requirement.

Self-Assessment Questions

1. What are the benefits of operating a pharmacy as a private company as opposed to a partnership?

   Answer: The main difference from the perspective of a pharmacist operating a pharmacy is the fact that the liability of the members of a partnership is unlimited whereas members of a private company can avail themselves of limited liability and the company has a separate corporate identity to its members.

This separate corporate identity is overlooked only in a few limited and well-defined statutory and judicial exceptions. However, a pharmacist has the option of entering into a limited liability partnership which is a separate legal entity in which the relations between the partners resemble that of a conventional partnership.

2. What is the significance of the Memorandum and Articles of Association of a company?

Answer: The Memorandum and Articles of Association are the governing documents of the company and contain basic information regarding the company as well as information as to how the company will operate. Prior to the Companies Act 2006, the objects of the company had to be contained in the Articles of Association because otherwise any contracts entered into which were not connected or in pursuance of the objects of the company were outside the capacity or *ultra vires* the powers of the company. This meant that such contracts were void and unenforceable.

This common-law position has changed under the Companies Act 2006, which effectively abolishes the doctrine of *ultra vires*. The objects of a company are unrestricted unless some specific restriction is included in the Articles of Association.

Chapter 29

The Sale of Goods

The range of transactions which can be described as a sale of goods is enormous, and includes sales of goods worth from a few pence to millions of pounds. Yet the basic legal framework governing this diverse range of transactions is the same.

This area of law affects the pharmacist in his dual role as purchaser and seller of medicinal and other products. As a purchaser, the pharmacist will come into daily contact with this area of the law when he purchases medicines and other products from his wholesaler suppliers. The same law will regulate the pharmacist's onward sale of these products to the customer. The object of this section of the book is to provide a synopsis of the relevant law, much of which is to be found in the Sale of Goods Act 1979.

Unless otherwise stated, references to statutory sections in this chapter will refer to the Sale of Goods Act 1979.

CONTRACT FOR THE SALE OF GOODS

The basic definition of a sale of goods is found in *Section 2(1)*, which defines it as a 'contract whereby the seller transfers or agrees to transfer the property in goods to the buyer for a money consideration, called the price'. 'Property in goods' is a way of describing what is commonly called ownership, but a sale of goods can include an agreement to sell whereby the ownership of the goods passes at a later date. 'Money consideration' generally means that the buyer must pay in money. A combination of money and goods in exchange, for example a trade-in on a new car, comes within this definition, but a pure exchange of goods does not.

Contracts for labour and materials supplied and contracts of hire purchase do not fall within the law on sale of goods. In the former, the principal object of the contract is the provision of services. In the latter, the hirer (the buyer) does not acquire the ownership, but merely an option to purchase when all the instalments are paid. There is statutory protection for the customer in these circumstances outside the sale of goods law.

Pharmacy Law and Practice. DOI: http://dx.doi.org/10.1016/B978-0-12-394289-0.00029-1

Formation of the Contract

The precise moment when the contract is formed is critical, in that before the contract is formed either party is free to withdraw. The contract is made when an offer made by one party is accepted by the other. An offer is an offer to buy. The display of goods for sale in a shop, for example, is merely an invitation to make offers. The customer makes the offer when he produces the goods to the cashier, and it is accepted when the cashier accepts payment.

The Carbolic Smoke Ball

One of the principal cases in the law of contract concerned a proprietor of a medicinal product. In *Carlill v. Carbolic Smoke Ball Co. (1893)*, the defendants, who were the owners of a medicinal product called 'The Carbolic Smoke Ball', issued an advertisement in which they offered to pay £100 to any person who succumbed to influenza after having used one of their smoke balls in a specified manner and for a specified period. They added that they had deposited a sum of £100 with their bankers to show their sincerity. The plaintiff, on the faith of the advertisement, bought and used the ball as prescribed, but succeeded in catching influenza. She sued for the £100. The defendants argued that the advertisement was a mere 'puff', never intended to create a binding obligation, that there was no offer to any particular person, and that, even if there were, the plaintiff had failed to notify her acceptance. The Court of Appeal rejected these arguments. Although the offer was made to the world, the contract was made with that limited portion of the public who came forward and performed the condition on the faith of the advertisement. Accordingly, the plaintiff recovered the £100.

Using the Post

When the buyer and seller transact a sale by post, special rules apply. Generally, when the means of communication is expected to be the post, the acceptance takes place when the letter of acceptance is posted; see *Household Fire & Carriage Insurance Co. v. Grant (1879)*. When the chosen means of communication is instantaneous, such as telephone or fax, the acceptance takes effect when it is actually communicated to the offeror; see *Brinkibon Ltd v. Stahag Stahl (1982)*.

Oral and Written Contracts

Section 4 provides that the contract of sale 'may be made in writing (either with or without seal), or by word of mouth, or it may be implied from the conduct of the parties'. Thus the form of the contract is something which is decided by the parties to it, and where the contract is not made in writing, a court may infer the existence of a contract from oral or any documentary evidence tending to show that a contract was made.

The Price to be Paid

The price to be paid is usually agreed between the parties, but *Section 8(2)* provides that 'where the price is not determined … the buyer must pay a reasonable price'. Sometimes, however, the price to be paid for the goods is so fundamental an aspect of the contract that a court will refuse to enforce a contract where none has been agreed. If none has been agreed it may often be the case that the parties have done no more than agree to contract at some later date, and have not concluded an enforceable contract of sale. When deciding upon such issues, the court will look to all the surrounding circumstances to determine the intention of the parties at the time of the agreement.

Cancelling the Contract

As a general rule, once a contract has been concluded it cannot be cancelled. There are certain exceptions under the Cancellation of Contracts made in a Consumer's Home or Place of Work Regulations 2008/1816, which apply to contracts between consumers and traders for the supply of goods and services and which are made either during a visit by the trader to the consumer's home or place of work, or to the home of another individual or during a meeting organised by the trader away from his usual business premises. The regulations also apply to a contract made between the two parties after the consumer has made an offer during a visit or meeting away from the trader's normal business premises and to consumer credit agreements   (Regulation 5).

Under these regulations, the consumer is able to cancel the contract once he serves notice within the cancellation period on either the trader or another person specified in the notice as a person to whom the notice should be given. The notice can be delivered or sent (including by electronic email)   (Regulation 8).

The consumer can exercise his right to cancel the contract at any time within 7 days of his receipt of the notice.

There are also exceptions for certain 'distance contracts' where agreements for goods or services are concluded exclusively by 'distance communication' – see the Consumer Protection (Distance Selling) Regulations 2000. The cancellation period is usually seven working days from receipt of the good or conclusion of the contract in the case of services. However, this period may be extended if the supplier does not give the requisite confirmatory information with details about the right to cancel. The cancellation of a contract under the regulations also has the effect of cancelling any 'related credit contract.'

There are exceptions to the consumer's right to cancel contained in Regulation 13 and these apply to:

(a) certain goods the price of which is dependent on fluctuations in the financial market which cannot be controlled by the supplier;
(b) the supply of goods made to the consumer's specifications or clearly personalised or which by reason of their nature cannot be returned or are liable to deteriorate or expire rapidly;
(c) the supply of audio or video recordings or computer software if they are unsealed;
(d) the supply of newspapers, periodicals or magazines; or
(e) gaming, betting or lottery services.

Where the purchase is made by the consumer with the assistance of credit, a separate statutory regime applies in the form of the Consumer Credit Act 1974 and the Consumer Protection Act 1987. This legislation falls outside the scope of this book.

The Passing of Property

The time at which ownership transfers from the seller to the buyer does not always coincide with the transfer of physical possession from one to another. Often, for example in shipping contracts, property passes before the buyer accepts delivery. It is important to determine when ownership vests in the buyer for a number of reasons:

(1) The 'risk' in the goods, that is the risk of them falling in value or perishing passes with ownership.
(2) The buyer cannot transfer ownership to a third party until such time as he has ownership himself.
(3) The seller cannot sue the buyer for the price of the goods until ownership has passed.
(4) If the buyer or seller become bankrupt, the rights of the other party will depend on who has ownership.

The rules governing the transfer of ownership are contained in *Sections 16–19* of the Sale of Goods Act 1979, and their application depends upon whether the goods are specified or unspecified at the time of making the contract. Specified goods are those which are identified and agreed on at the time the contract of sale is made. A branded bottle of cough mixture taken from a display is therefore specific, but 100 grams of aqueous cream taken from a larger quantity is not specific as it cannot be said which 100 grams have been sold.

Section 17 provides that ownership of specific goods passes to the buyer at such time as the parties intended it to be transferred. If no specific provision has been agreed between the parties, then the court will look at all the surrounding circumstances to see what their intention was. If none can be found, the rules in *Sections 16–19* apply.

Section 16 provides that 'where there is a contract for the sale of unascertained goods no property is transferred to the buyer unless and until the goods are ascertained'. Thus until the goods can be specifically identified as those forming the subject matter of the contract, ownership cannot pass. For example, an English buyer contracts to buy 100 tonnes of senna leaves from the cargo of the ship Empress and the ship leaves India with 500 tonnes, 400 of which are firstly being delivered to Lisbon. If the 100 tonnes is mixed in with the bulk, it does not become ascertained until the 400 tonnes is unloaded. Once the goods are ascertained, ownership passes in accordance with the intention of the parties.

Rules set out in *Section 18* of the Act apply where the intention of the parties cannot be ascertained.

Rule 1. Where there is an unconditional contract for the sale of specific goods, in a deliverable state, the property in the goods passes to the buyer when the contract is made, and it is immaterial whether the time of payment, or the time of delivery, or both be postponed.

Thus, when the goods are specific and ready to be handed over, the buyer becomes the owner the moment the contract is made. However, if the goods are not in a deliverable state and require something to be done to them before delivery, ownership cannot pass until they are in an appropriate condition (see below).

Rule 2. Where there is a contract for the sale of specific goods and the seller is bound to do something to the goods for the purpose of putting them in a deliverable state, the property does not pass until the thing is done, and the buyer has notice that it has been done.

'Notice' means actual knowledge that the goods are in a deliverable state.

Rule 3. Where there is a contract for sale of specific goods in a deliverable state, but the seller is bound to weigh, measure, test or do some other act or thing with reference to the goods for the purpose of ascertaining the price, the property does not pass until the act or thing is done and the buyer has notice that it has been done.

Rule 3 is self-explanatory, but it must be noted that it applies only where the seller is bound to do something to the goods.

Rule 4. When goods are delivered to the buyer on approval or on sale or return or similar terms, the property in the goods passes to the buyer:

(a) When he signifies his approval or acceptance to the seller or does any other act adopting the transaction.

(b) If he does not signify his approval or acceptance to the seller but retains the goods without giving notice of rejection, then if a time has been fixed for the return of the goods, on the expiration of that time and, if no time has been fixed, on the expiration of reasonable time.

In ascertaining whether the buyer has signified his approval or acceptance where he has not specifically stated to the seller that he has accepted the
goods, he will be taken to have done so if he does something which substantially impedes his ability to return the goods by the end of the period. Pledging
the goods to a pawnbroker for a period exceeding the time limit for refusal
would satisfy this test. However, if he cannot return the goods because, for
example, they have been stolen, this will operate as an excuse and property
will not pass.

Rule 5 (1). Where there is a contract for the sale of unascertained or future
goods by description, and goods of that description and in a deliverable condition are unconditionally appropriated to the contract, either by the seller with
the assent of the buyer, or by the buyer with the assent of the seller, the property in the goods then passes to the buyer; and the assent may be express or
implied, and may be given before or after the appropriation is made.

Rule 5 (2). Where, in pursuance of the contract, the seller delivers the
goods to the buyer or to a carrier or other bailee or custodian for the purpose
of transmission to the buyer, and does not reserve the right of disposal, he is
taken to have unconditionally appropriated the goods to the contract.

Thus, for the operation of Rule 5 it is necessary that goods complying with the contract be unconditionally appropriated to the contract, that is
they become specified by one of the parties, and that the other party assents.
Returning to the example of the cargo of senna leaves, if the contract was
merely for the delivery of 100 tonnes of senna leaves, the goods would not
become specified and accepted until the senna leaves were off-loaded and
accepted by the buyer. When goods have to be dispatched by a carrier, they
will normally be unconditionally appropriated when they are handed over to
the carrier. However, the same rules apply, and the goods must be specified in
order for ownership to pass.

Section 19 provides that, if the seller reserves the right of disposal until
certain conditions are fulfilled, ownership does not pass until those conditions
are fulfilled. For example, if a seller dispatches goods to the buyer through a
carrier with instructions that the goods cannot be handed over until the buyer
has paid, the goods will remain the seller's property until the buyer had paid
for them.

The Romalpa Clause

In the case of *Aluminium Industrie Vaasen BV v. Romalpa Aluminium Ltd
(1976)*, the Court of Appeal had to consider the situation where the seller had
sold a large quantity of materials to the buyer in the knowledge that the buyer
would only be able to pay the seller when the materials had been used to manufacture goods, and the finished product sold. Before full payment was made
the buyer became insolvent, some of the materials remained in their raw state,
and some had been processed and mixed with other substances. The Court of

Appeal upheld the validity of a clause in the contract of sale which reserved the ownership of the materials to the seller until they had been paid for or until they became processed with other materials, and which created a fiduciary duty (binding financial duty) on the buyer's part to repay the price of the raw materials out of the proceeds of sale of the manufactured product. Thus a seller in such a situation can reserve ownership of the goods until they become transformed or sold onto a third party, and can create a right to be paid out of the proceeds of the buyer's subsequent sale to a third party. Such clauses have become commonly known as Romalpa clauses. They are sometimes found in the standard contracts used by perfume and cosmetic manufacturers.

Transfer of Risk

As was stated above, the usual position is that the risk in the goods transfers with ownership unless the parties agree otherwise (*Section 20(1)*). Therefore, if the goods are damaged or stolen, the loss falls on the seller if it occurs before ownership is transferred, otherwise it falls on the buyer.

There are two limitations on this rule. The first is created by *Section 20(2)* which provides that '… where the delivery has been delayed though the fault of either the buyer or seller, the goods are at the risk of the party at fault as regards any loss which might not have occurred but for such fault'. The second is created by *Section 20(3)* which provides that 'nothing in this section shall affect the duties or liabilities of either seller or buyer as a bailee or custodian of the goods of the other party'. The effect of this section is that the party in possession of the goods must take reasonable care of them, and if the goods are damaged or lost as a result of his negligence, he will have to bear that loss.

If the buyer has to bear some loss because the risk in the goods has passed to him, he must still carry out all his obligations under the contract. Thus if he withholds some of the purchase price he is in breach of the contract and can be sued for the remainder by the seller.

Perishing of Goods

Section 6 provides that 'where there is a contract for the sale of specific goods, and the goods without the knowledge of the seller have perished at the time when the contract is made, the contract is void'. There can be no legally constituted contract for goods which have perished before the contract date. 'Perish' means more than slight deterioration not sufficient to change the commercial character of the goods. In *Asfar v. Blundell (1896)* it was held that dates which had been under water for two days and which had been contaminated with sewage had 'perished' and were no longer commercially valuable.

Section 7 provides that 'where there is an agreement to sell specific goods, and subsequently the goods, without any fault on the part of the seller or the buyer, perish before the risk passes to the buyer, the agreement is avoided'. This section applies the common law doctrine of frustration, whereby a contract is declared void if supervening events outside the control of either party render performance of the contract impossible. *Section 7* applies only to specific goods, but the same considerations apply to unspecified goods as apply in the case of goods perishing before the making of the contract. The contract will not be frustrated if the origin of the unspecified goods is not specified.

It follows from this that once the risk in the goods has passed to the buyer, the contract cannot be avoided by *Section 7*, or in the case of unspecified goods at common law by the doctrine of frustration. If the position were to be otherwise, the concept of the passing of risk would be meaningless.

When the contract is either avoided by the operation of *Section 6* or *7* or declared void at common law, the buyer need not pay for the goods and the seller need not deliver them. However, if the parties have provided for the eventuality which occurred, the terms of the contract will take precedence. In the case where the buyer has paid some of the purchase price before the goods perished, if the contract is avoided by operation of *Section 6* or *7*, then the buyer will recover the whole of the sums he has paid over. If the contract is frustrated at common law, that is the goods were unspecified, the Law Reform (Frustrated Contracts) Act 1943 empowers the court, before remitting the balance to the buyer, to deduct from the sums already paid to the seller a sum towards expenses incurred by the seller in performing the contract and to deduct any reasonable sum for any benefit the buyer has received under the contract.

Invalid Title

The situation often arises where the seller of goods does not have proper title to the goods. This may occur where the goods are not his to sell, or where the contract by which he originally acquired the goods is voidable (discussed below). The general principle is contained in the maxim *nemo dat quod non habet*, in other words, you cannot give what you do not own. *Section 2(1)* provides that: '... where goods are sold by a person who is not their owner, and who does not sell them under the authority or with the consent of the owner, the buyer acquires no better title to the goods than the seller had, unless the owner of the goods is by his conduct precluded from denying the seller's authority to sell.' Generally speaking, a seller cannot transfer to a buyer any better title than that which he already possesses. Where there has been a chain of sales, for example, where B, without authority, sells A's goods to C who in turn sells them to D, C and D have no better title to the goods than B had. In order to retrieve his goods A can take out an action (called an action for conversion) against D for the recovery of the goods. D may then sue C who may in turn sue B for breach of contract, for it will be an implied term of each contract that the seller had full title to the goods.

If, however, A represented by words or conduct that B had authority to sell his goods, then A will be prevented from asserting that the sale was unauthorized. For the representation to have this effect, it must have been made intentionally or negligently, it must have misled the innocent purchaser and the innocent purchaser must have bought the goods. For example, in *Eastern Distributors v. Goldring (1957)*, a customer who wished to raise some money against his van conspired with a motor trader by pretending that he was buying the van from the motor trader. Both of them filled out their portions of the hire purchase forms.

The customer subsequently sold the van to a third party and defaulted on the payments to the hire purchase company. The question then arose as to whether the hire purchase company had acquired title from the motor trader or the customer. It was held that as the customer had allowed the motor trader to represent the van as belonging to him, he was prevented from disputing that the title had passed to the hire purchase company.

Where the owner has signed a document purporting to transfer title, the document will usually be taken to have legal effect except in the rare circumstances where the owner can show both that he was radically mistaken about the nature and effect of the document, and where he can show that he was not careless in signing it.

Exceptions to the *nemo dat* Principle

Mercantile Agents

A mercantile agent is an independent agent to whom someone else entrusts his goods and to whom is usually transferred the authority to sell the goods, consign them, or to raise money on the security of the goods. Problems as to title may occur when the owner instructs the mercantile agent that his goods are not to be sold without his express authority. For example, a man may wish to place his sports car in the window of a car show room to see how many offers may be lodged, and to ascertain the level of offers made. The manager of the show room may be acting as a mercantile agent on a commission basis, but it may be agreed between the parties that the car is not to be sold without the owner's express permission.

Another exception to the *nemo dat* maxim is created by *Section 2(1)* of the Factors Act 1889, by which a mercantile agent in possession of goods with the authority of the owner, but without the authority to sell, may pass a good title to a purchaser from him if the purchaser buys from him in good faith and without notice that he does not have authority to sell. In this situation the burden is on the purchaser to prove that he was acting bona fide and bought without knowledge of the absence of authority. Thus a purchaser can acquire good title to the sports car if he innocently believes the mercantile agent to be the true owner. The owner must then sue the agent for the market value of the car.

Sale where the Owner's Title is Voidable

An exception to the *nemo dat* rule can occur where the owner's title is voidable. An example of what is meant by voidable title is where B has induced A to enter into a contract of sale by making some misrepresentation, for example that he is a respectable person whose cheque will be honoured, when in fact he is an impostor who has no funds to meet the cheque. Under these circumstances B has falsely induced A to enter into the contract and will acquire only a voidable title. A will retain the right to set the contract aside and claim his goods back.

However, if B sells the goods to C before A realises that he has been misled, C will get a perfect title (provided he buys in good faith and without notice of B's dishonesty) by virtue of *Section 23*.

Lawyers distinguish between a voidable contract and one which is void, that is not valid from the outset. Where the contract is void, C cannot acquire good title.

This will occur when the following two conditions are met:

(1) The identity of the buyer was an essential fact to A when selling to B.
(2) When making the contract A was intending to deal with someone other than B.

Thus in *Cundy v. Lindsay (1878)*, a rogue purchaser ordered goods from the seller, Lindsay, in the name of Blenkarn of 37 Wood Street. The signature was written in such a way that it looked like the name of the reputable firm Blenkirn & Co. Assuming that he was dealing with a reputable firm, Lindsay dispatched the goods to Blenkirn & Co. at 37 Wood Street. Blenkarn received the goods but never paid for them, and sold them to Cundy who knew nothing of the fraud. The House of Lords held that the contract between Lindsay and Blenkarn was void and therefore the goods still belonged to Lindsay.

Seller Retaining Possession Sells to Third Party

The situation may arise where the seller sells or agrees to sell goods to B and later sells or agrees to sell them to C. The question arises, to whom do the goods belong? Applying *Section 24* of the 1979 Act and *Section 8* of the Factors Act 1889, under certain circumstances C may acquire title to the goods following a previous sale to B. The conditions are as follows:

(1) A must have been in possession of the goods or documents of title at the time of the sale to C. The point of this condition is that B could have safeguarded his position by taking immediate possession of the goods or documents of title.
(2) There must be delivery to C of the goods or documents of title.
(3) C must be acting in good faith and acting without notice of the previous contract with B.

The purpose of these provisions is to safeguard the position of C. B obviously retains the right to sue A for breach of contract when the goods are not delivered.

Buyer in Possession Without Ownership Sells to Third Party

The buyer usually has ownership of goods when he takes possession, but in some circumstances he may have possession without ownership. For example, a buyer may take delivery, but the agreement is that ownership does not pass until payment is made. What is the position of the third party purchaser who buys before the original buyer has paid the original seller and thereby acquired title? The answer is that by operation of *Section 25* of the 1979 Act and *Section 9* of the Factors Act 1889, the subsequent purchaser will acquire good title where certain conditions are satisfied as follows.

(1) The person selling must be someone who has bought or agreed to buy the goods. Purchasing an option or purchasing goods on hire purchase is not sufficient for this condition to be met.

(2) The person selling the goods must have been a buyer in possession, in other words he must have obtained possession of, or documents of title to the goods with the consent of the seller.

(3) There must be a delivery or transfer of the goods or documents of title to the innocent sub-purchaser.

(4) The buyer in possession must have acted in the normal course of business of a mercantile agent. In other words the transaction with the sub-purchaser must be carried out in such a way as it would be carried out by a mercantile agent. This is a little absurd as the buyer in possession may not be a mercantile agent, but the requirement is implicit in the statutory section.

(5) The sub-purchaser must be acting bona fide and unaware that the original seller has any rights in respect of the goods.

All the above requirements must be fulfilled in order for the sub-purchaser to acquire a good title.

Misrepresentation

A misrepresentation occurs when one party is induced into entering a contract as a result of something which has been represented by the other party but is in fact false. Statements amounting to a misrepresentation may be made orally or in writing; the essential factor is that it operates on the mind of the other party. A distinction must be drawn between mere statement of opinion or trader's 'puff' and a genuine misrepresentation. A statement of opinion is something other than a statement of fact. Traders' puffs are, for example, claims that a particular product will 'cure smoking', or will 'protect against cardiac arrest', or some other serious illness.

The misrepresentation need not have been made fraudulently in order for it to be actionable; it may be made innocently or negligently. Accordingly, this area of the law may be particularly relevant to the community pharmacist who sells a product about which he has no personal knowledge. The misrepresentation must, however, be an influencing factor on the mind of the party induced.

The aggrieved party may succeed in rescinding the contract and/or in obtaining damages. The effect of rescission is to return the parties to the position they were in before the making of the contract. Thus goods and purchase price must be returned. Rescission is not available where to grant it would be unfair to one of the parties. For example:

(1) Where the parties cannot be returned to their pre-contract position, for example where the goods have been consumed or used in a manufacturing process.

(2) Where the goods of an innocent third party would be affected, for example where the goods have been sold on by the purchaser.

(3) Where an unreasonable length of time has elapsed since the date of the contract.

(4) Where the contract has been affirmed by the aggrieved party, for example where the purchaser of an unsound second-hand car restores the vehicle and drives it for six months before claiming rescission.

Damages may be available in addition to rescission to compensate any extra loss suffered by the aggrieved party, or they may be awarded as an alternative to rescission. However, damages are not normally allowable where the misrepresentation was wholly innocent, for example where the misrepresentation is made upon the basis of information honestly believed to be true and by a person who cannot be expected to have known otherwise. The seller of a nicotine patch who states, in reliance upon the manufacturer's claim, that the patch will cure the purchaser from smoking, would make a wholly innocent representation if in fact the properties of the particular patch have no effect on the purchaser who wishes to stop smoking.

Some contracts seek to exclude liability for misrepresentation by means of exclusion clauses. These are invalid unless they satisfy the requirement of reasonableness in the Unfair Contract Terms Act 1977. The circumstances in which such clauses will be valid will be rare and probably confined to specialized markets where the buyer and seller are both expert in the goods being sold.

Terms of the Contract

As a general rule, the parties to a contract will be bound by the terms they agree upon. However, in order for a term to be binding, it must be incorporated into the contract. This is often done by reducing the entire contract to writing, but contracts may be made orally. A written contract may also have terms incorporated into it by oral agreement. The requirement is either that the terms were expressly agreed by the parties, or that the party seeking to rely on the term took all reasonable steps to bring it to the attention of the other party. For example, one of the terms of a theatre-goer's contract with the theatre cloak-room may be that no liability is accepted for loss of or damage to coats. This term may be adequately incorporated by the position of a prominent notice which can be seen by potential customers.

Terms of the contract may be express or implied. Express terms are those specifically set out or agreed by the parties. Implied terms are those implied by operation of law. Terms may be implied by statute (see below), or they may be implied by the court to make sense of a contract, for example, where a contract makes no express stipulation as to the time in which goods must be delivered, a term will be implied whereby they must be delivered within a reasonable time.

Conditions and Warranties

Contractual terms are classified as either conditions or warranties. Conditions are terms of the contract which are so fundamental to its performance that breach of the term would go to the root or essence of the contract. Warranties are other terms which, although they must be performed, are not so fundamental that a failure to perform goes to the substance of the contract. For example, if a second-hand car is sold purportedly running in good order, if it is delivered without an engine, the absence of an engine would be fundamental to the contract and would constitute a breach of condition. If, however, it was delivered requiring minor adjustments to the carburettor, this would amount to no more than a breach of warranty. The significance of this difference is that a breach of condition entitles the other party to treat the contract as repudiated, to return the goods and to sue for damages for any further losses incurred, whereas a breach of warranty merely entitles the aggrieved party to sue for compensation in damages, for example the cost of employing a mechanic to adjust the carburettor.

Terms Implied by Statute

In contracts for the sale of goods, *Sections 12–15* of the Sale of Goods Act 1979 imply some important terms into contracts for the benefit of the purchaser. The terms implied are expressly stated to be either conditions or warranties: different remedies apply according to the nature of the term breached. *Section 12(1)* implies a condition on the part of the seller that he has a right to sell the goods. *Section 12(2)* implies warranties that

(a)   *the goods are free ... from any charge or encumbrance not disclosed or known to the buyer before the contract is made*

(b)   *the buyer will enjoy quiet possession of the goods ...'*

We have seen how issues are resolved when a bona fide purchaser buys goods from a seller with a questionable title. If the purchaser acquires ownership through the operation of those rules then there is no dispute with the seller. If, however, the original owner still has ownership, the buyer can sue the seller for breach of condition claiming damages and/or the purchase price.

Where a third party retains any rights over the goods, not amounting to ownership, which have not been disclosed to the buyer, the buyer may sue for damages for breach of warranty. This may occur, for example, where the goods are subject to a repairer's lien, that is a party who has carried out repairs to the goods may have acquired ownership of the goods in proportion to the sum outstanding for the cost of repairs carried out by him. In such a case the buyer can sue the seller for the sums still owed to the repairer and any additional sums incurred as a direct result.

Section 13 provides that:

(1) Where there is a contract for the sale of goods by description, there is an implied condition that the goods will correspond to the description.

This section is designed to cover the situation in which the buyer has not seen the goods for himself but has relied upon a description. Thus, where a car is described as a 'Herald, White Convertible 1961' when it emerges after the sale that in fact the vehicle is two cars welded together, one of which is older than 1961, a breach of condition occurs *(Beale v. Taylor (1967))*. Most packaged goods sold in pharmacies are sold by descriptions on the label; therefore, if the contents fail to match the label there is a breach of condition.

Section 14 implies two conditions. The first in *Section 14(2)* provides that:

'Where the seller sells goods in the course of a business, there is an implied condition that the goods supplied under the contract are of merchantable quality, except that there is no such condition:

(a) as regards defects specifically drawn to the buyer's attention before the contract is made; or

(b) if the buyer examines the goods before the contract is made, as regards defects which the examination ought to reveal.

It is important to note that this section applies only to goods sold in the course of a business. In a private sale, unless such a term is expressly included, there is no such term implying merchantable quality. Further exceptions to the application of the section are included in the section itself, namely that if the buyer examines the goods himself or has the defects drawn to his attention, he cannot then complain that the goods are sub-standard.

'Merchantable quality' is defined in *Section 14(6)* as meaning that the goods must be as fit for the purpose for which goods of that kind are commonly bought as it is reasonable to expect. Thus goods cannot be expected to be in immaculate condition, and the standard to be expected will vary according to the circumstances. For example, a second-hand car sold as 'in working mechanical condition' will not be of merchantable quality if the brakes fail immediately after purchase. If, however, the clutch needs replacing 500 miles after the purchase, the car will nonetheless be of merchantable quality as it can only be expected that parts will need to be replaced on second-hand cars.

Section 14(3) provides that:

'Where the buyer sells the goods in the course of a business and the buyer ... makes known to the seller ... any particular purpose for which the goods are being bought, there is an implied condition that the goods supplied under the contract are reasonably fit for the purpose, whether or not that is a purpose for which such goods are normally supplied.'

Section 14(3) could be particularly relevant to a pharmacist who counter-prescribes a product in circumstances where the product is not licensed for the condition in question.

The section applies to transactions carried out in the course of a business. The expression 'reasonably fit' does not require the goods to be of the highest quality, merely, that they are suitable for the job intended. This can cause difficulties for the purchaser where, for example, he has bought a washing machine which has cosmetic damage to it but which nonetheless functions perfectly in cleaning clothes. The retailer may in this situation be able to argue successfully that it is fit for its purpose. If the retailer is successful, the purchaser can then only sue for breach of an implied warranty that the machine would be in good cosmetic order. (The courts will only imply a term where it considers that term to have been intended to be included by the parties, or where the contract would not make sense without the inclusion of such a term.) It was established in *Slater and Slater (a firm) v. Finning Ltd (1996)* that where a purchaser fails to make known that goods are to be used for other than their normal purpose, the seller's obligation does not extend to anything beyond an assurance that the goods are fit for the purpose for which they would ordinarily be used. There is no breach of the implied condition of fitness where the failure of the goods to meet the intended purpose arises from an abnormal feature or idiosyncrasy, not made known to the seller, on the part of the purchaser or the use to which the goods are to be put.

Section 15 provides that where the contract is a contract for sale by sample, for example where a quantity of senna leaves are bought having examined a sample from the bulk, there is an implied condition that:

(1) The bulk will correspond to the sample in quality.
(2) The buyer will have reasonable opportunity of comparing the bulk with the sample.
(3) The goods will be free from any defect, rendering them unmerchantable, which would not be apparent on reasonable examination of the sample.

The bulk must correspond to the sample and, where it does not, the buyer may treat the contract as repudiated and sue for the price and/or damages.

Implied Terms in Contracts other than those for Sale of Goods

The Supply of Goods and Services Act 1982 creates implied terms similar to those in the Sale of Goods Act 1979, which apply to contracts closely related to the sale of goods such as barter, contracts for repair and contracts for the provision of services.

Sections 2–5 of the 1982 Act give to customers in contracts of barter and contracts for repair (e.g., a contract where a roofer repairs a roof and supplies the materials used), rights in relation to title, description, quality and sample which are identical to those conferred by the Sale of Goods Act 1979. These rights relate specifically to the goods/materials supplied under such a contract. *Sections 2–5* of the 1982 Act correspond only to *Sections 12–15* of the Sale of Goods Act 1979, and do not create any further rule concerning, for example, the passing of ownership and risk under a contract of barter.

Sections 6–10 of the 1982 Act imply similar conditions to those in *Sections 12–15* of the Sale of Goods Act 1979 into contracts of hire other than hire purchase agreements. Thus in contracts for the hire of cars, for example, similar terms relating to title, merchantable quality, fitness for purpose and correspondence to sample apply.

Sections 13–15 deal specifically with contracts for the supply of services, and are fairly self-explanatory.

Section 13 implies a term that '... where the supplier is acting in the course of a business, there is an implied term that the supplier will carry out the service with reasonable care and skill'. Where this term is breached, the customer can sue the supplier for damages, for example for the cost of having the defective work made good. A pharmacist would be caught by this section if, for example, he failed to take reasonable care in mixing solutions whilst dispensing a prescription for a patient.

Section 14 provides that where a time for performance of the contract for services is not specified in the contract, there is an implied term that the supplier will carry out the service within a reasonable time.

Section 15 provides that where the price is not specifically stated in the contract for services, there is an implied term that the customer will pay a reasonable price.

Exemption Clauses

Clauses which purport to exclude or restrict the liability of one or other of the parties to a contract are termed exemption clauses. The validity of many such clauses is governed by the Unfair Contract Terms Act 1977, but common law rules also apply.

A clause is of no effect unless it is incorporated as a term of the contract, and incorporation must occur at the time of contracting. If the exemption clause is brought to the attention of the purchaser after the time of contracting, it is of no effect. Thus exemption clauses printed on receipts are usually of no effect.

As with all contractual terms, an exemption clause must be specifically incorporated into the contract to be of effect. Where the contract is written and signed by the buyer, he will be presumed to be bound. Where a clause is contained in an unsigned document, the party seeking to rely upon it must prove that it was brought to the attention of the other party, or that all reasonably necessary steps were taken to draw the other party's attention to it.

Where the exemption clause is displayed on a notice, as in a cloakroom or car park, the clause will only be incorporated if at the time of contracting the customer already knew of the existence of the term, or reasonable steps had been taken to draw it to his attention.

Where there has been a course of dealing between the parties on the same terms, the same terms will be presumed to be incorporated into later contracts, including exemption clauses.

A party other than a party to a contract cannot rely on an exclusion clause in that contract. Thus a manufacturer cannot rely on an exclusion clause incorporated into the contract of sale between a retailer and consumer.

Exemption clauses are always construed narrowly and against the party seeking to rely upon them. In this respect the law is plainly weighted in favour of the person prejudiced by the operation of the clause.

The Unfair Contract Terms Act 1977 curbs the operation of exemption clauses in many respects.

Section 6 of the Act prevents a seller from avoiding any liability imposed by *Sections 12–15* of the Sale of Goods Act 1979, that is the terms as to title, description, merchantable quality, fitness for purpose and sample, where the buyer deals as a consumer. A buyer deals as a consumer where he is not acting in the course of business, but where the seller is, and where the goods are of a type normally supplied for private use. Purchases at auctions or by competitive tenders are excluded.

Where the buyer is not dealing as a consumer, the seller cannot exclude himself from the liability imposed by *Section 12* of the Sale of Goods Act 1979 (implied terms as to title), but he can exclude liabilities imposed by *Sections 12–15* insofar as the exemption clause satisfies the requirement of reasonableness. This is in order that businessmen maintain freedom to contract on whatever terms they choose. Exemption clauses can be unreasonable in certain circumstances, however, especially where the parties are not in equal bargaining positions. Thus in determining the reasonableness or otherwise of such a clause, under Schedule 2 of the Unfair Contract Terms Act 1977, the court can take into account the strength of the bargaining positions of the parties; whether the customer was acting under an inducement to agree to the term; whether the customer knew or ought to have known of the existence of the term; whether, where the term excludes liability for the breach of some condition, it was reasonable at the time of the contract to expect that condition to be complied with; and whether the goods were made specifically to the order or specification of the customer.

Where the clause seeks to exclude liability from terms other than those imposed by the Sale of Goods Act 1979, it will be subject to the requirement of reasonableness where:

(1) The seller's liability is a business liability; and
(2) In buying the goods the buyer deals as a consumer or on the seller's written standard terms of business.

Where neither of the above applies, the exemption clause will be valid. Where either of them do apply, *Section 3* of the Unfair Contract Terms Act 1977 applies, by which the seller cannot: 'when in breach of contract, exclude or restrict any liability in respect of his breach; or ... claim to be entitled

(i) to render a contractual performance substantially different from that which was reasonably expected of him; or
(ii) in respect of the whole or any part of his contractual obligation, to render no performance at all, except in so far as the contract term satisfies the requirement of reasonableness.'

The courts have a wide discretion in interpreting the reasonableness of exemption clauses in these circumstances, and each case will have to be considered on its facts bearing in mind the factors listed in Schedule 2 (see above).

Case Study

Facts: P wants to lease a photocopying machine and makes it clear that a certain feature is particularly important. However, the machine supplied does not have this feature. P finds out that the lease agreement was made with a finance company, L, as opposed to the supplier of the machine, as P originally thought. The lease excluded liability for representations made about the machine and P contends that this is unreasonable.

Question: Is the exclusion of liability for representations made about the goods supplied unreasonable?

Answer: Yes, the representations that the supplier made to P override the exclusion clause in the contract. The leasing agreement incorporated L's written standard terms of business which meant that *Section 3* of the Unfair Contract Terms Act 1977 applied to the contract. This means that liability could not be excluded or restricted except in so far as doing so would be reasonable.

This case study is based on the case of *Lease Management Services v Purnell Secretarial Services* [1994] C.C.L.R 127.

Where the contract purports to exclude liability for negligence, *Section 2* of the Unfair Contract Terms Act 1977 provides that liability for death or personal injury caused by negligence cannot be excluded. However, liability for other loss or damage can be excluded, but only insofar as the clause satisfies the requirement of reasonableness.

The Unfair Contract Terms Act 1977 applies to contracts generally, and is not limited in its application to contracts for the sale of goods.

The Unfair Terms in Consumer Contracts Regulations 1999

These regulations provide that in a contract between a business and a consumer an 'unfair term' will not be binding on the consumer. The regulations give illustrations of terms which will, *prima facie*, be regarded as unfair: relevant to clauses fixing damages is '(e) requiring any consumer who fails to fulfil his obligation to pay a disproportionately high sum in compensation.' So a consumer will be able to appeal to this standard, as well as to the common law on penalties.

REMEDIES AVAILABLE TO THE SELLER AND BUYER IN DEFAULT

When the buyer is in default, the seller has personal remedies exercisable through the courts and remedies exercisable against the goods.

Personal Remedies

The seller has two possible remedies under this head: damages for non-acceptance or an action for the price.

Section 49 of the Sale of Goods Act 1979 allows the seller to sue for the price of the goods where:

(1) The buyer has wrongfully refused or neglected to pay according to the terms of the contract; and
(2) Either the property has passed to the buyer or the price is payable on a certain day irrespective of delivery.

The most important thing to note about the above requirements is that the buyer's refusal to pay must be wrongful. If he has rightfully rejected the goods the seller's action fails. Furthermore, under *Section 28* the buyer is entitled to refuse payment until delivery (unless there has been a contrary agreement). If the specified date for payment has passed, however, the seller may bring an action.

Under *Section 37*, the seller may have a claim where the buyer does not take delivery of the goods within a reasonable time from when he has been informed that the seller is ready and able to deliver, and has been requested to take delivery. If for some reason the seller cannot maintain an action under *Section 49*, he may have a claim for damages under *Section 50* where 'the buyer wrongfully neglects or refuses to accept and pay for the goods'. Usually the damages under this head will be less than the price.

Remedies against the Goods

The three possible remedies against the goods are lien, stoppage in transit and resale. These are available to the seller who is owed the whole of the price.

The seller's lien is a right to retain possession of the goods when ownership of the goods has passed to the buyer. *Section 41(1)* enables this right to be exercised:

(1) Where the goods have been sold without any stipulation as to credit.
(2) Where the goods have been sold on credit, but the term of the credit has expired.
(3) Where the buyer becomes insolvent.

The seller loses his lien where any of the following occurs:

(1) The seller is paid by the buyer.
(2) An innocent third party acquires title under one of the *nemo dat* exceptions (see above).
(3) The seller delivers the goods to any seller or carrier for the purpose of transmission to the buyer without reserving the right of disposal of the goods. However, even when this occurs, the seller may still exercise his right to stoppage in transit.
(4) The buyer or his agent lawfully obtains title to the goods.
(5) The seller waives his lien.

Under *Section 44*, if the buyer has become insolvent and the goods are in transit, the seller can resume possession of the goods and retain them until payment is made. Transit ends when the buyer obtains delivery; the carrier acknowledges that he holds the goods on behalf of the buyer; or when the carrier wrongfully refuses to hand the goods to the buyer. The fact that part of the goods have been delivered does not stop the remainder being stopped in transit.

Under *Section 48*, the seller is allowed to resell the goods where:

(1) they are of a perishable nature and the buyer does not tender the price within a reasonable time of being told that the unpaid seller intends to resell; or
(2) the seller expressly reserves the right of resale in case the buyer should default, and the buyer defaults.

When the right of resale is exercised, the contract is rescinded. When it is rescinded, if the title has passed to the buyer, it reverts to the seller. By *Section 48(2)*, if an unpaid seller resells the goods when he has exercised his seller's lien or stopped the goods in transit, the subsequent buyer acquires a good title to them as against the original buyer. The original buyer then has to bring an action against the seller for non-delivery, provided the seller did not have the right to resell.

BUYER'S REMEDIES

Specific Performance

Section 52 allows the court to make an order that the goods be delivered to the buyer in the case of a contract to deliver specific or ascertained goods. Such an order can only be made where the specific goods are ascertained and where damages would not be an adequate remedy, for example when it is commercially essential that the buyer have the specific goods. When such an order is made, the seller does not have an option to deliver other goods or repay the price.

Rejection of the Goods

Where the seller has breached a condition of the contract, as well as a right to damages, the buyer has a right to reject the goods (to treat the seller's breach as a repudiation of the contract). The buyer need not deliver the goods to the seller, but may inform him that he rejects the goods. Any storage expenses reasonably incurred will be recoverable from the seller.

Breach of a warranty will not entitle the buyer to reject the goods, but gives him an action for damages.

Where there has been a breach of condition, the buyer loses his right to reject the goods once he has accepted them. By *Section 35* acceptance is constituted when:

(1) The buyer informs the seller that he has accepted the goods.
(2) If after taking delivery, and following a reasonable time in which to examine the goods, the buyer carries out some act inconsistent with the seller being owner of them (e.g. he uses them in a manufacturing process).
(3) The buyer retains the goods for more than a reasonable length of time without telling the seller that he has rejected them.

The buyer may lose his right to reject the goods by waiving the right. This may occur where he knows that the seller is in breach of a condition before the date of delivery, but nevertheless accepts delivery in spite of the breach. If the buyer rejects the goods, he can do so without treating the contract as repudiated, and therefore the seller remains at liberty to re-tender goods in accordance with the contract.

Damages

The buyer can claim damages for non-delivery or for breach of any other condition or warranty. This is in addition to any right to reject the goods and recover the purchase price.

The purchase price can be recovered where there has been a failure on the part of the seller to deliver. Where the buyer has rejected the goods or treated the contract as repudiated, he is entitled to the return of any payment made.

The Measure of Damages

In general, contract damages compensate any loss naturally arising from the breach, and any loss which, at the time of making the contract, the defendant could have predicted as likely to result from the breach of it. Some specific rules relate to contracts for the sale of goods.

Non-Acceptance

Section 50 of the Sale of Goods Act 1979 provides that:

> *(1) Where the buyer wrongfully neglects or refuses to accept and pay for the goods, the seller may maintain an action against him for damages for non-acceptance.*
>
> *(2) The measure of damages is the estimated loss directly and naturally resulting, in the ordinary course of events, from the breach of contract.*
>
> *(3) Where there is an available market for the goods in question, the measure of damages is prima facie to be ascertained by the difference between the contract price and the current market price at the time or times when the goods ought to have been accepted, or at the time of refusal to accept.*

The principle behind this section is that if the seller is able to resell the goods he will receive only nominal damages if he could get a good price on resale. This section does not, however, exclude any further loss which was reasonably foreseeable. So, for example, the seller will be able to recover any extra storage expenses he had to incur.

Non-Delivery

Section 51 provides that:

> *(1) Where the seller wrongfully neglects or refuses to deliver the goods to the buyer, the buyer may maintain an action against the seller for damages for non-delivery.*
>
> *(2) The measure of the damages is the estimated loss directly and naturally resulting, in the ordinary course of events, from the seller's breach of contract.*
>
> *(3) Where there is an available market for the goods in question the measure of damages is prima facie to be ascertained by the difference between the contract and market price or current price of the goods at the time ... when they ought to have been delivered ... or at the time of refusal to deliver.*

This is the converse of *Section 50*, and provides that where the buyer may buy the goods elsewhere, his damages are limited to the difference between the contract price and the price elsewhere, plus any other reasonably foreseeable loss.

Anticipatory Breach

Where one of the parties to a contract commits an anticipatory breach, for example before the date for performance of the contract the seller informs the buyer that he will not deliver, or the buyer informs the seller that he cannot pay, the other party has an option to treat the contract as repudiated immediately and to claim damages, or wait until there has been actual failure to perform and claim damages under the principles in either *Section 50* or *51*. If the former course is adopted, the innocent party is under a duty to minimize his loss by buying alternative goods at the best available price. If the price of the goods is currently rising, the damages will be assessed according to the best price the innocent party could have obtained as soon as reasonably practicable after the acceptance of the repudiation. However, if the innocent party refuses to accept the anticipatory breach as a repudiation, he is not under a duty to minimize his loss, and damages will be assessed according to the normal principles in *Section 50* or *51*.

Late Delivery

Late delivery by the seller will normally be a breach of condition. If the buyer rejects the goods for breach of condition, his damages are assessed as in the case of non-delivery. If it is only a breach of warranty or if the buyer accepts the goods, the damages are *prima facie* assessed according to the difference between the value of the goods on the date they should have been delivered and their value (if lower) when actually delivered.

Breach of Warranty

Section 53(2) and *(3)* provides:

'(2) The measure of damages for breach of warranty is the estimated loss directly and naturally resulting, in the ordinary course of events, from the breach of warranty. (3) In the case of breach of warranty of quality such loss is prima facie the difference between the value of the goods at the time of delivery to the buyer and the value they would have had if they had fulfilled the warranty.'

Under this section the buyer has a choice as to claiming his capital loss or his loss of profit. He cannot claim both. In *Cullinane v. British Rema (1953)* the sellers had warranted that a clay pulverising machine would process clay at six tons per hour. In fact it could not do so. The buyer claimed first for capital loss and secondly for loss of profits, being the difference between those profits actually made and those that would have been made had the machine performed as promised. The Court of Appeal held that both claims could not succeed, and disallowed the smaller of the claims. The Appeal Court also stated that loss of profits could have been claimed for the whole of the useful life of the machine.

Subsection 3 provides that only the *prima facie* amount can be claimed. In addition to the losses discussed above, the buyer may also claim any loss which could reasonably have been predicted by both parties as likely to occur in the event of the breach. The question is, 'had the seller been aware of the defect at the time of the contract, what type of damage could the seller at the time of contract have reasonably predicted?'

In *Parsons v. Uttley Ingham (1978)* the sellers sold a hopper to a farmer for the storage of pig nuts. When it was installed, the ventilator was not opened by the installers. As a result, the pig nuts became mouldy and the pigs died as a result of eating them. The sellers were held liable for the loss of the pigs, the Court of Appeal taking the view that the loss of the pigs was a reasonably foreseeable consequence of the failure to ensure that the ventilator was working correctly. Under *Section 55(1)*, the buyer may set off damages due to him for breach of warranty against the price he owes the seller, but retains the right to sue for any excess.

Mitigation of Loss

In all cases of breach of contract, whether or not in a contract for the sale of goods, the innocent party is under a duty to take reasonable steps to minimize his loss. Failure to do so will result in the loss which could have been avoided being deducted from the damages. The requirement is one to act reasonably in the particular circumstances. For example, if the seller delivers defective goods but offers to buy them back at a reasonable price, the buyer will normally be under a duty to accept the offer. This does not prejudice his claim for the excess. The seller cannot force the buyer to accept defective goods. If the buyer rejects the goods and the market price is climbing, the buyer will usually be under an obligation to minimize his loss by purchasing alternative goods as soon as reasonably practicable. However, if alternative goods are not available, for example the goods were being made especially for the buyer, the buyer cannot reasonably be expected to buy alternative goods which will not suit his purpose.

Penalty Clauses

Some contracts contain a clause which stipulates how much is to be paid by the party in breach; for example £50 for every day payment fails to be made after the due date. The general rule is that such a clause is binding on the party in breach if it is a genuine attempt by the parties to estimate the actual loss which will be caused to the innocent party during the period of breach. Thus, if the sum claimed is extravagant and unconscionable in comparison with the amount of the actual loss, the clause will be of no effect. However, if the penalty clause is void, the innocent party may nevertheless sue for his loss in the normal way.

PRODUCT LIABILITY

Fundamental to the English law of contract is the doctrine of privity of contract. This means that no one other than a party to a contract can sue on it. This has particular implications where damage has been caused by a product to a consumer or a third party. If damage is caused to a consumer, he can sue the retailer under one of the implied terms in the Sale of Goods Act 1979. He cannot, however, sue the manufacturer under normal contractual principles as he has no contract with him. In any event, the measure of damages under the contract is limited to putting the parties back into the positions they would have enjoyed had the contract never been made. If the product is, for example, a defective medicine, contractual damages will not cover damages for personal injury and loss of earnings incurred by the consumer. Furthermore, if the person harmed is someone other than the buyer, he has no right to sue on the contract of sale at all. The traditional remedy for such an occurrence was to sue for negligence in the law of tort. Damages in negligence compensate the aggrieved party for all the reasonably foreseeable losses incurred as a result of the negligence. The main problem for the consumer, however, is that he bears the burden of proving that the manufacturer was negligent, a task which is often by no means easy.

Consumer Protection Act 1987

The law in this area was considerably advanced by the Consumer Protection Act 1987, which implemented an EC (now EU) Directive on product liability. Under the Act, any person who is injured by a defective product can sue the manufacturer for compensation whether or not the manufacturer was negligent.

To succeed the consumer must establish four things:

(1) that the product contained a defect
(2) that the plaintiff suffered damage
(3) that the damage was caused by the defect
(4) that the defendant was producer, own-brander or importer into the EU of the product.

A product is defective if its safety is not such as persons generally are entitled to expect. Safety includes not only safety in the context of death or personal injury, but also the risk of damage to property. In determining the defectiveness of the product, *Section 39(2)* of the Act requires that the nature of the product, any instructions, what use might reasonably be expected for the product and the time when the product was supplied by the producer, must all be considered. The term 'product' is very wide and covers everything which can be considered a product, including gas and electricity. There are exceptions relating to land, some agricultural produce and game.

Under the 1987 Act damages may be claimed for death, personal injury or damage to property (including land) which is ordinarily intended for private use, occupation or consumption; and intended by the person suffering the loss or damage mainly for his private use, occupation or consumption. Thus damage to business property cannot be claimed under the Act (and must therefore be claimed for in negligence). Furthermore, only claims worth over £275 can be entertained. The final qualification is that under the Act a claim cannot be made for the cost of the defective product itself-this must be made under the contract of sale.

Claims can be brought against the manufacturer or, in the case of products which are abstracted from the earth such as coal, the abstracter. An 'own-brander' is someone who holds themselves out as a producer. Pharmacies which carry their own brand name on goods fall into this category. The only importers who are liable are those who import the goods from outside the EU into the EU.

Defences

Section 4 of the Act provides the following defences which, if relied upon, must be proved by the defendant:

(1) The defect is due to compliance with a statutory regulation or EU rule.
(2) The defendant did not supply the product.
(3) The defendant supplied the product otherwise than in the course of business and did not produce it with a view to profit, for example the defendant gave to friends a bottle of his home-made wine which had become contaminated.
(4) The defect did not exist in the product at the time of supply.
(5) The defect is in the design of the overall product and the defendant is merely the manufacturer of a component.
(6) The defect was such 'that the state of scientific and technical knowledge at the relevant time was not such that a producer of products of the same description as the product in question might be expected to have discovered the defect if it had existed in his products while they were under his control'. This 'state of the art' defence protects the producer who can show that the defect was not such that it could have been discovered at the time the product was made, abstracted or imported.

Case Study

Facts: A is injured when attaching a product made by M to a pushchair and as a result, A loses the sight in one of his eyes. M argues that since scientific and technical knowledge in the form of accident reports concerning the product did not exist at the time, M is entitled to rely on the 'state of art' defence on the basis that M could not have been aware of the defects in the product without notification of other accidents.

Question: Can M rely on the defence contained in the Consumer Protection Act 1987?

Answer: No. M's awareness of any defect is irrelevant to its liability because liability is determinable by reference to public expectations of safety and those expectations had not changed since the time of accident. Further, accident reporting does not constitute 'technical knowledge' for the purposes of this defence and there has been no relevant developments in this since the time of A's accident. It was irrelevant that M did not apprehend that there was a risk.

This case study is based on *Abouzaid v Mothercare (UK Ltd)*, Court of Appeal (Civ.), 21 December 2000.

Furthermore, it is open to the producer to argue that part of the damage was due to the contributory negligence of the consumer, for example when the purchaser of a lawn mower fails to read the safety instructions and suffers an injury which he would not have suffered if he had read the instructions. If this is proved, then the damages will be reduced in proportion to the culpability of the consumer. Under the Act the producer is prohibited from excluding liability imposed by the Act. However, any claim must be made within three years of the date of the injury or damage occurring, and in any event within ten years of the producer supplying the product.

Self-Assessment Questions

1. In order to assess whether goods supplied under a contract satisfy the implied term that they will be satisfactory, what criteria will the court be influenced by?

   Answer: Under *Section 14 (2)* of the Sale of Goods Act 1979, it is implied that goods sold in the course of business will be of satisfactory quality. Satisfactory quality is defined as a standard that a reasonable person would regard as satisfactory, taking account of any description of the goods, the price and all other relevant circumstances. In some cases it might also be appropriate to examine whether the goods in question are fit for all the purposes for which such goods are commonly supplied and this may involve reference to the appearance and finish, safety and durability of the goods.

   Where the buyer is dealing as a consumer, there are extra criteria to be taken into account in assessing whether the goods are satisfactory. These include any public statements on specific characteristics of the goods made about them by the seller, the producer or his representative including in advertising and labelling (*Section 14(2D)* Sale of Goods Act 1979).

2. What are the options available in the event that a supplier defaults?

   Answer: There are three possible remedies available to the buyer.

   First the buyer is entitled to seek specific performance of the contract under *Section 52* of the Sale of Goods Act 1979 where the goods in question are specific or ascertained and where damages would be an inadequate remedy.

   Secondly, the buyer can also reject the goods when the seller has breached a condition of the contract. This right of rejection is lost if the buyer accepts the goods or acts in a manner that is inconsistent with the seller retaining ownership. However, it should be noted that where the seller has breached only a warranty, the buyer is only entitled to damages.

   Thirdly, the buyer can claim damages for breach of warranty or a condition, in addition to rejecting the goods and recovering the purchase price. In the event that the buyer repudiates the contract, he is entitled to recoup any payments he has made.

Chapter 30

Employment Law

THE CONTRACT OF EMPLOYMENT

A pharmacist needs to be aware of the basic principles of employment law. He may employ members of staff, perhaps a locum pharmacist, dispenser or shop assistant; or alternatively he may himself be an employee of a limited company, sole trader or partnership.

A contract of employment is approached legally in the same way as any other commercial contract. Over the years, however, there have developed particular regulations relating to the formation of such a contract, the conditions of service and termination of the contract. Much of the law in this area is contained in the Employment Rights Act (ERA) 1996, though some common law rules remain. Thus contracts of employment are subject to rigorous controls from the beginning to the end of the employment. The rules are complex, and they need to be examined in considerable detail in order for their application to be fully grasped.

Statutory Controls on the Contents of the Contract

Statute law used to confine itself generally to termination of the contract of employment, that is unfair dismissal, redundancy and takeovers and to certain specific areas which cover employment as one among several areas of human activity, that is discrimination and health and safety.

The position has now changed considerably. In the National Minimum Wage Act 1998 and the Working Time Regulations 1998, we have for the first time a general statutory control of the two most basic elements of the contract of employment: how much employees are paid and how long they can be required to work in return. In addition 'family-friendly' measures have been introduced by the Employment Relations Act 1999 and the Employment Act 2002. The Employment Act 2008 contains a number of statutory reforms to these pieces of legislation, notably making provision for the resolution of employment disputes and to provide for compensation for financial loss in cases of unlawful underpayment or non-payment.

Pharmacy Law and Practice. DOI: http://dx.doi.org/10.1016/B978-0-12-394289-0.00030-8

Contract of Service or Contract for Services?

There is a fundamental difference between a contract of service (employment) and a contract for services, that is between the existence of an employer and employee relationship and the relationship between a party and a self-employed contractor. This distinction is important as most of the relevant legislation applies only to the employer/employee relationship. The Equality Act 2010 is a significant exception because it applies to both employees and contract workers (Equality Act 2010, Part 5).

The system of taxation is also different. The duties of the employer towards his employee are far more onerous. There are certain terms which are only implied into a contract of employment and which are not implied into a contract for services. Further, in some situations where the employee has committed an unlawful act, his employer will be vicariously liable for his wrongdoing; no such principle applies where the contract is merely one for services.

The ERA 1996, *Section 230*, defines an employee as an individual who has entered into or works under a contract of service. This is deliberately broad and in practice the distinction is not always an easy one to draw, and in the past the courts have experienced difficulty in devising a satisfactory test to discern the difference between a contract for service and a contract of service. Having tried tests which look to the level of control exercised by the employer, or the extent to which the employee is integrated into the employer's business, a three stage 'economic reality' test has been developed.

In *Ready Mix Concrete Ltd v. Minister of Pensions and National Insurance (1968)*, the court held that a contract of employment can only exist where:

(1) the employee agrees to provide his own work and skill;
(2) there is some element of control exercisable by the employer; and
(3) the other terms of the contract are not inconsistent with a contract of employment.

This case involved the question of whether the driver of a lorry who had obtained it on hire purchase from the plaintiff company was an employee. He was required to paint the lorry in the company livery but could use substitute drivers if he was unwell or away. The court found that the provision for the use of substitute drivers rendered the driver an independent contractor.

Form of the Contract of Employment

There is no formal requirement that the entire contract of employment be evidenced in writing: therefore valid contracts can be made orally. However, *Section 1* of the ERA 1996 requires the employer to produce a written statement within 2 months of the commencement of employment containing the following information:

(1) the names of the parties and the date upon which the period of employment began

(2) the rate of remuneration and the method for calculating it

(3) the intervals at which remuneration is to be paid

(4) the terms relating to hours of work

(5) the terms concerning entitlement to holiday

(6) terms relating to provision for inability to work through sickness and details of sick pay arrangements

(7) the periods of notice required for either party to terminate the contract

(8) the terms concerning pension arrangements

(9) the job title/description.

The employee must also be provided with details of:

(1) any applicable disciplinary rules

(2) the person to whom he can apply should he be unhappy with the operation of any disciplinary procedure

(3) the person to whom he can apply if he has any grievance with his employment generally

(4) whether a contracting-out certificate (under the provisions of the Pension Schemes Act 1993) is in force in relation to that employment.

All the above information may be included in one document to which the employer may then draw the employee's attention. The written statement is not itself the contract of employment but is strong prima facie evidence of the terms agreed upon by the parties. There is nothing to prevent the parties from altering the terms set out in the statement at a later date, in which case the subsequent agreement will take precedence. The significance of these written particulars from the perspective of an employee is that they provide the basis for any statutory based claims. For example, claims for unfair dismissal and redundancy require minimum periods of service before having leave to take a claim and compensation is calculated by reference to the number of years in employment. Thus particulars referring to the commencement of employment will be particularly important to establish the length of the term of employment.

Terms of the Contract of Employment

Apart from the conditions implied by statute, the contract of employment will usually consist of a written or an oral agreement between the parties setting out the basic conditions of employment. Express statements made prior to the contract may also be incorporated, and deviation from such statements will constitute breach of contract unless there has been specific agreement to be contrary. Attempts to vary the terms or conditions of employment after the contract has been made will only be effectual if they are specifically agreed to by the parties.

Collective Agreements

Many contracts of employment consist partly or wholly of terms which have been arrived at collectively by means of negotiations with a trade union. Such collective agreements may be incorporated into the contract of employment by express incorporation or may be implied by statute. Once a trade union receives the express consent of its members to act on their behalf as an agent, any agreement reached with the employer will be incorporated into each individual contract of employment. For example, under the ERA 1996 there is provision for collective agreements to replace the statutory provisions for the right to claim unfair dismissal or the right to claim statutory redundancy payment. Should the Secretary of State approve the collective agreement, the terms negotiated between the trade union and the employers will replace those created and implied by statute.

Company Rules

Where there is a company rule book, those rules may be incorporated into the individual contract of employment subject to the following principles.

(1) If the employee agrees before the making of the contract that the rules are to form part of the contract, then they are expressly incorporated into the contract.
(2) The rules may be incorporated if the employee is given other notice, that is the posting of a large notice that they are to be included in the contract. However, the matter is usually decided as a matter of custom and practice.
(3) Not all rules automatically become terms of the contract. This may be so where, for example, rules have become out of date. It is a matter of construction of the specific rules as to whether they are terms of the contract or merely guidelines as to how the work should be performed.

The nebulous nature of this area of law is further emphasized by the part which custom plays in determining terms of the contract of employment. In *Marshall v. English Electric Co. Ltd (1945)* it was stated as a matter of general principle that 'established practice at a particular factory may be incorporated into a workman's contract of service, and whether he knew it or not, it must be presumed that he accepted employment on the same terms as applied to other workers in the same factory'. The range of customs is potentially wide and may even relate to such matters as dismissals procedure. Examples of the incorporation of custom can be seen in case law. In *Sagar v. Ridehalgh and Son Ltd (1931)*, it was held that the customs of the Lancashire weaving trade were incorporated into the contract of employment of an individual weaver. Therefore customary deductions for faulty workmanship were held to be lawfully deductible. *Davson v. France (1959)* shows the operation of the principle in the converse manner. A musician who had received 1 week's notice to quit was held to have been wrongfully dismissed as the customary period in the trade was 14 days.

Continuity of Employment

Once an employee has commenced employment, he acquires various rights if continuity of employment is maintained. For example, although an employee is always entitled to sue for breach of his contract of employment in an action for wrongful dismissal (i.e., dismissal that is in breach of the terms of the contract of employment), the right to complain to an employment tribunal for unfair dismissal (a much wider concept the conditions for which are contained in the Employment Tribunals Act 1996 and discussed below) is only acquired after 2 year's continuous employment unless the employee is dismissed for a reason that specifically dispenses with this qualifying requirement such as dismissal on the basis of membership or non-membership of a trade union, maternity, health and safety complaints. The length of time an employer has spent with his employer has always been an important factor in determining whether or not he qualifies for unfair dismissal rights. The present position is contained in the Unfair Dismissal and Statements of Reasons for Dismissal (Variation of Qualifying Period) Order 2012, which came into force on 6 April 2012.

Part XIV of the ERA 1996 deals with the continuity of employment, and *Section 218(2)* prescribes that:

If a trade or business, or an undertaking (whether or not established by or under an Act) is transferred from one person to another:

(a)   *the period of employment of an employee in the trade or business or undertaking at the time of the transfer counts as a period of employment with the transferee, and*
(b)   *the transfer does not break the continuity of the period of employment.*

SPECIAL CATEGORIES OF EMPLOYEE

There are several categories of employee to whom special considerations apply.

Company Directors

Company directors are usually considered as employees if they have a written service contract with the company, but non-executive directors are usually not. The question as to whether such a person is or is not an employee is always a matter of law to be decided upon the test for the incidents of employment (see above). Where, for example, a non-executive director did not have anything in writing referring to him as an employee, and where he had not been paid remuneration for a period due to the financial condition of the company, the Employment Appeal Tribunal would be unable to find that he was an employee.

Partners

Partners in a firm are not employees. However, those employed by partnerships may be employees.

Civil Servants

Civil servants were long thought not to be employees, but the position now seems to be that they enjoy a relationship similar to that created under a contract of employment, subject to the right of the Crown to dismiss its servants at its pleasure. This is not as harsh as it sounds, as many of the legal protections accorded to other employees, including the ERA 1996 provisions for unfair dismissal, apply equally to Crown servants. The main exceptions are the right to a minimum notice period and statutory redundancy period. Police officers and prison officers are exceptions to this, however, and cannot claim unfair dismissal. Similarly, members of the armed forces are specifically excluded from statutory protection.

Minors

Minors (i.e., persons under the age of 18) are bound by the contract of employment subject to the same proviso affecting any other contract – that it must be substantially for their benefit when taken as a whole. This is a matter to be decided by the court and is a measure designed to stop an unfair advantage being taken of young persons.

Children under the age of 13 cannot be employed. Between the ages of 13 and 16 a minor may work part-time subject to a strict limit on hours. 'Young persons' between the ages of 16 and 18 may work subject to various restrictions, for example those in the Working Time Regulations 1998, Regulation 5A and Regulation 6A, which limit the hours of work and the nature of work which may be undertaken.

Temporary Staff

Temporary workers who are drafted in to replace regular employees, who are absent through illness or maternity leave, are not normally regarded as unfairly dismissed if the regular employee returns to work.

Probationary Staff

Probationary employees can be dismissed in accordance with the conditions of their probation, but if the probationary period extends to 2 year's of continuous employment, the statutory rights will be acquired and the employer will be subject to the statutory requirement of showing that the dismissal was fair.

Retirement Age

Retirement age in the United Kingdom has been subject to review in recent months. The age of retirement was traditionally determined by reference to the contract of employment. Where the employment contract was silent on this issue and there was no established custom or common practice upon which a contractual term could be implied, the employee was entitled to continue working until the employer terminated the contract or the employee chose to retire.

With the implementation of the Employment Equality (Age) Regulations 2006 on 1 October 2006, this position changed and the retirement age was set at 65 unless retirement before that age could be objectively justified. The implementation of the Equality Act 2010 did not alter this. Under the 2006 Regulations, an employee was entitled to request to work beyond the retirement age and the employer was obliged to consider the request. This remained the case with the implementation of the Equality Act 2010.

From 6 April 2011, the Employment Equality (Repeal of Retirement Age Provisions) Regulations 2011 revoked this national default retirement age of 65. Now, unless a retirement dismissal is objectively justifiable, any retirement dismissal is unlawful. The provisions permitting an employee to request to work beyond their retirement age have been repealed by the 2011 Regulations. Retirement is no longer grounds for fair dismissal and an employer will be liable for unfair dismissal unless it is justified by 'some other substantial reason'. A dismissal at any age is also potentially age discriminatory unless it is objectively justifiable (Employment Equality (Repeal of Retirement Age Provisions) Regulations 2011, Regulation 2(2)).

The old regime is still applicable where a notification of retirement was issued before 6 April 2011 where the employee turns 65 (or the normal age of retirement if older) before 1 October 2011. However this exception is limited because an employer cannot issue a notification on or after 6 April 2011 and an employee may not make a request to continue working past 5 January 2012.

EMPLOYEE'S DUTIES UNDER THE CONTRACT OF EMPLOYMENT

The duties upon the employee which are commonly implied into the contract of employment by historical operation of the common law are the duties:

- to be ready and willing to work
- to use reasonable care and skill
- to obey lawful orders
- to take care of the employer's property and
- to act in good faith.

The duty to be ready and willing to work needs little explanation. It is the duty of the employee to present himself for work and to abide by the terms of his employment. If the employee fails to attend for work, it constitutes a breach of the contract of employment and the employer may act accordingly. The employer may withhold pay with just cause if the employee is failing in his contractual duties, but withholding pay for no just cause is a breach of contract, giving the employee the option to repudiate the contract and sue for damages.

Reasonable Care

The duty to use reasonable care and skill can be described as a twofold duty, that is not to be unduly negligent and to be reasonably competent. Where a third party takes an action against an employer for the negligent act of an employee, the employer will be vicariously liable (liable on the employee's behalf), but if the employer can prove that the employee was in breach of the implied term in his contract not to be unduly negligent, the employee may be held liable to the employer for all or a portion of the damages. The duty to be reasonably competent requires that the employee is able and competent at the job. Therefore, if someone holds himself out as skilled in a trade in which he has no experience, the employer will be entitled to claim that the employee has breached his duty of competence.

Lawful Orders

Disobedience to orders that are in the scope of the contract of employment can amount to a breach of contract and may in certain circumstances justify summary dismissal. However, in order for such action to be justified, the order must have been within the scope of the contract. Although employees are not obliged to obey orders falling outside their contract, they will be obliged to adapt to new machinery and working techniques if the appropriate training is given. Whether the extent of the change is unreasonable is a matter that can only be decided in the circumstances. An employee may lawfully disobey an order which is *prima facie* within the scope of his contract if either the execution of the order involves exceptional danger for which there is no extra payment or the execution of the order constitutes a criminal offence. Most cases involving dismissal for disobedience to an order come before the employment tribunal. Under the ERA 1996 the employer must show that the dismissal was reasonable, therefore the nature of the order will be subject to the test of reasonableness (see below).

Care of the Employer's Property

The duty to take care of the employer's property is self-explanatory. Where the employee's breach of the implied term to take care of the employer's property results in the employer sustaining loss, the employee is liable to indemnify him.

Act in Good Faith

The duty to act in good faith towards an employer has several aspects. There is a duty not to make a secret profit, which entails an obligation on the employee not to make a personal profit in the course of his employment. If such profits are discovered, the employee will be liable to repay them.

There is a duty to disclose certain information. For example, in an action by the widow of an epileptic building worker, the court found that the employee had breached his duty to inform his employer of his condition. As the employee's death resulted from his suffering a fit at height, the claim for compensation failed.

There is a general duty on the employee not to disclose confidential information gained from his employer. Information is confidential if the owner believes that the release of the information could be injurious to him and if the information is not publicly known. Whether particular information satisfies these requirements will depend on the particular circumstances, including the availability of the information within the profession and generally. Contracts of employment relating to work in areas where confidential information is handled will usually contain a specific term dealing with the duty not to disclose. Problems often arise when employees leave their employment and seek to use information gained whilst employed. The duty not to disclose confidential information does extend to ex-employees, but it is not so wide as to extend to 'know-how'. In *Faccenda Chicken v. Fowler (1986)*, the Court of Appeal stated that the distinction between confidential information and know-how is based on:

(1) The nature of the employment, that is whether information known to be secret is dealt with by the employee.
(2) The nature of the information, that is whether it is such as to constitute a trade secret.
(3) Whether the employee was informed by the employer that the information was confidential.
(4) Whether the confidential information was easily distinguishable from other information that the employee was free to disclose. These are common sense principles, which will be applied to each specific situation.

Restraint of Trade Covenants

Employers are often keen that the employee does not use the expertise gained whilst in employment to aid competing concerns when he leaves his employment. Thus covenants in restraint of trade may be included in the contract of employment, whereby the employee promises:

- Not to establish a competing business within a certain distance from his former employer or within a specified period of time from terminating his employment.

- Not to use his expertise to the benefit of a competing concern within a certain period of the termination of his employment.

Such covenants (which are merely terms of the contract which have continuing effect after the termination of the period of employment) are subject to the requirement of reasonableness. If an employer sues a former employee for breach of his covenant, the issue of reasonableness will be decided by reference to the following factors:

(1) Time – the covenant will be held invalid if it purports to run for an excessive period of time.
(2) Area – the covenant must normally be limited to the area within which the former employee worked. (An action for breach of an express or implied term forbidding the former employee from using confidential information is distinct from an action for breach of restraint of trade covenant. In the former case the duty will attach notwithstanding the whereabouts of the former employee.)
(3) Nature of the competing business and the covenant must be limited to similar business in competition with the former employer.
(4) The public interest in not fettering the activities and marketability of a skilled man and thus a balance always has to be struck between the gaining of an unfair advantage by an employee, and the public interest in free trade and availability of services.

If an employee is thought by the former employer to be in breach of his covenant, an application may be made to the courts for an injunction restraining the employee from acting in continuing breach of the covenant.

If during the period of employment the employer breaches the contract of employment by unfairly dismissing the employee, the employee may thereafter disregard the effect of the restraint of trade clause.

EMPLOYER'S DUTIES UNDER THE CONTRACT OF EMPLOYMENT

Both common law and statute have created a variety of obligations, which must be fulfilled by the employer. The main obligations are as follows:

(1) The duty to pay remuneration.
(2) The duty to pay sick pay.
(3) The duty to treat the employee with trust and confidence.
(4) The duty not to require the employee to work beyond agreed hours or hours prescribed by statute.
(5) The duty to allow time off work for the purpose of carrying out certain public functions.
(6) The duty to indemnify legitimate expenses.
(7) The duty to provide a safe working environment.

Remuneration

This is normally determined by reference to the contract. Failure to pay
the agreed rate is a breach of contract that may entitle the employee in certain circumstances to claim constructive dismissal (see below under 'unfair
dismissal').

Minimum Pay

The National Minimum Wage Act 1998 came into force on 1 April 1999. Most
of the operational details of the national minimum wage are contained in the
regulations made under the 1998 Act, the most recent regulations at the time of
writing being the National Minimum Wage (Amendment) Regulations 2011.

From 1 October 2011, pursuant to the National Minimum Wage
(Amendment) Regulations 2011, the adult rate of the minimum wage (for
workers aged 21 and over) increased to £6.08 an hour from £5.93. For workers
aged 18–20 the minimum rate increased from £4.92 to £4.98. For workers who
have not reached the age of 18, the hourly rate of pay is now £3.68.

Although there are some exceptions (such as apprentices and 16 and 17
year olds), the Act's application to 'workers' goes beyond the unfair dismissal
legislation in applying to home workers and agency temps. In the context of
community pharmacy, this means that the legislation will apply to collection
and delivery drivers who may not be employed by a pharmacy under a formal
contract of employment.

Workers paid less than the minimum wage will be able to complain of an
unauthorized deduction in the employment tribunal or bring a civil action for
breach of contract. Workers are entitled to access records and have the right
not to be victimized for asserting their rights under this legislation in good
faith. The Employment Act 2008 amended the 1998 Act to entitle an employee
who has been paid less than the minimum wage to claim the difference. The
claim may be brought as either an unlawful deduction from wages or as a contractual breach. The 1998 Act also provides for enforcement by government
agency and for criminal penalties. The detailed provisions are complex and
may be found in the National Minimum Wage Regulations 1999. They address
situations where workers are paid by reference to output rather than time, are
on standby, etc.

Sick Pay

The contract of employment will normally specify the terms relating to the
payment of sick pay. If it does not do so, terms may be implied. There is no
general presumption that sick pay is to be paid, but the court or employment
tribunal will attempt to construe the intentions of the parties at the time of contracting. All employees apart from some exceptions are entitled to statutory
sick pay. Statutory provision for sick pay is contained in the Social Security

Contributions and Benefits Act 1992, subject to amending regulations made there under. To qualify for statutory sick pay the employee must be:

(1) At least 16 years of age and gainfully employed.
(2) He must have been incapable of work for a period of at least 4 consecutive days (including Sundays and holidays).
(3) He must supply evidence of inability to work (the form this evidence takes depends on the requirements of the employer). Commonly, an employer will accept a 'self-certificate' for periods of 4–7 days. For longer periods of incapacity (7 days or more) a doctor's certificate is required.

Examples of employees who are not entitled to receive statutory sick pay include:

(1) An employee who earns less than £102 per week (the weekly lower earning limit for National Insurance contribution liability).
(2) An employee who has not yet performed any work for the employer under the contract of service.
(3) An employee who is pregnant and falls ill during the period of maternity pay.
(4) An employee who has already received the maximum statutory sick pay of 28 weeks from his employer in any one period of incapacity for work ('PIW') or from two periods of incapacity for work that are separated by less than 8 weeks (in which case the two periods are 'linked' and counted as one period of PIW).
(5) An employee who claims incapacity with a new employer and who has already received the maximum statutory sick pay of 28 weeks from a former employer, with a gap of 8 weeks or less between the first day of incapacity with the new employer and the last day of statutory sick pay from the old employer.
(6) Agency workers on assignments of less than 3 months.

The weekly rate of statutory sick pay for the 2011–2012 tax year is £81.60 but it is computed at a daily rate. The daily rate may vary for different employees. It is calculated by dividing the weekly rate by the number of qualifying days in a week. For example, an employee with a 5-day working week would normally have a daily rate of £16.32 (2011–2012). Only qualifying days count for statutory sick pay and the first 3 days do not qualify. The maximum entitlement is 28 weeks in each period of sickness or linked PIW. Thus the amount payable for maximum statutory entitlement to sick leave is £2,284.80.

Should the employer fail to pay statutory sick pay, a complaint may be made to the employer. The employer must provide the employee with written reasons within a reasonable time. If the employee wishes to challenge the decision he can refer it to the Her Majesty's Revenue and Customs ('HMRC').

Trust and Confidence

This duty has grown up as a result of case law involving constructive dismissal, that is a claim by the employee that the behaviour of the employer was such that it left no reasonable alternative but to leave the employment. In *Courtalds Northern Textiles Ltd v. Andrew (1978)*, the Employment Appeal Tribunal held that in a contract of employment there was an implied term that an employer 'would not, without reasonable and proper cause, conduct (himself) in a manner calculated to be likely to destroy or seriously damage the relationship of trust and confidence between the parties'. Breach of such a term is likely only to be argued in a dismissal claim; in other words, when the relationship between the employer and the employee has broken down.

Hours of Duty

The hours to be worked will be included in the contract of employment. However, there are statutory maxima that apply to limit the total hours allowable.

Minimum Hours

The Working Time Regulations 1998 provide for:

- A minimum daily rest period of 11 consecutive hours
- An additional minimum weekly rest period of 24 h
- A rest break in any working day over 6 h
- Maximum average working week of 48 h (over a 4-month reference period)
- Maximum average working week of 40 h for a young worker
- Minimum of 4 weeks' annual paid holiday
- Night workers' normal working hours should not exceed eight in 24 h.

The average weekly working time is normally calculated over 17 weeks. This can be longer in certain situations (26 weeks) and it can be extended by agreement (up to 52 weeks). Workers can agree to work longer than the 48 h limit. An agreement must be in writing and signed by the worker. This is generally referred to as an opt-out. It can be for a specified period or an indefinite period. Workers can cancel the opt-out agreement whenever they want, although they must give their employer at least 7 days' notice or longer (up to 3 months) if this has been agreed.

The Working Time Regulations 1998 provide for enforcement by the Health and Safety Executive and local authorities. However, in *Barber v. RJB Mining (UK) Ltd (1999)* the High Court held that employees may also seek a declaration and injunction restraining their employer from requiring them to work an average of 48 h per week.

Time Off for Public Functions

These include being a magistrate, a member of a local authority, a member of a statutory tribunal, a member of a housing association, a member of the governing body of a local authority maintained establishment or being a member of a water authority. Time off must also be allowed for jury service. Under *Section 55* of the ERA 1996 a pregnant employee must also be allowed a reasonable amount of time off for the purposes of receiving antenatal care.

Incurred Expenses

There is a duty on employers to indemnify employees for expenses incurred in executing their duties.

SAFE WORKING ENVIRONMENT

Control of Substances Hazardous to Health Regulations 1988

The Control of Substances Hazardous to Health ('COSHH') Regulations 1988 came into force on 1 October 1989. These were subsequently amended and then replaced by 2002 Regulations of the same name, which came into effect from 21 November 2002. They affect the use of hazardous substances in a work situation, by laying down measures that an employer must take to control hazardous substances and to protect people who are exposed to such substances. Regulation 6 requires that an employer may not carry on any work that is liable to expose any person to any substance hazardous to health, unless a suitable and sufficient assessment of the risks has been made. A substance hazardous to health is defined as 'any natural or artificial substance: solid, liquid, gas, vapour or hazardous micro-organism, and certain dust levels'.

Substances hazardous to health can include:

(1) Any substance classed under the Chemicals (Hazard Information and Packaging) Regulations 2009, SI 2009 No. 716 as 'toxic, very toxic, harmful, corrosive, irritant, carcinogenic, mutagenic, toxic for reproduction, sensitizing'.
(2) Any micro-organism.
(3) Any dust.
(4) Any substance that has a prescribed maximum exposure limit, for example, formaldehyde.
(5) Any other substance that can adversely affect health.

In other words, any substance used or present at work.

Helpfully, the COSHH Regulations state that a substance is not hazardous when it is at a level that nearly all the population can be exposed to, repeatedly, without ill effect.

Exclusions

Certain situations are specifically excluded from COSHH:

(1) Those covered by the Control of Lead at Work Regulations 2002.
(2) Those covered by the Control of Asbestos at Work Regulations 2002.
(3) Coal Mines (Control of Inhalable Dust) Regulations 2007.
(4) When the hazard is radioactivity.
(5) When the hazard is the explosive or flammable properties of the substance.
(6) Medicines administered to patients.

EMPLOYER'S DUTIES

The employer must first of all decide whether or not any substance is potentially hazardous. This must be done by a competent person.

The employer must then:

(1) Assess the risk to health from the use of the substance in the workplace.
(2) Decide what precautions are needed.
(3) Introduce appropriate measures to control the risk.
(4) Inform and train employees about the risks and about the precautions to be taken.
(5) Ensure the measures are actually taken.
(6) In some cases, monitor any exposure of workers to hazardous substances.

Detailed guidance on such assessment is given in the Management of Health and Safety at Work Regulations 1999, SI 1999 No. 3242 which require all employers to assess the risk to employees while at work and are made under the Health and Safety at Work, etc. Act 1974.

Records

All records should be available for inspection by the Health and Safety Executive.

The Manual Handling Operations Regulations 1992

These require the employer to take steps to avoid hazardous manual handling operations, to assess the safety of any operations which are necessary and to reduce the risk of injury from those operations so far as is reasonably practicable. Employees are required to follow specified systems of work.

The Health and Safety (Miscellaneous Amendments) Regulations 2002 (SI 2002/2174) amends the 1992 Regulations by including factors to be considered in determining whether manual handling operations at work involve a risk of injury (Regulation 4(3)). Factors to be considered include physical suitability of the employee to do the task, the clothing and footwear of the employee, that employee's knowledge and training and the result of any relevant risk assessment.

The Electricity at Work Regulations 1989

These require employers to take all reasonably practicable steps to avoid danger from electrical installations. The Regulations do not specifically require annual tests of equipment, although this is one way of minimizing risk.

The Health and Safety (Display Screen Equipment) Regulations 1992

These implement a European Directive 90/270/EEC on health and safety. They require an employer to assess the risks in the use of computers and to minimize those risks. The employer must ensure that any workstation used for work complies with the requirements of this regulation. This is to be done by ensuring that equipment, including desks, hardware and software, is suitable and appropriate. Eyesight tests are to be provided for employees on request. Employees must also have periodic breaks from using the equipment.

The Safety Representative and Safety Committee Regulations 1977 and 1996

An employer must consult with all staff, either directly or where appropriate through a recognized trade union, on health and safety matters. This includes telling staff about new measures and taking account of their views. A 'competent person' must be appointed to liaise with staff. There are two regimes in place: one for workers whose union has recognition and another for those workers who are members of an unrecognised union.

WAGES ISSUES

Deductions

The Wages Act of 1986 regulated the payment of wages and created a system based upon the contract of employment. The Act abolished the old requirement that wages be paid in cash, thus permitting cashless payment. Now subsumed by Part II of the ERA 1996, deductions from wages can only be made in order to comply with statutory provision (e.g., tax or national insurance) or by prior agreement.

Itemized Pay Statement

An employee has a right to an itemized pay statement giving particulars of the amount of gross pay and deductions made.

Lay-Off Periods

During periods when an employee is laid off because there is no work, Part III of the ERA 1996 provides for a system of guaranteed payments during the period of the lay-off. In order to be eligible for such a payment the employee must have been continuously employed for at least 1 month when the lay-off occurs; he must have been laid off for the whole of his normal working hours on a day he is normally required to work; he must not have refused a reasonable offer of alternative employment; he must comply with any requirements imposed by the employer with a view to ensuring that his services are available; he must not have been laid off as a result of industrial action; and he must have been available for employment on the day.

If the above conditions are fulfilled, then the employee is entitled to be paid for the number of hours per day for which he was laid off, or £22.20 per day (from 1 February 2011), whichever is the lesser sum. There is limit on the number of days in respect of which these payments can be made. The current limit is 5 days in any period of 3 months. An employer's maximum liability is limited to £444. Failure to pay the guaranteed payment may be made the subject of a complaint to the employment tribunal.

If an employee is suspended from work as a result of the operation of certain statutory provisions (listed in *Section 64(3)* of the ERA 1996), for example, if his workshop is temporarily closed as a result of a notice served under the Health and Safety at Work Act 1974, he is entitled to remuneration. To qualify, the employee must have been continuously employed by the employer for 1 month, he must not be incapable of work through sickness; he must not have unreasonably refused suitable alternative work; and he must not have refused to comply with reasonable requirements imposed by the employer with a view to ensuring that his services are available. The maximum period for such pay is 26 weeks.

MATERNITY ISSUES

Maternity Pay

In order to qualify for maternity pay an employee:

- must have been employed by the same employer without a break for at least 26 weeks ending with the week immediately preceding the 14th week before the expected week of confinement but have ceased to work for him;
- must have weekly earnings not less than the lower limit for payment of National Insurance contributions (currently £102) for the period of 8 weeks ending with the week immediately preceding the 14th week before the expected week of confinement;
- must have become pregnant and reached, or been confined before reaching, the start of the 11th week before the expected week of confinement (Social Security Contributions and Benefits Act 1992, *Section 164(2)*).

Statutory maternity pay is payable for each week of the 'maternity pay period' which is currently 39 weeks. For the first 6 weeks it is at the rate of 90% of normal weekly earnings. For the remaining 33 weeks it is either 90% of normal weekly earnings or a prescribed rate reviewed annually (currently £128.73 per week) whichever of these is the lowest.

If an employee does not receive maternity payments that she believes are due to her then she may ask the employer to provide her with a written statement explaining the employers understanding of the situation. If the employer believes he has no obligation to pay maternity pay, he must provide the employee with the details and reasons for this and provide information about making a claim for a maternity allowance, incapacity benefit, employment and support allowance. If the dispute continues the employee can refer the matter to HMRC. It is an offence for an employer to refuse to pay when the employee is entitled. The employee is also entitled to look to the Secretary of State for payment where, for example, the employer has become insolvent.

Return to Work

The employee has the right to return to work after the birth if at least 21 days prior to her absence (or as soon as reasonably practicable thereafter), she informs the employer in writing of her expected absence, of her intention to return to work and of the expected week of confinement. Not later than 49 days after the start of the week of confinement, the employer may write to the employee asking for written confirmation of the intention to return to work. Confirmation must be made within 14 days of the request.

The right to return to work may be exercised before the expiration of 29 weeks from the actual week of confinement and includes the right to return to the same job on terms no less favourable than those previously enjoyed. If the employer can prove that by the time the employee intended lawfully to return there was no suitable position, she will be entitled to a redundancy payment. There will be no such entitlement if she refuses a suitable vacancy.

Unlawful Dismissal

If, in breach of her right to return, the employee is not allowed to return to work, or if she has been made redundant and not been offered a suitable available alternative position, the employee may claim to have been unlawfully dismissed, subject to the employer's defence that he acted reasonably because of something which happened in the employee's absence.

Case Study

Facts: An employee (R) claims she is unfairly dismissed. The employer (B) states that the reason for the dismissal was that R was unable or unwilling to perform routine tasks adequately. R is pregnant at the time of dismissal but has not informed B of this. She claims that she has been dismissed for a reason related to her pregnancy.

Question: Is this dismissal an unfair dismissal?

Answer: No. This dismissal is not unfair because B was not aware of R's pregnancy and it was not enough that R had symptoms of pregnancy. B cannot be held to have any knowledge, actual or constructive of the pregnancy, and the dismissal was unconnected with R's pregnancy. However, if B did suspect that R was pregnant and dismissed R based on those fears, it could possibly amount to an automatic unfair dismissal.

Reason: An employer cannot be liable for unfairly dismissing a pregnant employee where he was unaware she was pregnant. Otherwise there would be a very onerous burden on employers to make inquiries about whether female employees were pregnant. This is very unrealistic and could potentially invade an employee's right to privacy.

This case study is based on the case of *Ramdoolar v. Bycity Ltd (2005)*.

Postponed Return

The employer has the right to postpone the return of the employee for up to 4 weeks. The employee may postpone her return if either she is ill (in which case the postponement can be for up to 4 weeks) or if there is an interruption in work (such as a strike), which renders it unreasonable to expect the employee to return to work on that day.

Maternity Leave

Until the amendments under ERA 1999, the rules on maternity leave had become very complicated. We now find in Schedule 4 of ERA 1999 a complete replacement of Part VIII of ERA 1996, and in particular new *Subsections 71–75* setting out the structure of maternity leave. In addition one needs to take account of the Maternity and Parental Leave Regulations 1999 ('MPL Regulations 1999') as amended in 2002, which enlarge on the statutory framework.

Irrespective of any entitlement to maternity pay, *Section 71* of ERA 1996 as amended establishes a general right to 26 weeks' maternity leave (ordinary maternity leave) for all employees, regardless of length of service, hours of work or size of firm, during which an employee is entitled to the benefit of all her normal contractual rights, except for remuneration, which is specifically excluded. This right to maternity leave was introduced in 1993, implementing the requirements of a European Directive on the introduction of measures to encourage improvements in the safety and health at work of pregnant workers and workers who have recently given birth or are breast-feeding.

If an employee qualifies for ordinary maternity leave, she also automatically qualifies for additional maternity leave. The period of additional maternity leave commences the day after the final day of ordinary maternity leave and can be up to 26 weeks in duration. The employee is required to give no notice of her intention to return if she returns at the end of the 26-week period but must give 8 weeks' notice of an intention to return early (Regulation 11). An employer is no longer entitled to look for confirmation that the employee will be returning to work once the period of additional maternity leave ends (after 52 weeks).

An employee with a separate contractual right to maternity leave is entitled to exercise a 'composite' right by taking advantage of whichever right is, in any particular respect, the more favourable. However, the rights and duties of the parties during maternity and parental leave are much reduced. There is no right to remuneration or to fringe benefits. Under MPL Regulations 1999, Regulation 17, the only terms of the contract that apply for the benefit of the employee are the right to notice, the right to redundancy pay, access to disciplinary or grievance procedures and the employer's implied obligation of good faith.

Under MPL Regulations, Regulation 18, the employee is entitled to return after maternity and parental leave to do the same job or if it is not reasonably practicable for the employer to permit her to do that, to a job which is both suitable for her and appropriate for her to do in the circumstances and her terms and conditions of employment are to be the same as would have applied to her if she had not been absent. Her seniority on the day she returns is to be the same as it was when she started the additional leave. Thus the period of additional leave, unlike ordinary leave, does not count towards continuity of service in relation to any contractual right, for example service-related holidays. It counts under ERA 1996, *Section 212* towards continuity for statutory purposes.

INSOLVENT EMPLOYER

If an employer becomes insolvent, the Insolvency Act 1986 provides that the employee becomes a preferential creditor in respect of up to 4 months' wages from the period preceding the insolvency. There is a limit of £800 on the sum that is classed as preferential debt under the Insolvency Act 1986. Thus a claim for sums in excess of this must be pursued in accordance with the method set out in the Insolvency Rules 1986 (SI 1986/195). Other payments such as guarantee payments and payments for time off during antenatal care are also classed as preferential debts.

The employee may claim from the National Insurance Funds certain sums due from his employer, comprising arrears of up to 8 weeks' wages, 6 weeks' holiday pay and wages during the statutory minimum period of notice (ERA 1996, Part XII). The employee can choose the period of 8 weeks' wages he pursues. This allows him to maximise the value of his claim. The employee also has the right to ask the Secretary of State to pay pensions contributions, which have not been paid due to the employer's insolvency. If the employee does not receive the sums to which he believes he is entitled from the Secretary of State, he has the right to make a complaint to an employment tribunal. An employee is entitled to a maximum payment of £400 for any 1 week in respect of these debts or a proportionate sum for a period less than a week.

EQUAL PAY AND DISCRIMINATION

Equal Pay

Article 157 (formerly Article 141) of the Treaty of Rome, which was signed by the United Kingdom on joining the then EEC, provides that:

Each Member State shall … maintain the application of the principle that men and women should receive equal pay for equal work.
For the purpose of this Article, 'pay' means the ordinary basic or minimum wage or salary and any other consideration, whether in cash or in kind, which the worker receives, directly or indirectly, in respect of his employment from his employer.

The spirit of Article 141 was first embodied in the Equal Pay Act 1970 (as amended by the Equal Pay (Amendment) Regulations 1983, SI 1983 No. 1794). The Equality Act 2010 now makes provision for equal pay between men and women.

The 2010 Act repealed the 1970 Act and consolidated the provisions contained therein. Chapter 3 of Part V of the 2010 Act provides for equality of terms. Since most of the 2010 Act came into effect on the 1 October 2010, the 1970 Act is still of significance because it is the applicable legislation to cases brought prior to the implementation of the 2010 Act.

Like Work

The 2010 Act defines both equal work and like work (Equality Act 2010, Section 65). Equal work is work that is 'like', 'rated as equivalent' or 'equal in value'. 'Like' in this context means work that is broadly similar and if there are any differences, are insignificant. In assessing work to determine if it is 'like' the work of a contemporary, account must be taken of the nature, frequency and extent of any differences that exist (Equality Act 2010, Section 65(3)).

Where a woman claims to be entitled to equal pay on the grounds that her work is 'like work' with a man in the same employment, she must show that the work done by them both is of a broadly similar nature and that any differences are not of practical importance in relation to terms and conditions of employment.

The 1970 Act was so worded as to prevent irrelevant or insignificant differences in jobs from precluding equal pay. For example, in *Coombs Holdings v. Shields (1978)* a female teller in a betting shop claimed equal pay with a male employee doing the same job. On behalf of the employer it was urged that the male employee deserved greater remuneration because he was expected to deal with any trouble that arose. The tribunal found that the difference did not justify a finding that they were not doing like work.

Rated as Equivalent

A claim for equal pay based on a finding that the work carried out by the woman is rated as equivalent to that carried out by a male employee invariably follows a job evaluation study. An employer is not obliged to authorize or commission such a study, but once he does he will be bound by the findings.

Section 1(5) of the 1970 Act provided that

A woman is to be regarded as employed on work rated as equivalent with that of any men if, but only if, her job and their job have been given an equal value, in terms of the demands made on the worker … or would have been given an equal value but for the evaluation being made on a system setting different values for men and women on the same demand under any heading.

This position is maintained in the 2010 Act, which provides that work will be rated equivalent where a job evaluation study gives 'an equal value' to the jobs 'in terms of the demands placed on the worker' or would give an equal value but for 'a sex-specific system' Equality Act 2010, *Section 65(4)*. A sex-specific system is defined if 'for the purpose of one or more of the demands made on a worker, it sets values for men different from those it sets for women' (Equality Act 2010, *Section 65(5)*).

Equal Value

By an amendment made in 1983, *Section 1(2)(c)* of the 1970 Act stated that an equality clause is to be implied into a contract of employment:

Where a woman is employed on work which … is, in terms of the demand made on her (for instance under such headings as effort, skill and decision), of equal value to that of a man in the same employment.

The 2010 Act contains a provision to similar effect (Equality Act 2010, *Section 65(6)*).

This clause is operative only where the provisions relating to like work and work rated as equivalent have no application, for example, where a cook in a shipyard canteen claims to be entitled to equal pay with male shipyard workers (*Hayward v. Cammell Laird Shipbuilders Ltd (1984)*). In order to adjudicate on this matter the employment tribunal must first be satisfied that there are reasonable grounds for determining that the work is of equal value. If there are not, the claim will automatically be dismissed. Secondly, the tribunal must require a panel of experts (to be appointed by the Advisory, Conciliation and Arbitration Service (ACAS)) to compile a report on whether the work is of equal value. The tribunal will then consider the findings in the report in deciding whether the work is of equal value.

The general approach prior to the 2010 Act was for the work of the complainant to be compared with that of the 'comparator' male, with whom the complainant alleges she is entitled to equal pay. Percentage points are awarded, taking the output of the comparator as 100%. For example, in *Wells v. F. Smales and Son (Fish Merchants) Ltd (1985)*, there were 14 female applicants. The ACAS assessor said that nine of them scored higher than the comparator, but five scored lower (between 79% and 95% of the comparator's score). The tribunal found that they all scored so closely that they should all be entitled to equal pay. However, under the 2010 Act, absence of an 'actual' comparator will not preclude a woman bringing a direct sex discrimination claims (but it will prevent an indirect sex discrimination claim) (Equality Act 2011, *Section 71*).

The House of Lords in *British Coal Corporation v. Smith (1996)* ruled that common terms and conditions meant terms and conditions which were substantially comparable on a broad basis. It is sufficient for the applicant to show that her comparators at another establishment and at her establishment were or would be employed on broadly similar terms.

Employer's Defences

Section 1(3) of the 1970 Act provided a defence to an employer against a claim for equal pay where he can prove that the variation in pay is genuinely due to a material factor which is not the difference of sex. That factor *must* be a material difference between the woman's case and the man's, except where work is alleged to be of equal value, in which case the difference *may* be such a material difference. In other words, where there is a claim based on an allegation of equal value, the employer may be able to base his defence arguments on economics. For example, where there are existing females doing a skilled job and, in order to attract other skilled workers into the job, the employer offers more money to new employees who happen to be male, the employer may successfully defend the disparity in wages on the grounds of economic necessity. In the case of *Bilka-Kaufhaus GmbH v. Weber von Hartz (1986)*, the European Court of Justice held that the disparity in pay must be objectively justified and must be reasonably necessary in order to cope with a particular set of circumstances (like those previously described). Therefore, matters of mere convenience are prevented from justifying a departure from equal terms in a woman's contract.

This defence is still available under the 2010 Act. Where a 'responsible person' is able to demonstrate that any disparity is based on a material factor, the sex equality provisions will cease to have effect. A 'responsible person' for these purposes is the employer of a person or a person responsible for paying that person. The material factor cannot be either directly or indirectly discriminatory. It is important to note that an employer does not have to objectively justify every pay differential just those differentials that are based on a factor that appears indirectly discriminatory because it is disadvantageous to one sex over the other (Equality Act 2010, *Section 69*).

An employee wishing to make a complaint must do so by making an application to the employment tribunal. If the tribunal finds in the employee's favour, it may make a declaration to the effect that equal pay must be paid and up to 2 years of back pay may be awarded.

Sex Discrimination

The Sex Discrimination Act 1975 outlawed discrimination on the grounds of sex and/or the fact that a person is married. It did not provide any protection for unmarried people. The 1975 Act was amended to reflect the changes introduced by the Civil Partnership Act 2004. The 1975 Act was extended to include discrimination against people who are civil partners. There were certain exceptions to the prohibition on discrimination contained in the Act as follows:

(1) 'Special treatment' of women on the grounds of pregnancy and childbirth (*Section 2*).
(2) Discrimination in favour of members of a sex of which in the previous year there were few or no members in the particular job (*Section 48*).
(3) Discrimination in selection, promoting or training where being a man or a woman is a 'genuine occupational qualification'.
(4) Discrimination in certain specified professions such as the police and prison service (*Sections 17–20*).
(5) Discrimination in respect of provisions relating to death or retirement.

An exemption from the 1975 Act in respect of those employing five or less employees was repealed in 1986 and the 1975 Act subsequently applied to all employers regardless of number of employees.

The 1975 Act covered the following areas of employment:

(1) The selection, interviewing and offering of a job (*Section 6(1)(a)*).
(2) The terms upon which employment is offered (as opposed to the terms of employment once it has commenced) (*Section 6(1)(a)*).
(3) Access to promotion, training, transfer or any other benefit, facility or service (*Section 6(2)(a)*).
(4) Dismissal or the subjecting of any person to any detriment (*Section 6(2)(b)*).

Under *Section 38(1)* it was unlawful to publish any advertisement which might reasonably be taken as displaying an intention to commit an act which is contrary to the 1975 Act. Job descriptions that specify the sex of candidates were unlawful.

The Equality Act 2010 recognises both 'marriage and civil partnership' and 'sex' as protected characteristics. The reference to 'sex' as a protected characteristic is a reference to being a man or woman of any age. The protection available is confined to people who are married or are civil partners. There is no protection available for single people.

THE CATEGORIES OF DISCRIMINATION

There are two categories of discrimination contained in both the 1975 Act and the 2010 Act.

Direct Discrimination

An employer directly discriminates against an employee where, by virtue of sex or marital status, the employer is less favourable than he is with another employee or would otherwise be. Where the allegation of discrimination is gender-specific, a comparison between the treatment of men and women in the same employment is required. However, the 1975 Act was amended in 2005 and harassment was included as a separate form of unlawful discrimination, which reduces the need to rely on the offence of sex discrimination.

Under the 2010 Act, direct discrimination occurs where, by virtue of the one of the 'protected characteristics', an employer treats an employee less favourably than the employer treats or would treat others (Equality Act 2010, *Section 13(1)*).

Indirect Discrimination

Under the 1975 Act, a person discriminates against a woman if 'he applies to her a requirement which he applies or would apply to a man' but:

(i) which is such that the proportion of women who can comply with it is considerably smaller than the proportion of men who can comply with it, and

(ii) which he cannot show to be justifiable irrespective of the sex of the person to whom it is applied, and

(iii) which is to her detriment because she cannot comply with it.

This test was applicable in respect of both sex discrimination and discrimination on the basis of marital or civil partnership status, save references to men are replaced with references to 'unmarried persons' and references to women replaced with 'married persons'. Civil partners were also included under this.

An example of indirect discrimination would be where candidates are required to be at least 65 kg in weight where that requirement cannot be shown to be justifiable in order to fulfil (ii) above. For example, in *Price v.*

Civil Service Commission (1978) a condition that all job applicants be under 28 years of age was held to be discriminatory as many women have time off to have children in their late twenties.

Direct discrimination is unlawful per se, but indirect discrimination is not unlawful if it can be shown to be justifiable. 'Justifiable' was defined in *Panesar v. Nestle Co. Ltd (1980)* as 'reasonable commercial necessity' and not 'absolutely necessary'.

In *Ojutiku v. Manpower Services Commission (1982)* Lord Keith said: 'I decline to put any gloss on the word 'justifiable' … except that I would say that it clearly applies a lower standard than the word 'necessary'. There should be sound and tolerable reasons. Thus commercial considerations will often be capable of defeating a claim based on an allegation of indirect discrimination.

The 2010 Act provides a comprehensive test for indirect discrimination. An employer discriminates against an employee if the employer applies to that employee a provision, criterion or practice, which is discriminatory with respect to a relevant protected characteristic of the employee (Equality Act 2010, *Section 19(1)*). The cases under the 1975 Act are still of application.

Financial Compensation

When the sex and race discrimination legislation was enacted, Parliament provided that financial compensation may not be awarded in cases of indirect discrimination unless it is established that the discrimination was intentional. The law has been developed further in respect of sex discrimination by virtue of the Sex Discrimination and Equal Pay (Miscellaneous Amendments) Regulations 1996. These Regulations provide that employment tribunals in indirect sex discrimination cases may now award compensation regardless of whether or not the indirect sex discrimination is intentional or not. The Regulations were a response to criticism that the law was out of line with the requirements of the EC Equal Treatment Directive 76/207. As a consequence the provisions of the 1975 Act, which precluded the award of damages in cases of unintentional indirect sex discrimination, had to be read as amended by the Regulations. Under the 2010 Act, a tribunal can order the employer to pay compensation but only after it has considered making a declaration as to the rights of the employee in respect of the complaint or making a recommendation (Equality Act 2010, *Sections 124(2), (5)*).

Case Study

Facts: An employer, E, decides it needs to make a person from a particular team within its organisation redundant. E decides to base its decision on an assessment of two candidates, D and R. One of the criteria being assessed is called 'lock-up' which is the period of time between the completion of work and receipt of payment. R cannot be assessed on this ground as she has been away on maternity leave for 7 months. E gives her a notional maximum score for this assessment. Overall, R's scores are better than D's scores and D is made redundant.

Question: Has D been unfairly discriminated on the basis of his sex?

Answer: Yes. The means adopted by E to resolve the difficulty in assessing R's 'lock-up' rates because of her maternity leave was beyond what was reasonably necessary or proportionate.

Reason: The obligation of employers to accord special treatment to women who were pregnant had to be proportionate and did not extend beyond was reasonable in the circumstances to prevent them from being disadvantaged because of pregnancy or maternity. D had suffered as a result of the preferential treatment given to R as a result of her maternity leave.

This case study is based on *Eversheds Legal Services v. De Belin (2011)*

DISCRIMINATION ON THE GROUNDS OF RACE

The 2010 Act has repealed the Race Relations Act 1976 and instead recognises 'race' as a protected characteristic. For the purposes of the 2010 Act, 'race' is an umbrella term that includes colour, nationality and ethnic or national origins (Equality Act 2010, *Section 9(1)*).

The Race Relations Act 1976 rendered unlawful discrimination on grounds of 'colour, race, nationality or ethnic or national origin'. As with the Sex Discrimination Act 1975 there were defences available to an employer, for example, where it can be proved that being a member of a certain racial group is a 'genuine occupational qualification'. Thus it would not have been unlawful for the owner of an Indian restaurant to discriminate against applicants for the job of a waiter where the aim of the restaurant is to create a particular ambience (see *Section 5(2)* of the 1976 Act).

A person who wishes to make a complaint may complain to the employment tribunal. If the tribunal finds in the applicant's favour, it may make a declaration of rights of the respective parties and may order compensation. The employer may also be ordered to take certain steps to reduce the effect of the discrimination on the complainant.

The Commission for Racial Equality

The Commission for Racial Equality had extensive investigatory powers and could conduct formal investigations of employers. The Commission issued codes of practice for employers to encourage compliance with the terms of the 1976 Act. It also encouraged employers to adopt an equal opportunities policy. The Race Relations Act 1976 provided that, while failure to observe provisions of the code of practice did render an employer liable, it could be considered in evidence before an employment tribunal. The tribunal was permitted to take this into account when making a determination. From 1 October 2007, Equality and Human Rights Commission replaced the Commission for Racial Equality. The codes of practice issued by the Commission for Racial Equality continued in effect until the introduction of the Equality Act 2010. Codes of Practice made under previous legislation were revoked, effective from 6 April 2011 (*The Former Equality Commissions' Codes of Practice (Employment, Equal Pay, and the Rights of Access for Disabled Persons) (Revocation) Order 2011 (SI 2011/776)*). Since 1 October 2010 the relevant code of practice is the Equality Act 2010 Code of Practice on Employment and the Equality Act 2010 Code of Practice on Equal Pay.

DISABILITY DISCRIMINATION

The Disability Discrimination Act 1995 introduced new rights for disabled people where discrimination occurs during the course of employment. All employers were placed under a statutory duty to accommodate the needs of a disabled person at work, by considering any adjustments needed for a particular individual. The duty applied to the situation where a person became disabled during the course of his employment, as well as to the situation where an employer interviewed a disabled person at the recruitment stage.

A disabled person is one who has 'a physical or mental impairment which has substantial and long-term adverse affects on his or her ability to carry out day-to-day activities'. An 'impairment' was regarded as affecting normal daily activities if it affected mobility, dexterity, coordination, continence, ability to carry, speech, hearing, eyesight, memory, ability to concentrate and perception of the risk of personal danger. This included depression since it is a recognized clinical illness causing impairment.

Self-induced illnesses were specifically excluded from the 1995 Act. These included abuse of an addictive substance (alcohol, drugs, nicotine) and complications resulting from deliberate disfigurement (tattoos, body piercing).

In addition to accommodating the needs of a disabled person, the 1995 Act provided that reasons for dismissing an employee must not be discriminatory on the grounds of disability. However, this did not mean that employment could never be terminated on grounds of ill-health. If, for example, an employee developed multiple sclerosis or Parkinson's disease, it was acceptable for an employer to terminate the employment, but only where the illness made it impossible for an employee to perform the main functions of his job and it was not reasonable and practical for an employer to make an adjustment.

In this context the kind of adjustments that an employer should consider include adjustments to premises, re-allocating some of the disabled employee's duties to another employee, altering the employee's working hours, assigning the employee to a different place of work or a different activity at work, allowing the employee reasonable time away from work for rehabilitation and treatment, acquiring or modifying equipment, and where necessary providing supervision. A failure to make reasonable adjustments cannot be justified.

The 2010 Act repealed the 1995 Act and instead makes for 'discrimination arising from disability' (Equality Act 2010, *Section 15*). 'Disability' means any physical or mental impairment, which substantially and adversely affects the ability of an employee to carry out normal day-to-day activities (Equality Act 2010, *Section 9*)). The 1995 Act contained a similar definition. Cancer, HIV infection and multiple sclerosis are considered disabilities (Equality Act 2010, Scheme 1, paragraph 6). An employee who is certified as blind, severely sight impaired or partially sighted is deemed disabled.

The current regime is very similar to provisions of the 1995 Act and reference can be made to the case under the 1995 Act when approaching a claim under the 2010 Act.

Disability-Related Discrimination

Under the 2010 Act, an employer engages in disability-related discrimination if he treats an employee unfavourably because of something arising from that employee's disability and where the employer cannot justify the behaviour as proportionate with respect to a legitimate aim.

A reason relating to disability may include the disabled person's poor time-keeping due to lack of mobility. In *Clark v. Novacold Ltd (1999)*, the Court of Appeal confirmed that for a disabled person to establish that there has been less favourable treatment for a reason relating to disability there is no need to identify an able-bodied comparator (or a person with a different disability) who has or would have been treated differently. All that a disabled person has to show is that, for a reason related to his disability, he was treated less favourably than another to whom that reason, that is the reason for the treatment, does not apply.

Exceptions

Whilst there were certain exceptions under the Race Relations Act 1976 and the Sex Discrimination Act 1975 where the nature of the job required a particular kind of person, there were no equivalent exceptions under Disability Discrimination Act 1995 except for the armed forces.

Defence of Justification

Under the current legislation, the defence of justification is only available in cases of indirect discrimination on the basis of all 'protected characteristics', direct discrimination on the basis of age and discrimination arising from disability. In order to invoke this defence successfully, an employer will have to demonstrate that his actions are 'a proportionate means of achieving a legitimate aim' (Equality Act 2010, *Section 15(1)(b)*). This differs from the 'old' test and while the case law on the 'old' test is still used, care should be taken to ensure that the specific limbs of the defence in the 2010 Act are satisfied.

The case of *Matty v. Tesco Stores*, IDS Brief 609, is an example of a case where a defence of justification has been accepted: A failure to employ a diabetic as a fitter at a distribution centre was justified as a result of the risk of injury to a diabetic employee in the low-temperature environment which could not be reduced by supplying or modifying equipment.

Discrimination Against Part-Time Workers

A part-time 'worker' may complain to an employment tribunal where an employer discriminates against him because he is part-time. These provisions cover all those in the employment of the Crown, the House of Lords and the House of Commons. Regulation 5 of the Part-Time Workers (Prevention of Less Favourable Treatment) Regulations 2000 (as amended) gives a part-time worker a right not to be treated less favourably than the employer treats a comparable full-time worker as regards the terms of his contract, or by being subjected to any other detriment by any act or deliberate failure to act. The starting point for assessing whether a part-time worker is being treated less favourably is to determine who the correct comparable full-time worker should be. The regulations state that a full-time worker is comparable to a part-time worker if, at the time when the treatment alleged to be less favourable to the part-time worker takes place, both workers have been employed by the same employer doing the same work with similar levels of qualification, skills and experience and the full-time worker works or is based at the same place as the part-time worker.

The definition of a 'worker' for the purposes of the regulations is sufficiently wide to include a self-employed worker who does not genuinely run his own business. Moreover, there is no prescribed maximum number of hours to be worked by a part-time worker before he can be said to become a full-time worker for the purposes of the regulations. A worker is full-time if he is paid wholly or in part by reference to the time he works, and, having regard to custom and practice of the employer in relation to workers employed by him under the same type of contract, is identified as a full-time worker. There is no minimum number of hours to be worked before a worker qualifies as a part-time worker. Examples of where an employer in a pharmacy might treat a part-time worker less favourably are:

- where a part-time worker's workload is re-organised and he is given more or less work on a pro rata basis;
- where a part-time worker is not considered as a candidate for promotion because he is part-time;
- where a part-time worker's pay is less pro rata;

- where a part-time worker is not afforded equivalent contractual sick pay and maternity pay;
- where a part-time worker does not have equal access to an occupational pension scheme, or other benefits such as health insurance, staff discounts, etc.;
- where a part-time worker is not given equal access to training;
- where a part-time worker is selected for redundancy because he is part-time;
- where a part-time worker is not afforded his statutory entitlement to annual leave and parental leave.

BRINGING THE EMPLOYMENT TO AN END

Dismissal

The position at common law is that an employer can lawfully dismiss an employee by giving notice in accordance with the period prescribed by the contract of employment. To a certain extent this still remains the case, but as will be seen below, in a few circumstances an employee will be entitled to compensation for loss of his job even though notice was given.

The requisite period of notice required to effect a dismissal may be expressly stated in the contract of employment or may be implied into the contract by custom in the trade or profession. Where no such period can be implied, a court may arrive at a reasonable period which will be determined by taking all the surrounding circumstances into account, including the age of the employee and the length of service. As a fall-back, *Section 86* of the ERA 1996 provides a minimum period of notice of 1 week for an employee who has been continuously employed for between 1 month and 2 years, and for an employee who has been employed for over 2 years but less than 12 years, the period is 1 week for every full year of employment. However, after an individual has been employed for 13 years, the minimum notice of entitlement is 12 weeks. The statutory minimum period of notice therefore has a ceiling of 12 weeks.

Of note, the term 'not less than [x weeks]' is used under *Section 86*. This leaves the courts and tribunals open to awarding 'reasonable notice' instead of the minimum period. However, the courts will only turn to reasonable notice where either the contract has been unclear or the facts have been extreme.

Waiving Rights to Notice

The parties are also free to agree to give shorter notice than would normally be required or even to waive notice. Provided such variations are genuine there will be no breach of contract and no damages to pay: *Baldwin v. British Coal Corporation (1995)*.

Summary Dismissal

Where an employer dismisses an employee without notice, it is termed 'summary dismissal'. If there is no justification for the dismissal it is wrongful, and an action for damages may be brought in the county court for breach of the contract of employment. Alternatively, the dismissal may be sufficiently unjustified to merit a complaint of unfair dismissal to an employment tribunal (although both actions cannot be taken in respect of the same incident).

As a general rule, summary dismissal is only justifiable where the conduct of the employee is such that it prevents 'further satisfactory continuance of the relationship'. For example, in the case of *Sinclair v. Neighbour (1967)*, the manager of a betting shop borrowed some money from the till, without attempting to hide the fact and with every intention of paying it back. His summary dismissal was nevertheless justified, as he was also fully aware that the practice was forbidden.

Employers sometimes attempt to set out a right to dismiss without notice on the occurrence of certain events, other than gross misconduct. This is questionable practice in itself; but, certainly, the wording of such clauses will be construed *contra proferentem*: *T & K Improvements Ltd v. Skilton (2002)*, where a clause allowing dismissal 'with immediate effect' on failing to reach sales targets was held not to permit dismissal without notice.

Resignation

If the employee wishes to leave his employment, he must also comply with the notice procedures. An employee may resign at any time by giving proper notice under the contract. The minimum *Section 86* period is 1 week; and this does not alter with length of service. The contract may set any notice requirement.

In a situation where an employee feels forced to leave immediately through the behaviour of his employer, he may make a claim for 'constructive dismissal' (see below). The employment may be terminated by agreement, in which case the termination will not qualify as a dismissal for the purposes of an unfair dismissal or redundancy claim, although to achieve this result the employment must not be terminated as a result of pressure being applied to the employee to encourage him to leave. Further, the employment may come to an end where it is 'frustrated', that is where sickness or imprisonment prevents the employee from returning to work. However, the negative effect of finding a contract of employment frustrated through sickness is that frustration brings a contract to an end: therefore, the employee will not be entitled to statutory sick pay from his employer and will have to rely on state benefits.

Action for Wrongful Dismissal

Where an employee alleges that he has been wrongfully dismissed, that is, where he has been unjustifiably dismissed without, or without the requisite period of, notice by his employer, he may bring an action in the civil courts for wages lost through insufficient notice being given. For this purpose the wages are calculated in accordance with the amount the employee could reasonably be expected to have earned in the notice period (including income such as commission which does not come directly from the employer). Deductions will be made for:

(1) Other sums earned in alternative employment during the dismissal period.
(2) Any state benefits received during the same period.
(3) Sums representing the tax and national insurance contributions that would have been paid out of the wages in the notice period.

Unfair Dismissal

The most common form of action taken against an employer is an action for unfair dismissal in the employment tribunal. *Section 94* of the ERA 1996 gives every employee the right not to be unfairly dismissed. This applies whether the dismissal was in accordance with the contract of employment or not. (This procedure is open to all employees except for a few categories, the most important of which are persons over retiring age, policemen, employees on certain 'fixed term' contracts, share fishermen and employees who mainly work outside the United Kingdom.)

Proving Unfair Dismissal

In order to prove unfair dismissal, the employee must first show that there was a dismissal. In most cases this will be obvious. In some cases, however, the employee will have to allege 'constructive dismissal', that is the behaviour of the employer was such that the employee could not reasonably be expected to have continued in the employment.

For some time an employment tribunal would only find constructive dismissal where the employer could be shown to have breached the terms of the contract of employment. However, this was not adequate to cover situations where employers 'squeezed out' employees without committing any specific breach. The modern approach is therefore to imply a term that the employer will not breach the 'relationship of trust and confidence' between himself and the employee and to find constructive dismissal where that term is breached. In the case of *Woods v. W.M. Car Service (1981)* it was said that

… an employer who persistently attempts to vary an employee's conditions of services with a view to getting rid of the employee or varying the employee's conditions of service, does an act in a manner calculated to destroy the relationship of confidence and trust between [them].

Such an employer has therefore breached an implied term.

Unfairness

Having established dismissal, the tribunal must then decide the issue of unfairness. In order to determine the unfairness or otherwise of the dismissal, the reasonableness of the employer's actions are examined. It is for the employer to establish the reasons for the dismissal. *Section 98(4)* of the ERA 1996 provides that the tribunal must then decide whether:

in the circumstances (including the size and administrative resources of the employer's undertaking) the employer acted reasonably or unreasonably in treating it as a sufficient reason for dismissing the employee; and that question shall be determined in accordance with the equity and substantial merits of the case.

Thus the employer is under a duty to act reasonably both substantively and procedurally. In determining the reasonableness of the dismissal, the tribunal must consider the surrounding circumstances and the provisions of the ACAS code of conduct entitled 'Disciplinary and grievance procedures'. The code generally recommends the use of informal action to resolve matters followed by formal action and provides for various steps to be taken before dismissal such as warnings for offences, which are not of the utmost gravity, and a fair hearing before dismissal.

Reasonableness of the Dismissal

The employer may rely on one of five categories of reasons to justify the dismissal as reasonable.

Capability or Qualifications

The employer must establish an honest belief that the employee was incompetent or not suitably qualified for the employment, but even where this is proved, the employer remains under a duty to comply with the procedural requirements for dismissal in order to render the dismissal reasonable.

Conduct

Where there has been misconduct on the part of the employee, the employer may act reasonably in dismissing him. The ACAS code of practice deals with the procedures that should be adopted by employers and provides, for example, that only 'serious misconduct' justifies dismissal for a first breach of discipline. The categories of misconduct are wide but would include, for example, drunkenness, dishonesty, sexual harassment and criminal convictions outside the employment.

Redundancy

This is discussed in further detail below, but where an employer can show that the reason for the dismissal was that the employee had genuinely been rendered redundant, the dismissal will not be unfair. Dismissal for redundancy may be rendered unfair in certain situations where the procedure for choosing specific employees for redundancy in similar occupations may have been carried out unfairly. Thus employers are obliged to operate redundancy criteria and to apply the criteria fairly. Such criteria are often decided in conjunction with trade unions, and where this is the case, the tribunal may consider them.

Illegality of Continued Employment

Where it would be illegal for an employee to carry on his employment, for example where a solicitor has lost his practising certificate and so can no longer act for clients, dismissal may be justified on the ground of reasonableness. The ERA 1996, *Section 98(2)(d)*, states that such occurrences provide a fair reason for dismissal where the employee 'could not continue to work in the position which he held without contravention (either on his part or on that of his employer) of a duty or restriction imposed by or under an enactment' (thus statutory instruments are included in the definition).

Other Substantial Reasons

This is an open category to accommodate particular circumstances. Thus dismissal has been held as justified in cases where employees have unreasonably refused to agree to alterations in working arrangements and hours; where there has been an insurmountable conflict of personalities between employer and employee; and where the work was only of a temporary nature and came to an end.

Pregnancy

A dismissal on the grounds of pregnancy alone will be unfair. The employer can only justify a dismissal in such circumstances where he can show that the employee is, or will have become incapable of doing the work required, or that the employee will not be able to do the work without contravening a legal requirement.

Trade Union Membership

Except in certain limited circumstances, it is unfair to dismiss an employee for belonging to a trade union. However, membership of trade unions in specific employment is illegal, for example the security services.

Procedure

An employee who wishes to allege that a dismissal has been carried out unfairly must make a complaint to the employment tribunal on form ET1 within 3 months of the termination of employment (although this period is extendible at the discretion of the tribunal). A copy of the complaint is then sent to the employer who may contest the allegation by replying within 14 days. ACAS is also informed of the complaint and an attempt to organize reconciliation between the parties without the need for a formal hearing is made. The procedure governing applications to the employment tribunal is set out in the Employment Tribunals Act 1996.

Powers of the Tribunal

When a finding of unfair dismissal has been made, the tribunal has a number of remedies available. When the finding has been made, the employee has the option (where practical) to be reinstated (in the same job) or re-engaged (in similar employment). Where it is practicable to make such an order for re-instatement or re-engagement, and the employer only partially complies or fails to comply with the order, the tribunal may make an award of compensation of between 13 and 26 weeks' pay (and 52 weeks' pay in the case of sexual or racial discrimination). The existence of such compensatory awards is designed to encourage the employer to comply with the terms of the order.

Where re-instatement or re-engagement is not appropriate, an award of compensation will be made. The compensation will consist of a basic award and a compensatory award.

Basic Award

The amount of the basic award will, in most cases, be the same as that of a statutory redundancy payment; the principle difference is that in the case of redundancy payment employment prior to the 18th birthday is not counted. It depends upon basic weekly pay, length of service and age.

The maximum amount of a week's pay for the purpose of the calculation is £400 (for dismissals taking place after 1 February 2011) and the maximum number of years to be taken into account is 20. A week's pay is calculated in accordance with ERA 1996, *Subsections 221–229* and is based on gross pay. The Employment Relations Act 1999 provides that the maximum amount of the basic award is calculated by reference to the period, ending with the effective date of termination, during which the employee was continuously employed, by starting at the end of that period and reckoning backwards the number of complete years of employment falling within that period and allowing for the following:

Age of Employee Amount of Award (calculated in weeks' pay for each year of continuous employment):

18–21	0.5
22–40	1
41–65	1.5

Compensatory Award

The compensatory award will invariably be larger and is subject to a current maximum of £68,400 for dismissals on or after 1 February 2011. However, there is no maximum in health and safety cases (ERA 1996, *Section 100*), protected disclosure cases (ERA 1996, *Section 103A*), and selection for redundancy on protected disclosure grounds (ERA 1996, *Section 105(6A)*). In the case of a refusal to reinstate or reengage, the tribunal may exceed the normal maximum to the extent necessary fully to reflect the sums which would have been payable under its original order (ERA 1996, *Section 124(4)*).

The heads of loss compensated are as follows:

(1) Expenses directly incurred as a result of the dismissal including loss of perks and fringe benefits.

(2) Lost earnings up to the hearing date.

(3) Estimated future loss of earnings.

(4) The manner of the dismissal, that is if the manner of the dismissal will have made the employee less attractive to subsequent employers, compensation may be awarded.

(5) Loss of the protection afforded against unfair dismissal by 2 years of continuous employment, that is the risk of being unfairly dismissed during the first 2 years of subsequent employment without the protection of the ERA 1996 may be compensated for in small amount.

(6) Loss of pension rights.

There is no upper limit for the compensatory award in unfair dismissal proceedings where the dismissal is attributable to discrimination under the EEC Directive for equal pay and equal treatment for men and women, as regards access to employment, vocational training and working conditions; see *Marshall v. Southampton and SW Hampshire AHA (1993)*. The employee is under a duty to minimize his loss by taking all reasonable steps to find and accept offers of reasonable alternative employment. Further, if the tribunal finds that the employee contributed to the loss of his employment, it may make a deduction from the overall sum of the compensatory award.

Maximum Awards

The maximum basic award is $20 \times 1\frac{1}{2} \times £400 = £12,000$. The maximum compensatory award is £68,400. The minimum basic award in a case of unfair dismissal on the basis union membership, health and safety, working times and employee representation is £5000. An employee may also receive an award in respect of unfair dismissal, which is increased by £760 to £1520 (under EA 2002, *Section 38*) where the employment tribunal finds in his favour but fails to make an award. Any additional award will not be less than 26 weeks and not more than 52 weeks pay, the maximum being a total of £20,800. The maximum amount of a 'week's pay', which determines the maximum amount of a basic award, is revised annually and linked to the Retail Price Index.

Redundancy

Under the ERA 1996, all persons who work under a contract of employment are entitled to an award on being made redundant with exceptions as follows:

- Employees of less than 2 years' standing.
- Share fishermen.
- Persons normally working outside the United Kingdom.
- Some employees with fixed term contracts before 1 October 2002.
- Members of the armed forces.

An employee can only claim to have been made redundant where he can be shown to have been dismissed. Once dismissal has been proved, there is a presumption by virtue of *Section 163(2)* of the ERA 1996 that the reason for the dismissal was redundancy. It is then for the employer to show that the dismissal was for some reason other than redundancy (e.g., misconduct). By *Section 139(1)* of the ERA 1996, there is a redundancy where the dismissal is attributable to:

(a) the fact that the employer has ceased, or intends to cease, to carry on the business for the purposes of which the employee was employed by him; …

(b) the fact that the requirements of that business for employees to carry out work of a particular kind … have ceased or diminished or are expected to cease or diminish.

Where the employer has asked for volunteers for redundancy, and the employee accepts a redundancy package voluntarily, the right to claim a redundancy payment under the ERA 1996 is lost.

Where an employee is laid off or put on short time, and there is no provision for such an eventuality in the contract of employment, the employee is entitled to claim to have been made redundant. If the contract of employment does make provision for such eventualities, but the employee is laid off or on short time for 4 consecutive weeks or for six of the preceding 13 weeks, the employee may claim redundancy.

This is done by sending written notice of intention to claim redundancy to the employer. The employer then issues a counter-notice within 7 days stating that there is a reasonable chance within the following 4 weeks that the employee will commence a period of 13 weeks consecutive employment. If the promise is not fulfilled, the employee is entitled to a redundancy payment. If an employee is offered suitable alternative employment by his employer, he will lose his right to a redundancy payment if he unreasonably refuses it.

REDUNDANCY AWARDS

An employee who considers that he has been made redundant must make a written claim for a payment to his employer. If the employer refuses to make the payment, the employee can refer the matter to the employment tribunal within 6 months of the termination of the employment. Some large employers agree their own schemes for redundancy with employees and trade unions. With the consent of the Secretary of State, they can thereby contract out of the legislation.

Where the employee is a member of an independent trade union, the employer is usually under a duty to discuss proposed redundancies with a union representative. Particular rules requiring consultation apply when the number of employees facing redundancy is greater than 20. It is a statutory duty for an employer to consult employee representatives collectively under the Trade Union and Labour Relations (Consolidation) Act 1992, *Section 188* and any failure to do so may make dismissals unfair.

If the employer fails to carry out the necessary consultation process, the trade union may make a complaint to the employment tribunal and seek a declaration of the parties' respective rights. The tribunal may also make a 'protective award' whereby the employees concerned must be paid during a specific period not exceeding 90 days. This is designed to protect the employees' interests during the consultation period. If the employer fails to comply with an order for a protective award, the employee may make a complaint to the tribunal as an individual.

There is therefore fairly comprehensive provision for compensatory payments to employees who are made redundant, but unless the employee has been working for many years, the size of the statutory award is likely to be relatively small. An employee who has been notified of forthcoming redundancy is entitled to reasonable time off work in order to look for alternative employment, but only if he has been in continuous employment for 2 years.

Case Study

Facts: A company, X, decides to make a large number of its workforce redundant. X fails to comply with the statutory requirements to provide information to its employees or consult the employee representatives. Many employees make claims for protective awards to an employment tribunal but most of the claims are struck out or settled. However A's claim remains.

Question: Can A apply and obtain a protective award for himself and other employees similarly affected where there is no employee representative?

Answer: No. Representative rights were for elected representatives and trade unions and they were the only groups in a position to enforce these rights. The group of employees that A represented was too large and under the legislation A was only entitled to claim a protective award in his own right. Otherwise employees whose cases had either been struck out or dismissed would benefit and the intention of the legislation is that only those employees who were represented by a trade union and by an elected representative or acting in their own right could seek a protective award.

Reason: The Court found that if A had been granted a protective award then he would have been granted greater representative status for a wider pool of people than an elected representative or a trade union and that could not been the aim of the legislation. The Court stated that the legislation had to be interpreted in its context and that Parliament could not have intended an anomalous situation where an individual had greater rights than those elected groups but no corresponding duties.

This case study is based on *Independent Insurance Co. Ltd v. Aspinall (2011)*.

HUMAN RIGHTS AT WORK

One of the areas most affected by the Human Rights Act 1998 is employment law. Although the Act does not create direct obligations for an employer with respect to his employees, employment tribunals are required to interpret existing UK employment law in line with the principles of the European Convention on Human Rights and its associated case law.

Employee privacy is a key area, since Article 8 of the Convention provides for the right to respect for private and family life, home and correspondence. Interference with this right is only permitted if it is 'in accordance with the law' and 'necessary in a democratic society' and is effected for a legitimate purpose, such as the prevention of crime or the protection of health.

The case law under the Convention makes it clear that employees cannot complain if they are made aware that their employer reserves the right to conduct monitoring of telephone, e-mail and other communication facilities. Since working in a pharmacy exposes a dishonest employee to a vista of temptations (namely unlawful sales of medicines, fraudulent prescription claims, etc.), pharmacists would be well advised to insert a clause to this effect in an employee's contract of employment.

The use of CCTV and other monitoring equipment may be permitted; however, a crucial point is that measures conflicting with the right to privacy can only be taken where 'proportionate', in the sense that the interference must be reasonable and justifiable in the circumstances. Indiscriminate monitoring may not be permitted. Where an employer does engage in surveillance, Article 8 is engaged and there is a presumption in favour of a breach of privacy. An employer must be able to demonstrate that the action is proportionate and for a legitimate aim in order to justify surveillance of an employee.

Dress codes are frequently discussed in the light of Article 10 of the Convention, which guarantees freedom of expression. One of the leading cases on this point concerned an employee who was dismissed for insisting upon wearing a number of badges to work proclaiming that she was a lesbian. Her unfair dismissal claim failed on the basis that the employer could decide, after sensible consideration, what was likely to offend fellow customers and employees. The result of this case is unlikely to be different now that the Human Rights Act 1998 is in force. Community pharmacists have reasonable grounds to impose a sensible dress code to operate at their pharmacy, provided that the code is reasonable and justifiable, or proportionate, in all the circumstances.

Forced/Compulsory Labour Under Article 4 of the European Convention of Human Rights

No forced labour claim has succeeded to date, and speculations that working conditions, long hours and compulsory overtime amount to such a breach are not convincing. The employment relationship is a contractual one that both parties can terminate and, even within the relationship, existing legislation on working time, harassment, etc., cover these areas adequately.

Only time will tell how much the principles of the Act will affect the approach of employment tribunals to their application of UK employment law. Although many of the issues covered by the Act are already addressed by domestic law, inevitably there will be some cases where the Human Rights Act 1998 will give rise to some expanded arguments on the part of an aggrieved employee.

Self-Assessment Questions

1. In what circumstances can an employer now dismiss an employee who has reached the age of 65?

   Answer: An employer can dismiss an employee where he has served notice on or before 6 April 2011 and the employee was 65 or older before 1 October 2011. The default retirement age has recently changed and this means that an employee can effectively retire when he or she wants.

2. What are the right of an employee once he has been made redundant?

   Answer: An employee's rights vary slightly depending on the number of employees being made redundant. All employees are entitled to a consultation with the employer prior to redundancy but where more than 20 people are to be dismissed the employer is obliged to consult with the employees' representatives. If an employer fails to do this, the employees are entitled to make an application to an employment tribunal for a protective award for up to 90 days' pay. An employer is prohibited from basing redundancy on unfair or discriminatory reasons and if he does, that redundancy is automatically unfair and it is open to the employee to claim this before an employment

Pharmacy Law and Practice

tribunal. Finally, redundancy pay is determined by reference to the length of continuous employment, age and weekly pay (up to a maximum amount of £400 from 1 February 2011). Redundancy pay of less than £30,000 is not taxable. However, an employee is not entitled to redundancy pay where the employer has offered suitable alternative work and this has been refused without sufficient justification.

3. In the event of employer insolvency, how can an employee obtain payment of wages and statutory entitlements?

Answer: An employee is a preferential debtor in respect of up to 4 months' wages from the period preceding the insolvency of the employer. This priority is in respect of £800 only and any claims above that amount have to be pursued under alternative methods. There are arrangements in place when the employer cannot make these payments. Employees can claim from the National Insurance Fund for up to 8 weeks' wages, holiday pay of up to 6 weeks and compensatory notice pay (1 week after 1 calendar month's service rising to 1 week per year of service up to a maximum of 12 weeks). An employee cannot claim more than £400 as weekly pay (from 1 February 2011).

4. What are an employee's entitlements after having a baby?

Answer:

I. **Statutory Maternity Pay ('SMP')**

Once an employee has worked for the same employer for 26 weeks up until the 14th week before the expected birth of the baby and earns an average weekly amount of £102, then that employee is entitled to SMP. SMP is payable for 39 weeks and is paid at 90% of the employee's average weekly earnings for the first 6 weeks. The subsequent 33 weeks of SMP are payable at a rate of either £128.73 or 90% of the employee's average weekly earnings, depending on which of these is lower. If an employer cannot provide SMP, an employee can apply for Maternity Allowance instead.

II. **Statutory Maternity Leave**

An employee is also entitled to 26 weeks ordinary maternity leave and 26 weeks additional maternity leave. An employee is entitled to statutory maternity leave once they provide correct notice to the employer. This notice must be provided to the employer 15 weeks before the beginning of the week that the baby is due. The notice needs to confirm that the employee is pregnant and when baby is due and specify the date upon which the employee wants to commence maternity leave.

An employee can return to work before the 52 weeks of maternity leave have elapsed but it is compulsory to take 2 weeks leave immediately after the birth of the baby. Once an employee avails of the 52 weeks of maternity leave, she is not legally obliged to give notice to her employer of her return. However, it is advisable that she does so anyway.

Chapter 31

Human Rights

The Human Rights Act (HRA) 1998 creates a statutory general requirement that all legislation be read and given effect in a way that is compatible with the European Convention on Human Rights (ECHR). In all cases in
which Convention rights are in question, the Act gives 'further effect' to the
Convention, whether the litigants are private persons or public authorities.
There is no doubt that community pharmacists, alongside everybody else in the
United Kingdom, will be affected by the HRA 1998, and accordingly it is most
important that pharmacists know all about it. The Act takes effect in three ways:

(1) By obliging courts to decide all cases before them (whether brought under
statute or the common law) compatibly with Convention rights unless
prevented from doing so either by primary legislation or by provisions
made under primary legislation which cannot be read compatibly with the
Convention (*Section 6(1)–(3)*).
(2) By introducing an obligation for courts to interpret existing and future legislation in conformity with the Convention wherever possible (*Section 3*).
(3) By requiring the courts to take *Strasbourg* case law into account in all cases,
in so far as they consider it relevant to proceedings before them (*Section 2(1)*).

HUMAN RIGHTS AND PRIVACY

The incorporation of Article 8 of the ECHR (the Convention) into UK law by
the HRA 1998 creates a general right to respect for privacy where none previously existed. Article 8 offers general protection for a person's private and
family life, home and correspondence from arbitrary interference by the State
in the following terms:

Everyone has the right to respect for his private and family life, his home and his
correspondence.
There shall be no interference by a public authority with the exercise of this right
except such as is in accordance with the law and is necessary in a democratic society
in the interests of national security, public safety or the economic well-being of the
country, for the prevention of disorder or crime, for the protection of health or morals,
or for the protection of the rights and freedoms of others.

Pharmacy Law and Practice. DOI: http://dx.doi.org/10.1016/B978-0-12-394289-0.00031-X

The Duty of Public Authorities

The requirement on public authorities, such as the NHS, to act compatibly with Article 8 of the Convention is contained in *Section 6* of the HRA. *Section 6* provides that central government, local government and other public bodies such as the police and the courts must all act compatibly with human rights.

Horizontal Effect of the HRA 1998

Not only will the HRA 1998 affect public companies per se, but it will also affect the relationship between private companies (which are not public bodies) and individuals, because many of the protected rights have horizontal effect. For example, by reason of the horizontal effect, Article 8 will protect confidentiality of messages between Internet users (email, etc.).

Interferences with Rights to Privacy

This right affects a large number of areas of life. However, the right to respect these aspects of privacy under Article 8 is qualified. This means that interferences by the State can be permissible, but such interferences must be justified and satisfy certain conditions.

Article 8(2) provides that there can be no interference by a public authority with the rights protected by Article 8(1), except such as in accordance with the law and is necessary in a democratic society. An applicant, alleging a violation of Article 8, needs to show, first, that there has been an interference and, secondly, that the interference was by a public authority. An interference can be due to either an act of a public authority or its failure to act but establishing an interference will depend on the facts of each individual case.

The nature and extent of each interference must be judged against the end it is meant to achieve. Thus, any interference with rights under Article 8 that goes further than is necessary may well be unlawful. The more severe the infringement of privacy, the more important the legitimate objective in each case will need to be. In most cases, the interference will be judged against whether it meets a pressing social need, and the extent to which an alternative, less intrusive interference would achieve the same result.

In addition any interference must be in the interests of the legitimate objectives identified in Article 8(2). These objectives are widely drawn and it will often be possible for an interference to be categorised as being in pursuit of one of these legitimate objectives.

More difficult questions arise where there are competing interests at issue, such as balancing privacy rights. In some cases it will be important to distinguish between a lawful interference in someone's private life in the public interest, as opposed to an unlawful one which has occurred merely because it is something in which the public might be interested.

HUMAN RIGHTS AND PATIENT CONFIDENTIALITY

Patient confidentiality is a key example. The access to Health Records Act 1990 was passed as a result of the case of *Gaskin v. United Kingdom (1990)*, where the European Court of Human Rights held that the United Kingdom's refusal to grant a right of access by a patient to his health records was in breach of Article 8 of the European Convention.

The Data Protection Act 1998 has been designed to protect the right of individuals to privacy with respect to the processing of personal data. Under the Data Protection Act 1998, individuals are entitled to access their patient medication records or other personal information about them and can contact their pharmacist in order to do this. However, any right of access to medical records is subject to certain exclusions.

The public expects pharmacists and their staff to respect and protect privacy. This duty extends to any information relating to an individual, which pharmacists or their staff acquire in the course of their professional activities. Confidential information includes personal details and medication, both prescribed and non-prescribed.

Pharmacists must ensure that:

The confidentiality of information acquired about an individual in the course of their professional activities is respected and protected, and is disclosed only with the consent of the individual other than in the circumstances defined below in (2).

It may be appropriate to disclose information without the patient's consent in the following circumstances:

- Where the patient's parent, guardian or carer has consented to the disclosure and the patient's apparent age or health makes them incapable of giving consent to disclose. Pharmacists should not normally disclose information about services provided to adolescent patients to their parents.
- Where disclosure of the information is to a person or body empowered by statute to require such disclosure (e.g., the Royal Pharmaceutical Society of Great Britain (RPSGB) Inspector or a Controlled Drugs Inspector).
- Where disclosure is directed by a coroner, judge or other presiding officer of a court, or the Crown Prosecution Office in England and Wales.
- Where a police officer or NHS Fraud Investigation Officer who provides in writing confirmation that disclosure is necessary to assist in the prevention, detection or prosecution of serious crime.
- Where it is necessary to prevent serious injury or damage to the health of the patient, a third party or to public health.

Pharmacists should not disclose information relating to the prescribing practices of identifiable prescribers or their practices, for example, to sales representatives, other than for the necessary purposes of the NHS or other health care provider, unless the prescriber has given his or her written informed consent to the disclosure. This does not interfere with a pharmacist's right to disclose information to an appropriate body where he or she has reasonable concerns for the well-being of a patient or the public.

Access to confidential information within the pharmacy must be restricted to those who require access to that information and who are themselves subject to an obligation of confidentiality.

The requirements of data protection legislation for data collection and use must be complied with. Confidential information must be protected effectively against improper disclosure when it is stored, transmitted, received or disposed of.

Pharmacy computer and manual systems which include patient specific information must incorporate access control systems to minimise the risk of unauthorised or unnecessary access to the data. Pharmacy computer systems, which include patient specific information and which are linked to the Internet or other networks must incorporate measures such as encryption to eliminate the risk of unauthorised access to confidential data.

Case Study

Facts: R applies for the disclosure of a medical report by the NHS Trust ('N'). R has been the subject of a hospital and restriction order and has been admitted to a high-security hospital that N runs. A hearing before the Mental Health Review Tribunal has been listed. A psychologist prepares a report about R, which is presented to N but N expresses concern at the content and nature of this report. R requests for the disclosure of this report but it is refused. R applies to the tribunal for disclosure but his application is refused because N does not intend to rely on the report at the forthcoming hearing as it will rely on a report from another psychologist. R has permission to rely on his own psychology report and would have a fair opportunity of challenging N's evidence and presenting his own evidence. The hearing is adjourned while R's expert evidence is prepared.

Question: Is R entitled to disclosure pursuant to the Data Protection Act 1998 and the ECHR?

Answer: No. N had produced clear and cogent reasons why the report should not be released and stating the justification for that was unnecessary. R was not prejudiced in the tribunal hearing without the report, as N did not intend to rely on it.

Reason: The guarantee to a fair trial in Article 6 of the ECHR did not provide an unqualified right to every piece of documentation.

This case study is based on the case of *Roberts v. Nottinghamshire Healthcare Trust (2008) EWHC 1934 (QB)*.

HUMAN RIGHTS AND EMPLOYMENT ISSUES

The important articles of the HRA 1998 which are most likely to have an impact in the employment field include Article 4 (right not to be held in slavery and to be protected against forced or compulsory labour), Article 5 (right to liberty and security of the person), Article 6 (right to a fair and public hearing within a reasonable period of time), Article 8 (right to respect for private and family life), Article 9 (right to freedom of religion), Article 10 (right to freedom of expression), Article 11 (right to peaceful assembly and the freedom of association with others) and Article 14 (prohibition of discrimination).

Many of the rights and fundamental freedoms under the Convention are qualified (e.g., Articles 8–11) and as such many cases have failed because of the exceptions – for example, for public safety or for the protection of health.

Under the Convention employment cases have not been particularly successful. Future developments will depend on a number of factors including more flexible courts. Article 6 (right to a fair and public hearing within a reasonable period of time) may be the most useful, in challenging the conduct of court and tribunal processes. This is because 'public authorities' are defined to include courts and tribunals.

However, Article 6 does not usually apply to internal disciplinary hearings though it may apply to those held by professional bodies which can affect a worker's right to practice unless there is a subsequent right of appeal to a court (see *Tehrani v. UK Central Council for Nursing, Midwifery and Health Visiting (2001)* and *Preiss v. General Dental Council (2001)*).

Case Study

Facts: R is employed as a superintendent pharmacist for a chain of pharmacies owned by his employers. R is investigated following the receipt by RPSGB('S') of an email alleging that R's employers had been involved in deliberately reusing patient returned medication and resupplying it to customers. Solicitors instructed by R write to S stating that this is damaging to R and seek information about the investigation. After a delay of 2 years and 8 months, S's registrar refers the allegations against R to an investigating committee (the first decision). R is not given notice of the referral for another 6 weeks thereafter. The original allegations made against R's employers are not pursued, and the misconduct alleged against R is different in nature, relating to the way pharmacy stock was dealt with at the warehouse.

Question: Is the registrar under an implied statutory duty to make a referral to the investigating committee within a reasonable time and is it necessary for R to show that he has been prejudiced by the failure to do so readily?

Answer: Yes there had been an inexcusable delay in making a referral to an investigating committee, but this was not sufficient to quash the referral and stay the proceedings unless R could demonstrate that he had been prejudiced by it.

Reason: R would need to demonstrate that the delay would result in an unfair disciplinary process or that it would be unfair for the process to continue. Delay alone was insufficient to halt the disciplinary process.

This case study is based on the case of *R (on the application of Rycroft) v. The Royal Pharmaceutical Society of Great Britain (2010) EWHC 2832 (Admin)*.

HUMAN RIGHTS AND PROPERTY INTERESTS

Under the Convention, the human right relating to property is not a right to have or acquire property but a right to the protection of a person's existing property. By protecting property rights as a human right, the Convention, and the HRA 1998, empowers an individual to utilise the judicial arm to seek to prevent interferences with property which may be aimed at advancing the public interest.

Protocol 1, Article 1, ECHR protects peaceful enjoyment of possessions:

Every natural or legal person is entitled to the peaceful enjoyment of his possessions. No one shall be deprived of his possession except in the public interest and subject to the conditions provided for by law and by the general principles of international law. The preceding provisions shall not, however, in any way impair the right of a State to enforce such laws as it deems necessary to control the use of property in accordance with the general interest or to secure the payment of taxes or other contributions or penalties.

The term 'possessions' in Protocol 1, Article 1, has a very wide meaning, including all property and chattels and also acquired rights with economic interest such as:

- Leases
- Planning consents
- The vested interests of a doctor in private practice
- Goodwill (e.g., the ability to retain clientele or the goodwill of customers).

In order to show that Protocol 1, Article 1, has been violated, it must be shown that:

The peaceful enjoyment of the applicant's possessions has been interfered with (Rule 1); or The Applicant has been deprived of possessions by the state (Rule 2); or The Applicant's possessions have been subject to control by the state (Rule 3).

The essence of Article 1, Protocol 1, is that it provides a guarantee for the right of property. It provides not only a positive guarantee to the peaceful enjoyment of possessions, which embraces the right to own, possess, use, lend or dispose of the property, but also a negative guarantee that no one shall be deprived of their possessions by the state except in certain circumstances. This is clearly a valuable protection that all community pharmacists who have a freehold or leasehold ownership of a property should be aware of.

FREEDOM OF INFORMATION

The Freedom of Information Act (FOIA) was passed on 30 November 2000. It is challenged with the task of reversing the working premise that everything is secret, unless otherwise stated, to a position where everything is public unless it falls into specified excepted cases.

From 1 January 2005 the FOIA 2000 has obliged pharmacies to respond to requests about information held about NHS pharmaceutical services and creates a right of access to that information subject to some exemptions, which have to be taken into consideration before deciding what information can be released.

The FOIA 2000 recognises that members of the public have the right to know how public services are organised and run, how much they cost and how the decisions are made. In addition to accessing the information identified in the Publication Scheme, members of the public are entitled to request information about an individual pharmacy under the NHS Openness Code 1995. The 2003 NHS Openness Code notes that pharmacists dispensing more than 1500 prescriptions a month generally provide practice leaflets.

The FOIA does not, however, change the right of patients confidentiality in accordance with the HRA 1998 Schedule 1 Article 8, the Data Protection Act 1998 and at common law.

Types of Information That Can Be Requested Under the FOIA 2000

The type of information that can be requested must be the type that authorities believe will not cause significant harm. For example, *Section 38* of the Act provides a qualified exemption from the duty to provide information if its disclosure under the Act would or would be likely to endanger the physical or mental health of any individual, or endanger the safety of any individual.

Insofar as the information under request involves living individuals it will be covered by *Section 40* relating to personal information. The focus of *Section 38* will be on other information whose disclosure might pose a risk and this may include:

- Information about sites of controversial scientific research which may be targets for sabotage. There may be well-founded fears that if the location of such sites were disclosed to individuals or groups opposed to the research, there would be risks to the physical safety of staff.
- Information relating to the dead (not therefore covered by the personal information exemption) whose disclosure might endanger the mental health of surviving relatives.
- Information whose disclosure might have an adverse effect on public health.

In such cases, the information will be withheld under the appropriate exemption of the code of practice. It also places a number of obligations on public authorities about the way in which they provide information. Subject to the exemptions, anyone making a request must be informed whether the public authority holds the information and, if so, be supplied with it – generally within 20 working days. There is also a duty to provide advice or assistance to anyone seeking information (e.g., in order to explain what is readily available or to clarify what is wanted).

Complaints Procedure

The best policy is to be as open as possible and supply the information that has been requested. If the release of that information is considered to cause significant harm then the information may be withheld. The Information Commissioner might later force the disclosure of the information.

In the case where information is requested and there are sections of the information that are exempt, then the document should be clearly marked to show where exempt information is withheld. If all information is withheld, then the public body will have to give full reasons as to why the information has been withheld. If the person requesting access is not satisfied with the reasons, they have the right to appeal. They may also appeal if they think that the charges for information are unfair. The FOIA will be enforced by the Information Commissioner, formerly, the Data Protection Registrar.

FOIA is openness with teeth. The maximum sentence punishable under the FOIA is 2 years imprisonment for the accountable officer of the public body. A practice recommendation can be issued that outlines the steps to help the authority with compliance. These must be given in writing and refer to the relevant section of the code of practice with which the authority does not comply.

If a member of the public feels that they have not had their request for information dealt with in accordance with the Act, they may apply to the Commissioner for a decision. If the complainant has exhausted all internal procedures, the Commissioner either informs the complainant that no decision will be made and the reason for that or serves a decision notice on the complainant and the public authority.

When the Commissioner has received an application for a decision notice or requires more information to consider whether compliance has been achieved with the code of practice and the Act, he or she can serve an information notice. This is time limited and again, must be in writing and must say why the notice has been issued.

If the authority fails to comply with any of its duties under the Act, it may be served with an enforcement notice. Failure to comply with any of the notices may result in the Commissioner certifying this to the court who may ultimately deem non-compliance as Contempt of Court.

Self-Assessment Questions

1. What information is a pharmacist obliged to keep confidential?

   Answer: A pharmacist is obliged to keep confidential all patient information which he or she becomes aware of in the course of business. This obligation also applies to members of staff of the pharmacy and applies to information such as contact details, medical information and prescriptions details. There are instances in which this duty of confidentiality is limited and these exceptions are contained in the Data Protection Act 1998.

2. What legal protections are available in the event a pharmacist is subject to disciplinary procedures?

Answer: Throughout the professional disciplinary process, a pharmacist is protected by a number of well-established common law rules. However, it is necessary to look at the disciplinary process as a whole and whether the process as a whole operates justly. Where, for example, there is no right of appeal to a court or where, for example, the applicant is not present to challenge the evidence presented, Article 6 of the ECHR will be engaged (see e.g., *Brabazon-Drenning v. United Kingdom Central Council for Nursing, Midwifery and Health Visiting (2000)*).

Index

Note: Page numbers followed by "*b*" refer to boxes, respectively.

Lightning Source UK Ltd.
Milton Keynes UK
UKOW04f0400100514

231441UK00001B/22/P